Living with Art

REPRODUCED ON THE COVER:

Henri Matisse.
Odalisque with a Red Coat. 1937
Oil on canvas, $21\frac{5}{8} \times 18\frac{1}{8}''$.
Private collection.
Succession H. Matisse/ARS.

Living with Art

THIRD EDITION

RITA GILBERT

McGraw-Hill, Inc.

New York   St. Louis   San Francisco   Auckland   Bogotá   Caracas   Lisbon   London   Madrid
Mexico   Milan   Montreal   New Delhi   Paris   San Juan   Singapore   Sydney   Tokyo   Toronto

Living with Art

3 4 5 6 7 8 9 0 KGP KGP 9 0 9 8 7 6 5 4 3 2

ISBN 0-07-023454-X

Publisher and Acquiring Editor: Roth Wilkofsky
Editing Supervisor: Curt Berkowitz
Assistant Editor: Nancy Blaine
Designer: Wanda Siedlecka
Layout Designer: Wanda Lubelska
Production Manager: Richard A. Ausburn
Picture Editor: Kathy Bendo
Picture Researcher: Jacquelyn Wong

Line illustrations by Bill Evans, Denton, Texas;
and Vantage Art Studios, Massapequa, NY.
This book was set in Aster by York Graphic Services, Inc.
Color separations by York Graphic Services, Inc., York, Pennsylvania;
and Chanticleer Company, Inc., New York/Switzerland.
Maps by Kelley Graphics, New York.
Arcata Graphics/Kingsport was printer and binder.

Library of Congress Cataloging-in-Publication Data

Gilbert, Rita, (1942–).
    Living with art / Rita Gilbert.—3rd ed.
     544 p.   27.75 cm.
    Includes bibliographical references and index.
    ISBN 0-07-023454-X
     1. Art appreciation.   I. Title.
N7477.G55   1992
701'.1—dc20   91-32780

Preface

Living with Art is a basic art text for college students and other interested readers. It offers a broad introduction to the nature, vocabulary, media, and history of art, drawing on examples from many cultures.

Structure of the Book

As in the two previous editions, I have divided *Living with Art* into five major parts. Part One serves as a general overview of the subject of art and its study. In the opening chapter are discussions about what it means to live actively with art and the importance of art in today's world; the basic impulse for art as exemplified in prehistoric art, children's art, and folk art; and the roles of the three essential participants in art—the artist, the patron, and the observer. Chapter 1 also presents material about creativity and perception and concludes with guidelines for art criticism and understanding.

Chapter 2 poses the question "What Is Art?" and gives readers criteria for answering it within their own frames of reference. The chapter considers "motel" or "sofa" art; art funding and censorship; and the relationship art has to the audience, to the artist's intention, to beauty, and to the "real" world. This chapter also introduces important concepts of form and content, style, and iconography. Chapter 3 presents several broad themes that run through the entire history of art and notes the various purposes art has served and continues to serve.

Part Two is a thorough analysis of the elements and principles of design in art, with detailed explanations and many illustrations. The part concludes with a more comprehensive list of guidelines for art criticism. Part Three covers the two-dimensional media, and devotes a full chapter to each of the major categories—drawing, painting, prints, the camera arts, and graphic design. In Part Four the same detailed coverage is applied to three-dimensional media—sculpture, crafts, architecture, and environmental design. No comparable text, I believe, gives such in-depth treatment to these important modes of expression. Techniques and materials are explained in relation to their expressive possibilities and, wherever possible, in relation to the visual elements and principles.

Part Five is a brief, but complete, chronological history of Western art from earliest times to the present. The three chapters comprising this part include chronologies and maps, which I hope will provide a clearer context for works of art illustrated throughout the book.

The Epilogue, dealing with conservation and restoration, is perhaps the most important section of *Living with Art*. Artworks around the world are in constant danger from many sources—natural disasters, wars, pollution, theft, vandalism, simple neglect. Students who learn to love art should also learn to share the global responsibility for addressing these problems. Otherwise, there will soon be no more need for books like *Living with Art*, because we will lose the precious art we live with.

Illustrations and Feature Boxes

I have a 1936 edition of Gardner's classic *Art Through the Ages*, bought at a library book sale. Even after more than half a century, Helen Gardner's intelligence in writing about art remains impressive. The look of the text, however, makes one wonder how *any* reader could get a sense of what art is about without taking the Grand Tour. Five color plates of dubious quality are inserted at intervals through the book's 800 pages. The remaining illustrations are in very fuzzy black and white and generally of postage-stamp size. Yet for its time this *Art Through the Ages* must have been the latest word in art-book production. The author writes proudly in her Preface of changes from the 1926 edition that have "not only improved the book as an example of the bookmaker's art but have greatly facilitated the ease of reference to the illustrations." It is therefore with a wry sense of comradeship that I prepare to say the same thing—knowing that rapidly advancing technology will make this *Living with Art* seem quaint long before another fifty years have passed.

No illustration can substitute for the experience of actually seeing works of art. At best, a picture in a book acts as a kind of "shorthand" for the true appearance of a work. Still, my publisher and I have tried hard to make the shorthand as meaningful as possible. This new edition of *Living with Art* has 650 illustrations, and 300 of them are printed in full color—a 65 percent increase in color over the previous edition. Great care has been taken to ensure that the color reproductions are as nearly faithful to the original works of art as four colors of ink on paper can be.

Throughout the production process I have worked alongside the layout designer. Our goals were: to give as generous a size as possible to the illustrations; to place the pictures exactly with their text discussions; and to keep related items (such as comparisons) together. It is a credit to the designer's skill and our shared perseverance that we nearly always succeeded.

Such a large number of illustrations permits flexibility. Readers will find works of art from many different cultures, works made by women and by men, works as old as civilization and others barely dry. Historical periods have been documented thoroughly. However, because I feel that students often connect particularly well with the art of their own time, more than one hundred of the works shown in *Living with Art* date from the 1980s and 1990s.

The artists' biographies in *Living with Art* are both the hardest work and the most pleasurable for me to write. Hard, because it is a real challenge to distill a person's whole life into one page and get down not only the facts but also the *flavor* of the person. Pleasurable, because artists are interesting people. I chose the 38 individuals represented by biographies in this edition for various reasons: they are important to the history of art, or they led fascinating lives, or I found a powerful or amusing image of the artist—frequently all three. Each biography includes a portrait of the artist, a brief life history, and a quotation. For me, knowledge of the artist's own story makes the art more meaningful—brings it to life, so to speak.

This edition continues the feature called "Art People"—one-page stories about people who generally are not professional artists but who have had major impact on the world of art. They include several collectors, a dealer, a biographer, an artist's relative, two art patrons, even a forger and a thief.

A new feature box for the third edition, "Artists on Artists," will be described in the following section.

New to This Edition

The third edition of *Living with Art* has been changed from the previous book by about 20 percent, in both text and illustrations. There is something new in every chapter—sometimes a little, sometimes a lot.

The most substantive changes will be found in Part Five, the chronological history of Western art. While I do not want *Living with Art* to become an art history text, or even a history-intensive art appreciation text, neither do I want to short-change students for whom this may be the only exposure to formal art studies. Therefore, I have added new material and illustrations, especially in Chapter 15, "The Ancient World to the Middle Ages." Portions of the chapter dealing with Egyptian, Greek, and Roman art have been expanded, and I have written wholly new sections about Early Christian art, animal-style and Carolingian art, and Romanesque and Gothic styles. Chapter 17, "The Modern World," has been revised to bring it into the 1990s.

Beyond these textual additions, there are two new features in the history chapters. Detailed chronologies of styles, events, and artists—previously at the back of the book—have been moved into the chapters for easier reference. A series of seven four-color maps, specially designed for *Living with Art*, show geographical regions at significant points in history, highlighting places and monuments discussed in the text.

Earlier parts of the book also have been revised. Chapter 2 now has a section dealing with censorship and public funding for the arts, beginning with a discussion of the controversy surrounding Robert Mapplethorpe's photographs. I've added a new theme to Chapter 3, "Themes and Purposes of Art." The chapter now considers how artists of different times have treated the milestones of birth, marriage, and death; the latter section provides coverage of the Vietnam Memorial and the AIDS Quilt. Chapter 13, "Architecture," has been expanded with a comparison of three hotels (including Michael Graves' hotels at Disney World) and three apartment buildings (including Gaudí's Casa Milá and Safdie's Habitat).

A special interest of mine prompted the new feature box in this edition, called "Artists on Artists." Perhaps students will be as intrigued as I am in seeing how certain artists have adapted the work of their admired predecessors. The six examples include one of Picasso's great studies after Velázquez and Marisol's three-dimensional version of Leonardo's *Last Supper*. Three biographies have been added to the book: Andy Warhol, Elisabeth Vigée-Lebrun, and Christo. There is also a new "Art People" story, telling of that unsurpassed patron of the arts, Pericles.

Finally, two new study aids have been incorporated in this edition of *Living with Art*. Throughout the text, key terms are now highlighted in boldface italic. A Pronunciation Guide for unfamiliar names and words appears at the back of the text, just after the last chapter.

One never stops writing a textbook. There is always some other thing the author can do to make the book more informative, more appealing, more accessible to the students who will use it. Echoing Helen Gardner's sentiments of half a century ago, I think my publisher and I have "improved the book as an example of the bookmaker's art" and made it much stronger and better than the previous edition. I hope its readers will agree.

Additional Resources

A number of additional resources have been provided for *Living with Art*. As noted earlier, a Pronunciation Guide for unfamiliar names and words appears at the end of the text. There is a bibliography with suggestions for further reading. A glossary of terms summarizes definitions given in the text.

An Instructor's Manual is available, providing teaching strategies, sample tests, student projects, suggestions for further illustrations, and a list of teaching resources, emphasizing audio-visual materials. A set of slides of illustrations in the book can be purchased from an independent supplier, either as a set or individually.

Acknowledgments

Being a person much involved with theater, especially musical theater, I love ensemble work. I love to be part of a group of individuals—each talented, each master of a specialized craft—all contributing to the creative whole. *Living with Art* has the great advantage of such an ensemble.

Numerous reviewers have helped to shape this text. I am especially indebted to the three readers who contributed so much to revisions in the history chapters: Kathy Flores of New Mexico State University at Alamogordo, Pamela Patton of Northeastern University, and David Cooper of Butte College. I received excellent advice about the first two chapters from Paul Grootkerk of Mississippi State University (member in good standing of the ensemble since the very beginning) and Pamela Lee of Washington State University. The following people also gave valuable suggestions: David Bertolotti, GMI Engineering and Management Institute; Shelley Cordulack, Millikan University; Dwaine Greer, University of Arizona; Ralph Jacobs, Mankato State University; Karen Kietzman, College of St. Francis; Walter Martin, Concordia University; Timothy McNiven, Ohio State University; John Shaak, California State University, Long Beach; and Ray Sonnema, Georgia Southern University.

I do not forget the readers of previous editions, because their counsel continues to enlighten the text. They include: Mary Alice Arnold, Appalachian State University; Michelle R. Banks, Memphis State University; Ross Beitzel, Gloucester County College; Carole Calo, University of Massachusetts; George Arnott Civey, III; Jerry Coulter, James Madison University; Betty Disney, Cypress College; Richard T. Doi, Central Washington University; Henry Drewal, Cleveland State University; Steve Eliot, Broward Community College; Robert N. Ewing, California State University, Fullerton; Lynn Galbraith, University of Nebraska; Douglas George, University of New Mexico; Larry Gleeson, University of North Texas; Janice Hardy, Georgia College; Sharon K. Hopson; Susan Jackson, Marshall University; Jan Koot, California State University, Long Beach; Nell Lafaye, University of South Carolina; Kathleen Lobley, Butler University; Carolyn Loeb, Central Michigan University; Joseph Molinaro, Broward Community College; Tim Morris, University of Central Arkansas; Jo Anne Nix, Georgia College; Christie Nuell, Middle Tennessee State University; Helen Phillips, University of Central Arkansas; Dominic Ricciotti, Winona State University; John C. Riordan, State University of New York, College at Potsdam; Barbara Kerr Scott, Cameron University; Claire Selkurt, Mankato State University; Michael J. Smith, Southern Illinois University; Thomas Turpin, University of Arkansas; Barbara von Barghahn, George Washington University; Randy Wassell, Colorado State University; Kenneth Weedman, Cumberland College; and Rochelle Weinstein, Borough of Manhattan Community College of the City University of New York.

Since the second edition of *Living with Art* was published, I have made the transition to a new publishing house. This could be difficult, but many of the same people are still part of the ensemble. My publisher, Roth Wilkofsky, gave his usual meticulous attention to every line of the manuscript and every aspect of the revision.

I do not have enough superlatives in my personal dictionary for the staff and free-lancers at McGraw-Hill who worked on this edition. Short of gushing at length, I can only salute: the design skills and superb taste of Wanda Siedlecka and Wanda Lubelska; the production wisdom of Rich Ausburn; the creative picture editing and research of Kathy Bendo, Jacquelyn Wong, and Erica Demme, assisted by Rita Geffert; the marketing savvy of Alison Husting; and the dedicated research and help-of-all-kinds from Nancy Blaine. Majordomo of this crew was Curt Berkowitz, whose title of "editing supervisor" doesn't tell the half of it. Besides coordinating the efforts of the team, Curt has been my goad, my conscience, my father confessor, my tour guide, my ally, and my best pal. They are champions, every one of them.

Finally, I give my special thanks to two extraordinary friends, Diane Damerau and Fred Damerau, who sustain me in many endeavors, including this one. I have dedicated this book to them.

North Salem, New York, July 1991   RITA GILBERT

Contents

PART TWO

THE VOCABULARY OF ART   98

Chapter Four

The Visual Elements   99

Chapter Five

Principles of Design in Art   147

Living with Art

PART ONE

INTRODUCTION

1. Henri Matisse. *Pianist and Checker Players*. 1924. Oil on canvas, 29 × 36⅜".
National Gallery of Art, Washington, D.C. (collection of Mr. and Mrs. Paul Mellon).

Chapter One

Living with Art

Enter the world of Henri Matisse. It is a world of color and pattern and beautiful things. A world of lovely women and wonderful indoor spaces **(1)**. Two boys have a game of checkers at a table draped in a printed cloth; they are the artist's sons. A young woman plays at a piano that seems to float upward on a wall of vividly patterned wallpaper; she is the artist's daughter. In the background are a sculpture and paintings displayed against the furnishings of a French gentleman's home. This is Matisse's world.

Matisse chose to live with art, and he shows us his world through his own artistic vision. His eye sought the beautiful, the color against color, the pattern on pattern, the lushness of everyday life. He might pose a model in a coat of brilliant scarlet and flowing pink trousers **(cover)** and call her an *odalisque,* a harem woman. He sets her against a background of lush plants, so that she herself seems an exotic plant to be admired for her colors and shapes. She is ordinary life made extraordinary, life made into art.

Or, if you prefer, enter the world of Vincent van Gogh. Follow him as he takes up residence in the little yellow house on a street corner in the southern French town of Arles **(2)**. The artist was so eager to settle in this house that he began sketching it immediately, as soon as the rental was assured. Then he turned the sketches into an important painting, called *Vincent's House at Arles.* Later he made another painting of his bedroom inside the house **(532)**. Van Gogh chose to live with art, and he spent most of his adult life painting images *of* his life—his own likeness, his friends, the landscape he inhabited, his house, his special chair. For Van Gogh, *living* and *art* were practically the same thing. This is Van Gogh's world.

Relatively few of us will commit a lifetime to art, as Matisse and Van Gogh did, but that doesn't mean we are not involved with art. Who lives with art? You do. Everybody does. It would be impossible *not* to live with art, because art is inextricably connected to human existence. Art has been with us since the earliest cave dwellers made their first steps toward civilization, and will be with us as long as civilized life continues on our planet.

You probably have more art in your life than you realize. If you live in a city or town, artists have designed almost everything in your environment. The buildings in which you live and work, the furniture inside those buildings, the clothes you wear—all were designed by artists in specialized fields. Very likely the walls of your home are decorated with posters, prints, photo-

2. Vincent van Gogh.
Vincent's House at Arles. 1888.
Oil on canvas, 30 × 37".
Vincent van Gogh Foundation,
Rijksmuseum Vincent van Gogh,
Amsterdam.

graphs, maybe original paintings, that you have hung to give personal meaning to your world. Perhaps your school or office building has a large-scale sculpture out front, or a fabric hanging or mural inside.

Whether we know it or not, all of us make choices—every day, every minute—with respect to art. We choose one product over another, one garment over another, one way to walk from place to place, basing our decisions largely on the visual attractiveness of the preferred option. We choose to study and enjoy particular works of art or to ignore them. We choose to plan encounters with art, as in museums and galleries, or not to do so. Some people choose to devote their entire lives to the pursuit of art, thereby acquiring the designation of "artist."

Whatever our degree of involvement with art, we must remember that it *is* a choice. We can go through life like sleepwalkers, ignoring or taking for granted the art around us. Or we can enrich our lives by developing a more active appreciation of the art we live with. This book is about the appreciation of art, which means a combination of understanding and enjoyment. It is possible to heighten our appreciation of art, to learn to see, to take an active interest in the visual world. When we do so, we are only following a basic *aesthetic impulse*—an urge to respond to that which we find beautiful.

The Impulse for Art

A few paragraphs ago we said that art is inextricably connected to human existence. Before going on, it might be well to challenge this statement. Is it true? Do we really need art in the same way that, for instance, we need language? In fact, why is there art? Are such things as paintings and sculptures necessary to human life?

The history of civilization suggests that we do need art, that it is basic to human expression. This seems equally true for those who make art, those who buy or support it, and those who simply admire it. To begin with the people who make art, there are three areas we might consider to see how the artistic impulse works. In none of them have the artists always been aware of making "art." They have simply done what seemed to them perfectly natural, and it remained for others, outsiders, to declare that their efforts constitute art. The three areas are prehistoric art, children's art, and folk art.

PREHISTORIC ART

The earliest people made art—whether they called it that or not—as evidenced by the cave paintings found in various parts of the world (3). Archaeologists tell us that in the Ice Age, about 35,000 years ago, Cro Magnon peoples in Europe "suddenly" began making objects that we would describe as art. (The word "suddenly" must be understood in the context of thousands of years, the point being that all the earliest known works date from roughly the same time.) They painted the walls of their caves, carved figurines, decorated their tools and everyday implements with fine designs (4), and even made musical instruments.

As primitive peoples advanced and learned to make more sophisticated objects for their daily use, they nearly always embellished them with art-

above: 3. Cave painting of horses.
c. 15,000–10,000 B.C.
Lascaux, France.

left: 4. *Romping Ibexes,*
detail of a spear-thrower.
c. 20,000 B.C.
Carved reindeer horn, length 3⅝".
Musée de l'Homme, Paris.

5. *Calle de Sueños (Dream Street)*. 1989. Mural, mixed media; 100 × 50'. East 124th Street, East Harlem, New York. Project of the Creative Arts Workshop in affiliation with Sheltering Arms Childrens Services 1989.

work. A pot will hold water or cook food over the fire just as well if it is plain. Why decorate it? A plain garment will keep the wearer warm. Why make it fancy? A shelter needs only to keep out the rain and wind. Why ornament it? Nevertheless, our long-ago ancestors did all these things. A partial explanation assumes that the life-and-death struggle for survival had eased off just enough to allow time for artistic expression, but it does not tell us why the spare time was actually used for artistic expression. We like to think that Cro Magnon humans "suddenly" developed a sense of themselves as being human, of being unique in the order of the universe, different from animals or trees. A work of art declares to the world: "I am here. I am unlike anyone else. I am special." If true, this theory supports the conclusion that there is an inborn human urge to create and enjoy art, to be "special."

CHILDREN'S ART

Children come to art as readily as they do to play. For them, painting and drawing are play activities, not much different from building with blocks (a kind of architecture) or playing with dolls (a kind of theater). No one is likely to tell children their artistic efforts aren't good enough to qualify as "real" art, so they can create spontaneously, happily. Given the opportunity and the right materials, they will draw and paint and sculpt and build—and have a wonderful time doing it.

Our next illustration shows a group effort—many children working together to make art. In 1989 seventy-five children collaborated to paint the mural *Calle de Sueños (Dream Street)* on a blank Post Office wall in the East Harlem section of New York City **(5)**. The children ranged in age from five to fifteen, and most of them were homeless, living in city shelters or welfare hotels. Their mural project was supported by New York artist Brookie Maxwell, who had founded the Creative Arts Workshop for Homeless Children.

The children were as free with their colors and forms as with their dreams. A magical Oz-like urban landscape fills the mural, its buildings cheerfully topsy-turvy, its sunny colors as far as possible from the drab surroundings of the real inner city. And what were their dreams for the Calle de Sueños? The dreams of these children were straightforward: McDonald's; unlimited skateboards; free apartments, some meant only for children; no bedtime; no drug dealers; everyone friendly and happy; and, most poignant for these young artists, "Daddy Home." The Harlem children cannot create the world they dream of in real life, but they readily embrace the impulse to create that world in art.

FOLK ART

Folk art is a term applied to works made by individuals with no academic training in art and often with little or no formal education. Folk art exists outside the mainstream of Western art; you will rarely find it included in official surveys of art history, like the one comprising Part Five of this book, nor occupying the main galleries of important museums. Nevertheless, this art has a living current of its own. Some folk artists work within a longstanding tradition. Skills are handed down from parent to child over many generations. Other such artists are true "originals" who begin to make art even though it might be considered a strange pursuit by their families and friends.

So much about folk art is appealing. Like the art of children, it often reveals a quite direct expression. Most folk painters and sculptors would become impatient if someone tried to tell them how art is "supposed" to look. They form images of what they see, colored by their feelings about what they see, and they are satisfied. They invent, they play with forms, they delight in colors and shapes, they decorate—free of the inhibition that comes from being told "That's not *real* art."

Ralph Fasanella's *Family Supper* (6) is characteristic of much folk art in that it has a strong narrative content, it tells a story, and that story is impor-

6. Ralph Fasanella. *Family Supper.* 1972. Oil on canvas, 5'10" × 4'2". Courtesy the artist.

tant to the artist's life experience. Fasanella's family were immigrants from Italy who arrived in the United States in 1910. His father was an iceman—a deliveryman who carted blocks of ice to people's kitchens in the days before electric refrigeration—and his mother was a buttonhole maker. Like many poor immigrant families of the time, they lived in cramped quarters in a tenement building. *Family Supper* depicts their home.

The artist's style shows his lack of formal training, but at the same time the folk painter's sure eye for telling detail. Even if the drawing seems crude and simple, we miss nothing, we understand the scene. Each family member is portrayed as an individual, and each object in the room is given its special identity—the pots on the stove, the Singer sewing machine, the gas meter on the wall, all the little artifacts of home life. Fasanella paints with the affection and memory of a natural artist.

Folk sculpture is equally spontaneous and personal. In the depressed area of Los Angeles known as Watts, an immigrant tile setter, Simon Rodia, built a fantasy-land construction that has come to be called the Watts Towers **(7)**. Working with bits of bottle glass, broken dishes, shells, pieces of mirrors, and other debris from the streets, Rodia patiently created a thing of beauty—a very personal expression of art, in monumental form—in his backyard. He labored over the towers for about thirty years, feeling that he thus paid a debt to the country that had given him a home and a living. But the Watts Towers are not just the obsession of an eccentric laborer. They are the product of a creative artist who has found a unique way to use his gift.

So we return to our initial question: Is art necessarily connected to human existence? The groups just considered—prehistoric people, children, and folk artists—suggest that it is, that art is a natural form of expression.

left: 7. Simon Rodia. Watts Towers, Los Angeles, detail. c. 1921–54 (now partially destroyed).

above: 8. Rembrandt Peale. *Thomas Jefferson.* 1805. Oil on canvas, 28 × 23½″.
New-York Historical Society, New York.

But suppose one does not choose to *make* art. Many people don't, yet they still can participate in the artistic impulse. This chapter began with the premise that *everybody* lives with art, artist and nonartist alike. There are three different ways in which people can live with art—by making it, by supporting it, and by observing and enjoying it. The balance of this chapter considers these three roles: artist, patron, observer.

The Role of the Artist

Nobody questions the role farmers play in society. They produce the food necessary to sustain life. Much the same is true of furniture makers, car and clothing manufacturers, and nowadays computer programmers and bankers. But what of artists? What role do they fill? What do they contribute to society, and do we really need them? Would our world be seriously diminished if there weren't any artists? To answer these questions, let us focus briefly on those people who live actively with art every day of their lives—the artists themselves.

Throughout history artists have filled many different kinds of social roles. In ancient Egypt, Greece, and Rome, artists usually had very low social status, and some were actually slaves whose task was to carry out the artistic requirements of their masters. During the Middle Ages the artist moved into the realm of the craftsman, occupying a social level roughly equivalent to that of today's fine cabinetmaker. Only by the time of the Renaissance, the 15th century, were artists accepted in "good" society, and still their creations were under the rigorous control of wealthy patrons. Today's artists in most countries enjoy a social status like that of Renaissance artists—a special elite apart from class—but their freedom of expression is greater than that of artists even a few generations ago.

WHAT DO ARTISTS DO?

The social role of artists has changed over time, but their function remains basically the same. Like their counterparts in earlier times, contemporary artists fulfill a practical function, designing virtually every structure and object in the environment. Today this practical role is carried out by artists with specialized, often technical, training—industrial and graphic designers, architects, craft artists, and fashion designers, among others. But what about the painters and sculptors, the photographers and cinematographers? What needs do they meet in our computer age? We can identify at least four basic functions for the artist—all of them age-old, all expanding in complexity.

First, artists *record*. They give us visual images that can be preserved for historical reference. This idea is so obvious that we take it for granted, forgetting how overwhelming our ignorance otherwise would be. Were it not for artists, we would have no idea what people from the past looked like. Thomas Jefferson was one of the founders of our country, principal author of the Declaration of Independence, and third president of the United States. He is well known to us from his extensive writings. His splendid architecture (436) stands today and is still admired. But Jefferson died more than a decade before the invention of photography, and were it not for artists' portraits, including the sensitive one by Rembrandt Peale (8), we would have no visual image of the man to match the achievement. Nor could we form any visual image of historical places and events. Before the invention of the camera in the early 19th century, artists recorded images mainly through painting and sculpture. Today we rely more heavily on photography, cinema, and television to keep our history, but of course the people behind these media are also artists. Even with the prevalence of mechanical recording, there is a renewed interest in the painted portrait, and a great many well-known artists are thriving on portrait commissions.

Second, artists *give tangible form to the unknown.* In other words, they attempt to record what cannot be seen with the eyes or what has not yet occurred. This role has been important throughout the history of art, and it is no less vital today. Ancient artists had a somewhat different list of unknowns to contend with. They puzzled over and feared such things as tornadoes, floods, eclipses, and the wrath of spirits. Even in an age when satellites predict the weather and spirits have been tamed, there still are certain unknowns, and artists still are struggling to give them tangible form. What would a nuclear holocaust be like? We do not know and dare not find out. What exists at the edge of our universe? Scientists will know eventually, but not soon. What do our dreams and nightmares really mean (9)? None of us can analyze them definitely. These unknowns are frightening to us, just as the Thunder God must have been to our ancestors. If artists can present them to us in some concrete form, we can tame them and go about our business.

Third, artists *give tangible form to feelings.* These may be the artist's own feelings that are expressed in paint or marble or whatever the medium. But surely they are feelings shared by many people—love, hate, despair, fear, exhilaration, anger, admiration. When we respond to a work of art, when we pay attention to the emotions it evokes, we are communicating in a way with the artist and with other people who share these responses.

Fourth, artists *offer an innovative way of seeing,* a unique visual perspective. When we experience a work of art, we confront the artist's perspective, compare it to our own, and take note of both the similarities and the differences. Art encourages us to think, to question, to imagine, to explore, to dream. It stretches our own horizons by confronting us with someone else's.

To sum up, then, artists perform at least four important functions in society: they record, they visualize the unknown, they portray feelings, and

9. Phyllis Bramson.
Metaphysical Drama 2. 1983.
Oil on canvas, 5′ × 6′ × 4″.
Courtesy Dart Gallery Incorporated,
Chicago.

10. Pablo Picasso.
Bull's Head. 1943.
Bronze cast of bicycle seat
and handlebars, height $16\frac{1}{8}''$.
Courtesy Chevojon Frères, Paris.

they stretch one's ability to see. All of these functions have to do with communication. Artists are able to fill these roles because they *create* new visual images. The words *creative* and *creativity* will come up often in this book, so it might be well to pause a bit and consider what they really mean.

CREATIVITY

Who is creative? Are artists more creative than other people? If so, how did they get that way? What is creativity? Does everyone start out having it and do some people then lose it? Is there any way to get it if you don't have it? Can a person become more creative? Less creative? These are fascinating questions to which, unfortunately, there are no definite answers. We can approach the problem by looking at examples and perhaps gain some insight, but nobody will ever write the rules of creativity.

The illustration (**10**) shows a work by Pablo Picasso entitled *Bull's Head*, which consists entirely of the seat and handlebars of a bicycle. No doubt every one of us has seen a bicycle, and we are familiar with the shapes of seat and handlebars. Picasso, however, looked at these shapes and saw something else—saw it in his creative imagination. He saw the head of a bull. By putting the two shapes together in a special way, he made something of them that had not been there before. In other words, he created. What's more, he created so persuasively that, if you hadn't been told what the shapes were and had not read the caption, you might not recognize the bicycle seat and handlebars for what they are. You would instead see a bull's head, because that is what Picasso has caused us to see. It is important to note that Picasso was a great fan of the bullfight. His creativity in this instance was filtered through his life's experiences and interests—his own *references*. Another creative artist might have combined the two shapes into something different. (Numberless other creative artists have seen bicycle seats and handlebars and paid no attention to them.)

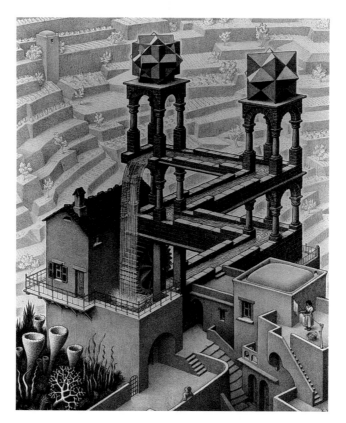

11. M. C. Escher. *Waterfall.*
1961. Lithograph, $14\frac{7}{8} \times 11\frac{3}{4}''$.
Escher Foundation,
Haags Gemeentemuseum,
The Hague.

The Dutch artist M. C. Escher was a lover of visual puzzles. He enjoyed tricking the viewers of his art. In *Waterfall* **(11)** we see an elaborate, fantastic structure and landscape; the trick comes when we look more closely. The waterfall of the title spills down normally in the center of the picture. Then the water proceeds back and forth, somehow running uphill to the top! We stare at the drawing, trying to figure out what is wrong with it. At any given point it *looks* all right, but we know it cannot be. Our brains are sure that water does not flow uphill; our eyes see that the water gets to the top, flows down, then goes around again. Escher has created an intriguing image. His creativity makes us see something that could not possibly be true. More to the point, his creativity let him imagine that water might run uphill, then figure out a way to make it happen.

The last example in this section is a painting by André Derain, called *The Turning Road, l'Estaque* **(12)**. In every respect but one this seems a fairly straightforward landscape. The one exception, needless to say, is the color. Trees and grass in our world are not blood red, nor are people. Clouds and shadows are not vivid purple. Roads seldom are bright yellow. Derain, a member of the Fauve group in France at the early part of this century (Chapter 17), painted in *arbitrary* colors, or colors unrelated to the natural world. He chose to depict nature not as we see it through the window, but as he wanted to see it in his painting. Such disregard of natural colors requires a creative leap of the imagination that was shocking to art viewers of the time.

These three works—the Picasso, the Escher, and the Derain—have certain characteristics in common. All three involved the making of something that had not been before. All three resulted from the artists' suspending judgment about what should be or actually is, in favor of what might be. All three developed as they did because of certain personal preoccupations: for Picasso, the bullfight; for Escher, a puzzle; for Derain, color as pure color. Taken together, they give us clues about the nature of creativity.

The literature on creativity is plentiful. Many writers and educators have tried to analyze creativity and determine what makes a person creative.[1] While the exact nature of creativity remains elusive, there is general agreement that creative people tend to possess certain traits, including:

- *Sensitivity*—heightened awareness of what one sees, hears, and touches, as well as responsiveness to other people and their feelings.
- *Flexibility*—an ability to adapt to new situations and to see their possibilities; willingness to find innovative relationships.
- *Originality*—uncommon responses to situations and to solving problems.
- *Playfulness*—a sense of humor and ability to experiment freely.
- *Productivity*—the ability to generate ideas easily and frequently, and to follow through on those ideas.
- *Fluency*—a readiness to allow the free flow of ideas.
- *Analytical skill*—a talent for exploring problems, taking them apart, and finding out how things work.
- *Organizational skill*—ability to put things back together in a coherent and logical order.

This list is helpful in identifying the characteristics and behaviors of creative people, but it doesn't really tell us how creativity *works*, a subject that has engrossed scientists for decades. One theory, popular in the 1960s and 1970s, suggests that the right half of the human brain is more creative than the left half, or at least that the right brain has greater responsibility for *visual* creativity. According to this theory, the left brain is the custodian of words and logic, the right brain the keeper of images and analogies. Proponents of the theory believed that artists, when they set out to work, could somehow "turn on" the right brain and thus tap into its creative potential.

New research indicates that the two halves of the brain are more interdependent than had been believed. Rather than having sole charge of a particular set of functions, they are specialists, using each other's abilities as needed. If indeed the right brain is more image-oriented and the left brain more word-oriented, it stands to reason that the creative experience will be heightened if one uses *both* sides of the brain to their fullest capabilities.

Are artists more creative than other people? Maybe, maybe not. The profession of artist is not the only one that requires creativity. Scientists, mathematicians, writers, teachers, business executives, doctors, lawyers, librarians, computer programmers—people in every line of work, if they are any good, look for ways to be creative. The football coach who invents a new play is being creative, as is the plumber who devises an innovative way to keep the washing machine from leaking. Artists occupy a special place in that they have devoted their lives to opening the channels of *visual* creativity.

12. André Derain. *The Turning Road, l'Estaque.* 1906. Oil on canvas, 4'3" × 6'4¾". Museum of Fine Arts, Houston (John A. and Audrey Jones Beck Collection).

13. Sandro Botticelli. *Primavera.* c. 1478. Tempera on panel, 6'8" × 10'3¾". Uffizi, Florence.

Can a person become more creative? Almost certainly, if one allows oneself to be. Being creative, as we said, means making something new. It means learning to trust one's own interests, experiences, and references, and to use them to enhance life and work. Above all, it means discarding rigid notions of what has been or should be in favor of what *could* be. For both the artist and the observer of art, creativity develops when the eyes and the mind are wide open.

The Role of the Patron

A patron is a person who buys or commissions works of art. Without patrons, artists could not prosper, for there would be no one to finance their endeavors. The first section of this chapter presented the idea that people have an inherent impulse to make art. It seems equally true that people have an inherent impulse to collect and support art. The patron of art may be a private individual, a political or religious leader, a business or government body, even a whole culture.

Patrons may have any number of motivations for supporting art. Perhaps art is meant to show the patron's wealth or prestige. Perhaps the patron simply loves the experience of being surrounded by art and can afford to indulge that love. In the case of an establishment—a monarchy, a government or religious body, or a business firm—art may embody the ideals and principles of that establishment, may express what it feels about itself and wishes to communicate to the world. The same may be true when art is integral to a whole culture.

Looking back into history, we find that many of the cultures we admire as high points in the world's progress also were great patrons of art. Among them we could include the Classical civilizations of Greece and Rome, the

Gupta period in 5th- and 6th-century India, the Song dynasty in China, and the Renaissance in 15th-century Europe. History tells us that art thrives in an atmosphere fostering the highest ideals and the greatest energy. Art grows alongside achievements in science, government, and commerce.

There are records to show how highly art was valued in some of these exemplary cultures. For instance, in 15th-century Italy, in the prosperous city-state of Florence, one family reigned supreme for three generations—the Medici. The Medici were bankers and, although not of noble blood, ruled as virtual kings. They were also great patrons of art and supported Raphael, Michelangelo, Sandro Botticelli, and many other artists whose works appear in this book. Botticelli's *Primavera* **(13)**, one of the loveliest paintings from the Renaissance, originally was created to hang in a villa belonging to the Medici. Lorenzo de' Medici had this to say about his vast expenditures for art: "Many deem that it would have been preferable to keep part of the funds in the treasury; I think that our patronage was the great splendor of our regime and, in my opinion, the money was well spent."[2] Five centuries later we can only agree: The money was *very* well spent. Our artistic heritage would be much the poorer without works commissioned by the Medici.

We can find a surprisingly true echo of Lorenzo's ideals in our own national history. Writing for *The New York Times*, historian Arthur Schlesinger, Jr., tells us:

> In the third year of the Civil War, President Abraham Lincoln ordered that construction of the Capitol dome be completed. When critics objected to the diversion of labor and money from the prosecution of the war, President Lincoln said, "If people see the Capitol going on, it is a sign that we intend this Union shall go on."

Nearly a century later, Schlesinger continues, "President Franklin D. Roosevelt recalled this story in 1941 when, in a world ablaze with war, he dedicated the National Gallery of Art in Washington." We can only marvel at these stories. Why should political leaders, fighting for the very survival of their nations and people, pay attention to art? Perhaps they felt that, somehow, art is important *for* survival. Perhaps they understood that art will endure long after the details of battle and politics are forgotten. As Schlesinger says, "If history tells us anything, it tells us that the United States, like all other nations, will be measured in the eyes of posterity less by the size of its gross national product and the menace of its military arsenal than by its character and achievement as a civilization."[3]

From the words and actions of Lorenzo, of Lincoln and Roosevelt, of many other government leaders like them, we may conclude that the purpose of official art patronage is to show contemporaries "This is who we are," and to show future generations "This is who we were." No doubt the same purpose underlies patronage by a new breed of patrons—the corporate giants.

Once a sculptor's masterpiece might have adorned the private sitting room of a king or dictator or cardinal. Today it is more likely to rest in the lobby of an office building or in the street outside **(14)**. Some corporations,

14. Jean Dubuffet.
Monument with Standing Beast.
1984. Fiberglass, height 29'.
Commissioned by the Illinois
Capital Development Board;
given by the Leonard J. Horowich
Family Foundation in memory
of Leonard J. Horowich
with additional funding
by the Graham Foundation
and an anonymous donor.

15. Alberto Giacometti.
*Large Standing Woman II
(Grande femme debout II)*. 1960.
Bronze, height 9'1½".
*Large Standing Woman III
(Grande femme debout III)*. 1960.
Bronze, height 7'8⅞".
Courtesy PepsiCo Inc.,
Purchase, N.Y.

such as IBM and PepsiCo, invest very heavily in art, particularly contemporary art **(15)**. Their reasons for this patronage are diverse. Certainly prestige is among their motivations; the chief executive of PepsiCo Inc., which maintains a large sculpture garden at its headquarters, has said, "I don't think anybody could walk away from here without being impressed."[4] Another reason may have to do with productivity—productivity of the most inventive sort. We said earlier that art stretches people's horizons, encourages them to think and explore. Apparently, the large corporations of the United States agree. But the kind of intellectual and emotional stimulation afforded by art need not be restricted to our working lives. Art can give us new ways of seeing in our social, leisure, and personal lives. There are gains for the self, not just for the employer, in becoming an active observer of art.

The Role of the Observer

There is a difference between being merely an observer and being an intelligent, *informed* observer. Observers walk through the world letting their eyes record art while their brains are occupied elsewhere. Informed observers, by contrast, have spent the time and energy needed to educate themselves so that their exposure to art will be meaningful. They don't just coexist with art; they live with it.

How, then, do observers of art proceed to educate themselves? As with most areas of life, the more one puts into it, the more one will get out of it. You can observe and enjoy art at many different levels. Some art is "easy." Advertising layouts, magazine covers, record-jacket designs—these make good examples. The graphic design is bright, colorful, and attractive. Its main purpose is to appeal superficially to the eye—and to encourage you to buy the product. Nearly anyone can admire the cleverness of the design without spending a lot of time studying it.

Other kinds of art are more "difficult" for the untrained observer. This could be said of the two paintings illustrated next **(16,17)**. If you are not familiar with works of art in these particular styles, you may think that the first, a painting by Alma Thomas, is little different from a computer printout, perhaps in Arabic; and the second, a painting by Alex Katz, may strike you as resembling a poster or magazine advertisement. If you turn away from them quickly, the paintings may communicate nothing to you. But if you have seen a range of work in these styles, if you have learned the process by which the two artists arrived at these kinds of expressions, then you may find some thread of communication.

In other words, there are two specific things that can enhance your appreciation of art: exposure and study. *Exposure* means looking at art, as much as possible, and really seeing it. You should be familiar with this process from your experience with music. The first time you hear a song or a symphony you may find it appealing. But when you have listened to the same piece of music over and over, you begin to greet it like an old friend. You hear patterns and rhythms and harmonies that you didn't notice before. Whereas the first exposure gave you sensory pleasure, repeated exposures bring emotional and perhaps intellectual pleasure. This in turn gives you greater appreciation of similar music by the same composer and by others.

Another benefit of exposure to art—of looking at art and really seeing it—is that we heighten our perceptions of art. Perception is a complicated process, and if we do not understand its intricacies, a lot of our visual world can slip past us.

PERCEPTION

Our appreciation of art is directly tied to our individual *patterns of perception*—the specific ways in which we experience the world around us. In most cases art depends primarily on visual perception—the process by which our minds interpret the information that we collect with our eyes.

In visual perception our eyes take in information in the form of light patterns. Through a complex interaction that scientists do not entirely understand, the brain processes these visual images to give them meaning. The mechanics of perception work in much the same way for everyone, yet in a given situation, we do not all see the same things. The human eye simply cannot take in all available visual information. Our world is too complex, and we are constantly bombarded with an incredible range of visual images.

left: 16. Alma Woodsey Thomas.
Light Blue Nursery. 1968.
Acrylic on canvas, 4'2" × 4'.
National Museum of American Art,
Smithsonian Institution, Washington, D.C.
(gift of Alma W. Thomas).

below: 17. Alex Katz. *Impala.* 1968.
Oil on canvas, 6 × 8'.
The Cleveland Museum of Art
(Mr. and Mrs. William H. Marlatt Fund
and gift of the Eppler Family Foundation
and Agnes Gund Saalfield).

above: **18.** E. G. Boring's Object-Ambiguous Mother-in-Law.

below: **19.** The Circle That Isn't There.

20. Vincent van Gogh. *The Starry Night* (detail).

If the mind recorded all the visual detail that our eyes see at any given moment, it would "blow a fuse." To avoid overloading our mental circuits, the brain responds only to that visual information required to meet our needs at one moment.

Suppose you are driving along a busy street, assailed on all sides by demanding visual images. Your eyes "see" everything. But what does your brain register? If you are behind the wheel of the car, you will see the traffic signs and lights, because awareness of such details is necessary to survival. If you are very hungry, your attention may be attracted by fast-food signs and restaurants. But if you are looking for a specific address—the home of a friend or the place where you have a business appointment—then you will focus on building numbers and block out nearly everything else. It is easier to cope with life and with our complex visual world if we simplify our perceptions and see according to our immediate needs.

Studies indicate that the brain is often more important than the eyes in determining what each of us sees as we move through the world. The brain's ability to control perception is obvious when we study ambiguous figures, such as the classic one reproduced here **(18)**. When you first look at this drawing, you may see a young woman turning away from you so that only her cheek line, the top of her nose, and her eyelashes are visible. Or you may see a toothless old woman with a large, warty nose, whose chin is buried in a dark collar. For you to be able to see both images, your brain must reorganize the lines in the drawing.

Even after you have been made aware of the two images, you must consciously work at going back and forth between them. You can feel your brain shifting as it organizes the visual information into first one image and then the other. The important thing to remember as you shift your perception back and forth from the young woman to the old is that the visual image *always stays the same*. It is only your perception that changes.

While perception can cause us to miss seeing what is actually present in the visual field, it can also do the reverse: cause us to "see" what is *not* present. In the illustration of wavy forms **(19)** you may see a perfect white circle, but there is no circle. There is only the illusion of a white circle created by breaks in the wavy forms. (If you doubt this, cover up any two adjacent forms and look at the space between them.) This is just another trick our brains play on us as part of the phenomenon of perception. The brain supplies information to create a kind of order it requires, even though that information may not be recorded by the eyes.

Some understanding of perception is extremely helpful to the appreciation of art. When you look at a painting, for example, at least three factors always are operating: the actual, physical substance of the painting; the artist's intention in making the painting; and your own perception of the painting. Each person who looks at that same painting will bring a different perception, so you can see how complex is the communication we call art. To get an idea of how this works, let us study one well-known painting.

When you look at the image shown at left **(20)**, you will see a layer of paint on canvas, the individual strokes of a brush. This is what you would see if you stood very close to the painting and focused on one area—globs of inert pigment attached to a canvas backing.

Now pull back farther and consider the whole painting **(21)**. You see a brilliantly colored landscape with a tree, a village, a church, and a turbulent sky. This is Vincent van Gogh's masterpiece, called *The Starry Night*. If we limit ourselves to absolute scientific observation, no night sky ever looked like this. Stars do not race about in frenzied whirlpools. What was Van Gogh's perception of the scene that caused him to paint it this way? We know that he was a tormented, intense, and mystical man. Some of the torment, and a kind of ecstasy, are built into the painting.

And what is the viewer's perception? That depends, to a large extent, on the individual's perceptual habits and biases and on past experience. The cosmologist might think *The Starry Night* alludes magnificently to the formation of the universe. A Londoner who experienced the German blitz in World War II might see a bombing raid. Someone who has been in a fever or taken drugs might see a hallucinatory vision. A person with a certain visual disorder might think this is the way a sky always looks. And the individual who views nature in a scientific way might think that Van Gogh was crazy.

The message Van Gogh (or any other artist) sends cannot be precisely the message you receive. Van Gogh brought to his work a whole set of experiences and emotions; no one else can duplicate them exactly. However, if you open yourself to looking at the art, to receiving whatever message it may have for you, then a communication exists. Communication, as we all know, is a two-way process. Two people cannot hold a conversation if one is doing all the talking and the other is sitting there dumbly. Van Gogh poured a lot of himself into *The Starry Night*. If you want to understand and enjoy—to appreciate—his art, then you also must bring something to the experience. This is where *study* comes in.

STUDYING ART

Art requires intellectual as well as sensory involvement. Your appreciation of art can be greatly improved by knowing how a work of art was made, why it was made, what went before and came after.

The understanding of process—the *how*—often contributes quite a lot to our appreciation of art. Parts Three and Four of this book are largely concerned with this issue. If you understand why painting in watercolor may be different from painting in oil, why clay responds differently to the artist's hands than does wood or glass, why a stone building has different structural needs than one made of poured concrete—you will have a richer appreciation of the artist's expression.

Vincent van Gogh

1853–1890

The appeal of Van Gogh for today's art lovers is easy to understand. A painfully disturbed, tormented man who, in spite of his great anguish, managed to create extraordinary art. An intensely private, introspective man who wrote eloquently about art and about life. An erratic, impulsive man who had the self-discipline to construct an enormous body of work in a career that lasted only a decade.

Vincent van Gogh was born in the town of Groot-Zundert, in Holland, the son of a Dutch Protestant minister. His early life was spent in a variety of roles, including those of theological student and lay preacher among the miners of the region. Not until the age of twenty-seven did he begin to take a serious interest in art, and then he had but ten years to live. In 1886 he went to stay in Paris with his brother Theo, an art dealer who was always his closest emotional connection. In Paris Vincent became aware of the new art movements and incorporated aspects of them into his own style, especially by introducing light, brilliant colors into his palette.

Two years later Van Gogh left Paris for the southern provincial city of Arles. There he was joined briefly by the painter Paul Gauguin, with whom Van Gogh hoped to work very closely, creating perfect art in a pure atmosphere of self-expression. However, the two artists quarreled, and, apparently in the aftermath of one intense argument, Van Gogh cut off a portion of his ear and had it delivered to a prostitute. Soon after, Van Gogh realized that his instability had gotten out of hand, and he committed himself to an asylum, where—true to form—he continued to work prolifically at his painting. Most of the work we admire so much was done in the last two and a half years. Vincent (as he always signed himself) received much sympathetic encouragement during those years, both from his brother and from an unusually perceptive doctor and art connoisseur, Dr. Gachet, whom he painted several times. Nevertheless, his despair deepened, and in July of 1890 he shot himself to death.

Vincent's letters to his brother Theo represent a unique document in the history of art. They reveal a sensitive, intelligent artist pouring out his thoughts to one especially capable of understanding. In 1883, while still in Holland, he wrote to Theo: "In my opinion, I am

often *rich as Croesus*, not in money, but (though it doesn't happen every day) rich, because I have found in my work something to which I can devote myself heart and soul, and which gives inspiration and significance to life. Of course my moods vary, but there is an average of serenity. I have a sure *faith* in art, a sure confidence that it is a powerful stream, which bears a man to harbour, though he himself must do his bit too; and at all events I think it such a great blessing, when a man has found his work, that I cannot count myself among the unfortunate. I mean, I may be in certain relatively great difficulties, and there may be gloomy days in my life, but I shouldn't want to be counted among the unfortunate nor would it be correct."[5]

Vincent van Gogh. *Self-Portrait.* 1889. Oil on canvas, $25\frac{1}{2} \times 21\frac{1}{2}''$. Musée d'Orsay, Paris.

An artist may create a specific work for any of a thousand reasons, and awareness of the *why* can also give the viewer greater understanding. We show here a late work by the American artist Charles Willson Peale (**22**). Peale was born in the colony of Maryland in 1741 and saw active service in the Revolutionary War. He is best known, perhaps, for his many portraits of George Washington, but they represent only a small portion of his achievement. Few other individuals typify so well the ambition of a new nation.

Charles Willson Peale was passionately devoted to the pursuit of art and its development in the new country. (He named several of his seventeen children, including Titian, Raphaelle, and Rembrandt, after artists; we saw Rembrandt Peale's fine portrait of Thomas Jefferson earlier in this chapter.) Beyond this, he was a talented inventor, a scientist, and an organizer of the first museum in the United States. *The Artist in His Museum*, painted when Peale was eighty-one, was done for a specific purpose. It is a kind of summing up of his lifetime achievements. He lifts the curtain on his museum and, with quiet pride, invites the viewer to share his pleasure. In the foreground are symbols of his various careers—his artist's palette, the tools of the taxidermist, the bones of a mastodon, which he excavated. Beyond the curtain, in the museum, are stuffed animals and portraits by the artist and his sons. Peale might be saying, "Here are the fruits of my life, and they are good."

The historical place of a work of art—*what went before and came after*—can be most interesting. Artists borrow and learn from each other all the time. The myth of the lonely artist—starving in a garret, isolated from human contact, leaving behind a mass of brilliant work that no one had suspected—is mostly that, a myth. There have been a few such cases, but not many. On the whole, artists study each other's work carefully, adapt ideas to serve their own needs, and then bequeath those ideas to future generations of artists. The more you know about this living current of artistic energy, the more interesting will be any specific work of art.

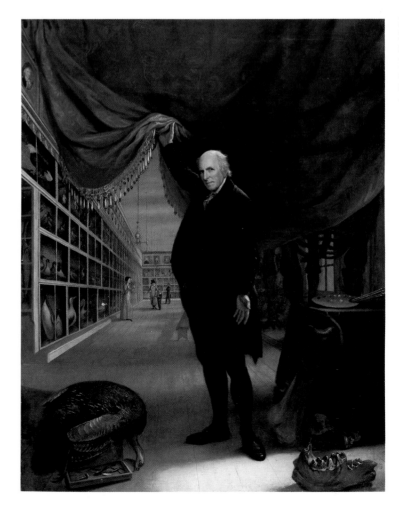

22. Charles Willson Peale.
The Artist in His Museum, 1822.
Oil on canvas, 8'7¾" × 6'7⅞".
Pennsylvania Academy
of the Fine Arts, Philadelphia
(gift of Mrs. Sarah Harrison;
the Joseph Harrison, Jr., Collection).

21

above left: 23. Henri de Toulouse-Lautrec. *L'Estampe originale,* cover. 1893. Color lithograph, 17¾ × 23¾".
The Metropolitan Museum of Art, New York (Rogers Fund, 1922).

above right: 24. Chobunsai Eishi. *Komurasaki of Kodatoma-ya,* from the series *Greenhouse Beauties as the Six Poets.* c. 1795. Woodcut, 15¼ × 10¼".
Art Institute of Chicago (Clarence Buckingham Collection).

left: 25. David Hockney. *Celia.* 1973. Lithograph, 42½ × 28½".
© David Hockney/Gemini G.E.L., 1973.

The three pieces illustrated here **(23,24,25)** have two things in common: each is a picture of an elegant woman, and each is a *print*—a work designed for multiple reproduction (Chapter 8). But far more than that connects them to the artistic chain letter of seeing, adapting, and passing along.

The first print **(23)** is by the French artist Henri de Toulouse-Lautrec. Lautrec was an unexcelled master of the color lithographic poster for advertising. The illustration shown here is essentially a print about a print. It shows the entertainer Jane Avril, a close friend of the artist's, examining a freshly printed proof of a poster advertising her performance at the Moulin Rouge. In this lithograph Lautrec reveals his debt to Japanese art. In 1853 Commodore Matthew Perry, an American naval officer, had sailed with his fleet into Tokyo Bay and thereby "opened" Japan to the West, ending two centuries of that country's isolation from the rest of the world.

Soon afterward Japanese prints **(24)** began to flow into Europe, and artists studied them avidly. Lautrec took from them the ideas that were most useful for his own vision, especially the large flat areas of color and the elegant, flowing silhouette lines. If you compare *L'Estampe originale* with the Japanese print made a century earlier, you will see that both have a sharply drawn, curving outline around the rather flat figure.

And a century *after* Lautrec these influences—explored by him and by other artists of his time—have made their way into contemporary art **(25)**.

Henri de Toulouse-Lautrec

1864–1901

Henri Marie Raymond de Toulouse-Lautrec Monfa was born at Albi, in the south of France, son of an aristocratic French family. From early childhood he showed talent for drawing and painting—a talent his family encouraged. The events that probably shaped the rest of his life and his career as an artist began at the age of thirteen, when he broke his left thigh in a fall. A year later he broke the other thigh. Although he recovered from the injuries, his legs never grew again. As an adult he stood just over 5 feet tall, with a fully developed body but shrunken legs, and he walked with difficulty and pain. In photographs, like the one here, he often stressed his odd appearance.

By the age of seventeen Lautrec had begun serious art studies in Paris. He had also gotten his first taste of Montmartre—the rather seedy part of the city where writers, painters, and students congregated; where the brothels were located; and where soon would open the famed cabaret, the Moulin Rouge. At that time he wrote to his grandmother, "I am against my will leading a truly Bohemian life and am finding it difficult to accustom myself to this milieu." Later, that milieu would be the only one in which he seemed to belong.

The artist gradually began to achieve modest success with his paintings. He also began to accumulate a circle of friends—other artists, writers, intellectuals, performers—who were attracted by his great wit and unflagging high spirits. In 1889 the Moulin Rouge opened and quickly became the focus of this social life, as well as of Lautrec's art. Singers and dancers, prostitutes and poets, the highborn and the lowborn who came to the Moulin Rouge—Lautrec drew them all, with a style and originality that captured the essence of Paris nightlife.

After two years of popularity the Moulin Rouge fell upon hard times, and its owner decided to regroup. He hired new talent, planned a grand reopening, and asked the all-but-resident artist to create a poster announcing the event. The poster Lautrec designed was unlike any Paris had ever seen—colorful, immediate, full of life, focusing on the image, not the printed words. Once again the Moulin Rouge was a sensation, and so were the artist and his poster.

In the years following his triumph as a graphic artist, Lautrec often had no regular home. He lived for

periods of time at one or another of the brothels, among the prostitutes. Some of the women were his lovers, many were his friends, and all were potential subjects, whom he painted with sympathy and warmth. His dissipated life notwithstanding, he continued to work prolifically. Little by little, however, he began to drink more and work less, until the situation became so grave his family placed him in a sanitarium. A brief recovery was followed by yet more drinking, and at last the illness took over. In September of 1901, two months short of his thirty-seventh birthday, Lautrec died at his family's estate.

Lautrec's art is above all an art of people and life. He explained this after a brief visit to the countryside, meant to improve his health: "Only the human figure exists; landscape is, and should be, no more than an accessory; the painter exclusively of landscape is nothing but a boor. The sole function of landscape is to heighten the intelligibility of the character of the figure."[6]

Maurice Guilbert. *Lautrec par lui-même.* 1890.
Photographic montage. Musée Toulouse-Lautrec, Albi, France.

David Hockney's *Celia*, done in 1973, shows the same rather flat figure, the same elegant, curving silhouette line. Hockney has adapted the style for his own needs, but he has also tapped into the vibrant artistic current that inspired those earlier works.

As an observer, you will find that familiarity with this artistic current contributes quite a lot to your appreciation of art. Combined with the "how" and the "why" it will move you closer to being an intelligent, informed observer. That is what this book is all about. It will give you a sample of the how, the why, and the when. With this knowledge you should have a much more active enjoyment of the art around you, the art you live with. And, in turn, you may find that you want to live much more actively with art.

There are great observers as well as great artists, each with his or her own special tendencies and interests. Whatever artists may say, their art is not done just for themselves. It is done for serious observers who, through education and experience, have made themselves sympathetic receivers of the messages of art. In the end, it is for these observers that artists create.

OBSERVATION AND CRITICISM

You may be thinking to yourself, it is all well and good to say, "Be an intelligent observer," but how does one get started? If we all live with art every day, is there not some way to enjoy the art right now before devoting months or years to studying art? Yes, of course there is. Even taking a little time and paying a little more attention can enhance one's appreciation of art.

When you walk into a museum, or into someone's home where art is displayed, or down a street where there is sculpture or a new building, try to approach the art as a unique visual experience. Give some time to thinking about it and trying to analyze it. To get you started, we list below six questions you might ask yourself when you encounter any new work of art. At the end of Chapter 5 you will find an expanded list of questions, a more detailed method of approaching art criticism.

1. Do I know where this work fits into the history of art? Does it remind me of any others I have seen, and in what way? Can I make any connection between this piece and others?
2. What do I know about the artist? Is there anything about his or her background that would influence my reaction to this work?
3. When and where was this work made? What else was going on in the world at the same time? What are the characteristics of the culture from which it emerges?
4. Does this work depict any particular subject—a story, a person, a place, or an event? If so, how is that subject treated?
5. What feelings, memories, or associations does this work evoke in me? Does it make me feel happy, angry, sad, frightened, disgusted, uplifted, inspired? Can I imagine the artist felt the same way? Do I feel any sense of kinship with the artist?
6. What is this work of art made of? Are the materials important to the type of expression and the overall effect of the work?

You probably will not be able to answer all these questions about every work of art you see, but at least the process will start you thinking. And after a bit of practice this six-step procedure—which sounds long in the telling—will become almost automatic. You will not have to think about it, because the questions will arise, and be answered, whenever you give serious attention to a new work of art.

Living with art—living with it actively and positively—does involve some effort, but the effort is worth it. Art stretches our intellectual horizons. It taps our emotions. It deepens our humanity and makes us less alone in the world. It makes us more alive.

ART PEOPLE *Gertrude Stein*

Practically no one ever has lived with art so wholeheartedly as Gertrude Stein. Students of literature remember her as a daringly experimental writer, most closely associated with the line: "Rose is a rose is a rose is a rose." But the influence of Gertrude Stein extends far beyond her literary efforts, for she was one of the most ardent collectors of art—and of artists—who ever lived.

Born in Allegheny, Pennsylvania, in 1874, Stein spent her childhood in Europe and in San Francisco. Both parents died when she was a teenager, and thereafter her intimate family would consist of her brother Leo, her oldest brother Michael, and Michael's wife, Sarah—all soon to be art collectors of great importance. Young Gertrude attended Radcliffe and then undertook medical studies at Johns Hopkins, but she never quite finished her medical degree.

In 1903 Gertrude took up residence with Leo at his new apartment in Paris. Their address—27, rue de Fleurus—was destined to become famous in the history of arts and letters. From their combined home and studio, Gertrude and Leo embarked on a fabulous career of buying innovative art. Their special pets were Pablo Picasso, Henri Matisse, and the Spanish artist Juan Gris, but they also invested in works by Cézanne, Renoir, and others. Perhaps more important, their home soon became a gathering place for the artists and art lovers of the time. Everybody who was anybody came to 27, rue de Fleurus. The Saturday night "at-homes" brought out painters, sculptors, composers, writers, poets, dealers, critics, and all those who wished to meet the foregoing. Picasso and Matisse often came to dine. In later years Gertrude Stein welcomed the American writers Ernest Hemingway and F. Scott Fitzgerald.

Among those who came to the rue de Fleurus was an American named Alice B. Toklas, and, as it turned out, she had come to stay. By 1910 Alice Toklas had moved into the apartment, serving Gertrude Stein as secretary, household manager, and all-purpose useful helpmeet. The two women became inseparable and remained lifelong companions. Some four years later Leo Stein moved out of rue de Fleurus, taking half the

art collection with him. The close relationship between brother and sister was over.

World War I brought new adventures to Gertrude Stein. France had gone to war, and so did Miss Stein and Miss Toklas. In a ragtag Ford van nicknamed "Auntie," they traveled all over the countryside delivering supplies in behalf of the American Fund for French Wounded. Stein drove the car. Toklas navigated and handled all necessary paperwork. After the war, most of the women's efforts were directed toward getting Gertrude Stein's writings published—no easy feat, considering their individual and often maddeningly repetitive style. Actually, Stein's only commercial literary success was *The Autobiography of Alice B. Toklas*, which was in fact Gertrude Stein's own autobiography.

When Gertrude Stein died of cancer in 1946, she left her art collection to Alice Toklas, who lived on, with the paintings and her memories, until 1967. The two women are buried together in Paris. After Miss Toklas' death, the Stein family regained control of the collection and sold it for many millions of dollars.

Gertrude Stein (**right**) with Alice B. Toklas in the studio at 27, rue de Fleurus, Paris, 1922, photographed by Man Ray.

Chapter Two

What Is Art?

U ntil about a hundred years ago almost no one would have thought to ask the question "What is art?" People who considered art at all assumed they knew what it was. In the 20th century, however, the problem of definition, of deciding what is and what is not art, has become far more complex, and this is true for several reasons.

For one thing, people today are exposed to art from many different times and places—an available body of art far more varied than at any other period in history. If you walk into a large museum, you will see on display works of art from literally all over the world, and covering a time span of some 15,000 years. Magazines, newspapers, and television also bring us into contact with different types of art. Each work of art we see is the product of its own culture, with its own prevailing standards of taste. Each represents what the person who made the work—and those for whom it was made—considered to be art.

The citizen of ancient Athens might have said that art is a sculpture, perhaps depicting a goddess, modeled to look very much like a living woman, yet taller and more beautiful than life (26). The tribal member from the Baluba area in Africa might have said that art is a wood figurine, stylized and exaggerated in its features, that symbolizes the human figure (27). Each of these works met the standards of acceptable art for its audience, yet we cannot apply the same standard to both. We cannot even be sure that all the objects now housed in our art museums—the Baluba figurine, for example—were considered by their makers to be art in the sense that we mean it.

Before our age of easy worldwide communication, the art produced by any specific culture tended to be relatively homogeneous—much the same in style and expression. Of course, there always has been cross-fertilization of styles among cultures, and styles have changed over the years, but generally we can point to a pattern. We can say, "These are the general characteristics of 4th-century B.C. Greek art" (or Italian Renaissance art or Song dynasty Chinese art), and then proceed to list them. Now, not only are we confronted with art from many different cultures, but the art of our own time defies such classification. If you were to tour the art galleries in any major city today, and look at all the different works on display, you would be hard-pressed to formulate a definition of art suitable for all of them. How, for example, do we categorize a work that consists of the artist and another figure, spray-painted in black and hung (literally, by harness and hook) from a "canvas" of simulated drapery (28)? This "painting" can move, shake hands with onlookers, even react to its own shenanigans.

To further complicate the problem, we now have works of art created in media undreamed of a mere thirty or forty years ago. Electronic images of all kinds are made and accepted as art. Often there is no concrete "object," nothing you could hang on the wall or place on a pedestal. Some types of contemporary art are preserved only in the memory banks of computers, and some disappear forever within minutes or hours after they are created. Little wonder, then, that in our century, for the first time, we need to stand back and ask, "What exactly *is* art? How can we tell what is and what isn't?"

This book will not give the definitive answer to either question, about any particular work or about art in general. What it will do, however, is present some guidelines that will help individual viewers to make up their own minds. It will show what some people have considered to be art in different times and places, and what some people consider to be art now. With this information, the viewer should be able to make a better judgment about "What is art *for me*?"

Art and the Eye of the Beholder

There are any number of diagnostic tests we could apply to the question "What is art?" None of them is infallible, but all raise interesting issues about the nature of art and its place in society. This section considers three of the possible areas we might explore in evaluating a particular work: What do observers think about it? Who made it? Why was it made?

above: 26. *Aphrodite of the Cnidians.* Roman copy after an original of c. 330 B.C. by Praxiteles. Marble, height 6'8".
Vatican Museums, Rome.

right: 27. *Kneeling Woman Presenting a Bowl,* from Luba, Zaire. Wood, height 17⅞".
Royal Museum of Central Africa, Tervuren, Belgium.

below: 28. Stephen Taylor Woodrow. *The Living Paintings.* The artist, spray-painted and hung on a simulated backdrop. Installation view at the New Museum of Contemporary Art, New York, February 1988.

29. Richard Serra. *Tilted Arc.*
1981. Corten steel,
12′ × 120′ × 2½″.
Installed at Federal Plaza,
New York;
removed March 15, 1989.

ART AND THE AUDIENCE

THE PUBLIC PERCEPTION Rarely has the question "What is art?" caused such a public uproar as in a controversy that erupted in New York City in the early 1980s. At the center of the drama was a sculpture by Richard Serra, entitled *Tilted Arc* **(29)**, a 12-foot-high, 120-foot-long steel wall installed in a plaza fronting a government building in lower Manhattan.

Commissioned by the Art-in-Architecture division of the General Services Administration, *Tilted Arc* was part of a program that allocates 0.5 percent of the cost of federal buildings to the purchase and installation of public art. Soon after the sculpture's installation, however, the public for whom it was intended spoke out, and their message was a resounding, "*That's* not art!" More than 7,000 workers in surrounding buildings signed petitions demanding the sculpture's removal. Opponents of the work had numerous complaints. *Tilted Arc*, they maintained, was ugly, rusty, and a target for graffiti. It blocked the view. It disrupted pedestrian traffic, since one had to walk all the way around it rather than straight across the plaza. It ruined the plaza for concerts and outdoor ceremonies. At a public hearing, one man summed up the opposition view: "I am here today to recommend its relocation to a better site—a metal salvage yard."[1]

Artists, dealers, and critics rushed to the sculpture's defense. The sculptor himself argued vehemently against any attempt to move *Tilted Arc*, maintaining that it had been commissioned specifically for that site and any new location would destroy its artistic integrity. Even former Senator Jacob K. Javits, for whom the building in question had been named, wrote eloquently in support of *Tilted Arc*. He said:

> Art requires freedom for the artist to make his statement about the life and time in which the artist lives. It is an expression of the deepest values of our society. The purpose of the program as I understood it when I voted as a member of the United States Senate to authorize it, was essentially to express the commitment of our country to artistic expression as a vital element of our culture.[2]

The battle raged for many months, and, while there were dissenting voices from all sides, it shaped up principally as a struggle between the art establishment (pro) and the general public (con). Finally, in an unusual editorial, *The New York Times*—a newspaper that heavily supports the arts—took a stand. "One cannot choose to see or ignore 'Tilted Arc,' as if it were in a museum or a less conspicuous public place. To the complaining workers in Federal Plaza, it is, quite simply, unavoidable. . . . The public has to live with 'Tilted Arc'; therefore the public has a right to say no, not here."[3] This time the public won. *Tilted Arc* was dismantled and removed in March of 1989.

So the question "What is art?" has, in at least one case, been answered by a kind of public referendum, a majority decision. This does not mean that *Tilted Arc* is not art, nor that it is inferior art. Majority decisions are not infallible. As we shall see throughout this book, some of the finest masterpieces in the history of art were initially scorned by the public.

CENSORSHIP The Serra controversy had barely abated when another took its place—a controversy provoking far more heated debate and with far more wide-ranging implications. In this instance the question became not "Is it art or junk?" but rather, "Is it art or pornography?" The issues involved include public support of the arts, freedom of expression, sexually explicit subject matter, and, above all, censorship. These issues will no doubt henceforth be linked with the name Robert Mapplethorpe.

Mapplethorpe was a photographer known primarily for his portraits, among them numerous self-portraits **(30)**; for his still lifes, often of flowers **(31)**; and for his nude figure studies. His style emphasizes elegance of composition and dramatic contrasts of light and dark (p. 232). Starting in 1976, with his first exhibition, Mapplethorpe gained considerable fame, but that fame acquired a troublesome edge when the public at large became aware of his "X Portfolio." For the "X Portfolio" contains images of sadomasochism and homoeroticism, images so frank as to be profoundly disturbing to many (even most) viewers.

Mapplethorpe died of AIDS in the spring of 1989. Soon after, an exhibition of his work was organized, including several examples from the "X Portfolio." The show was planned to tour the United States. Here the saga

left: **30.** Robert Mapplethorpe. *Self-Portrait.* 1988. Photograph. Copyright © 1988 The Estate of Robert Mapplethorpe.

right: **31.** Robert Mapplethorpe. *Orchid, 1987.* 1987. Photograph. Copyright © 1987 The Estate of Robert Mapplethorpe.

begins, and it probably will be discussed and debated in art circles for many years to come.

The Mapplethorpe show was scheduled to open at Washington's Corcoran Gallery of Art, a public museum, in the summer of 1989. Before the opening, however, it came to the attention of Senator Jesse Helms, Republican of North Carolina, who denounced the photographs as obscene. Senator Helms' chief objection was that part of the funding for the exhibition had come from the National Endowment for the Arts—in other words, from American taxpayers. His attempt to persuade Congress to prohibit funding for work he considered obscene caused a furor, with intense argument on both sides. In the heat of this controversy, the Corcoran canceled, but the show later opened at Washington's Project for the Arts.

After Washington, the Mapplethorpe show moved to Hartford, Connecticut, and Berkeley, California; in both places it ran without major incident or protest. Next on the itinerary, however, was a city well known for its strict opposition to pornography: Cincinnati. And in Cincinnati the controversy became an uproar. No longer was the issue merely public funding. Now it became: Should these photographs be shown at all?

On opening day in Cincinnati, police closed the Contemporary Arts Center while they videotaped the exhibition for evidence. Then the exhibition was reopened, and it played to huge crowds for the duration of its stay. But a grand jury indicted both the gallery and its director on obscenity charges. If convicted, the gallery's director could serve up to a year in jail.

Before discussing the outcome of the trial, it might be well to pause and consider some of the issues involved. Is the Mapplethorpe case really a matter of censorship, and what, in fact, is censorship?

For our purposes here, we will define **censorship** as the supervision by one individual or group over the artistic expression of another individual or group. This definition assumes that person or group A has the power to *control* the expression of person or group B. Usually, the power is exerted for political, religious, or moral reasons. In other words, A can prevent B from making or showing work that conflicts with A's political, religious, or moral point of view.

We expect to find censorship in totalitarian societies, and we are seldom disappointed. Absolute rule survives only *because* it is absolute, so it cannot tolerate other points of view. But in the United States today censorship for political reasons is far less an issue than censorship concerning religious or moral standards. We have a pluralistic society, representing many religions, many moral points of view. People of goodwill and thoughtful convictions disagree about what is "right" or "wrong," what should be allowed or not allowed. One of the most explosive areas of disagreement concerns the issue of free expression, specifically as it pertains to the arts. Should artists, writers, and performers be allowed to express whatever they wish? Or should there be limits on that expression to control material that large segments of society consider morally wrong?

Proponents of free expression cite the First Amendment to the Constitution, which states in part: "Congress shall make no law . . . abridging the freedom of speech." Yet that amendment does *not* give you the right to say anything you please. You cannot, for example, deliberately tell a lie about another person, either verbally (slander) or in print (libel), because the other person could sue you. In a classic example from the early part of this century, Supreme Court Justice Oliver Wendell Holmes, Jr., said, "No one has a right falsely to shout 'fire' in a crowded theatre." So freedom of speech is *not* absolute, it has limits. Moreover, the Supreme Court historically has held that it is permissible to ban obscene speech, obscene writing, obscene imagery. The problem lies in deciding just *what* is obscene.

As of this writing the Supreme Court standard for obscenity comes from a 1973 case called *Miller v. California*, which held that something is obscene if the "average person applying contemporary community standards" would find it so, and if "the work taken as a whole lacks serious literary, artistic, political or scientific value." Obviously, this judgment raises more questions than it answers. Who is the average person? Which community? Who decides whether the artistic value is serious?

Further complicating the problem is the issue of public funding for the arts. Many people feel that taxpayers' money should not be used to support the arts at all. Others think the government should finance the arts, but not "obscene" art—whatever that is. Those who oppose limits on spending fear that such limits would lead to a situation like the one that has existed in totalitarian societies, where government controls the arts rigidly.

In our system we pay our taxes and allow our elected representatives to decide how the money should be spent. And in 1965 Congress passed the National Foundation on the Arts and Humanities Act, whose declaration of purpose includes this statement: "It is necessary and appropriate for the Federal Government to help create and sustain not only a climate encouraging freedom of thought, imagination and inquiry, but also the material conditions facilitating the release of this creative talent."

Again as of this writing, funding for the National Endowment for the Arts will continue, but the question of funding for "obscene" art—and the method of determining what is "obscene"—remains vague. Of course, there will *never* be absolute answers to any of these questions, answers acceptable to everyone. Readers of this book must make up their own minds, as the courts continue to grapple with these complex issues. And that brings us back to the Mapplethorpe case.

Six months after the Cincinnati gallery and its director were indicted on obscenity charges, a jury of local citizens found them not guilty. The jurors were not art experts; most of them had never been in an art museum, knew nothing about art and cared little about it. Yet they were willing to be guided by the opinions of people who were presented to them as experts, art professionals brought in by the defense. As one juror said afterward, "We had to go with what we were told. It's like Picasso. Picasso from what everybody tells me was an artist. It's not my cup of tea. I don't understand it. But if people say it's art, then I have to go along with it."

Another juror explained his decision this way: "We thought the pictures were lewd, grotesque, disgusting. But like the defense said, art doesn't have to be beautiful or pretty."[4]

The Mapplethorpe jurors were "average persons" who, even when applying the standards of a rather conservative "community," found that the works in question *did* have "serious artistic value." That was the resolution of one case, but there will be many cases, and the question of censorship can never have a definite answer.

ART AND THE ARTIST

It is tempting to speculate whether *Tilted Arc* or the Mapplethorpe pictures would have attracted such a storm of criticism if the name "Michelangelo" or "Picasso" had been attached to them. Michelangelo's frescoes in the Vatican have, in other generations, been described as lewd, but they are admired by millions of tourists each year. A huge Picasso sculpture installed outside Chicago's Civic Center in 1967 caused almost as much commotion as the Serra, but it is still there. By now, Michelangelo and Picasso are accepted as Great Artists, and the general public will give them any benefit of the doubt. Serra and Mapplethorpe, though known in art circles, were not familiar to the general public until their scandals broke out. Whether for good or ill, the verdict on "Is this art?" has much to do with another question: Who made it?

In the summer of 1954 artist Willem de Kooning (48) took the three toilet seats from an outhouse on a summer property he was renting and painted the seats in a "marbleized" effect. Apparently, the painting was meant as a joke—whipped off in a few minutes before a croquet party with friends **(32)**. The artist then forgot about it, and so did everyone else. Some thirty years later the summer house was to be sold and the contents dispersed at auction. The auctioneer sensed a good thing and arranged to have the toilet-seat painting authenticated by Elaine de Kooning, Willem de Kooning's wife. The auctioneer therefore had in his possession a certified Willem de Kooning painting, and de Kooning paintings sell for millions of dollars. The toilet seats were exhibited and offered for sale. But wait a minute. Is a row of toilet seats, painted just for fun, a work of art because a master artist painted them? Some people think so. Others are outraged.

To consider the opposite extreme, is a work *not* great art because a master artist *didn't* paint it? For generations a painting called *The Polish Rider* **(33)** was thought to be a work by Rembrandt and was considered one of the jewels of the Frick Collection, a distinguished small museum in New York City. But now Rembrandt's authorship of this painting—and of numerous other paintings—is in question.

left: 32. Three toilet seats from an outhouse, said to have been painted by Willem de Kooning in 1954.

below: 33. Rembrandt (?). *The Polish Rider.* c. 1655. Oil on canvas, 3'10" × 4'5⅛". Copyright The Frick Collection, New York.

ARTISTS ON ARTISTS *Rivers on Rembrandt*

Throughout history artists have been fascinated by the work of their predecessors. Many artists learn their craft by copying others' creations, but some take the process one step further and *adapt* a favorite work, placing their own imaginative stamp on the forms of an artist they admire.

Contemporary painter Larry Rivers has long been interested in Dutch art and particularly Rembrandt (if it *is* Rembrandt). His own version of *The Polish Rider* is called *Rainbow Rembrandt* for obvious reasons. Rivers has overlaid a sunburst of bright colors on the familiar depiction of a young man on horseback, thus turning the proud 17th-century warrior into a 20th-century pop hero.

Rivers' rendering of the original painting is quite faithful, but a close look shows us some differences. The drawing of the horse is smoother, not so lifelike, so the animal becomes almost a carrousel horse. (This is particularly apparent in the hooves.) The looming background recedes, as our hero rides forth bathed in a multicolor spotlight—an actor at center stage. *Rainbow Rembrandt* is both a tribute to the old master and a clever stroke by the new one.

Larry Rivers. *Rainbow Rembrandt I*. 1977.
Acrylic on canvas, 5'6" × 6'4". Hirshhorn Museum and Sculpture Garden, Smithsonian Institution, Washington, D.C.
(the Joseph H. Hirshhorn Bequest, 1981).

Over the years various experts have tried to determine how many genuine Rembrandts there are in the world. Estimates have ranged from a high of 614 to a low of 48. Since 1982 a group of five scholars known collectively as the Rembrandt Research Project, based in Amsterdam, have been at work trying to find a definitive answer. Using modern scientific methods, considering such subtleties as brushwork, use of colors, and handling of anatomical forms, the R.R.P. studies each painting thought to be by Rembrandt and presents its conclusion. And for many a museum and private collector the news has been bad: The R.R.P. has "deattributed" their prized Rembrandts. As of this writing the Frick Collection awaits a verdict about *The Polish Rider*, but—gossip in the art world being active—their painting seems to be on the R.R.P.'s "hit list." (Some art historians refer to them as the "Amsterdam Mafia.") When the project is done, it will probably certify about three hundred Rembrandts.

Among the deattributed paintings, there is no question of forgery or attempt to deceive. With older paintings it is simply difficult to know for sure who painted them and when. A pupil of Rembrandt's, Willem Drost, is now thought a likely candidate as artist of *The Polish Rider*. Whatever the truth, the effect of deattribution is dramatic. Another Rembrandt work, which came up for auction in 1988, was expected to bring ten million dollars. After the R.R.P. turned its thumbs down, the painting was sold for $800,000—or 8 percent of its previous value.[5]

Through all this questioning, we must remember, *the paintings remain the same.* No matter who painted *The Polish Rider*, it is a splendid, masterful picture. Yet crowds of tourists, who once would have elbowed each other to get a glimpse of it, will now pass it by, looking for the "real" Rembrandts. The student and lover of art should consider seriously how much impact the authorship of a work has to do with one's appreciation of that work.

Another element we might take into account is the artist's intent. Willem de Kooning, by all reports, had no intention of making art with his toilet seats. He was just having a good time on a summer afternoon. But the artist of *The Polish Rider* clearly meant to paint a wonderful picture, took great pains to do so, and succeeded. Is this factor—the artist's intent and effort—a criterion for deciding what is art?

ART AND INTENTION

In many parts of the United States today you will encounter the phenomenon known as "motel art." This will be a large inventory of original oil paintings, turned out by assembly-line methods and sold on weekends at bargain prices in suburban motels—hence the name. You may also hear this work called "sofa art," because the most popular item is the 2-by-3-foot painting considered "correct" for hanging over a sofa. As a potential buyer you are encouraged to bring your wallpaper samples, your upholstery swatches, your paint chips when shopping. This will ensure that the painting you select "goes with" your décor. If you like the painting of the flowers but its colors clash with your sofa, chances are you can find the same flowers in a different range of hues. Your sofa is unusually small or large? No problem. That same bowl of flowers comes in various sizes, like shirts or shoes.

The people who paint these pictures do so on commission from an entrepreneur, who often tells them what to paint and which colors to use. When they gear up, they turn out thirty or forty paintings in a week. Of one such sale *The New York Times* reported: "Most of the paintings on display . . . were landscapes and seascapes with little detail. While each was an original, many were markedly similar, some virtually identical." The *Times* quoted one dealer as saying his artists "prefer doing landscapes, probably because if you make a mistake on a landscape, who can tell?" Moreover, "after a while [the artists] can do them in their sleep—with their eyes shut."[6]

Are these people making art? Certainly it is billed as art by the sellers, and many buyers would agree. A buyer might say, "I like it because it looks nice on my wall and makes me happy. *For me*, this is art." We should not disparage this point of view. What is art for one person may not be art for somebody else, and that is exactly the problem we are addressing in this chapter.

Other critics might insist that the "motel artists" are not making art but are making *money*—and by a far safer system than printing up counterfeit bills in the basement. People on this side of the argument are disturbed by the concept of paintings that their makers can turn out "in their sleep."

The issues raised by motel art are those of motivation and satisfaction. What motivates the artist to make art? If money is the *primary* motive, can the result be art? If money is a *secondary* motive and the artist's expression comes first, is the product "more" art? Also, who is supposed to be satisfied by the art—the commissioner, the buyer, the artist, or all three? Again, there are no absolute answers to these questions. They raise issues for consideration and debate, and the answers each of us decides upon will help to clarify our own opinions about what is art.

We might compare the factory approach of motel art to a statement by the sculptor Reuben Nakian: "In art you have to shoot your grandmother. You can't compromise. I'll compromise in life. I'll clown, I'll get drunk. But not in art, which is a life-and-death matter. If it isn't 100 percent right, zing, I'll smash it."[7]

When Nakian said, "You have to shoot your grandmother," he meant that the artist is searching for an ultimate truth, an ultimate perfection, an ultimate confrontation with the self and the art. Nothing short of this will do. By this definition, a work that is tossed off quickly to please someone else's specifications—the entrepreneur or the potential buyer—cannot possibly be considered art. Others will judge the merits of the work, but the first and most demanding judge is the artist.

This does not mean that art commissioned by someone else is necessarily inferior to art originated by the artist. As we saw in Chapter 1, artworks have always been commissioned, and throughout history there have been patrons with strong ideas about what they wanted. The ceiling of the Sistine Chapel in the Vatican—undoubtedly one of the best-known works of art in the Western world—was painted by Michelangelo on commission from Pope Julius II **(34)**. What's more, Michelangelo undertook the project with great reluctance. Despite these facts, the ceiling of the Sistine Chapel is not, to say the very least, in any way comparable to "sofa art." Michelangelo spent four years of arduous labor on the ceiling paintings, and many art historians consider it miraculous that he finished them in that time. Throughout his career the artist set for himself almost inhumanly high standards. (One of his sculpture commission contracts specified that he would carve the most beautiful statue ever made.) The original idea for the Sistine ceiling might have come from Julius, but the conception and execution were all Michelangelo's—at the height of his artistic powers. Figuratively speaking, Michelangelo "shot his grandmother," and in so doing produced one of the artistic masterpieces of all time. The artist satisfied his patron only after he had satisfied himself.

But what of the viewer? What does it take to satisfy the viewer and to convince him or her that a certain piece is art and is good art? Most people

34. Michelangelo. *Creation of Adam*, detail of Sistine Chapel ceiling. 1511. Fresco. Vatican, Rome.

bring to art a set of aesthetic *values*, a collection of likes and dislikes that predispose their judgments about what art should be. Usually, these values are instilled during childhood. One person, fond of graphic detail, likes the painting that shows every blade of grass; another admires all paintings that have a lot of blue in them, because blue is a favorite color; and so on.

To study art on a more formal basis, however, you should try to suspend these value judgments for a little while. If you set aside preconceived ideas about art and open your awareness to other possibilities, you may find that your own area of "likes" has broadened considerably. At the very least you will have a sounder basis for your value system. As a first step toward a heightened appreciation of art, let us look at two of the most common preconceptions about art and see if they hold up.

Art and Beauty

Many people take for granted that all art should be beautiful. They think of art as something to ornament one's home, like "sofa art." This line of thinking may cause trouble if you visit a museum exhibit, especially an exhibit of 20th-century art. You are almost certain to find a few things that you consider plain ugly. Why are they there?

We may as well face the question squarely, since it is basic to our whole attitude toward art. Why are there so many "ugly" works of art? There are several possible answers. We might reply that "beauty is in the eye of the beholder." In other words, beauty is subjective, and your personal taste leads you to reject things that might be beautiful to others. Both "beautiful" and "ugly" imply aesthetic value judgments.

Another possibility is that the ugly works of art are failures, which were hung because the museum director didn't look at them carefully or because the artist had a famous name. You might even imagine that you are the victim of a great plot designed to make a fool of you by showing you ugly things as if they were art. All these possibilities depend on the assumption that the artist's proper aim is the creation of beauty.

But there is another possibility. Perhaps the works are successes by artists who were sincerely aiming at something *other than* conventional, physical beauty.

The issue of conventional beauty almost cannot help but come up when we view a painting like Quintin Massys' *Grotesque Old Woman* (35). Even the title challenges our notions about art and beauty with the word "grotesque." Why would an artist paint a subject so ugly, and why would viewers want to look at it? To get an interesting perspective on this problem, we might consider the opinions of people who live with art all day long. For a 1988 feature article in *Art & Antiques* magazine, writer Catherine Barnett interviewed the guards at several large museums—those whose job it is to protect the art. Here is what two different guards at the National Gallery in London had to say about the Massys painting:

MARGARET: Generally I prefer portraits, but I can't say anything too nice about this one, Quintin Massys's *Grotesque Old Woman*. Visitors walk by and they just say how horrible she is, and I'm inclined to agree. She must be the result of the artist's nightmarish fantasy. . . . It's a bit unnerving. When you dislike a portrait, you feel its eyes on you.

MARIE: When I'm sick I miss the paintings here, especially the *Grotesque Old Woman*. She's one of my favorites and I love her very much. She's very sympathetic. She's got beautiful eyes. Have you ever noticed her eyes? And her hands are lovely. The visitors are always ridiculing her, and that hurts me.[8]

So there we have the opinions of two "experts," who see Massys' work every day. Notice that even Margaret, who doesn't like the portrait, refers to it as "she" and feels the power of the eyes. Neither of the guards is indifferent; both feel some strong connection to the painting. Whether for good or ill, the work evokes a response.

We do not mean to imply that art should *not* be beautiful in the more conventional sense. Many artists aim at creating this kind of beauty. If that is their goal, then we measure their success according to how well they achieve it. The important point for the student of art to learn from the *Grotesque Old Woman* is that art can be many things, and "beautiful" is only one of them.

The observer of art should be open to the widest possible range of experience. Art that momentarily pleases the eye offers only one level of experience. Art that touches the intellect and the emotions ultimately brings far greater satisfaction.

Art and the "Real" World

Just as many people expect all art to be beautiful, many people expect all art to mimic the real world, to duplicate as closely as possible the appearance of nature. This is another preconception we might examine. If duplicating the natural world is the *only* thing art is supposed to do, why should artists bother? We already have the natural world, so why make another? No one expects this kind of fidelity from the other arts. If, for instance, all works of literature were restricted to a faithful duplication of the real world, there could not be any novels or poems or fairy tales. There probably never was any real Cinderella or Anna Karenina or Tom Sawyer, and if there actually was a King Arthur we're not sure what he did in his life. The great works of literature are not real, they are made-up stories. It has been said that in fictional literature you "have to tell a lie to tell the truth." In other words, a made-up story can touch basic truths more vividly than can a strict recitation of facts. In a sense, this is what artists are doing: looking for a basic truth that is more "real" than the everyday world we perceive with our eyes.

Have you ever heard someone say, "That guy's a terrible artist. He can't even draw!" There is a strong feeling among much of the public that a "good" artist should be able to draw well—to make pictures of horses or dogs or people that look like the real thing. To be sure, some modern artists cannot draw lifelike images. But far more of them can—and choose not to. Picasso is a prime example of this situation. By anyone's standard, he was one of the greatest draftsmen who ever lived (36). Nevertheless, through most of his long career he produced works that did not look anything like the "real" world (37).

Picasso himself addressed this problem. He said: "They speak of naturalism in opposition to modern painting. I would like to know if anyone has ever seen a natural work of art. Nature and art, being two different things,

left: 36. Pablo Picasso. *Olga Picasso in an Armchair.* 1917. Oil on canvas, 4'3¼" × 2'10⅝". Musée Picasso, Paris.

right: 37. Pablo Picasso. *Dora Maar Sitting.* 1939. Oil on canvas, 28⅝" × 23½". Courtesy Perls Galleries, New York.

Pablo Picasso

1881–1973

The life of Picasso defies summary in a one-page biography. Few artists have lived so long; none have produced such an immense volume of work in so diverse a range of styles and media; and only a rare few can match him in richness and variety of personal history.

Pablo Ruiz y Picasso was born in the Spanish city of Málaga. He attended art schools in Barcelona and Madrid but became impatient with their rigid, academic approach and soon abandoned formal study. After two trips to Paris—where he saw the work of Van Gogh, Gauguin, and Lautrec—he settled permanently in that city in 1904 and never again lived outside France.

Although Picasso worked in many different styles throughout his life, much of his art is classifiable into the well-known "periods": the "Blue" period, when his paintings concentrated on images of poverty and emotional depression; the "Rose" period, whose paintings included depictions of harlequins and acrobats; the Cubist period, when he worked with the painter Georges Braque; and the "Neoclassical" period, in which the figures took on qualities resembling ancient Greek and Roman sculptures.

Success came early to Picasso. Except for brief periods when he was short of funds (usually because of some romantic entanglement), he lived well and comfortably, traveled widely, and enjoyed a large circle of friends. His work was always in demand, whether in painting, sculpture, prints (of which he made thousands), theatrical design, murals, or ceramics (he took up ceramic art in 1947 and decorated some two thousand pieces in a single year).

It would be impossible to discuss Picasso's life without reference to the women who shared it, because they are a constant presence in his art. Picasso married only twice, but he maintained long, occasionally overlapping, liaisons with several other women. His attachments included Fernande Olivier; Eva Gouel; Olga Koklova, his first wife and the mother of his son Paulo; Marie-Thérèse Walter, mother of his daughter Maïa; Dora Maar; Françoise Gilot, who bore him Claude and Paloma, then later wrote a scandalous memoir of her years with the artist; and finally Jacqueline Roque, whom he married in 1961, in his eightieth year.

Despite his international celebrity, Picasso gave almost no interviews. One of the few took place in 1935 and included this insight into the nature of art: "Everyone wants to understand art. Why not try to understand the song of a bird? Why does one love the night, flowers, everything around one, without trying to understand them? But in the case of a painting people have to understand. If only they would realize above all that an artist works of necessity, that he himself is only a trifling bit of the world, and that no more importance should be attached to him than to plenty of other things which please us in the world, though we can't explain them. People who try to explain pictures are usually barking up the wrong tree."[9]

Pablo Picasso. *Self-Portrait.* 1906.
Oil on canvas, $36\frac{1}{4} \times 28\frac{3}{4}''$.
Philadelphia Museum of Art (A. E. Gallatin Collection).

cannot be the same thing. Through art we express our conception of what nature is not."[10]

In looking at any work of art, we must always keep in mind that it *is* a work of art. A painting of a horse is not a horse, but daubs of pigment on a backing. A sculpture of a horse is not a horse, but a chunk of metal or wood or stone. The way these works should look is dictated by the artist's aesthetic sense, not by biological laws. Artists are looking for the "lie that tells the truth," for something "realer than real."

Only in Western culture has it been supposed that art should always duplicate the natural world and, at that, only during certain periods of Western culture. We owe this idea to the ancient Greeks and Romans. Plato put forth the notion in *The Republic*, written in Athens in the 4th century B.C. He believed that the aim of painters is to create imitations of objects they see before them, as a mirror reflects the appearance of its surroundings. Even the ancient Greeks, however, were capable of attempting something "realer than real." The Greek statue at the beginning of this chapter **(26)** looks like a human being, but probably not like any human being you know. Plato to the contrary, the Greek sculptor was more interested in the *ideal* than the real. The statue is a little taller than a person, a little more perfectly proportioned, a little more beautiful than nature usually manages to be.

We tend to think that this goal of imitating the natural world carried through from the Greeks to almost our own time, when 20th-century artists broke abruptly with tradition. However, this isn't really true. From the beginning of the Christian era in Europe until the 14th century, naturalism in art was not so highly valued. Much of medieval art is decorative and abstracted, symbolic rather than naturalistic **(476)**. Should we assume that medieval artists "forgot" how to draw, were not as good at it as their ancient counterparts? Definitely not. The artists of the Middle Ages simply did not care all that much about creating a faithful imitation of the natural world. Their concerns were above all spiritual, so their eyes focused on the heavens, not the earth.

The Renaissance revived the idea of naturalism as a goal for art. This period began in Italy around 1400 and gradually spread to the rest of Europe. The word **renaissance** means "rebirth," and the rebirth in question was that of ancient cultures—specifically, the cultures of Classical Greece and Rome. Artistic leaders of the Renaissance took a good look at Classical art and said, in effect, "This is the best that art has ever been."

During the Renaissance the imitation of nature in art became not a goal but a passion. Treatises were written. Artists made all kinds of mathematical studies to better simulate "reality." In some cases this resulted in great masterpieces, such as Michelangelo's **(34)**. In others, it created works that are meticulously real—and also static and lifeless **(150)**. The trouble is, those of us who have inherited the Western tradition of art—people in North America and Europe—have gotten "stuck" at the Renaissance. Many of us look back to 16th-century Italy, to Michelangelo and Leonardo and their ilk, and say in turn, *"That* is the best that art has ever been—and let's keep it that way!" Such a point of view ignores most of the world's art and much of the living flow of history, culture, and style.

Outside the European tradition there was no similar progression away from naturalism and back again. The great artists of the Orient, of Africa, of pre-Columbian America generally had less interest in reproducing the real world. Like so many artists today, they were seeking something "realer than real." In the 15th century the Japanese artist Sesshu painted a study of *Daruma*, the first Zen Buddhist patriarch **(38)**. We may hope this is not what Daruma really looked like. The stark brushwork and the horribly staring eyes are meant to show Daruma's ardent devotion to the Buddha. (Legend tells us that Daruma, while meditating on the Buddha one day, accidentally fell asleep. To punish himself, he cut off his eyelids, so that his eyes could never again close on the Buddha.)

We might compare Sesshu's painting to a self-portrait by Picasso, done in 1901 (39). There is an extraordinary resemblance—not in the features, but in the effect. We know that Picasso did not actually look just like this. He did have unusually piercing black eyes, and here he has emphasized that feature. He has also made his face gaunt and almost corpselike. Perhaps we are seeing the intensity of passion in a young man absorbed in his art, just as Daruma was absorbed in his adoration of the Buddha. Both paintings have given us a reality beyond mere illusion.

If we demand realism, therefore, we deny ourselves the pleasure of enjoying a huge portion of the world's art. We would even dismiss a type of art that nearly everyone finds appealing—so-called naive art. Naive art, as the term implies, is made by people who are unsophisticated, lacking in formal art training, simple and fresh in their approach to art. They are not unlike the folk artists discussed in Chapter 1 (p. 7), except that they concentrate on paintings (sometimes sculptures). Best known of the naive artists was a man named Henri Rousseau, whose translation into paint of the "real" world was eccentric at best.

Rousseau worked in France during the late 19th and early 20th centuries. He was acquainted with all the up-and-coming artists of the Parisian scene, and sometimes he exhibited with them. In Rousseau's case, the naiveté of his expression came not so much from ignorance of formal art traditions as

left: **38.** Sesshu. *Daruma.*
Japan, Ashikaga Period,
15th century. Hanging scroll,
ink on paper.
Yoshinari Collection, Tokyo.

right: **39.** Pablo Picasso.
Self-Portrait. 1901.
Oil on canvas, $31\frac{1}{2} \times 23\frac{5}{8}''$.
Musée Picasso, Paris.

from indifference to those traditions. His last work, *The Dream* **(40)**, combines typical elements: a monumental nude perched on a sofa that has no seat; improbable wild animals and birds that never coexist in nature; lush foliage no botanist ever identified; and a dark-skinned "native" (of where?) playing a musical instrument. Rousseau loved to copy plants and animals from books, to fill in from his imagination, to mix and match in a picture as the inspiration took him. He labored over the meticulous rendering of every leaf and stem, yet the rendering is not lifelike at all, for the landscape does not exist; it is a fantasy land. Rousseau's world—which was apparently very real for him—is the paint on canvas that makes a rich, complex design for the viewer's pleasure.

Before we leave this subject of art and the real world, it will be useful to discuss a few terms that will come up throughout the book. All have to do with the relationship between the artistic image and the appearance of objects in the natural world.

REPRESENTATIONAL ART   Representational or **naturalistic** images in art are those that look very much like images found in the natural world. Picasso's portrait of Olga **(36)** fits this category. You may also encounter the term **illusionistic,** which means images that are so natural they trick us into thinking they are real.

An extreme of illusionism is referred to as **trompe-l'oeil,** the French term for "fool the eye." We generally use this expression when the eye is being fooled into thinking there are three dimensions in a work that is flat.

Trompe-l'oeil illusionism has been out of fashion during most of this century, but recently there has been a revival of interest, due largely to the work of Richard Haas. In a number of U.S. cities Haas has used his almost

40. Henri Rousseau. *The Dream.* 1910. Oil on canvas, 6'8½" × 9'9½". Collection, The Museum of Modern Art, New York (gift of Nelson A. Rockefeller).

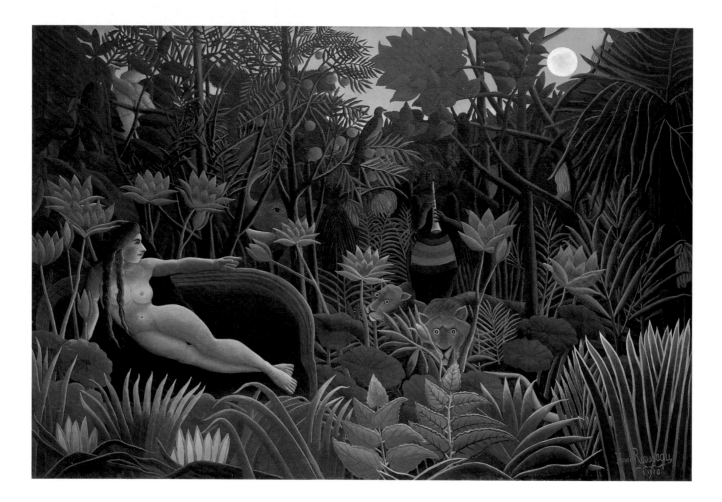

Henri Rousseau

1844–1910

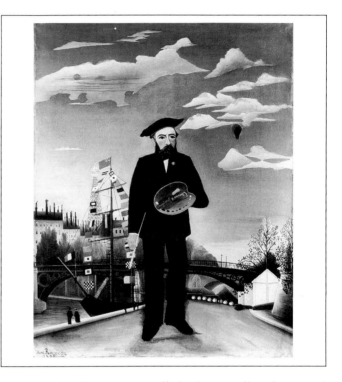

On the surface Rousseau was a ridiculous figure. One writer has observed that in the movies he would have been played by Charlie Chaplin. Like the eccentric who thinks he is Napoleon, Rousseau was convinced he was the master painter of his time. He was forever making up stories about his life, and eventually he came to believe them himself. He mingled with the pioneering artists of the day—Picasso, Braque, Kandinsky—who made him rather a pet, an object of half-real/half-mock admiration. Now, of course, the paintings of Picasso and the others are displayed in the world's great museums. So are the paintings of Henri Rousseau.

Born in a town in northwestern France, Rousseau completed secondary school and then enlisted in the army. Later he circulated the story that he had traveled with the infantry to Mexico, where he observed the tropical foliage seen in his mature paintings, but in fact he never left France. After military service, he became a toll collector for the city of Paris, and this too he exaggerated. Because he preferred the much higher rank of *douanier*, or customs inspector, he promoted himself and is often known as "le Douanier Rousseau."

Rousseau began as a Sunday painter, daubing away in his spare time. Then in 1884, at the age of forty, he took a small pension and retired to devote his life to painting. He never had any formal training in art. Instead, he set about teaching himself—copying paintings in the Louvre, studying nature at the botanical gardens in Paris, observing the work of other artists. When drawing figures he would carefully measure the features of his subjects with a tape measure, even though the results never seemed to reflect such precision. Rousseau liked to say that the great and famous art teachers had warned him never to lose the naive quality of his work. And he never did.

In specific details Rousseau's life was a harsh one. He married twice, and both of his wives died early, as did eight of his nine children. He rarely had any money, and sometimes he had to beg for food. Curiously, he seems never to have been unhappy. So convinced was he of his great talent, so caught up in his wonderful visions, so enthralled with the life he had invented for himself—that he floated serenely through the world, much as he appears to float in the self-portrait shown here. Rousseau's death, on the other hand, was a miserable one. A cut on his leg became infected and then gangrenous. "Le Douanier" died virtually alone and was buried in a pauper's grave.

Who was Rousseau? He was a fabulous romantic, a master of the naive, a stolidly middle-class clerk, a disciplined and hard-working painter, a dreamer, a man of simple tastes and magnificent visions. His friend Picasso, even while making jokes at Rousseau's expense, admired and respected the distinctive talent. The highlight of Rousseau's life was a banquet, held in his honor, at Picasso's studio in 1908. All the bohemian artistic world of Paris turned out. Rousseau, enthroned on a chair set atop a packing case, played a composition of his own on the violin. Many toasts were drunk, and the party became quite lively. Near the end, as the story goes, Rousseau staggered up to Picasso and paid what was for Rousseau a splendid tribute: "My dear Picasso," he said, "we are the two greatest painters of our time—you in the Egyptian style and I in the modern style."

Henri Rousseau. *Myself, Portrait-Landscape.* 1890.
Oil on canvas, 4'8¼" × 3'7¼". National Gallery, Prague.

left: **41.** Richard Haas.
Trompe-l'oeil mural on Brotherhood
Building, The Kroger Company,
Cincinnati. 1983.

below: **42.** Comparison of abstract
and naturalistic figures.

left: *Statuette of a Woman.* Cycladic,
c. 3000 B.C. Marble, height 24¾".
The Metropolitan Museum of Art, New York
(gift of Christos G. Bastis, 1968).

right: Jean Antoine Houdon.
La Frileuse (Winter). 1787.
Bronze, height 4'9".
The Metropolitan Museum of Art, New York
(bequest of Kate Trubee Davison, 1962).

devilish skill to transform blank, depressing, flat walls into fantasy murals that make us question our own senses over and over again. His mural on the Brotherhood Building in Cincinnati (41) offers a spectacular example. Only the windows and the left cornice (roof ornament) are real. Apart from those elements the wall is absolutely flat. The soaring half-dome and columns, projecting porch, and curving stairways are all a painted illusion.

ABSTRACT ART We call a work of art abstract when the art has reference to the natural world but does not try to duplicate it exactly. In the illustration opposite (42) the figure at right is naturalistic. The figure at left, a sculpture from the ancient culture of the Cyclades Islands, off the coast of Greece, is highly abstract. We have no doubt that the Cycladic image is meant to portray the nude female figure, yet the form has been abstracted to an extreme. The face is a rough triangle, with another jutting triangle for the nose. The crossed arms are flat and geometric. Knees, pubic area, and the curve of the abdomen are suggested by simple incised lines. In a sense, the sculptor of this figure has given us the minimum visual information we need to identify the form. The sculpture thus becomes not any particular female figure, but the *essence* of the female figure.

Stylized is a term closely related to abstract; you may have difficulty separating the two words until you become accustomed to hearing them applied to specific works of art. We are more likely to call a work of art stylized when it shows certain features of a natural form—features closely associated with that form—exaggerated in a special way. In Rousseau's painting (40), for instance, the two big cats, presumably lions, are stylized—their round staring eyes and prominent whiskers not lifelike but a kind of artistic shorthand for "cat." The leaves and flowers are similarly stylized.

NONREPRESENTATIONAL ART Nonrepresentational art has no reference to the natural world of images. It does not show people or animals or mountains, but simply shapes and sometimes colors (43). This art bypasses known forms and touches our senses and emotions directly. It does not "represent" anything but itself. If, for instance, you were to see a painting that was entirely red, you might suppose it to be about fire or sunsets or a volcano. It might, however, be "about" *red*, and nothing else.

43. Ellsworth Kelly. *Red White.* 1962. Oil on canvas, 6'8⅛" × 7'6". San Francisco Museum of Modern Art (T. B. Walker Foundation Fund Purchase).

Despite the apparent dissimilarities in these kinds of art, they all share a common trait. They are expressions of the artists who made them.

Art as Expression

Until now we have been talking about things that art can be but need not be. Now at last we come to something that art is always—the expression of the artist. By **expression** we mean the artist's unique view of art and of the world, an outward manifestation of the artist's emotions, thoughts, feelings, fears, dreams, and observations. We have got to the root of what Nakian meant when he talked about shooting his grandmother.

Expression means that the artist is always present in the work of art. No matter how straightforward a work may seem, it is influenced tremendously by the artist's own perspective and by his or her culture. This may be a difficult idea to grasp at first. We look at a portrait, for example, especially one painted in earlier centuries, and think, "But that's just the way the person *looks*. The artist isn't expressing anything." Is this really true? To find out, we might compare two portraits of the same person.

The paintings illustrated next (**44,45**) were done in the same year, and both are portraits of Vincent van Gogh. The first is by Van Gogh's friend Paul Gauguin, and the second is a self-portrait. Without the titles and the background information, almost no one would identify these works as portraits of the same man at the same time. Each expresses what the artist felt about the subject—in one case, about the self.

Gauguin shows us a rather ordinary, heavy-set, middle-class man at work, delicately painting sunflowers. The subject is shifted far to the right in the composition and balanced against the sunflowers, which assume equal importance. It is as though Van Gogh and his sunflowers are two sides of the same coin. How different is Van Gogh's self-portrait! The artist strips away all background details and presents himself as a gaunt, brooding, almost monklike figure—totally introspective, totally isolated.

We may be tempted to ask ourselves, which of these two portraits is the more "real"? And the answer must be: both of them. Gauguin's portrait is the

44. Paul Gauguin. *Vincent van Gogh.* 1888. Oil on canvas, $28\frac{3}{4} \times 35\frac{7}{8}''$. Rijksmuseum Vincent van Gogh, Amsterdam.

left: **45.** Vincent van Gogh. *Self-Portrait Dedicated to Paul Gauguin.* 1888. Oil on canvas, 24⅜ × 20½″. The Fogg Art Museum, Harvard University, Cambridge, Mass. (bequest, collection of Maurice Wertheim, class of 1906).

below: **46.** Käthe Kollwitz. *Self-Portrait.* 1938. Lithograph, 18¾ × 11¼″. National Gallery of Art, Washington, D.C. (Rosenwald Collection).

real Van Gogh as perceived by Gauguin, sifted through his friendship, memories, emotions, and indeed all of Gauguin's life experiences. Van Gogh's self-portrait is equally the real Van Gogh, as perceived by himself, sifted through the mental torment we know he endured, colored by the self-image he wanted to express to the world.

Two periods in the recent history of art have so intensely shown us the artist's expression that they have been labeled with the term. ***Expressionism,*** sometimes called ***German Expressionism*** because most of the leading artists worked in Germany, was a movement of the late 19th and early 20th centuries. Above all, this was an art that looked inward, to the soul and psyche. Expressionist artists sought to explore their own emotions, their own passions and terrors. Among the most moving of these artists was Käthe Kollwitz, who worked chiefly in prints. Kollwitz drew images based on her own anguish to express her feelings about a world in which there could be war and brutal death. Throughout her difficult life she maintained a fascination for the self-portrait. The lithograph shown here (46) portrays an old woman beyond pain and despair, a woman reduced to an exhausted kind of acceptance. The artist is expressing her utter weariness in a stark and poignant image.

Another movement closely linked with the artist's expression came in the mid-20th century and was known as ***Abstract Expressionism*** (Chapter 17). Artists identified with this style also looked inward and sought a direct expression of their emotions. This expression, however, took the form of abstract—sometimes nonrepresentational—images: colors, shapes, lines.

One of the best-known Abstract Expressionists was Jackson Pollock. In the late 1940s and early 1950s Pollock began showing works like *Convergence* (**47**). His style of painting was unusual, even revolutionary. Pollock set his huge canvases on the floor, stood above them (sometimes walked on them), and flung the paint from brushes, sticks, drippers, and even from the paint can itself. The result was an intricate web of lines and colors, with no beginning and no end. A viewer, once drawn into the painting, is led around and through it, with the eye moving continuously through a network of forms. What does the painting express? Movement, color, action, life, vitality—the spirit of the artist. As a matter of fact, many critics referred to this style as **action painting.** The artist's action in making the painting is communicated directly to the viewer. If you stand for a while in front of one of Pollock's paintings, you almost want to conduct it, as if it were an orchestra. The expression is available to anyone who is willing to receive it.

An interesting point about Pollock's art is that its *form* and its *content* are hard to separate. Indeed, the two are almost identical. Form and content are important ideas for the study of art. An understanding of how they work together will bring us closer to answering the question "What is art?" These terms are also indispensable for communicating about art to other people.

47. Jackson Pollock.
Convergence. 1952.
Oil on canvas, 7′11½″ × 12′11″.
Albright-Knox Art Gallery,
Buffalo, N.Y.
(gift of Seymour H. Knox, 1956).

Form and Content

If a good idea were all it took to be a famous artist, we all would be famous. The world is full of people who are carrying around in their heads great ideas for novels, symphonies, and paintings. What is lacking is form. Unfortunately for the dreamers, form is essential to any work of art.

Jackson Pollock

1912–1956

Jackson Pollock was born on a sheep ranch in Cody, Wyoming, the youngest son in a family of five boys. During his youth the family moved around a good deal and led a fairly unstable existence. By the age of fifteen Jackson had begun to show signs of the alcoholism that would plague him all his life.

In 1930 Pollock went to New York to study at the Art Students League. His principal teacher there was Thomas Hart Benton, a realistic painter of regional Americana, best known for his murals. Later, Pollock would say he was glad to have had the experience with Benton, because he then had to struggle all the harder to make art so very different from that of his mentor.

Money was a critical problem throughout the early years in New York. By 1935 Pollock was employed on the Federal Art Project of the Works Progress Administration—a Depression-era program meant to provide employment for artists. He was required to turn out, every four to eight weeks, one painting suitable for installation in public buildings, for which he was paid a stipend of about $100 a month. Frequent alcoholic binges often interfered with this work, and in 1937 Pollock began psychotherapy in an attempt to overcome his addiction.

Pollock's work was first exhibited in 1942, as part of a group show that also included the work of painter Lee Krasner. Krasner and Pollock soon formed a close relationship, and they were married in 1945. Gradually, Pollock's work began to change, to be freer and more spontaneous, to contain fewer and fewer figural elements. During the late 1940s he began exhibiting works in his mature style.

Some critics praised Pollock as the greatest of all American artists, but the general public was very slow to accept his revolutionary art. *Time* magazine epitomized the bewilderment of the popular press, dubbing him "Jack the Dripper." Nevertheless, there were some collectors willing to invest, so finances became less pressing.

The years 1948 to 1952—Pollock's late thirties— were the artist's prime, when he was at the height of his creative powers. After that, he seemed less sure where to go with his art, and even the sympathetic critics were not so responsive to the work. Pollock began to paint less and drink more. On the night of August 11, 1956, Pollock—along with two young women friends— was driving his convertible near his home when he lost

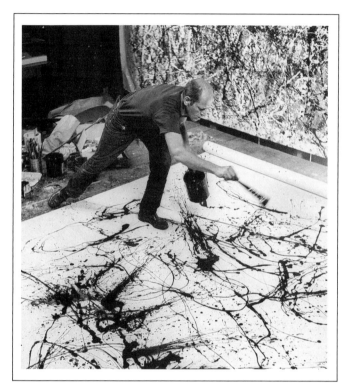

control of the car and rammed into a clump of trees at high speed. Pollock and one of the women were killed instantly. The artist was only forty-four years old.

Pollock drunk could be violent and brutish; Pollock sober was shy, introverted, and uncommunicative. Few ever succeeded in getting him to talk about his art, but there is one quote, reprinted many times, that gives voice to his truly remarkable vision: "On the floor I am more at ease. I feel nearer, more a part of the painting, since this way I can walk around it, work from the four sides and literally be *in* the painting. . . . When I am *in* my painting, I am not aware of what I'm doing. It is only after a sort of 'get acquainted' period that I see what I have been about. I have no fears about making changes, destroying the image, etc., because the painting has a life of its own. I try to let it come through. It is only when I lose contact with the painting that the result is a mess. Otherwise there is pure harmony, an easy give and take, and the painting comes out well."[11]

Jackson Pollock in his studio at East Hampton, N.Y., 1950, photographed by Hans Namuth.

In simplest terms, **form** is the way a work of art looks; and **content** is what a work of art says. Form includes everything from the material the artist uses (oil paint, stone, paper, whatever), to the style in which the artist works, to the shapes and lines and colors in the art. It also includes how a work of art is put together—its **composition.**

Content refers to the message communicated by a work of art—what the artist expresses. Sometimes content begins with a story or an event or an image of something we recognize, which we could call the **subject matter.** For instance, in a painting called, say, *The Battle of Bull Run,* the subject matter would be a battle scene. The content would be a battle scene *and* what the artist wanted to communicate about that battle scene. (You can guess that the content would likely be very different if a Union sympathizer and a Confederate artist were painting the same scene.) Similarly, in a portrait, as in the two portraits of Van Gogh, the content begins with the subject and includes whatever the artist wishes to communicate about the subject.

In other types of art, however, the content may not be so clear. It could be anger or fear or loneliness or joy or, as in the Pollock, action and vitality. For an interesting study in form and content, we might look at Willem de Kooning's *Woman and Bicycle* **(48)**, one of a series of "woman" paintings the artist did during the early 1950s. In form *Woman and Bicycle* is an oil painting in an abstract style, consisting mainly of harsh, savage brush strokes.

As to the painting's content, we have a clue in the title "woman," but that is only a starting point. De Kooning's women throughout this series are predatory monsters—all eyes and teeth and huge, engulfing breasts. The artist himself said that he always began with an image of a young, beautiful woman, only to see it transformed on canvas, as he worked, into a hideous nightmare creature. We have a sense of de Kooning struggling against the women in his paintings, struggling to carve them up and subdue them, while at the same time the painted women become more and more menacing, in danger of destroying the artist. The content of *Woman and Bicycle,* then, is not simply a woman, but de Kooning's conscious and unconscious feelings about women.

48. Willem de Kooning.
Woman and Bicycle. 1952–53.
Oil on canvas, 6'4½" × 4'1".
Collection, Whitney Museum
of American Art, New York
(purchase).

Throughout the preceding discussion the word *style* has been used a number of times. Style is a term familiar to us from everyday conversation, but because it is so crucial to an understanding of art, we might consider its meaning as specifically related to art.

Style

There are styles of music, styles of dress, styles of interior design, even styles of speaking and walking. When an automobile manufacturer changes the way its cars look from year to year, we speak of the "new style." If a person we know always wears jeans and cowboy boots, or always wears long flowing dresses and flowered prints, we identify that person with his or her particular style of dress. Furthermore, we may say of someone, "She really has style!" Or we might describe the décor of a particular home as "stylish." In the latter two cases, we mean the person or place shows a *desirable* style, one we admire, because everybody and everything has *some* style or other. But what exactly *is* style?

Above all, **style** is a characteristic or group of characteristics that we can identify as constant, recurring, or coherent. For instance, suppose you have a friend who has very long hair and always wears it in braids; then your friend gets a short haircut. You would call this a sudden change of style. Or perhaps you know a family whose home is entirely decorated with antiques, except for one very modern chair and table in the living room. You would recognize a mix of styles—not necessarily bad, but obvious.

In the visual arts, just as in any other area of life, style indicates a series of choices an artist has made. **Artistic style** is the sum of constant, recurring, or coherent traits identified with a certain individual or group. In painting, for example, a particular style could be composed of many elements—the materials used, the type of brush strokes, the colors, the way forms are handled, the choice of subject matter, the degree of resemblance to the natural world (representational versus abstract style), and so on.

Style may be associated with a whole artistic culture (the Song dynasty style in China); with a particular time and place (the early Renaissance style in Rome); with a group of artists whose work shows similar characteristics (the Abstract Expressionist style); with one artist (Van Gogh's style); or with one artist at a certain time (Picasso's Blue period style). In all these instances there are common elements—constant, recurring, coherent—that we can learn to recognize. Once you become familiar with Van Gogh's mature style **(21)**, with its licking, flamelike brush strokes and vivid color, you will probably be able to identify other paintings by Van Gogh, even if you have never seen them before. Some artists develop a style and stick to it; others work in several styles, simultaneously or sequentially.

One way to think of style is to consider it an artist's personal "handwriting." You know that if you give ten people identical pieces of paper and identical pens and tell them to write the same sentence, you'll get ten very different results, because no two people have the same handwriting. Penmanship styles are interesting. Each is absolutely unique, yet there are characteristics we can identify, even if we don't know the person who did the writing. If you study handwriting at all, a given sample should be able to tell you if the writer is male or female, old or young, American or European, and so forth. Much the same is true of artistic styles. Every one is individual, but we may find similarities among artists of a particular time, place, or group.

To get a sense of style variations in art, let us consider three paintings **(49,50,51)** with similar subject matter. Each depicts a woman in profile, from the waist up, but the paintings are very different. Even someone who knows practically nothing about art would observe differences in style, although he or she might not be able to articulate those differences. The first, by Alesso

above left: **49.** Alesso Baldovinetti.
Portrait of a Lady in Yellow. c. 1463.
Wood panel, 24¾ × 16″.
National Gallery, London
(reproduced by courtesy of the Trustees).

above: **50.** *Lady with a Bird*, from Hyderabad,
India. c. 1730. Gouache on paper, 13 × 8½″.
Victoria & Albert Museum, London.

left: **51.** Joshua Reynolds.
Mrs. Mary Robinson (Perdita). 1784.
Oil on canvas, 30½ × 25″.
The Wallace Collection, London
(reproduced by permission of the Trustees).

Baldovinetti, was painted in Italy in the 15th century **(49)**. It shows the woman in sharp outline, against a plain blue background, almost as flat as a silhouette. The drawing is lifelike but probably idealized, made to look more beautiful than the subject actually was. All is elegance, from the pure features to the long neck to the prominent leaf pattern on the sleeve.

The second painting **(50)** was made in India in the 18th century. Again the outline is sharp against a plain background, but the subject's pose is even more rigid, almost ritually frozen. The woman holds a bird in one hand and, presumably, the bird's treat in the other, but these are really ornaments for the carefully posed hands. She does not look at the bird but instead stares off into an unseen distance. Following the artistic style of that culture, the artist has bared the woman's breasts and exaggerated her enormous, almond-shaped eyes.

Our third example **(51)**, painted at almost the same time as the Indian picture, is by the great English portraitist Sir Joshua Reynolds. Here we see no flat background, but rather the illusion of deep space—a vague and romantic seascape toward which the woman seems to be gazing. Unlike the first two artists, Reynolds invites us into the sitter's mind. She is pensive, perhaps a little sad, perhaps daydreaming or remembering. Her pose is more relaxed than either of the previous two, more dramatic, even a bit theatrical. Colors are softer, the forms slightly blurred.

Three lovely portraits, each by a skilled artist, but markedly different from one another—that is the nature of style. In every case the artist's style will be influenced by choices related to time, place, and the artist's expressive needs.

We said at the beginning of this chapter that many periods in the history of art have been marked by a cohesive style, common to much or all of the art produced then. Such cohesion may occur whenever artists are strongly influenced by their societies or when they work closely together. An extreme example of style similarity occurred in the early part of this century. From 1908 to about 1912 the artists Pablo Picasso and Georges Braque worked virtually side by side in developing the style that would come to be called **Cubism** (Chapter 17). So harmonious were their efforts that, in some cases, only experts can definitely tell their paintings apart **(52,53)**. Later, the artists' styles diverged, but for a time they painted almost as one.

left: **52.** Pablo Picasso.
The Accordionist. 1911.
Oil on canvas, 4'3¼" × 2'11¼".
Solomon R. Guggenheim Museum,
New York (gift, 1937).

right: **53.** Georges Braque.
Man with a Guitar. 1911–12.
Oil on canvas, 45¾ × 31⅞".
Collection, The Museum of Modern Art,
New York (acquired through
the Lillie P. Bliss Bequest).

In a sense, this whole book—or any book about art—is really about style. Part Two will discuss how an artist's choices of elements affect style, Parts Three and Four will consider styles in the various media, and Part Five will survey styles in Western art throughout history.

Before going on to these broader issues, however, we should introduce one more term that is important for the study of art. The term is related to style, because if we are to fully understand an artist's style we must know what is being depicted in a work of art and why—the work's iconography.

Iconography

Loosely, iconography is the "story" within a work of art. Many people find the term confusing, because both subject matter and content could be described in much the same way as iconography. An example may help to clear up the confusion among the three terms. Suppose you see a painting of a boy and a dog. The *subject matter* of that painting is simply "a boy and a dog." Its *content* might be "the love between a boy and his dog." But if you, the observer, see that the dog is a collie, realize that the dog is Lassie, and know the Lassie stories—know that Lassie is an intelligent and heroic dog who often saves people from danger—then you have caught the painting's *iconography*.

Artists around the world always have assumed a certain iconographical knowledge on the part of their audiences. A viewer's comprehension of the iconography includes familiarity with the people, places, and events that are depicted, as well as any symbolism intended by the artist. Much of the history of art has some literary or historical or religious reference. Quite a lot of Western art is based on the Bible. Most of the time an artist's immediate circle of patrons and viewers will grasp the iconography at once. Problems arise, however, when we confront art from other times and places.

left: **54.** Fra Filippo Lippi. *Nativity*. c. 1459. Tempera on wood, 4'2" × 3'10". Staatliche Museen, Berlin.

right: **55.** Albrecht Dürer. *The Fall of Man*. 1504. Engraving, $9\frac{7}{8} \times 7\frac{5}{8}''$. The Metropolitan Museum of Art, New York (Fletcher Fund, 1919).

56. *Sita in the Garden of Lanka with Ravana and His Demons.* Guler School, India, c. 1720. Gold and color on paper, $22\frac{3}{4} \times 33\frac{1}{4}''$. The Cleveland Museum of Art (gift of George B. Bickford).

Christians around the world are familiar with the story surrounding the birth of Christ. When a person with this background looks at Fra Filippo Lippi's *Nativity* **(54)**, certain things are immediately apparent. There is the child Jesus, watched over by his mother Mary (who wears a halo symbolic of her perfect sinlessness). To the left is a praying saint and, just below, Jesus' cousin John the Baptist, identified by his staff. And at the top are God the Father and the Holy Ghost in the form of a dove, completing the Trinity. Someone with no knowledge of the Christian tradition, however, would probably see a lovely mother-and-child scene and wonder who those other people are and why they are wearing such funny hats. We can try to imagine what an Inca in 15th-century Peru or a Samurai in 15th-century Japan (both contemporary with this painting) would see in Filippo Lippi's scene.

Even in the Western culture we have inherited, the iconography can sometimes be unfamiliar. Albrecht Dürer, who worked in Germany during the late 15th and early 16th centuries, was a Christian. Much of his iconography is biblical, but it is overlaid with mystical northern European symbolism. In *The Fall of Man* **(55)** we see Adam and Eve about to be banished from the Garden of Eden after their sin of eating the forbidden fruit. Dürer has included symbols of the four humors, or temperaments, which were thought to rule the human body: the elk symbolizes gall; the ox, phlegm; the cat, choler; and the rabbit, blood. Each of these humors, in turn, was associated with a particular sin—avarice, gluttony, cruelty, and lechery—sins to which the fallen Adam and Eve were now susceptible. Dürer's iconography is incredibly rich, and we can only begin to explore it here. For the artist's learned contemporaries it was understandable; for us it is new territory.

Now let us consider a work even further outside the experience of most of us—a painting that portrays an episode from the *Ramáyana*, the classic epic poem of India **(56)**. Probably composed in the 3rd century B.C., the *Ramáyana* is an integral part of daily life in India even today. Every character, every incident in the tale is as well known to the Indian public as the details of the Nativity are to practicing Christians.

Briefly, the *Ramáyana* tells the adventures of Rama—a prince who was the seventh incarnation of the god Vishnu—and his beautiful, faithful wife, Sita. Through a trick, the demon-king Ravana manages to abduct Sita and carry her off to his splendid palace at Lanka, which we see in the left half of this illustration. Ravana is so demonic, and so powerful, that he can assume any form he chooses—the worst one being a monster with ten heads and

Albrecht Dürer

1471–1528

Albrecht Dürer is the first of the northern European artists who seems to us "modern" in his outlook. Unlike most of his colleagues, he had a strong sense of being an *artist*, not a craftsman, and he sought—and received—acceptance in the higher ranks of society. Moreover, Dürer appears to have understood his role in the history of art—sensed that his work would exert great influence on his contemporaries and on artists of the future. This awareness led him to date his works and sign them with the distinctive "AD" (visible in the left background of his self-portrait)—a fairly unusual practice at the time.

Born in the southern German city of Nuremberg, Dürer was the son of a goldsmith, to whom he was apprenticed as a boy. At the age of fifteen young Albrecht was sent to study in the workshop of Michael Wolgemut, then considered a leading painter in Nuremberg. He stayed with Wolgemut for four years, after which he began a four-year period of wandering through northern Europe. In 1494 Dürer's father called him back to Nuremberg for an arranged marriage. (The marriage seems not to have been a happy one and produced no children.) Soon afterward Dürer established himself as a master and opened his own studio.

Dürer made a great many paintings and drawings, but it is his output in prints (engravings, woodcuts, and etchings) that is truly extraordinary. Many people would argue that he was the greatest printmaker who ever lived. His genius derived partly from an ability to unite the best tendencies in northern and southern European art of that period, for Dürer was a well-traveled man. In 1494 he visited Italy, and he returned in 1505, staying two years in Venice, where he operated a studio. This second trip was a huge success, both artistically and socially. The artist received many commissions and enjoyed the high regard of the Venetian painters as well as of important patrons in the city. Upon his return to Germany Dürer took his place among the leading writers and intellectuals of Nuremberg, who seem to have valued him for his knowledge and wit, as well as for his art. In 1515 he was appointed court painter to the Holy Roman Emperor Maximilian I.

The last years of Dürer's life were devoted largely to work on his books and treatises, through which he hoped to teach a scientific approach to painting and drawing. As a Renaissance artist, he was fascinated by

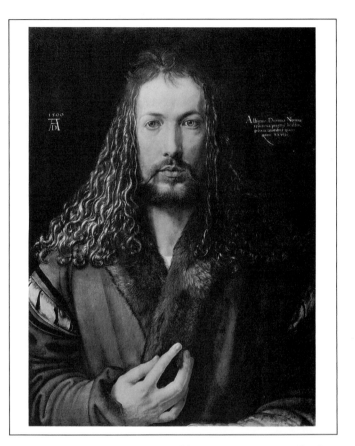

perfection and by an ideal of beauty. He wrote: "What beauty is, I know not, though it adheres to many things. When we wish to bring it into our work we find it very hard. We must gather it together from far and wide, and especially in the case of the human figure throughout all its limbs from before and behind. One may often search through two or three hundred men without finding amongst them more than one or two points of beauty which can be made use of. You, therefore, if you desire to compose a fine figure, must take the head from some, the chest, arm, leg, hand, and foot from others; and, likewise, search through all members of every kind. For from many beautiful things something good may be gathered, even as honey is gathered from many flowers."[12]

Albrecht Dürer. *Self-Portrait.* 1500.
Wood panel, $25\frac{5}{8} \times 18\frac{7}{8}$".
Bayerische Staatsgemäldesammlungen, Munich.

57. Audrey Flack. *Marilyn.* 1977. Oil and acrylic on canvas, 8' square. University of Arizona Museum of Art, Tucson (Museum purchase with funds provided by the Edward J. Gallagher, Jr., Memorial Fund).

twenty arms. After kidnapping Sita, he gives her one year to renounce Rama and become his consort, and he exiles her to the forest in the keeping of demon-handmaidens. In this episode Ravana is paying Sita a visit to see if she has yet relented, but Sita remains steadfastly true to Rama.

Without this background information we find the painting lovely and exotic, but how much more interesting it becomes when we understand its iconography. Nowadays all of us are exposed to art from cultures other than our own, and it is well worth the effort to learn more about them.

We should also remember that our own culture could be equally mystifying to those outside it. What would Filippo Lippi or Dürer or the painter of the *Ramáyana* make of Audrey Flack's *Marilyn* (57)? The details of the tragic film star's life are well known to most Americans, and so we readily accept the symbols of glamour, of artifice, of lushness, and especially of time running out (the candle, watch, calendar, and egg timer). But to someone who has never heard of Marilyn Monroe, the painting would seem a meaningless jumble. A knowledge of any work's iconography, therefore, can enhance our appreciation, as can acquaintance with the culture that produced the art.

And so, to return to the title of this chapter: What is art? It is the "lie that tells the truth." Sometimes it is beautiful, but it may be ugly. It can look like things in the natural world, but frequently it does not. It is always the expression of the artist. It is always a product of the culture that produces it. It is the artist showing us something, telling us something, making us experience something. It is communication—if we but look, listen, think, and feel.

ART PEOPLE *Theo van Gogh*

We think of Theo van Gogh as the sensible one. Mentor and benefactor of his brother, the tormented artist Vincent van Gogh, Theo was nearly everything his brother was not—successful in business, financially solvent, steady and dependable, easy in friendship, a serious family man. Sometimes it is hard to remember that Vincent was the *older* brother, Theo younger by four years. The relationship between them was extraordinary. Without Theo, Vincent van Gogh probably could not have survived as an artist, or survived at all. Without Vincent, Theo probably would have lacked the grand purpose of his life.

Theo was born at the family home in Holland in 1857. When he was a teenager his uncle arranged for him to be apprenticed to a firm of international art dealers, Goupil & Co., as Vincent had been before him. Here the brothers' characters diverged. Vincent soon drifted out of the business. Theo became well established and fairly prosperous, eventually settling in as an art dealer in Paris. From a young age Theo assumed principal responsibility for Vincent's financial support, and he continued in this role through Vincent's life. Both accepted the arrangement as natural.

The Van Gogh brothers maintained a remarkable intimacy of spirit—surprisingly so, in view of the fact that, except for brief visits, they spent relatively little time in each other's company. They were together in their boyhood, then for two years in Paris, when Vincent stayed with Theo before moving to the south of France. This latter period exhausted Theo; Vincent was never an easy person to live with. Theo described Vincent's presence in the Paris apartment as "unendurable" and was relieved when the artist finally journeyed to Arles.

The thread of Theo and Vincent's connection depended on an immense volume of correspondence. Vincent was compulsive in writing to Theo—his subjects ranging from intensely personal thoughts and emotions through minute descriptions of work in progress. Theo was always there for Vincent. When Vincent finished a series of paintings, he shipped them off to Theo, who did his best to promote and sell the work (with little success). When Vincent was irresponsible, Theo lectured. When Vincent was in financial crisis, Theo sent money. When Vincent was in emotional crisis, Theo arrived to pick up the pieces. Although under no illusion about his brother's difficult temperament,

Theo seems to have known from the beginning that Vincent was a brilliant painter, and to have considered it his mission to sustain the painter's career.

Theo's marriage to Johanna Bonger in April of 1889 caused a brief strain in the Van Gogh bond. What had been a straight line became a triangle. Vincent suffered over having any of Theo's emotional energy diverted from himself to the new wife. Before long, however, he came to be fond of his sister-in-law and rejoiced in the birth of his nephew.

Vincent shot himself in July of 1890, and Theo was summoned to the deathbed. Three days later Theo wrote to his mother: "One cannot write how grieved one is nor find any solace. . . . Oh, Mother! He was so my own, own brother."[13] Vincent's death left Theo, only thirty-three years old, broken in health and spirits. Within six months he too was dead. The brothers are buried side by side. Afterward, the work of establishing the art of Vincent van Gogh was carried on by Theo's wife and his only child, a son, named Vincent.

Photograph of Theo van Gogh. c. 1888–90.
Amsterdams Historisch Museum.

Chapter Three

Themes and Purposes of Art

There are several ways to approach the study of art. A popular one is to trace its history chronologically, from the earliest cave paintings of the Stone Age to the art of our own time. This method offers great advantages, because it places works of art in the context of the cultures from which they emerged and allows one to follow the development of art over the centuries. Part Five of this book will present a brief chronological survey of art in Western civilization.

The chronological approach has one drawback, however, in that we may lose sight of the characteristics that works made by different cultures have in common. For instance, a sculpture produced today and one produced ten thousand years ago may seem very different, and a chronological approach emphasizes the differences by focusing on the cultural aspects that influenced each. But suppose the two sculptures are images honoring political leaders; then we would say they have the same *theme*, so we can make interesting comparisons between them. While it is useful to understand how and why works of art differ, it is also helpful to see how much they are alike, even when thousands of miles and years separate them.

In Chapter 2 we discussed content—the subject matter of a work of art and what the artist means to convey about that subject matter. Content can be considered as theme whenever similar material is treated by many artists at various times and places. A theme is therefore like a thread running through the entire history of art, and there are many such threads. No doubt every person setting out to name the important themes in art would produce a different list. We have chosen to consider these: magic and survival; religion; pride and politics; art as the mirror of everyday life; art and nature; imagination and fantasy; birth, marriage, and death.

The *purpose* of a work of art is what the artist hoped to achieve (or in some cases what the art patron hoped to achieve by commissioning it). Sometimes the two factors—theme and purpose—overlap, so it is difficult to tell them apart, but in other instances we can identify a separate purpose. For example, the theme of a landscape painting would probably be nature, and the purpose simply to depict some aspect of nature. But if the artist's goal in painting a landscape is to show the glory of God's creation, then the theme is still nature but we might consider the purpose to be religion. Let us therefore examine the seven themes mentioned, with several examples of each, and see how they lend themselves to various purposes. We begin with what was probably the first preoccupation of artists and indeed of all people in early cultures.

Magic and Survival

Our illustration shows a little statuette that is nearly everybody's favorite way to begin studying art history **(58)**. She is made of stone, was formed about twenty-three thousand years before the birth of Christ, and was found near a town in Austria. Her name: the *Venus of Willendorf*. At first her title of "Venus" may seem strange, given our usual image of the Goddess of Love. The name, of course, was applied by modern scholars, possibly supposing that people many thousands of years ago considered this sort of figure a sexual ideal. It seems clear that the little *Venus* was a fertility image, perhaps meant to be carried around as an *amulet*, or good-luck charm (the *Venus* is less than 5 inches tall). Only the features associated with childbearing have been stressed—the belly, breasts, and pubic area. Venus' face is obscured, her arms, crossed above the breasts, are barely defined, and her legs taper off to nothing. If we take this figure literally, she could not see or speak or walk or carry; what she could do was bear and nurture children.

How difficult it is for us living now to imagine what childbirth meant all those millennia ago. On the one hand it must have been a pressing necessity. Children were needed to help in the task of survival, and there may also have been an instinct to continue life through future generations. On the other hand, however, the process by which children are conceived and born was a mystery to these early peoples. The ovum and the sperm were unknown. Bringing forth a child must have seemed very much like the magician's trick of pulling a rabbit out of a hat. No wonder elements of magic became associated with childbirth. Many scholars assume that fertility figures like the *Venus of Willendorf*, which are extremely common in early art, were meant to play a cause-and-effect role. The sculptor would form an image of a woman with exaggerated reproductive features, and this figure would *result* in a child (or children) being born. To primitive peoples this sequence must have made as much sense as any other.

Much primitive art seems to have been created for this purpose—to make sense out of the universe and to exert some control over the forces of nature. Today we have weather forecasters and meteorologists and seismologists and orbiting satellites and computers—but we still are not absolutely sure whether it will rain tomorrow. Early peoples had none of these, but they made the best out of what they had. Some of their arrangements startle us with their ingenuity.

On a plain in the south of England stand the enormous megaliths known as Stonehenge **(59)**, much as they have stood for more than three thousand years. Stonehenge was built over a period of centuries, perhaps beginning as early as 2000 B.C. It consists of four concentric rings of stones, the outermost ring being 100 feet in diameter. The basis of the structure is *post-and-lintel* construction (Chapter 13), in which two uprights are surmounted by a horizontal crosspiece, the *lintel*. One of the most fascinating aspects of Stonehenge is the puzzle of *how* it was built. The stones, some weighing 50 tons or more, were quarried many miles away and dragged to the site by whatever primitive means may have been available. Next came the staggering feat of raising the lintels into position, without benefit of the cranes and other modern devices we take for granted. There is no mortar holding up these immense rocks. The method used by Stone Age peoples to erect them has stood up ever since.

Even more interesting is the problem of *why* Stonehenge was created. What purpose can have been so compelling as to stimulate this tremendous human effort? For centuries art historians debated the question. Then in

58. *Venus of Willendorf.*
c. 23,000 B.C.
Limestone, height 4⅜".
Natural History Museum, Vienna.

1964 a theory was advanced by astronomer Gerald S. Hawkins that appears to have solved the riddle of Stonehenge. By feeding complex measurements into a computer, Hawkins found that, at the moment of sunrise on the summer solstice (usually June 21), the sun shines through a key opening directly to an altar at the center. Similar computations showed that the position of the stones was organized to predict the winter solstice, the spring and autumnal equinoxes, and even eclipses of the sun and moon. In other words, Stonehenge apparently functioned as a giant calendar, codifying the mysterious changes of seasons and stars. Is Stonehenge a tool of magic, or the beginning of science, or a link between the two? Whichever the case, it provided the means by which its makers could plan for survival.

Whenever we talk about survival among these early peoples, we must remember that the concept probably represented far more than an individual fending off death. Survival of the *group*—of the tribe or clan—always was precarious, and this consideration may well have taken priority over all others. Magic therefore would be directed toward the endurance of the tribe. We see this tendency in "primitive" cultures of the past and present.

In many cultures throughout Africa, in the Pacific islands, and among native peoples of the Americas there has been a long tradition of making masks. These masks, often worn in the dance, are usually ceremonial, magical, and related to such basic aspects of survival as birth, healing, puberty, marriage, fertility, success in the hunt, and death. (Death, seen as the transition to the afterlife, can be considered an aspect of survival.) Our illustration **(60)** shows a splendid example from Bella Coola, on the Pacific Coast of British Columbia, in Canada. Representing the sun—the source of warmth and therefore all life—this mask has a central face surrounded by upraised hands, presumably symbolizing the sun's rays.

Art whose theme is magic and survival has as its purpose the establishment of some sense of control. For nearly everyone, it seems, the most terrifying situation is that of being helpless, out of control, at the mercy of forces much bigger than we are. Worst of all, many psychologists contend, is the fear of *random* disasters. It is safer to believe that lightning strikes a particular spot because a spirit is angry than to know that lightning's path is arbitrary. At least a spirit can be placated, but randomness leaves us defenseless. Therefore, even if the control we take is imaginary—wearing a mask honoring the sun or beating a drum to quiet the lightning-god—we are comforted.

above: 59. Stonehenge.
c. 2000–1500 B.C.
Height of stones 13'6".
Salisbury Plain, England.

below: 60. Bella Coola mask representing the sun, from British Columbia.
Before 1897.
Wood, diameter 24¾".
© American Museum of Natural History, New York.

61. Leonora Carrington.
The Magic Witch. 1975.
Gouache on vellum,
47¾ × 32⅜″.
The National Museum of Women
in the Arts (gift of Wallace
and Wilhelmina Holladay).
© Leonora Carrington.

Today's world is far more complex and calls for different kinds of control over powerful forces—the "magic" of the physicist, the neurosurgeon, the cosmologist, the mathematician. Even with all these specialists, there still are a great many areas of mystery in our world. Although we have learned much about the principles of birth and crop raising and healing, we do not really know much about the nature of our universe. For most of us quasars and black holes do not seem any less magical than the idea that forming an image of a pregnant woman could produce a child. Perhaps that is why some artists today endow their work with magical qualities.

Today's magical art is less apt to be cultural or tribal, more likely to be personal, with symbolism meaningful to the individual artist. So it is with Leonora Carrington's *Magic Witch* **(61)**, a work so filled with mystical forms and cryptic signs that it tempts us to study the composition in close detail. Is the "magic witch" the central figure with a snake arm inside the blue circle, or is it the larger grayish figure with outstretched hands—or both? Carrington is much involved in the exploration of mystic rituals and ceremonies. She is fascinated by metamorphosis—forms that change into other forms. An arm becomes a snake, a head slips into a kind of onion shape, a fish tail grows into . . . what? The artist does not tell us what the symbols in this work mean, so we are free to apply to them our own interpretations, our own personal magic.

Art in the Service of Religion

Since earliest times art has served religion in two important ways. First, artists have erected the sacred temples where believers join to profess their faith and follow the observances faith requires. Second, art attempts to make specific and visible something that is, by its very nature, spiritual, providing images of the religious figures and events that make up the fabric of a faith. In this section we shall explore how the theme of religious art has been adapted for different purposes, for different faiths, in different parts of the world.

A very large portion of the magnificent architecture we have was built in the service of religion. Naturally the architectural style of any religious structure reflects the culture in which it was built, but it is also dependent on the particular needs of a given religion. Three examples will show this.

On a high hill, the Acropolis, overlooking the city of Athens stands the shell of what many consider the most splendid building ever conceived: the Parthenon **(62)**. The Parthenon was erected in the 5th century B.C. as a temple to the goddess Athena, patroness of the city, and at one time its core held a colossal statue of the goddess. However, the religion associated with the Parthenon was not confined to worship of a deity. In ancient Greece, veneration of the gods was closely allied to the political and social ideals of a city-state that celebrated its own greatness.

Rising proudly on its hill, visible from almost every corner of the city and for miles around, the Parthenon functioned as a symbol of the citizens' aspirations. Its structure as a religious shrine seems unusual for us in that it turns outward, toward the city, rather than in upon itself. Worshipers were not meant to gather inside the building; actually, only priests could enter the inner chamber, or *cella*, where the statue of Athena stood. Religious ceremonies on festal occasions focused on processions, which began down in the city, wound their way up the steep path on the west side of the Acropolis, and circled the Parthenon and other sacred buildings at the top.

Most of the Parthenon's architectural embellishment was intended for the appreciation of the worshipers outside. All four walls of the exterior were decorated with sculptures high up under the roof, and originally portions of the marble facade were painted a vivid blue and red **(583)**. In Chapter 13 we shall consider details of the Parthenon's structure; here we concentrate on the theme of religion and on the Parthenon's purpose, which is both religious *and* political exaltation.

62. Ictinus and Callicrates. The Parthenon. 447–432 B.C. Acropolis, Athens.

At about the same time the Parthenon was being constructed in Athens, but half a continent away, one of the world's great religions was developing and beginning to form its own architecture. Buddhism derives its principles from the teachings of Gautama Siddhartha, later known as the Buddha, who was born in India about 563 B.C. Although of noble birth, the Buddha renounced his princely status and life of ease. When he was about twenty-nine he began a long period of wandering and meditation, seeking enlightenment. He began with the supposition that humans are predisposed to live out lives of suffering, to die, then to be reborn and repeat the pattern. Ultimately, he worked out a doctrine of moral behavior that he believed could break the painful cycle of life and death, and he attracted many followers.

Buddhism is predominantly a personal religion, and its observances depend less on communal worship than on individual contemplation. It places great emphasis on symbolism, much of it referring to episodes in the Buddha's life. Both of these aspects—the personal and the symbolic—are evident in one of Buddhism's finest early shrines, the Great Stupa at Sanchi, in India (63). Like the Parthenon, the Great Stupa turns more outward than inward, but its moundlike form is more sculptural, intended as a representation of the cosmos. At the very top is a three-part "umbrella," symbolizing the three major aspects of Buddhism—the Buddha, the Buddha's Law, and the Monastic Order.

Buddhist shrines—the word *stupa* means "shrine"—often housed relics of the Buddha, and worship rituals called for circumambulation ("walking around") of the stupa. Thus, on the outside of the Great Stupa we see a railed pathway, where pilgrims could take the ritual clockwise walk following the Path of Life around the World Mountain. Elsewhere the stupa is embellished richly with carvings and sculpture evoking scenes from the Buddha's life. Every part of the stupa is geared to the pursuit of personal enlightenment and transcendence.

If the Buddhist temple is dedicated to private worship, then its extreme opposite can be found in the total encompassment of a community religious experience: the medieval Christian cathedral. And the supreme example of that ideal is the Cathedral of Notre Dame de Chartres, in France (64). Chartres Cathedral was built, rebuilt, and modified over a period of several hundred years, but the basic structure, which is in the Gothic style (Chapter

63. The Great Stupa. Sunga and early Andhra periods, 3rd century B.C.–A.D. 1st century. Sanchi, India.

64. Chartres Cathedral, France, view from the southeast. c. 1194–1260.

15), was established in the 13th century. A cathedral—as opposed to a church—is the bishop's domain and therefore always in a town or city. This one fact is crucial to understanding the nature of Chartres and the role it played in the people's lives.

Our illustration shows that the cathedral towers magnificently over the surrounding city, much as the Parthenon does over Athens, but here the resemblance ends. Whereas the Parthenon is above and apart from the city, accessible only by a steep path, Chartres Cathedral is very much a living presence *within* the city. In the Middle Ages houses and shops clustered right up to its walls, and one side of the cathedral formed an edge of the busy marketplace. The cathedral functioned as a hub of all activities, both sacred and secular, within the town.

Medieval France had one dominant religion, and that was the Christianity of Rome. One could assume that almost every resident of the town of Chartres professed exactly the same faith, and so the church was an integral part of everyday life. Its bells tolled the hours of waking, starting work, praying, and retiring for the evening rest. Its feast days were the official holidays. Chartres Cathedral and its counterparts served the populace not only as a setting for religious worship but as meeting hall, museum, concert stage, and social gathering place. Within its walls business deals were arranged, goods were sold, friends met, young couples courted. Where else but inside the cathedral could the townsfolk hear splendid music? Where else could they see magnificent art?

Three religious structures: the Parthenon, the Great Stupa, and Chartres Cathedral. Each was built in the service of religion but for each we can find another slightly different purpose. For the Parthenon the purpose is also *political;* for the Great Stupa there is the purely *private* observance of religion; and for Chartres the *social* role is as important as the religious.

Similarly interesting comparisons can be made in the other major aspect of religious art, the creation of imagery. Art provides images of Christ, the Buddha, the whole galaxy of Greek and Roman gods, the saints and angels, and other figures. It portrays the legends, stories, and events connected with a particular faith. Each of these depictions, of course, is the artist's own interpretation of what a certain being or situation looked like. But by giving the faithful an image to focus on, the artist makes religion more concrete, less abstract. Again we will look at art from three faiths—the old Greek religion, Buddhism, and Christianity.

We have already seen in this book an example of religious art from ancient Greece, the sculpture by Praxiteles of the goddess Aphrodite **(26)**. To modern eyes this seems a very odd sort of religious statue—a nude woman, undeniably sensuous, shown in a provocative pose. To understand it, we must know something about the Greek deities. The gods and goddesses of ancient Greece were grander and stronger than humans, and they possessed powers that humans do not. But they also displayed (to a godlike degree) distinctly human traits, including pride, anger, jealousy, and—yes— sexuality. In this context, Aphrodite, the Goddess of Love and Beauty, would naturally be portrayed in the nude, and with a body as lovely as the great sculptor could make it. The Greeks worshipped her *for* her beauty, and they relished her numerous romantic adventures.

Our next two examples, one Buddhist and one Christian, are very different from the Aphrodite, and also different from each other in content. What may surprise us is how much alike they are in *form*. The works were made at approximately the same time but some four thousand miles apart.

An image of the Buddha from Tibet or Nepal **(65)** shows the Buddha seated in the pose of meditation, his hands in a classic *mudra*, or hand posture, symbolizing the dispensing of gifts. Arranged around him are *bodhisattvas*, or would-be Buddhas, who have deferred their ultimate goal of *Nirvana*—

65. *A Tathagata Buddha,*
from Tibet. 13th century.
Opaque watercolors on cloth,
$36\frac{1}{4} \times 26\frac{7}{8}''$.
Los Angeles County Museum of Art
(Nasli and Alice Heeramaneck
Collection, Museum Associates
Purchase).

66. Cimabue.
Madonna Enthroned.
c. 1280–90. Panel,
12′7½″ × 7′4″.
Uffizi, Florence.

freedom from the cycle of birth, death, and rebirth—in order to help others attain that goal. All wear halos signifying their holiness. The Buddha, being the most important of the personages depicted, dominates the painting and is much the largest figure. Typically, he faces straight front, in a pose of tranquility, while the others around him stand or sit in relaxed postures.

The second example, painted by the 13th-century Italian master Cimabue, depicts the Virgin Mary, mother of Christ, with her son **(66)**. Mary sits tranquilly on her throne, her hand in a classic gesture indicating the Christ child, who is the hope of earth's salvation. On both sides of her are figures of angels, heavenly beings who assist humankind in its quest for Paradise. Again, all these wear halos symbolizing their holiness. Yet again, the Virgin, being the most important figure in this painting, dominates the composition, is the largest, and holds the most serenely frontal posture.

We should not conclude from the remarkable structural similarity of these works that any communication or influence took place between Italy and central Asia. A safer assumption is that two artists of different faiths independently found a format that satisfied their pictorial needs. Both the Buddha and the Virgin are important, serene holy figures. Bodhisattvas and angels, who are always more active, attend them. Therefore, the artists, from their separate points of view, devised similar compositions.

So we see that religious art is deeply affected by many forces: when it was made, where, why, by whom, and for what purpose. The same is true of art that deals in more earthly matters.

Pride and Politics

It has been said that everything in life comes down to politics. All the worthy emotions—love, honor, patriotism, charity—have at their root a concern with politics, which means simply possessing the power to achieve one's desired goal. This is not the place to debate whether that theory holds true or not, but it is certainly clear that a great portion of the world's art has had political implications. The queen or pope or president who commissions an artist to make a particular work may have a true love of art, but that patron surely knows that a great masterpiece will enhance the patron's prestige and therefore increase his or her power.

Political art, and those who make it, can be divided between the "ins" and the "outs." The "ins" want to be even more in—to consolidate their power and enhance their prestige. The "outs," by and large, are unhappy with the existing political situation (whatever it may be) and hope to dislodge the "ins" and replace them. Art has traditionally served both ends; we will look at a bit of each.

The structures that many consider to be the ultimate in kingly pride, the height of political power, were built four and a half millennia ago and have never been surpassed. At Giza in Egypt rise the three great pyramids, tombs of the pharaohs Mycerinus, Chefren, and Cheops **(67)**. Only an immensely prideful king would divert thousands of workers to the massive chore of erecting a burial mound on this scale. Cheops' pyramid, the largest of the three, is about 450 feet tall (roughly the height of a fifty-story building), covers more than 13 acres, and consists of some 2.3 million blocks of stone. Each of these blocks had to be quarried with hand tools, dragged to the site, and assembled without mortar.

Perhaps even more interesting than the difficulty of the task is the grandiosity of the kings who willed it. The pharaohs planned these pyramids as

67. The Great Pyramids: Pyramid of Mycerinus (c. 2500 B.C.); Pyramid of Chefren (c. 2530 B.C.); Pyramid of Cheops (c. 2570 B.C.). Giza, Egypt.

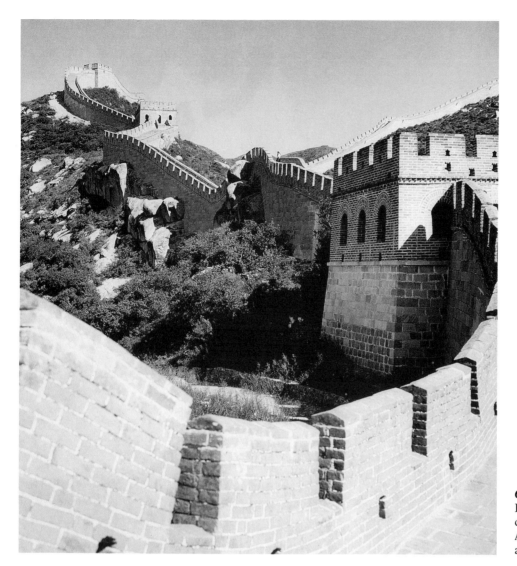

68. Great Wall of China.
Begun c. 228 B.C.,
completed A.D. 17th century.
Average height 25′,
average thickness at base 25′.

safe and permanent resting places for themselves and their families in the afterlife. By their logic, the more powerful an individual had been in life, the more dramatic a mark that individual's tomb should make upon the landscape. The great pyramids, therefore, represent an extreme of kingly pride, of a pharaoh saying, in effect, "*My* name will never be forgotten; *my* monument will endure through all the generations to come." And so far, despite the wars and political upheavals and natural disasters that the earth has witnessed, they have been right.

We assume the pharaohs, in building their pyramids, were motivated by pride. However, we *know* what motivated another great ruler to undertake an even more amibitous project. The Great Wall of China **(68)** was built along the northern borders of China to repel invasion by barbarians from outside the empire. Sections of the wall may have existed as early as the 5th century B.C., but the greatest spurt of building took place by order of Shi Huang Di, the first emperor of China, between about 228 and 204 B.C. Constructed entirely by hand of stone and earth, the wall eventually reached a length of more than two thousand miles, curving to follow the contours of rivers, deserts, and mountains. (For comparison, imagine a wall 25 feet high and about 25 feet thick at the base stretching from New York to Denver.) Today much of the Great Wall has crumbled, and what remains is basically a tourist attraction. But in an era before airplanes and missiles, Shi Huang Di and those who followed him could hope to keep themselves politically "in" by keeping everybody else *out*.

69. *Augustus of Prima Porta.*
c. 20 B.C. Marble, height 6'8".
Vatican Museums, Rome.

Given what we know about the spread of the mighty Roman Empire in the few centuries surrounding the birth of Christ, it is not surprising that some of the most prideful and political art was created at that time. The Roman emperors, who eventually conquered most of the civilized world they knew of, understood the political value of celebrating themselves and their achievements. An example of this approach to art is the statue of Augustus, which is known as the *Augustus of Prima Porta* **(69)**.

Augustus came to power in Rome in 31 B.C. by virtue of his military successes, and he reigned unchallenged for forty-five years—the first of the great Roman emperors. Under Augustus the empire enjoyed peace, prosperity, administrative order, and a flowering of the arts. In those times the line separating admiration for the ruler and worship of a deity was a fine one; emperors and heroes took on the attributes of gods. (The little figure accompanying Augustus is a cupid, symbol of Venus, the goddess from whom the emperor was supposedly descended.) That Augustus deliberately sought to enhance this godlike image is clear, and recent scholarship provides fascinating clues about how this statue and others played a role in his "public relations" campaign.

Considerable evidence supports the theory that Augustus was in fact much less attractive than he appears here. In life he had unruly hair, a small chin, small eyes, big ears, a bony face, and thin lips. Scholars now believe that in about 27 B.C.—seven years before the presumed date of the Prima Porta figure—the emperor commissioned an idealized portrait head, which was to be used as a model for all later sculptures, regardless of the emperor's advancing age. The Prima Porta head was based on this model; it is not only beautiful and godlike but also resembles the idealized Greek style. What were Augustus' motives for promoting this idealized self-portrait? According to those who have studied the question, "the portrait was supposed to show that he had ideal human qualities and, at the same time, that he stood for a culture that combined the best traditions." Also, the Prima Porta style head "was part of a representational program which gave Romans hope for the future under Augustus, as a divinely inspired leader. He claimed to be acting as the agent of the gods on earth."[1] In other words, the emperor's purpose in commissioning this art was a political one—an attempt to consolidate his power and ensure its continuity.

For the ultimate in a political portrait, however, we must look several hundred years later, to a king who so wholeheartedly embraced his role as divine ruler that he dared to say "L'état, c'est moi" ("I am the state")—Louis XIV of France. Hyacinthe Rigaud's portrait (70) captures all the pageantry of a reign that was built on drama as carefully as any full-scale operatic performance might be.

Louis himself commented on the value of visible symbols: "Those who imagine that these are merely matters of ceremony are gravely mistaken. . . . The peoples over whom we reign, being unable to apprehend the basic reality of things, usually derive their opinions from what they can see with their eyes."[2] Louis ruled as the "Sun King" for an amazing seventy-two years, and during that time France experienced a period of political, social, and artistic achievement without parallel. At his death the nation was only seventy-five

70. Hyacinthe Rigaud. *Louis XIV*. 1701. Oil on canvas, 9'1½" × 6'2⅝". Louvre, Paris.

years away from revolution—a revolution that would bring down the monarchy—but while Louis sat on the throne he kept all eyes focused on himself as the personification of France in her glory.

To the modern viewer Louis's costume seems absurd, his pose more than a little affected, but his subjects must have found the picture inspiring. No detail that might have contributed to the king's grandeur has been spared, from the lavish ermine-lined robes, to the lush canopy of the backdrop, to the classical Greek column at left. Louis obviously realized that political power rests on illusion. Art that fostered the illusion helped to maintain the power.

So far in this section we have focused on the person who was the *patron* of political art, rather than the artist who made it. Let us turn our attention now to the artist who chooses a specific political ideal and uses his or her talent to realize it. More often than not, such artists are allied with the "outs," not the "ins," of the political scene. Among the most famous of these was the 19th-century French artist Honoré Daumier.

Daumier was a painter, but he achieved greater renown as a political cartoonist, and he possessed all the traits necessary for the latter occupation— righteous anger, an eye for the telling detail, and a pen that could strike like a stiletto. In the early 1830s Daumier's harsh political criticism brought him fame but also got him into trouble with the authorities. One image in particular, widely distributed as a print (Chapter 8), caused official wrath, and that was *Murder in the rue Transnonain* **(71)**.

The title of Daumier's work was enough for his contemporary audience to understand the subject. In 1834 France was rocked by a popular uprising against the government of King Louis Philippe. Working-class people who lived on a certain street in Paris, the rue Transnonain, were suspected of taking part. On April 15 shots were fired from one tenement building, whereupon the civil guard broke in and killed an entire family—without determining their guilt or innocence. Daumier has portrayed the chilling aftermath of that slaughter. The father lies sprawled against a disarrayed bed, nearly covering the body of a dead child. A woman's body, graceless in sudden death, fills the shadows at left, while an old man's blood-spattered head projects into the picture at right.

Daumier's harsh realism gives this image its poignancy. We can't help wondering what these people were doing just a few moments ago, before they were murdered. Were they sleeping? Was the old man sitting in the chair,

71. Honoré Daumier. *Murder in the rue Transnonain.* 1834. Lithograph, $11\frac{1}{4} \times 17\frac{3}{8}$". The Metropolitan Museum of Art, New York (Rogers Fund, 1920).

now overturned? The father's body, bathed in light, has a heroic quality despite the clumsy pose (or perhaps because of it). Daumier's art turned this poor family into martyrs for the cause—as the authorities well knew when they confiscated the artist's original and destroyed most of the copies.

Our next example also was created by an artist whose sympathies lay with those not in power, an artist who took up his brush with a sense of fury at the "ins" who caused devastation. From his fury came one of the great masterpieces of 20th-century art. The artist was Picasso, and the painting is called *Guernica* **(72)**.

It is necessary to know the story behind *Guernica* to understand its power. In 1937 Europe was moving toward war, and a trial run, so to speak, occurred in Spain, where the forces of General Francisco Franco waged civil war against the established government. Franco willingly accepted aid from Hitler, and in exchange he allowed the Nazis to test their developing air power. On April 28, 1937, the Germans bombed the town of Guernica, the old Basque capital in northern Spain. There was no real military reason for the raid; it was simply an experiment to see whether aerial bombing could wipe out a whole city. Being totally defenseless, Guernica was devastated and its civilian population massacred.

At the time Picasso, himself a Spaniard, was working in Paris and had been commissioned by his government to paint a mural for the Spanish Pavilion of the Paris World's Fair of 1937. For some time he had procrastinated about fulfilling the commission; then, within days after news of the bombing reached Paris, he started *Guernica* and completed it in little over a month. Despite the speedy execution, however, this was no unreasoning outburst of anger. Picasso controlled his rage, perhaps knowing that it could have better effect in a carefully planned canvas, and he made many preliminary drawings **(225)**. The finished mural had a shocking effect on those who saw it; it remains today a chillingly dramatic protest against the brutality of war.

At first encounter with *Guernica* the viewer is overwhelmed by its size; it is more than 25 feet long and nearly 12 feet high. It dominates any space in which it is hung and seems to reach out and engulf the observer. Picasso used no colors; the whole painting is done in white and black and shades of gray, possibly to create a "newsprint" quality in reporting the event. Although the artist's symbolism is very personal (and he declined to explain it in detail), we cannot misunderstand the images of extreme pain and anguish throughout the canvas. At far left a shrieking mother holds her dead child and at far

72. Pablo Picasso. *Guernica.* 1937. Oil on canvas, 11'5½" × 25'5¾". Museo del Prado, Madrid.

right another woman, in a burning house, screams in agony. The gaping mouths and clenched hands speak of disbelief at such mindless cruelty.

Another victim is the dying horse to the left of center, speared from above and just as stunned by the carnage as any of the human sufferers. Various writers have interpreted the bull at upper left in different ways. Picasso drew much of his imagery from the bullfight, an ingrained part of his Spanish heritage. Perhaps the bull symbolizes the brutal victory of the Nazis; perhaps it, like the horse, is also a victim of carnage. There is even more confusion about the symbols of the lamp and the light bulb at top center. These may be indications that light is being cast on the horrors of war, or they may be signals of hope. Picasso did not tell us, so we are free to make our own associations.

With *Guernica* Picasso, like Daumier a century earlier, functioned as an artist of the "outs"—a voice crying against those who had power to do something of which he disapproved vehemently. Much political art of our time has this purpose. In the United States one group, black Americans, has a long history of being "out"—out of power, out of work, out of schools, out of the material pleasures of society. No wonder, then, that oppression of blacks should have found expression in art.

Jacob Lawrence, who is himself black, took up this theme in the early 1940s with an ambitious sixty-panel series called *The Migration of the Negro.* We illustrate here the best-known panel from the series, *One of the Largest Race Riots Occurred in East St. Louis* **(73)**. As a work of social protest, Lawrence's painting can be compared, in concept if not in style, to Picasso's *Guernica.* Rather than depicting realistically the bloody violence of a race riot, Lawrence has transformed the action into a stylized ballet of flat, abstract shapes. Interpreted this way, the conflict takes on universal implications, revealing not just a vicious clash of individuals, but the underlying hatreds of "us" against "them" that mark a pattern throughout human history. Lawrence's composition is a masterful geometric arrangement, all forms leading to the clenched fist holding a knife—the one form silhouetted above the horizon line.

73. Jacob Lawrence.
One of the Largest Race Riots Occurred in East St. Louis,
Panel 52 from *The Migration of the Negro.* 1940–41.
Tempera on composition board, 12 × 18".
Collection, The Museum of Modern Art, New York (gift of Mrs. David M. Levy).

Jacob Lawrence

b. 1917

The name "Harlem" is associated in many people's minds with hardship and poverty. Poverty Harlem has always known, but during the 1920s it experienced a tremendous cultural upsurge that has come to be called the Harlem Renaissance. So many of the greatest names in black culture—musicians, writers, artists, poets, scientists—lived or worked in Harlem at the time, or simply took their inspiration from its intellectual energy. To Harlem, about 1930, came a young teenager named Jacob Lawrence, relocating from Philadelphia with his mother, brother, and sister. The flowering of the Harlem Renaissance had passed, but there remained enough momentum to help turn the child of a poor family into one of the most distinguished American artists of his generation.

Young Lawrence's home life was not happy, but he had several islands of refuge: the public library, the Harlem Art Workshop, and the Metropolitan Museum of Art. He studied at the Harlem Art Workshop from 1932 to 1934 and received much encouragement from two noted black artists, Charles Alston and Augusta Savage. By the age of twenty Lawrence had begun to exhibit his work. A year later he, like so many others, was being supported by the federal WPA Art Project, a government-sponsored program to help artists through the economic void of the Great Depression.

Even this early in his career, Lawrence had established the themes that would dominate his work. The subject matter comes from his own experience, from black experience: the hardships of poor people in the ghettos, the violence that greeted blacks moving from the South to the urban North, the upheaval of the civil rights movement during the 1960s. Nearly always his art has a narrative content or "story," and often the titles are lengthy. Although Lawrence does paint individual pictures, the bulk of his production has been in series, such as *The Migration of the Negro*, some of them having as many as sixty images.

The year 1941 was significant for Lawrence's life and career. He married the painter Gwendolyn Knight, and he acquired his first dealer, when Edith Halpert of the Downtown Gallery in New York featured him in a major exhibition. The show was successful, and it resulted in the purchase of Lawrence's *Migration* series by two important museums.

From that point Lawrence's career prospered. His paintings always have been in demand, and he is

sought after as an illustrator of magazine covers, posters, and books. His influence continues through his teaching—first at Black Mountain College in North Carolina, later at Pratt Institute, the Art Students League, and the University of Washington. In 1978 he was elected to the National Council on the Arts.

Many people would call Lawrence's paintings instruments of social protest, but his images, however stark, have more the character of reporting than of protest. It is as though he is telling us, "This is what happened, this is the way it is." What happened, of course, happened to black Americans, and Lawrence the world-famous painter does not seem to lose sight of Lawrence the poor youth in Harlem. As he has said, "My belief is that it is most important for an artist to develop an approach and philosophy about life—if he has developed this philosophy he does not put paint on canvas, he puts himself on canvas."[3]

Jacob Lawrence. *Self-Portrait*, detail. 1977.
Gouache on paper, 23 × 31".
National Academy of Design, New York.

74. Robert Rauschenberg. *Bach's Rocks*. 1990. Acrylic and fabric collage on plywood panels, 8'3¼" square. National Gallery of Art, Washington, D.C. (gift of Robert Rauschenberg in honor of the Rauschenberg Foundation).

What happens when the "ins" become "outs," and when the politically unacceptable becomes acceptable? This situation occurred in the late 1980s, when the communist regimes of Europe fell one after another. For decades Europe had been split in two, with democratic and free-market countries in the West, totalitarian and communist countries in the East. A symbol of this division was Berlin—previously one city, then two, cut down the center by the infamous Berlin Wall erected in 1961. How rigid was this division between free West and communist East—and how quickly it changed—can be shown by the experience of one artist, the American Robert Rauschenberg.

For nearly a decade Rauschenberg, through his Rauschenberg Overseas Culture Interchange project (ROCI), had tried repeatedly to mount a show of his work in Berlin. But the exhibition could never be arranged because of the artist's one stipulation: that the show run simultaneously in West Berlin and East Berlin, with access by people from both sides of the wall. The West Berlin museum was willing. The East German government said no, refusing to let its people cross into the western sector.

Then, suddenly, the world changed. On November 9, 1989, the Berlin Wall was opened and began to come down. Rauschenberg hurried to get his exhibition ready, incorporating into works like *Bach's Rocks* **(74)** local references like an image of the Brandenburg Gate, the most famous gate in the wall. The show was planned for East Berlin. No other site was necessary because, astonishingly, Berlin was one city again and everybody could come. As an East German cultural spokesman put it, "An artist—who would be surprised at this?—couldn't breach the wall; a citizens' movement did. But I want to thank [Rauschenberg] for his readiness not to abandon the project despite many failures."[4]

Robert Rauschenberg

b. 1925

Born in Port Arthur, Texas, Milton Rauschenberg—who later became known as Bob and then Robert—had no exposure to art as such until he was seventeen. His original intention to become a pharmacist faded when he was expelled from the University of Texas within six months, for failure (he claims) to dissect a frog. After three years in the Navy during World War II, Rauschenberg spent a year at the Kansas City Art Institute; then he traveled to Paris for further study. At the Académie Julian in Paris he met the artist Susan Weil, whom he later married.

Upon his return to the United States in 1948, Rauschenberg enrolled in the now-famous art program headed by the painter Josef Albers at Black Mountain College in North Carolina. Many of his long-term attachments and interests developed during this period, including his close working relationship with the avant-garde choreographer Merce Cunningham. In 1950 Rauschenberg moved to New York, where he supported himself partly by doing window displays for the fashionable Fifth Avenue stores Bonwit Teller and Tiffany's.

Rauschenberg's work began to attract critical attention soon after his first one-man exhibition at the Betty Parsons Gallery in New York. The artist reports that, between the time Parsons selected the works to be exhibited and the opening of the show, he had completely reworked everything, and that "Betty was surprised." More surprises were soon to come from this unpredictable artist.

The range of Rauschenberg's work makes him difficult to categorize. In addition to paintings, prints, and combination pieces, he has done extensive set and costume design for dances by Cunningham and others, as well as graphic design for magazines and books. "Happenings" and performance art played a role in his work from the very beginning. In 1952, at Black Mountain College, he participated in *Theater Piece #1*, by the composer John Cage, which included improvised dance, recitations, piano music, the playing of old records, and projected slides of Rauschenberg's paintings. Even the works usually classified as paintings are anything but conventional. One has an actual stuffed bird attached to the front of the canvas. Another consists of a bed, with a quilt on it, hung upright on the wall and

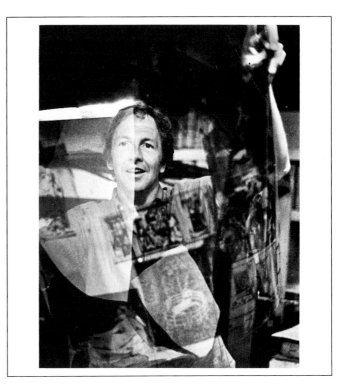

splashed with paint. Works that might be called sculptures are primarily assemblage; for example *Sor Aqua* (1973) is composed of a bathtub (with water) above which a large chunk of metal seems to be flying.

In recent years the artist has devoted much of his time to ROCI (pronounced "Rocky"), his Rauschenberg Overseas Culture Interchange, which has as its goal promoting international friendship, understanding, and peace. Through ROCI he has brought his work to Mexico, Chile, China, Venezuela, Japan, Cuba, the Soviet Union, and the newly liberated city of Berlin.

We get from Rauschenberg a sense of boundaries being dissolved—boundaries between media, between art and nonart, between art and life. He has said: "The strongest thing about my work . . . is the fact that I chose to ennoble the ordinary."[5]

Robert Rauschenberg, photographed by Hans Namuth.

Art as the Mirror of Everyday Life

When children start to draw and paint, they deal in the images they know best: mother and father, sisters and brothers, the teacher, the house, the dog. Many artists never lose their preoccupation with everyday things, and so we have a rich heritage of art depicting those concerns that are closest to the artist's personal world.

Art that depicts the little moments of everyday life and its surroundings is known as *genre.* Often, its purpose is a simple one—to record, to please the eye, to make us smile. Images like this occur throughout the entire history of art, in all cultures and parts of the world. A charming example from China is *Ladies Preparing Newly Woven Silk* **(75)**, part of a handscroll made in the 12th century but copied from an 8th-century painting. No grand political or social issues are at stake here. Rather, the artist has captured a delightful scene of daily activity: three women and a girl stretch and comb the length of silk, while a little girl peeks underneath as though to see what is going on. The fresh pastel colors of the kimonos, the women's quiet poses, the atmosphere of pleasant shared work—all these elements combine to give us a gentle masterpiece of genre.

A series of equally charming genre paintings occurs in an early French manuscript, one page of which we shall examine here. During the Middle Ages wealthy patrons customarily would commission artists to *illuminate,* or hand-illustrate, books, particularly prayer books. In the early 15th century a close relationship existed between the Duc de Berry, brother of the French king, and three artist brothers, the Limbourgs. The Limbourgs painted for the duke what has become one of the most famous illuminated books in the history of art, *Les Très Riches Heures* ("the very rich book of hours"). It contains a calendar, with each month's painting showing a typical seasonal activity of either the peasantry or the aristocracy.

The *February* page, shown here **(76)**, focuses on a small peasant hut with its occupants clustered around the fire, their garments pulled back to get maximum benefit from the warmth. (Underwear as we know it had not yet been invented, and so this forthright image has occasionally been censored.)

75. *Ladies Preparing Newly Woven Silk,* from China, Northern Song Dynasty. Attributed to Emperor Hui-zong (1082–1135) but probably by a court painter. Section of a handscroll; ink, colors, and gold on silk; 1'2½" × 4'9¼". Museum of Fine Arts, Boston (Chinese and Japanese Special Fund).

76. Limbourg Brothers. *February* page, from *Les Très Riches Heures du Duc de Berry*. 1416. Illumination, $8\frac{7}{8} \times 5\frac{3}{8}''$. Musée Condé, Chantilly.

With a touch of poetic license, the artists have removed the front of the hut so that we may look inside. Outside the hut we see what may be the earliest snow-covered landscape ever painted. Sheep cluster in their enclosure, a peasant comes rushing across the barnyard pulling his cloak about his face to keep in the warm breath. From there the movement progresses diagonally up the slope to a man chopping firewood, another urging a donkey uphill, and finally the church at the top. Such was the everyday life of the lower classes in medieval France, and the Limbourgs have left us a capsule picture of it.

Genre painting has been important in the United States since colonial times. One of its greatest practitioners was Missouri-bred George Caleb Bingham, who in the mid-19th century portrayed scenes of what was then the American frontier. Bingham's most famous picture, *Fur Traders Descending the Missouri*, shows us an apparently simple subject—a man, a boy, a pet fox, a flat boat floating placidly down the river. At one level we can read the painting as simply capturing a slice of life in the untamed American Midwest

77. George Caleb Bingham.
*Fur Traders Descending
the Missouri.* 1844.
Oil on canvas, 29 × 36½″.
The Metropolitan Museum of Art,
New York
(Morris K. Jesup Fund, 1933).

(77), but such is Bingham's skill that we find more in the scene as we continue to study it. The serene horizontal of the boat barely making a ripple in the still water, the tranquil poses of the fur traders, the misty (almost mystical) island glimpsed behind them, the cottony clouds in the sky—all these combine to create a poetic vision of people in harmony with nature. One strangely eerie note is the fox, black and motionless, reflected in the mirrorlike river.

French artists of the period were equally interested in portraying life's little moments, the fleeting experiences that last for an instant and then are gone. This type of subject was a particular favorite with the Impressionist painters of the late 19th century, whose goal was to record that which is transitory—an impression (Chapter 17). In Pierre-Auguste Renoir's *Le Moulin de la Galette* **(78)** young couples meet at the outdoor café, they dance, they fall in love. The viewer has a quick impression of the most delightful of all ways to spend a summer day. As observers, we seem to have glanced briefly at the scene and absorbed its essence, rather than its details. We can almost hear the bright music (a waltz tune unquestionably), feel the warm breezes, sense an atmosphere of innocent flirtation and fun.

Everyday life in the late 20th century may take on a different kind of quality, as evidenced by the sculptures of George Segal **(79)**. In 1982 Segal set up three of his life-size figures in New York City's Port Authority bus terminal, ostensibly waiting in line to buy a ticket. The figures are naturalistic, having been cast from living models (Chapter 11 and **360**), but they are made of unpainted white plaster. And they wait. Patiently, eternally, they wait in line, much as the modern-day individual has to wait for the bureaucratic realities of life to sort themselves out. Commuters moving through the bus terminal were much taken by Segal's waiting people. Some good-humored passersby fell casually in line behind them, as though prepared to stand immobile as long as they did, amused by this image of themselves. Segal, himself a commuter, managed to capture what is for the urbanite, unfortunately, a faithful mirror of everyday life.

above: **78.** Pierre-Auguste Renoir.
Le Moulin de la Galette. 1876.
Oil on canvas, 4'3½" × 5'9".
Musée d'Orsay, Paris.

right: **79.** George Segal. *Next Departure.* 1979.
Bronze, metal, plaster, wood, paper, and vinyl;
7 × 6 × 8'. Installation 1982 at Port Authority
of N.Y. and N.J. Bus Terminal, New York.

Art and Nature

If art is the mirror of everyday life, it is also the mirror of everyday surroundings. Drive out into the country on a splendid autumn day, and along the road you are likely to see cars parked, easels set up, amateur painters trying to distill, on canvas or watercolor paper, the glories of the natural landscape. Throughout history professional artists, too, have responded to this impulse and have turned their eyes to nature as an engrossing subject for art. What they have seen depends on many things, including the cultures in which they worked and their own artistic visions.

Our first example, a miniature from 16th-century India, is part of the *Akbar Nama,* or history of Akbar. The Mughal emperor Akbar, who ruled

right: 80. Lal and Sanwlah.
Akbar Hunting with Trained Cheetahs,
from the *Akbar Nama.*
c. 1590. Gouache on paper,
height 15″.
Victoria & Albert Museum, London
(courtesy of the Trustees).

below: 81. John Constable.
The White Horse. 1819.
Oil on canvas, 4′3⅝″ × 6′2⅛″.
The Frick Collection,
New York (copyright).

India from 1556 to 1605, was both a powerful leader and an enthusiastic patron of the arts. He attracted to his court both Indian and Persian artists, providing them not only with his royal patronage but also with the finest painting materials available, including powdered gold. *Akbar Hunting with Trained Cheetahs* **(80)** shows the emperor at middle right, on a rearing brown horse, watching his cheetah bring down an antelope. The landscape teems with activity. Horses, men, and game rush through the trees and brush, in and around the bulbous, knobby outcroppings of rock. In fact, the trees and rocks themselves seem to be in motion, caught up in the frenzy of the hunt. There is no area of rest for our eyes in this scene. Every inch of the painting is filled with decorative detail and bursting with energy. Were it not for the dominance of natural forms in the composition, we might be tempted to call this a genre scene. But here even the powerful emperor is rendered small amid the turbulence of the landscape.

England in the first half of the 19th century produced two preeminent landscape artists who were only a year apart in age but light years apart in their approach to the painting of nature. John Constable was concerned with absolute naturalism, a sense of what—for him—the landscape *really* looked like. In a Constable painting, such as *The White Horse* **(81)**, the viewer seems to be surrounded by the natural scene, inside it without taking a step. To stand before this huge canvas is to be transported to another world, a peaceful corner of the rural English countryside. Constable was meticulous about recording details of foliage and other features, but his main fascination lay in transitory effects of light and changing patterns in the sky. The sunlight dapples through the leaves, reflects off the water, and picks out the white horse that gives the painting its name. Clouds scuttling across the sky seem actually to be in motion; we know that a second earlier or later the effect would be different. For all their serenity, Constable's visions capture a moment that will never come again.

Landscapes in the later work of Joseph Mallord William Turner would never be called serene. To be sure, Turner also strove to capture the transitory moment, but his moments are those at the height of the storm, so to speak. Cyclones at sea, huge fires on land, blizzards and tempests and outbursts of *Rockets and Blue Lights* **(82)**—these are the subjects of a Turner

82. J. M. W. Turner. *Rockets and Blue Lights*. 1840. Oil on canvas, 3'⅛" × 4'⅛". Sterling and Francine Clark Art Institute, Williamstown, Mass.

83. Paul Cézanne. *Mont Sainte-Victoire.* 1902–04. Oil on canvas, $27\frac{1}{2} \times 35\frac{1}{4}''$. Philadelphia Museum of Art (George W. Elkins Collection).

landscape, so transformed by the artist's abstraction as to become studies in light and air. Turner's paintings are whirlpools of energy, so compelling we seem to hear dramatic music crashing in the background.

Yet another approach to the theme of nature can be found in Paul Cézanne's *Mont Sainte-Victoire* (83), one of many versions the artist painted of a mountain near his home in Provence. We may be amazed to see that less than a hundred years and only the breadth of the English Channel separate Cézanne's landscape from those of Constable and Turner. Through the later years of Cézanne's life Mont Sainte-Victoire obsessed him, but his interest was less in recording nature than in searching for a solidity and unity of form in nature, an inherent order that he saw with his painter's eye. To Cézanne, geometry served as the basis for all forms, including those in the landscape. He sought to discover the forms of geometric solids—the cone, the sphere, the cylinder—in nature and to record them in his paintings.

Absolute naturalism, a lifelike recording, is not the goal of Cézanne's expression. His purpose was to explore the landscape as a vehicle for the study of forms in space, much as he would study a group of objects on a table for a still life painting. Here he has reduced the vista of Mont Sainte-Victoire to a pattern of color patches, with individual brush strokes defining planes and surfaces. Details are generally obscured. One does not walk through this landscape or repose within it; one stands back and considers it as a perfect realization of form.

Paul Cézanne

1839–1906

Paul Cézanne remains one of the most enigmatic figures in modern art history, even though the details of his life are well known. A word often used to describe his personality is "difficult." Clearly, he was a man of intelligence and great sensitivity, yet he could be rude to strangers and boorish with his friends. Although he was acquainted with most of the leading artists then working in Paris, he spent the greater part of his life in isolation in the southern French town of Aix-en-Provence, where he was born.

Cézanne's banker father tried to steer his son into his own profession or the law, but the young man showed so little talent and inclination for either that eventually the father gave up and permitted him to undertake art studies. Cézanne's first attempts at exhibiting his work met with disastrous results; the critics' reactions ranged from ridicule to outrage. Nevertheless, he persevered, struggling on alone to achieve the form in art that was his vision. Cézanne's paintings are difficult to date, because he worked on many canvases at once and often labored over the same painting for several years. So demanding was he with live models that few sitters were willing to pose for him. One who did pose, the art dealer Ambroise Vollard, reported that he was forced to endure 115 sittings, some lasting three hours or more.

In 1869, while visiting Paris, Cézanne met a young woman, Marie-Hortense Fiquet, and they became lovers. Some three years later their son Paul was born. Cézanne went to extraordinary lengths to conceal this liaison from his domineering father, for fear his allowance would be cut.

For most of Cézanne's life only the very discerning—and they were few—recognized the genius of his art. After his initial disappointments, the artist stopped exhibiting in Paris for twenty years. Then in 1895 Ambroise Vollard decided to mount a show—Cézanne's first one-man exhibition—and asked the artist to send all available work. Cézanne bundled up 150 canvases and shipped them off to Paris from Aix. The show took Paris completely by surprise and was an immediate sensation. From that time until his death the artist gradually acquired the recognition he deserved; ironically, he had become so embittered by long neglect that the acclaim gave him little pleasure.

While alternatively mocked and ignored by critics and the general public, Cézanne never lost faith in himself and his art. In 1874 he wrote this to his mother: "I am beginning to find myself stronger than any of those around me. . . . I must go on working, but not in order to attain a finished perfection, which is so much sought after by imbeciles. And this quality which is commonly so much admired is nothing but the accomplishment of a craftsman, and makes any work produced in that way inartistic and vulgar. I must not try to finish anything except for the pleasure of making it truer and wiser. And you may be sure that there will come a time when I shall come into my own, and that I have admirers who are much more fervent, more steadfast than those who are attracted only by an empty outward appearance."[6]

Paul Cézanne. *Self-Portrait with a Beret.* c. 1906.
Oil on canvas, 25¼ × 21".
Museum of Fine Arts, Boston
(Charles H. Bayley Picture and Painting Fund
and partial gift of Elizabeth Paine Metcalf).

84. *The Five-Colored Parakeet,* from China, Northern Song Dynasty. Before 1126. Detail of a handscroll, ink and colors on silk, height 21". Museum of Fine Arts, Boston (Maria Antoinette Evans Fund).

Nature on a grand scale inspired the artists we have considered so far in this section, but nature on a small scale can be as compelling. *The Five-Colored Parakeet* **(84)**, a Chinese scroll attributed to the same artist who painted the genre scene we saw earlier **(75)**, selects just a few elements from nature to create this delicate composition. A bird perched on a blossoming branch—beautiful and perfect forms are studied for their pleasing contrasts of color and texture. The bird is drawn with meticulous realism, each feather carefully delineated, and the delicate blossoms and rough bark of the tree branch receive graceful attention.

Our next artist zooms in on natural forms even more tightly. The flower paintings of Georgia O'Keeffe, such as *Black Hollyhock, Blue Larkspur* **(85)**, are extreme close-ups, almost to the point of abstraction. O'Keeffe examines every nuance of the form minutely, as though a whole universe were unfolding within the flower. Much has been made of the apparent sexual symbolism in these paintings, and, although the artist denied it, there is surely a sensuous quality to the flower's lush opening.

O'Keeffe's flowers fill nearly every square inch of her canvas, leaving only a little background (non-flower) at the upper edges. For a contrast, we might look at Joan Nelson's *Untitled #227* **(86)**, which seems to have nothing *but* upper edges. A quick glance gives the impression that Nelson used only the space O'Keeffe had left over. Almost the whole of Nelson's tiny painting consists of sky, showing just a hint of organic forms at the top. The observer of this scene could be in a cave, looking up and out at the clouds, so that the upper rim of the cave obscures the view slightly.

Why did the artist choose such an unusual angle? Why is there much more sky than landscape? The answer gives us clues to the essence of art. In Chapter 2 (p. 40) we said that a painting of a horse is not a horse; horses are flesh and blood, paintings are daubs of paint on a background. Nelson amplifies this idea. She chooses an image that looks like an unimportant detail from the upper section of, say, a Constable **(81)** and makes it the center of attention. Then she works over her paintings heavily, coating them with wax or varnish, scarring and scraping them to get the quality of an "Old Master" painting that has hung in a museum for generations. Nelson wants us to see that her work is "about" the subject of painting, not "about" the subject of nature. It is the artist's creation, daubs of paint on a background. Of course, every other version of nature painting is the same—as is every painting of every kind. But Nelson drives the point home.

above: **85.** Georgia O'Keeffe.
Black Hollyhock, Blue Larkspur.
1929. Oil on canvas, 36 × 30″.
The Metropolitan Museum of Art,
New York (George A. Hearn Fund,
1934).

left: **86.** Joan Nelson.
Untitled (#227). 1988.
Oil and wax on wood, 12″ square.
Courtesy Robert Miller Gallery,
New York.

Georgia O'Keeffe

1887–1986

"At last! A woman on paper!" According to legend, this was the reaction of the famed photographer and art dealer Alfred Stieglitz, in 1916, when he first saw the work of Georgia O'Keeffe. Whether accurate or not, the quote sums up Stieglitz' view of O'Keeffe as the first great artist to bring to her work the true essence and experience of womanhood. Ultimately, much of the critical art world came to share Stieglitz' opinion.

O'Keeffe was born on a farm in Wisconsin. She received a thorough, if conventional, art training at the School of the Art Institute of Chicago and the Art Students League in New York. During the early years she supported herself by teaching art in schools and colleges. By 1912 she was teaching in Amarillo, Texas—the beginning of a lifelong infatuation with the terrain of the Southwest.

In the winter of 1915–16 O'Keeffe sent a number of drawings to a friend in New York, asking her not to show the drawings to anyone. The friend violated this trust—and no doubt helped to set the path for O'Keeffe's entire life and career. She took the drawings to Stieglitz.

By 1916 Stieglitz had gained considerable fame, not only as a photographer but, through his "291" Gallery, as an exhibitor of the most innovative European and American painters. He was stunned by O'Keeffe's work. Later that year he included her in a group show at "291," and in 1917 gave her a solo exhibition. This was the beginning of an extraordinary artistic and personal collaboration that would last until Stieglitz' death in 1946.

O'Keeffe moved to New York. Stieglitz left his wife and lived with her. O'Keeffe painted; Stieglitz exhibited her work and made hundreds of photographs of her. The couple married in 1924, but their union was always an unconventional one. For more than a quarter-century their paths crossed and separated. Stieglitz was most at home in New York City and at his family's summer place at Lake George. O'Keeffe was drawn increasingly to the stark landscapes of Texas and New Mexico. O'Keeffe treasured her husband's presence but could paint at her best only in the Southwest. Stieglitz longed for her company but also needed and wanted her paintings for his gallery.

O'Keeffe gained critical acclaim with her first exhibition, and it never entirely left her. Although major showings of her work were rare after Stieglitz died, no one forgot Georgia O'Keeffe. She was part of

no "school" or style. Her work took an exceptionally personal path, as did her life. She dressed almost exclusively in black. She came and went as she pleased and accepted into her world only those people whom she found talented and interesting. More than most, O'Keeffe marched to her own drummer.

After 1949 O'Keeffe lived permanently in New Mexico, the area with which she is most closely associated. In 1972, when she was eighty-four years old, a potter in his twenties, Juan Hamilton, came into her life, and they became close companions. Rumors that they married are probably unfounded, but Hamilton remained with the increasingly feeble, almost-blind artist until her death.

Early on, in her thirties, O'Keeffe had expressed her impatience with other people's standards for life and art: "I decided I was a very stupid fool not to at least paint as I wanted to and say what I wanted to when I painted as that seemed to be the only thing I could do that didn't concern anybody but myself—that was nobody's business but my own."[7]

Alfred Stieglitz. *Georgia O'Keeffe*. 1932. Photograph.
The Metropolitan Museum of Art, New York
(Alfred Stieglitz Collection, lent by Georgia O'Keeffe).

Nelson's art, like all the rest we have seen in this chapter, looks primarily to the outside for inspiration. Our next thematic category focuses on artists who turn inward, looking instead to their own brains and psyches, for the genesis of their art.

Imagination and Fantasy

The purposes of imaginative art are as complex and as individual as imagination itself. An artist may look inward and paint what he or she sees in an attempt to understand this inner life, to purge it of its terrors, or simply because the products of the imagination seem more interesting than the realities of every day. We may be tempted to think of imaginative art as a purely 20th-century phenomenon, a product of the Freudian era or even of the "me generation." Looking closely at one's dreams and fantasies—and then recording them as art—does indeed seem to be a peculiarly modern preoccupation. Nevertheless, we can trace imaginative art back at least to the 16th century, where it flourished in the hands of the extraordinary Netherlandish artist Hieronymus Bosch.

When we first encounter *The Garden of Earthly Delights* **(87)**, we might think we have wandered into a fun house of a particularly macabre kind. Bosch's large **triptych** (a three-section panel, of which we show only the middle portion) is like a peep into Hell—but this is an X-rated earthly Hell. Hundreds of nude human figures cavort in a fantasy landscape peopled also by giant plants, animals no biologist ever classified, and strange creatures

87. Hieronymus Bosch.
The Garden of Earthly Delights,
center section. c. 1505–10.
Panel, 7'2⅝" × 6'4¾".
Museo del Prado, Madrid.

that are part human, part vegetation. Humans ride upon, emerge from, are devoured by, or become part of the plant and animal forms. Bosch has let his imagination and perhaps his dream imagery go wherever it might. He drew upon many sources for his creations, including folklore, literature, astrology, and religious writings, but only his own inventiveness could have constructed an amazing fantasy land like this one.

Artists who deal in the realm of the imagination are often quite interesting as personalities. This was true of Bosch, and it was true also of an English artist/poet who worked during the late 18th and early 19th centuries. William Blake was, by the standards of his time and most others, a thoroughgoing eccentric. He was foremost a poet and will be remembered by generations of college literature students for the lines "Tyger! Tyger! burning bright/In the forests of the night." Much of Blake's production as an artist involved the illustration of books, not only of his own volumes of poetry but also of the Bible, Shakespeare, and Dante. In these he expressed a kind of personal theology, which he claimed had been revealed to him in visions of God, Christ, various angels, and certain notable personages from history.

Typical is his *Satan Watching the Caresses of Adam and Eve* **(88)**, an illustration for John Milton's epic poem, *Paradise Lost*. The scene depicted does not appear in the Scripture, nor in Milton's poetic version of the fall from grace of Adam and Eve. According to standard Christian doctrine, Adam and Eve were innocent and free of carnal desire before eating the forbidden fruit. William Blake, however, had other ideas, and he followed his own theological and sexual interpretation in this work. Years later, in discussing the illustration, he insisted: "I saw Milton in imagination, and he

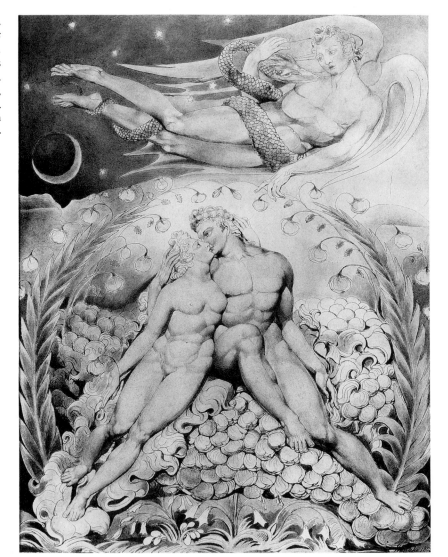

88. William Blake. *Satan Watching the Caresses of Adam and Eve*, illustration for Milton's *Paradise Lost*. 1808. Pen and watercolor on paper, $19\frac{7}{8} \times 15''$. Museum of Fine Arts, Boston (gift by subscription, 1890).

89. Salvador Dali.
The Temptation of St. Anthony.
1947. Oil on canvas, 35¼ × 47".
Musées Royaux des Beaux-Arts
de Belgique, Brussels.

told me to beware of being misled by his *Paradise Lost*. In particular he wished me to shew the falsehood of his doctrine that the pleasure of sex arose from the Fall. The Fall could not produce any pleasure."[8]

Blake's picture, therefore, shows the first couple, still not having touched the apple, still in the Garden of Eden, engaged in a decidedly erotic pursuit. They are enveloped in a lush circle of fantasy foliage, and their bodies are muscular and full-fleshed in the manner of Dürer or Michelangelo, both of whose works were known to the artist. Floating above the pair is the figure of Satan—part angel (it must be remembered that Satan was the fallen angel Lucifer) and part serpent. Soon afterward, Satan, in the guise of a serpent, will tempt Eve to eat the apple, resulting in banishment from the Garden of Eden. Blake's Satan looks down upon the lovers with something rather like jealousy, which gives new meaning to the story of the temptation. The artist's imagery comes not from the Bible, not from Milton, but from Blake's own imagination.

Imaginative treatment of a religious subject also appears in the work of the 20th-century Spanish artist Salvador Dali. In *The Temptation of St. Anthony* **(89)** Dali addresses a subject that had been popular throughout the Middle Ages and early Renaissance. The story concerns efforts by the holy man, St. Anthony, to fend off temptations of the flesh that tormented him in his thoughts and dreams. Earlier representations showed the saint being assailed by all manner of hellish demons and often being lured by a lustful woman or women. Dali has perhaps come closer to the truth by reinterpreting the temptation as a dream/nightmare landscape.

Dali's art, often identified as **Surrealism** (Chapter 17), is predominantly an art of the unconscious. The artist explored his own dreams, studied case histories of psychotic individuals, and even toyed with waking hallucinations, which he claimed he could summon on command. In *The Temptation* St. Anthony appears as a gaunt figure, besieged yet strong, holding off a nightmare parade of fantastic creatures stalking across an endless plain on giant insect legs. Dali's demons are not actual monsters from Hell, but the demons of the mind.

right: **90.** Marc Chagall. *I and the Village.* 1911.
Oil on canvas, 6'3⅝" × 4'11⅝".
Collection, The Museum of Modern Art, New York
(Mrs. Simon Guggenheim Fund).

below: **91.** Judy Chicago. *Birth Trinity*,
from *The Birth Project.* 1983.
Needlepoint on 6-mesh canvas, from color study;
3'6" × 10'6". Needlework by "The Teaneck Group."
Collection Through the Flower,
a nonprofit organization.

Another 20th-century artist who explored the mysteries of the mind was
the Russian-born painter Marc Chagall. In his most famous work, *I and the
Village* **(90)**, Chagall interweaves many diverse memory images from his
childhood to evoke a warm and happy picture of village life. At right we see a
green-faced young man, at left a transparent cow through which is visible a
milkmaid tending another cow. A farmer carrying a scythe strides toward an
upside-down peasant woman against a background of colorful Russian provincial architecture. All conventions of realistic color, size, and placement
have been abandoned in favor of an inner reality—the reality of the mind.
Chagall chooses and arranges his elements according to their importance for
him, his private associations, and the structural needs of the painting as he
conceives it.

From the imaginative and fantastic, we turn to the concrete and everyday: the milestones of life. Years ago it was said that a respectable person's

name should appear in the newspaper only three times—at birth, marriage, and death. Today other lifetime events are considered properly newsworthy, but those three remain paramount. Two are universal, the third prevalent. And all are valid subjects for art.

Birth, Marriage, and Death

It may surprise us to discover that the subject of birth appears so rarely in Western art—the art derived from European traditions (Part Five). Everybody is born, and it is the most important thing that ever happens to us. Many children being born now are photographed and videotaped in the act, and some doctors even provide videotapes of the baby *in utero* through the miracle of ultrasound. But, except for religious pictures—images of the birth of Christ are plentiful—birth has not captured the attention of many artists.

Contemporary artist Judy Chicago believes this is so because, historically, most artists have been men, and men do not have babies. Her large-scale enterprise called *The Birth Project* (91) was planned to remedy this absence of birth imagery. Its approximately one hundred individual pieces were designed by Chicago, then executed in various forms of fiber craft by 150 volunteer needleworkers, nearly all women. Most forms of traditional "women's craft" are represented—embroidery, quilting, weaving, crochet, petit point—with the needleworkers following Chicago's lushly colored and often anatomically graphic designs.

Artists outside the European tradition are more likely to accept birth and infancy as fit subjects for their expression. The "primitive" art of Africa, Oceania, and Central and South America includes numerous mother-and-baby figures. Our example from the Bambara tribe in Mali (92) shows the mother protectively cradling her newborn child, the infant giving every sign of safety and warmth pressed against its mother's belly.

For a similar treatment in Western art—a rare one—we turn to a painting by Paula Modersohn-Becker, called *Mother and Child* (93). What might have been simply a woman nursing her baby has been given a universal quality by Modersohn-Becker, so that the image seems to be *all* mothers nursing all babies since time began. The mother's body, heavy and solid as the earth itself, curves protectively around the child, who in turn curves into

above: **92.** *Mother and Child*, Bambara tribe, from Mali. Wood, height 4'5⅝".
The Metropolitan Museum of Art, New York (The Michael C. Rockefeller Memorial Collection, bequest of Nelson A. Rockefeller, 1979).

left: **93.** Paula Modersohn-Becker. *Mother and Child.* 1906. Oil on canvas, 2'10½" × 4'1". Sammlung Böttcherstrasse, Bremen.

the mother's belly. Both figures are anonymous; the baby's face is obscured, and the woman's barely articulated. Modersohn-Becker's picture speaks not just of childbearing but of the unbreakable attachment, the love, between mother and child.

Marriage is popular with artists from all cultures; in fact, it is the subject of one of the most famous works in Western art, *Giovanni Arnolfini and His Wife* (94). Painted in the 15th century by the northern European artist Jan van Eyck, the "Arnolfini Wedding," as it is sometimes called, is believed by many experts to have had a specific purpose. It apparently served as a marriage document, made to record and legitimize the nuptials between the merchant Arnolfini and his bride, Giovanna Cenami. At center in the painting is a mirror reflecting the artist, who has come to bear witness to the ceremony, adding his signature "Jan van Eyck was here, 1434." To reinforce the solemn nature of the occasion, the artist has included many symbols, such as the little dog at the couple's feet—an emblem of fidelity. Arnolfini has removed his shoes to indicate that he is standing on sacred ground—the ground on which are pledged the holy vows of matrimony. Other symbols relate to the potential fruitfulness of marriage, from the actual fruits on the windowsill to the marriage bed in the background. In fact, some observers have concluded that the new wife is already pregnant, but her gesture and rounded form are probably due mostly to the fashions of the day.

Henri Rousseau's *Wedding in the Country* (95) is certainly not the solemn marriage document Van Eyck's was meant to be. Futhermore, given what we know about Rousseau's free exercise of imagination (p. 43), we might take the scene depicted in his painting with a grain of salt. Rousseau poses the bridal couple stiffly—he with his relatives at left, she supported by her relatives at right. The groom gazes fondly at his new wife, but no one, least of all the bride, looks particularly happy on this gala occasion. The two families, in fact, are eyeing each other suspiciously. As though to highlight their wariness, the artist has given each family its own personal forest—two clumps of

94. Jan van Eyck.
Giovanni Arnolfini and His Wife.
1434. Oil on wood, 33 × 22½″.
The National Gallery, London
(reproduced by courtesy
of the Trustees).

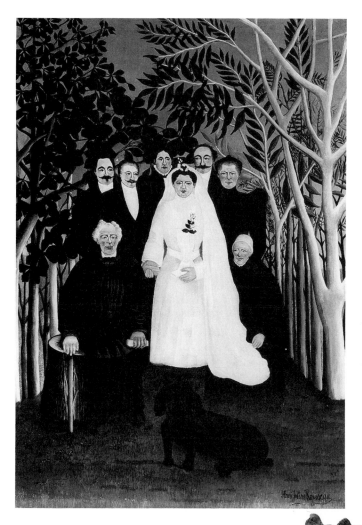

left: 95. Henri Rousseau. *A Wedding in the Country.* 1904–05. Oil on canvas, 5′4¼″ × 3′8⅞″. Musée d'Orsay, Paris.

below: 96. *Sarcophagus of the Spouses,* from Cerveteri. c. 520 B.C. Terra cotta, length 6′7″. Museo Nazionale di Villa Giulia, Rome.

trees with decidedly different foliage. Can these family trees grow together through the union of marriage? Not even the minister, with his worred frown, would depend on it. Rousseau's painting style may be naive, but he has captured a situation that prevails at all too many weddings.

There is no shortage of death imagery in the history of art. From all times, from all cultures, artworks commemorating death are abundant. We have already seen one such example, the Great Pyramids of Egypt, but the scale of those funeral structures is so grandiose that we placed them in the category of political art. Personal mementos of death are more common, and often they take the form of tomb imagery.

Our first illustration shows a **sarcophagus,** or burial coffin, from the ancient Etruscans—the people who inhabited the Italian peninsula from about the 7th century B.C. until the rise of the Roman Empire. From this example **(96)** and many others, we can deduce that the Etruscans held a more serene view of death than most cultures before and after. A couple, presumably husband and wife, recline comfortably on the lid of their sarcophagus, their demeanor suggesting that not only their spirits but their bodies are enjoying the hereafter. Their expressions are those of people at a pleasant dinner party, engaged in animated conversation with other guests, whom we cannot see. This tomb sculpture has a reassuring quality, comforting those left behind with the thought that their loved ones are happy, that the afterlife is not a bad place to be.

The final two works of art in this chapter have much in common. Both commemorate death on a hideously large scale. Both are memorials to *unexpected* death—not the anticipated rest after a long life, but death coming prematurely, striking mostly the young. And both are meant to personalize *each* death among the many, to celebrate the individual life that was amid the mass tragedy that is.

The Vietnam Memorial in Washington, D.C. **(97)**, is the most-visited spot in the nation's capital. Completed in 1982, the memorial was designed by Maya Ying Lin, who was just twenty-two years old when her entry was selected from more than 1,400 submitted for this government commission. When first unveiled to the public, Lin's design was highly controversial. It is, after all, nothing more than two long walls of polished black granite, set into the earth so as to form a V. Many viewers felt "the Wall," as it has come to be called, flaunted tradition, that it was not sufficiently respectful of those who fought the bloody Vietnam war. Many thought a statue of a heroic soldier marching off to battle would be more appropriate.

But public opinion changes. In time the American public came to accept this memorial—with its 58,000 names carved into the stark granite walls—as the most fitting tribute to those who died. Visitors from all over, visitors who had no connection with the war, even young people who cannot remember the war stand quietly before the roster of names—names on a mass tombstone. Many come to find their own personal name, the name of a dead relative chiseled forever into the rock and not to be forgotten. They leave flowers and poems, teddy bears and ribbons, photographs and letters, reminders of the past. Mostly the relatives touch the Wall, running their fingers over the carved letters as though to touch once again the life that is gone.

The Vietnam War is long over; no more names will be added to the Wall. But another wave of unexpected death has swept the nation and the world,

97. Maya Ying Lin. Vietnam Memorial, Washington, D.C. 1982. Black granite, length 492′.

also striking primarily the young, and it will not pass soon. The wave of death from AIDS has not even crested. In the United States, San Francisco has been especially hard-hit by the epidemic, and it was there that the Names Project began. The purpose of the Names Project is simple: to memorialize as *individuals* those who have died from AIDS, to remember that each was a unique human being, though all are bound together by a common death. No better means could have been chosen than the AIDS Quilt **(98)**.

The AIDS Quilt consists of hand-sewn panels, each of them 3 by 6 feet, each commemorating one person who has died from AIDS. Some of the panels have a name and a photograph, others just initials or forms symbolizing that person's interests, abilities, and achievements. Most important, each panel tells a story, a story ended too soon, therefore all the more precious in the telling. The choice of a quilt format is especially meaningful. Historically, quilts have often told lifetime stories, incorporating bits of fabric from important life events. Quilts make us think of warmth and protection and nurturing. And quilting has traditionally been a community activity, so it is only natural that a community should form among those grieving a death from common illness.

Unlike the Vietnam Memorial, the AIDS Quilt cannot possibly remember all who have died. Only those whose friends or families chose to be involved in the Names Project are represented. Tragically, that number has already grown so large that the quilt is too big to be displayed in one place (although sections of it are sometimes on view). By late 1989 the AIDS Quilt had 10,848 panels and weighed 13 tons. It was exhibited in its entirety for the last time outdoors in Washington, D.C. But the *idea* of the quilt lives on, as do those people whose death inspired a very special kind of art.

98. The Names Project, San Francisco. *AIDS Memorial Quilt.* Displayed on the Ellipse facing the White House, October 6–8, 1989.

PART TWO

THE VOCABULARY OF ART

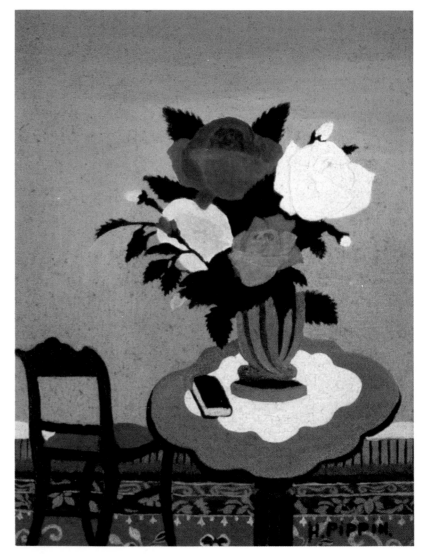

99. Horace Pippin.
Roses with Red Chair. 1940.
Oil on canvas, 14 × 10″.
Private collection.

The Visual Elements

If somebody asked you what you see in our first illustration (99), you might say something like "a picture of a vase of flowers on a table." You know it isn't a real vase of flowers or a real table, but a representation in paint on canvas. This is a painting by the American artist Horace Pippin.

Now look closer and observe how the painting is constructed. You will see that Pippin has used *lines* to draw the scalloped edge of the tabletop, the vertical design in the vase, the tracery of flower petals, and the patterns and fringe of the rug. He has created the *shapes* of flowers, vase, table, and chair, and set them off against the plainer *space* of the wall behind. The flowers and leaves have a ruffled *texture*, contrasted with the smooth wall and tabletop. The painting is full of *light*, which illuminates this cheerful indoor scene. Pippin employs a range of *colors*—red and yellow for the roses, dark green for the leaves, brown for the rug, a rich turquoise blue for the background wall. There is also a range of *values*, from lightest in the doily on the table and the pale rose to darkest in the chair and leaves.

These seven things Pippin used to construct his picture—line, shape, texture, light, value, color, and space—are the ingredients an artist has available in making any work of art. They are called the *visual elements*. (As we shall see, some works of art also involve time and motion, so these two are often added to the list.) No matter what kind of art, no matter where or when it was made, the character of these elements and the way they are organized determine what the work of art will be like.

In this chapter we shall look closely at the visual elements—what they are, how they are used, and how they affect a work of art. Chapter 5 deals with organization of these elements according to the principles of design.

Line

By conventional definition, a line is the path left by a moving point. You put down your pencil on a sheet of paper and *move* its point across the paper to make a line. We can also think of line as an extended mark. Line is so basic to art that it is difficult to conceive of any work of art *not* having lines.

When you sit down to write a letter or an examination paper or a note to yourself, you are making lines, whether you think of it that way or not. The letters of the alphabet are lines, and they are also symbols of sounds. Artists, too, use lines as symbols. In Pippin's painting of the flowers, the heavy line around the table edge, for example, acts as a symbol. Tables don't actually have lines separating them from their surroundings. But at the point where table visually meets wall or floor, our eyes "see" an imaginary line, so Pippin has drawn that line in his painting. This task of symbolically outlining form is only one of the many functions line performs in a work of art.

FUNCTIONS OF LINE

OUTLINE AND FORM In Ellsworth Kelly's drawing *Apples* (100) a thin, elegant line describes the shape of the fruit. This is called an ***outline drawing.*** There is no shading, no interior detail, and no background. By this amazingly economical line Kelly convinces us that we see a group of rounded apples resting on an invisible surface. As in Pippin's painting, the line creates a boundary. It marks the point where the apples stop and the surrounding area begins. This function of line as outline is extremely important to art.

Whereas Kelly uses line to create the illusion of three-dimensional form, Alexander Calder in his *Cow* (101) works with line to create a form that is

left: 100. Ellsworth Kelly. *Apples.* 1949.
Pencil, $17\frac{1}{8} \times 22\frac{1}{8}''$.
Collection, The Museum of Modern Art,
New York (gift of John S. Newberry).

below: 101. Alexander Calder. *Cow.* 1929.
Wire construction, $6\frac{1}{2} \times 16 \times 4\frac{1}{4}''$.
Collection, The Museum of Modern Art,
New York (gift of Edward M. M. Warburg).

actually three-dimensional. This witty little sculpture consists of a few pieces of wire welded and twisted together—the wire drawing lines in space. Somehow, Calder makes these few thin lines suggest a cow, placidly standing in the pasture, turning her head to gaze with little interest at us, who have interrupted her grazing. Details drawn in line are the key to this sculpture—one great swoop to show the udder, squiggle lines for the dangling teats, the little curl of hair at the end of the tail, the clumsy feet, the . . . well . . . *cowlike* expression on the face. Line alone, in the hands of a master like Calder, conveys the essence of the beast.

Line as outline and form is also central to art by Keith Haring, who began his career as a subway graffiti artist. Long before his name was known, Haring's bold outline drawings on blank poster spaces in the New York subways attracted wide attention **(102)**. The drawings are simple, like cartoons, and they feature instantly recognizable images—a barking dog, a spaceship, a television set, outline people and babies. Short, choppy lines radiating from the figures—a Haring trademark—suggest noise, energy, happiness, movement, a general exuberance. There is no deep meaning in these drawings. They are supposed to be fun, to give immediate visual pleasure to the people who see them, as they did to the artist in making them. As his work progressed, Haring was represented by major New York galleries and appeared in important exhibitions, but he continued to draw in the same forceful linear style we see in this example.

102. Keith Haring.
Subway Drawing. 1983.
Chalk on black paper.
© The Estate of Keith Haring 1991.

above: 103. Alberto Giacometti.
The Nose. 1947.
Bronze and steel wire,
$32 \times 28\frac{1}{2} \times 15\frac{3}{8}''$.
Hirshhorn Museum and Sculpture Garden,
Smithsonian Institution, Washington, D.C.
(gift of Joseph H. Hirshhorn, 1972.)

left: 104. Paul Cézanne.
The Large Bathers. 1906.
Oil on canvas, 6'10" × 8'3".
Philadelphia Museum of Art
(purchased: W. P. Wilstach Collection).

MOVEMENT AND EMPHASIS Line often implies movement, and this is another of its functions. Every line goes somewhere, so the viewer's eye naturally follows it. Alberto Giacometti's *Nose* **(103)** gives us a particularly compelling sculptural line in the form of a Pinocchio figure who has told many lies indeed. The head and torso are suspended, possibly trapped, inside a cage, with only the elongated nose—symbol of the liar—projecting outside. No matter how many times we as viewers try to focus on the face, the sharp line of the nose keeps pulling us away again.

Line also plays a role in creating emphasis in a work of art. In Paul Cézanne's painting *The Large Bathers* **(104)** diagonal lines of trees bend inward to form a triangle in the center of the canvas. The figures lean in such a way as to echo the diagonal line. By means of this triangle Cézanne focuses attention on the main figures at the bottom center of the composition. His diagonal lines create a frame-within-a-frame, so we concentrate on forms within the triangle.

PATTERN AND TEXTURE   Yet another function of line in art is the creation of pattern and texture. Saul Steinberg has used line to great effect in creating the ornate texture of chicken feathers in his ink drawing *Hen* **(105)**. Repeated, interwoven squiggly lines, drawn in a decorative pattern, suggest a fabulous plumage that any bird would be proud of. The face and feet of the hen seem almost an afterthought to this rich display of texture. Later in the chapter (p. 128) we will consider pattern and texture in more detail.

SHADING AND MODELING   One very important function of line, especially in drawing and printmaking, is the creation of shaded effects. Shading is natural to some media, like pencil; the artist can simply use the side of the pencil instead of the point. But with a more "linear" medium, such as pen and ink, this is not possible. Instead the artist will create shaded effects by means of closely spaced short lines **(106)**. There are three basic techniques. *Hatching* is an area of closely spaced parallel lines. *Cross-hatching* is similar except that the parallel lines intersect like a narrow checkerboard. *Stippling* means that the lines are reduced to dots and spaced closer together or farther apart.

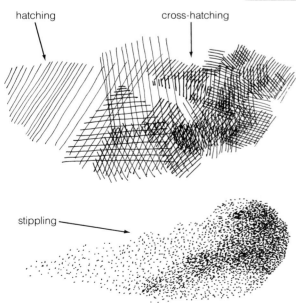

above: **105.** Saul Steinberg. *Hen.* 1945.
Pen, brush, and India ink; $14\frac{1}{2} \times 23\frac{1}{8}''$.
Collection, The Museum of Modern Art, New York (purchase).

left: **106.** Line techniques to create modeling: hatching, cross-hatching, and stippling.

107. Michelangelo.
Head of a Satyr.
Pen and ink over chalk,
$10\frac{5}{8} \times 7\frac{7}{8}''$.
Louvre, Paris.

Often, the goal of shading is to ***model,*** or to create the illusion of round-ness, of three-dimensionality on a flat surface. We can see this in Michelan-gelo's *Head of a Satyr* **(107).** Michelangelo has drawn some areas of hatching, especially in the hair at the right side of the drawing, but most of the model-ing is accomplished by cross-hatching. Areas we are meant to perceive as hollows, or depressions in the face, have the densest cross-hatching: the socket of the eye, the back of the nostril, the jawline below the ear, and so forth. Conversely, where we are meant to see a raised area, such as the cheek-bone, there is no cross-hatching at all. (If you put your finger over the high-light of the cheekbone, you will see that the face seems flatter.) By the skillful use of line Michelangelo persuades us that the head is three-dimensional.

TYPES OF LINES

The preceding sections have dealt primarily with actual lines—visible marks made in pencil or paint or some other medium. In studying art, however, we often have to take into account other types of lines **(108).** Actual lines are the most familiar, so we begin with them.

ACTUAL LINES Actual lines are obvious in Roy Lichtenstein's *Still Life with Crystal Bowl* (**109**). In fact, they are the dominant element in the composition. Thick parallel bands create a background; the fruits are outlined in bold strokes, while finer lines delineate the shape of the bowl. Working in the Pop Art style with which he is associated (p. 483), Lichtenstein has chosen a familiar item, one that could be found in a great many homes, and transformed it into a precious object, like the gem displayed in a jeweler's window. The strong linear treatment takes the bowl of fruit, so to speak, "outside" itself. We as viewers *must* look at it with fresh eyes, must respond to it for its own sake, rather than as a casual accessory to decorate a dining room table.

above: 108. Actual line (**a**), implied lines (**b,c**), and line created by edge (**d**).

left: 109. Roy Lichtenstein. *Still Life with Crystal Bowl.* 1973. Oil and magna on canvas, 4'4" × 3'6". Collection, Whitney Museum of American Art (purchase, with funds from Frances and Sydney Lewis).

Raphael

1483–1520

According to the 16th-century biographer Giorgio Vasari, we find in Raphael "an artist as talented as he was gracious," possessed of unbounded "grace, industry, looks, modesty, and excellence of character." Whereas both Michelangelo and Leonardo da Vinci emerge as rather moody, solitary figures, their younger colleague seems to have been the sort of person who charms everybody and to whom success comes as naturally as breathing.

Born in the town of Urbino, Raffaello Sanzio received his first art training from his father, then later became an assistant to the early Renaissance master Pietro Perugino. At twenty-one Raphael struck out on his own, but he continued to study avidly the work of other artists—including Leonardo and Michelangelo, both of whom influenced him greatly. (Vasari claims that Raphael was secretly let into the locked Sistine Chapel when Michelangelo had temporarily stopped work on the ceiling frescoes so that he could get an advance look at the figures.)

Raphael established his reputation early and throughout his career never lacked for patrons. A major preoccupation was the Madonna-and-child group, of which he made numerous versions. In 1508 Pope Julius II called Raphael to Rome, where the artist began the fresco decoration of four rooms in the Vatican. Among these frescoes was the famous *School of Athens* **(233)**.

By his early thirties Raphael had become a busy person indeed, testing his artistic skills in many areas. Increasingly, the work of carrying out his commissions was delegated to assistants. He had been named chief architect of Saint Peter's Basilica in the Vatican and was also director of excavations for ancient Greek and Roman art in and around the city of Rome. On commission from Pope Leo, Julius' successor, Raphael designed ten huge tapestries for the Sistine Chapel and perhaps executed the cartoons (drawings to guide the weavers) himself, although this point is in dispute.

Raphael's private life seems to have been as full and satisfying as his artistic career. At home in any social situation, sought after as a friend, he played as energetically as he worked. He never married—possibly because he hoped to be made a cardinal of the Church—but he lived for many years with the same woman. The

biographer Vasari refers to "secret love affairs" and comments that the artist "pursued his pleasures with no sense of moderation." If we are to believe Vasari, Raphael's death at the tragically premature age of thirty-seven came as the aftermath of such lack of moderation, which brought on a "violent fever" made fatal by unwise medical attention.

Among Raphael's great talents was the ability to please his patrons while at the same time fulfilling his own ideals of art. In about 1514 he wrote this to a noble client: "I should consider myself a great master if [a drawing of Galatea] had half the merits you mention in your letter. However, I perceive in your words the love that you bear me; . . . I am making use of a certain idea which comes into my mind. Whether it is possessed of any artistic excellence I do not know. But I do strive to attain it."[1]

Raphael. *School of Athens,*
detail with presumed self-portrait **(left)**. 1510–11.
Fresco. Stanza della Segnatura, Vatican, Rome.

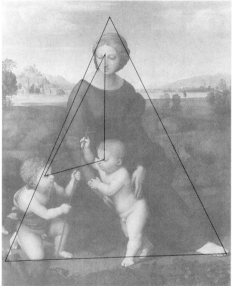

left: 110. Raphael.
The Madonna of the Meadows.
1505. Oil on panel, 44½ × 34¼".
Kunsthistorisches Museum, Vienna.

right: 111. Line analysis
of Raphael's *Madonna of the
Meadows.*

IMPLIED LINES   When a person stops on a street corner and gazes upward, other passersby will also stop and look up, following the "line" of sight. When someone points a finger, we automatically follow the direction of the point. Artists often exploit this natural response by using implied lines in their work. In Raphael's painting *The Madonna of the Meadows* (110), implied lines of sight between the Virgin and the two children help to pull the composition together and direct the eyes of the viewer to the most important figure in the painting—the child Jesus (111). The Madonna casts her eyes downward toward John the Baptist, who, in turn, gazes upward at the baby Jesus, establishing a triangular flow. As observers, we unconsciously follow these lines of sight around and through the painting, just as we would glance upward if we saw someone in the street staring up. Implied lines here give both coherence and a subtle sense of movement to the painting.

LINES FORMED BY EDGES   If you press the palms of your two hands flat together in a praying gesture, you will see that a "line" seems to form where they meet. There is no line, in reality, but the point where the edge of one form meets the edge of another form creates the impression of a line. This can

112. Claes Oldenburg and Coosje van Bruggen. *Stake Hitch.* 1984. Painted epoxied aluminum, urethane foam, polyester resin, and fiberglass; height 53′6″. Dallas Museum of Art (commissioned to honor John Dabney Murchison, Sr., for his arts and civic leadership and presented by his family).

happen in two-dimensional art as well, wherever one shape or color area meets another shape or color area. The line created by edge is evident in our next illustration—a sculpture by Claes Oldenburg in the Dallas Museum of Art **(112)**. *Stake Hitch*, with its giant "rope" stretched from floor to ceiling, is actually a three-dimensional form, but in contrast to the light-colored background we perceive a wavy, scalloped line on either side of the rope. The edges of buildings, of sculptures, of any shapes isolated against a plain background fool the eye into seeing lines where none exist.

CHARACTERISTICS OF LINES

When someone mentions the word "house," everyone who hears it forms a different mental image. Listeners might picture anything from a small cabin in the woods to Buckingham Palace, depending on their frame of reference. So it is with line. Line is such a broad term that it can encompass everything from Lichtenstein's heavy black strokes to the delicate pencil marks of Kelly's *Apples* **(100)**. The characteristics of any given line have much to do with how that line performs in a work of art. Two important characteristics are direction and linear quality.

DIRECTION Most of us have instinctive reactions to the direction of line, which are related to our experience of gravity. Flat, horizontal lines seem placid, like the horizon line or a body in repose. Vertical lines, like those of an upright body or a skyscraper jutting up from the ground, may have an assertive quality; they defy gravity in their upward thrust. But the most dynamic lines are the diagonals, which almost always imply action. Think of a runner hurtling down the track or a skier down the slope. The body leans forward, so that only the forward motion keeps it from toppling over. Diagonal lines in art have the same effect. We sense motion because the lines are unstable; we half expect them to topple over. (One exception is the diagonal line that makes up part of a triangle or pyramid, as in Cézanne's painting **[104]**; such lines are very stable because the triangle form is closed and solid.) To see how linear direction works, let us compare two paintings that both show a boat in the water.

In Thomas Eakins' *The Biglen Brothers Racing* **(113)** nearly all the lines are horizontals. The two boats, the shoreline, the ripples on the river, the treetops, even the clouds scuttling across the sky are horizontal. Only the diagonal lines of the oars and rowers' arms and bodies suggest that this is a race. Why should a race be so placid? Eakins has captured the essence of sculling, races involving flat, long-oared boats powered by one or two rowers. Usually done on calm bodies of water, sculling has an odd, streamlined quality in the way the boats knife through the still water. The only apparent motion is in the bodies of the rowers, whose brisk, automaton movements in tandem make them seem, from a distance, like little mechanical toys. Eakins, therefore, has given his painting an overall serenity, broken only by the diagonals of the men.

A diagram **(114)** will help to show the great differences in linear direction, and thus in emotional effect, between Eakins' work and our next illustration. Serenity was the last thing Théodore Géricault wanted for his painting *The Raft of the Medusa* **(115)**. Géricault's work is based on an actual event—the wreck of the French government ship *Medusa* off North Africa in 1816. Only a few of those on board survived, some by clinging to a raft. The artist has chosen to depict the dramatic moment when those on the raft sighted a rescue ship. Virtually all the lines in the composition—the men straining forward, the arc of the sail, the bodies of the dead and dying in the foreground—are diagonal. Their thrust reinforces the sense of a desperate situation as the raft plunges toward safety. And all these exciting diagonals build toward the climax of the one vertical—the man signaling to the rescue ship. The use of line direction may be overt or subtle, but we nearly always respond to it.

a

b

top: **113.** Thomas Eakins.
The Biglen Brothers Racing.
1873. Oil on canvas, $24\frac{1}{8} \times 36\frac{1}{8}''$.
National Gallery of Art,
Washington, D.C. (gift of Mr.
& Mrs. Cornelius Vanderbilt
Whitney, 1953).

above: **114.** Line analyses
of Eakins' *The Biglen Brothers
Racing* **(a)** and Géricault's
The Raft of the Medusa **(b)**.

left: **115.** Théodore Géricault.
The Raft of the Medusa. 1818–19.
Oil on canvas, $16'1\frac{3}{8}'' \times 23'9''$.
Louvre, Paris.

LINEAR QUALITY As with direction, an artist's choice of linear quality does much to influence the overall impact of the work, including the viewer's emotional response. Lines can be any length, thick or thin or tapered, straight or curved or angular. For example, we might compare the linear quality in three works reproduced here.

A drawing by Vincent van Gogh, *Cypresses with Two Women* **(116)**, consists almost entirely of short, wavy, flamelike lines—a style characteristic of Van Gogh's later drawings. The cypress trees seem to be in undulating motion, their leaves perhaps shivering in the wind, and this movement is differentiated from the more stable foreground foliage defined in curling lines.

Henri Matisse's lithograph has a very different subject—the curve of a woman's back **(117)**. The artist has employed a long, elegant, gently curving line to convey the sensual, ripe quality of the form. So delicate is the line that in places it disappears altogether, leaving a space—and an implied line to connect the two sections.

How different is the linear quality of the lines in Eugène Delacroix's drawing **(118)**. The lines in *Study for the Death of Sardanapalus* swoop and swirl with tremendous energy. Just by looking at these turbulent lines we know that Delacroix made them swiftly, not with studied deliberation. The emotional tumult all but leaps out of the boundaries of the paper, carrying the viewer along with it.

This brief discussion of linear quality ends our discussion of line. We turn next to a second vital element in art—shape, and its three-dimensional counterpart, mass. However, it must be remembered here and throughout the chapter that all the elements are interdependent and affect each other continually. The quality of line, for example, will influence the quality of a shape it produces.

left: 116. Vincent van Gogh. *Cypresses with Two Women.* 1889. Reed pen and ink, chalk, and touches of oil; $12\frac{5}{8} \times 9\frac{1}{2}''$. Rijksmuseum Kroller-Müller, Otterlo, The Netherlands.

right: 117. Henri Matisse. *Study: A Woman's Back.* 1914. Lithograph, $16\frac{1}{2} \times 10\frac{1}{2}''$. The Metropolitan Museum of Art, New York (Rogers Fund, 1921).

118. Eugène Delacroix.
*Study for the Death
of Sardanapalus.* 1827–28.
Pen, watercolor, and pencil;
$10\frac{1}{4} \times 12\frac{1}{2}''$.
Musée Bonnat, Bayonne.

Shape and Mass

A *shape* is a two-dimensional area with identifiable boundaries. A *mass* is a three-dimensional solid with identifiable boundaries. These definitions are correct as far as they go, and they will make sense to anyone who has studied geometry. Circles and squares are shapes; spheres and cubes are masses. So far, so good. Confusion arises, however, when we try to move beyond these bare-bones statements, and for two reasons. First, there is little consistency in the way the terms are used in everyday conversation; people are just as likely to call a three-dimensional object a "shape." Second, there are at least two other terms—*form* and *volume*—that have similar meanings and overlap the first two. In this section we will try to provide workable definitions that will serve for analysis of the art elements.

A **shape** is a two-dimensional area. Shapes are created by lines, by color areas, by contrasting textures, or by some combination of these. If the artist draws a circle and colors it red inside the line, the result is a round red shape. Even if there is no line, just a roundish daub of red paint, we still perceive a circular red shape set off from the surrounding space by its red edges.

A **mass** is a three-dimensional solid. It has actual depth in space. An orange is a piece of fruit, and it is also a spherical orange mass. Sometimes the word "mass" implies bulk, density, and weight. We might speak of the mass of a heavy paperweight or the mass of a natural rock formation.

Volume may be synonymous with mass, except that volume can also refer to a void, an empty but enclosed space, whereas mass usually refers to a solid. For example, we might refer to the mass of the Rock of Gibraltar (we might also refer to its volume), but inside a large building, such as the Guggenheim Museum **(143)**, we would talk about the volume enclosed and created by the structure.

Form is the trickiest term of all, because it has so many meanings. It can mean shape or mass. As mentioned in Chapter 2, it can refer generally to the way a work of art looks or the way it is put together. It can also mean composition or structure or even style.

For this discussion of the art elements we have chosen to focus on the terms "shape" and "mass." These two have the most easily restricted definitions and lend themselves more readily to analysis.

It is customary to distinguish two broad categories in both shapes and masses: organic and geometric. **Geometric shapes**, based on the mechanically drawn line, include the square, the rectangle, the circle, and the triangle. **Organic shapes** are based on the forms of nature, which are usually rounded, irregular, and curving. Many works of art combine these two categories, but often one or the other will predominate.

One artist who devoted a career to exploring the potential of geometric shape was the Dutch painter Piet Mondrian **(119)**. Mondrian's *Composition with Red, Yellow, and Blue* is typical of his mature work and represents the artist's search for what he called a "pure reality." Mondrian felt that certain things are universal, common to all people—the rectangle, the vertical and horizontal, the primary colors red, yellow, and blue, plus black and white. By these means he hoped to cut through cultural and emotional differences among people and make a visual statement that would be meaningful to all. Mondrian's canvases, apparently so simple, rest on the hair's-breadth balance of line, shape, and color—the dynamic equilibrium Mondrian achieved with geometric shapes.

Organic shapes prevail in Pedro Perez' *Los Marielitos* **(120)**. This painting has almost no straight lines; it is rather an assemblage of natural forms—animal, human, humanoid, plantlike. Moreover, the forms are interconnected, as though all were branches of a vivid tropical plant. Perez, who was born in Cuba, takes his title from the wave of refugees who entered the United States in 1980 from the Cuban port of Mariel. His picture may recall Picasso's *Guernica* **(72)**, in the sense that we know something has *happened* to a group of people, and we feel the magnitude of the event without really understanding the individual symbols.

Before we complete our discussion of two-dimensional shape, we should touch upon one more aspect of it, and that is the concept of positive/negative shape, sometimes called ***figure-ground relationship.*** A painting or other work of two-dimensional art usually has one or more shapes meant to be perceived as positive. In a representational work, they are the shapes of the subject; in a nonrepresentational work, they are the shapes that seem active or dominant. For instance, in Pippin's painting of the vase of flowers at the beginning of this chapter **(99)**, the vase of flowers, the table, and the chair are positive

119. Piet Mondrian.
Composition with Red, Yellow, and Blue. 1928.
Oil on canvas, 4'$\frac{3}{4}$" × 2'7$\frac{1}{2}$".
Collection Stefan Edlis, Chicago.

left: 120. Pedro F. Perez.
Los Marielitos. 1983.
Oil pastel on black wove paper,
3'8¼" × 5'.
The Museum of Fine Arts, Houston
(Museum purchase with funds
provided by Drexel Burnham
Lambert Incorporated).

below left: 121. M. C. Escher.
*Study of Regular Division
of the Plane with Horsemen.*
1946. India ink and watercolor.
Collection, Haags Gemeentemuseum,
The Hague.

below: 122. George Sugarman.
Yellow Spiral. 1970.
Metal, height c. 10'6".
Installed in Rodney Square,
Wilmington, Del.

shapes, or figure. Everything else is negative shape, or background. If you compare this to a work by M. C. Escher (121), you will find it hard to decide which are the positive shapes and which are the negative ones. Focus your eyes on the dark figures, and the light ones become ground; focus on the light ones, and the opposite is true. Escher meant this to be a clever visual puzzle, but it makes an important point about art in general. What Escher's drawing emphasizes is that both positive and negative shapes are dynamic elements.

Three-dimensional mass also can be considered either geometric or organic. George Sugarman's *Yellow Spiral* (122) consists of a series of shallow, hollowed-out cubes (a geometric mass) arranged in a broken spiral. Although the plain shape of the cube can seem static, even boring, this work is full of movement. No single cube stands flat on its side; all are caught in a precarious teetering pose and dependent on their neighbors for stability. The sculpture seems particularly effective in contrast to the traditional equestrian statue in the background—an organic mass.

Light, Value, and Color

Light, value, and color are intimately connected elements. Color is a function of light and therefore directly dependent on its presence. Value, being a measure of lightness or darkness, plays a role in our perception of light and color.

Apart from the purely sensory pleasure we derive from it, color helps to define shape and mass. For example, we notice that the *green* hills are set off against the *blue* sky. In a nonobjective painting color may be the only means by which we identify shapes and spaces. Color is also used by artists to convey emotion. Value defines shape when, for instance, we see a light shape against a dark background, and it too carries emotional impact. We speak of "dark, brooding" paintings or "light, airy" ones.

In this section we take up the subjects of light, value, and color insofar as they affect our response to art. All involve complex sciences, but only a little of the science is necessary to understand how these elements operate.

LIGHT

ACTUAL LIGHT In architecture and in sculptures meant to be exhibited outdoors we are particularly aware of the influence of natural light. The architect of an old cast-iron building in New York, photographed by Evelyn Hofer **(123)**, probably realized how important would be the play of light and shadow on its ornate façade. The photographer has seen this too and has captured a moment when patterns of light are especially dramatic. One could say that this photograph is "about" light, as light interacts with three-dimensional mass.

Dazzling natural light admitted by a glass roof is virtually the most important element in the great hall of Vancouver's courthouse **(124)**. Reacting against the usual image of a courthouse as stuffy and claustrophobic, architect Arthur Erickson has "turned the traditional courthouse inside-out." Shadow patterns over the course of the day make a fascinating, ever-changing mosaic on the floors and throughout the interior. Erickson welcomed light as an important part of his design, but any artist whose work will be exposed to natural light must take it into account.

left: 123. Evelyn Hofer. *Cast-Iron Building, Broadway and Broome Streets, New York.* 1965. Photograph. Courtesy the photographer.

right: 124. Arthur Erickson. Great Hall, Courthouse, Vancouver, B.C. Completed 1979.

THE ILLUSION OF LIGHT Artists working in two-dimensional art—painting or drawing or prints, for instance—often wish to create the impression of light illuminating their subjects. This apparent light may be daylight evenly illuminating a scene or dappling the leaves in a landscape or the light cast by a lamp, candle, or fire. In some cases the supposed light source is included in the image, as when a painter depicts figures clustered around a lamp. At other times the light source is assumed to be outside the frame of the picture, but we see its effects clearly. A subject bathed in light from a definite angle, with the resultant shadows, may seem more lifelike and three-dimensional. (When light is general and comes from no specific source, figures tend to be flattened.)

We can see how light enhances the sense of depth in Thomas Eakins' painting *The Concert Singer* (**125**). This work shows the singer Weda Cook in a solo performance. The strong light coming from below and to her left is apparently from a footlight on the concert stage. Eakins obviously was intrigued with the effects of light on form. The lower part of the gown is the most brilliantly illuminated, while more than half the face remains in shadow. Light picks out folds in the dress, hollows in the singer's throat, the musculature of the arms—all of these details contributing to the roundness of the figure.

VALUE

The term *value*, as we have said, means relative lightness or darkness, whether in color or in black and white. Values are perhaps easier to see in black and white than in color; we are accustomed to their effects in black-and-white television, photography, and reproductions, such as the ones in this book. When *The Concert Singer* is reproduced in black and white (**126**), the pale pink on the near side of the dress is seen as a very light gray, the singer's illuminated arm and cheek slightly darker grays, and so on, to the

left: **125.** Thomas Eakins. *The Concert Singer.* 1892. Oil on canvas, 6'3⅛" × 4'6¼". Philadelphia Museum of Art (given by Mrs. Thomas Eakins and Miss Mary A. Williams).

right: **126.** Eakins' *The Concert Singer* reproduced in black and white, to show gray values.

white

high
light

light

low
light

medium

high
dark

dark

low
dark

black

above: **127.** Value scale in gray.

top: **128.** Lorenzo di Credi.
*Drapery for a Standing Man,
Represented Frontally.*
Late 15th–early 16th century.
Brush and gray wash
on brown paper, $15\frac{1}{4} \times 10\frac{5}{8}''$.
Louvre, Paris.

very dark grays that represent the shadows behind the singer and on her right side. Color values are translated into values of gray. In black and white, then, lacking the color cues we have in most situations, we rely to a large extent on contrasts of grays to help us distinguish one form from another.

For purposes of analysis, value is usually considered in terms of a value scale **(127)**, ranging from white (the lightest) to black (the darkest), with several gradations in between. (The same value scale can be applied to colors, as we shall see.) Works of art in which light values predominate are called *high-key;* those in which dark values predominate, *low-key.*

Value contrasts—contrasts of light and dark—may be used in a painting or drawing to create the effects of light and shadow in the natural world. This technique is called **chiaroscuro,** which literally means "light/dark." In Lorenzo di Credi's *Drapery for a Standing Man* **(128)** there is no explicit light source, such as a lamp or candle, yet the figure has clearly been modeled as though light were coming from somewhere beyond the man's right shoulder (our left as we look at the drawing). The lightest values are reserved for folds of drapery at the left side of the drawing and on the out-thrust knee. Much darker values appear in folds of drapery that are supposed to be in shadow. These contrasts and gradations of value give a sense of depth and three-dimensionality to the drapery study. In fact, one of the reasons why the head and torso seem so flat by comparison is that chiaroscuro is not used for this area. The figure seems linear; the drapery looks almost sculptural.

Lorenzo's drawing is primarily black and white. The effects of value, light, and contrast become even more complex when we add color.

COLOR

It is probably safe to say that none of the visual elements give us so much pleasure as color. You will understand this if you have ever been restricted to watching an old black-and-white television and then suddenly have access to a color set. For the same reason certain entrepreneurs have acquired the rights to classic films like *Casablanca,* and "colorized" them—applied color by painstaking computer methods to what was originally a black-and-white movie. The debate about whether this practice is acceptable, ethically and aesthetically, will continue for many years, but obviously the "colorizers" are hoping to tap a segment of the market that demands full color.

Various studies have demonstrated that color affects a wide range of psychological and physiological responses. Restaurants often are decorated in red, which is believed to increase appetite and therefore food consumption. A common treatment for premature babies born with potentially fatal jaundice is to bathe them in blue light, which, for reasons not fully understood, eliminates the need to transfuse their blood. Blue surroundings also will significantly lower a person's blood pressure, pulse, and respiration rate. In one experiment subjects were asked to identify, by taste, ordinary mashed potatoes colored bright green. Because of the disorienting color cues, they could not say what they were eating. And in one California detention center violent children are routinely placed in an 8-by-4-foot cell painted bubblegum pink. The children relax, become calmer, and often fall asleep within ten minutes. This color has been dubbed "passive pink." The mechanism involved in these color responses is still unclear, but there can be no doubt that color "works" on the human brain and body in powerful ways.

In this book you will find nearly 300 works of art reproduced in full color. This color does not exactly duplicate the colors you would see if you stood in front of the actual works, because mechanical reproduction on paper is never wholly accurate. But you will no doubt look at these color reproductions first and will look at them more often. Color always draws the eye.

At the beginning of this section we said that color is a function of light. Without light there can be no color. The principles of color theory explain why this is so.

COLOR THEORY Much of our present-day color theory can be traced back to experiments made by Sir Isaac Newton, who is better known for his work with the laws of gravity. In 1666 Newton passed a ray of sunlight through a prism, a transparent glass form with nonparallel sides. He observed that the ray of sunlight broke up or **refracted** into different colors, which were arranged in the order of the colors of the rainbow **(129)**. By setting up a second prism Newton found he could recombine the rainbow colors into white light, like the original sunlight. These experiments proved that colors are components of light.

In fact, all colors are dependent on light, and no object possesses color intrinsically. You may own a red shirt and a blue pen and a purple chair, but these items have no color in and of themselves. What we perceive as color is reflected light rays. When light strikes the red shirt, for example, the shirt absorbs all the color rays *except* the red ones, which are reflected, so your eye perceives red. The purple chair reflects the purple rays and absorbs all the others, and so on. Both the physiological activity of the human eye and the science of electromagnetic wavelengths take part in this process.

129. Sketch of colors separated by a prism.

white light

prism

violet
blue
green
yellow
orange
red

yellow

yellow-orange

yellow-green

orange

green

red-orange

blue-green

red

blue

red-violet

blue-violet

violet

130. Color wheel.

If we take the colors separated out by Newton's prism—red, orange, yellow, green, blue, and violet—add the transitional color red-violet (which does not exist in the rainbow), and arrange these colors in a circle, we have a *color wheel* **(130)**. Different theorists have constructed different color wheels, but the one shown here is fairly standard.

Primary colors—red, yellow, and blue—are labeled with the numeral 1 on the color wheel. They are called primary because (theoretically at least) they cannot be made by any mixture of other colors.

Secondary colors—orange, green, and violet—are labeled with the numeral 2. Each is made by combining two primary colors. For most of us this information is not new. Even in kindergarten children working with poster paints learn to make green by mixing yellow and blue.

Tertiary colors, labeled number 3, are the product of a primary color and an adjacent secondary color. For instance, mixing yellow with green yields yellow-green.

Complementary colors are those directly opposite one another on the color wheel. They are assumed to be as different from one another as possible. The relationship between complementary colors, as we shall see, is extremely important in such areas as the optical and emotional effects of color.

COLOR PROPERTIES Any color has three properties: hue, value, and intensity.

Hue is the name of the color—green or red or violet-blue. In any serious discussion of color it is important to avoid the poetic color names promoted by the fashion industry, such as "fuchsia" or "topaz." The hues listed on the color wheel and the designations on the color chart **(131)** are meant to be

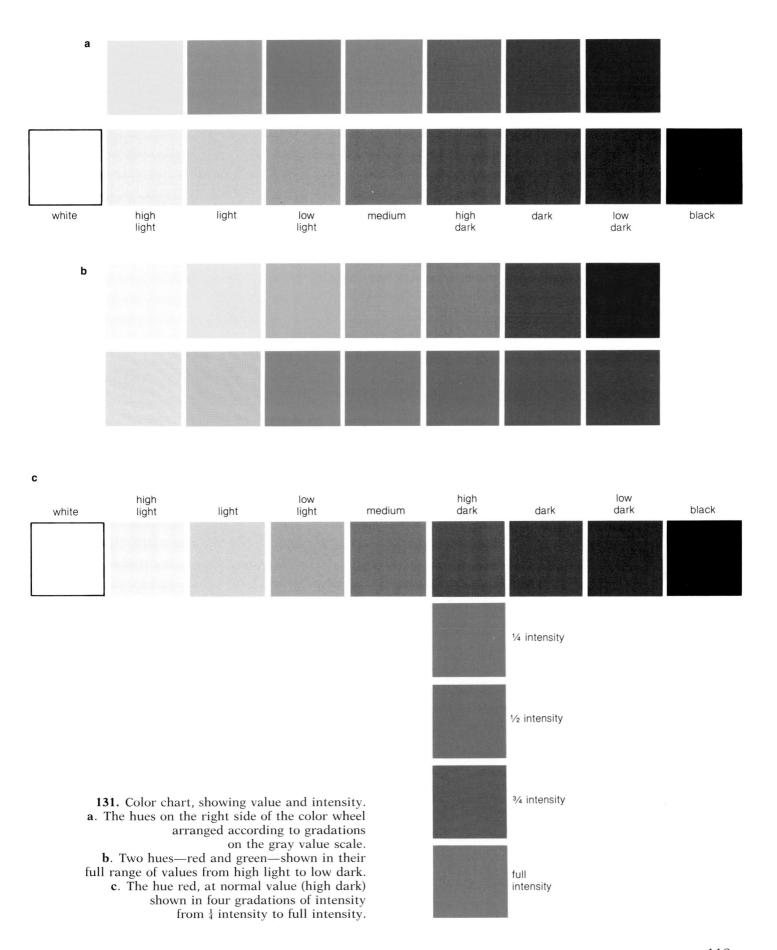

a

| white | high light | light | low light | medium | high dark | dark | low dark | black |

b

c

| white | high light | light | low light | medium | high dark | dark | low dark | black |

¼ intensity

½ intensity

¾ intensity

full intensity

131. Color chart, showing value and intensity.
a. The hues on the right side of the color wheel
arranged according to gradations
on the gray value scale.
b. Two hues—red and green—shown in their
full range of values from high light to low dark.
c. The hue red, at normal value (high dark)
shown in four gradations of intensity
from ¼ intensity to full intensity.

standard, so that people can agree on their meanings. "Autumn red" could mean many things to many people, but "red, high dark, ¾ intensity" is precise; you could pick the correct color out of a box of standard color chips.

Value, again, refers to relative lightness or darkness. Most colors are recognizable in a full range of values; for instance, we identify as "red" everything from palest pink to darkest maroon. In addition, all hues have what is known as a ***normal value***—the value at which we expect to find that hue. We think of yellow as a "light" color and violet as a "dark" color, for example, even though each has a full range of values. The top section of the color chart (**131a**) shows the hues on the right side of the color wheel organized according to their normal values in relation to the gray value scale. We could do the same with the left half of the wheel, pairing yellow-orange with light, and so on. The middle section of the color chart (**131b**) shows a full range of values, from high light to low dark, for two hues: red and green.

A color lighter than the hue's normal value is known as a ***tint;*** for example, pink is a tint of red. A color darker than the hue's normal value is called a ***shade;*** maroon is a shade of red. (This terminology is specific to color theory and differs from everyday usage of the word "shade" to mean any variation of a color, as in "My coat is a lovely shade of blue.")

Intensity—also called **chroma** or **saturation**—refers to the relative purity of a color. The difference between intensity and value can be a bit difficult to understand until you see how it works on the color chart (**131c**). Colors may be pure and saturated, as they appear on the color wheel, or they may be grayed and softened to some degree. The purest colors are said to have high intensity; grayer colors, lower intensity. In the color chart (**131c**) we show four intensity gradations of the hue red at normal value. We could construct the same intensity scale for any other hue. To lower the intensity of a color when mixing paints or dyes, the artist may add a combination of black and white (gray) or may add a little of the color's complement.

LIGHT AND PIGMENT Colors behave differently depending on whether the artist is working with light or with pigment. In light, as we said, white light is the sum of all colors. In other words, if you combine all colors, you will get white. This is not true for pigment—artists' colors or dyes. If you mix all these colors together, you will get a **neutral**—either black or an almost colorless brownish-gray.

Artists who work in light need to master a complex technology of light-and-color dynamics. This science applies to photographers, filmmakers, video and computer artists, anyone whose medium involves color as a component of light. One of the fastest-growing areas in art today is the field of computer art, and among its most fascinating branches is fractal imagery.

132. Benoit B. Mandelbrot. *A Fractal Dragon.* 1982. Computer-generated image. Copyright © 1982 by Benoit B. Mandelbrot.

133. Arnaldo Roche-Rabell. *The Spirit of the Flesh*, 1980. Oil pastel on paper, 4'2" × 3'4". Collection Myrna Baez, Hato Rey, Puerto Rico.

A *fractal* picture is a computer-generated representation of a complex mathematical formula **(132)**. According to Benoit B. Mandelbrot, the pioneer of fractal mathematics, "Fractals are geometric shapes that are equally complex in their details as in their overall form. That is, if a piece of a fractal is suitably magnified to become of the same size as the whole, it should look like the whole."[2] For the mathematically inclined, fractals are an exciting new world to explore, but considered purely on artistic terms, fractal images are intricate, elegant, usually colorful, and often quite beautiful. Even without understanding their mathematical properties, we can appreciate their visual expressiveness.

Artists using real light usually select their colors mechanically, at a distance, by pushing buttons or choosing filters or adjusting dials. Their work requires a sophisticated knowledge of color science. By contrast, artists who work in pigments—watercolors or oil paints or similar media—usually blend their colors by trial and error, using their own hands. In both cases, familiarity with the color wheel and the color properties can help.

COLOR HARMONIES A color harmony, sometimes called a **color scheme** is the selective use of two or more colors in a single composition. We tend to think of this especially in relation to interior design; you may say, for instance, "The color scheme in my kitchen is blue and green with touches of brown." But color harmonies also apply to the pictorial arts, although they may be more difficult to spot because of differences in value and intensity.

Usually, an artist's choice of colors is intuitive, so it is only after a work of art has been completed that observers can identify the color harmony involved. These harmonies do, however, help us to understand why certain combinations of colors produce certain visual effects. There are several categories of color harmonies.

Monochromatic harmonies are composed of variations on the same hue, often with differences of value and intensity. A painting all in reds, pinks, and maroons would be considered to have a monochromatic harmony. Arnaldo Roche-Rabell's *Spirit of the Flesh* **(133)**, for instance, is painted entirely in subtle variations of the color blue, to create an eerily brooding, disturbing image of the man's face.

Complementary harmonies involve colors directly opposite one another on the color wheel. The most obvious pairings are red and green, violet and yellow, blue and orange. Complementaries "react" with each other more vividly than other colors. They set up a tension, a dynamic bond of opposites. Marc Chagall's *Painter and His Wife* (134) demonstrates just such a forceful complementary scheme. Chagall has divided his canvas into two sections—the "painter" side, represented by a vase of flowers, in an intense green; the "wife" side in saturated red. The two sections vibrate against one another, suggesting a clear duality, and yet they do not appear to be at war. They seem, in fact, to complement one another, to be two halves of the whole.

Analogous harmonies combine colors adjacent to one another on the color wheel, such as red, red-orange, and orange. In *Portrait of Madame Renoir with Bob* (135) Renoir holds to this scheme to create a warm and charming image of his wife with their small dog. Except for touches of white, nearly all the colors in this work can be found in the upper left third of our color wheel (130), from yellow through the oranges to red. Even the puppy sports a golden orange.

Triad harmonies use three colors equidistant on the color wheel. The most obvious combination is red, yellow, and blue, as in Mondrian's painting (119). In addition, there are several more complicated color harmonies that are significant mainly to color theorists. For our purposes here it is enough to know that such harmonies exist and that they may sometimes help us to understand why particular colors work together.

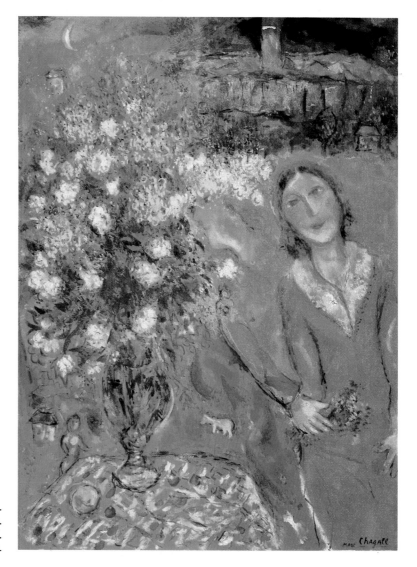

134. Marc Chagall.
The Painter and His Wife. 1969.
Oil on canvas, 36¼ × 28¾".
Collection the artist's estate.

left: **135.** Pierre-Auguste Renoir.
Portrait of Madame Renoir with Bob.
c. 1910. Oil on canvas, 31⅞ × 25⅝".
Wadsworth Atheneum, Hartford, Conn.
(Ella Gallup Sumner and Mary Catlin Sumner Collection).

below: **136.** Demonstration of the effects of afterimage
in colors. Stare at the dot in the center of the flag
for at least 30 seconds. Then quickly turn your eyes
to a white paper or a white wall. The flag should appear
in its usual colors, which are complementary
to those shown here.

OPTICAL EFFECTS OF COLOR Certain uses and combinations of colors can "play tricks" on our eyes, or, more accurately, on the way we perceive colors registered by our eyes. For one thing, there is the phenomenon known as *simultaneous contrast.* If you place two complementary colors next to each other, both of them will seem more brilliant: red seems redder, green greener, and so forth. Food merchandisers understand this well. Strawberries are nearly always packaged in green, the complement of red, and the meat counter in a grocery store often will have some touch of green. Both the fruit and the meat therefore seem redder and more appetizing. Similarly, the home decorator might create an instant "still life" by piling fresh oranges into a blue bowl on the table; the two colors spark against each other and dazzle the eye.

Another phenomenon associated with complementary colors is *afterimage.* If you stare fixedly at the color areas in the illustration (136) for half a minute, and then turn your eyes quickly to a white page or wall, you will see a faint afterimage of the color patches in their complementary colors.

137. Georges Seurat.
Study for Le Chahut. 1889.
Oil on canvas, 21⅞ × 18⅜″.
Albright-Knox Art Gallery,
Buffalo, N.Y.
(General Purchase Funds, 1943).

left: detail
right: entire work

Some colors seem to "advance," others to "recede." Interior designers know that if you place a bright red chair in a room it will seem larger and farther forward than the same chair upholstered in beige or pale blue. Thus, color can dramatically influence our perceptions of space and size. In general, colors that create the illusion of large size and advancing are those with the warmer hues (red, orange, yellow), high intensity, and dark value; small size and receding are suggested by colors with cooler hues (blue, green), low intensity, and light value.

Colors can be mixed in light or pigment, but they can also be mixed by the eyes. When small patches of different colors are placed close together, the eye may blend them to produce a new color. This is known as *optical color mixture,* and it is an important feature in the painting of Georges Seurat. Seurat's style of painting, known as **pointillism,** depends on the painstaking arrangement of many, many tiny dots of color very close together. From a distance of a few inches a Seurat painting looks like a meaningless jumble of color dots **(137).** But as the viewer moves back, the dots merge to form soft, subtly graduated colors. Although Seurat's work is the epitome of optical color mixture, many artists use the effect in less extreme forms.

EMOTIONAL QUALITIES OF COLOR Endless studies have been undertaken in an attempt to explain the emotional effects of color. Why does a bull chase something red? Why does a person wearing a red shirt or dress immediately attract our attention? Why are red, white, and silver status colors for an automobile, whereas orange is not? Whatever the reasons, one group of experts—packaging designers—have been aggressive in exploiting these qualities. If you scan the shelves of the supermarket, you will discover that few packages are entirely free of red, because red seems to attract attention better than any other color. (One exception is foods promoted as being "natural," whose packages usually feature beige and brown.)

In our language we have given specific emotional symbolism to the different color names. Green is associated with envy; blue, with sadness; red, with anger; yellow, with cowardice; and so on. Beyond this, we think of colors as having different "temperatures," as suggested earlier. Red and orange are thought of as being "warm" colors, perhaps because of their association with fire, sunsets, and the like. Blue and green are considered "cool."

An artist choosing colors for a particular work will expect those colors to have some emotional impact on the viewer, an impact that supports the intent in that work of art. We can see this by comparing three paintings with very different emotional qualities.

Jean-Honoré Fragonard's *Love Letters* (138) is a masterpiece of the mid-18th-century style known as Rococo (Chapter 16). Fragonard's work celebrates an ideal of frivolous, light-hearted love, frolicking play, and gentle

138. Jean-Honoré Fragonard. *Love Letters.* 1771–73. Oil on canvas, 10'4¾" × 7'1⅛". Copyright The Frick Collection, New York.

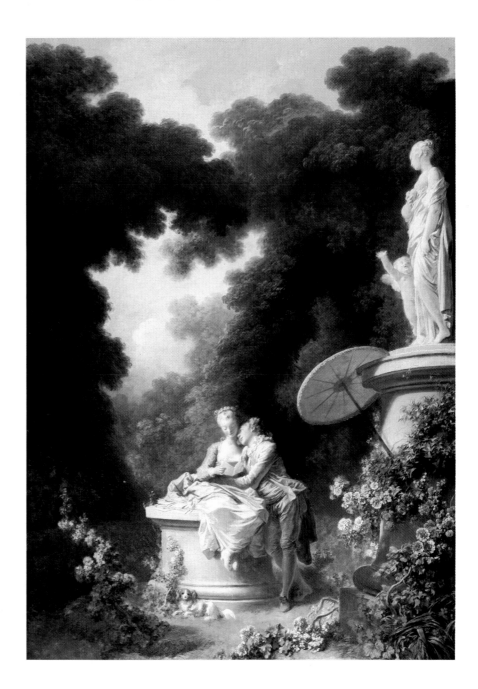

sensuality. No serious concerns intrude in this artist's world. His people might have moved straight into adulthood from the nursery and simply incorporated the pleasures of romantic love into their play. Nature is a picture-postcard scene, with every leaf and flower arranged to best effect. Nearly all the colors in the painting are soft pastels, with an emphasis on pinks and yellows. The mood is supposed to be light and charming, and Fragonard's colors foster this.

Our second example, a painting from late-18th-century India, shows the Hindu god Krishna in a rendezvous with his beloved, Radha **(139)**. In keeping with the poetic, idyllic mood of the scene, the dominant colors are misty blues and greens, with delicate touches of pink. The shadowy colors also convey an aura of secrecy; this is a clandestine meeting, a few precious moments alone, when no one else is looking. Krishna and Radha seem to float in their own dream landscape, a landscape blurred by soft-focus filters. The only bright colors are in the lovers' garments, suggesting that they alone are real in this magical world.

How different is *Incident at the Café Tintoretto* **(140)** by the contemporary Italian artist Sandro Chia. Often identified as a **Neo-Expressionist** artist (Chapter 17), Chia paints simple everyday events and yet gives them cosmic importance. The "incident" depicted here might be an ordinary fight in a café, but it has all the drama of a scene from Dante's *Inferno*. Part of the

139. *Krishna and Radha in a Grove.* c. 1780. Gouache on paper, $4\frac{3}{4} \times 6\frac{3}{4}''$. Victoria & Albert Museum, London (by courtesy of the Board of Trustees).

reason for its impact is the dense, seething composition, but another part is the color. Chia's color absolutely *shrieks* at us, compelling attention with its vividness and "clash."

These three examples should be enough to demonstrate how potent a force color can be in a work of art, just as it is in life. Our next element is also a major factor in the experience of everyday life, and artists have learned to explore its power in art.

Texture

Texture refers to surface quality—a perception of smooth or rough, flat or bumpy, fine or coarse. Our world would be bland and uninteresting without contrasts of texture. Most of us, when we encounter a dog or cat, are moved to pet the animal, partly because the animal likes it, but also because we enjoy the feel of the fur's texture against our hands. In planning our clothes we instinctively take texture into account. We might put on a thick, nubby sweater over a smooth cotton shirt and enjoy the contrast. We look for this textural interest in all facets of our environment. Few people can resist running their hands over a smooth chunk of marble or a glossy length of silk or a drape of velvet. This is the outstanding feature of texture: it makes us want to touch it.

ACTUAL TEXTURE

All the textures referred to above are *actual* or *tactile;* we experience them through the sense of touch. The rougher the texture, the greater is the difference in surface elevation. If we cannot touch these surfaces, as it is forbidden to touch most sculptures in museums, we understand their actual textures by remembering similar objects we *have* touched.

Actual texture in art is associated with sculpture, architecture, and the crafts. But many paintings also have actual texture. When an artist lays on the paint in thick layers (a technique known as **impasto**), with some areas thicker than others, the painting may have actual surface texture (237). Sometimes, too, an artist may attach three-dimensional objects to a canvas, giving it actual surface texture. More often, of course, the textures we see in a painting are visual.

140. Sandro Chia.
Incident at the Café Tintoretto.
1981. Oil on canvas, 8′5″ × 11′2″.
Courtesy the artist.

141. Raoul Dufy.
Visit of the English Squadron to Havre. c. 1928.
Gouache, $18\frac{3}{4} \times 25\frac{1}{2}''$.
Searle Collection.

VISUAL TEXTURE

Raoul Dufy's *Visit of the English Squadron to Havre* **(141)** illustrates the concept of visual texture. If you could touch the paper, you would find it to be primarily flat. Nevertheless, the eye perceives a texture because of the closely spaced, small forms and brush strokes, especially the waves in the sea. This work reminds us of forms in the natural world that do in fact have texture, so we apply remembered perceptions of tactile texture to the visual expression.

We saw another type of visual texture in Steinberg's *Hen* **(105)**. In this drawing Steinberg used ink lines to evoke a tactile texture from the natural world—the feathers of a hen. Throughout history artists have attempted to simulate, on the flat surface of a canvas, natural textures—textures of fur and hair and fabric, for example, or textures of fruits and vegetables in a still life.

A visual texture, therefore, may be aimed at creating an illusion, or it may exist simply for its own sake, to provide visual interest. Either way, the texture helps to enliven a work of art.

PATTERN

As was mentioned in the section dealing with line, pattern is any decorative, repetitive motif. What is the difference between texture and pattern? Pattern nearly always creates visual texture, but texture may not be seen as pattern all the time. When a visual texture is decorative, highly repetitive, and evenly spaced over an area, we are more likely to call it pattern. A good example is the drawing by Gustav Klimt **(142)**. Klimt's subject in this work, a common one for him, is a woman in a long, flowing dress. The dress has been fragmented into a series of irregular triangles. Only this pattern separates the figure from its background, which consists of spiraling plantlike tendrils—another pattern. The figure, then, becomes a point of departure for the overall decorative patterns.

Klimt's drawing is full of movement and energy, thanks to the background spirals, which seem to spin like whirlpools. It is meant to be decorative, not naturalistic. You may observe that there is no impression of roundness in this figure, no distinction of foreground and background, no sense of looking through the "window" of the picture area into a real world. Klimt meant his picture to be "flat," but other artists have had very different goals. This brings us to consideration of the most complex visual element—space.

Space

The word "space," especially in our technological world, sometimes conveys the idea of nothingness. We think of outer space as a huge void, hostile to human life except when protected by complex support systems. A person who is "spaced out" is blank, unfocused, not really "there." But the space in and around a work of art is not a void, and it is very much there. It is a dynamic visual element that interacts with the lines and shapes and colors and textures of a work of art to give them definition. Consider space in this way: How could there be a line if there were not the spaces on either side of it to mark its edges? How could there be a shape without the space around it to set if off?

In this section we will look at the different types of space an artist deals with and how these spaces affect the other elements.

THREE-DIMENSIONAL SPACE

Sculpture, architecture, and all forms with mass exist in three-dimensional space—that is, the actual space in which our bodies also stand. These works of art take their character from the individual ways in which they carve out sections of space within and around them.

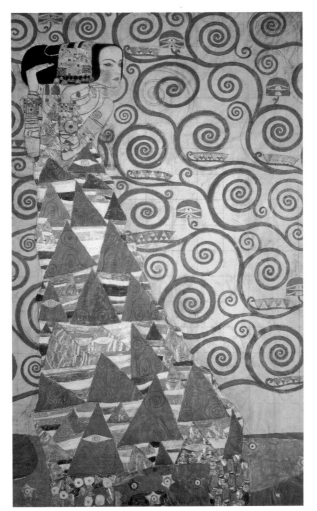

142. Gustav Klimt. *Expectation.* c. 1905–09. Mixed media with silver and gold leaf on paper, 6'4" × 3'9⅜". Osterreichisches Museum für Angewandte Kunst, Vienna.

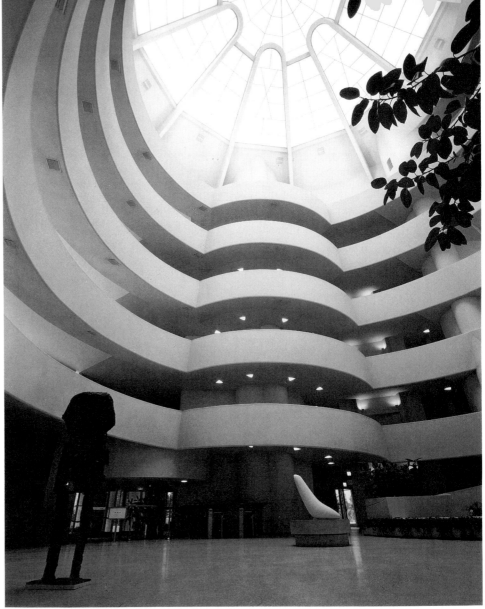

right: **143.** Frank Lloyd Wright. Solomon R. Guggenheim Museum, New York, interior view.

below: **144.** Barbara Hepworth. *Single Form (Memorial).* 1961–62. Bronze, height 10'3". Battersea Park, London.

Architecture, in particular, can be thought of as a means of carving space. Without the walls and the roof of a building, the space would be limitless; with them, the space has boundaries and therefore has volume. For instance, in a very simple house, say a shoebox-shaped house, the walls and roof create a "cube" of space that could be measured in terms of its volume. If the house is subdivided into rooms, then several smaller cubes of space have been created. The interior of the Solomon R. Guggenheim Museum in New York, designed by Frank Lloyd Wright **(143)**, provides a more complex example. Inside the building Wright constructed a huge bubblelike volume enlivened by curved forms cutting in and out and culminating in the skylight dome overhead. Because of this unusual treatment, Wright makes us think of space as active rather than passive, something rather than nothing. From outside we might view the Guggenheim Museum as a *mass;* inside we experience it as *shaped space.* The mass and the space are equal partners, since neither could exist without the other.

Space is also a vital element of sculpture. In Barbara Hepworth's *Single Form* **(144)** the focus of attention is likely to be the rounded opening near the top, which we might be tempted to call a "hole." Certainly it is a hole in the bronze, but we can also consider it from the opposite point of view, as a space *encircled* by the bronze. The space is not passive; it plays an active role in giving this sculpture its interest and power.

TWO-DIMENSIONAL SPACE

Two-dimensional space refers to the space in a painting, drawing, print, or other type of flat art. As the name implies, this kind of space has only height and width, no actual depth. There are two major considerations in dealing with this kind of space. The first is the way in which shapes, lines, and other elements are arranged vertically or horizontally within the space. The second is the possibility of visual depth, or the *illusion* of three-dimensional space on a two-dimensional surface.

SPATIAL ORGANIZATION Working on a picture surface that is flat, the artist has to decide where to place forms in that flat space—high or low, left or right, centered or off to one side. Each time the artist makes a mark of any kind, the space is divided into segments that were not there before.

In Jean Arp's collage *Arrangement According to the Laws of Chance* (145) the square forms have been organized more or less evenly throughout the space. The spaces between squares are similar, as are the top and bottom spaces. Now let us compare the spatial organization in Edgar Degas' *Dancers Practicing at the Barre* (146). The two major forms are crowded into the upper right quadrant of the painting, leaving the rest of the canvas as open space. Why would Degas design such an unusual division of space? Partly because he was influenced by Japanese art, in which asymmetrical balance is common (184). Also partly because he was fascinated by the unexpected angle of vision, such as a viewer might catch by peeping in a window or over a balcony. Even with the eccentric placement of the dancers at upper right, the space below and to the left does not seem "dead." Quite the opposite—the daring composition and sharp diagonal bring the whole space to life.

left: **145.** Jean Arp. *Arrangement According to the Laws of Chance.* 1916–17. Torn and pasted paper, $19\frac{1}{8} \times 13\frac{5}{8}''$. Collection, The Museum of Modern Art, New York (purchase).

right: **146.** Edgar Degas. *Dancers Practicing at the Barre.* 1877. Oil, freely mixed with turpentine, on canvas; $29\frac{3}{4} \times 32''$. The Metropolitan Museum of Art, New York (H. O. Havemeyer Collection, bequest of Mrs. H. O. Havemeyer, 1929).

ILLUSION OF DEPTH In some works of art the artist will try to create on a flat surface the illusion of three-dimensional space, as one might see in a natural landscape. This space appears to go backward in depth "behind" the front surface of the painting, which is referred to as the **picture plane.** When artists establish illusionary depth, they create the impression that some forms in the composition are farther away than others, and that some forms are in front of or behind others in space.

At different times in history and in different cultures there have been several methods used to create the illusion of depth on a two-dimensional surface. One of the simplest of these is **overlapping.** If one form overlaps another, that form appears to be in front of the other one. We see this effect in Marie Laurencin's painting, *Group of Artists* **(147)**. Laurencin portrays herself, at top left, standing beside her lover, the poet Guillaume Apollinaire (seated, center), along with Pablo Picasso and his dog, Frika (left), and Picasso's lover, Fernande Olivier (right). The space in this group scene is quite shallow, and even the figures are flat, seeming more like cutouts than flesh-and-blood people. Laurencin has slyly given Picasso an "Egyptian" eye, looking straight front in a profile head, much like the eyes he had experimented with in his own paintings. But in spite of the pervasive flatness, we sense some depth because the figures are overlapped. Laurencin is farthest back, overlapped by Picasso and Apollinaire, who are in turn overlapped by the dog and by Fernande Olivier (in her amazing hat) at the picture plane. These layers of depth are very slight, but Laurencin makes them real in the way she arranges her figures.

Another device to show spatial depth is **position.** In this method, pictorial figures that are meant to be understood as farther away are placed *higher* in the composition. We can see this effect clearly in a painting by Chiu-Tah, of the Taos Pueblo, depicting the *Taos Round Dance* **(148)**. All the figures in the circle are essentially the same size (except those meant to be children), yet because of their ingenious placement—lowest in the "foreground" gradually moving to highest in the "background," we have a compelling impression of a circle of people receding into deep space.

During the 15th century in Italy artists perfected the science of **linear perspective**—the most "realistic" method of portraying in two dimensions the visual depth of the natural world. Although linear perspective can be extremely complex and mathematical, it is based on the application of two simple, observable phenomena. In linear perspective:

147. Marie Laurencin.
Group of Artists. 1908.
Oil on canvas, 25½ × 31⅞".
The Baltimore Museum of Art
(The Cone Collection, formed
by Dr. Claribel Cone and Miss Etta Cone
of Baltimore, Maryland).

left: **148.** Chiu-Tah, Taos Pueblo. *Taos Round Dance*. 1938. Tempera. Present whereabouts unknown.

below: **149:** Sketches of linear and isometric perspective.

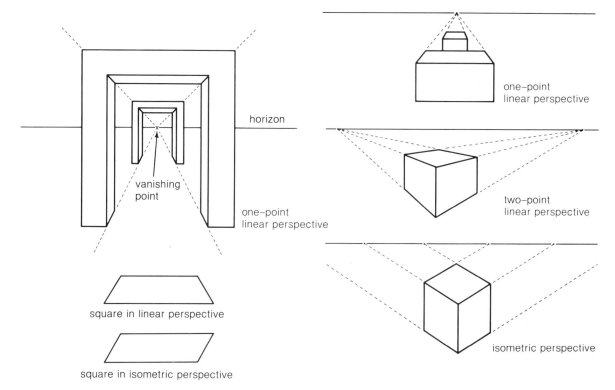

1. Forms that are far away from the viewer seem smaller than those that are close up.
2. Parallel lines receding into the distance seem to converge, until they meet at a point on the horizon line where they disappear. This point is known as the **vanishing point.**

You can visualize this second idea if you remember gazing down a straight highway. As the highway recedes farther from you, the two edges seem to come closer together, until they disappear at the horizon line **(149)**. Linear perspective is a translation into drawing principles of these two ideas.

Renaissance artists took up linear perspective with as much delight as a child takes up a new toy. For the first time in the history of civilization (as far as they knew) they could depict absolutely naturalistic scenes, and this was an important goal at the time. Several paintings were done as academic exercises to test the new science of perspective, including *View of an Ideal City* **(150)**. In this work the ground lines, the façades of the buildings, the roof lines, and the protruding architectural elements recede in a perfectly contrived scheme toward a vanishing point somewhere behind the circular building **(151)**. Also, the buildings get smaller and smaller as they go back into space.

Once artists had learned to depict deep space in a convincing manner, they could apply that knowledge to their own aesthetic purposes. Some four decades after the *Ideal City* was painted, the great Renaissance artist Leonardo da Vinci used linear perspective to enhance the dramatic and narrative thrust of his masterpiece, *The Last Supper* **(152)**. (*The Last Supper,* as we

ARTISTS ON ARTISTS *Marisol on Leonardo*

The imagery is late 16th century, but the expression is late 20th century, and that contrast provides the fascination of artists looking at artists. In the example shown here, the artist quite literally "looks" at the work of one of her great predecessors. The sculptor called Marisol has made a portrait of herself (seen from the side in this view) contemplating Leonardo da Vinci's *Last Supper*—or, more accurately, contemplating Marisol's version of Leonardo's *Last Supper*.

Marisol's sculptures are nearly always figural, and they typically show a blend of two-dimensions and three. The figures are cut from thin plywood, so they have little depth—just a back and front with no real sides—but they are arranged in full three-dimensional space. For *The Last Supper* Marisol built a construction that is almost the same size as Leonardo's mural in

height and width. But where Leonardo created the illusion of deep space on his flat wall, Marisol sets her figures in an actual space about 5 feet deep.

All the same characters present at Leonardo's *Last Supper* are duplicated by Marisol, but the sculptor has stylized her figures—simplified the forms and exaggerated their poses and gestures. Most important, Marisol has added another layer of experience. We as viewers cannot just see this *Last Supper*. We must see it through the sculptor's eyes, because she is there.

Marisol. *Self-Portrait Looking at The Last Supper.* 1982–84.
Painted wood, plywood, brownstone, charcoal, plaster, and aluminum; 10′1″ × 29′10″ × 5′7″.
The Metropolitan Museum of Art, New York
(gift of Mr. and Mrs. Roberto C. Polo, 1986).

shall see in the Epilogue [p. 504], is in extremely poor condition and has been undergoing a major restoration. Nevertheless, the details of Leonardo's perspective rendering should be clear.)

Painted on a monastery wall in Milan, *The Last Supper* depicts the final gathering of Jesus Christ with his disciples, the Passover meal they shared before Jesus was brought to trial and crucified. Leonardo captures a particular moment in the story, as related by the Gospel book of Matthew in the Bible. Jesus, shown at the center of the composition, has just said to his followers: "One of you shall betray me." The disciples, Matthew tells us, "were exceeding sorrowful, and began every one of them to say unto him, Lord, is it I?"

Leonardo portrays each of the disciples as individuals, each reacting differently to the terrible prediction. Some are shocked, some dismayed, some puzzled—but only one, only Judas, knows that indeed, it is he. Falling back from Jesus' words, the traitor Judas, seated fourth from the left with his elbow on the table, clutches a bag containing the thirty pieces of silver, his price for handing over his leader to the authorities.

To show this fateful moment, Leonardo places the group in a large banquet hall, its architectural space constructed in careful perspective. Cloth hangings on the side walls and panels in the ceiling are drawn so as to recede into space. Their lines converge at a vanishing point behind Jesus' head, at the exact center of the picture. Thus, our attention is directed forcefully toward the most important part of the composition, the face of Jesus. The central opening in the back wall, a rectangular window, also helps to focus our attention on Jesus and creates a "halo" effect around his head.

Leonardo's perspective performs another function as well, in making the scene believable. When thirteen people sit down to dinner, they do not usually cram themselves all on one side of the table, leaving the opposite side empty. But Leonardo needed this odd arrangement to show the personalities and reactions of his characters. Placing the line of figures in deep space helps to take away the oddness, to make the grouping seem more natural. It gives them, pictorially, "more room." You can see how this effect works if you cover up the section of picture above the heads. Without the illusion of space afforded by the perspective, Leonardo's figures would look artificially crowded together.

Linear perspective may seem "correct" to our eyes because of our experience with photographs. Many photographs, especially of architecture, resemble a drawing in careful linear perspective (153,154). Nevertheless, it is

left: 153. Berenice Abbott. *Canyon, Broadway and Exchange Place.* 1936. Photograph. Courtesy Berenice Abbott/ Commerce Graphics Ltd., Inc.

right: 154. *Canyon, Broadway and Exchange Place,* with linear perspective lines.

not the magic key to perfect art, as some Renaissance artists thought. The perspective works only if the viewer stands motionless and fixes his or her eyes (or, even better, one eye with the other closed) on a particular spot. For this reason the results of academically perfect linear perspective may appear static and lifeless—much like the *Ideal City,* which reminds us less of a living metropolis than of a ghost town. Expanding the perspective to include two or more vanishing points **(149)**, a more complex form of perspective, helps to give a more vital image, but the results may still be rather rigid. As with any artistic element, perspective is a tool, and its use depends on the artist.

The 18th-century Italian painter Canaletto understood the mathematical precision of linear perspective very well, and he employed that precision to give depth to his many views of Venice. Moreover, he knew how to use it without being rigid or lifeless. In a typically dense canvas, *View of Venice: Grand Canal, Looking Southwest from Near the Rialto Bridge* **(155)**, the expanse of the vista plunges so far into deep space that the vanishing point never quite seems to "vanish." We imagine that if only our vision were sharper, we could see *beyond* what Canaletto has showed us to yet more buildings, more boats, more people farther down the canal. Much of the life in a Canaletto landscape comes from the thousand details the artist provides: people in all guises and occupations, gondolas in motion or tied up, laundry flapping out of windows, endlessly varied architecture, a little dog barking. For Canaletto, linear perspective creates the framework, but the exuberant life of Venice is the picture.

In Eastern art linear perspective has played much less of a role. Instead, artists often have relied on a system of ***isometric perspective,*** in which distant forms *are* made smaller but parallel lines do not converge. The Shinto

155. Canaletto (Giovanni Antonio Canal). *View of Venice: Grand Canal, Looking Southwest from Near the Rialto Bridge.* c. 1730. Oil on canvas, 19¼ × 29". The Museum of Fine Arts, Houston (The Robert Lee Blaffer Memorial Collection, gift of Sarah Campbell Blaffer).

left: **156.** *Kumano Mandala*, Japan.
Kamakura Period, c. 1300.
Color on silk, 4'4¾" × 2'⅜".
The Cleveland Museum of Art
(John L. Severance Fund).

right: **157.** *Kumano Mandala*,
with isometric perspective lines.

shrines depicted in the *Kumano Mandala* **(156)** might be considered the Japanese equivalent of a Renaissance "ideal city." As usual in isometric perspective, lines that would be perpendicular to the picture plane are drawn as sharp diagonals **(157)**. Whereas linear perspective turns the square into a trapezoid, isometric perspective turns the square into a parallelogram **(149)**. Architects and industrial draftsmen often use this type of perspective for their drawings, because it allows them to indicate accurate measurements.

In conjunction with linear or isometric perspective, the artist may employ the device of ***atmospheric perspective.*** This means that forms meant to be perceived as far in the distance are blurred, indistinct, and misty—much as the eye perceives distant forms in nature. You can see this effect in many landscape paintings reproduced throughout this book.

To sum up, then, artists can draw upon several devices to create the illusion of three-dimensional depth on a two-dimensional surface. Here are some of the major ones:

Seen as Foreground	Seen as Background
large size	small size
set low in the picture	set high in the picture
parallel lines far apart	parallel lines converging
overlapping other forms	overlapped by other forms
sharply defined forms	blurred forms
intense colors	grayed colors
rough textures	smooth textures

When linear perspective is applied to human or animal forms or to objects receding into depth, the result is called **foreshortening.** Literally, the body, or part of it, is "shortened" from its normal vertical height to better convey the appearance of figures that are perpendicular to the picture plane. A classic example of foreshortening is Andrea Mantegna's *Dead Christ* **(158)**. If you could lift this figure out of the painting and stand it upright, its proportions would seem very strange indeed. The legs are far too short for the body, and the entire figure would be absurdly short compared to its breadth. Mantegna's composition, however, seems entirely believable given the unusual angle of vision. And his choice of this angle makes the body of the dead Christ all the more poignant and vulnerable.

The aim of all perspective systems, including the device of foreshortening, is to create the impression of realism. Yet once the artist has the *ability* to convey the idea of depth on a flat surface, the question remains, how much sense of depth does he or she want in any given work? Most Renaissance

158. Andrea Mantegna. *Dead Christ.* After 1466. Tempera on canvas, $26\frac{3}{4} \times 31\frac{7}{8}''$. Brera Gallery, Milan.

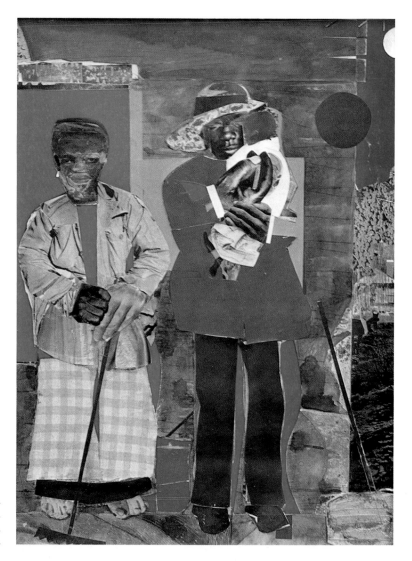

159. Romare Bearden.
Miss Bertha & Mr. Seth. 1978.
Collage, $25\frac{1}{2} \times 18\frac{1}{2}''$.
Private collection, New Jersey.

artists would have answered this question by saying "the more the better," the more depth in a painting, the better the artist has succeeded. Later artists, however, have had many different goals, and illusion of depth is only one of them.

The space in Romare Bearden's *Miss Bertha & Mr. Seth* **(159)** is almost entirely flat. The figures stand flush at the picture plane, and the backdrop pushes up very close behind them. Moreover, the figures themselves have no full-bodied roundness; they are more like paper dolls or the large cardboard cutouts one might see in a shop window. Only in the extreme right-hand side of the composition has Bearden given us a suggestion of depth. We see a hint of a deep landscape, but this serves to make the space of the entire work even more complicated. Bearden knew how to draw deep space, but in this case he chose not to. He stands his figures flat at the front of the canvas, thereby giving them an importance and a dignity they might not have had were they worked into a conventional landscape.

The French artist Suzanne Valadon also knew how to draw deep space, but for her *Reclining Nude* **(160)** she has chosen to keep the space of the painting quite shallow. The figure is posed rather awkwardly on a too-small sofa, with legs crossed and one arm clutched across the breast in a self-protective gesture. This model presents herself for our inspection, but at the same time she pulls away and keeps to herself. Valadon has outlined the figure in a strong black line and concentrated especially on the powerful volumes of thigh and belly and upper arm. But the most fascinating aspect of this painting is its claustrophobic space. We as viewers seem to be very close to the model, who is hemmed in on three sides by the sofa. The tight space creates a tension, a psychological confrontation, between the viewer and the model. She is naked but private; the viewer is perhaps embarrassed and sympathetic, surely intrigued.

So we see that pictorial depth, or the lack thereof, is a powerful tool that an artist can use for whatever effect is desired. Once the skill is acquired, the possibilities are endless. Yet no matter how skilled the artist, it is not possible to make a painted scene look exactly like a real scene for one simple reason: our world does not stand still. At every moment there is the sense of passing time, the sense of movement. Some works of art, however, do deal in time and motion. We turn finally to a consideration of these two factors.

Time and Motion

The ancient Egyptians undoubtedly would have been puzzled to find time and motion included in a discussion of art. In Egyptian culture, and in many others, art was supposed to be time*less*, motion*less* for all eternity. Our own world, however, is considerably more dynamic. Most of us, especially in the industrialized nations, are obsessed with time, and motion is a fact of everyday life. Both time and motion have come to be recognized as important elements in art.

ELAPSED TIME

In the three-dimensional arts, especially sculpture and architecture, time is always a factor in the observer's reaction. When you walk through a building or walk around a sculpture, your viewpoint changes with every split second

160. Suzanne Valadon.
Reclining Nude.
Oil on canvas, $23\frac{5}{8} \times 31\frac{11}{16}''$.
The Metropolitan Museum of Art, New York (Robert Lehman Collection, 1975).

Suzanne Valadon

1867–1938

In 1867, in a small town in central France, was born an illegitimate child named Marie-Clémentine Valade. When Marie was three years old her mother brought her to Paris, where they lived in extreme poverty, subsisting on vegetables discarded as garbage at the market. Little Marie worked as a laundress and, later, joined a circus as animal rider and trapeze artist. At the age of eighteen she, in turn, gave birth to an illegitimate child, who would become the painter Maurice Utrillo. During her childhood she taught herself to draw—first with cinders given to her by a coal hauler, then with whatever drawing materials she could find. After an accident at the circus, she became an artist's model, posing for Degas, Renoir, and the young painter Henri de Toulouse-Lautrec. The latter formed a friendship, perhaps a romance, with Marie, and is said to have given her a new name—Suzanne Valadon.

Although she never had a formal lesson, Valadon received much encouragement from her artist-patrons, whose work she was able to study at close range. She began to paint, and then to make prints. By the time she was twenty-eight she had had her work exhibited by an important dealer and had sold many drawings and etchings. Some compared her painting to that of Paul Gauguin, whom she much admired, yet always she retained an originality and reliance on her own artistic instincts, especially in her use of the bold, definitive outline.

In 1894 Valadon took up with a rich banker, Paul Mousis, and spent the next fourteen years living as his wife—they never were married legally—in a large house in the Paris suburbs. Despite the slightly scandalous nature of their unwed relationship and the presence of Valadon's illegitimate (and alcoholic) son, this proved to be the *least* bohemian period in her colorful life. Valadon continued to work and to exhibit, and she taught Maurice to paint, apparently in the hope that it would help him to overcome his alcoholism. But in 1908 Valadon herself slipped back into what most people considered a bohemian life style. She fell in love with a young painter, André Utter, a friend of Maurice's who was twenty-one years her junior, and went to live with him. On one occasion the three—Valadon, Utter, and Utrillo—held a joint exhibition in Paris, but the public was more interested in the trio's sins than in their art.

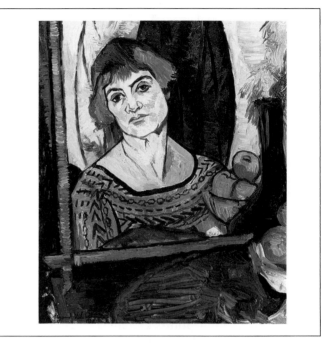

Toward the end of her life, Valadon achieved some measure of fame and considerable financial security. Until her last year she continued to paint and to show, in both solo and joint exhibitions. Indeed, death came, in the form of a stroke, while she was at her easel working on a new painting. The mourners at her funeral included virtually the whole Parisian art community, among them Picasso.

Certainly the details of Valadon's life are interesting, and they mark her as a genuine individual. In her life, as in her art, she followed her own path, copying no one, offering no explanation. She seldom spoke, and never wrote, about her art, but one comment that was recorded seems to sum up her faith in her own vision: "I don't understand the experts, neither their explanations, nor their comparisons. When they speak of technique, balance and values they simply make me dizzy. Only two things exist for me and all others who paint: good pictures and bad pictures, that's all."[3]

Suzanne Valadon. *Self-Portrait*. 1927.
Oil on wood, $24\frac{1}{2} \times 19\frac{3}{4}''$.
Courtesy Paul Petrides, Paris.

that elapses. Usually, you *cannot* experience every aspect of the structure from one vantage point or at one moment. You must expend time to accumulate all the different points of view and assemble them into an understanding of the whole. The architects of the great cathedrals knew this, and so did the architect of one of the great modern churches.

Set high in the Vosges Mountains of eastern France, near Switzerland, is the Chapel of Notre-Dame-du-Haut (Our Lady on High), designed by the contemporary architect known as Le Corbusier. The little church sits atop a pinnacle, overlooking the town of Ronchamp (161). There is only one access road, so the visitor's viewpoint while approaching the church is controlled at every turn. Having reached the summit, the visitor finds no obvious entrance to the church on the facing side, and so must walk all around to enter. The exterior of Notre-Dame-du-Haut is endlessly unpredictable. Each new viewpoint, each moment of elapsed time, brings a different perspective.

The inside of the chapel (162) is equally unusual. Irregular openings cut into the thick walls admit light according to a constantly changing pattern— a pattern affected by time during the day. No one vantage point will reveal everything about the chapel. The visitor must walk around, move from spot to spot, draw closer and then pull away to get a full sense of the building's architecture. Notre-Dame-du-Haut is as much a masterpiece of time as it is of mass and space and light.

ACTUAL MOTION

When time is a factor in art, it is often assumed that the viewer is in motion. In some cases, however, the work of art is also in motion. One sculptor whose special preoccupation has been forms in motion is George Rickey. In any Rickey sculpture the shape of the object is less important than the movements that may be produced by that shape. *Two Rectangles Vertical Gyratory*

left: **161.** Le Corbusier. Notre-Dame-du-Haut, Ronchamp, exterior. 1950–55.

right: **162.** Le Corbusier. Notre-Dame-du-Haut, Ronchamp, interior. 1950–55.

(163) floats above the streets of Rotterdam, its two rectangular slabs set in constant, nonrepetitive motion by the wind. The balance of these slabs makes them receptive to any passing breeze, but no one can predict exactly what configuration they will take at any moment. Their polished surfaces reflect light from above, the street scene from below, in an ever-changing pattern.

ILLUSION OF MOTION

Just as artists have long attempted to create the illusion of deep space on a flat surface, so have they often tried to create the illusion of motion where there is none, and, as with spatial depth, the artist has a choice. Some works of art are planned to be rather static and motionless, and a sense of movement would actually be harmful to the artist's intent. Valadon's *Reclining Nude* **(160)** fits this category. In other cases a sense of movement contributes much to the success of the work. Gericault's *The Raft of the Medusa* **(115)** seems dynamic because the artist has created an illusion of the raft plunging through the water, an illusion of motion. We could find many other examples of this situation. Indeed, in Gustav Klimt's drawing **(142)** the illusion of motion—caused by the repetitive pattern of spirals that seem to spin—becomes one of the most important elements in the composition.

The same is true for the three works illustrated here. Bridget Riley's *Current* **(164)**, an example of the style known as **Op Art,** has as its theme the illusion of motion caused by optical effects, a direct response by the retina of the eye to lines and colors arranged in certain ways. The lines in this painting are just that—precisely drawn lines on flat canvas—but as we stare at them they begin to swim before our eyes, and the painting actually seems to be in

above: 163. George Rickey. *Two Rectangles Vertical Gyratory.* 1969. Stainless steel, height 45'. Collection City of Rotterdam, courtesy the artist.

right: 164. Bridget Riley. *Current.* 1964. Synthetic polymer paint on composition board, 4'10⅜" square. Collection, The Museum of Modern Art, New York (Philip Johnson Fund).

motion. Some viewers have experienced vertigo or even nausea after spending time in front of an Op canvas, so powerful is the effect on one's central nervous system.

Giacomo Balla's *Dynamism of a Dog on a Leash* (165) shows another way in which motion can be suggested. Balla was a member of the **Futurist** group that flourished in Italy during the second decade of this century. An important (though short-lived) movement, Futurism, as the name implies, rejected the art forms of the past, which it considered static, in favor of images that conveyed movement and energy. In *Dog on a Leash* Balla has blurred the forms of dog, leash, and dog walker, repeating the feet, tail, and leash many times to set them in motion across the canvas. When we look at this charming painting, we might almost swear we see the dog's tail wagging, its little feet scampering along.

Seventy years later Andy Warhol employed a similar technique to suggest motion in his screenprint *Superman* (166). The ghost image to the right of Superman's full-color form creates the impression of him streaking through the sky so fast that he registers as a blur. Here Warhol is capitalizing on our familiarity with motion photography to present an image of believable motion.

Line, shape and mass, light, value, color, texture, space, time and motion—these are the raw materials, the elements, of a work of art. Some people are troubled by this approach to works of art, taking them apart and putting them back together again like jigsaw puzzles. And how can we justify discussion of the art elements in the face of utterly down-to-earth and commonsensical remarks like Suzanne Valadon's declaration that such analyses made her "dizzy"?

Whether she cared to talk about it or not, Valadon understood the art elements. She had absorbed them into her eye and her hand and her soul as an artist. For the rest of us, a discussion of the elements gives systematic and intellectual order to our aesthetic appreciation of art. With a knowledge of the elements, we begin to understand *why* we love one work of art, why we do not much like another. And then we—along with Valadon—can make intelligent judgments about "good pictures and bad pictures, that's all."

left: 165. Giacomo Balla. *Dynamism of a Dog on a Leash.* 1912. Oil on canvas, $35\frac{3}{8} \times 43\frac{1}{4}$". Albright-Knox Art Gallery, Buffalo, N.Y. (bequest of A. Conger Goodyear and gift of George F. Goodyear, 1964).

right: 166. Andy Warhol. *Superman*, from the series *Myths.* 1981. Silkscreen, 38" square. Courtesy Ronald Feldman Fine Arts, New York.

A biographer is by nature a gossip. We value the art of biography because it enables us to better understand the work of noted individuals through knowing their histories. At a more basic level, however, nearly all of us love to learn the details of other people's lives—in other words, gossip. And one of the most delightful gossips in history was Giorgio Vasari.

Vasari was a painter and architect of considerable skill. Born in Arezzo, in the Italian province of Tuscany, in 1511, he pursued the career of artist throughout his life. Many of his paintings still exist, and his major work as an architect, the Uffizi Palace in Florence, is now an important museum. But for two facts, Vasari might today be known as a prominent artist of the Renaissance. The facts are these: Vasari was inevitably overshadowed by the giants at work in Italy at the same time, notably Leonardo da Vinci, Michelangelo, and Raphael. And Vasari's artistic production was overshadowed by his own brilliant literary endeavor—a comprehensive biography of the outstanding Renaissance artists.

The first edition of his masterwork, *Lives of the Most Excellent Architects, Painters, and Sculptors,* was published in 1550, after seven years of hard work. (A revised and expanded edition of the book was published in 1568.) Although other biographies had been written, nothing on this scale had ever been completed. Reading the *Lives* today, we may find the style a trifle precious, but at the time Vasari's approach was considered natural and conversational. For his research, Vasari traveled constantly (on horseback, over bad roads), spoke with anyone he could, viewed works of art whenever possible. Some of his subjects, including Raphael, were long dead when he began the *Lives,* so he depended on secondhand sources. Others, like Michelangelo, were close and respected friends. It is on Michelangelo that Vasari pours out the extremes of his flowery admiration.

Everyone seems to have liked Vasari. He had a vast network of friends, a huge correspondence, a long list of patrons. His genial temperament gave him access to information about all the leading artists. In the *Lives,* Vasari's style is so charming, so enthusiastic, so *cheerful,* that reading him now, more than four hundred years later—we like him too.

Against his extremely busy public life, Vasari's personal life was uneventful. Under pressure from one

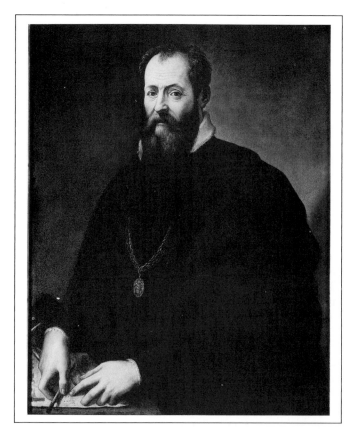

of his patrons, a cardinal of the Church, he "resolved to do something, which hitherto I had not wished to do, that is to take a wife." In 1550 he married Niccolosa Bacci, always called Cosina, for whom he seems to have had a rather absent-minded affection but little passion. The couple had no children.

As historian and biographer, Vasari must be taken with a grain of salt. His grasp of dates is particularly casual. We should remember, however, that Vasari was breaking new ground. In his day there were no reference books to check facts, no encyclopedias, no public libraries. Under the circumstances, the *Lives* must be viewed as a staggering achievement, giving us a picture of Renaissance artists that is true in its quality if shaky in some specifics. For without Vasari, we would have had little picture at all.

Giorgio Vasari. *Self-Portrait.* c. 1571.
Uffizi, Florence.

Principles of Design in Art

When an artist sets about making any work, he or she is faced with infinite choices. How big or small? What kinds of lines and where should the lines go? What kinds of shapes? How much space between the shapes? How many colors and how much of each one? What amounts of light and dark values? Somehow, the elements discussed in Chapter 4—line, shape, light, value, color, texture, space, and possibly time and motion—must be organized in such a way as to satisfy the artist's expressive intent. In two-dimensional art this organization is sometimes called **composition,** but the inclusive term, applicable to all kinds of art, is **design.** The task of making all the decisions involved in designing a work of art would be paralyzing were it not for certain guidelines that, once understood, become almost instinctive. These guidelines are usually known as the *principles of design.*

All of us have some built-in sense of what looks right or wrong, what "works" or doesn't. Some—including most artists—have a stronger sense of what "works" than others. If two families each decorate a living room, and one room is attractive, welcoming, and pulled together while the other seems drab and uninviting, we might say that the first family has better "taste." Taste is a common term that, in this context, describes how some people make visual selections. What we really mean by "good taste," oftentimes, is that some people have a better grasp of the principles of design and how to use them.

The principles of design are a natural part of perception. Most of us are not conscious of them in everyday life, but artists usually are very aware of them, because they have trained themselves to be aware. These principles codify, or explain systematically, our sense of "rightness" and help to show why certain designs work better than others. For the artist they offer guidelines for making the most effective choices; for the observer an understanding of the principles of design gives greater insight into works of art.

It must be stressed that the principles of design are not rules or laws. If they were, nearly every great artist would have been guilty of breaking them at one time or another. They are, as we said, guidelines that apply in most situations. There are circumstances, however, in which an artist may choose to violate or ignore these guidelines to achieve a particular effect.

The principles of design most often identified are unity and variety, balance, emphasis and focal point, proportion and scale, and rhythm. This

167. Ben Jones.
Black Face and Arm Unit. 1971.
Painted plaster, lifesize.
New Jersey State Museum,
Trenton (purchase).

chapter illustrates some forty works of art that show these principles very clearly. But *any* work of art, regardless of its form or the culture in which it was made, could be discussed in terms of the principles of design, for they are integral to all art.

Unity and Variety

Unity is a sense of oneness, of things belonging together and making up a coherent whole. Variety is difference, which provides interest. We discuss them together because the two generally coexist in a work of art. A solid wall painted white has unity for sure, but it is not likely to hold your interest for long. Take that same blank wall and ask fifty people each to make a mark on it and you will get plenty of variety, but there probably will be no unity whatever. In fact, there will be so *much* variety that no one can form a meaningful visual impression. Unity and variety exist on a spectrum, with total blandness at one end, total disorder at the other. For most works of art the artist strives to find just the right point on that spectrum—the point at which there is sufficient visual unity enlivened by sufficient variety.

Ben Jones' *Black Face and Arm Unit* **(167)** illustrates the way unity and variety work together. This wall-mounted sculpture consists of several units of a painted masklike face above a decorated arm. We get the impression of a whole personality from each of the units; each face-and-arm pair stands for an entire human being. There is unity in the basic forms—face above arm—and in the spacing of the forms. Yet the artist has provided great variety in facial expressions, decorative motifs, even the direction in which the arms are bent.

How does an artist achieve unity? One way is by holding one or two elements constant and varying the others. Jones, in his sculpture, kept the elements of shape and space constant and varied the lines, colors, and visual textures. Similarly, in Stuart Davis' *Ready to Wear* **(168)** shape is the unifying element. Nearly all the shapes in Davis' painting are roughly geometric, and most are variations on the rectangle or oval or triangle. We imagine that the artist drew his outlines with a tool, rather than freehand. Yet despite this unity of shape we see great variety in size, placement, angle, color, and overlapping of the shapes. The composition is coherent yet excitingly diverse.

Henri Matisse used color to unify *The Red Studio* **(169)**. Walls and floor are saturated with a vivid scarlet, and some of the furniture is drawn as though transparent to let the red show through. By this method Matisse pulls

left: **168.** Stuart Davis. *Ready to Wear.* 1955.
Oil on canvas, 4'8¼" × 3'6".
The Art Institute of Chicago (gift of
Mr. and Mrs. Sigmund Kunstadter and Goodman Fund, 1956).

below: **169.** Henri Matisse. *The Red Studio.* 1911.
Oil on canvas, 5'11¼" × 7'2¼".
Collection, The Museum of Modern Art, New York
(Mrs. Simon Guggenheim Fund).

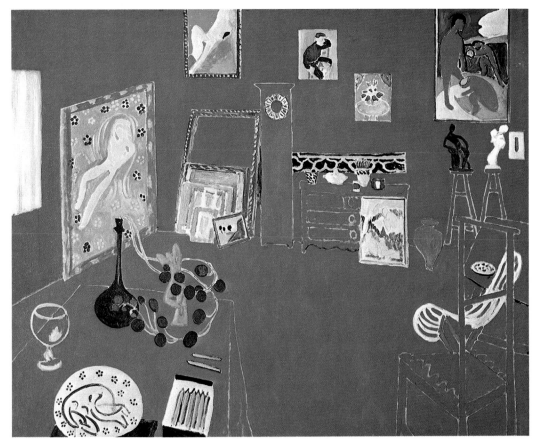

together the variety of what might be any artist's home studio—paintings displayed and stacked against the wall, a clock and bureau, drawing and eating utensils. Although the spatial organization may at first glance seem random, we get a strong sense of unity due largely to the color.

Unity is especially important in architecture, because one is working on such a grand scale. Think how unsettling it would be to see a large building in which the parts didn't seem to belong together. Not only the major forms but also the decorative design should contribute to the overall effect intended by the architect. In Moscow, which we often consider to be a stronghold of stern, bureaucratic drabness, stands one of the most delightfully ornate churches in the world, the Cathedral of St. Basil **(170)**. Many domes—some of them called "onion" domes because of their bulbous shape—crown this magnificent structure. The amazing richness of detail makes us think more of a fairy-tale castle than a Christian church. Points and arches, triangles and half-circles and zigzags, round and square and octagonal shapes—everything the creative imagination can dream up has been lavished on this design. A major factor in pulling it all together is a unifying texture. Although the shapes are riotously varied, their surface texture, which catches the light and casts shadows, creates a harmonious pattern.

The classic exercise in achieving unity-with-variety is the still-life painting. To make a still life, the artist brings together a number of diverse objects having different colors, shapes, sizes, and textures, and arranges them into a pleasing composition. The usual goal is to make these forms belong together, to harmonize with and yet play against one another. Chardin's glorious *Kitchen Still Life* **(171)** consists of homely objects one might expect to find in an 18th-century kitchen—earthenware jugs, a casserole, a deep cooking pot, a bit of raw meat, some fish, two eggs. Shape is a unifying

170. Cathedral of St. Basil, Moscow. 1555–60.

left: 171.
Jean Baptiste Siméon Chardin.
Kitchen Still Life. c. 1730–35.
Oil on canvas, $12\frac{1}{2} \times 15\frac{1}{4}''$.
Ashmolean Museum, Oxford.

below: 172. Miriam Schapiro.
Children of Paradise. 1984.
Color lithograph with collage,
$31\frac{1}{2} \times 47\frac{1}{4}''$.
University of South Florida
Art Museum, Tampa, Fla.

element here, as most of the forms are round or curves, including the table edge. But beyond this, Chardin has made the curves echo and overlap one another, resulting in a gentle, rhythmic motion. For the viewer there is little "stillness" in this still life. Our eyes move up and around and down, following the rounded shapes. Each object is treated as though it were perfect, the most beautiful form in the world, yet all are drawn together in a unified composition.

The five works we have just considered show a primarily *visual* unity— unity of shape or space or color or texture or pattern. We should also take into account the potential for *conceptual* unity, or unity of ideas, which may enhance or even replace visual unity. For instance, if Miriam Schapiro's *Children of Paradise* (**172**) reminds you of a patchwork quilt, that is no accident.

right: **173.** Joseph Cornell. *The Hotel Eden*. 1945. Assemblage with music box, $15\frac{1}{8} \times 15\frac{1}{8} \times 4\frac{3}{4}''$. National Gallery of Canada, Ottawa.

below: **174.** Andy Warhol. *200 Campbell Soup Cans*. 1962. Casein on canvas, $6' \times 8'4\frac{1}{8}''$. Courtesy Leo Castelli Gallery, New York.

The quiltlike quality is a major factor in unifying the composition; we perceive all the forms as being of cloth, and we identify the decorative fabric-type designs we would see in a quilt. Even though the little boy's suit and the little girl's dress are not alike in shape or color, we look at them and think "child's outfit." Schapiro is much interested in the handcrafts of 19th-century American women, and she has used this idea to unify her composition. Visual unity is provided by the repeated heart and house motifs, but variety abounds in the colors, patterns, positions, and overlapping of forms.

Conceptual unity predominates in the works of Joseph Cornell, such as *The Hotel Eden* (173). Cornell devoted most of his career to making boxlike structures that enclosed many dissimilar but related objects. Contained within the boxes, these objects build their own private worlds. Cornell collected things, odds and ends, wherever he went. His studio held crates of stuff filed according to a personal system. There were even crates labeled "flotsam" and "jetsam." When making his box sculptures, Cornell would select and arrange these objects to create a conceptual unity that was meaningful to him, based on his dreams, nostalgia, and fantasies. This is not sufficient to provide a *visual* unity, and so the boxed enclosure and the smaller boxes within it take care of the latter.

All the works illustrated so far strike a balance between unity and variety, and this is most often the artist's goal. Sometimes, however, an artist will aim at extreme unity or extreme variety. Andy Warhol's *200 Campbell Soup Cans* (174) is an example of the first. No one would question that this composition has unity. What little variety Warhol gives us comes in the different soup names, and this is a subtle variety to say the least. Warhol, like many Pop artists of the 1960s, is commenting on the packaged uniformity of our society. He might be saying that we have sacrificed variety for efficiency, in manufacture and in life, so that this has become our world—row upon row of sameness.

When a composition is as unified as the *200 Campbell Soup Cans*, there is likely to be a side effect in the automatic achievement of compositional balance. In most works of art, however, balance is more subtle and somewhat more difficult to create.

Balance

How can a ballet dancer stand, poised on the toes of one foot, with arm and chest thrust out in one direction, extended leg thrust out in the other direction? The answer, of course, is balance. The dancer has instinctively calculated bodily weight so it is dispersed and balanced perfectly around the supporting leg.

If our bodies were not balanced in standing and walking and running, we would topple over. We have an innate desire for balance and stability. Maybe that is why we seek balance in a work of art, why we feel threatened by instability when balance is absent. *Actual weight*, physical weight in pounds, is important in some types of art, such as sculpture and architecture. All art, however, must deal with the concept of **visual weight.** Visual weight refers to the apparent "heaviness" or "lightness" of forms arranged in a composition. When two sides of a flat composition have the same visual weight, the composition is in balance. Let us see how this works by considering the three types of balance—symmetrical, asymmetrical, and radial.

SYMMETRICAL BALANCE

Symmetry in art means that forms in the two halves of a composition—on either side of an imaginary vertical dividing line—correspond to one another in size, shape, and placement. Sometimes the symmetry is so perfect that the two sides of a composition are mirror images of one another; more often the correspondence is very close but not exact—a situation some writers have called *relieved symmetry*. In either case we consider the composition symmetrically balanced. Since the two sides are identical or nearly so, they have the same visual weight, and therefore they are balanced. The Matisse collage above: **175.** Henri Matisse. *Large Composition with Masks.* 1953. Collage, paper on canvas; 11′7¼″ × 32′8⅛″. National Gallery of Art, Washington, D.C. (Ailsa Mellon Bruce Fund, 1973).

right: **176.** Frida Kahlo. *The Two Fridas.* 1939. Oil on canvas, 5′8½″ square. Museo de Arte Moderno, Mexico City.

(175) is symmetrically balanced; if you were to fold this image down the middle and match the two sides, they would fit almost exactly. Except for color variations, the forms on one side of the center axis correspond to those on the other side.

Symmetrical balance served the artist Frida Kahlo with exceptional force in *The Two Fridas* **(176)**, for she used it to express the warring duality of her own nature. Kahlo was born in Mexico in 1907, the child of a Hungarian/Jewish father and an Indian/Spanish mother. These two influences—the European and the Mexican—coexisted uneasily in her psyche and her art as long as she lived. We might almost say that Frida Kahlo was Siamese twins who didn't get along. *The Two Fridas* shows this graphically. At left is the "European Frida," dressed in an elegant white gown; at right, the "Mexican Frida" wears a costume suited to that country's natives. Both have their hearts exposed in gory anatomical detail, with veins connecting them. The Mexican Frida holds a tiny portrait of the artist Diego Rivera, to whom Kahlo was married. The European Frida snips the vein connected to the portrait, allowing blood to fall on her skirt. This picture's symmetrical format gives a chilling interpretation to the double identity of its maker.

Henri Matisse

1869–1954

How ironic it is that Matisse, of all people, should have provoked a critic to call him a "wild beast," for, while his art may indeed have seemed a bit wild at first, the artist himself could scarcely have been less so. Cautious, reserved, cheerful, a hard worker, dedicated family man, frugal, painstaking—these are the qualities that describe Matisse. His longtime friend and rival Picasso captured more of the headlines, but the steadfast Matisse created art no less innovative and enduring.

Matisse's father intended him to be a lawyer, but a severe bout of appendicitis at the age of twenty-one changed his life—and changed the course of all modern art. Henri's mother bought him a box of paints as a diversion, and, for once, Matisse reacted strongly. Much later he said of this experience, "It was as if I had been called. Henceforth I did not lead my life. It led me."[1]

Matisse enrolled at the Ecole des Beaux-Arts in Paris and studied with the painter Gustave Moreau, a brilliant teacher who is said to have told his young pupil, "You were born to simplify painting." After a period of experimentation in various styles, Matisse exploded onto the Parisian art scene at the Salon d'Automne (autumn salon) in 1905, when he exhibited, along with several younger colleagues, works of such pure, intense, and arbitrary color that a critic labeled the artists *fauves*—wild beasts. In these early years Matisse did not fare much better with the general public. However, he had the good fortune to attract the attention of certain wealthy Americans who have achieved fame as inspired collectors, including the Stein family (Gertrude and her brothers) and the eccentric Cone sisters of Baltimore.

Considering the period in which he lived, encompassing two world wars, Matisse kept himself remarkably outside the fray. His art did not touch upon politics or social issues. Throughout his life, his favorite subjects remained the human body (usually a beautiful female body) and the pleasant domestic interior. The joys of home life, of family, of cherished objects dominate his expression. In 1898 Matisse married Amélie Parayre, with whom he maintained a contented rela-

tionship for many years. Mme. Matisse was lovely, a willing model, charming and lively, and devoted to her husband's career. Their three children all chose art-related lives, Pierre becoming a prominent art dealer in New York.

We think of Matisse as a painter, but he worked in many fields—sculpture, book illustration, architectural design (of a small, jewel-like chapel near his home), and finally in *découpage*. By the early 1930s Matisse had begun to use cut-up paper as a means of planning his canvases, and a decade later the cut paper had become an end in itself. When he was very old and could no longer stand at his easel, Matisse sat in his wheelchair or in his bed, cutting and arranging segments of prepainted paper into compositions, some of mural size.

Perhaps it was at the end that he came nearest to his goal: "What I dream of is an art of balance, of purity and serenity, devoid of troubling or depressing subject matter, an art which might be for every mental worker, be he businessman or writer, like an appeasing influence, like a mental soother, something like a good armchair in which to rest from physical fatigue."[2]

Henri Matisse, photographed by Robert Capa.

177. Paul Gauguin.
Day of the God (Mahana no Atua).
1894. Oil on canvas, 27¾ × 35⅝".
The Art Institute of Chicago
(Helen Birch Bartlett Memorial
Collection, 1926).

The symmetrical balance in Paul Gauguin's *Day of the God* **(177)** is a little more subtle, but it is nonetheless clear when we study the painting. Here the "god" is centered at the top of the composition, with the main figure directly below flanked by two curled-up reclining bodies. In the background paired figures stand at either side of the god. These major forms establish the symmetry and therefore the essential balance.

When you stand with your feet flat on the floor and your arms at your sides, you are in symmetrical balance. But if you thrust an arm out in one direction and a leg out in the other, your balance is asymmetrical (*not* symmetrical). Of the two, asymmetrical balance is often considered to be the more dynamic.

ASYMMETRICAL BALANCE

An asymmetrical composition has two sides that do not match. If it seems to be balanced, that is because the visual weights in the two halves are very similar. What looks "heavy" and what looks "light"? Unfortunately, there are no mathematical formulas to follow. The drawing **(178)** illustrates some very general precepts about asymmetrical or ***informal balance:***

1. A large form is visually heavier than a smaller form.
2. A dark-value form is visually heavier than a light form of the same size.
3. A textured form is visually heavier than a smooth form of the same size.
4. A form placed close to the central axis may be visually heavier than a similar form placed near the outer edge of the composition.
5. Two or more small forms can balance a larger one.
6. A smaller dark form can balance a larger light one.

These are only a few of the possibilities. Keeping them in mind, you may still wonder, but how does an artist actually go about balancing a composition? The answer is unsatisfactory but true: The composition is balanced when it looks balanced. An understanding of visual weights can help the artist achieve balance or see what is wrong when the balance doesn't work, but it is no exact science.

A fairly straightforward example of small forms balancing a large one (#5 in the drawing) can be found in Paul Klee's *Costumed Puppets* (**179**). The single large form to the right of the center axis is offset by two smaller forms at the left. Because Klee was a brilliant draftsman and designer, the balance does not seem static. The lower small figure curves in toward the center, and Klee's endlessly inventive pen line animates the entire composition.

A photographic postcard from the early 1900s (**180**) has much more complicated balance, involving placement, size, value, and several other variables. The man sitting just to the right of the center axis provides most of

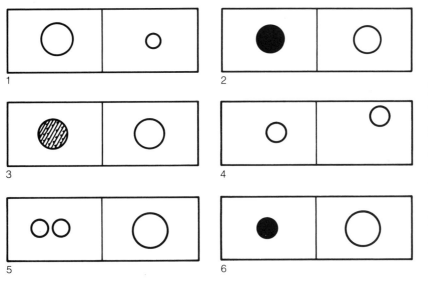

left: 178. Sketch showing some of the different factors in visual balance.

below left: 179. Paul Klee. *Costumed Puppets.* 1922. Ink on paper, mounted on board; $9\frac{1}{2} \times 6\frac{3}{4}''$. Solomon R. Guggenheim Museum, New York.

below: 180. Photographic postcard. Early 1900s. Gotham Book Mart Collection.

the visual weight in the right side of the composition. Not only is he the largest form and placed close to the center axis, but he is a human being. People attract our attention, thereby gaining a lot of visual weight. To balance this weight on the right, the photographer has made the crescent moon (a large form and light value) curve upward on the left side and also placed the flag on the left. The hat perched on the tip of the crescent is crucial; it finishes the perfect balance. Our eyes are drawn to it immediately because, after all, it's rather silly to have a hat on the point of a moon. If you put your finger over the hat, you'll find that the balance is upset and the composition tilts to the right.

An equestrian sculpture from Africa also reveals an elegant asymmetrical balance **(181)**. The upraised horse's head and longer front legs balance the form of the rider, who is mounted very far to the rear. Obviously, the Dogon sculptor who made this figurine knew that horses do not have much longer front legs, that people do not have arms twice the length of their legs, and that riders do not sit just over the horse's tail. These features have been adjusted and stylized to create a sculptural balance.

left: 181. *Equestrian Figure*, Prim-African, Dogon tribe, Mali. Wood, height 27⅛″. The Metropolitan Museum of Art, New York (Michael C. Rockefeller Memorial Collection, bequest of Nelson A. Rockefeller, 1979).

below: 182. Albrecht Dürer. *Reclining Female Nude (Proportion Study).* 1501. Pen and brush on green paper, 6¾ × 8⅝″. Albertina, Vienna.

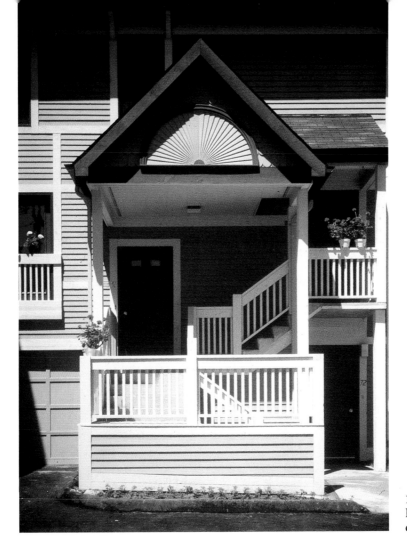

183. Zane Yost & Associates. Riverplace, New Haven, Conn., detail of townhouse entryway.

At first glance we might think that Dürer's *Reclining Female Nude* **(182)** is out of balance. Nearly the whole figure, and most of its bulk, lies in the right half of the composition. But the subtitle, *Proportion Study,* gives us a clue to Dürer's intent. He was undoubtedly studying not only the proportions of the human body but also the placement of a figure within the picture space. The figure gazes to the left, and we, as observers, follow her gaze. Thus we find a center of interest in the left side of the drawing when nothing is there! In our minds we fill in the blank of whatever the woman is looking at. This is not imbalance but a daring balance created by conceptual rather than visual cues.

Balance in architecture has special importance because of the size of the object. Any flaws in balance will be greatly enlarged and evident to all passersby. Moreover, unlike a painting or sculpture or print, architecture often changes over the years, especially the architecture of houses. A wing may be added, a garage tacked on, a porch removed. With any such changes the balance of the whole structure must somehow be maintained.

Like any other work of art, a building can be balanced symmetrically or asymmetrically. Our illustration, a detail of the entrance to a Connecticut townhouse **(183)**, shows a graceful combination of the two. The projecting porch of the dwelling is symmetrical, including its pedimented (triangular) roof and the fan ornament inside the triangle. But inside the little porch the architect has employed a strong asymmetrical balance. The door, which is painted a dark color, is thrust far to the left and balanced against the stairway cutting diagonally upward to the right. Both the angle of the stair railing and the visual texture of openwork slats counter the visual weight of the dark door at left. (For this picture the photographer has added an extra touch of asymmetrical balance in the potted geraniums.)

We said at the beginning of this discussion that an artist may choose deliberately to violate the principles of design. Occasionally, asymmetrical balance may be carried to such an extreme that the composition appears unbalanced. We find this often in the work of Chinese and Japanese painters. Nonomura Sotatsu's *Zen Priest Choka* **(184)** shows the priest perched in a tree that barely makes it into the composition. In Asian art as much importance may be placed on what is *not* there as on what is there. The empty space to the right and below may be visually empty, but it is animated by the daring unbalanced design. In looking at this work we feel a tension, a lack of resolution or closure. Imbalance might be compared to someone's starting a story "Once upon a time . . . ," but never getting to ". . . and they lived happily ever after." We are left feeling keyed up, waiting for something to happen.

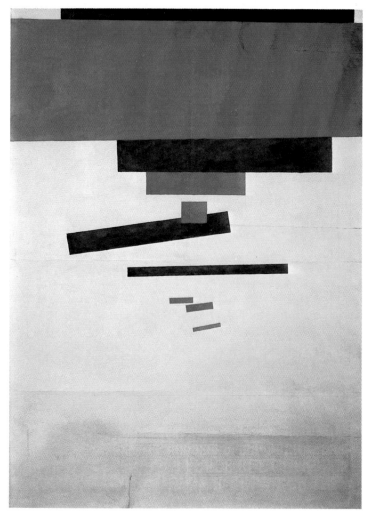

left: 184. Nonomura Sotatsu. *Zen Priest Choka.*
Late 16th–early 17th century.
Hanging scroll, ink on paper; $37\frac{3}{4} \times 15\frac{1}{4}$″.
The Cleveland Museum of Art (purchase, Norman O. Stone
and Ella A. Stone Memorial Fund).

above: 185. Ilya Chashnik. *Floating Suprematist Forms.*
1922. Watercolor, $29 \times 20\frac{7}{8}$″.
Courtesy Leonard Hutton Galleries, New York.

Another painting **(185)**, this one by a Western artist, is balanced (asymmetrically and perfectly) from left to right, but it seems unbalanced vertically. Nearly all the forms appear in the top half of the composition. This is the reverse of what we expect. We are used to gravity, to heavy things being down. In most works of art of all kinds you will find the greatest weight—visual or actual—toward the bottom, so that the composition is firmly rooted in the ground. Ilya Chashnik's watercolor catches us, quite literally, off balance. We get a sense of the rectangular shapes falling continuously. The forms never actually fall, of course, but against all reason we feel that they are doing so. By using imbalance artists are able to make us see movement where none exists.

186. *Baptism of Christ and Procession of Twelve Apostles,* dome mosaic.
c. 520. Arian Baptistry, Ravenna.

RADIAL BALANCE

There is a third possibility for balance, which is more common in architecture and the crafts than in the pictorial arts. Radial balance means that elements in the composition radiate outward from a central point. A frequent expression of this is the architectural dome **(186)**. The dome of the Arian Baptistry in Ravenna, Italy, has the scene of Christ's baptism in the center with the twelve apostles arranged in a radial pattern around the outside. Radial balance works especially well with a circular format, and it nearly always focuses attention on the central point.

Emphasis and Focal Point

Emphasis means that the viewer's attention will be centered more on certain parts of a composition than on others. A focal point is a specific spot to which one's attention is directed. Our everyday perception is structured around focal points. Walking down a crowded street, we naturally pick out from the throng the person who is dressed bizarrely, the one person who is exceptionally tall, the person who is waving to attract attention. Not all works of art have a focal point—Warhol's *Soup Cans* **(174)** does not—but the vast majority do have areas of greater emphasis and one or more focal points. Without them, the composition might seem bland and repetitive.

There are numerous methods by which an artist can create a focal point or center of emphasis in a work of art. Grant Wood used several of them in his painting *Parson Weems' Fable* **(187)**. The fable in question is the story of a young George Washington chopping down the cherry tree, then admitting to the evil deed because he "could not tell a lie." Although the boy George is one of the smaller elements in the picture, we have no doubt that he is the center of interest. For one thing, Wood has employed strong directional lines. George's father gestures directly at the boy, and Parson Weems' pointing finger also carries our attention to him. Moreover, the curve of the drapery at right and the opposing curve of the half-chopped tree frame little George between them. In case we still miss the point, the artist has placed George almost precisely in the middle of the composition and given him a white shirt—the lightest value in the painting. (Although this has little to do with emphasis, we might notice for fun that Wood has painted George's head like that of a full-grown man, the Father of his Country, and put that venerable head atop the body of a boy caught red-handed.)

Another device for creating emphasis is the manipulation of light. We see this in Henry O. Tanner's sensitive portrait of his mother **(188)**, in which the artist uses a strong light—cutting through prevailing shadow—to focus attention on the woman's face, with its pensive, perhaps weary expression. This light seems to be coming from a source above and outside the picture. It falls also on the drape of a shawl behind the chair, possibly an emblem of motherhood. Because of the subject matter and the pose, we cannot help but be reminded of Whistler's painting of *his* mother **(534)**, but they are very

187. Grant Wood.
Parson Weems' Fable. 1939.
Oil on canvas, 3'2⅜" × 4'2⅛".
Amon Carter Museum, Fort Worth.

different pictures. Whistler, as we shall see in Chapter 17 (p. 464), was primarily interested in the arrangement of compositional elements. His lighting is general, not focused. Tanner, on the other hand, seems intent on showing the character of his model, and so he shines his clearest light on her face.

Both directional lines and light create the focal point in Francisco de Goya's *Executions of the Third of May, 1808* **(189)**. The event Goya depicted was the invasion of Spain by Napoleon's armies and their savage execution of Spanish resisters. Our interest is centered on one heroic but doomed Spaniard, his arms raised in a pose of crucifixion. This tragic figure is bathed in

Francisco de Goya

1746–1828

Writers on Goya have long been fascinated by the close friendship between him and the Duchess of Alba, the powerful aristocrat whom many considered the most beautiful woman of her time in Spain. It is a measure of this artist's complexity and uniqueness that the haughty duchess should form a special bond with one who emerged from quite humble origins, whose temperament was often morose and reclusive, and whose imagery could be shockingly gruesome.

Francisco José de Goya y Lucientes was born in a village in the bleak northeast section of Spain. While a young man Goya may have supported himself partially as a bullfighter, but this is one of many unverifiable stories about his intriguing life. By the age of twenty he was in Madrid.

Goya's earliest commissions were for church murals and tapestry cartoons. In 1783 he was launched in one of the two artistic arenas for which he is best known—portraitist to the nobility. Within a few years he was active at the royal court, and in 1799 he was appointed court painter to Charles IV, King of Spain. Some of Goya's portraits, including two of the Duchess of Alba, are exquisitely lovely; others have a darker side to them. According to some critics, Goya's pictures of the royal family, while appearing to flatter, were actually subtle revelations of the subjects' greed, stupidity, and corruption.

Goya's other major field of expression was prints, of which he was an unexcelled master. Two major series, each having about eighty images, constitute the bulk of his work: *Los Caprichos*, in which the many follies of human nature are satirized; and *The Disasters of War*, an often brutally explicit catalogue of the cruelties prevalent in wartime.

Goya achieved both fame and financial success relatively early. While his career prospered, however, his personal life was repeatedly marked by tragedy. His marriage to Josefa Bayeu seems to have been more of a convenience than a passion. She bore him many children—perhaps as many as twenty—but only one survived to maturity. In 1792 the artist was struck by a severe illness that left him almost totally deaf. Another near-fatal illness in 1819 increased his isolation and pessimism; Goya bought a home outside Madrid, known as La Quinta del Sordo ("The House of the Deaf Man"), to which he retired and painted a series of

works known as the "Black Paintings," for their dark tonality and aura of despair. After all, the artist's relationship with the Duchess of Alba, whatever it might have been (some maintain that they were lovers), seems to have been one of few bright periods in his life.

Goya's education was sketchy, and as an adult he read and wrote with some difficulty. An announcement for *Los Caprichos* probably was written with the help of a friend, but it captures Goya's attitude toward his art: "Painting, like poetry, selects in the universe whatever she deems most appropriate to her ends. She assembles in a single fantastic personage circumstances and features which nature distributes among many individuals. From this combination, ingeniously composed, results that happy imitation by virtue of which the artist earns the title of inventor and not of servile copyist."[3]

Francisco de Goya. *Self-Portrait.* 1815.
Oil on canvas, 18¼ × 15¾".
Museo del Prado, Madrid.

light, while most of the rest of the painting remains in shadow. Moreover, the faceless figures of the soldiers point their rifles at him, and even the stance of their bodies focuses our attention on the victim. Goya's sympathies clearly lay with the killed, not the killers. He therefore emphasized the poignant sacrifice of one man, to deemphasize the mechanical slaughter by the others.

Emphasis by placement is evident in Grandma Moses' painting, called *Hoosick Falls, N.Y., in Winter* (190). In this tranquil town landscape Grandma Moses has chosen to emphasize the locomotive of the train steaming across the picture. To accomplish this, she has placed the locomotive just on the bridge crossing the river, with the pale tone of the water acting as a contrasting background. The horseshoe curve of the river also helps to direct our attention to the train.

A variation on emphasis by placement is emphasis by isolation. In Joan Brown's *Out on a Limb* (191) we see the traditional Three Wise Monkeys, who "hear no evil, see no evil, speak no evil," clustered together in a fearfully

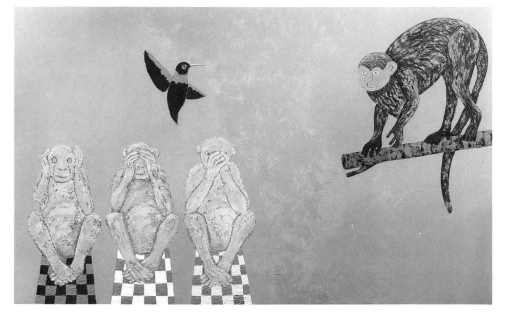

above: 190. Anna Mary Robertson ("Grandma") Moses. *Hoosick Falls, N.Y., in Winter.* 1944. Oil, $19\frac{3}{4} \times 23\frac{3}{4}''$. Phillips Collection, Washington, D.C.

left: 191. Joan Brown. *Out on a Limb.* 1986. Acrylic on canvas, 6 × 10'. Courtesy Frumkin/Adams Gallery, New York.

192. Marc Chagall.
Woman, Flowers, and Bird. 1952–53.
Gouache, $25\frac{3}{4} \times 19\frac{7}{8}''$.
Stedelijk Museum, Amsterdam.

submissive group. We know from their poses and their timid conformity to the group that they are afraid, perhaps of life itself. All alone and daring is the one active monkey, literally out on a limb, precariously supported and ready to take risks. By isolating this one monkey, the artist emphasizes the freedom and danger of being up in the air, on one's own.

Emphasis by contrast works much the same way. Contrast can mean any obvious distinction—dark against light, big against small, textured against smooth, color against gray. Marc Chagall's painting *Woman, Flowers, and Bird* **(192)** is done almost entirely in a neutral bluish gray, with touches of white and pale green leaves at the center. There are only two spots of vivid color, the two bright pink flowers, and they attract our attention immediately. This painting is interesting, however, in that the colorful flowers are *not* the main focal point, although they are certainly areas of emphasis. In effect, they are "assistant" focal points. They claim our interest and direct it toward the area they frame—the woman's face, which is the real focal point.

Finally, we should mention emphasis by content. Regardless of other focal devices employed by an artist, certain visual images, when included in a composition, will draw the viewer's attention. Blood and gore attract attention; anything shocking or surprising will act as a focal point. In a figural work the face is nearly always the major focal point, because we are used to looking at people's faces rather than their elbows or hips. And in general, as mentioned earlier, the human figure will tend to draw the viewer's eye.

Proportion and Scale

Proportion and scale both have to do with size. Sometimes the two words are used interchangeably, but there is a difference. **Scale** means size in relation to some constant or "normal" size. Normal scale is the size we expect something to be. For example, a model airplane is small-scale in relation to a real airplane, or to the usual size for an airplane. The 10-pound tomato that wins a prize at the county fair is large-scale.

Proportion, on the other hand, refers to size relationships between parts of a whole, or between two or more items perceived as a unit. Proportion can also mean the size relationship between an object and its surroundings. A very large chair in a very small room seems "out of proportion." René Magritte played with the idea of proportion in *La Folie des grandeurs* **(193)**. The three sections of the nude torso are in different proportions, so they do not fit together at all. Magritte, of course, used this jarring disproportion on purpose to create a startling image.

There are many reasons an artist may choose to violate normal proportions in a work of art. In Morris Hirshfield's *Boy with Dog* **(194)**, for instance, the disproportion was undoubtedly made to serve decorative purposes. Hirshfield, known as a folk or "naive" painter, relished decorative pattern. Here the boy's dog, even if it is a toy poodle (though it looks a bit like a miniature horse), is much too small in relation to the boy. And the boy's arms, hands, and feet are far too small for his body. Yet there is a pleasing sense of flow in the figures of the boy and dog—a flow that echoes the rhythm

left: 193. René Magritte. *La Folie des grandeurs.* 1948. Oil on canvas, 39⅛ × 32⅛". Hirshhorn Museum and Sculpture Garden, Smithsonian Institution, Washington, D.C. (gift of Joseph H. Hirshhorn Foundation, 1972).

right: 194. Morris Hirshfield. *Boy with Dog.* 1945. Oil on canvas, 32 × 23". Courtesy Sidney Janis Gallery, New York.

above: **195.** *Poseidon* or *Zeus.*
c. 460–450 B.C.
Bronze, height 6'10".
National Museum, Athens.

below: **196.**
Sketches of proportions
in the golden section.

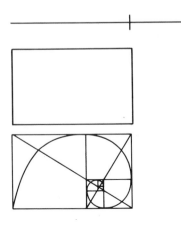

of the wavelike background. The boy's tiny right arm curves downward in an arc, is met by the opposing arc of the leash, and then again by the arc of the dog's body. From head to shoulder to tail we can draw a lovely, undulating S-curve—all of which is mirrored in the background. Similar curving lines move from the boy's hair down through the shirt and coat tails to the legs, and terminate gracefully in the boy's minute feet. If the proportions had been accurate, this decorative effect would have been lost.

The two preceding illustrations both show proportions that are "wrong"—that is, proportions that seem inappropriate, based on our experience of the natural world. In a sense, it is easier to understand the usual applications of proportion by studying the *un*usual, the exceptions. But most artists, most of the time, seek to find the "right" proportions for their work, and the great majority of illustrations in this book have proportions that seem harmonious, seem to mesh with our impressions of the natural world.

Since the time of the ancient Greeks people have been seeking the "ideal" proportions in art. Much classical Greek figure sculpture was based on a *canon*, or set of rules, of ideal proportions in which the figure's head was to be one-eighth of the total height, the width of the chest one-quarter of the total height, and so on **(195)**. (These proportions would remain the same regardless of the figure's scale.) Similarly, in Greek architecture, vase-making, and painting, proportions derived from what is known as the ***golden section,*** or ***golden mean.*** Algebraically, the golden mean **(196)** says that a:b = b:(a + b). If *a* is the width of a temple and *b* is its length, then the ratio of width to length should be the same as the ratio of length to width-plus-length. For those not mathematically inclined, we can translate this formula into an example. Suppose you want to build a house, and you want it to be 40 feet wide. How long should the house be to fit the "ideal" proportions of the golden section? The answer is about 65 feet. Your house would end up being a rectangle rather like the one shown in the drawing **(196)**.

For mathematicians the golden section, sometimes known as *phi,* has far-reaching implications. The illustration **(196)** shows that every time you cut off a square from one end of a golden rectangle, you are left with another golden rectangle, and so on indefinitely. For artists, as the Greeks knew 2,500 years ago, the golden section "feels right," and to the viewer it "looks right." Many objects in our daily life approximate the golden section in their proportions. The standard 3 × 5 index card is an almost perfect golden rectangle, and the standard playing card comes close. If you were to measure the illustrations in this book, you would find that a large number of them approach the golden mean in their dimensions. Piet Mondrian, that most precise and mathematical of artists, worked within a perfect golden rectangle for his *Composition with Red, Yellow, and Blue* **(119)**. Even the "motel art" we discussed in Chapter 2 (p. 34) holds close to the golden mean in its typical 2 × 3 format. Whatever the reason, this proportion is one we find inherently pleasing and satisfying.

For an entertaining exercise in scale and proportion, we might look at the next illustration, a photograph by Annie Leibovitz **(197)**. Noted for her striking—often startling—portraits of well-known personalities, Leibovitz here brings together the jockey Willie Shoemaker and the basketball star Wilt Chamberlain in a double image that is bound to cause a doubletake. The photograph is real, not distorted or composite. What makes it remarkable is the contrast of proportion and scale. Both men are "correctly" proportioned as individual people; each has a head and arms and legs suited to the body. But Shoemaker is a very small-scale human, and Chamberlain a very large-scale one. Side by side, and dressed alike, they are wildly out of proportion, a jarring unit. It is as though nature was playing a game of scale with these two men, so Leibovitz caught the fun and played a proportion game of her own.

Like proportion, scale is most noticeable when it is "wrong," when it is not what we expect. One artist who is well known for experimenting with distortions of scale is the sculptor Claes Oldenburg, and his approach to scale can only be described as grand. Oldenburg's *Knife Ship* **(198)** is a giant representation in steel of an ordinary pocket knife, with double blade and corkscrew, motorized so that the blades move up and down and the corkscrew turns. The huge size of the sculpture—it is 40 feet long—requires exhibition outdoors or in a large enclosed space, such as the interior of the Guggenheim

198. Claes Oldenburg, Coosje van Bruggen, and Frank O. Gehry. *The Knife Ship from "Il Corso del Coltello."* 1985. Steel, 26 × 40'. Installed at the Solomon R. Guggenheim Museum, New York.

Museum shown here. By taking an ordinary object, blowing it up to massive scale, and setting it in a public place, Oldenburg makes the form heroic. In effect the artist is saying, "Look at this form, look at it in the new way I have shown it to you." Now, many people have a pocket knife, perhaps a Swiss army officer's knife, and normally this object would not command our attention. But a pocket knife a hundred times the usual size, painted bright red, and equipped with "oars" to make a "ship"—*that* catches our attention. Manipulation of scale—or, for that matter, of any design principle—can make us look at form with fresh perspective.

Proportion and scale must be considered together because they nearly always operate simultaneously. A painting that is, say, 10 feet by 15 feet is certainly large-scale; it is larger than most of the paintings we have seen. We must also take into account, however, where the painting is to be hung. If it

above: 199. Nicholas Africano. *Whiskey per tutti!* 1980–81. Oil, acrylic, and magna on enamel on Masonite; 4 × 7'. Courtesy Holly Solomon Gallery, New York.

right: 200. Pieter Bruegel the Elder. *Wedding Dance.* c. 1566. Oil on panel, 3'11" × 5'2". © The Detroit Institute of Arts (City of Detroit Purchase).

is hung in a small house, it will be out of proportion to its surroundings. But if it is hung in a huge auditorium, the proportions may be just right.

Scale and proportion can work side by side *within* a work of art. The figures in Nicholas Africano's *Whiskey per tutti!* **(199)** and the figures in Pieter Bruegel's *Wedding Dance* **(200)** are all small-scale. If you were standing in front of the actual paintings, the figures would be just a few inches tall. The proportions in the two paintings, however, are quite different. Africano's little people are set in a huge, almost empty canvas, so they seem tiny and lost. They are out of proportion to the field they inhabit. Bruegel's painting has many figures, arranged to fill the composition, so its proportions seem perfectly normal. The reason for this discrepancy lies in the different intents of the two artists. Bruegel was drawing a naturalistic festive scene. Africano is aiming at a grand theatrical image, a vision of tiny people lost on an enormous opera stage.

Rhythm

People who are totally deaf can learn to dance. No one is quite sure how they keep time when they cannot hear the sounds, but they do. Apparently, they have some perception of rhythm that is independent of aural cues. All of us are accustomed to rhythm in music, in dance, in poetry (where it is called meter), in other aspects of life. Intuitively, we seek rhythm in the visual arts.

Visual rhythm depends upon the repetition of accented elements, usually shapes. In Edward Hopper's *Early Sunday Morning* **(201)** we find several different rhythms moving horizontally across the canvas **(202)**. At top there is the rhythm of the eaves under the roof, and below that the strong rhythmic pulse of the second-story windows alternating with plain wall. At bottom the rhythm of the repeated storefronts counters the two patterns above. Although this is a very repetitive rhythm, we do not find it boring, because there is enough variation of color and light to create interest. The two focal points of fire hydrant and barber pole punctuate the rhythm.

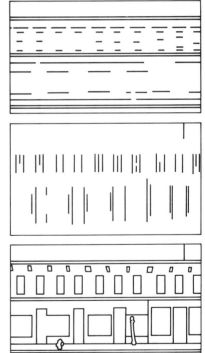

top: 201. Edward Hopper. *Early Sunday Morning.* 1930. Oil on canvas, 2′11″ × 5′. Whitney Museum of American Art, New York.

above: 202. Sketch of the visual rhythms in Hopper's *Early Sunday Morning.*

The rhythm in Piet Mondrian's *Composition in Blue B* (**203**) is sharp and staccato. Rectangles of color, many of them overlapping, intersperse with smaller black rectangles that act as weaker beats in the pulse. There is so much energetic movement in this work that it could almost be set to music.

Rhythm is crucial to Van Gogh's *Starry Night* (**204**)—a swirling, swooping rhythm made up of both the pattern of lighted forms and their frenzied circular motion. An important function of rhythm in art is that it keeps the viewer's eye moving through the composition. Nowhere is this more evident than in *The Starry Night*. Our eyes follow the tumbling shapes up, around,

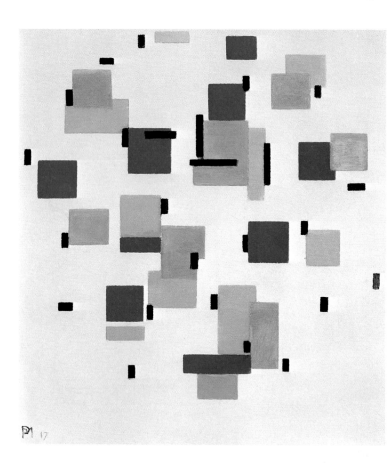

left: 203. Piet Mondrian. *Composition in Blue B.*
1917. Oil on canvas, 24 × 19″.
Rijksmuseum Kroller-Müller, Otterlo, The Netherlands.

below: 204. Vincent van Gogh. *The Starry Night.*
1889. Oil on canvas, 29 × 36¼″.
Collection, The Museum of Modern Art, New York
(acquired through the Lillie P. Bliss Bequest).

bottom: 205. Wang Yani. *A Hundred Monkeys.* 1984–85.
Handscroll (detail), ink and color on paper;
height 1′⅝″, overall length of scroll 34′9⅜″.
Collection the artist.

down, and back again in a constant motion. Even the vertical tree form at left participates in this, as it carries the eye upward to start the roller-coaster ride all over again.

Do artists deliberately "put" rhythm into their work, or is that rhythm a natural component of the creative process? Probably some of both, but in the case of our next illustration we might lean toward the latter. Wang Yani, a remarkable artistic prodigy from China, has attracted worldwide fame for the sophisticated brilliance and spontaneity of her painting. Having begun to paint at age two and a half, she had her first one-artist show at four. *A Hundred Monkeys* (**205**), a long handscroll of which we show just a small detail, was painted when Yani was nine and has a favorite theme. Even in this little section, the joyful rhythm is immediately evident. Yani's monkeys roll and tumble over themselves and one another. The line of the monkeys' bodies swoops up and down rhythmically. We can almost hear happy circus music in the background. Now a teenager, Yani has traveled widely and often gives public demonstrations of her painting. (If she did not, few would believe such astonishing skill had come from a child.) She works rapidly, her brush moving across the page without indecision. Merely from seeing the results we sense the rhythmic flow of her arm and brush, her internal rhythms translated onto paper.

As in music, there are different kinds of rhythm in the visual arts. One is simple repetition of regular beats, visible in Hopper's painting. Another is alternating rhythm—stronger beats alternating with weaker ones, as in Mondrian's painting. Van Gogh's *Starry Night* has a circular rhythm, Wang Yani's a combined circular and up-and-down rhythm. Yet a fifth type of rhythm is *progression*. Progression means that the visual beats gradually increase (or decrease) according to a definite pattern. We see this in Pat Steir's *Yellow Chrysanthemum* (**206**). Steir's triptych (three-part work) is obviously meant to be "read" from left to right. Moving our eyes across the canvas, we almost cannot help but think "flower . . . FLOWER . . . FLOWER!" The composition climaxes at right with a giant close-up chrysanthemum, much as a symphony might climax with full sound and all the instruments playing.

206. Pat Steir.
Yellow Chrysanthemum. 1981.
Oil on canvas; three panels,
each 5′ × 6′8″.
Private collection, New York.

Elements and Principles: A Summary

In this chapter and the preceding one we have focused one by one on the elements of art and principles of design, isolating each for individual scrutiny. Every member of the ensemble, so to speak, was brought before the curtain and allowed to take a separate bow. Now, to finish this section, we should put the actors back together, reunite the company into a performing unit. By analyzing one work of art in some detail, we can begin to see how the elements and principles interact. It should be clear that we cannot easily talk about one element or principle without involving several of the others. The painting we will analyze is Pablo Picasso's *Girl Before a Mirror* **(207)**.

In *Girl Before a Mirror* a young woman—probably inspired by Picasso's lover at the time, Marie-Thérèse Walter—contemplates her nude image in a mirror (at right) just at the time when she is reaching maturity and realizing her sexual and childbearing capabilities. The reproductive organs are therefore prominent in the image. This is a very brief summary of the painting's content. Now let us consider its visual design.

Unity is achieved in several ways, including the dominance of curved lines **(208a)**. The straight lines, horizontals and diagonals **(208b)**, serve as a kind of background "filler" to the large swooping curves, and they also provide linear variety. Unity of shape is particularly important to this work; the circle motif—be it face, breast, womb, or buttock—recurs in a rhythmic pattern **(208c)**. The concept of unity with variety becomes clearer when we put together the straight lines and curved shapes **(208d)**.

Colors are brilliantly varied, but they fall generally in the same range of values and intensities, thus contributing unity. A skeleton of dark, almost black values in shape and line provides the structure on which the picture is "hung" **(208e)**, much as the human body is hung on its bony skeleton.

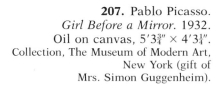

207. Pablo Picasso. *Girl Before a Mirror.* 1932. Oil on canvas, 5′3¾″ × 4′3¼″. Collection, The Museum of Modern Art, New York (gift of Mrs. Simon Guggenheim).

208. Linear analyses of Picasso's *Girl Before a Mirror.*

The balance of *Girl Before a Mirror* is predominantly symmetrical **(208e)**. Picasso has even provided a vertical line in the center of the composition to divide the two halves. Subtle differences between the girl's body and her mirror reflection enliven and relieve the symmetry. There is almost a pendulum effect as our eyes shift back and forth rhythmically between one side and the other—a pendulum effect enhanced by the curve of the arm.

There are several areas of emphasis in *Girl Before a Mirror*, most of which can be found in the shapes painted with the lightest values **(208f)**. Also, the two faces—the light face of the girl and the darker and more menacing one of the reflection—are emphasized by their colors, their placement, and simply by the fact that they *are* faces. Secondary areas of emphasis are the reproductive organs below, shown in a kind of X-ray vision, which gain emphasis by their brightness and by the repetition of the round form. Even with these areas of emphasis, however, it should be borne in mind that the background of this painting is almost as important as the figures. There is no "dead" space, no area of rest for the eyes; every inch of the canvas is important to the artist's expression.

In scale the *Girl Before a Mirror* is rather large, but not unusually so. The proportions are more interesting. Picasso has filled almost the entire space of the composition with the two figures; they jam the picture space from top to bottom and left to right. Also interesting are the proportions of shapes to one another. Small circles and ovals play off against larger and larger circles, to the oval of the mirror image.

Finally, we have alluded before to the rhythms in this work—the rhythm of echoing curved lines, of repeated circular forms, of the pendulum swing from side to side **(208g)**. Besides the pendulum swing, there is a figure-eight rhythm that swoops us through the two figures. By introducing these rhythms Picasso has made what might have been a static image—a girl facing a mirror in a flat space—assume qualities of almost dancelike grace.

Picasso had no program when he painted *Girl Before a Mirror*. He did not stand before his easel with a checklist and make sure that all the visual elements had been accounted for in the proper amounts of unity, variety, balance, scale, proportion, and rhythm. He *knew* what he was doing, but he would not have spelled it out in these terms. Being able to articulate the elements and principles does, however, help the viewer to better understand works of art, and to penetrate, a little, the genius of those who make them.

Observation and Criticism

Having considered the art elements and principles of design, we are now ready to formulate a slightly more detailed plan for seeing and criticizing art—for becoming an intelligent observer—than was outlined in Chapter 1. As before, the main point is to take a little time and pay more attention than usual to any new work of art you encounter. While you look, ask yourself the following questions and do your best to answer them. Some of the questions given below duplicate those listed in Chapter 1; others are based on increased art-critical skills you have gained from reading Chapters 2 through 5.

Naturally, you will not ask yourself every one of these questions about every single work of art, from pencil drawing to skyscraper. Rather, the questions are to be filed away in the back of your mind, to be called up as needed for a given situation.

1. Where does this work fit into the history of art? Does it remind me of any others I have seen, and in what way? Can I make any connection between this piece and others?
2. What do I know about the artist? Is there anything about his or her background that would influence my reaction to this work?
3. Does this work fall into any particular theme in the history of art? If so, how does it echo or contradict other works done in the same theme?
4. When and where was this work made? What else was going on in the world at the same time? What are the characteristics of the culture from which it emerges, and how does the work reflect those characteristics?
5. What is the form of this work? What is the work made of, and how is it organized?
6. What is the content of this work? What do I know about its iconography? Is there a recognizable subject, and, if so, how is that subject treated? Are there symbols, and can I decode them?
7. What are the most prominent art elements in this work? Lines? Shapes? Values? Colors? How do these elements influence my reaction to the work? How does the artist use space? What is the quality of the texture? Are time and motion factors in my appreciation of this work?
8. Does this work seem unified, and is there enough variety to sustain interest? How has the artist balanced the composition? What is the focal point or points, and how did the artist create them? What roles do proportion and scale play, and how are they handled? Do I sense a particular kind of rhythm?
9. Are the materials of this work important to its type of expression and its overall effect? Does this work seem well crafted? If so (or if not), does it matter?
10. What feelings, memories, or associations does this work evoke in me? Does it make me feel happy, angry, sad, frightened, disgusted, uplifted, inspired, depressed? Can I imagine the artist felt the same way? Do I feel any sense of kinship with the artist?

And finally:

11. Do I like it? Could I live with this art?

By answering these questions—or as many of them as seem applicable—about a new work of art you encounter, you give what every serious artist deserves: an intelligent, thoughtful, informed appraisal of the work. If, after such consideration, you don't like the work of art, that is nobody's business but your own. If you do like it, you have given something to yourself as well as to the artist—another small spot of satisfaction for your life. Indeed, you have enriched your own life.

Claribel

and Etta Cone

To the family of Helen and Herman Cone in the latter part of the 19th century were born thirteen children, ten boys and three girls. The boys were expected to go into business; the girls were expected to be sweet and demure and to make good marriages. One of the girls performed as anticipated. The other two—Claribel and Etta—were hardly demure, never married, and became, in time, the most endearingly eccentric collectors of art one could imagine. They are the extraordinary Cone sisters of Baltimore.

Claribel launched the sisters on the path of unpredictability in 1882, when she announced her desire to become a doctor—an almost unheard-of role for a woman at the time. She undertook studies at the Women's Medical College in Baltimore and earned her license. Dr. Claribel treated one private patient, declared that was sufficient, and never saw another.

Meanwhile, Etta proved equally unpredictable. A small event in 1896 set the stage for the Cones' lifelong adventure. The oldest Cone brother had given Etta $500 to enhance the family parlor, assuming she would buy rugs or furniture. Instead, Etta bought four shockingly modern paintings. It was a modest beginning, but the Cone sisters were on their way.

Soon after the turn of the century began the pattern of many long trips to Europe. Separately or together, Claribel and Etta traveled constantly. Often their base was Paris, where they had close contact with another noted pair of collectors, Gertrude and Leo Stein. It was the Steins who introduced them to two young, struggling, unknown artists: Pablo Picasso and Henri Matisse. With Gertrude Stein, Etta paid her first visit to Picasso's studio, which she found hopelessly cluttered. Drawings and watercolors littered the floor. Etta scooped up handfuls, chose two, and bought them for $20. Eventually the sisters would buy many Picassos, at ever-increasing prices, but their favorite was Matisse, who became a close friend. Bit by bit they amassed a world-class collection of his art.

As their tastes and financial resources expanded, the Cones bought works by Cézanne, Van Gogh, Degas, Gauguin, Chagall—virtually a catalogue of modern art. Always compulsive shoppers, they also invested heavily in antiques, textiles, and fine laces. These they shipped back to their apartments in Baltimore, which soon resembled a packed museum.

Dr. Claribel and Miss Etta were as remarkable for their personalities as for their collecting. Claribel, older by six years, always dominated the pair. A huge woman with a spellbinding manner of speaking, Claribel held forth in company while Etta kept to the background and attended to all the housekeeping details of their complicated lives. Their friends thought of Etta as the "wife." Both sisters dressed flamboyantly, usually in long black gowns topped with wildly colorful shawls and exotic jewelry. Both also had a passion for food—high in quality, vast in quantity. This had the inevitable result, and, according to their great-niece, they had to be pushed in and out of taxicabs backwards with a special stick that had a carved hand on the end.

When Dr. Claribel died in 1929, she left her collection to Miss Etta, who kept it intact. At Etta's death twenty years later the joint collection went to the Baltimore Museum of Art. In 1949 it was valued at three million dollars. Now, of course, it is priceless.

left: Claribel Cone, c. 1915–16 (age 51–52).
right: Etta Cone, c. 1890 (age 20?).
The Baltimore Museum of Art (The Cone Archives).

PART THREE

TWO-DIMENSIONAL MEDIA

209. Michelangelo. *Arm Studies for the Lord, and Studies for Angels in the Creation of Adam*, preparatory drawings for Sistine Chapel ceiling. 1511. Red chalk over black chalk, 8⅜ × 11″. Teylers Museum, Haarlem, The Netherlands.

Drawing

Everybody draws. There can scarcely be a person above the age of two who has never made a drawing. Many people take photographs, some paint, a few make sculpture, and a very few may even design a building. But everybody draws. You see a patch of wet sand at the beach, a dusty tabletop, or a blank notepad while you are sitting in class or at a business meeting—and your natural impulse is to draw something.

Children begin to draw long before they begin to write, sometimes before then can talk intelligibly. In drawing far more than in speech, children reveal their fantasies and their fears. Whatever the content, nearly all children draw, which shows how truly universal is this method of expression.

Two qualities often associated with drawing are familiarity and intimacy. Drawing is familiar in that it uses the materials we all are accustomed to—the pencil, the pen, the stick of chalk. There are no mysterious or exotic ingredients. You can pick up a pencil and draw somebody's likeness on paper and so can a great draftsman like Ingres (211). Your drawing almost certainly will not look as good as his, but it is the same kind of expression.

Drawing seems intimate because it is frequently—although not always—the artist's private note-taking. Many drawings are not intended for exhibition and therefore are not shown publicly during the artist's lifetime. They may be preliminary sketches for some other work of art or just the artist's refined doodling. We think of such drawings as direct expression—from brain to hand—without the intervening censor of desired public approval. In looking at a sketch by Michelangelo (209), for example, we can speculate about what he was actually thinking as he drew those lines.

The drawing illustrated here is a notebook page showing studies for the ceiling paintings of the Sistine Chapel (34). When we look at the finished paintings, they seem so perfect that we cannot imagine the forms being any other way. It is almost as though the composition sprang fully realized from Michelangelo's brush. But, of course, it did not. The artist tried and rejected forms repeatedly, as this drawing demonstrates. Here he is testing various poses for the arm of God in the act of creating Adam, one of the best-known painted forms in Western art. Through the drawing Michelangelo becomes more human to us, as we watch him experimenting, correcting, playing with new shapes. Drawings give a clue to the often agonizing path of genius.

Other factors may contribute to drawing's sense of intimacy. Most drawings are relatively small (compared to paintings), and many are exe-

210. Page from a Koran, from Persia. 11th century. Ink and colors on paper, height 7½".
Victoria & Albert Museum, London (by courtesy of the Board of Trustees of the Victoria & Albert Museum).

cuted quickly. Drawings are often made in great quantities; some artists do hundreds of drawings for every "finished" work. There are exceptions to this generalization, drawings that are large and/or are executed with painstaking attention to detail, including several examples in this chapter. But part of the charm of drawing as a medium must surely be the fact that, even when a work *is* intended for exhibition, it still retains an air of intimacy.

We usually associate drawings with paper, but, historically, many other surfaces have been used to draw upon. The oldest artworks we know of are the cave drawings found in southern France and in Spain **(3)**. (These images are often referred to as paintings, but many have a strong linear quality that would more accurately categorize them as drawings.) The artists who made the cave images worked directly on the stone walls of the caves; archaeologists speculate they drew the outlines either with mats of hair or with charred sticks, then filled in by blowing colors through a hollow pipe. Some 5,000 to 10,000 years after the cave drawings were done, nomadic peoples developed the technique of pottery making. A number of later cultures had strong pottery traditions, including the ancient Greeks **(453,454)** and native peoples of Central and South America. Other cultures worked on papyrus (a paperlike material made from pressed plant stems) or on parchment (treated animal skins). The ancient Chinese drew on silk, their special material, and many Chinese artists still do. However, it is the Chinese who are credited with providing the most common surface for drawing.

According to legend, the Chinese invented paper in A.D. 105. Centuries later the Moslems spread the knowledge of papermaking from the East through Europe and the Mediterranean world. A page from a manuscript of the Koran **(210)**, dated to the 11th century, shows how the Persians of that era developed *calligraphy,* or "beautiful writing," into an art form. The Koran is, of course, the holy book of Islam, the Moslem faith, and the purpose of writing manuscript copies—in this age long before the printed book—was to spread and teach the faith. Yet that higher goal does not preclude giving the sacred words all the decorative beauty at the calligrapher's command.

Nowadays, the artist who wants to make a drawing has a dizzying array of surfaces and materials to choose from. Some materials are ancient, while others depend on space-age technology. In this chapter we shall look first at the range of materials used for drawing and the effects each can produce. Then we will explore the various purposes for which a drawing can be made

Materials for Drawing

Some artists draw almost exclusively in one favorite material, whereas others experiment widely and are eager to try each new medium that comes along. It would be difficult to say how much a choice of material influences the resulting work. Of course, the potential for expression comes from within the artist, not from any substance, but it is nevertheless true that different materials tend to produce particular effects. By "playing" with many tools and papers the artist may be inspired to create new types of imagery.

All drawing media (and, for that matter, all painting media) are based on *pigment*—coloring material in a neutral or some version of a hue that has been ground and mixed with a substance that enables it to adhere to the drawing surface. Drawing materials generally are divided into two categories—dry media and liquid media. The dry media tend to be abrasive. They "scratch" across a paper or other surface, depositing particles wherever they come in contact with the surface. Liquid media, in contrast, have particles of pigment suspended in fluid, so they flow onto the surface much more freely.

DRY MEDIA

PENCIL The graphite pencil, sometimes called a "lead" pencil, probably has made more drawings than any other medium. Pencils are cheap, readily available, and easy to work with. Mistakes can be erased. If the drawing turns out badly, it can be thrown away at no great expense.

In spite of the pencil's humble status, however, some of the most sensitive, elegant drawings we know have been done with graphite pencil. The acknowledged master of this technique was Jean Auguste Dominique Ingres. In the work shown here **(211)** Ingres used the sharp point of a pencil to draw

211.
Jean Auguste Dominique Ingres.
*Madame Reiset
and Her Daughter.*
1844. Graphite pencil, $12 \times 10\frac{1}{2}''$.
Museum Boymans-Van Beuningen,
Rotterdam.

an exquisite portrait of a woman and her daughter. The figures are idealized—cool, pale, reserved, and aristocratic—and the delicate pencil line is perfectly suited for rendering this ideal.

Pencil can also be a warm medium, especially the colored pencils that some artists favor. David Hockney's portrait of *Marinka Nude* **(212)** exemplifies this quality; it is wonderfully vibrant. The artist has reserved his strongest colors for the model's hair and eyes, making her head the focal point. Marinka is naked and thus, we might think, exposed; but she holds her body primly, and her expression is very private. In Hockney's interpretation, the body, the chair, and the background all focus attention on the face.

METALPOINT Metalpoint, the ancestor of the graphite pencil, is an old technique that was especially popular during the Renaissance. Few artists use it now, because it is not very forgiving of mistakes or indecision. Once put down, the lines cannot easily be changed or erased. The drawing material is a thin wire of metal, often of pure silver (in which case the medium is called *silverpoint*), mounted in some kind of holding device, such as a wooden shaft or a modern mechanical pencil. The drawing surface must be specially coated with white poster paint or a similar ground—historically, the coating was bone dust and glue—and the lines produced by the metalpoint are thin and of uniform width.

Metalpoint drawings are characterized by a fine elegance, a finished perfection. Because of the thin, uniform lines it is somewhat difficult to model rounded forms, so artists often highlighted their drawings in white paint to enhance the illusion of depth, as in Perugino's magnificent *Man in Armor* **(213)**. This drawing undoubtedly was meant to be a finished work, not a preliminary sketch. It is as carefully planned as any painting in its subtle effect of gray line against lovely blue ground.

CHARCOAL Charcoal's effects are almost the exact opposite of those offered by metalpoint. Where metalpoint produces a thin, delicate line, charcoal's line is dark, sometimes very soft, occasionally harsh. Charcoal is actually burned sticks of wood—the best-quality charcoal coming from special vine wood heated in a kiln until only carbon remains. Charcoal lines can be thin or thick, pale to velvety black. If charcoal is used on a paper with a "tooth," or heavy grain, the results are textured. Honoré Daumier used charcoal to create the drawing called *Fright* (214). The undulating charcoal line and repeated form make the figure seem actually to be trembling in fear. No delicate medium could so easily have produced this chilling image.

CHALK AND CRAYON A wide range of chalks and crayons are available to the artist, and nearly all of them offer color effects. We consider them together here, because there is not always agreement among manufacturers or artists (or even textbook writers) about what to call a given product. Generally speaking, the main difference between chalks and crayons is the **binder**—the substance that holds particles of pigment together. Chalks have nonfat binders, whereas crayons have a fatty or greasy binder, so there is considerable variation in the way these materials react to contact with paper. If you imagine blackboard chalk and ordinary children's crayons, this difference should be clear.

Chalks and crayons vary in several characteristics. Artists need to experiment with specific products from specific manufacturers to find the effects they want. We can, however, make certain generalizations, bearing in mind they are not hard-and-fast rules. Chalks, being drier and more crumbly, blend well and can be overlaid (two or more colors on top of one another) to produce shaded effects. They usually require a paper with some tooth, are relatively fragile unless covered by a fixative, and offer a limited range of colors. The greasier crayons adhere well to paper and are more permanent, but they are difficult to blend with one another for subtle tones and gradations. (However, the newer oil-based crayons can be finger-blended almost as easily as oil paints blend.) Crayons usually offer a wider choice of colors than do chalks, and they come in varying degrees of hardness to permit sharp lines or tonal areas.

Crayon can mean anything from the wax crayons used by children through the lithographic crayon meant for drawing on stone in printmaking (Chapter 8). But the commonest drawing material is **conté crayon**—a fine-textured stick medium available in shades of red, brown, and black.

214. Honoré Daumier. *Fright.*
19th century.
Crayon and charcoal on ivory laid paper, 8¼ × 9⅜".
The Art Institute of Chicago (gift of Robert Allerton).

The artist who comes to mind most readily in discussing conté crayon drawings is Georges Seurat. In Chapter 4 we looked at Seurat's painting technique, called *pointillism,* in which tiny dots of color are massed together to build form **(137)**. Seurat also did many drawings. By working in conté on rough-textured paper he could approximate the effect of color dots in paint. *Seated Boy with Straw Hat* **(215)** is a preliminary study for Seurat's large painting *Une Baignade.* Unlike Michelangelo's rough sketches for the arm of God, however, this drawing, along with many of Seurat's studies, is a fully realized work of art. The figure is shown in soft silhouette, blending into the even softer background. It was Seurat's practice to work out his figures very completely as separate units in drawing, and then to transfer them to the painted canvas.

A harder crayon and smoother paper resulted in the much more detailed modeling in Dante Gabriel Rossetti's portrait of *Jane Burden* **(216)**. Rossetti was one of a group of mid-19th-century artists known collectively as the "pre-Raphaelites." One characteristic of their art is concentration on a specific ideal of female beauty—thick, flowing hair, enormous eyes, and a pursed rosebud mouth. Jane Burden was the perfect embodiment of this type. In the drawing Rossetti has taken advantage of the precision afforded by the hard crayon, which can produce either a sharp line or a shadowy gray one. He has left the figure and gown pale and only slightly defined, to focus on the model's haunting pre-Raphaelite face.

One other medium that should be mentioned along with the chalks and crayons is *pastel.* Because it is very soft and offers a full range of colors, pastel is often considered a borderline medium, somewhere between painting and drawing. Being fine-textured, it lends itself especially well to the kind of blending of hues that creates gradated tones. Pastel was a favorite medium of the American artist Mary Cassatt, no doubt because this soft drawing material provided an intimacy suitable for the mother-and-child scenes Cassatt liked to depict. In *Woman with Baby* (**217**) an intense, vibrant orange warms the whole page, contradicting our everyday use of the term "pastel" to mean a pale, light-value color.

LIQUID MEDIA

PEN AND INK Ink flowing onto paper gives a smooth, uninterrupted line. As with other relatively permanent media, such as silverpoint, there is little possibility for correction once the lines have been inscribed. A major variable in the ink drawing, however, is the relative thickness or thinness of lines, which depends on the pen point used. The lines can be all one width, ranging from fine to heavy, or they can vary. A single line may change, perhaps starting as a fine thread, broadening into thickness, and then tapering down again to a slender mark. Such thick-and-thin lines are often referred to as *calligraphic* or *gestural.*

As crayon makes us think of Seurat, pen and ink makes us think of Rembrandt—one of the greatest draftsmen who ever lived. Rembrandt made thousands of drawings during his long career, and he drew almost everything imaginable. But it is his landscapes that perhaps more than any other theme

217. Mary Cassatt.
Woman with Baby.
Pastel on gray paper, $28\frac{3}{8} \times 20\frac{7}{8}''$.
Sterling and Francine Clark
Art Institute, Williamstown, Mass.
(gift of the Executors of Governor
Lehman's Estate and the Edith
and Herbert Lehman Foundation).

reveal Rembrandt's personal "handwriting." In *A Thatched Cottage by a Tree* **(218)** the curling penwork in the trees and foreground foliage, drawn with a reed pen, is typical of his rapid, sketchy style. The stiff reed point yields a rather bold line with much visual character. We know that trees have leaves, not swirling shapes, and yet ever since Rembrandt this curving line seems to us the very essence of "tree." The drawing may seem sketchy and quick, but the artist has given us a strong sense of forms in space.

Another artist who achieved a distinctive style in pen and ink—quite a different style—was Van Gogh. In *A Peasant of the Camargue* **(219)** the pen

above: 218. Rembrandt. *A Thatched Cottage by a Tree.* c. 1652. Reed pen and bistre, $6\frac{7}{8} \times 10\frac{1}{2}''$. Devonshire Collection, Chatsworth (reproduced by permission of the Chatsworth Settlement Trustees).

left: 219. Vincent van Gogh. *A Peasant of the Camargue.* 1888. Quill and reed pen and brown ink over soft graphite, $19\frac{1}{2} \times 15''$. The Fogg Art Museum, Harvard University, Cambridge, Mass. (bequest of Grenville L. Winthrop).

opposite above: 220. Alexander Calder. *Somersaulters.* 1931. Pen and ink, $22\frac{3}{4} \times 30\frac{3}{4}''$. Collection Mr. and Mrs. Alvin S. Lane, Riverdale, N.Y.

opposite below: 221. Katsushika Hokusai. *Woman Fixing Her Hair.* Early 19th century. Ink on paper, $16\frac{1}{4} \times 11\frac{5}{8}''$. The Metropolitan Museum of Art, New York (Charles Stewart Smith Collection, gift of Mrs. Charles Stewart Smith, Charles Stewart Smith, Jr., and Howard Caswell Smith, in memory of Charles Stewart Smith, 1914).

Calder 1931

marks are massed together to produce visual texture. Van Gogh combined a reed pen with the more flexible quill to obtain quite varied lines—fine and thready in the face, heavy in the shirt and around the hat, short and choppy in the background. All the splendid modeling in the face is accomplished by patterning of thick and thin lines. The background texture of dots and tiny strokes makes the figure stand out plainly. Van Gogh did this drawing as a study for a painting, using the different types of pen marks and textures to represent contrasting colors he would employ in the later work.

Still another use of the pen line can be seen in Alexander Calder's circus drawings of the 1930s **(220)**. These drawings are related to Calder's thin wire sculptures from that period **(101)**, and they are just as economical in form, just as uniform in line as the three-dimensional wires. The artist gives us only the barest outlines of the figures, the minimum needed to show shape and position. This type of drawing is a kind of visual shorthand, energetic and playful. The figures are transparent, as they would be when done in wire, but we have no doubt about their arrangement in space. Only a skilled draftsman can give us so much sense of place with so little.

BRUSH AND INK The brush has long been the favorite drawing tool of Asian artists. Because in the East the brush is commonly used for writing, its handling seems as natural there as using a pencil does to Westerners. When the brush is manipulated in the Asian way, it is the ideal tool (better than a pen) for producing the calligraphic line—thin at the beginning, broadening along its length, and then tapering again to very thin. We see this effect in a marvelous drawing by the Japanese artist Katsushika Hokusai **(221)**. The woman's body is sketched in a few quick calligraphic lines, yet it seems round and full-bodied. One deft stroke down the center of the back, combined with the curve of breast and belly, and Hokusai has made us believe in the three-dimensional form.

When ink is diluted with water and applied with a brush, the result is called a **wash** drawing. Käthe Kollwitz combined touches of wash and thick, aggressive lines of pure black for the powerful image of a *Fettered Man* (222). Kollwitz made a great many drawings, and nearly all of them are charcoal, a softer medium. For this anguished figure she chose the bolder black ink.

Kollwitz' drawing shows plainly the interaction between drawing medium and imagery. In this case we might suspect that the artist had an image in mind and selected the medium that would best fit that image. Other times the reverse may occur: an artist experiments with a particular medium and thus is inspired with an image idea.

NEW DRAWING MEDIA

Artists today have a broad spectrum of drawing media to work with, and they do not limit themselves to the traditional materials we have just described. In this electronic age drawings are made by computer, by video technology, by all kinds of sophisticated equipment. For instance, if we came upon a reproduction of Barbara Nessim's *Two Shadows Outside Two Women* (223), without looking at the caption we might speculate about what materials the artist used. Perhaps chalk or crayon for the lines, and maybe a colored wash for the pink and blue and purple tones, but how did she get the very fine stippled (dotted) effects in the figures? Actually, this drawing was made on an IBM PC computer terminal, then printed for permanence. Many of us associate computer graphics with flowcharts and other business applications, but this delicate and lovely image shows how artists can tap the advanced image-making abilities of the computer.

Side by side with the computer in today's office is the fax machine, and its possibilities for artistic expression have not been neglected. David Hockney, an artist fully comfortable with traditional media (212), also loves to experiment with new ones. In the late 1980s Hockney began sending fax drawings to his friends. He made the drawings solely for this purpose, so his

above: 222. Käthe Kollwitz.
Fettered Man. 1927.
Pen and wash, 17½ × 14½".
Private collection, New York.

right: 223. Barbara Nessim.
Two Shadows Outside Two Women.
1985. Computer drawing,
Cibachrome print, 16 × 20".
© Barbara Nessim, 1985.

Käthe Kollwitz

1867–1945

In a time when the word "artist" usually meant a painter or a sculptor, Kollwitz did the bulk of her work in prints and drawings. In a time when vivid, sometimes startling color was preoccupying the art world, Kollwitz concentrated on black and white. And, in a time when nearly all artists were men, Kollwitz was—triumphantly—a woman, a woman whose life and art focused on the special concerns of women. This combination of oddities might have doomed a lesser artist to obscurity, but not one of Kollwitz' great gifts and powerful personality.

Käthe Schmidt was born in Königsberg (then in Prussia, now part of the U.S.S.R.), the second child in an intellectually active middle-class family. Her parents were remarkably enlightened in encouraging all their children to take an active part in political and social causes, and to develop their talents—in Käthe's case a talent for drawing. Käthe received the best art training then available for a woman, in Berlin and Munich. In 1891, after a seven-year engagement, she married Karl Kollwitz, a physician who seems to have been equally supportive of his wife's career. The couple established themselves in Berlin, where they kept a doctor's office and artist's studio for fifty years.

During her student days Kollwitz had gradually focused on line and had come to realize that draftsmanship was her genius. Her conventional artistic training must have intensified the shock when she "suddenly saw that I was not a painter at all."[1] She concentrated then on drawings and prints—etchings and woodcuts early on, lithographs when her eyesight grew weaker.

Five major themes dominate Kollwitz' art: herself, in a great many self-portraits and images for which she served as model; the ties between mothers and their children; the hardships of the working classes, usually interpreted through women's plight; the unspeakable cruelties of war; and death as a force unto itself. As a socialist Kollwitz identified passionately with the sufferings of working people; as a mother she identified with the struggle of women to keep their children safe.

Kollwitz bore two sons—Hans in 1892 and Peter in 1896. The first of many tragedies that marked her later life came in 1914, with the death of Peter in World War I. She lived long enough to see her beloved grandson, also named Peter, killed in World War II. During

the almost thirty years separating those losses, she continued to work prolifically, but her obsession with death never left her.

Few artists have so touchingly described their attempts to achieve a certain goal, and their continual frustration at falling short. In Kollwitz' case, the artistic goals were generally realized, but the emotional and political goals—never: "While I drew, and wept along with the terrified children I was drawing, I really felt the burden I am bearing. I felt that I have no right to withdraw from the responsibility of being an advocate. It is my duty to voice the sufferings of men, the never-ending sufferings heaped mountain-high. This is my task, but it is not an easy one to fulfill. Work is supposed to relieve you. . . . Did I feel relieved when I made the prints on war and knew that the war would go on raging? Certainly not."[2]

Käthe Kollwitz. *Small Self-Portrait, Facing Left.* 1922.
Lithograph, 13⅝ × 9⅞".
National Gallery of Art, Washington, D.C. (Rosenwald Collection).

work cannot be called finished until it has been faxed (224). Of these drawings the artist says, "I realized that if you draw especially for the fax, the prints are perfectly good. The medium is the fax, and if the fax can't read the image, you don't use those techniques."[3] Hockney delights in the fact that these works have no material value; the very act of transmission causes them to "dematerialize." Drawings of this sort force us to reconsider and stretch our definitions of art, because where, after all, *is* the art? In the original drawing? In the recipient's fax print? Or somewhere in the atmosphere?

Purposes of Drawing

PRELIMINARY STUDY

Many of the drawings reproduced in this chapter—including those by Michelangelo, Seurat, and Van Gogh—were done as preliminary studies for paintings. Before committing time and material to a finished painting, the artist will often sketch and experiment until the form seems exactly right. Artists working in all fields do the same thing. Sculptors, architects, interior designers, printmakers, landscape architects, and industrial designers—all make preliminary drawings.

In Chapter 3 we examined Picasso's great painting *Guernica* (72), the artist's outraged response to the bombing of a defenseless Basque town by the Nazis in April of 1937. We pointed out that Picasso did not merely spew out his anger onto canvas, but planned the large picture carefully, through many preliminary drawings. It is known that Picasso worked on *Guernica* from May 1 to June 4, 1937. On May 24 he made the drawing shown here (225). We see a disembodied head drawn in heavy pencil, a head all but exploding in violent rage and terror and sorrow. The eyes, transformed into teardrop shapes, are displaced, with one located in the position of an ear. The nose is fragmented, and the mouth gapes open in a soundless shriek. You will not find this head in the finished painting, although there are similarities in the screaming woman with a dead baby at far left. Picasso tried this expression in a sketch and then did not use it. It is as though he needed to explore the many faces of anguish before choosing those that satisfied his vision.

Whenever we encounter an artist who is noted in some particular field, such as sculpture or architecture, and then discover that the artist has an unusual flair for drawing, we may feel we have earned a bonus—a gift on top of a gift. The public works are out in the world for all to see; we study the drawings quietly, more privately, as though we were having a personal conversation with the artist.

Architects use drawing throughout the process of designing a building. At the beginning they may make very rough sketches, which they gradually refine as the idea takes shape. They may also make detailed sketches of certain parts of the building. Finally they make a finished drawing for presentation to the client, to sell the idea. Most architects get by with basic drafting skills, but a few have delighted in drawing for its own sake. One such architect was Frank Lloyd Wright. Wright liked to work in colored pencils, and he nearly always sketched in much of the landscape surrounding the proposed building, in keeping with his belief that a structure should be integral with its environment. His project drawing for a hunting lodge at Lake Tahoe **(226)** is almost as lyrical as a Chinese landscape painting. Wright has sketched this tree-house-among-trees as though the house had simply grown there, just like any other natural element. For this master builder, at least, drawing was not only a means to an end but an end in itself.

What was true of Wright is true for many artists. A drawing that is preliminary to something else is not necessarily trivial. For any artist who enjoys drawing, each drawing is potentially a perfect work of art.

ILLUSTRATION

Another purpose for drawing is illustration, and this field is enormous. Illustrations are made for books, for magazines, for newspapers, for advertising, for fashion displays. Before the advent of the camera, drawn illustrations were the only kind available. Illustrators today still make drawings to record events where the camera is not permitted, such as at many courtroom trials.

One of the most famous illustrators of all time was the 19th-century English artist Aubrey Beardsley. Beardsley was a fascinating character who achieved international recognition by the age of twenty, was enormously productive, and died of tuberculosis at twenty-six. His style is distinctive, bringing together elements of the erotic and the grotesque with ornate, free-flowing decoration. The style has influenced many later illustrators but has never quite been imitated. Beardsley's illustrations for books and magazines **(227)** have strong contrasting areas of black and white. The drawing is broad

left: **226.** Frank Lloyd Wright. Project drawing for Hunting Lodge, Tahoe Summer Colony, Lake Tahoe, Calif. 1923. Pencil and colored pencils on tracing paper, $21\frac{7}{8} \times 15\frac{1}{8}''$. Frank Lloyd Wright Memorial Foundation, copyright © The Frank Lloyd Wright Foundation, 1957.

right: **227.** Aubrey Beardsley. *Ali Baba*, cover design for *The Forty Thieves*. 1897. Pen and black ink, white gouache, and graphite; $9\frac{7}{16} \times 7\frac{13}{16}''$. The Fogg Art Museum, Harvard University, Cambridge, Mass. (bequest of Grenville L. Winthrop).

191

and exaggerated—in this example almost a caricature. Like any great illustrator, Beardsley went beyond the story he was illustrating to create a whole new world from his own imagination. Once you get to know Beardsley's style, you cannot fail to recognize it. For an illustrator, the style, the personal view of the world, is all important.

There are some areas in which drawn illustration has never given way to the camera but is still used extensively, such as cartoons and the illustration of children's books. These fields have enjoyed unwavering popularity, and their styles have kept pace with other types of art.

Illustration for children's books has been greatly influenced by the innovative work of Maurice Sendak. Sendak's drawings are not the gentle, benign images that several previous generations had thought appropriate for children. Sendak draws monsters, monsters who dwell somewhere between the naughty and the truly wicked. In his book *Where the Wild Things Are* (228) the artist gives concrete form to the dreadful creatures that inhabit children's fantasies. Some critics have attacked the drawings as being too frightening for children. Others suggest that the drawings have psychological value, in that Sendak's stories allow children to confront their monsters and conquer them. From the audience, however, there has never been any argument. Children love the drawings, scary though they be.

There is one more type of drawing associated with illustration—the cartoon. Cartooning is a terrifically demanding art. Most cartoons have specific narrative content, which may be amusing, dramatic, satirical, political, or a combination of these. The artist has to convey this content in one drawing, or, in the case of a comic strip, in a few economical drawings. If the cartoon has a caption, it too must be economical. Perhaps more than any other art, the cartoon must live up to the old saying, "One picture is worth a thousand words." Often, the successful cartoon depends on an audience's specialized knowledge; they are made to feel "in on" the joke. For example, it is assumed that readers of *The New Yorker* know that Rembrandt made a great many self-portraits (514, p.205), and that he did indeed pose himself in some "funny" hats (229).

EXPRESSION

All drawings are made for the expression of the artist, regardless of any other purpose they might serve, and self-expression was a key motivation for most of the drawings we have seen in this chapter. Artists record on paper what they see, in the unique way they see it. Drawing is just one way in which the imagination takes concrete form.

Contemporary artists have expanded the potential for expression in drawing, as in every other artistic medium. For example, the work by Julian

"Hendrickje, I feel another self-portrait coming on. Bring in the funny hats."

top: 228: Maurice Sendak. Drawing from *Where the Wild Things Are*. 1963. Courtesy Harper & Row Publishers, Inc., New York.

above: 229. "Hendrickje, I feel another self-portrait coming on. Bring in the funny hats." Drawing by Handelsman. © 1987 The New Yorker Magazine, Inc.

Schnabel **(230)**, which many people would call a painting, actually contains a great many areas that resemble drawing, particularly the nude figure at left. Schnabel's materials—oil and modeling paste on velvet—are not those of drawing; they are not even the materials of conventional painting. But Schnabel's imagery, with its sketchy, linear quality, clearly derives from the world of the sketchbook. Above all, his work shows that the line between drawing and painting, at least for certain artists, has all but disappeared.

With the work of Jonathan Borofsky we have come full circle from the cave drawings of earliest history. Borofsky often draws directly on the walls of a room, and his images are those remembered and recorded from dreams **(231)**. Some historians speculate that the cave artists as well were recording dreams, and their surfaces too were the walls around them. In bypassing conventional surfaces, such as paper, Borofsky shows us that drawing today need accept no limits, no restrictive sizes or shapes. Drawing is so much a natural impulse that it can be around us in the most natural way.

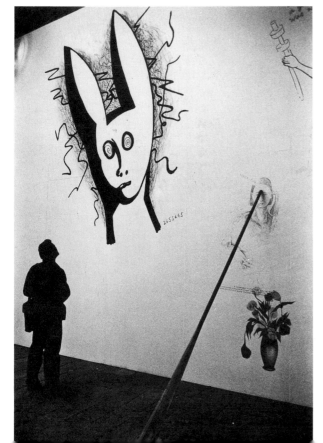

above: 230. Julian Schnabel.
Nicknames of Maitre d's. 1984.
Oil and modeling paste on velvet, 9 × 21'.
Courtesy Pace Gallery, New York.

left: 231. Jonathan Borofsky. Installation on four walls, floor, and ceiling, Venice Biennale, 1980.
Mixed media, wall height 20'.
Courtesy Paula Cooper Gallery, New York.

ART PEOPLE *Leo Castelli*

"I wanted to be the perfect Renaissance man." This is the way art dealer Leo Castelli recalls the ambitions of his youth—to be multitalented, well-versed in arts and letters, comfortable in many languages and places, proficient in many realms, from music to art to athletics. Few people attain such lofty youthful goals, but Castelli did. He is the perfect Renaissance man.

Artists today rarely sell their works directly to collectors. Instead, the transactions are carried out through a dealer, the owner of an art gallery, who agrees to handle a particular artist's work for commission. Among dealers in New York and the world, Leo Castelli stands with the elite, the best of the best.

Castelli was born in Trieste, in northern Italy, in 1907. His banker father encouraged a wide-ranging education, including art-historical studies and languages, then sent Leo to the University of Milan, where the youth acquired a law degree. Leo then embarked upon a career in banking, which took him to many parts of Europe. One of his posts was Bucharest, in Romania, where he met and married Ileana Sonnabend. The couple continued to move about, and eventually they arrived in New York.

Leo Castelli was nearly fifty years old before he launched the career for which he will always be known. He and Sonnabend occupied an apartment on East 77th Street in Manhattan, and from their living quarters, in 1957, they began to exhibit and to sell contemporary art. Both had an eye, a knack, almost a sixth sense about how the artistic winds were blowing. Pop Art was about to soar to the top of prevailing fashion, and the Leo Castelli Gallery was in at the beginning. Later, Castelli would take the lead in the ensuing trends of Minimal Art, Conceptual Art, and Neo-Expressionist Art. Although he does not take credit for discovering or establishing any artist, there can be no doubt that Castelli was vital to the careers of numerous important artists—Robert Rauschenberg, Jasper Johns, Frank Stella, Andy Warhol, Roy Lichtenstein, Ellsworth Kelly, Claes Oldenburg, and many others.

Castelli and Sonnabend divorced (both remarried), but they remain close professional colleagues. Sonnabend operates her own gallery, while Castelli maintains two important gallery spaces in New York. Castelli the dealer wields enormous power, yet he is

known for his integrity and generosity. His relationships with his artists have been marked by an exceptionally high degree of warmth and friendliness. From the beginning he established the unusual practice of paying each young artist a monthly stipend, a kind of allowance, so the artist could devote full time to art and not have to worry about putting food on the table. Castelli the man is known for his charm, his intriguing personality, his multilingual poise and good manners—the Renaissance man. Small and slight and wiry, he has been called "Mighty Mouse."

Mighty is indeed the word for this elegant old-world gentleman whose impact on the new world of 20th-century art has been incalculable. Castelli himself summed it up best: "It makes me very happy that any important contemporary collection would have to include 15 or 20 of my artists."[4]

Andy Warhol. *Portrait of Leo*, detail. 1973.
Acrylic and silkscreen on canvas, 40⅜" square.
Courtesy Leo Castelli Gallery, New York.

Painting

Painting is the queen of the arts. Ask ten people to form a quick mental image of "art," and nine of them are likely to visualize a painting on a wall. There are several reasons for the prominence of painting. For one thing, paintings usually are full of color, and, as was noted in Chapter 4, color is a potent visual stimulus. For another, paintings usually are framed, some quite elaborately, so that one has the impression of a precious object set off from the rest of the world for our visual excitement. Even without a frame, a painting may seem a thing apart—a focus of energy and life, a universe unto itself. Whatever the painting shows, it establishes its own visual scope, sets its own rules.

If we consider some of the earliest cave images, especially the more elaborate and colorful ones, to be paintings, then the art has been practiced for at least twelve thousand years. During that long history the styles of painting have changed considerably, as have the media in which paintings are done—the physical substances the painter uses. In the latter case it might be more accurate to say broadened, rather than changed, for few media have been completely abandoned while many new options have been added to the painter's repertoire.

To begin this discussion of painting, we should define certain terms crucial to the understanding of how, physically, such a work of art is put together. As with drawing media (Chapter 6), the color element in paint is the ***pigment,*** which consists of natural or synthetic color particles. Pigments usually come in the form of a powder, which by itself cannot be spread or made to adhere to the painting surface.

The ***medium*** or ***binder*** is the substance in which the pigment is suspended. ("Suspension" here means that the particles are mixed with a liquid or semiliquid material without dissolving or changing chemically.) Linseed oil—as in oil paint—is the best-known medium, but there are many others. A successful medium allows the painter to spread the colors on a surface as desired and, when it dries, adheres securely to the surface. The name of the medium of a particular work is often used to describe the work: an oil painting, a watercolor painting, and so on.

The ***solvent*** or ***vehicle*** enables the artist to thin the paint so as to control its flow and also to clean the brushes. A solvent is selected according to whether the paint is ***aqueous*** (water-solvent) or ***nonaqueous*** (dissolved by other than water). Most of us are familiar with the distinction used for house paints—water-base or oil-base. For water-base paints you can wash the brushes with tap water, but for oil-base paints you need to use turpentine. Much the same distinction applies to artists' paints.

Finally, there is the painting **support,** which is the canvas, paper, wood panel, wall, or other surface on which the artist works. The painter may first apply a preliminary coating known as a **ground** or **primer** to make the support more receptive to the paint and/or to create certain effects.

As suggested earlier, practically every painting medium ever invented is still in use somewhere, by somebody. Artists interested in history or chemistry love to experiment with obscure techniques that went out of fashion centuries ago. Most of the painting media that have fallen out of favor have been abandoned because they were cumbersome or because they were replaced by similar media that had certain advantages—lower cost, clearer colors, easier preparation, better adherence to the support, quicker drying time, slower drying time—whatever artists might wish.

It is impossible to tell which painting medium is the oldest, but we know that ancient peoples mixed their pigments with such things as fat and honey. Apparently, the first widespread and well-perfected technique came into use in the Classical period, the few hundred years surrounding the year 1 of our era. This was encaustic painting.

Encaustic

For encaustic, the pigment particles are suspended in hot beeswax, which must be kept at the proper temperature for spreading on a support (often a wood panel). Encaustic is an extremely demanding medium, and few contemporary artists want to cope with its difficulties. However, the wax gives a clear, luminous quality that almost no other medium can rival. The early Christians in Egypt, the Copts, were especially proficient at encaustic painting, and their works retain a splendid brilliance even two thousand years later **(232).**

Fresco

To make a fresco the artist paints in water-suspended pigment on a surface of freshly spread plaster. As the plaster dries, the colors are absorbed into it, so that the two substances—paint and plaster—fuse. The painting will survive in good condition as long as the plaster remains intact.

Fresco is above all a wall-painting technique, and it has been used for large-scale murals since ancient times. Probably no other painting medium requires such careful planning, such meticulous attention to the chemical properties of the medium, and such hard physical labor. The plaster can be painted only when it has the proper degree of dampness; therefore, the artist must plan each day's work and spread plaster only in the area that can be painted in one session. (Michelangelo could cover about 1 square yard of wall or ceiling in a day.)

There is nothing tentative about fresco. Whereas in some media the artist can experiment, try out forms, and then paint over them to make corrections, every touch of the brush in fresco is a commitment. The only way an artist can correct mistakes or change the forms is to let the plaster dry, chip it away, and start all over again. Usually, the artist begins with a preliminary drawing called a **cartoon.** This may be a scaled-down or full-size version of the finished painting. If the cartoon is full size, the artist may cut it up into pieces, each the size of a day's work. Next the artist outlines major forms by

232. *Portrait of a Man* (mummy portrait), from Fayum, Egypt. A.D. c. 117–161. Encaustic on wood, $15\frac{1}{2} \times 7\frac{1}{8}''$. The Metropolitan Museum of Art, New York (Rogers Fund, 1909).

placing the cartoon on the surface and poking through its lines with a sharp tool to leave a row of pinholes in the plaster.

There have been three great eras of fresco painting in the history of art: the Classical period in the Aegean and Rome, the Renaissance in 15th- and 16th-century Italy, and the early 20th century in Mexico. Only a few of the Classical frescoes have survived (465); as buildings become ruins, so do their frescoed walls. But among the works we consider the greatest of all in Western art are the magnificent frescoes of the Italian Renaissance.

While Michelangelo was at work on the frescoes of the Sistine Chapel ceiling (34,495), Pope Julius II brought in Raphael to decorate the walls of several rooms in the Vatican Palace. Raphael's fresco for the end wall of the Stanza della Segnatura, a room that may have been the Pope's library, is considered by many to be the summation of Renaissance art. It is called *The School of Athens* (233) and depicts the Greek philosophers Plato and Aristotle, centered in the composition and framed by the arch, along with their followers and students. The "school" in question means the two schools of philosophy represented by the two Classical thinkers—Plato's the more abstract and metaphysical, Aristotle's the more earthly and physical.

Everything about Raphael's composition celebrates the Renaissance ideals of perfection, beauty, natural representation, and noble principles. The towering architectural setting provides an arena for quiet intellectual debate, and it is drawn in masterful linear perspective (Chapter 4, p. 133; the vanishing point is between the heads of the two philosophers). The figures, perhaps influenced by Michelangelo's figures on the Sistine ceiling, are idealized—more perfect than life, full-bodied and dynamic. *The School of Athens* reflects Raphael's vision of one Golden Age—the Renaissance—and establishes its kinship with the Golden Age of Greece two thousand years earlier.

233. Raphael.
The School of Athens. 1510–11.
Fresco, 26 × 18'.
Stanza della Segnatura,
Vatican, Rome.

234. Diego Rivera. *Detroit Industry*, detail. 1932–33. Fresco, 17′8½″ × 45′ (north wall, central panel). The Detroit Institute of Arts (Founders Society Purchase, Edsel B. Ford Fund and gift of Edsel B. Ford).

The era that spawned the great fresco artists of Mexico, while scarcely "golden," was a fertile and turbulent one. The Mexican Revolution began in 1911 and continued for twenty years. It launched a period of great economic and social upheaval, overlapping with the social upheaval of the Depression in the United States. A number of Mexican artists, trained in Mexico but influenced by European art of the time, sought to revive fresco painting, and in this they were supported by the Mexican government.

Diego Rivera's enormous frescoed murals in many public buildings in Mexico and the United States typify this style. *Detroit Industry* (**234**), an ambitious four-wall panorama at the Detroit Institute of Arts, illustrates the grand scale and monumental quality that often characterize mural painting. Conceived as a tribute to the city and the worker, Rivera's mural has a complex iconography. The detail shown here portrays the manufacture of the 1932 Ford V-8 automobile. Every step of the job, every event in the worker's day is represented, from the punching of the time clock through steel processing, molding, welding, drilling—even the lunch break. The mural treatment bestows a grandeur on the everyday operations of the assembly line. In fact, the frescoed mural probably served Rivera's expressive needs better than any other medium could have done.

Egg Tempera

Anyone who has washed breakfast dishes knows about the adhesive strength and quick drying of egg yolk. A painting medium based on egg yolk, called tempera, was preferred by artists throughout the medieval period, until the introduction of oil paint. Egg tempera's yellow color, surprisingly, does not distort a pigment color, and, also surprisingly, tempera works tend to yellow less with age than do those in oil. Paintings done in tempera hundreds of years ago retain their brilliant glow and clear colors. The one disadvantage is that tempera is not as flexible as oil or the synthetics, not nearly as convenient in the application. Oils or acrylics can be laid on in large strokes, small strokes, thick or thin. But in tempera forms must be built up slowly, with small, individual brush strokes. For those few contemporary artists who care to take the trouble, the rewards are gratifying.

Among 20th-century artists one painter in particular has made tempera his own medium—Andrew Wyeth. Wyeth's painting *Braids* **(235)** shows the luminous technique at its best. *Braids* is part of a large cache of paintings and drawings that Wyeth had kept secret from most of the art world for fifteen years until a surprise showing in 1986. Nearly all the works depict a woman known as Helga. *Braids* shows Helga's face and upper torso painted in the most painstaking tempera technique. Individual brush strokes highlight single strands of hair, eyelashes, and threads in the sweater, and the face has an almost claylike texture from innumerable tiny strokes of paint. Helga seems natural and lifelike, yet we do not expect her to come to life, to move or turn her head. She is frozen in time by the meticulous rendering of the paint.

Oil

A popular legend says that oil painting was invented early in the 15th century by the great Netherlandish artist Jan van Eyck, who experimented with it for this portrait **(236).** However, Van Eyck probably learned the technique

235. Andrew Wyeth. *Braids.* 1979.
Tempera on canvas, $16\frac{1}{2} \times 20\frac{1}{2}''$.
Copyright © 1986 Leonard E. B. Andrews.

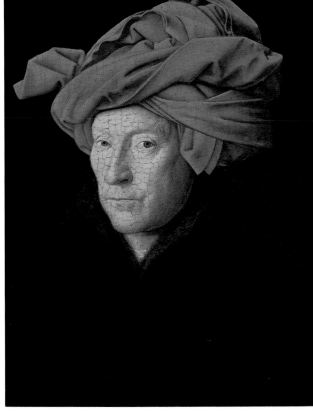

236. Jan van Eyck.
Man in a Red Turban (Self-Portrait?). 1433.
Oil on panel, $10\frac{1}{4} \times 7\frac{1}{2}''$.
The National Gallery, London
(reproduced by courtesy of the Trustees).

from another artist and merely perfected it himself. From that time and for about five hundred years the word "painting" was virtually synonymous with "oil painting." Only in the 1950s, with the introduction of acrylics (plastic resin paints), was the supremacy of oil challenged, and even then many artists clung to their oil paints.

The outstanding characteristic of oil paint is that it dries very slowly. This creates both advantages and disadvantages for the artist. On the plus side, it means that colors can be blended very subtly, layers of paint can be applied on top of other layers with little danger of separating or cracking, and the artist can rework sections of the painting almost indefinitely. This same asset becomes a liability when the artist is pressed for time—perhaps when an exhibition has been scheduled. Oil paint dries so *very* slowly that it may be weeks or months before the painting has truly "set."

Another great advantage of oil is that it can be worked in an almost infinite range of consistencies, from very thick to very thin. The German Expressionist painter Oskar Kokoschka often used thick oil paints straight from the tube, occasionally squeezing them directly on the canvas without a brush **(237)**. He could then mold and shape the thick paint with a palette knife (a spatula-shaped tool) to create actual three-dimensional depth on the canvas. Any thick application of paint is referred to as **impasto,** and

237. Oskar Kokoschka. *Self-Portrait.* 1917. Oil on canvas, $31\frac{1}{8} \times 24\frac{3}{4}''$. Von der Heydt Museum, Wuppertal, Germany.

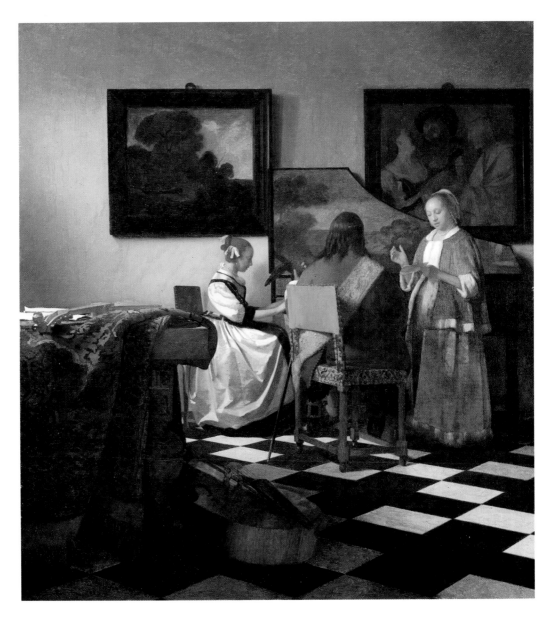

238. Jan Vermeer. *The Concert.*
c. 1660. Oil on canvas, 28 × 24¾″.
Isabella Stewart Gardner Museum, Boston.
(Stolen from the museum March 18, 1990;
not recovered as of this writing.)

Kokoschka's is an extreme version of this. The ability to use paint in this way was important for Kokoschka's expression, because the sinewy coils of paint in the *Self-Portrait* trace the artist's passionate exploration of his inner self. A smoother medium could not so define his anguished personality.

Oil paint can with equal ease be diluted and applied in very thin layers called **glazes.** By painting glaze upon glaze the artist can achieve a sense of depth, a subtle coloration, and a luminous quality that are very different from the effect of impasto application. This was the technique of many European artists during the 16th and 17th centuries. We find a masterful example in Jan Vermeer's *Concert* **(238).** The warm, rich glow of this work comes from the application of many glazes and is intensified by Vermeer's method of placing tiny light dots of opaque paint as highlights. Like many artists of his time, Vermeer was much concerned with naturalism, and the thin application of oil paint in layers lends itself to lifelike portrayal.

239. Alice Neel.
Westreich Family. 1978.
Oil on canvas, 3'11" × 5'8".
Collection Mrs. T. Westreich,
Washington, D.C.

The huge number of "old master" paintings in museums may lead us to think of oil as an old-fashioned medium—out of style and not relevant for artists of the late 20th century. Alice Neel's picture of the *Westreich Family* **(239)** challenges this notion. If we did not know this painting's medium, we might be tempted to say it was one of the newer synthetic paints, especially seeing it in reproduction. The rather flat color areas and sharp defining lines around the figures, the arbitrary blues and greens on flesh—these seem too "modern" somehow for oil paint. But that is just the point: oil has the flexibility to be a great many things. In this thoroughly contemporary painting, oil seems every bit as modern as any substance invented by chemistry.

As is typical of a Neel portrait, this image gives a portrait of the whole body, not just the face, and the group portrait is particularly interesting for its psychological insights into the family dynamic. Neel invites us to study these people and speculate about their relationships. How do these family members feel about each other? Are they close or distant? Are some members bound together while others stand outside the family group? Who are the dominant members? The artist provides us with a number of clues. Notice how the various members of the family hold their hands, their arms, their shoulders, their legs and feet. Observe the ways their bodies lean and the direction of their gaze. See how each of the subjects is dressed. Considered this way, a modern portrait in oil becomes a fascinating study in character.

Before we leave the topic of oil paints, we might mention one more interesting fact about the medium. Oil paintings very often are coated with a top layer of varnish to protect the painted forms underneath. Although many types of paintings and drawings are framed behind glass, oils seldom are. The varnish therefore serves roughly the same purpose as glass would in preserving the artwork. Sometimes the varnish does more to distort the artist's imagery than it does to protect. This was the case with one of Rembrandt's most famous paintings.

Alice Neel

1900–1984

When an acquaintance once remarked that Alice Neel painted "like a man," the artist retorted, "No, I don't paint like a man; but I don't paint like they expect a woman to paint." As a matter of fact, this extraordinary woman spent a long lifetime doing the unexpected, with cheerful disregard for the prevailing mores and fashions.

Alice Neel was born in Merion Square, Pennsylvania, the daughter of a proper middle-class family that she described as "anti-bohemian." She studied at what was then the Philadelphia School of Design for Women—"a school where rich girls went before they got married"—and received a thorough, if conventional, grounding in art.

Her personal life, too, was conventional up to that point, but soon it changed drastically. Neel referred to the men who played important roles in her life by stereotype, rather than by name. Upon leaving art school she married "the Cuban." The couple moved to Havana, where Neel continued to paint and had her first exhibition in 1926. The Cuban marriage eventually broke up, after which Neel returned to New York and worked on the W.P.A. project—the government-sponsored Depression program to help support artists. Along the way she took up with "the sailor," with whom she lived until he cut up and burned all her work. ("You know how men are, they get jealous, they're possessive.") With "the Harvard man" she maintained a friendship for decades, but she claimed he was most useful in the thirties, because, when everyone was very poor, he took her to expensive places to eat. There was also "the Puerto Rican singer."

From the beginning Neel was a portraitist, although she preferred to call herself a "people painter," feeling that portraitists are looked down on. This assessment actually proved correct through most of her career. Just at the point when Neel should have been in her artistic prime—the 1940s and 1950s—abstraction had completely taken over the art world. The painter of figures was out of fashion and remained so for at least twenty years. Not until 1974, at the age of seventy-four, did Neel have her first important show—at the Whitney Museum in New York. The show included some fifteen pictures that had not previously been "off the shelf." Alice Neel waited a long time to hear an impor-

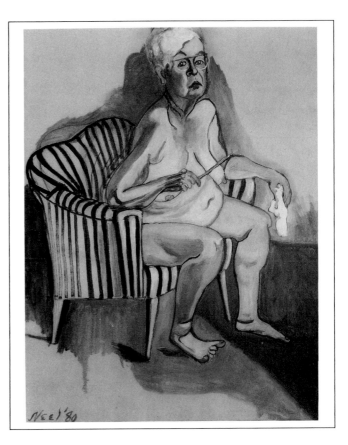

tant critic name her as the best portrait painter of the 20th century, and then she herself did not contradict that statement. The pictures, however, have transcended portrait status in the sense of recording someone's looks. They are major paintings that happen to have people as their subjects.

Quite obviously, Alice Neel was an original, an exceptionally self-directed artist and human being. Neither her personal life nor her career was modeled after any example, nor did she follow anything but her own inclinations: "When they asked me if I had influences I said I never copy anybody. I never did, because I feel that the most important thing about art and in art—and I tell students this—is to find your own road."[1]

Alice Neel. *Nude Self-Portrait.* 1980. Oil on canvas, 4'6" × 3'4". National Portrait Gallery, Washington, D.C.

Sortie of Captain Banning Cocq's Company of the Civic Guard **(240)** shows a kind of private elite militia guard going out on an exercise. In the center is Captain Cocq, giving orders to his lieutenant, and grouped around are members of the company, who seem especially pleased to be dressed up and playing war games. For many years Rembrandt's painting was known as *The Night Watch*, and it still is informally called by this name. The reason has nothing to do with the artist's intent. A heavy layer of varnish applied on top of the oil paint, combined with smoke from a nearby fireplace, had gradually darkened the painting's surface until it seemed to portray a nighttime scene. No one alive remembered it any differently.

During World War II Rembrandt's masterpiece was put away for safe-keeping. Before it was returned to exhibition after the war, the varnish was removed and the surface thoroughly cleaned. What emerged was a painting very different from the one art lovers had become accustomed to. *The Night Watch* is shot through with light and is, in fact, a daytime scene. Details that had long been obscured were once again visible. The painting was to have still more adventures, as we shall see in the Epilogue **(577)**.

Watercolor

Watercolor is thought of as an intimate art, usually small in scale and executed with great freedom and spontaneity. Watercolor straddles the border between painting and drawing.

The pigments for watercolor are suspended in gum arabic (a gummy plant substance), thinned with water, and painted with a flowing motion onto paper of good quality. Generally, the watercolor is translucent, so that much of the white paper shows through. Watercolors are meant to be done quickly, according to the inspiration of the moment. Mistakes cannot easily be corrected, and overworking spoils the spontaneity of the medium.

240. Rembrandt. *Sortie of Captain Banning Cocq's Company of the Civic Guard (The Night Watch).* 1642. Oil on canvas, 12'2" × 14'7". Rijksmuseum, Amsterdam.

Rembrandt

1606–1669

Of the few artists classified as "greatest of the great," Rembrandt is the most accessible to us. Through more than one hundred self-portraits, we follow his path from the brashness of youth to the high good spirits and prosperity of middle life to the melancholy loneliness of old age. Rembrandt's penetrating self-portraits represent a search for the self, but to the viewer they are a revelation of the self.

Born in the Dutch city of Leiden, Rembrandt Harmensz van Rijn was the son of a miller. At fourteen he began art lessons in Leiden and later studied with a master in Amsterdam. By the age of twenty-two he had pupils of his own. About 1631 he settled permanently in Amsterdam, having by then attracted considerable fame as a portrait painter. Thus began for Rembrandt a decade of professional success and personal happiness—a high point that would never come again in his life.

In 1634 Rembrandt married Saskia van Uijlenburgh, an heiress of good family, thus improving his own social status. The pair must have been rather a dashing couple-about-Amsterdam. The artist's portraits were in demand, his style was fashionable, and he had money enough to indulge himself in material possessions, especially to collect art. One blight on this happy period was the arrival of four children, none of whom survived. But in 1641 Rembrandt's beloved son Titus was born.

Rembrandt's range as an artist was enormous. He was master not only of painting but of drawing and of the demanding technique of etching for prints. (It is said that Rembrandt went out sketching with an etcher's needle, as other artists might carry a pencil.) Besides the many portraits, the artist displayed unparalleled genius in other themes, including landscapes and religious scenes.

In 1642 Rembrandt's fortunes again changed, this time, irrevocably, for the worse. Saskia died not long after giving birth to Titus. The artist's financial affairs were in great disarray, no doubt partly because of his self-indulgence in buying art and precious objects. Although he continued to work and to earn money, Rembrandt showed little talent for money management. Ultimately he was forced into bankruptcy and had to sell not only his art collection but even Saskia's burial

plot. About 1649 Hendrickje Stoffels came to live with Rembrandt, and she is thought of as his second wife, although they did not marry legally. She joined forces with Titus to form an art dealership in an attempt to protect the artist from his creditors. Capping the long series of tragedies that marked Rembrandt's later life, Hendrickje died in 1663 and Titus in 1668, a year before his father.

Rembrandt's legacy is almost totally a visual one. He does not seem to have written much. Ironically, one of the few recorded comments comes in a letter to a patron, begging for payment—payment for paintings that are now considered priceless and hang in one of the world's great museums. "I pray you my kind lord that my warrant might now be prepared at once so that I may now at last receive my well-earned 1244 guilders and I shall always seek to recompense your lordship for this with reverential service and proof of friendship."[2]

Rembrandt. *Self-Portrait*, detail. 1652. Oil on canvas, 44½ × 31⅞" (entire work). Kunsthistorisches Museum, Vienna.

top: 241. Maurice Prendergast. *Sunlight on the Piazzetta, Venice.*
c. 1888–89. Watercolor over graphite, $12\frac{1}{2} \times 20\frac{5}{8}''$.
Museum of Fine Arts, Boston (gift of Mr. and Mrs. William T. Aldrich).

left: 242. Sesshu. *Autumn Landscape.* Late 15th century.
Ink and color on paper, height $18\frac{1}{8}''$.
National Museum, Tokyo.

above: 243. John Marin. *From the Bridge, New York City.* 1933.
Watercolor on paper, $21\frac{7}{8} \times 26\frac{3}{4}''$.
Wadsworth Atheneum, Hartford (The Ella Gallup Sumner
and Mary Catlin Sumner Collection).

Maurice Prendergast's painting *Sunlight on the Piazzetta, Venice* **(241)** illustrates the watercolor technique at its most vibrant. Prendergast, an American artist who worked at the turn of the 20th century, was much influenced by the French Impressionists. His style is filled with light and color—the quick blink-of-an-eye impression of life in motion. Watercolor captures the immediacy of the moment, the gaiety and fleeting charm of a sunlit outdoor scene.

Watercolor has been an important part of traditional Japanese painting, where it is often combined with ink or ink washes (sweeps of diluted ink). Japanese brushwork lends itself especially well to a rapid, assured execution. In 15th-century Japan, landscape painting in watercolor and ink reached a high point of development, and the great master of the style was Sesshu. His *Autumn Landscape* **(242)** is a wonderfully composed arrangement of diagonals—one from the trees at upper right to the ground at lower left, another cutting from middle left to intersect with the first and focus attention on the pagoda near the center of the painting. Throughout the painting Sesshu's brushwork is sharp and assured. Only a few strokes are needed to show us the essence of forms.

Like oil, watercolor is a flexible medium, capable of yielding very different effects in the hands of different artists. Two American painters in particular, John Marin and Winslow Homer, were noted for their watercolors; in fact, Marin worked primarily in this medium. Their careers overlapped in time, and both were active at the beginning of this century. But if you compare their paintings, you will see a contrast and understand how each artist drew from the watercolor technique the expression he wanted.

Marin's cityscapes, such as *From the Bridge, New York City* **(243)**, capture the essence and the spirit of the metropolis, rather than its actual appearance. Full of vigor and energy and exciting diagonals, they make us feel the city's pulse, its movement. The brushwork is loose and free, with form only barely sketched in. Marin's style exploits the fluidity of watercolor to the fullest extent.

Homer's watercolor style, while retaining the freedom and spontaneity of the medium, is far more contained. In *For To Be a Farmer's Boy* **(244)** the forms are defined by small color patches—in contrast to Marin's long sweeps of liquid paint. Homer was certainly capable of dramatic diagonals, but here there is a predominance of serene horizontal lines, broken only by the vertical of the boy's figure. Homer's more controlled handling of watercolor in this work shows us the pleasures of a peaceful summer afternoon on the farm.

244. Winslow Homer.
For To Be a Farmer's Boy. 1887.
Watercolor, 14 × 20".
The Art Institute of Chicago
(gift of an anonymous donor
in memory of Edward Carson Waller).

Gouache

When opaque (nontranslucent) white is added to watercolors, the result is known as gouache. The white may be either mixed with the paints or coated on the support before the watercolors are applied. Because gouache is exceptionally quick-drying, it is well suited for sketches and preliminary drawings, but this also means that brush strokes do not blend well. The artist must adapt to this characteristic by placing colors and forms side by side, rather than overlapping them or blending them into one another. Wassily Kandinsky has exploited this quality splendidly in *Russian Beauty in a Landscape* **(245)**. Individual daubs of flat, opaque paint are laid down like the tiles in a mosaic to create a shimmering, exotic image. The effect is not naturalistic, not like the real world at all, but rather more like an illustrated book of fairy tales, so that the woman is transformed into a beautiful princess, the landscape into a magical kingdom.

Distemper

Distemper, commonly known as poster paint, is a medium based on water-soluble glue into which pigments are mixed. Like gouache, it dries very

left: 245. Wassily Kandinsky.
Russian Beauty in a Landscape. 1904.
Gouache, $16\frac{1}{4} \times 10\frac{5}{8}''$.
Städtische Galerie in Lenbachhaus, Munich.

above: 246. Edouard Vuillard. *The First Steps.*
1902. Distemper, $19\frac{1}{2} \times 13\frac{3}{4}''$.
Private collection, U.S.A.

247. David Alfaro Siqueiros. *María Asúnsolo as a Child.* 1935. Duco on plywood, $39\frac{3}{4} \times 29\frac{1}{2}''$. Collection María Asúnsolo, Mexico City.

quickly, so the blending of brush strokes or the glazing of colors is almost impossible. We often think of distemper as a good painting medium for children because it is inexpensive, covers mistakes solidly, and cleans up easily. But it is also a respectable medium for adult artists who are willing to adjust to its difficulties. The French artist Edouard Vuillard, who began his career painting stage flats for the theater, developed an affinity for this fast-drying medium and later adapted it to his easel paintings, such as *The First Steps* **(246)**. As in Kandinsky's gouache painting, this work has many individual, unblended brush strokes, but here they are smaller, with subtle gradations of value areas. Under Vuillard's expert handling the sturdy medium of distemper seems to flicker and pulsate with life.

Synthetic Media

The enormous developments made in chemistry during the early 20th century had an impact in artists' studios. All painting media available up to that time had certain limitations. Oil, the most widely used, had the disadvantage of excessively slow drying time. The new synthetic media offered the promise of more control—control of fluidity, color fidelity, drying time, and durability. It should be noted, however, that there is still no *one* perfect medium for all types of expression and for all artists. The introduction of synthetic media, especially the acrylics, has simply expanded the range of possibilities.

By the 1930s the chemical industry had learned to make strong, weatherproof paint based on plastic resins, as well as new fade-proof colors for use in industry. The first painter known to have adapted these paints to art was the Mexican artist David Alfaro Siqueiros. In Los Angeles in 1932 Siqueiros organized his students into an industrial crew to paint outdoor murals with plastic resin paints, using slide projectors to transfer designs to the walls and spray guns to apply the paint. The murals, like those of Rivera, were meant to convey a social message. But the most revolutionary part of Siqueiros' work was the way the murals were made. The acrylic paints many artists use today are a development of these early synthetic resins, with similar characteristics of quick drying and resistance to weather and fading.

Siqueiros also pioneered in the use of synthetic paints for smaller works, such as the portrait illustrated here **(247)**. The quick-drying Duco paint allowed him to build up rich surface textures, strong value contrasts, and an almost sculptural quality—all of which would be possible but far more laborious in oil.

Synthetic paints were still a novelty in the 1930s, but within twenty years they had become a fact of everyday life and work for artists. The most popular synthetic paints are the water-base acrylics, which were introduced in the 1950s. Acrylics offer quick drying time (though not as unmanageably quick as that of the earlier synthetic resins), pure and intense colors, and great flexibility in methods of application. While many artists still paint with conventional brushes, others have adapted the acrylic medium to pouring, throwing, or dripping. Thinned down, acrylics can be shot through an air-brush—a tool that sprays a controlled mist of paint—as in the work of Audrey Flack (57). It has been suggested that the "hard-edge" painting of the 1960s (559) could not have been developed without acrylic paints, because they permit the artist to block off areas with masking tape to achieve an absolutely straight line. The masking tape could not be put down on top of slower-drying oils or most other media.

Helen Frankenthaler's painting *Nature Abhors a Vacuum* (248) shows how acrylic can behave when it is thinned to the consistency of a dye or stain and poured onto canvas, which partially absorbs the color. In this work there is little actual surface texture; any suggestion of pictorial depth comes from the interplay of colors, not from recognizable shapes. The forms are organic, creating a color landscape of their own within the rectangle of the painting, but they make no specific reference to the natural landscape. Free-flowing

248. Helen Frankenthaler.
Nature Abhors a Vacuum. 1973.
Acrylic on canvas, 8'7½" × 9'4½".
Private collection, courtesy
André Emmerich Gallery, New York.

249. Faith Ringgold.
The Purple Quilt. 1986.
Acrylic on cotton canvas,
tie-dyed, printed, and pieced
fabrics; 7'7" × 6'.
Collection Bernice Steinbaum.

washes of paint spread and overlap on the canvas in what appears to be an immediate, spontaneous burst of imagery and color. Like Jackson Pollock **(47,549)**, Frankenthaler often places her canvases flat on the floor, the better to control the flow of paint.

Acrylics also can be applied to many kinds of supports (not just canvas), and they combine well with other techniques and media. For example, Faith Ringgold's *Purple Quilt* **(249)** is actually what the title says—fabrics pieced together and quilted, serving as a framework for the artist's rows of figures painted in acrylic. *The Purple Quilt* is a tribute to Alice Walker's novel *The Color Purple.* One of a series of "painted story quilts," it is meant to celebrate not only women's experience but also black experience. For Ringgold, the quilt format ties contemporary art into the long tradition of (women's) handcraft work, thus breaking down the barrier between "fine" and "applied" arts. This format also provides a grid structure to unify the rows of people, all staring straight ahead, who inhabit the artist's quilts and who, she reports, are representative of the faces she sees while walking through Harlem. Ringgold intends the viewer to "read" her quilt, as one would read a book or play. And, like many contemporary artists, she is pushing out the boundaries of conventional painting media in order to tell her story.

This brief survey should have demonstrated that the various painting media and the artists who use them yield endless possibilities. It would be difficult to say which comes first—the artist's imagery or the material. Did the first cave artist have the impulse to paint something and search about for a material with which to do it? Or did the cave artist find some pigmented material and then speculate about what would happen if the substance were applied to a wall? The answer is not important, but the two aspects—idea and medium—feed upon each other. No visual image could be realized without the medium in which to make it concrete. And no medium would be of any consequence without the artist's idea—and the compelling urge to paint.

Han van Meegeren based his career—if we may properly call it a career—on revenge. Born in Holland in 1889, Van Meegeren was a painter who, by his early forties, had achieved some modest success. Unfortunately, the success was all too modest for Van Meegeren. Furious at the lukewarm reception to what he considered a great talent, he set out to prove that the critics and art experts were fools. Van Meegeren began to forge brand new "old masterpieces."

After trying his hand at the styles of various Dutch masters, he decided upon Vermeer as the most likely candidate for forgery. This was a happy choice for several reasons, but mainly because Vermeers were scarce. Jan Vermeer, who worked in Delft during the 17th century, was not prolific and left fewer than forty paintings definitely by his hand. Anyone who could produce a "lost" Vermeer could name the price. So Van Meegeren did just that.

No slipshod, third-rate forger was he. Not content merely to copy the master's style, this intelligent crook painted the pictures that Vermeer *might* have painted if he'd got around to it. Knowing that Vermeer, in his youth, had painted religious subjects, Van Meegeren painted a new "Vermeer" with a religious theme.

The forger's preparations were meticulous. He labored for four years, experimenting with various paints and techniques, aiming at a result that would fool even the most careful eye into thinking the painting was three hundred years old. He bought an old picture—a genuine work by a minor artist—and carefully rubbed off the paint to use the canvas. He even devised a special oven to bake the finished work and harden the paint. Then he took another six months to paint his "Vermeer." When done, he concocted a story that a family of his acquaintance had owned the painting for centuries and wished now to sell it—with Van Meegeren as agent.

And it worked. The art world was at first stunned, then rapturous. The "Vermeer" was subjected to many tests of its authenticity, and it passed them all. The Boymans Museum in Rotterdam bought the painting for $285,000. Initially, Van Meegeren planned to confess his hoax soon after the sale and thus thumb his nose at the experts. But he hesitated. Always extravagant, always unable to hold onto money, the artist had made a tidy sum from his forgery. Soon he settled down to produce yet more "Vermeers," and eventually

he turned out six of them. By 1945 he was an immensely wealthy man.

The art critics never unmasked Van Meegeren; it was politics that brought about his downfall. During World War II one of the fake Vermeers was acquired by Hermann Goering, Hitler's close deputy. The Dutch people, outraged that a national treasure, a Vermeer, had fallen into the hands of the Nazis, denounced Van Meegeren—the supposed agent—as a traitor. The artist was arrested and subjected to intense questioning. Finally, he burst out: "Fools! You are fools like the rest of them! I sold no Vermeer to the Germans! I sold no treasure! I painted the picture myself!"[3]

In a supreme twist of irony, nobody believed him. To prove the truth, Van Meegeren had to paint yet another "Vermeer" under the watching eyes of his accusers. He was tried for forgery in 1947 and sentenced to a year in prison, but before the sentence could be carried out, he died of a heart attack.

In a way, perhaps, the forger's goal was realized. His motivation was to outsmart the world, and he nearly succeeded. Han van Meegeren may not be esteemed as a master painter, but he remains the master forger of them all.

Han van Meegeren at his trial.

Prints

If you have ever received a handmade greeting card for Christmas, for a birthday, or as an invitation to a party, then you will appreciate the difference between an art print and a mass-produced reproduction. Commercial greeting cards are cranked out by the thousands, even millions, by the major card manufacturers. But many people like to make their own cards with their own original designs. Usually they will *print* the cards by some type of stamping process. The design is carved out on a printing block made of wood, linoleum, or even the cut side of a potato, leaving some areas raised as in a rubber stamp. Then the printing block is coated with ink and pressed carefully onto paper to make the card.

An image made this way is special. For one thing, the design is unique—a personal expression of the individual who conceived it. Also, each card will be slightly different from all the others because of variations in pressure, inking, placement on the paper, and steadiness of the hand. There is a human touch, which we find missing from commercial products. For each separate image, *one* person made it, judged its quality, and was satisfied. All these factors apply equally to art prints.

Prints differ from most other works of art in two important respects. First, they are made by an indirect process. The artist does not draw or paint directly on the work of art, but instead creates the surface that *makes* the work of art. (In some cases the artist may add special touches to each print, but this is not the most common practice.) Second, the printing process results in many nearly identical images, which is the reason it is called an art of **multiples.** Each image—called an impression—is considered an original work of art. This latter point is crucial to an understanding of art prints, so we need to discuss it more fully.

Before the 1950s there were no strict guidelines for what could genuinely be labeled an "original" print. In the past several decades, however, certain criteria have been established, and the value of contemporary prints has much to do with their adherence to these criteria. The guidelines were set up in an attempt to avoid abuses that had crept into the print market, such as inferior, shoddy, or inauthentic works being passed off as fine art.

Printmaking procedures now are rigidly controlled. The artist works on a plate or stone or some other surface to make the image. Then the image is printed on paper, by hand or by a hand-operated machine, either by the artist or by someone under the artist's immediate supervision. Each print is examined to make sure it meets the artist's standards, and any faulty impressions are destroyed. Usually the artist and printer decide in advance how many impressions will be made—ten, fifty, a hundred or more—and this number is referred to as the **edition.** The size of the edition may be determined by the material used for printing. Hard metal can print many perfect impressions, but a softer material, such as linoleum, will begin to wear down, resulting in a blurred image. Once the planned number of prints has been made, the plate or block is *canceled* (by scratching cross marks on it) or destroyed, so that no more prints can be struck. Finally, the artist signs each print individually and numbers each one. For example, if you buy a print marked 10/100, you will know you have the tenth print made in an edition of one hundred. Prints made earlier in the edition are sometimes considered more valuable.

The type of print we are talking about must be distinguished from posters and other reproductions made by mechanical or photographic processes, such as the illustrations in this book. You can buy a color reproduction of a Rembrandt or Picasso painting, or a poster featuring a rock star or film personality, but these are not prints in the sense that we are discussing in this chapter, not original works of art. The artist who made the images has no supervision over the printing process and may not even know about it. The quality of the reproduction is nowhere near as meticulously controlled as that of an art print. Such reproductions are useful for study purposes and they often give pleasure, but they have little artistic or monetary value.

Today's art print, above all, is designed to *be* a print. It is not a copy of a work done in some other medium, although it may be adapted from an image in another medium. Some artists, for instance, will take a theme they have used in painting and explore its possibilities in prints, but in this case the artist adjusts the image to fit the physical qualities and expressive potential of the particular print medium chosen.

Like drawings, prints are a great boon to the art lover and the collector. At a time when original paintings by well-known artists are beyond the means of any but the very rich, prints by established artists often can be purchased for just a few hundred dollars. (The most fashionable artists command many thousand dollars for each print, but this price range is limited to a small group.) Young collectors starting out, and even large corporations with huge resources, have eagerly taken to buying prints. They may be a sound financial investment, but far more important is the fact that they give aesthetic pleasure and the joy of owning original art.

There are four basic methods for making an art print **(250)**—relief, intaglio, lithography, and screenprinting. In this chapter we shall look at each in turn and then consider a few advanced and combined techniques.

250. The four basic print methods: relief, intaglio, lithography, and screenprinting.

ink

raised areas hold ink

RELIEF

ink

incised areas hold ink

INTAGLIO

image area holds ink; non–image areas repel ink

LITHOGRAPHY

ink passes through areas of screen that are not blocked

paper with screened image

SCREENPRINTING

Relief

The term *relief* describes any printing method in which the image to be printed is *raised* from a background **(250)**. Think of a rubber stamp. When you look at the stamp itself, you may see the words "First Class" or "Special Delivery" standing out from the background in reverse. You press the stamp to an ink pad, then to paper, and the words print right side out—a mirror image of the stamp. All relief processes work according to this general principle.

Any surface from which the background areas can be carved away is suitable for relief printing. Eskimo artists in Canada's Northwest Territories work with flat stones, cutting and chipping away the background until only the image areas remain in relief. Then the stone is inked and paper is laid on top and wiped by hand to make the print.

Stone provides an extremely durable printing surface, capable of yielding a virtually endless number of clear impressions. However, the difficulty of carving stone hampers the creation of fine details. Eskimo prints are valued for their bold and stylized designs (251). When printmakers seek greater flexibility in cutting and image-making, they generally turn to the material most commonly associated with relief printing: wood.

WOODCUT

To make a woodcut the artist first draws the desired image on a block of wood. Then all the areas that are not meant to print are cut and gouged out of the wood so that the image stands out in relief. When the block is inked, only the raised areas take the ink. Finally, the block is pressed on paper, or paper is placed on the block and rubbed to transfer the ink and make the print.

Woodcut is the oldest of the printmaking methods, having been developed in the Western world as soon as paper became available, about 1400. In fact, even before papermaking techniques were introduced in Europe, wood blocks were used to stamp designs on textiles. It was a simple transition from cloth to paper, and so the new art form advanced rapidly.

Early woodcut prints were used for both religious and secular purposes. Until the 15th century only the very rich could afford to own religious pictures, which had to be drawn by hand. Prints put such images into the reach of anyone who wanted them. Similarly, woodcuts ended the upper classes' monopoly on certain games of amusement. Playing cards made from wood blocks were now accessible to the common people. Our illustration (252) shows part of the earliest surviving woodcut "deck" of cards. An anonymous master from south Germany or Austria made these cards about the middle of the 15th century. They depict the various trades—barber, baker, metalsmith—which must have made their users feel right at home while playing games of chance. The little figures, going about their work, are cheerful and charming. And, while the drawing style is simple, the bodies and clothing of the tradesmen seem animated, their faces suggest individual personality.

left: 251. Mungituk.
Man Carried to the Moon. 1959.
Stone relief print in black
and gray-orange, 19¼ × 15″.
The Brooklyn Museum, New York
(Dick S. Ramsay Fund).

above: 252. "Steward"
and "barber," playing cards
of a courtly pack
with illustrations of trades,
from south Germany or Austria.
1453–57. Hand-colored woodcuts,
each 5⅜ × 3⅞″.
Kunsthistorisches Museum, Vienna.

The woodcut print reached a high point in Germany and northern Europe during the 15th and 16th centuries, with the work of such masters as Albrecht Dürer. Dürer's *Rhinoceros* (253) represents an attempt by a highly imaginative artist to depict a beast he had never seen, but knew only from description. The artist must surely have amused himself very much in creating such wonderful decorative detail, and his results amuse us equally today. (Dürer also worked in other print media; we saw one of his engravings in Chapter 2, **55**.)

By the 17th century prints began appearing in Asia, where Japanese artists, in particular, experimented with the new medium. In the mid-18th century Japanese printmakers perfected the technique of full-color woodcut printing, using several blocks. This method required careful planning in the design and cutting of the wood blocks.

For color printing the artist usually must cut one block for each color that is to appear in the print. On the "red" block, for instance, only the areas that are to print in red are raised; on the "blue" block only the blue areas are raised; and so forth. Then the blocks are printed one color at a time on each sheet of paper in the edition. The impressions made by the various color blocks must be lined up very carefully, one on top of the other, so there are no unintended gaps or overlapping in the finished print. This process is known as **registration.**

The two names most often associated with masterful Japanese woodcut prints are Hiroshige and Hokusai. Ando Hiroshige was renowned for his landscapes, such as *Rain Shower on Ohashi Bridge* **(254).** As in many of

below: **253.** Albrecht Dürer.
Rhinoceros. 1515.
Woodcut, 8¾ × 11⅝".
The Metropolitan Museum of Art,
New York
(gift of Junius S. Morgan, 1919).

right: **254.** Ando Hiroshige.
Rain Shower on Ohashi Bridge.
19th century.
Woodcut, 13⅞ × 9¼".
The Cleveland Museum of Art
(gift from J. H. Wade).

ARTISTS ON ARTISTS *Van Gogh on Hiroshige*

During the two years he spent in Paris, from 1886 to 1888, Vincent van Gogh became an avid collector of Japanese prints. Many artists working in France at that time admired the Japanese woodcuts, but Van Gogh, never one to do things by halves, acquired hundreds of them, hung them in his studio and in a nearby café, and made direct copies of several. One such copy is *The Bridge*, after Ando Hiroshige.

We know that Van Gogh actually traced the image from the print directly onto his canvas; some of his tracing papers have been found. This explains the very close replication of Hiroshige's forms. But what of the differences between the two works? Most obviously, the Van Gogh is an oil painting, the Hiroshige a print. On closer inspection we see that Van Gogh's brushwork has finely drawn details, especially in the water and background landscape, that do not appear in the Hiroshige.

The most striking difference, of course, is the decorative border of the painting, which was purely Van Gogh's invention. The artist filled his border with Japanese characters (including the words for "water," "again," and "auspicious"), probably copying them at random from his collection of prints and very likely without knowing their meanings. We can only guess about the aesthetic reasons for this addition. Perhaps Van Gogh wanted to make his painting "more" Japanese. The practical reason, however, was simple: Van Gogh used a standard-size French canvas, $28\frac{3}{4}$ by $21\frac{1}{4}$ inches, and he needed something to fill up the spaces around Hiroshige's image area.

Vincent van Gogh. *The Bridge.* 1887. Oil on canvas, $28\frac{3}{4} \times 21\frac{1}{4}''$.
Vincent van Gogh Foundation,
National Museum Vincent van Gogh, Amsterdam.

Hiroshige's prints, the work is composed primarily of diagonals—the bridge slanting from lower left to middle right, the rain slashing down at a different angle, the riverbank cutting across at yet another diagonal. The figures crossing the bridge are small and are depicted not as individuals but as people responding to, and buffeted by, the weather. In a Hiroshige landscape nature is grand and people are small. The long parallel lines of the rain give this print a wonderful rich visual texture.

Katsushika Hokusai also made many landscapes during his prolific career. Best known are his numerous views of Mount Fuji—the cone-shaped above: **255.** Katsushika Hokusai. *View of Fuji from Seven-Ri Beach.* 1823–29. Color woodcut, $10\frac{1}{8} \times 15''$. The Metropolitan Museum of Art, New York (Rogers Fund, 1914).

below: **256.** Emil Nolde. *The Prophet.* 1912. Woodcut, $12\frac{5}{8} \times 8\frac{5}{8}''$. National Gallery of Art, Washington, D.C. (Rosenwald Collection).

volcano that is the highest mountain in Japan and is considered a sacred spot to the Japanese. Hokusai drew Fuji in all seasons, in all weathers, and from many vantage points. *View of Fuji from Seven-Ri Beach* **(255)** presents a vista that seems not entirely of this world. The white cone of the mountain hovers tranquilly in a realm of puffy green foliage and vivid blue clouds.

As was mentioned in Chapter 1, Japanese woodcut prints were imported to Europe in great quantities during the latter part of the 19th century. Many artists were influenced by aspects of their style, including the emphasis on diagonals, the subtle use of asymmetrical balance (note that Fuji is thrust far to right in the composition and balanced by the calligraphy at upper left), and the areas of flat, unshaded color in many prints. These style characteristics have been absorbed into the mainstream of contemporary art, so they no longer seem "Japanese" but are part of a universal visual expression.

The German Expressionist artists of the early 20th century found in woodcut a medium uniquely compatible with their style. A splendid example is Emil Nolde's *The Prophet* **(256)**. Expressionist imagery is stark, somewhat primitive, and occasionally shocking. Woodcut readily lends itself to this style by allowing harsh contrasts of black and white as well as broad—even crude—drawing and cutting. Expressionism is just what its name implies— expressive, and also brooding, emotional, uncompromising. Of all the print methods, woodcut offers the greatest possibilities for that expression.

LINOCUT

A linoleum cut, or linocut, is very similar to a woodcut. The major difference is that the material is much softer than wood, which makes it both easier to carve and less durable in printing multiple impressions, resulting in smaller editions. Linoleum has no grain, so it is possible to make cuts in any direction with equal ease. Some artists dismiss linoleum as being suitable only for

Katsushika Hokusai

1760–1849

One of the most delightfully eccentric figures in the history of art is the Japanese painter and woodcut designer who has come to be known as Hokusai. During his eighty-nine years Hokusai lived in at least ninety different houses and used some fifty names. The name that stuck for posterity—Hokusai—means "Star of the Northern Constellation."

Hokusai was born in the city of Edo (now Tokyo), the son of a metal engraver. At the age of eighteen he was sent as an apprentice to the print designer Katsukawa Shunsho. So impressed was the master with his pupil's work that he allowed the young man to adopt part of his own name, and for several years Hokusai called himself "Shunro." Later the two quarreled, and Hokusai changed his name.

Even in his early years Hokusai always worked very quickly, producing huge quantities of drawings. As he finished a drawing, he would toss it on the floor, until there were papers scattered all over the studio, making cleaning impossible. When the house got too filthy and disorderly, he would simply move to another, followed by his long-suffering wife.

Hokusai's first book of sketches was published in 1800 and showed various scenes in and around Edo. That same year the artist produced a novel, which he sent off to a publisher accompanied by the self-portrait here. (Hokusai's head is shaved in the manner of Japanese artists and writers of that time.) Both books achieved a popular success, but, characteristically, Hokusai never bothered to open the packets of money sent by his publisher. If a creditor stopped by, he would hand over a packet or two without counting it. Throughout his life he remained indifferent to money and despite his accomplishments was usually at the brink of starvation.

As Hokusai's fame spread he was often invited to give public drawing demonstrations. Legends of his virtuosity abound. On one occasion, the story goes, he stood before the assembled crowd outside a temple and drew an immense image of the Buddha, using a brush as big as a broom. Another time he drew birds in flight on a single grain of rice. Hokusai's sense of humor, never far below the surface, came bubbling out when he was asked to perform for the Shogun (the military governor). As onlookers gathered at the palace, Hokusai spread a large piece of paper on the floor, painted blue watercolor waves across it, then took a

live rooster, dipped its feet in red paint, and allowed it to run across the painting. Bowing respectfully, he announced to the Shogun that this was a picture of red maple leaves floating down the river.[1]

Though well aware of his own skill, Hokusai often amused himself by pretending modesty. In the preface to one of his books he wrote: "From the age of six I had a mania for drawing. At seventy-three I had learned a little . . . in consequence when I am eighty I shall have made still more progress, and when I am a hundred and ten, everything I do . . . will be alive." But the artist did not make it quite that far. As he lay on his deathbed, he cried out: "If Heaven would grant me ten more years!" And then: "If Heaven would grant me *five* more years, I would become a real painter."[2] His grave is marked by a slab on which is carved the last of his names: Gwakio Rojin—Old Man Mad About Drawing.

Katsushika Hokusai. *Self-Portrait,*
from *The Tactics of General Oven.* 1800. Woodcut, $5\frac{7}{8} \times 8\frac{7}{8}''$.
The Art Institute of Chicago (Ryerson Collection).

257. Pablo Picasso.
Seated Woman (after Cranach).
1958. Color linoleum cut,
$25\frac{11}{16} \times 21\frac{5}{16}''$.
Collection, The Museum
of Modern Art, New York
(gift of Mr. and Mrs.
Daniel Saidenberg).

schoolchildren (or for greeting cards), but Picasso never let such preconceived ideas interfere with his creativity. His color linocut depicting a *Seated Woman (after Cranach)* **(257)** is, as the title implies, an interpretation of a painting by the 16th-century German artist Lucas Cranach, but a more abstract treatment than Cranach could ever have imagined. The splendid colors result from printing with several linoleum blocks, just as is done with color wood blocks. The richly detailed textures in the hair, arm bands, and jewelry may have been made easier to achieve by the relatively soft linoleum.

WOOD ENGRAVING

Wood engraving differs in several aspects from woodcut. For one thing, it is done on the end grain of the wood. If you imagine a board, say a 2 × 4, the long, smooth plank sides would be used for woodcut, but the grainy cut end would be used for wood engraving. The end grain can be cut in any direction without chipping or splintering, unlike the plank sides.

A distinctive characteristic of wood engraving is that it is a "white-line" technique. The tool used for cutting makes fine, narrow grooves in the wood, and these grooves, which do not take the ink, result in white lines when the inked wood block is pressed to paper. Woodcut, by contrast, usually has larger, broader, more irregular uninked white areas because of the coarser tools that gouge out background areas.

During the 19th century wood engraving was used widely for printing books and journals. The cut end of the wood could easily be prepared to be "type high"—the same height ($\frac{7}{8}$ inch) as the wooden alphabet letters that printers worked with at the time. Therefore, both images and text could conveniently be printed together. Photography was a young art, and methods for reproducing photographs had not been perfected. Most illustrations still were made in the form of prints. In the United States this art of illustration was dominated by Winslow Homer, who worked for several periodicals during the latter half of the 1800s. Homer depicted events of the Civil War, important political figures, and scenes of everyday life (258).

Intaglio

The second major category of printmaking techniques is *intaglio* (from an Italian word meaning "to cut"), which includes several related methods. Intaglio is exactly the reverse of relief, in that the areas meant to print are *below* the surface of the printing plate (250). The artist uses a sharp tool or acid to make depressions—lines or grooves—in a metal plate (259). When the plate is inked, the ink sinks into the depressions. Then the surface of the plate is wiped clean. When dampened paper is brought into contact with the plate under pressure, the paper is pushed into the depressions to pick up the image.

There are five basic types of intaglio printing: engraving, drypoint, mezzotint, etching, and aquatint.

ENGRAVING

The oldest of the intaglio techniques, engraving developed from the medieval practice of incising (cutting) linear designs in armor and other metal surfaces. The armorer's art had achieved a high level of expertise, and it was just a short step to realizing that the engraved lines could be filled with ink and the design transferred to paper.

left: 258. Winslow Homer. *In Came a Storm of Wind, Rain and Spray—and Portia.* Illustration in *The Galaxy,* December 1869. Wood engraving, $4\frac{3}{8} \times 6\frac{1}{2}''$.

above: 259. Plate-making methods for intaglio printing: engraving, drypoint, mezzotint, etching, aquatint.

260. William Hogarth. *The Marriage Contract,* from *Marriage à la Mode.* 1745. Engraving, $13\frac{15}{16} \times 17\frac{1}{2}''$.

The basic tool of engraving is the ***burin,*** a sharp, V-shaped instrument used to cut lines into the metal plate **(259)**. Shallow cuts produce a light, thin line, while deeper gouges in the metal result in a thicker and darker line. Engraving is closely related to drawing in pen or sharp pencil in both technique and the visual effect of the work. Looking at a reproduction it is hard to tell an engraving from a fine pen or pencil drawing. As in these drawing media, modeling and shading effects usually are achieved by hatching, cross-hatching, or stippling **(106)**.

From the beginning of the 16th century one great benefit of engraving was the dissemination of artistic ideas and innovations. Because prints were circulated throughout Europe, noted artists were able to study each other's work and learn from one another with far greater ease than ever before. Previously, an artist's masterworks were known only to those who lived in the city where a given work was kept or who traveled to that city. Journeys to Italy from the northern countries were common; those from south to north less so. Engraved copies enabled artists to examine the work of their distant colleagues without leaving home, and soon influences among artists occurred more rapidly. Art styles of the various regions gradually became less distinctly different.

During the 18th century engraved copies of well-known paintings became sought-after items for middle-class people. This development came about largely through the efforts of the English artist William Hogarth. Hogarth is best known for three large series of paintings—*The Rake's Progress, The Harlot's Progress,* and *Marriage à la Mode.* Each series was a "picture story" with a moral, and each portrayed the progress of an individual (or in the last case, a couple) from innocent beginnings through increasing sin to complete ruin. Being short of funds, Hogarth hit on the idea of making engraved copies of the paintings, copyrighting the engravings, and selling them cheaply in great quantities. This plan worked splendidly. (It also formed the basis for English copyright law in regard to art.)

The first scene in *Marriage à la Mode* **(260)** sets the stage for eventual disaster. A poverty-stricken nobleman is marrying off his son to the daughter of a rich but middle-class merchant. The two fathers settle the details of the marriage contract as they would any business deal. Meanwhile, the engaged couple, at left, ignore each other. Hogarth is not subtle in pointing out that this is not a love match. In fact, the future bride is already responding to the attentions of Counsellor Silvertongue, the lawyer, who will soon become her lover. Later scenes in the series portray infidelities by both partners, great excess of all kinds, a duel, and ultimately the death of the husband.

Hogarth's satire may seem a bit heavy-handed to us today, but his eye for the telling detail—such as the groom's father having a bandaged foot as a result of gout, a disease supposedly caused by excesses of food and drink—must have greatly amused his public. Engraving was the ideal technique for Hogarth, for its precision enabled him to capture a wealth of detail. Not surprisingly, Hogarth's satirical prints were extremely popular with members of the working class.

DRYPOINT

Drypoint is similar to engraving, except that the cutting instrument used is a drypoint needle. The artist draws on the plate, usually a copper plate, almost as freely as one can draw on paper with a pencil. As the needle scratches across the plate, it raises a *burr*, or thin ridge of metal **(259)**. This burr holds the ink, making a line that is softer and less sharply detailed than an engraved line. If engraving is like fine pen drawing, sharp and distinct, then drypoint is more like drawing in soft pencil or crayon, with slightly blurred edges. This soft, sketchy quality is obvious in the figures of Reuben Nakian's drypoint *Myths and Legends* **(261)**.

MEZZOTINT

Mezzotint is a reverse process, in which the artist works from dark to light. To prepare a mezzotint plate, the artist first roughens the entire plate with a sharp tool called a *rocker.* If the plate were inked and printed after this stage, it would print a sheet of paper entirely black, because each roughened spot would catch and hold the ink. Lighter tones can be created only by smoothing or rubbing out these rough spots so as not to trap the ink. To do this, the artist goes over portions of the plate with a burnisher (a smoothing tool) and/or a scraper to wear down the roughened burrs **(259)**. Where the burrs are partially removed, the plate will print intermediate values. Highlights—very light values—print in areas where the burrs are smoothed away.

The major advantage of mezzotint is that it is capable of subtle gradations from dark to light. Whereas engraving and drypoint are predominantly line techniques, mezzotint is based on values. We see this effect in Peter

261. Reuben Nakian. *Myths and Legends.* c. 1980. Drypoint, $19\frac{3}{4} \times 25\frac{5}{8}''$. Courtesy DiLaurenti Gallery, New York.

Pelham's portrait *Cotton Mather* (**262**), one of the earliest prints made in the American colonies. So finely modeled is this portrait of the great Puritan leader that, in reproduction, we might almost mistake it for an oil painting. The face, in particular, is wonderfully naturalistic because of the skillful use of values. This naturalism would be hard to achieve in an engraving or in one of the relief processes.

ETCHING

Etching is done with acids, which "eat" lines and depressions into a metal plate much as sharp tools cut those depressions in the other methods. To make an etching the artist first coats the entire printing plate with an acid-resistant substance called a **ground,** made from beeswax, asphalt, and other materials. Next, the artist draws on the coated plate with an etching needle. The needle removes the ground, exposing the bare metal in areas meant to print (**259**). Then the entire plate is dipped in acid. Only the portions of the plate exposed by the needle are eaten into by the acid, leaving the rest of the plate intact. Finally, the ground is removed, and the plate is inked and printed. Etched lines are not as sharp and precise as those made by the engraver's burin because the biting action of the acid is slightly irregular.

Rembrandt, who was a prolific printmaker, made hundreds of etchings. Unfortunately, many of his plates were not canceled or destroyed. Long after his death, and long after the plates had worn down badly, people greedy to produce yet more "Rembrandts" struck impressions from the plates. These later impressions lack detail and give us little idea of what the artist intended. To get a true sense of Rembrandt's genius as an etcher, we must look at prints that are known to be early impressions, such as the magnificent portrait of *Arnold Tholinx* (**263**). In this work the artist brought to bear his most refined skills, accomplishing the fully rounded modeling entirely with hatching and cross-hatching (**106**). The face is serious, the man almost severe, possibly impatient with having his portrait done. Rembrandt's triumph is in conveying not just the physical image but the personality as well. Perhaps no one else could give us such insight into character in this demanding medium.

Another master of the etching technique was the Spanish artist Francisco de Goya. Goya made several ambitious series of prints, and he worked in all the various print media, sometimes, as here, in more than one tech-

left: 262. Peter Pelham. *Cotton Mather.* 1727. Mezzotint, 11 × 15″.

right: 263. Rembrandt. *Arnold Tholinx.* c. 1656. Etching, drypoint, and engraving; 17 13/16 × 5 7/8″. Musée de la Ville de Paris, Musée du Petit-Palais, Paris.

224

nique for a single print. The soft, occasionally irregular line of etching gives it a rather "dark," brooding quality, suited to Goya's political and social satire. *Hasta la Muerte* (*Until Death*, **264**) is from one of his major series, called *Los Caprichos*, meaning caprices, whims, eccentricities, freakishness. We see a grotesque old woman primping absurdly for her seventy-fifth birthday party, reflected even more horribly by her mirror. The look of satisfaction on her face suggests that *she* does not see the ugliness that we and the mocking onlookers see. Goya is poking none-too-gentle fun at her vanity, her girlish costume, her attempt at painting a very faded lily. The message of this print might be: "We do not see ourselves as others see us."

If etching can produce the dark, gruesome qualities that Goya was looking for, it is also capable of more delicate effects, as in the work of contemporary artist Donald Saff. *Our Lady of Sarcasm* (**265**) presents an airy female figure apparently floating in a garden of pale flowers. There are many ambiguities in this etching. Is the woman reclining, or is she drifting gently from right to left? Why are the beautifully drawn flowers at left canceled out by the harsh black scribbling at right? Why is the woman's expression so melancholy, why is her form barely suggested, and what is the round ball halfway down her figure? Above all, what is the meaning in the title *Our Lady of Sarcasm*? These mysteries draw us back again and again to study the print. We may understand imperfectly and yet be hypnotized by the elusive image.

AQUATINT

A variation on the etching process, aquatint is a way of achieving flat areas of tone—gray values or intermediate values of color. To understand why this is desirable, we need only look back at the portrait of *Arnold Tholinx* (**263**). In that etching Rembrandt created the *illusion* of tone and shading by means of lines, hatched and cross-hatched. But aquatint allows the intaglio printmaker to produce real, not simulated tone.

left: 264. Francisco de Goya. *Hasta la Muerte*, from *Los Caprichos*. 1797–98. Etching and aquatint, first edition; $8\frac{1}{2} \times 6''$. Meadows Museum, Southern Methodist University, Dallas (Algur H. Meadows Collection).

right: 265. Donald Saff. *Our Lady of Sarcasm*. 1978. Etching with hand coloring, $24 \times 19''$. Collection the author.

To prepare the plate, the artist first dusts it with particles of resin. Several methods are available to control where and how thickly the resin is distributed on the plate. Then the plate is heated, so the resin sticks to it. When the plate is dipped in acid, the acid bites everywhere there is no resin, all around the particles **(259)**. For instance, if the particles are thinly dusted and far apart, the acid will be able to bite into larger areas of the plate, but if the particles are close together the acid will have limited space to penetrate. Different tones, from light to dark, can be produced depending on the density of the particles, the length of time the plate is held in the acid, or the strength of the acid bath.

Because aquatint does not print lines but only areas of tone it is nearly always combined with one or more of the other intaglio techniques—drypoint, etching, or engraving. The 19th-century American artist Mary Cassatt, who was much influenced by the flat areas of color in Japanese woodcuts, adopted aquatint for a great many of her prints. *In the Omnibus* **(266)** has broad areas of soft tone in the women's dresses, the baby's bunting, and part of the background, but the faces and other details have been precisely rendered in drypoint and etching.

By combining techniques the intaglio artist can get almost any result he or she wishes. Because the artist can achieve effects ranging from the most precisely drawn lines to the most subtle areas of tone, the possibilities for imagery are much greater than in the relief methods. We turn now, however, to a branch of printmaking that is even more flexible in its effects.

Lithography

All the major printmaking categories except one have origins going far back into history, having developed from other art forms, such as decoration of armor, printing on fabrics, and so on. That one exception is lithography. Lithography was invented in a particular place at a particular time by a particular individual—a man named Alois Senefelder.

Senefelder was a young German actor and playwright living in Munich during the 1790s. Frustrated by the expense of publishing his plays, he began experimenting with variations on the etching process as a cheap method of reproducing them. He was too poor to invest much money in copper plates, so he tried working on the smooth Bavarian limestones that lined the streets of Munich, which he excavated from the street and brought to his studio. One day, when he was experimenting with ingredients for drawing on the stone, his laundress appeared unexpectedly, and Senefelder hastily wrote out his laundry list on the stone, using his new combination of materials—wax, soap, and lampblack. Later, he decided to try immersing the stone in acid. To his delight he found that his laundry list appeared in slight relief on the stone. This event paved the way for his development of the lithographic process. While the relief aspect eventually ceased to play a role, the groundwork for lithography had been laid.

Lithography is a ***planographic*** process, which means that the printing surface is flat—not raised as in relief, or depressed as in intaglio **(250)**. It depends, instead, upon the principle that oil and water do not mix. To make a lithographic print the artist first draws the image on the stone with a greasy material—usually a grease-based lithographic crayon composed of such materials as wax, soap, and shellac. (Senefelder's Bavarian limestone is still in use as a surface, but aluminum plates are also common.) Then the whole stone is treated with a light acid bath to fix the image and is soaked in water. Water is absorbed by the stone only in the areas *not* coated with grease. When the stone is inked, the greasy ink sticks to the greasy image areas and is repelled by the water-soaked background areas. Although the printing surface, stone or plate, is flat, only the image areas print. (This book was printed by a mechanical version of lithography, known as ***offset lithography***.)

The potential of lithography was recognized almost immediately. By this method artists could create a wide range of effects, both linear and tonal, with relative ease and consequently low cost. The general public thus could be supplied with inexpensive, high-quality prints suitable for framing. Many companies on both sides of the Atlantic went into the business of making lithographs, but in the United States one firm so dominated the market that its name became almost automatically associated with the word "lithograph." That firm's name was Currier & Ives.

Nathaniel Currier established his lithographic company in New York City in 1834, and in 1857 James Merritt Ives joined him as a partner. During the nearly seventy years the firm was in business it produced an estimated seven thousand lithographs on a wide variety of subjects. There was something for every taste—Civil War battles, landscapes, religious themes, famous disasters (especially fires, which allowed for lurid red effects in the sky), great trains and ships, scenes from the American West, sports (from prize fighting to fishing), and many other categories.

Currier & Ives devised an ingenious system for manufacturing the prints. They employed a great many artists to do the original drawings, after which the image was transferred to stone by professional lithographers. Although color printing, which required several stones, was feasible, Currier & Ives rarely used this expensive method. Instead, after the prints had been run off in black and white, each one was individually hand-colored in assembly-line fashion by platoons of young women sitting at long tables—one color per person. The colorists were supposed to follow color keys supplied by the artist, but quite often—perhaps to break the tedium of the job—they would select colors according to the whim of the moment. A catalogue from 1860 lists prices ranging from 8¢ to $3.75 for each print. In today's auction market a good Currier & Ives lithograph might sell for many thousands of dollars.

One of the most talented and certainly the busiest of Currier & Ives' artists was Flora Bond (Fanny) Palmer. During her career with the firm Palmer made an astonishing number of prints, on all the various subjects. Her detailed drawing style, plus an instinct for what the public would like, put her work greatly in demand. *American Express Train* (267) shows a favorite subject, drawn with her usual attention to detail.

left: **266.** Mary Cassatt.
In the Omnibus. 1891.
Color aquatint with drypoint and soft-ground, $14\frac{15}{16} \times 10\frac{1}{2}''$.
The Cleveland Museum of Art (bequest of Charles T. Brooks).

below: **267.** Flora Bond Palmer, for Currier & Ives.
American Express Train. 1864.
Lithograph.
Museum of the City of New York (Harry T. Peters Collection).

Most of the Currier & Ives artists were anonymous. It was the firm name that mattered, not the names of individual artists. Even Fanny Palmer signed few of her lithographs; later experts have identified her prints by analyzing the drawing style. By the end of the century, however, a number of well-known artists, especially in Europe, had taken up the new process. The Frenchman Henri de Toulouse-Lautrec has become closely identified with the lithograph because of one of those rare perfect convergences: He had the right artistic style for the right medium at the right time.

As we saw in Chapter 1, Lautrec practically invented the color lithographic poster, with the designs he made to advertise the Moulin Rouge nightclub and its performers. *La Goulue at the Moulin Rouge* (268) is a superior example. One of the featured dancers at the Moulin Rouge, La Goulue (the glutton) is shown doing the can-can before an audience rendered in silhouette. Lautrec understood well that a poster must, above all, catch the eye. Its message is simple: Come to the Moulin Rouge, where you will have a good time. The influence of Japanese prints is obvious in the flattened forms, the broad color areas, and the sharply uptilted perspective, which is visible especially in the floorboards. Despite the apparent foreground (the man in silhouette), middle ground, and background, we get little sense of spatial depth. The composition is meant to be flat and decorative. Lithography provided Lautrec with the means to achieve, with relative ease, both the definite outline and the flat areas of tone. In all, the effect is frivolous, bohemian, and just a trifle sinister—like the Moulin Rouge itself.

Lithography also was well adapted to the stark, intense, brooding imagery of the Norwegian artist Edvard Munch (269). Munch's lithograph *Sin* is

left: 268.
Henri de Toulouse-Lautrec.
La Goulue at the Moulin Rouge.
1891. Color lithograph,
5′5″ × 3′10″.
Philadelphia Museum of Art
(given by Mr. and Mrs.
R. Sturgis Ingersoll).

right: 269. Edvard Munch.
Sin. 1901.
Color lithograph, 27¾ × 15½″.
Rijksmuseum, Amsterdam.

Edvard Munch

1863–1944

The picture reproduced here, *Self-Portrait between Clock and Bed*, was completed by Edvard Munch two years before his death. Munch chose to portray himself in light of the short time left to him (symbolized by the clock), beside the bed on which he would die. It is not surprising that a man in his eightieth year was anticipating death, but for Munch it was nothing new. Death obsessed him throughout his life and was an ongoing presence in his art.

Born in a small town in Norway, Munch was raised in Christiania, as Oslo was then called. When he was five his mother died, and nine years later his beloved older sister died of tuberculosis. These events haunted the artist and no doubt contributed much to his extreme anguish and anxiety. At seventeen he began art studies in Christiania, becoming involved as well in the rather morbid, sexually permissive bohemian life of the city. In 1885 Munch paid the first of many visits to Paris. There he saw, and was influenced by, the work of the Impressionists and Post-Impressionists, especially that of Paul Gauguin. Although Munch borrowed aspects of painting techniques, his themes remained personal ones—death and dying, generalized anxiety, the despair of loneliness and abandonment, the passions between men and women, the sexual force of Woman as a source of terror.

Munch's first one-artist show, in Berlin in 1892, was a disaster. His powerful subject matter and (to onlookers) harsh painting style caused an uproar, and the show was closed within a week. Nevertheless, the artist decided to take a studio in Berlin, where he remained for several years. The sixteen years following the Berlin exhibition, spent mainly in Germany and Paris, were Munch's most fertile period. It was then that he developed his interest in prints—woodcuts, lithographs, etchings—of which he eventually made more than seven hundred. Prints allowed him to explore, in many variations, the subjects that absorbed him. Often a subject he had tried in painting became starker, more disturbing, more intensely colored in print versions.

By 1908 Munch had become internationally famous, but his personal life was far from tranquil. Alcoholic, worn out with hard work, overstimulated by the bohemian clique in Berlin, tormented by at least one miserable love affair—Munch suffered a nervous

breakdown and checked himself into a sanitarium in Copenhagen. There he underwent electric shock therapy to counteract effects on his brain of "persistent battering from an obsessive idea."[3]

If there is such a thing as a "Norwegian temperament"—brooding, melancholy, dark as the long nights of northern winter—Munch had it. Certainly it is difficult to visualize imagery like his coming from a French or Italian artist. After the breakdown, Munch's torments eased. However, the output from his later years lacks the power of the Berlin/Paris period. It is as though the therapy that healed him took away all the passion, and the passion was necessary to his art. Perhaps he understood this. As he himself said, "I shouldn't like to be without suffering. How much of my art I owe to suffering!"[4]

Edvard Munch. *Self-Portrait between Clock and Bed.*
c. 1942. Oil on canvas, 5'7⅜" × 3'11⅝".
Oslo Kommunes Kunstsamlinger.

270. Jim Dine.
The Yellow Robe. 1980.
Lithograph, 4'2" × 2'11".
Courtesy Pace Prints, New York.

done almost entirely in red, symbolic of the title, and we find it shocking to see such an intense color used so freely. Because the green eyes are the only contrast, they rivet our attention. (Red and green, being complementary colors, jar against one another to increase the tension in this print.) The woman's eyes seem at once to be looking inward and gazing at some dreadful horror. This image associates female sexuality with evil and shame—a theme that obsessed Munch throughout his life. Of course, the sense of evil and shame is inherent in the artist, not necessarily in his subjects. Women's hair, especially in quantity as here, was seen by Munch as both an allurement and a potential danger for men. This effect of voluptuous hair—gorgeous yet menacing—was enhanced by the free-drawing capabilities of the lithographic crayon on stone.

A number of contemporary artists who are best known as painters have taken up lithography as a means of broadening their range of expression. Among them is Jim Dine. In recent years Dine has used lithography and other printmaking media to explore the expressive possibilities of a series of motifs, or repeated images. During the late 1970s and early 1980s his motif often was a disembodied bathrobe, representative of himself **(270)**. Celebrated in an oversized print (there are woodcut versions as well as lithographs), the bathrobe seems a commanding presence, a personality and force unto itself.

Lithography has been a favorite technique of contemporary artists because it offers so much freedom in drawing and design. The technical limits of the medium are few. Our final branch of printmaking, however, gives even greater freedom in one particular respect—the use of color.

Screenprinting

To understand the basic principle of screenprinting, you need only picture the lettering stencils used by schoolchildren. The stencil is a piece of cardboard from which the forms of the alphabet letters have been cut out. To trace the letters onto paper, you simply place the stencil over the paper and fill in the holes with pencil or ink.

Today's art screenprinting works much the same way. The screen is a fine mesh of silk or synthetic fiber mounted in a frame, rather like a window screen. (Silk is the traditional material, so the process is often called **silkscreen** or **serigraphy**—"silk writing.") Working from drawings, the printmaker blocks (*stops out*) areas in the screen that are *not* meant to print by plugging up the holes, usually with some kind of glue, so that no ink can pass through. Then the screen is placed over paper, and the ink is forced through the mesh with a tool called a **squeegee.** Only the areas not stopped out allow the ink to pass through and print on paper **(250)**.

To make a color screenprint, the artist prepares one screen for each color. On the "blue" screen, for example, all areas not meant to print in blue are stopped out, and so on for each of the other colors. The preparation of multiple color screens is relatively easy and inexpensive. For this reason it is not unusual to see serigraphs printed in ten, twenty, or more colors. This color flexibility would be very difficult to achieve in any of the other methods. (Imagine preparing twenty-five Bavarian limestones, each weighing many pounds, for a single color lithograph!)

Andy Warhol's portrait of *Marilyn* **(271)** exploits another capability of screenprinting—its potential for flat areas of color. A broad area of unshaded color can be achieved simply by not stopping out the screen in that area. In this portrait of Marilyn Monroe—a favorite and recurring theme—Warhol paints the film star's face in one flat wash of color to emphasize the eyes and especially the mouth. The background also is flat color, throwing the head into stark contrast, drawing our attention to the famous blond hair and the seductive mouth. Some critics have suggested the colors are meant to show the artificiality of Monroe as sex goddess, the tinsel in the "Tinseltown" of Hollywood. But Warhol himself said this: "As for whether it's symbolical to paint Monroe in such violent colors: it's beauty, and she's beautiful and if something's beautiful it's pretty colors, that's all."[5]

271. Andy Warhol. *Marilyn.* 1967. Serigraph on paper, 36″ square.
Copyright 1991 the Estate and Foundation of Andy Warhol/ A.R.S., New York.

Andy Warhol

1928–1987

When friends recall the most visible and colorful of the Pop artists, they often remark that he was two people. There was Andy Warhol—media celebrity, high priest of commercial and show-business imagery, wearer of bizarre white wigs, leader to an entourage of quirky New York types, maker of sexually explicit cult films. Then there was Andrew Warhola—child of struggling Czech immigrants, devout Roman Catholic, prolific worker, introvert often paralyzed by shyness, adoring son who, as an adult, brought his mother to live with him for twenty years.

Warhol, born Warhola, grew up in Pittsburgh and attended Carnegie Institute of Technology. After graduation in 1949 he moved to New York, where he launched what would become a highly successful career as a commercial artist. Over the next ten years his employers included most of the chic fashion magazines and elegant Fifth Avenue stores, for which he designed advertisements, promotional pieces, and window displays. He was also—ironically, in view of his later adventures—one of the illustrators for the first edition of *Amy Vanderbilt's Complete Book of Etiquette.*

By 1960 the artist and his style had found each other. Warhol, the gifted commercial artist, slipped into Pop, the "fine art" style of commerical images, without missing a beat. For a decade Pop would remain a dominant art wave in the United States, and Warhol sailed on the crest of that wave. The themes with which he is most closely associated appeared repeatedly in prints and paintings: Marilyn Monroe, Elizabeth Taylor, Jackie Kennedy, and of course the famous Coke bottles and Campbell's soup cans **(174)**.

A turning point in Warhol's career occurred in 1963, when the artist moved into a new studio in New York. A friend decorated the entire space in silver paint and aluminum foil, a large group of acquaintances and admirers and hangers-on converged, and thus was born—the Factory. At the Factory Warhol continued his enormous output of prints, paintings, and sculptures. At the Factory he directed the production of many avant-garde (some would say outlandish) films, featuring actors with names like Viva, Ultra Violet, and International Velvet. And at the Factory, in 1968, a

woman who announced herself as the founder of SCUM (Society for Cutting Up Men) shot Warhol and nearly killed him.

Many observers felt that Warhol ran out of steam after the shooting, that his art no longer showed the edge and excitement it once had. Nevertheless, he worked steadily, developing his familiar themes and some new ones, until his death at age fifty-eight, of complications following gall bladder surgery.

Warhol often liked to say he was a "machine." He claimed to be devoid of emotion or feeling, just a machine that produced a product, called art, in a place called a Factory. One of his much-quoted statements sums this up. "If you want to know all about Andy Warhol, just look at the surface: of my paintings and films and me, and there I am. There's nothing behind it."[6]

Robert Mapplethorpe. *Andy Warhol.* 1986. Photograph. Copyright © 1986 The Estate of Robert Mapplethorpe.

Special Techniques

There is one major exception to the rule, stated at the beginning of this chapter, that prints are an art of multiples. That exception is the **monotype,** or **monoprint.** Monotypes are made by an indirect process, like any other print, but, as the prefix "mono" implies, only one print results. To make a monotype, the artist draws on a metal plate or some other smooth surface, often with diluted oil paints. Then the plate is run through a press to transfer the image to paper. Or the artist may simply place a sheet of paper on the plate and hand-rub it to transfer the image. Either way, the original is destroyed or so altered that there can be no duplicate impressions. If a series of prints is planned, the artist must do more work on the plate.

Monotype offers several technical advantages. The range of colors is unlimited, as is the potential for lines or tones. No problems arise with cutting against a grain or into resistant metal. One can work as freely as in a direct process like painting or drawing. You may wonder, then, why *not* simply draw or paint? Why bother with the indirect touch of the print? There can be as many reasons as there are monotype artists, but we might list a few. Monotype offers the "accidental" quality of the press as intermediary; even when the original is finished, one cannot be quite sure how the print will look when it comes through the press. Colors absorb into the paper differently, giving a "printed" effect many artists seek. There is the potential for working over the printed image to create a "layered" appearance. Probably the best reason is the simplest: artists love to experiment with techniques that expand their expressive range.

The French artist Edgar Degas **(146)** was particularly fond of the monotype and made hundreds of such prints. In the last decade or so the technique has enjoyed a new surge of popularity, encouraging many contemporary artists to explore the monotype. In Sam Francis' *Untitled* work **(272)** the splashes and splotches and swirls of lush color show the exuberance that can be conveyed by this indirect medium.

While some contemporary artists are drawn to relatively simple printing methods, others are pursuing ever more complex techniques. The ability

272. Sam Francis. *Untitled.* 1981. Monotype in oil and dry pigments, 22″ square. Courtesy Christie's, New York.

to combine several print processes in the same image broadens the artist's options significantly. Frank Stella's *La penna di hu* (273), for instance, was made by combining etching, relief, woodcut, screenprint, and other stencil techniques, in twenty-nine colors. Although not actually three-dimensional (unlike many of Stella's works, which have areas projecting forward in depth), *La penna di hu* has an exceptionally rich surface texture and creates a strong sense of visual three-dimensionality.

above: **273.** Frank Stella. *La Penna di hu*. 1988. 29-color etching, relief, woodcut, screenprint, stencil, hand-colored on TGL handmade paper; $4'7\frac{1}{2}'' \times 5'6''$. Collection, Walker Art Center, Minneapolis, courtesy Tyler Graphic Archives.

right: **274.** Mary Frank. *Untitled*, from *The Atelier Project*. 1985. High-relief cast-paper multiple, $21\frac{3}{4} \times 29''$. Collection, Neuberger Museum, State University of New York at Purchase (gift of Division of Visual Arts, State University of New York at Purchase).

275. Red Grooms. *Gertrude.*
1975. Color lithograph
on Arches-Cover, cut out, glued,
and mounted in Plexiglas box;
$19\frac{1}{4} \times 22 \times 10''$.
© 1991 Red Grooms/A.R.S.,
New York.

Stella's work is printed on handmade paper—an increasingly common practice. We may find it difficult to think of paper as being "made." For most of us, paper comes in tablets or sheets or rolls, and we don't give much thought to how it got that way. But paper is composed of vegetable fibers, pounded into a pulp and then pressed into sheets. There is no reason why it cannot be pressed into other forms—forms that are quite different from the pages of this text or a memo pad.

One artist who has explored the realm of cast paper is Mary Frank, whose untitled print **(274)** has been further embellished with imagery that may remind you of the early cave drawings **(3)**. Like most other prints, these cast-paper works can be duplicated for an edition, because the mold (usually of rubber) is reusable. The image consists not only of lines and colors, but is an actual three-dimensional impression.

Once prints start expanding into the third dimension, there is no stopping them. Contemporary printmakers are masters of the "why not try . . . ?" Take an artist whose imagination and sense of humor are manic, who understands the lithographic process, who appreciates pop-up books and paper dolls—and you get *Gertrude* **(275)**. Red Grooms made *Gertrude*—the writer and art collector Gertrude Stein (p. 25)—from two lithographic prints, cut, folded, and mounted in three dimensions within an acrylic box. She (we cannot think of the work as "it") is a multiple, but she might just as well have fit into the sculpture chapter of this text. There she sits, pudgy in her flowered blouse in her pudgy flowered chair—an example of where prints can go if artists don't take themselves too seriously.

If you had any doubt at the beginning of this chapter that printmaking is a lively art, chances are you have changed your mind by now. In some ways it is an art ideally suited to our life style. The painter, the sculptor, the architect—all these make *one* work of art at a time, that will reside in one place. People who want to see the original must journey to do so. But the print made in an edition of a hundred will reside in a hundred different places and be enjoyed by thousands of people. Truly, the print allows nearly anyone to corner a small piece of the world of art.

The Camera Arts: Photography, Film, and Video

A room with a view. This phrase may make you think of real estate or of a classic novel, but we may borrow it here, because it describes the essence of a camera. *Camera* is the Latin word for "room," and it is not farfetched to think of any camera as being a little room with a view—real or imaginary—of the outside world.

The desire to record and preserve images is probably as old as civilization. In the 4th century B.C. the Greek philosopher Aristotle understood the most basic principle of the camera, for he noted the ability of light, under controlled circumstances, to duplicate an image. Aristotle lacked the technology to exploit this phenomenon, and so did many generations after him. In fact, not until the 16th century did anyone construct a practical device to harness the image-transferring property of light. That device came to be known as the **camera obscura.**

You can make a *camera obscura* yourself. Find a light-tight room, even a closet or a very large cardboard box. Arrange for a small hole, no bigger than the diameter of a pencil, in one wall of the room to admit light. Inside, hold a sheet of white paper a few inches from the hole. You will see an image of the scene outside the room projected on the paper—upside-down and rather blurry, but recognizable. That is the principle of the *camera obscura*, which simply means "dark room."

Artists of the Renaissance welcomed the *camera obscura* with enthusiasm, because it aided them in achieving a major goal—to reproduce the natural world as accurately as possible, with correct proportions and perspective. By the 16th century the mechanism had come into use as a drawing tool; once an image had been captured in the *camera obscura*, the artist could trace over it, thus ensuring an accurate rendering of the scene. A portable shack serving as a *camera obscura* was sketched in cutaway (one wall and the roof removed for illustration purposes) in the 17th century **(276)**.

Today we have come a long way from the *camera obscura*, but its principles remain intact. The modern camera is still dependent on controlled light, and it is still a room with a view. That view, however, may be anything the artist chooses to make it, from a straightforward recording of the natural scene to the most elaborate special effects the mind can conceive. Let us now consider the camera arts—photography, film, and video—and their unique view of the world.

Photography

Photography is the art form that best demonstrates a basic truth: Artistry resides not in the hands but in the head. People who cannot draw well sometimes think that painters have some unusual skill in their hands, just as a singer may have an exceptional voice. But while some art forms do demand manual skill, the difference between a merely competent mechanical performance and a great work of art lies not in the artist's hands but in the brain—in the artistic inspiration that tells the hands what to do.

It is this confusion between mechanical skill and inspiration that has caused some people to question photography as an art form. After all, painters and sculptors *create* forms; photographers only *find and record* forms. Nevertheless, just as the painter's brain tells the hands what marks to make on canvas, so the photographer's brain interprets what is seen by the eyes and tells the camera what to do. Whereas the average person walks through the world seeing trees and buildings and people, the creative photographer walks through the world seeing compositions—possible photographs. We might almost say that the photographer has an invisible frame somewhere behind the eyes—a frame that is constantly composing pictures.

The photo-collages of David Hockney help to show how dependent an image may be on the creative instincts of the artist. In *The Scrabble Game* **(277)** Hockney portrays an ordinary scene, a scene duplicated in thousands of

right: 276. *Camera obscura,* in cutaway view. 1646. Engraving. International Museum of Photography at George Eastman House, Rochester, N.Y.

below: 277. David Hockney. *The Scrabble Game, January 1, 1983.* 1983. Photographic collage, 3'3" × 4'10". © David Hockney.

living rooms every day. Four people play a game of Scrabble. (The fourth is the artist himself, who slyly introduces his presence by showing his left hand, his cigarette in the ash tray, and his rack of letter tiles.) To capture the little drama of the game, Hockney combines dozens of photographs, each showing a portion of the scene. He has said, "It's our movement that tells us we're alive."[1] And so he follows the movement—the players thoughtful, stumped, triumphant, pleased, the hands tense or jumping to fill in a word, the cat at far left briefly interested then turning away to wash its face—the collage of moments that make up a friendly game.

But Hockney doesn't show us everything. He doesn't show us much of the room in which the game takes place. He doesn't include the lower halves of the players' bodies. (Are their feet tensed and twisted in concentration?) He doesn't tell us about the relationship of the players, or who is winning, or even whose turn it is. He doesn't tell us what he is going to do with his high-scoring letter "Q." He leaves out a thousand details that might have been included.

An old adage says that "the camera can't lie," and perhaps that is so, but the photographer can. To state that idea more positively, the photographer can show us whatever truth he or she wishes to show, and that is what Hockney has done with *The Scrabble Game.* The "truth" of his picture is what he has chosen to include.

We can apply this same idea to a single photographic image, because every situation in the visible world contains many truths, many thousands of details. Each time the photographer points a camera, he or she makes a great many decisions: what to include in the picture, what to leave out beyond the edges, what to emphasize, which angle to shoot from, where to give the sharpest focus. As we shall see throughout this chapter, the truth of a picture is whatever the creative photographer selects for us to see, selects as one particular view of the world.

THE STILL CAMERA AND ITS BEGINNINGS

Despite the amazing sophistication of modern photographic equipment, the basic mechanism of the camera is simple, and it is no different in theory from that of the *camera obscura.* A camera is a light-tight box **(278)** with an opening at one end to admit light, a lens to focus and refract the light, and a light-sensitive surface (today it is usually film) to receive the light-image and hold it. The last of these—the holding of the image—was the major drawback of the *camera obscura.* It could capture an image—and later versions of the *camera obscura* had a lens to focus the image and make it sharp—but there was no way to preserve the image, much less walk away with it in your hand. It was to this end that a number of people in the 19th century directed their attention.

One of them was Joseph Nicéphore Niépce, a French inventor. Working with a specially coated pewter plate in the *camera obscura,* Niépce managed, in 1826, to record a fuzzy version of the view from his window after an exposure of eight hours. Although we may consider Niépce's "heliograph" (or sun-writing), as he called it, to be the first permanent photograph, the method was not really practical.

Niépce was corresponding with another Frenchman, Louis Jacques Mandé Daguerre, who was also experimenting with methods to fix the photographic image. The two men were cagey with one another, each knowing that whoever was first to develop a simple, inexpensive process would strike a commercial gold mine. Daguerre won the contest. In 1837 he recorded an image of his studio that was clear and sharp, by methods that others could duplicate easily. Daguerre's light-sensitive surface was a copper plate, and he christened his invention the **daguerreotype.** Other pioneers worked with light-sensitive paper (the **calotype**), glass (the **ambrotype**), and dark metal (the **tintype**).

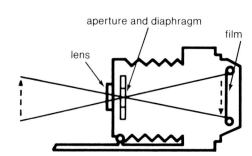

aperture and diaphragm

lens

film

278. The basic parts of a camera.

Daguerre's invention caused great excitement throughout Europe and North America. Entrepreneurs and the general public alike were quick to see the potential of photography, especially for portraits. It is hard to realize now, but until photography came along only the rich could afford to have their likenesses made, by sitting for a portrait painter. Within three years after Daguerre made his first plate, a "daguerreotype gallery for portraits" had opened in New York, and such galleries soon proliferated. To our eyes the portraits seem stiff and posed, which they were. Subjects had to remain motionless, without blinking, for between half a minute and a full minute—the minimum exposure time needed. (If this doesn't seem long to you, try doing it.) What's more, the idea of sitting for an "official" portrait was very new to most of these subjects. The sitters look awkward, and the results are often amusing—and charming **(279)**.

The desire to record what people look like remains an important function of photography, for professionals and amateurs alike. Nearly everyone has a drawerful of photographs and slides, recording significant events from birth (some have been photographed *during* birth) through childhood, adolescence, romance, marriage, parenthood, and old age. Despite the popularity of amateur photography, the professional still plays a role in recording what people look like. Portraits comprise a major category in photography.

SUBJECT MATTER IN PHOTOGRAPHY

PORTRAITS The professional portrait, at its best, goes beyond merely recording the subject's physical attributes. Like any other photograph, it tells one "truth"—a selected version of all the possible things one could record about the subject. And, like any other portrait—an oil painting, for example—it may serve as a revelation of the subject's character. Certain photographers have demonstrated a particular genius for portrait photography.

In the mid-19th century one man, by virtue of creative talent, enterprise, and sheer hard work, dominated the field of photography in the United States. That man was Mathew Brady. Brady opened a daguerreotype studio in New York in 1844, at the age of twenty-one. Later there was a studio in Washington and more studios in New York. From these bases he set out to photograph all the illustrious people of the time, and he very nearly succeeded. He employed many assistant photographers, called "operators," including Timothy O'Sullivan, whose work we shall see later in the chapter **(285)**. In many cases it is impossible to tell which pictures Brady himself took, because his name appears on all products of his studios.

The photograph shown here, however, almost certainly came from Brady's own camera. In 1860, when Abraham Lincoln was running for election to the presidency, he arrived in New York to make a speech at Cooper Union, an important college. During his visit he presented himself at Brady's studio, where this sensitive portrait was made **(280)**. Brady shows us a young Lincoln, clean-shaven, not yet torn by the heartache of war, fresh out of the back country of Illinois. His suit is obviously new, bought for the occasion, with the shirt cuff hanging down awkwardly from the jacket sleeve. Lincoln's facial expression is stern and dignified, but we also sense a bit of apprehension—perhaps caused by the leap into national politics, perhaps caused by the novel experience of having his portrait done.

Lincoln's Cooper Union speech was a success. Brady's photograph was in great demand, and thousands of copies were sold. After the election, Lincoln said, "Brady and the Cooper Union speech made me President."

Another famous portraitist of the 19th century—and an equally fascinating personality—was Frances Benjamin Johnston, who, without benefit of multiple assistants, was almost as prolific as Brady. Like Brady, she photographed an extraordinary range of subjects. Johnston was a niece of Mrs. Grover Cleveland, so she had access to the White House and, by extension, to many illustrious people, and she photographed them all. One of her most

top: **279.** Anonymous photographer, Great Britain. *An Elderly Veteran of Waterloo Posed with His Wife.* c. 1885. Hand-colored ambroytpe, $4\frac{3}{4} \times 3\frac{1}{2}''$. Rubel Collection, courtesy Thackrey and Robertson, San Francisco.

above: **280.** Mathew Brady. *Cooper Union Lincoln Portrait.* 1860. Photograph. Library of Congress, Washington, D.C.

left: **281.**
Frances Benjamin Johnston.
Self-Portrait. 1895. Photograph.
Library of Congress,
Washington, D.C.

below left: 282.
Edward Steichen.
Carl Sandburg. 1936.
Montage, gelatin-silver print;
$13\frac{11}{16} \times 16\frac{7}{8}''$.
Collection, The Museum of Modern Art,
New York (gift of the photographer).

below right: 283. Gordon Parks.
American Gothic. 1942.
Photograph.
Courtesy the photographer.

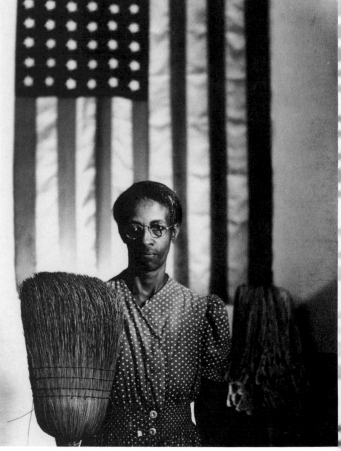

memorable works, however, is her portrait of herself **(281)**. As we can see, Johnston was a strong personality who flouted convention. This seems to have helped rather than hindered her career. She has chosen to portray herself with a beer stein in one hand and a cigarette in the other—both virtually unheard of for a woman in 1895. Most shocking of all, though her costume is in line with the demure fashions of the day, her pose is decidedly "unlady-like." She leaves us with the impression of a woman who lives and works exactly as she wishes, does it well, and answers to no one.

As we have said, the true photographic portrait is not just an accurate likeness but an interpretation of character. The poet Carl Sandburg inspired photographer Edward Steichen to create a multiple image **(282)**. It is as though Sandburg was so alive, so animated, so full of wisdom and charm that one likeness alone would not do justice to his character. Moreover, the repetition of Sandburg's head creates a visual rhythm that suggests the cadence of his poetry. Steichen's trademark was the dramatic use of light, especially of light-and-dark contrasts, and nowhere did he put it to better effect than in this portrait. Only the head is lighted, sometimes only the face. It is easy to imagine how much *less* striking this photograph would have been if the whole figure had been included.

Some might argue that our next image is not a portrait at all, but rather a documentary photograph—a photograph documenting a *situation*, in this case the harshness of life at the bottom of the economic ladder. But that is not the way the photographer has handled his subject. Gordon Parks' picture called *American Gothic* **(283)** shows a careworn black woman posed, solemn-faced, in front of an American flag. She stands rigidly between her broom and her mop, almost as though she were just another instrument for cleaning. Yet Parks gives the image so much dignity that the woman, Ella Watson, faces us as an individual. Her work is respectable and important; her broom and mop are the tools of her trade, every bit as appropriate to her portrait as a brush and palette would be to the portrait of an artist.

We expect a portrait to reveal individual personality, and so we automatically associate this type of photography with people, but there are exceptions. Fay Ray is an exception. She is an individual, she has a lot of personality, she even has star quality. The only thing a little exceptional is that Fay Ray is a dog. Photographer William Wegman has made a great many portraits of Fay **(284)**, his own Weimaraner, posed in whimsical situations,

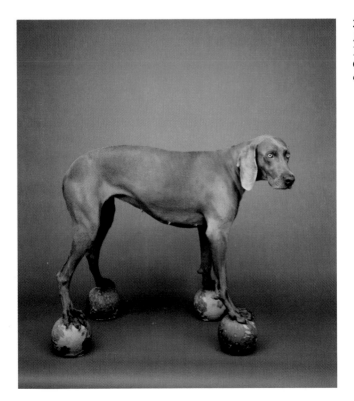

284. William Wegman.
Foot Upholstery. 1987.
Photograph, 24 × 20".
Collection Robert Reitzfeld,
copyright William Wegman.

PHOTOGRAPHY **241**

often with a prop or costume. The photographs are spare and elegant, the situations silly, the dog maintaining her elegance in spite of the silliness. Only the most stony-hearted dog hater would deny that Fay understands she is "sitting" for her portrait, and responds to the camera accordingly.

LANDSCAPE From the first, landscape has been a popular subject for photographers, whether it was the natural beauty of the countryside or the constructed landscape of the city. Some early photographers, like Timothy O'Sullivan, went to great extremes to capture nature's forms. Hauling what was then very cumbersome photographic equipment through mountains and desert presented a real challenge, but the results were well worth the effort.

In 1867 O'Sullivan signed on as official photographer to an expedition commissioned by the federal government to explore the territories of Nevada and Colorado. One of his most dramatic photos from this trip **(285)** shows the mule-drawn ambulance O'Sullivan had hired to carry water for his traveling darkroom. Tiny and stark against the vast shifting dunes, the vehicle looks like a dignified toy. We imagine that the footprints and grooves left by the wheels were the first marks ever made in this spot by anything but the wind.

The acknowledged master of 20th-century landscape photography was Ansel Adams. Our illustration **(286)** shows one of his most famous pictures, *Moon and Half Dome.* Although the scene that Adams chose to photograph is undeniably dramatic, that alone does not account for the artistry of this picture. Adams had "set up" the shot by choosing a precise vantage point; by *framing* the photo precisely (that is, including just the portion of landscape he wanted and no more); and by waiting until the moon, light, and shadows seemed just right. The composition is perfectly balanced, with the dark foreground rock at left and the dark shadow at right framing the lighted expanse of the rock known as Half Dome. The brilliant moon at top not only completes the balance of the picture but is its major focal point. Light is used to define the natural forms, to create contrast, to pick out textures and details; indeed, light structures the entire photograph. Adams demonstrates that the successful landscape photo, far from being a happy accident of nature, is a demanding art.

GENRE In the visual arts, as we have seen, the theme of genre focuses on everyday life. Usually people are included, but the intention is not to make a portrait of individuals. Instead, a genre photograph captures one of life's "little moments," as in André Kertész' *Couple in the Park* (287). The young couple, strolling through a park in Budapest, have paused for a moment to kiss. Who they are is not important; what matters is the sweetness of life and of young love. We see both tenderness and sensuality in this picture, heightened by the dark background and the light falling on the woman's face. Is she pulling away slightly? Perhaps, but her hands are clasped firmly behind her lover's back.

Our next photographer's pictures, while not strictly genre, expand that theme. The work of Diane Arbus concentrated on people who are unusual, apart from the norm—some would say "freaks." Arbus photographed a sword swallower, aging nudists, and people with physical abnormalities of all kinds. Her goal was to look directly, unflinchingly, at that which others turn away from. Often, her pictures reveal jarring incongruities. *The King and Queen of a Senior Citizens Dance* (288) shows a couple decked out in absurdly elaborate robes and crowns, which seem all the more absurd against their banal street clothing. Presumably this is meant to be a festive occasion, but the "king" and "queen" have such mournful expressions that we doubt any pleasure in their monarchy. Their postures are weary, and the woman in particular looks as though she has just plopped herself down in exhaustion. Arbus might be showing us that any attempt to impose gaiety or celebration on this couple will be futile.

above: 287. André Kertész.
Couple in the Park. 1915. Photograph.
© Estate of André Kertész.

left: 288. Diane Arbus.
*The King and Queen of a Senior Citizens Dance,
New York City.* 1970. Gelatin-silver print, $15 \times 11\frac{3}{8}''$.
Copyright © The Estate of Diane Arbus, 1971.
Collection, The Museum of Modern Art, New York
(Mrs. Armand P. Bartos Fund).

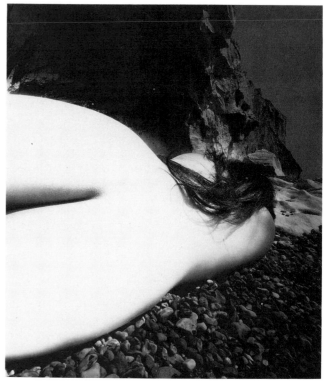

ABSTRACTION As has been noted before, abstraction is a process by which natural forms are simplified and reduced to their most characteristic aspects. We might think the camera, which tells only the "truth," cannot do this, but indeed it can. Abstraction in photography can result from viewpoint, angle, distance (including close-up), special lenses, darkroom techniques, or any combination of these.

Many of Edward Weston's photographs are extreme close-ups of familiar objects, such as the *Artichoke, Halved,* shown here **(289)**. Without the title, you might not be able to identify the picture's subject matter. By moving in close and picking up the exquisite detail of the vegetable, Weston gives it a majestic quality. All sense of scale is destroyed; this could just as easily be a huge underground cavern or a mysterious growth in a tropical rain forest— or a modern abstract painting. In creating this abstraction Weston challenges our preconceived notion of what an artichoke looks like. He may also encourage us to look beyond the familiar appearance of other common objects and consider their possibilities for abstraction of line, form, and texture.

A special lens known as a wide-angle lens produced the dreamlike abstraction of Bill Brandt's *Nude on a Pebbled Beach* **(290)**. Under some circumstances the wide-angle lens distorts what it records, stretching out shapes horizontally. Here the photographer has manipulated it in such a way that the nude figure takes on a monumental quality. Only the most essential features give us clues to the identity of this subject—the flow of hair, the swell of the hips, and the line between the buttocks. The last is most important. If the left quarter of the picture is covered up, the form could be almost anything.

From a straightforward portrait to a naked monolith on a beach, the subject matter of photography includes everything in this world and—since the advent of space travel and sophisticated telescopes—more than a few things that are out of our world. The choice of imagery is limited only by the limits of the photographer's imagination. In some cases, however, the choice of subject matter may be influenced by the photographer's circumstances. Like drawings, photographs often are made for specific applications. The following section explores some of the purposes of photography.

PURPOSES OF PHOTOGRAPHY

Many photographs are made for specific commercial applications, such as publication in books, magazines, and newspapers, and their purpose is primarily illustrative or documentary. Other pictures have no external incentive beyond the photographer's expressive impulse. The dividing line between these two categories is not a rigid one. The photographer on assignment from a magazine may make an image that survives for its artistic qualities long after that issue of the magazine has been forgotten. And, of course, art photographs often are reprinted in books and magazines. Nevertheless, our appreciation of photographs can be enhanced by considering the primary purpose for which each was taken, because this strongly affects the photographer's expression.

THE "ART" PHOTOGRAPH By art photograph, we mean a picture that is specifically intended for exhibition as art. Such photos are appreciated for their formal qualities and for their expressiveness, rather than for any illustrative value. Almost since the beginnings of the medium photographers have explored the purely expressive potential of the camera. But what we think of as today's art photography owes a great deal to the influence of one man in particular, both because of his own work and because of his efforts to promote photography as an art form. That man was Alfred Stieglitz, and his most famous picture is *The Steerage* (291).

The story of how *The Steerage* was made illustrates our point about photographers moving through the world with an invisible frame behind their eyes. In 1907 Stieglitz was aboard ship on his way to Europe, traveling first class. One day as he was walking the deck, he happened to look down into the steerage section—that portion of the ship where the poorest passengers, paying the lowest fares, were herded together like cattle. Before him he saw a perfectly composed photograph—the smokestack leaning to the left at one end, the iron stairway leaning to the right at the other, the chained drawbridge cutting across, even to such details as the round straw hat on the man looking down and the grouping of women and children below. Stieglitz knew he had only one unexposed plate left (the equivalent of one exposure at the end of a roll of film). He raced to his cabin to get his camera. When he returned, the scene was exactly the same; no one had moved. That one plate became *The Steerage*.

291. Alfred Stieglitz.
The Steerage. 1907. Photograph.
The Art Institute of Chicago
(Alfred Stieglitz Collection).

Alfred Stieglitz

1864–1946

If one had to choose the individual most responsible for establishing photography as an art form, the strongest candidate probably would be Alfred Stieglitz. Born in Hoboken, New Jersey, Stieglitz was the eldest child of German parents. His youth was spent in travel between Europe and the United States, and he studied at both the City College of New York and the University of Berlin. In 1883, at the age of nineteen, Stieglitz bought his first camera in Berlin; thereafter his life's work seems never to have been in doubt.

Stieglitz settled more or less permanently in New York in 1890, although he continued to travel widely. The first of his major efforts to promote photography as an art form came in 1896, when he was instrumental in founding the Camera Club of New York. The following year he became editor of its quarterly publication, *Camera Notes.* But the group most closely associated with his name was the "Photo-Secession," founded in 1902. A loosely structured national organization of photographers, the Photo-Secession was devoted to promoting exhibitions of photographers, later of contemporary painters and sculptors as well. Stieglitz served as editor of its quarterly, *Camera Work,* which maintained extremely high standards for photographs published and reproduction quality.

As a photographer, Stieglitz dedicated his talents to demonstrating that the medium was accessible to anyone, even those with unsophisticated equipment and little training. He often worked with the simplest cameras, had his photographs printed commercially, and delighted in shooting under difficult conditions—in rain, fog, and darkness. His pictures were exhibited widely and were collected by major museums.

In 1905 Stieglitz, along with photographer Edward Steichen, opened the Little Galleries of the Photo-Secession at 291 Fifth Avenue in New York, usually called "291." There the American public viewed the work of "art" photographers and also had its first opportunity to see the paintings of Picasso, Matisse, Cézanne, and other avant-garde European artists, as well as the most innovative of the Americans. Through his gallery Stieglitz had considerable influence on the spread of modern art.

Among the artists showing at 291 was the painter Georgia O'Keeffe. In 1918 Stieglitz left his first wife and moved in with O'Keeffe, whom he married after

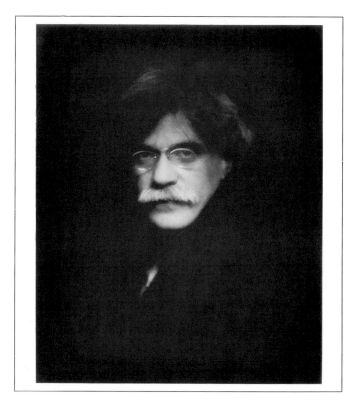

his divorce became final. His photographic portraits of O'Keeffe, including many close-up studies of her hands, are among his most sensitive and striking images. Although Stieglitz and O'Keeffe were frequently apart, often at different parts of the globe (their chronology for the next twenty years or so reads like a travelogue), they remained married until his death at the age of eighty-two.

Stieglitz wrote extensively about his work, but perhaps the most characteristic statement can be found in his catalogue notes for an exhibit of his photographs in 1921: "My teachers have been life—work—continuous experiment. Incidentally a great deal of hard thinking. Any one can build on this experience with means available to all. . . . I was born in Hoboken. I am an American. Photography is my passion. The search for Truth my obsession."[2]

Alfred Stieglitz. *Self-Portrait.* Photograph.
Philadelphia Museum of Art (Dorothy S. Norman Collection).

By the 1950s photography had definitely come into its own as an art medium, and among those recognized as master photographers was Harry Callahan. Over the years Callahan has made many pictures of his wife, Eleanor, but they are in no sense portraits. Some are quite abstract, and many, like *Eleanor, Port Huron* (292), show her distant and alone in a large, tranquil landscape. Callahan's photographs are very personal, a direct expression of his emotions. Their trademark is the use of strong contrasts between light and dark values, as here. If you squint your eyes, the brilliant white form of the woman's body almost seems to be floating in the lush dark background foliage. This image conveys utter serenity. Perhaps it speaks of Callahan's love for his wife, better than any portrait could do, in a grander way—as part of his love for life and nature.

One model also dominates photographs by Cindy Sherman, but in this case the model is the photographer herself, disguised in each picture so that her work presents an extremely varied cast of characters. Since her early college days Sherman has been preoccupied with makeup, wigs, costumes, props—all the elaborate trappings of theatrical presentation. Soon she began not only dressing herself up, but photographing the results. In early work Sherman cast herself as characters reminiscent of television programs, films, even commercials. Then, for a recent exhibition, she turned her ironic eye to the history of art, specifically to traditional portraits in art history. Transformed by the costumes and wigs—sometimes by fake body parts—Sherman parodied the extremes of high-style portraiture, as in her version of the Marquise de Pompadour (293; compare 520). According to the artist, "All the women in those paintings were the wives or mistresses of the artists, or the wives of [their] rich patrons. And there was a convention of portraying

left: 292. Harry Callahan.
Eleanor, Port Huron. 1954.
Photograph, $6\frac{5}{8} \times 6\frac{1}{2}''$.
Copyright Harry Callahan.

right: 293. Cindy Sherman.
Untitled. 1988.
Color photograph, $42\frac{1}{2} \times 28\frac{1}{2}''$.
Courtesy the artist
and Metro Pictures, New York.

women that was not real."[3] Sherman thinks of herself as a performance artist (p. 496), because, in a way, she is giving a performance every time she steps in front of her own camera. Her pictures document that performance.

Artist Barbara Kruger is usually associated with the photographic medium, but she does not take photographs in the usual way. Kruger quite literally "takes" photos—appropriates them—from other sources, such as magazines and newspapers, and blows them up to billboard size. She then overlays the photographs with messages drawn from advertising, politics, or popular jargon. *Are We Having Fun Yet?* **(294)** juxtaposes that ironic question with an anguished picture of hands pressed to a face. Kruger's images are stark and even shocking, especially so in view of their size. There is a tension, a biting clash between picture and words, a mockery of mass-produced values like "having fun." Today's art photograph often carries a message well beyond aesthetic satisfaction.

PHOTOJOURNALISM AND EDITORIAL PHOTOGRAPHY Until the 19th century the only pictures that ever appeared in newspapers and magazines were made from drawings or from prints, usually engravings **(258)**. Then photography came along, opening the potential for actual documentation of events. Mathew Brady, whose portrait of Lincoln we saw earlier **(280)**, was among the first to exploit the potential of photographs for journalism. When North and South went to war in 1860, Brady and his team also went to war, carrying their equipment in peculiar horse-drawn wagons that the soldiers dubbed "Whatsits." Because his photos still required a fairly long exposure time at sittings, Brady could not photograph actual battles (which obviously would not stand still for the camera), but he recorded scenes of camp life, important generals and their aides, and especially the poignant aftermath of battle. The American Civil War, therefore, was the first major war photographed for posterity.

Because no method had yet been perfected to reproduce the photographs accurately and clearly, early photographs like Brady's were first translated into drawings and then into woodcuts for reproduction. Then, about 1900, the first process for photomechanical reproduction—high-speed printing of photographs along with type—came into being.

Today nearly every event that might remotely be considered newsworthy is covered by photojournalists, from the carnage of war to the escape of a

left: 294. Barbara Kruger. *Untitled (Are We Having Fun Yet?).* 1987. Photographic silkscreen/vinyl, 12'3½" × 8'7". Courtesy Mary Boone Gallery, New York.

right: 295. Sam Shere. *Explosion of the Hindenburg, Lakehurst, New Jersey.* 1937. Photograph.

296. Dorothea Lange. *Heading West, Tulare Lake, California.* 1939. Photograph. Library of Congress, Washington, D.C.

pet snake in a residential neighborhood. News photographers must depend to a certain extent on luck. Their best pictures result when they are in the right place at the right time, when some extraordinary event occurs. Nevertheless, it is the photographer's skill that turns a record of an event into a great picture.

On May 6, 1937, the enormous German airship *Hindenburg* was scheduled to land at Lakehurst, New Jersey. Even though it was the dirigible's seventh transatlantic crossing, the arrival was still considered remarkable enough that a crowd gathered, and twenty-two photographers from the New York and Philadelphia papers had been sent to cover the landing. The photographers were set up to compose shots for feature stories. Just as the giant silver balloon was about to be secured to the mooring tower, it exploded and burst into flames. Of the ninety-two people on board, thirty-six were killed. Every one of the photographers, despite the tremendous heat and danger, managed to snap a few pictures before dashing to cover. Sam Shere's photo, with the tower silhouetted in front of the inferno, is memorable (295).

The burning of the *Hindenburg* was the first disaster to be thoroughly documented in photographs. During the decade of the thirties, however, another kind of disaster—not a sudden one, but a long and painful one—was covered in depth by the most creative photographers of the time. The Great Depression, which began in 1929 and lasted until the onset of World War II, caused hardships for photographers as well as for the population as a whole. To ease the first problem and document the second, the Farm Security Administration (FSA) of the U.S. Department of Agriculture subsidized photographers and sent them out to record conditions across the nation. One of these was Dorothea Lange.

Lange devoted her attention to the migrants who had been uprooted from their farms by the combined effects of Depression and drought. *Heading West, Tulare Lake, California* (296) shows a mother and her two children, dirty and disheveled, in a battered truck. Despair is written on all three faces, as the eyes stare off at some distant point that may offer no relief from misery. Lange's masterful composition gives an importance, a universal quality, to the tragedy of one family. The picture's basic structure is a triangle, with the boy's head at the apex, one side running down through his leg, the other diagonal through the mother's head and the younger child, and the base resting on the bottom of the photo. (Compare Raphael's *Madonna*, 110.) FSA photos like this one were offered free to newspapers and magazines.

Dorothea Lange's travels for the FSA took her to nearly every part of the country. In one summer alone she logged 17,000 miles in her car. Photojournalism is hard work. It may also be dangerous, as when the *Hindenburg* exploded. But the most difficult and dangerous job is that of war photographer.

The 1991 war in the Persian Gulf was the most media-intensive conflict in history. Among those covering its aftermath was photographer Fred R. Conrad, whose picture shows how war comes to people, not to armies (297). As battle raged in Iraq, Kurdish families in the north fled to the mountains. Only when their territory had been secured could they return. A young Kurdish girl, framed by Conrad's lens, shows the pure joy of homecoming. Beyond capturing the happiness on the girl's face, Conrad has made a masterful picture. His composition is basically triangular, leading from the face down to the two lower corners. There we see the more subdued pleasure of the woman at left, the apprehensive gaze of the child at right. A nooselike curl of rope beside the girl provides a grim symbol of death—but now it is death conquered by liberation.

The photojournalist, as we said, needs a certain amount of luck. He or she must wait for the picture to happen. There is another branch of journalistic photography, however, that *makes* pictures happen. This is editorial photography. Editorial photographers may deal in fashion, in architecture, in food, or many other areas. Their goal is to make the subject attractive and appealing, or possibly to interpret an idea photographically. Their pictures are "set up" very deliberately to achieve this purpose.

Fashion photography, like fashion illustration, usually aims at creating an illusion—the illusion of an impossible, idealized beauty that the viewer will feel compelled to emulate. No one has mastered this art of illusion better than Irving Penn. Penn's *Woman in Black Dress* (298) is almost an abstraction. The model, impossibly tall and thin, does not seem to resemble any living creature. We cannot imagine her walking or moving. If you cover up the head, you might be hard-pressed to identify the rest as a human body. What matters here is not reality but a glimpse of unearthly elegance.

Despite its unreal quality, Penn's photograph is essentially "straight," as are most of those we have seen so far in this chapter. The camera clicks, and the photograph essentially is made. For other photographers, however, the click of the shutter is only the beginning of a process that will create an image very different from that viewed outside the little room of the camera.

SPECIAL EFFECTS AND TECHNIQUES

The idea of using the photographic image only as a starting point is not a new one. We have already explored the question of photography as truth teller. The visual "truth" of a photograph may be influenced by a photographer's inner vision, by prevailing art styles, even by the culture in which photographs are made. We encounter the last of these in seeing how photography developed in a culture apart from Western traditions.

Photography reached India in the 1840s and was eagerly adopted by the populace. The Indian approach to the medium was very different from that in the West, however. Europeans, steeped in Renaissance concepts of depth and perspective, greeted photography as an ever more "real" depiction of the natural world. The Indians, by contrast, had a tradition of miniature painting in which the illusion of deep space was irrelevant. Paintings were flat, all in one plane, and highly decorative. So when they took up photography, the Indians painted over the camera image until it looked "correct" to *them*.

Our illustration shows a splendid example **(299)**. This portrait of a landowner, taken about 1900, has been meticulously painted all over. While the subject's face and hands retain a suggestion of roundness from the photograph, the rest of his body is flat, thanks to the painting. The chair seems to float in space, while the meeting of patterned rug and wall is just a vertical division of the picture plane, not an indication that the rug is perpendicular to the picture plane. (Possibly the rug was a plain floor in the photograph; it has been painted with no perspective at all, as though it were parallel to the picture plane.) The background wall—which in the photo must have showed

299. Anonymous photographer, India. *Portrait of a Landowner.* c. 1900. Photograph, painted. Smithsonian Institution, Washington, D.C., and American Institute of Indian Studies.

another room opening to the left and a vista out the window at right—now seems more like a painted backdrop for the theater.

There is a lesson to be learned from this approach to photography. Our understanding of how things "are" and how things "should be" has much to do with cultural conditioning. The Indians' cultural heritage predisposed them to the belief that a flat, decorative image is the ideal expression of art; Western cultural heritage predisposes us to believe that the illusion of depth on a flat surface is superior. Actually, neither is right or better. Through understanding and exposure, we can learn to appreciate aesthetic values different from our own. This applies to all aspects of art and culture, not just to photography.

Half a century later and half a world away, the American photographer Jerry Uelsmann created *his* personal reality by combining images, one on top of another. *Apocalypse II* **(300)** was printed from three negatives—two for the ghostlike white tree and a third for the silhouetted children on the beach. Cleverly, the photographer has made it seem that the figures are staring at the tree as though it were some mysterious cosmic force. You may be reminded of horror movies in which children possess demonic powers.

The Surrealist artist Man Ray experimented with several unusual photographic techniques in the 1920s and 1930s. One of them was **solarization,** a process by which an exposed negative is briefly reexposed to light during development. This causes chemical changes in the photographic emulsion—the light-sensitive coating on film. Actually, although Man Ray's name is usually associated with solarization, it may have been his companion at the time, photographer Lee Miller, who discovered the effect—albeit accidentally. She has written:

> Something crawled across my foot in the darkroom and I let out a yell and turned on the light. I never did find out what it was, a mouse or what. Then I realized that the film was totally exposed: there in the development tanks, ready to be taken out, were a dozen practically fully developed negatives of a nude against a black background. Man Ray grabbed them, put them in the [fixer solution] and looked at them.[4]

Miller's own portrait of a woman shows the effect that can be produced when the "accident" is controlled **(301)**. This image combines the visual appearance of a photographic negative *and* a positive print. The ghostly dark shadows around the hand and parts of the face give the woman's portrait a slightly surreal quality.

302. Doug and Mike Starn. *Double Stark Portrait in Swirl.* 1985–86. Toned silver print and tape, 8'3″ square. Collection Randolfo Rocha, courtesy Stux Gallery, New York.

At the beginning of this chapter we saw a photo-collage by David Hockney **(277)**, made up of many individual photographs joined to create a composite image. The technique of assembling pieces into a whole also underlies the work of two artists, identical twins, who function as a team—Doug and Mike Starn. The Starn twins are interested in process, in showing the process and the raw materials of photography as a painter might show the process of brush strokes. Their *Double Stark Portrait in Swirl* **(302)**, a portrait of themselves, consists of many pieces of photographic paper, cut and hacked irregularly, taped together (the Scotch tape is usually very obvious), then framed into a composition 8 feet square. Neatness and precision are not what the Starns are about. They smudge and tear and wrinkle their photographic fragments for a deliberate "scarred" effect. Sometimes their works are merely tacked or taped to the wall. Although they may be the art conservator's nightmare of the future, the Starn twins are today's photographic vanguard.

We might very well ask, then, what will photography do next? It is now possible to photograph the vastness of the universe through telescopes and the most minute forms of life through electron microscopes. Just as quickly as scientists have developed new techniques for their studies, creative artists have adapted those techniques for aesthetic purposes. In a mere century and a half photography has come farther and faster than any of the media that have been with us for thousands of years. Where does the camera go now?

One of the places the camera can go is into a realm we have not yet touched upon in this chapter. This realm is not really a new one. It was first explored about a hundred years ago, but progress since that time has been extraordinary. The camera can seek to capture motion.

PHOTOGRAPHY AND MOTION

Throughout history artists have tried to create the illusion of motion in a still image. Painters have drawn galloping horses, running people, action of all kinds—never being sure that their depictions of the movement were "cor-

303. Eadweard Muybridge. *Woman Kicking*, Plate 367 from *Animal Locomotion.* 1887. Collotype, $7\frac{1}{2} \times 20\frac{1}{4}''$. Collection, The Museum of Modern Art, New York (gift of the Philadelphia Commercial Museum).

rect" and lifelike. To draw a running horse with absolute realism, for instance, the artist would have to freeze the horse in one moment of the run, but because the motion is too quick for the eye to follow, the artist had no assurance a running horse ever does take a particular pose. In 1878 a man named Eadweard Muybridge addressed this problem, and the story behind his solution is a classic in the history of photography.

Leland Stanford, a former governor of California, had bet a friend twenty-five thousand dollars that a horse at full gallop sometimes has all four feet off the ground. Since observation by the naked eye could not settle the bet one way or the other, Stanford hired Muybridge, known as a photographer of landscapes, to photograph one of the governor's racehorses. Muybridge devised an ingenious method to take the pictures. He set up twelve cameras, each connected to a black thread stretched across the racecourse. As Stanford's mare ran down the track, she snapped the threads that triggered the cameras' shutters—and proved conclusively that a running horse does gather all four feet off the ground at certain times. Stanford won the bet, and Muybridge went on to more ambitious studies of motion.

In 1887 Muybridge published *Animal Locomotion*, his most important project. Somehow, he persuaded a great many of his friends to take off their clothes and move about doing specific physical activities—in this case, inexplicably, kicking a pith helmet—while he photographed them **(303)**. There were 781 plates in the series—many of nude people, some of clothed people, some of animals—all in motion. For the first time ever the world could see what positions living creatures really assume when they move.

Undoubtedly, Muybridge's experiments whetted the public's appetite. The little room with a view had glimpsed a different world, a world that does not stand still but spins and moves and dances, and the public wanted more of this. The public did not have long to wait.

Film

On the night of December 28, 1895, a small audience gathered in the basement of a Paris café, which was to become the first commercial movie theater in history. The audience viewed several very short films, including one of a baby being fed its dinner, another of a gardener being doused by a hose. One film in particular caused a strong reaction. *L'Arrivée d'un train en gare (The Arrival of a Train at the Station)* set the audience to screaming, ducking for cover, and jumping from their seats, because it featured a train hurtling directly toward the viewers. Never before, except in real life, had people seen anything of the kind, and they responded automatically. We may laugh at their naiveté—until we remember that contemporary horror films often have the same effect on today's far more sophisticated viewers. From the beginning, motion pictures could make an image on a screen seem real indeed.

THE ORIGINS OF MOTION PICTURES

Film depends on a phenomenon called **_persistence of vision._** The human brain retains a visual image for a fraction of a second longer than the eye actually records it. If this were not true, your visual perception of the world would be continually interrupted by blinks of your eyes. Instead, your brain "carries over" the visual image during the split second while the eyes are closed. Similarly, the brain carries over when still images are flashed before the eyes with only the briefest space between them. Motion-picture film is not real motion but a series of still images projected at a speed of 24 frames per second, which makes the action seem fluid and continuous.

Interest in moving pictures really predates the development of the still camera. As early as 1832 a toy was patented in Europe in which a series of drawn images, each slightly different from the next, was made to spin in a revolving wheel so that the image appeared to move. Eadweard Muybridge later applied this principle to his multiple photographic images, spinning them in a wheel he called the _zoopraxiscope._

Commercial applications of the motion picture, however, awaited three major developments. In 1888 the American George Eastman introduced celluloid film, which he intended for the Kodak still camera but which made it possible to string images together, rather than using the individual photographic plates required by early cameras. Another big step was taken by Thomas Edison, the famous American inventor better known for his development of the electric light bulb and the phonograph (precursor of the stereo). It was in Edison's laboratory, in 1894, that technicians created what was apparently the first genuine motion picture. Lasting only a few seconds, the film was made on celluloid. Its "star" was one of Edison's mechanics, a man who could sneeze amusingly on command. Its title: _Fred Ott's Sneeze._

Edison's filmmaking project had been directed by his brilliant assistant, W. K. L. Dickson, and Dickson had solved many of the problems involved in turning films into a commercial enterprise. One major drawback remained. There was no satisfactory method for projecting the films to an audience. Here the challenge was taken up by two Frenchmen, brothers appropriately named Lumière (_lumière_ means "light"), who in 1895 succeeded in building a workable film projector. The films shown in that Paris café were made by the brothers Lumière. From that point the motion-picture industry was off and running.

Film technology advanced rapidly. Almost overnight, it seemed, film companies sprang up on both sides of the Atlantic. Once the novelty of viewing motion pictures had passed, simple everyday events—such as a man sneezing or a baby eating—no longer satisfied. Filmmakers cast about for more dramatic and entertaining episodes to capture in the camera. Trained stage actors found themselves in great demand, and stories became more complex. The earliest movies were in fact rather "stagy." Actors entered and exited as they would in a theater, and all the action occurred in a shallow plane. Soon, however, filmmakers discovered the far greater flexibility of the movie arena. People could move, cameras could move, space need not be restricted, time could be expanded or compressed at will.

The fabulous era of silent films began with the Lumières' movie snippets in that Paris basement in 1895, and it lasted for just over thirty years. During that time a wholly new creature—the movie star—came into being, and the names from that generation live in legend: Rudolph Valentino, Mary

Pickford, Douglas Fairbanks, Lillian Gish, and perhaps the greatest of them all, Charles Chaplin. Silent-film stars filled a gap in the American consciousness. In a time when studio salaries were huge and income tax a trifling matter, they lived and behaved like royalty. Some would have long careers in the cinema. Others fell victim to the next major breakthrough in film technology. Sound film was introduced in 1927, and not all stars of the silent era could make the transition, for their voices did not match their physical attributes. Those who did pass muster vocally were launched into another great period of film history. By the late 1920s the camera—the little room with a view—had come of age. It not only had eyes, but ears as well. Soon it would see and hear things undreamed of theretofore. Filmmaking of the twenties and thirties seems amazing in at least three respects: the tiny budgets; the rapid production times—perhaps just two or three weeks of shooting for a full-length film; and the relatively small number of people involved. Today a major film may cost tens of millions and be in production for a year or more. Moreover, as we watch the credits roll by on the movie screen nowadays, it seems that a large number of people are needed to make a film, and certainly this is true. But from the beginning of motion-picture history the greatest films, the classic films, have often been the product of one creative imagination. Usually, though not always, the creative force behind an important film is its director. Let us turn now to a brief survey of classic films and the creative artists who made them.

FILMS AND FILMMAKERS

The word "epic," in films, suggests a picture that is long, crowded, and grand. Usually, an epic film has a story taken from some significant point in history, or perhaps from the Bible. It will employ many actors—the proverbial "cast of thousands"—in climactic scenes with considerable action, such as battles, riots, or natural disasters. Often, the epic film has a moral to preach to its audience. Through the history of film there have been many epics, but the pioneer of the form was a man named David Wark Griffith.

D. W. Griffith began his movie career in 1908 as a director of very short (10-minute) silent films cranked out at the rate of two a week. This apprenticeship taught him much about the mechanics of filmmaking, so that by the time Griffith had attained greater creative independence, he was ready for it. In 1914 the producer-director shot his first feature-length picture, and even its title proclaims an epic: *The Birth of a Nation* **(304)**. Griffith took his story from a contemporary novel. *The Birth of a Nation* is set in the American South before, during, and after the Civil War. In a now-familiar device, it

304. Scene from
The Birth of a Nation
directed by D. W. Griffith.
Released 1915.

interweaves the histories of two families—one northern, one southern—whose paths cross and whose members fall in love with one another. The plot allowed for many battle scenes and a particularly effective staging of President Lincoln's assassination. We must remember that this was a *silent* film. All action, all plot, all emotions had to be conveyed by visual images only, without dialogue or sound effects. (There was usually live musical accompaniment in the early movie theaters.)

Most viewers today would find it difficult to sit through *The Birth of a Nation,* for when it is not exaggerated in style it is offensive in its racial prejudice and simplistic morality. Even in its day some audiences reacted strenuously to these aspects of the movie. Reviewing the film on March 4, 1915, *The New York Times* complained about "melodramatic and inflammatory material." The *Times,* however, went on to evaluate "the film as a film" and deemed it "an impressive new illustration of the scope of the motion picture camera."[5] So it was, for Griffith had revolutionized the mechanics of filmmaking.

Each unbroken sequence of movie frames, with the camera rolling, is called a **shot.** Before Griffith, the standard in films had been the **full shot,** showing actors from head to toe as a theater audience would view them. Griffith preferred to experiment with a full range of shots for dramatic effect: the **medium shot** (from the waist up), the **close-up** (head and shoulders), the **extreme close-up** (part of a face), and the **long shot** (seen from the distance). Dissatisfied with the camera as immobile observer of a scene, Griffith developed the **pan shot** (camera moving from side to side) and the **traveling shot** (camera moving from back to front on a track). He also perfected the technique of **cross-cutting,** in which two or more scenes are alternated to advance the action of the film. For example, he might film scenes of a heroine in distress and her hero rushing to save her, then cut back and forth rapidly between the two in order to build suspense.

This last shows Griffith's mastery of film **editing,** or assembling the film creatively after all scenes have been photographed. In *The Birth of a Nation* Griffith also made effective use of the **iris shot (304),** in which the edges of the film are blacked out to create a circle of interest, as though one character in the film is looking at the events on the screen. *The Birth of a Nation* even has **flashbacks,** or cuts to episodes that are supposed to have taken place before the main action of the film. To sum up, Griffith had virtually written a menu of possibilities for future filmmakers.

The mechanics of filmmaking being in place, other creative movie people could focus on story line. Griffith's plots, obviously, had been dramatic. They could move audiences to tears or anger or patriotism. But film audiences also wanted to laugh, and filmmakers of the silent era gave them plenty of opportunity. The next great genius of the film was a man who tapped the endlessly entertaining possibilities of the human condition—of laughing at oneself and the ridiculous situations one encounters in daily life. His name was Charles Chaplin.

Chaplin began his career as an actor. Sometime in the years 1913–14 he began to develop the character of "Charlie," the Little Tramp, whom he played in most of his films. Physically, Charlie was what today we might call a "wimp"—undersized, clumsy, comical in appearance, wearing shoes and trousers far too big for him, sporting an absurd derby hat and a cane. Charlie was inevitably the one who got the pie in the face, the splash of slush from a passing streetcar, the foot caught in a goldfish bowl. He was the perennial outsider, always looking in wistfully at people who were rich, graceful, beautiful, and successful. But Charlie had courage, and he had a heart of gold. He would rush to save a maiden in trouble, only to lose her affections to the handsome leading man. Charlie was Everyman adrift in a world where anything could go wrong, anybody could trip him up.

Through many silent films Chaplin refined the character of Charlie and also honed his skills as a filmmaker. Soon he was not only acting but writing, directing, and producing the films, often creating the musical accompaniment as well. By the 1930s Chaplin was at the top of his form. Sound had been introduced, and although the Little Tramp did not speak (which would have been contrary to his mime-type character), Chaplin allowed for sound effects and had Charlie sing a kind of nonsense song. *Modern Times* (305) is considered by many to be Chaplin's greatest film. In this movie Chaplin pits himself against the modern assembly line and, predictably, loses the contest. Chaplin's inventive genius goes into high gear, so to speak, as Charlie struggles against the machine and the machine fights back. *Modern Times* continues the battle of the odd little hero against adversity, but now his opponents are mechanical, not human. As with all his films, Chaplin concealed a message in *Modern Times*—that our fast-paced world is hard on innocent nonconformists—but that message is presented with side-splitting humor.

From the beginnings of movie history the prospect of filming in color had been on filmmakers' minds. Black and white has its virtues. So many of the all-time classic films were shot in black and white, and certain filmmakers, for certain films, prefer to work in that medium even today. But color adds an extra dimension, an extra lushness. There are some films we cannot imagine *except* in color, and probably the earliest is *Gone with the Wind.*

Color photography for films was feasible in the early 1930s. By the end of that decade it had been perfected sufficiently to be available to master producer David O. Selznick when he set out to reproduce in film Margaret Mitchell's spectacularly best-selling novel of the Civil War. *Gone with the Wind* was not unlike *The Birth of a Nation* in its story line or its epic proportions, but for the filmmaker there was a difference. Mitchell's book had so thoroughly captivated the imaginations of millions of readers that a potential audience *knew* exactly what a film based on the novel should look like. The filmmaker who let them down would do so at great peril. Selznick as producer took full charge of the movie, overwhelming writers (there were several) and directors (also several), even the stars. And Selznick delivered. The movie of *Gone with the Wind* was, and remains, a tremendous success with audiences.

The color effects in *Gone with the Wind* are always vivid (306). For the most intense scenes, such as the burning of Atlanta, Selznick poured on a saturated red. Red worked for Selznick and the film on different levels. It is associated with the clayey soil of Georgia, where the story takes place. It is inherently dramatic. It often symbolizes passion, in this case the passions of war and the passion between those two classic lovers, Scarlett O'Hara and Rhett Butler. To our eyes now, accustomed to color films, the "scorched" effects of *Gone with the Wind* may seem a little exaggerated, but for that time and that movie they were exactly right.

305. Charles Chaplin as "Charlie," the Little Tramp, in a scene from *Modern Times*, directed by Charles Chaplin. 1936.

Selznick's control of *Gone with the Wind* was considerable, but it may
seem modest compared to the creative involvement by the next filmmaker
we shall study. In 1941 R.K.O. released a film created almost single-handed
by a twenty-six-year-old "boy genius" who played the starring role, produced
and directed the film, co-authored the screenplay, supervised the editing and
set design, and, it is said, even sewed some of the costumes himself. The film
was not a success with contemporary audiences or critics. It did not win any
major Academy Award. Today, however, when movie people compile lists of
the "ten best" filmmakers and films, we are sure to find the names of Orson
Welles and his masterpiece, *Citizen Kane* (**307**).

Welles based his story, loosely, on the life of the newspaper publisher
William Randolph Hearst, here renamed Charles Foster Kane (played by
Welles). What could have been a simple biography of a powerful man was
turned by Welles into a startling cinematic achievement. *Citizen Kane* was
innovative on a number of levels. Its structure, at first glance an ordinary
flashback, begins with Kane's death, then traces his life from childhood and
youth up through old age and back to his death again. But the actual telling
of the story is far more complex than that. Kane's life on film is divided into
five sections—the first played out in blaring newsreel films, the other four
narrated in turn from the points of view of four people involved with Kane.
Welles begins with a superficial outside view of the brash, successful young
Kane, then gradually probes deeper and deeper into Kane's psychic center,
as that center slowly disintegrates into lonely, bitter old age.

Cinematically, the movie opens the filmmaker's grab bag of tricks—all meant to highlight Kane's personality. There are **low-angle shots** (to show a towering Kane), dramatic long shots, extreme contrasts of light and dark, and many traveling shots intended to convey physical and emotional separation. For instance, as Kane's relationship with his first wife becomes cooler, the camera shows the couple farther and farther apart at the ends of an ever-lengthening dinner table. The introduction of garish newsreel-type footage, used for scenes of Kane's public life, contrasts with the brooding quality of the main story line. Welles calculated every shot to convey the mood, the emotional symbols, the portrait of a character he intended. *Citizen Kane* could not be a stage play. It is too dependent on film techniques for its impact. More than any filmmaker before him, Welles had shown what the camera, used imaginatively, could do.

With a few exceptions, American filmmakers dominated the movie industry in the early days, but starting in the 1920s they were challenged seriously from abroad, as creative artists in France, Germany, Russia, and other countries began to build their own styles for the motion picture. Increasingly the word "movie" ceased to be synonymous with "Hollywood." By the 1950s and 1960s, when Hollywood was investing heavily in musicals and light comedies, critical attention began to focus on European filmmakers with more serious aims. Two of these—one Swedish, one Italian—attracted special attention in the United States: Ingmar Bergman and Federico Fellini.

Ingmar Bergman's first internationally successful film, and some would say his greatest, was *The Seventh Seal*, made in 1957. *The Seventh Seal* is an allegory, a story filled with religious and macabre symbolism, a kind of morality play, set in the 14th century apparently in Sweden. As it begins, a knight returning from the Crusades is met on the beach by the figure of Death (**308**), who announces that the knight's time has come. Stalling for time, the knight challenges Death to a game of chess, and they agree that Death will not claim him until the game is over. The knight hopes to use this borrowed time to find some meaning in life, to accomplish some deed that he cannot name. As the game goes on intermittently, the knight and his squire, with other characters they meet, journey toward the knight's castle. Along the way they encounter a young couple, Jof (Joseph) and Mia (Mary) and their baby son—undoubtedly symbolic of the Christ child and his parents. In the end Death wins the chess game and calls the knight and his party to darkness, but the knight tricks Death into sparing the innocent couple and their baby.

Bergman, who both wrote and directed *The Seventh Seal*, was able to put an unusually personal stamp on this and all his films, because over the years he developed a close-knit repertory company of actors and supporting crew, accustomed to him and to one another. His actors, camera crews, and other associates became almost extensions of himself. They worked together on film after film, and some formed close relationships with the director.

308. The figure of Death in an early scene from *The Seventh Seal*, directed by Ingmar Bergman. 1957.

309. Opening sequence of *La Dolce Vita*, directed by Federico Fellini. 1959.

Of the filmmakers we have considered so far, Bergman is the best example (though many would argue that Welles also qualifies) of what is called an **auteur**. The French word *auteur* translates literally as "author," but in relation to films it implies a great deal more. A cinematic *auteur* has maximum control over a film's production and imparts an individual style to a film or series of films. He or she often writes the screenplay—or closely supervises its writing—and may draw upon personal imagery, dreams, obsessions, fears, memories, beliefs, or loves as subject matter. This was certainly true of Bergman, and it is equally true of his counterpart in Italy, Federico Fellini.

Where Bergman is somber and melancholy, Fellini is flamboyant. His films may at first seem light-hearted, but there is a darker quality beneath the surface. A good example of this complexity is found in one of Fellini's best-known films, *La Dolce Vita*. The title, translated as "the sweet life," surely is ironic, for Fellini's camera zeroes in on people for whom life has become a series of superficial, momentary pleasures, carried to the extreme of depravity. Contrasts are made throughout the film between the old, stable values and society's new focus on instant sensual gratification. Fellini establishes this in his opening sequence, when a huge Christ figure is carried dangling from a helicopter over the city of Rome **(309)**. A number of young women in bikinis, sunbathing on a rooftop, rise to wave at it. The symbolism is apt. Rome is, after all, a city of many churches, the seat of the Roman Catholic Church. But the Romans caught by Fellini's camera are more interested in indulgences of the flesh. They are rich, privileged, idle, and dissolute. Major events in the film include a suicide and an orgy. Fellini's message seems to be that this "sweet life" is not sweet at all, but poisonous; its participants not alive, but acting out a living death.

Despite the prominence of European filmmakers, not all serious films of this period were made outside Hollywood, and not all Hollywood films were musicals or frothy comedies. Long after Welles' *Citizen Kane*, Hollywood still could support a serious filmmaker, indeed an *auteur*, and it found its own in the person of a transplanted English director named Alfred Hitchcock. We might describe Hitchcock as the "purest" of filmmakers in the sense that his fascination lay almost entirely with the techniques of the camera, the view from the little room. Hitchcock had limited interest in story line, even less in dialogue, and he did not much care to direct his performers in interpreting their lines. Actually, by the time the cameras were ready to roll and the actors were in position, most of his creative work was over—a remarkable stance for a director. For Hitchcock, by then, would have plotted every shot to the last detail, established the camera angles and cuts, visualized the completed film. No editor could tamper with his work afterward, because he did not—as is the usual practice—shoot several versions of each scene. He shot only what he wanted in the film, what he had determined beforehand.

310. Cary Grant in a scene from *North by Northwest*, directed by Alfred Hitchcock. 1959. © 1959 Loew's Incorporated.

We see Hitchcock's masterful control of visual imagery in a classic scene from his thriller *North by Northwest*, released in 1959 **(310)**. The hero, played by Cary Grant, has been duped into riding a bus to an isolated spot in the middle of a cornfield. There he stands, waiting for a supposed meeting with a man he does not know (and who, it turns out, does not exist). As Grant waits in the hot sun, there is no sound but the scrunch of his feet on the ground. Hitchcock gives no "meaningful" background music. Then a small airplane appears in the distance, flies closer, and heads directly for Grant. We realize the plane is trying to mow him down, either with its landing gear or with gunshots fired from the plane. Again, there is no sound but the airplane's engine and Grant's breathing as he runs this way and that, trying to elude the plane. The scene is eerily terrifying, not least because viewers are unprepared for the spectacle of a man in a business suit, stranded in flat country, trying to escape death from a dive-bombing airplane. We never see the pilot or any other occupant of the plane. Considered logically, this scene is absurd; businessmen do not get attacked by murderous airplanes. Considered cinematically, it is a triumph—a life-and-death struggle of man against anonymous machine. Hitchcock spoke of how he planned this scene to be the *opposite* of what normally we would expect to be a menacing situation. Most filmmakers, setting up danger, would show darkness, looming buildings, mysterious figures peering from windows. Not Hitchcock. He gave us: "Just nothing. Just bright sunshine and a blank, open countryside with barely a house or tree in which any lurking menaces could hide."[6] That is the genius of Hitchcock's technique. Menace drops out of the sky into ordinary life.

In today's world of dazzlingly high-budget films, with their consequent monetary risk, it is unusual for a filmmaker to have the kind of absolute creative freedom that Hitchcock did—or Welles or Bergman or the others we have discussed. Films are giant corporate productions, with artistic decisions influenced by committees and financial administrators. One filmmaker who has escaped this bureaucratic control, who has managed to maintain the position of *auteur* right up to the present, is Woody Allen. Allen, who first achieved both critical and commercial success with *Annie Hall* in 1977, makes films that are nearly always loosely autobiographical and usually set in the artistic-literary world of New York City. An Allen film tests the viewer's command of trivia in such areas as film history, popular music, literature, New York gossip, and Jewish culture. Nevertheless, one can enjoy a Woody Allen film without fully understanding its iconography; probably no one could catch *all* his references, simply because they are special to him.

Radio Days, released in 1987, is a sentimental memoir of Woody Allen's youth, of the days before television when the radio provided the key to a world of glamour and excitement. The film has very little story line. Most of the events that take place are world events, such as the bombing of Pearl

Alfred Hitchcock

1899–1980

In the first scene of the film *North by Northwest* a man misses a bus and the doors slam in his face. He appears on screen for only a few moments and is never again seen in the movie. But in a very real sense the man missing the bus is the star of the picture. Making the "cameo" appearance that was his trademark in nearly every film, that man is the director—Alfred Hitchcock.

Born in a poor section of London, Hitchcock—who as an adult was always called "Hitch"—was the son of a greengrocer and his wife. His formal schooling ended at age fourteen, after which he worked at assorted jobs to help support his family. When he was twenty he got a job with an American film company based in London. The film industry then was very new, and the roles of participants tended to overlap. Hired as a designer of title cards, Hitchcock soon found himself filling in as scriptwriter, set designer, supervisor of costumes, production manager, and director. No better apprenticeship could have been planned for the man who would later be acclaimed as the technical virtuoso of filmmaking.

As the film industry expanded, so did Hitchcock's fortunes. Eventually he would direct nine silent films and fourteen sound features in London. With *The Lodger*, a silent film of 1927, Hitchcock already had begun to attract critical notice. Meanwhile, he had married Alma Reville, who would remain his lifelong creative partner. Their daughter Pat was born in 1928.

By the late 1930s the British film business was faltering. Hollywood had become the colossus of the film world. For a time Hitchcock and Hollywood played out a sort of mating dance. Then they were wed. In March of 1939 the Hitchcocks sailed for the United States, which would become their permanent home. During the balance of that year Hitchcock worked on the first, and one of the most famous, of his American films, *Rebecca*.

Not until 1954, however, did Hitchcock truly hit his stride. Most of the pictures that established his filmmaking genius were made in the decade starting with that year: *Rear Window*, *To Catch a Thief*, *Vertigo*, *North by Northwest*, *Psycho*, and *The Birds*. Hitchcock's themes were usually macabre, featuring suspense, murder, psychosexual madness, or (in *The Birds*) placid nature turned to mayhem. During this decade, too, Hitchcock's major preoccupations got their fullest indulgence. He was a demon practical joker, often turn-

ing rather cruel pranks against his actors on the set. His devotion to gourmet foods and fine wines sent his weight soaring over 300 pounds. And he indulged another passion (always intense, always platonic) in his choice of female stars for his films—the cool, distant, aristocratic blonde exemplified by Grace Kelly, the first of Hitchcock's favorites.

After 1964 Hitchcock's concentration seemed to fail. Though he made several more films, almost none attained the quality of those from his prime. Still, until his death, neither the world nor the man himself lost the sense of Hitchcock as the consummate director. As early as 1925 Hitchcock had predicted his role as a creative force in filmmaking. Addressing a meeting of his colleagues, he said, "*We* make a film succeed. The name of the director should be associated in the public's mind with a quality product. Actors come and actors go, but the name of the director should stay clearly in the mind of the audience."[7]

Photograph of Alfred Hitchcock.

Harbor by the Japanese in 1941, conveyed through radio broadcasts and the characters' reactions. Many of the characters are set up as types rather than individuals, with names like "Bea's Third Date," "Deranged Man," "Sophisticated Songstress," and "Naked Lady." But *Radio Days* is far more than a simple recollection. Allen constructed every shot as though it were a painting (311), and his effects are endlessly lovely and rich. Reviewing the film, *The New York Times* wrote that *Radio Days* "is so densely packed with vivid detail of place, time, music, event, and character that it's virtually impossible to take them all in in one sitting."[8] For Allen, obviously, the "radio days" were a magical time, so he has translated his internal magic into a glittery visual feast for the viewer.

Like most of the films we have considered so far, *Radio Days* is essentially "straight." Its view is of a world that *could* be real, even if it isn't exactly real. Before closing our brief discussion of the film, we should look at another kind of world that is often captured by the camera—a world in which dogs talk, giant apes climb on buildings, creatures from other planets land in the suburbs of California, and galaxies go to war with one another. This is the world of special effects and animation.

SPECIAL EFFECTS AND ANIMATION

King Kong was not the first film to employ special effects, but it was certainly one of the more memorable. Made in 1932, *King Kong* is an adventure story concerning a giant gorilla, some 50 feet tall, which is captured in Africa and somehow transported to New York for display as a curiosity. Also, the film is an odd kind of love story, because when Kong inevitably escapes from his captors he falls in love with a normal-sized woman and carries her around with him. Mostly, though, *King Kong* was an opportunity to try some of the most imaginative and startling visual effects yet attempted on film.

The model of Kong used for filming was about 18 inches tall. Through trick photography the figure was transformed into a monster capable of climbing the Empire State Building and grabbing at the airplanes that try to shoot him down (312). Effects like these were achieved because filmmakers had become more comfortable with the potential of the camera. No longer need anyone's imagination be limited by physical constraints. A filmmaker could daydream, "What if a giant ape climbed the Empire State Building?" and then proceed to make it happen on film. In life or on the stage, such a feat would present staggering difficulties. In film, anything is possible.

Animation is another tool that expands the filmmaker's range of possibilities. The word **animation** means "bringing to life," and that is precisely what the filmic animator does with drawings of people, animals, and inanimate objects. Animated films are, in principle, little more than sophisticated

left: 311. Scene from *Radio Days,* directed by Woody Allen. 1987. Courtesy Orion Pictures.

right: 312. Scene from *King Kong.* 1932.

left: 313. Scene from
the animated film
Lady and the Tramp. 1955.
Copyright © 1955
Walt Disney Company.

right: 314. Scene from
Who Framed Roger Rabbit? 1987.
Combined live action
with animation.
© Touchstone Pictures/Amblin
Entertainment.

versions of Muybridge's sequential photographs (303) made to spin in a wheel. They involve a series of drawings or cartoons, each slightly different from the next, arranged on film and projected at a speed that makes the drawn figures seem to move. The classic method of animation was perfected by Walt Disney Studios in the late 1920s. You can appreciate how time-consuming this was if you realize how much your body moves just in walking two steps, and consider how many drawings it would take to capture that movement. If the motion is not to seem jerky and unnatural, every shift of position by the merest fraction of an inch requires a new drawing. The smoothest animation, therefore, demanded about 24 different drawings per *second* or some 130,000 drawings for a feature-length film. In its heyday, the 1930s and 1940s, Disney Studios employed armies of illustrators.

Through animation, the improbable becomes commonplace. Dogs talk and have unlikely adventures and fall in love, as in Disney's 1955 classic *Lady and the Tramp* (313). Puppets come to life, as in *Pinocchio.* Actually, any object that can be drawn can be made to move, dance, grow, shrink, or do whatever the filmmaker's creativity can devise.

Today the mechanics of animation have been simplified by computers. Modern animation is accomplished directly at the computer terminal, using light rather than paint. The artist draws an original picture on the display screen and then programs the computer to "draw" the changing images that simulate action. Images and colors can be varied at will, live action can be combined with animation—the possibilities are literally endless.

Who Framed Roger Rabbit?, made in 1987, set a new standard for animation-with-live-action (314), thus raising the stakes on any potential competitors. So convincing is the blend of cartoon figures (or "toons") with live humans, that half the fun of the movie is wondering, "How did they *do* that?" An animated figure can be handcuffed to a human, and somehow the two are struggling against each other realistically. The marriage of two disparate media is seamless, and hilarious.

Roger Rabbit may serve as a bridge to our final section in the discussion of camera arts, for it represents an application of technology that had been used in television for some time. The video arts—of which television is most prominent—probably touch more people more significantly than any other visual medium. How extraordinary this seems when we remember they have existed for barely fifty years.

Video

All art is about communication, but the video arts in particular are about *mass* communication. No other medium even approaches television in its potential for presenting to millions of people the same visual experience at the same moment. A national or international event—such as a grand wedding in the British royal family or the Olympic Games—is telecast simultaneously into homes around the globe, complete with the graphics and other visual trappings devised by the networks to capture our attention. Viewers can, if they wish, compare their responses to an identical visual stimulus. This holds true not only for dramatic one-of-a-kind events, but also for the recurring fare of television. In offices, in supermarkets, in schools across the United States, conversations start with, "Did you see [name a popular show] last night?" For anyone alive now this is normal, but for all the billions of people who populated the earth before the 1950s it would be almost incomprehensible. Thanks to television, living with art has acquired another dimension: It is a mass visual experience.

Video is an electronic medium. Cameras record images, break them down into tiny dots, then transmit the dots electronically to receivers where the images are reassembled. The first official television broadcast in the United States took place in 1939, in connection with the opening of the New York World's Fair. Few people noticed, however, because there were practically no television receivers to accept the transmission. Americans were still under the spell of the "radio days" chronicled in Woody Allen's film (311).

It is difficult to date the beginning of television precisely, considering the number of elements needed to complete the package. The technology had to be perfected, television stations and networks had to be established, and the public had to be persuaded to buy television sets for their homes. By the season of 1949–50 these ingredients were pretty well in place. Technological advances had improved the quality of the images, the networks were broadcasting a full schedule of evening programs, and television sets had begun to appear in living rooms—enough of them to make broadcasting profitable.

From its beginnings television covered the full range of areas we take for granted today. NBC telecast a regularly scheduled sports program as early as 1944, and boxing soon became a favorite television diversion. (There were, of course, no instant replays at the time.) Television news—now a fact of life enhanced by on-the-spot interviews and sophisticated graphics—also

315. Ricky (Desi Arnaz),
Ethel (Vivian Vance),
and Lucy (Lucille Ball)
in a scene from "I Love Lucy." 1953.

was in place by 1944, using a straightforward speaking style carried over from radio. Only very gradually did news telecasts expand to the ballyhoo we expect for a presidential inauguration, an election, or a major sports event.

The word "sitcom" (situation comedy) did not appear until much later, but starting in 1951 CBS had on the air the first blockbuster sitcom, "I Love Lucy" (315). Across the United States ordinary life came to a halt at 9:00 P.M. on Mondays, when Lucy Ricardo (Lucille Ball) and her friends played out their amusing adventures. When Lucy supposedly gave birth to "Little Ricky" on the program in January 1953—the same day the actress gave birth to a son in real life—untold millions tuned in to watch, and the event completely eclipsed the inauguration of President Dwight D. Eisenhower the next day. "I Love Lucy" served as a model for sitcoms up to the present; it appears in reruns all over the world.

Although television is a visual medium, its chief legacy is from radio, rather than from film. Long into its history, television carried over the "mind-set" of radio—adding the extra dimension of visual imagery but not really exploiting it. The game show, a radio standard, is enhanced by our ability to see the players, but we could enjoy the show almost as much with our eyes closed. Much the same is true of soap opera, which has a long radio history. The characters walk on, play out their endless dramas and intrigues, and exit. Certainly we enjoy seeing what they look like, what they're wearing, and how their houses are decorated, but we could follow the story without. "Twin Peaks" (316), starting in 1990, was among the first to carry the soap opera truly into the visual realm, possibly because its director, David Lynch, is a filmmaker. Visual jokes, odd camera angles, and all sorts of cinematic techniques built the surreal quality of the show and made it genuinely tele*vision*.

Soap operas, news and sports, comedy and drama, game shows, adventure shows, variety shows—all these have been staples since the advent of television. One type of programming, however, is a relatively new entry into the world of television, having become common only in the 1980s, and that is music video (317). Music video is difficult to categorize and to illustrate with one example, because it includes so many different types of expression. The lowest common denominator inheres in its name: There is music (often throbbing rock music) and there is video imagery. Some music videos dramatize the words of a song or even create brief visual dramas that are only vaguely related to the music. Some offer a message or statement. Some are

318. Nam June Paik. *Fin de Siecle II*. 1989. Video installation: approximately 300 television sets, 3-channel color video with sound. Collection Laila and Thurston Twigg-Smith; installed at Whitney Museum of American Art, New York, November 9, 1989 to February 18, 1990.

relatively straightforward recordings of the performers at work. What we might call the "purest" of music videos have no story or plot line but instead present color and movement and visual stimulation to complement the music. This last category reaches directly for the senses—sight and hearing.

Music video has great appeal and attracts a wide audience. The lure of constantly changing, constantly exciting and colorful visual imagery is very much a part of today's world. It should come as no surprise, therefore, that music video for the home television screen has a close cousin in the museums and art galleries, where we find the work of serious video artists.

In *video art* the image is actually created on the television screen by manipulating dials, selecting colors, combining figures and other elements. Many artists believe this type of expression to be the most valid for our electronic age. Foremost among today's video artists is Korean-born, New York-based Nam June Paik. Paik envisioned a new art of video technology as early as 1960. He does not *reproduce* images electronically, as network television might show an image of a painting by Picasso or Renoir. Rather, the image is *produced* and controlled by means of the electronic equipment itself **(318)**. What is especially exciting about this approach is its immediacy, its "aliveness." According to Paik, "Most paintings reflect light. So when it's white paint, for example, you see the white light. Whereas television pictures are glowing light. Light is coming out, sprouting out. So it is much more intense physically. . . ."[9] Paik's video installations are expensive and take up space; they are not the sort of art that most collectors could expect to have in their homes. Still, they draw large crowds at museum exhibitions. We have grown accustomed to television. The fascination of flickering, transitory images is inherent in our world. Click—the art is there; click—it's gone; click—it's back again.

A room with a view—the camera. What do we see through the peephole of the room? Images from the past, images of the present, images of a possible future. Our fondest memories and our most horrifying nightmares. Colors and shapes known or imaginary. The artistry of those who direct the camera's view need accept no limitations whatever, for the view outside grows bigger all the time.

Graphic Design

All art has to do with communication, but this is uniquely true of graphic design. Graphic design has as its goal the communication of some *specific* message to a group of people, and the success of a design is measured by how well that message is conveyed. The message may be, "This is a good product to buy," or "You will want to read this book/magazine/article," or "This is an important, respected company," or "This way to the elevators (or rest rooms or newsstand)" or any of countless others. If it can be demonstrated that the public received the intended message—because the product sold well or the company's stock went up or the traveler found the right services—then the design has worked.

Not all graphic design has to do with selling, but much of it does, and so for a long time it was known as "commercial art." The term "graphic design" is more inclusive and describes more accurately what artists in this field really do. They create a visual image by some combination of words and/or pictures to communicate a message quickly and effectively. Graphic artists design books and packages and advertisements. They devise the trademarks and symbols (logos) that construct a special corporate identity for firms doing business around the world. They invent symbols that have the same meaning to people who speak different languages. They provide the colorful images that introduce television programs and movies.

Printed words play an important role in many graphic designs, but designers rely heavily on recognizable visual images as well. Certain images have longstanding and almost universal familiarity. For instance, the skull-and-crossbones has been associated for centuries with pirates and pirate ships (319), so that by extension it has come to mean danger and is often used on bottles containing poison.

The art of the graphic designer rarely involves subtle, complicated symbolism, as is often true of painting. The image presented must have instant *shared* impact on a large number of people in order for the communication process to work. Seldom are these designs meant to be savored, studied, or enjoyed at leisure—although they can be. The effect on the observer is supposed to be immediate and lasting.

Because of our constant exposure to television commercials as well as sophisticated magazine advertisements, graphic design seems very much

"If you don't mind my saying so, Captain, I love your graphics."

319. "If you don't mind my saying so, Captain, I love your graphics." Drawing by Lorenz. © 1982 The New Yorker Magazine, Inc.

320. Hobo signs, United States.

a phenomenon of the 20th century, but in fact it has existed almost since the beginning of civilized life. Street and shop signs were used in ancient Rome and, presumably, continued through subsequent centuries. Most graphic images were undoubtedly made in wood and other perishable materials, so we have little concrete evidence, but it is clear that graphic design gradually took hold until it became a central part of urban life.

Three factors are ultimately responsible for the growing influence of graphic design: the invention of the printing press in the 15th century; the Industrial Revolution in the 18th century; and the revolution in travel and communication in the 20th century.

Anyone can paint one sign, or two or three. The printing press, however, made it possible to reproduce a graphic image many hundreds or thousands of times. This gave designers the *ability* to communicate with a broad public. The *need* for such communication was largely a result of the Industrial Revolution, which began in Europe in the latter part of the 18th century. Before that time, most products were grown or made locally to serve a local population. The person who wanted, say, a new pair of shoes could walk down the road to the village cobbler, or perhaps wait for the monthly fair at which cobblers from the neighboring towns might appear, but the choices were fairly limited. With the advent of machines huge quantities of goods were produced in centralized factories for wide distribution, and competition between producers became intense. It was necessary, therefore, to inform the buying public about the availability of certain goods and their relative merits. Graphic design in the form of advertising filled that need.

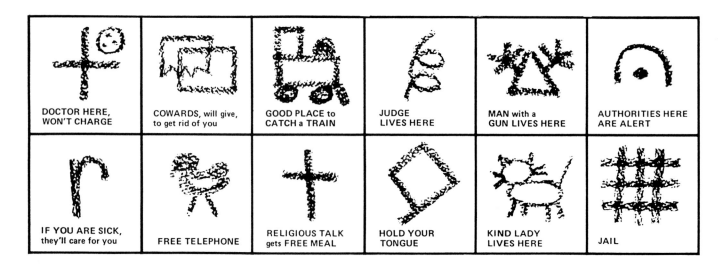

DOCTOR HERE, WON'T CHARGE	COWARDS, will give, to get rid of you	GOOD PLACE to CATCH a TRAIN	JUDGE LIVES HERE	MAN with a GUN LIVES HERE	AUTHORITIES HERE ARE ALERT
IF YOU ARE SICK, they'll care for you	FREE TELEPHONE	RELIGIOUS TALK gets FREE MEAL	HOLD YOUR TONGUE	KIND LADY LIVES HERE	JAIL

The history of graphic design for travelers is interesting, too. Some of it is speculative; we wonder, for instance, whether Robin Hood followed signs leading to Nottingham, or whether the pilgrims Chaucer wrote about found signs pointing the way to Canterbury. One of the more intriguing of travelers' communication systems was the one traditionally practiced by hobos in the United States. "Hobo signs" were simple, graphic images, usually scratched in chalk on a fence or post or sidewalk (320). The casual passerby probably would not have noticed them, but for those intrepid souls who rode the freight trains, slept under bridges, and caught a meal wherever they could, these signs had meaning. Some were *pictographic*, or visually suggestive of what they meant ("good place to catch a train"), while others were purely arbitrary and conveyed meaning from hobo to hobo because they had been learned. The message conveyed by "hobo signs" was a message of comradeship: "This is the experience I had here, and I want you to profit by it."

In the last few decades international travel has increased dramatically. People journey to foreign countries, without knowing the local language, and expect to get around comfortably and safely. Such travel has opened up a whole new realm for the graphic designer. Nowhere, perhaps, is the need to communicate without words more evident than at the Olympic Games, which draw athletes from scores of countries into one location. Somehow all the athletes must be housed, must find the places where they are supposed to be at various times, and must obtain the services they need. Preparing signs written in all the languages represented would be tedious and cumbersome. So whenever the games are held, graphic images are designed to mark basic areas and functions. The images are designed anew each time, but always they are simple, straightforward, and free of cultural biases (321). Even without captions you should have no difficulty identifying the sports they portray.

So in international travel as well as international commerce the need for graphic design has burgeoned. Fortunately, the *ability* to communicate graphically has also increased, thanks to new mechanical and electronic processes. Together, need and ability have yielded an unprecedented outpouring of graphic design. With this background, let us look first at the tools used by the graphic designer and then at some of the categories of graphic design.

The Tools of the Graphic Designer

Regardless of the kind of graphic design or the method of reproduction, the graphic designer works with three tools: **type** (printed letters), **photography**, and drawn or painted **illustration.** Every design has at least one of these resources and usually has two or more in combination. We must also take into account the variable of color, because color is often responsible for much of a design's impact. And motion—whether in television or in computer graphics—can dramatically influence the way these three elements operate.

Type design has come a long way since the invention of movable type about 1450. Contemporary graphic designers have a bewildering array of typefaces and styles to choose from, in an infinite range of sizes. This book, for instance, is printed in a typeface known as *Aster*, which is popular for books because it is easy to read, legible in fairly small sizes, and not tiring to the eyes.

With so many typefaces and sizes to choose from, the designer can select one that best fits the character of the design and the tone of the message to be communicated. Moreover, type design itself has changed radically. In earlier times the letters of type were painstakingly carved out of wood or cast in

321. Graphics from the 1984 Summer Olympic Games, Los Angeles.
Courtesy Los Angeles Olympic Organizing Committee.

metal. Today, type is "set"—or created and placed in position—by computer and photographic methods, so it is relatively easy to design an original typeface for a specific purpose. The designer can make a "word picture" that symbolizes the idea of the graphic design **(322)**.

A major decision for any graphic designer is whether to use photography or drawn illustration. In either case the options are limitless, so the choice becomes one of finding the image that will best present the idea for a particular audience.

One instance in which a drawn illustration proved compelling came in a *Boston Globe Magazine* article about veterinary medicine **(323)**. Here the art director *could* have used a standard photograph of a veterinarian treating someone's pet dog. Instead, illustrator Seymour Chwast was called in to do this charming drawing of a large animal (a cow?) in a wheelchair, blanket up to its chin, icebag on its head, looking very much under the weather. This illustration would attract almost anyone's attention to the article.

We used the term "drawn illustration" to distinguish from photography, but not all illustrations are actually drawn with a pen or crayon. One of the most sought-after illustrators today, Stephen Kroninger, does his "drawing" with scissors. His illustrations for many popular magazines and newspapers are made in the form of collage—cut-up pieces from magazines and other bits of paper, assembled into odd and playful portraits **(324)**. The collage form gives a three-dimensional feel to these illustrations, making them seem like pop-up figures jumping off the page.

Sometimes a photograph is the better choice for a particular design situation, but then the question becomes, "What sort of photograph?" To promote an upcoming art exhibition, for instance, the designer might choose to work with a photo of some painting in the exhibition, or a photograph of a featured artist. Our illustration shows a different approach **(325)**. For an exhibition sponsored by the Kentucky Arts Commission, the designers used a photograph of eggs, beautifully arranged and lighted, with three of the eggs apparently broken to produce "yolks" in brilliant primary colors. The idea of "fresh paint" suggests new paintings come to town, and a viewer might well be eager to see the exhibition that inspired such a splash of hues.

These three tools, then—type, photography, and illustration—lend themselves to literally infinite combinations. The following brief survey of graphic design categories should give some idea of the scope and variety in this field. We begin with the most pervasive design category of modern times.

322. Wanda Siedlecka. *Wordplay.* 1990. Type designed to create "word pictures."

Advertising

Imagine you have bet someone that you could get through an entire day without being exposed to a single advertisement. How would you go about winning the bet? You couldn't watch television or listen to the radio, of course, nor could you read any magazines or newspapers. You'd have to be careful about the food you ate; so many packages and cans have advertising

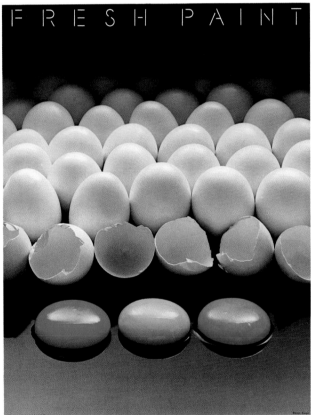

top left: 323. Seymour Chwast.
"Cow in Wheelchair," illustration for a story
in *Boston Globe Magazine*. 1983.
Pen and ink on newsprint with Cello Tak.
Art director: Ronn Campisi.

left: 324. Stephen Kroninger.
Michael Jackson. 1990. Collage illustration.
Courtesy the artist.

above: 325. Poster for an exhibition
of the Kentucky Arts Commission.
Art directors and designers: Julius Friedman
and Nathan Felde; photographer: Warren Lynch;
design firm: Images.

on them, for themselves or for some other product. You couldn't go to work or to class: too many billboards on the street, advertising posters on the bus, people handing out flyers on street corners. Should you settle down with a good book? Many books carry advertising for other books, either on the back cover or bound inside. A day at the beach? No, there's a skywriting airplane flying overhead and somebody's radio turned up loud. Perhaps a walk in the woods. But will it rain? You decide to call the weather service on the telephone. You've lost the bet! The weather report now includes commercials.

More than any other time in history we are bombarded from every side by advertising. So many products are made, so many consumers are there to buy them, so many millions of dollars are at stake in bringing the two together. Oftentimes the success of a product has more to do with the advertising campaign than with the product's intrinsic worth. This is especially true when products are alike. How different, really, are household cleaners? All have more or less the same ingredients, and all will get the sink clean. The manufacturer's job, therefore, is to fix the product name in the consumer's mind and have that consumer *perceive* a difference. For this the manufacturer relies on advertising.

The question then arises, what makes a successful advertisement? Why do some ads work better than others? Countless books have been written on this subject, and the answer sometimes involves complex psychological responses. Certain key factors can be identified, however, as contributing to an advertisement's effectiveness.

First of all, the ad must be noticed. Getting the viewer's attention is the advertising designer's first task, especially given the huge number of commercial messages constantly assailing us. One very popular technique for getting attention is consumer identification, as in ads for expensive items. While flipping through a magazine or newspaper, you see a picture of an elegant person or group and think to yourself, "I want to be just like that." After a barrage of such ads, you associate the product name with that desirable image.

A related approach is to take the expected, the familiar, and do something unexpected with it. Practically everyone knows the *Mona Lisa,* for example, but when she turns up in an unusual form—or many unusual forms—we are likely to take notice and look more closely.

Yet another method of attracting attention is by sheer size. Levi Strauss & Company tapped an unexpected resource when it decided to turn its three hundred trailer trucks into "moving billboards," with huge 6-by-8-foot decal advertisements on the sides **(326)**. In the language of the market researchers who participated in this ad campaign, each truck-billboard would garner seventy "consumer impressions" for every mile the truck was driven. Consumer impressions, naturally, translate into purchases—or so it is hoped.

326. "Moving billboard" truck advertising for Levi's. Courtesy Levi Strauss & Co.

Everybody on Leonardo

A popular song of the 1950s inquired whether *Mona Lisa* might be "just a cold and lonely, lovely work of art." Cold is in the eye of the beholder. But *lonely*? Hardly. She has too many sisters to be lonely.

Leonardo da Vinci painted the *Mona Lisa* (493) in the early 16th century, and for a long time there was just the one of her. Then came the graphics revolution of the 20th century, and *Mona Lisa* began to replicate, growing virtually out of control into the millions of Monas. She has appeared in advertisements, on posters, on stamps. Her face adorns billboards and matchbooks and packaging for every imaginable product. She is done up in eyeglasses, fright wigs, swimsuits, funny hats. One designer, doing a promotional ad for a television station, lined up twenty-five Monas in various guises, including a gorilla mask.

The obvious question is, *why*? Why this painting instead of some other one? What makes *Mona Lisa* so special that graphic designers around the world want to borrow her famous face? We might speculate about two reasons.

First, Leonardo's painting is the best-known image in Western art. Even people who care little about art usually recognize *Mona Lisa*. By transforming her—into a kimono-clad Japanese woman, a Lone Ranger impersonator, a gorilla—the designer attracts our attention, and that is the first goal of an advertisement.

Second, the *Mona Lisa* is considered to be the most *valuable* painting in the Western world. By putting this image on packaging, designers may hope that consumers will judge the contents—whether coffee or chocolates or spaghetti or olive oil—to be similarly valuable, the best product available.

Part of the phenomenon is that we tend to think of *Mona Lisa* not as *it*, but as *she*, with a personality of her own. Who knows what the original thinks about all this attention? After nearly five hundred years, she is still smiling.

left: "Looking Good Mona," generic image promotion for WHAS-TV, Louisville, Ky. Designer: Teresa Heintzman.

right: Bernadette Contensou. Collection of *Mona Lisa* images. Photograph.

ASK YOUR GROCER FOR IT.

Buy ARBUCKLES' UNGROUND ROASTED, as I do, and you will have no trouble.

Oh, I have Burnt my Coffee again!

ARBUCKLES' AIIOSA COFFEE

ARBUCKLES' UNGROUND ROASTED COFFEE.

AIR-TIGHT. Self Settling. Full Weight. 1 lb. PACKAGES

Fame has its price.

"Doctor, it's gotten to the point where people are constantly asking for my autograph. I can't even eat my chorizos in peace."

These words recently came from the fatigued form of Juan Valdez. Along with his partner he's starting to feel the pressure of success.

The cause of it all, of course, is their huge television exposure for Colombian Coffee. In fact this year alone, Juan and his friend will be seen almost 2 billion times in American living rooms.

Frankly they've proven to be successful spokesmen. A recent survey indicates that most Americans now believe that Colombian Coffee is the best in the world. Which, unfortunately for Juan, makes him even more popular.

What this means to you is that if you're not making shelf space for 100% Colombian Coffee brands, it's time to start. Every day you delay you're losing potential profits.

And if you let that happen you'll end up like Juan. Spilling the beans to a psychiatrist.

100% Colombian Coffee

above: 327. Chromolithograph poster, advertisement for Arbuckle's Coffee. 1880s. New-York Historical Society (Bella C. Landauer Collection).

right: 328. Advertisement for the National Federation of Coffee Growers of Colombia. 1983. Art director: Mark Hughes; copywriter: D. J. Webster; photographer: Larry Robbins; agency: DDB Needham Worldwide.

Most advertisements, regardless of what they are selling, are planned to appeal to the self-interest of the people at whom they are directed. The viewer is supposed to think, "This would be good for *me*." Advertising designers have known this for at least a hundred years. An ad for Arbuckles' coffee, dating from the 1880s **(327)**, suggests that home-roasting of coffee beans in those days was both a common practice and a "burning issue." The little dialogue in the ad is straightforward. It presents the problem in such a way that consumers can perceive a need, and then it offers a solution in comforting terms: "You will have no trouble." Since everybody wants "no trouble," the ad probably succeeded.

Coffee advertisements have changed rather a lot in the last century, as we can see by comparing the Arbuckles' ad with one from the 1980s **(328)**. Here is "Juan Valdez," the fictional representative of Colombian coffee growers, stretched out on an analyst's couch with his burro on another couch beside him. Both are presumably suffering from the effects of fame—so many autographs to sign, so much attention—caused by the popularity of Colombian coffee. We cannot doubt the attention-getting qualities of this ad; few people could miss the image of a burro on a couch, its legs waving in the air. And how does this advertisement appeal to the consumer's self-interest? Well, after all, don't most people want to associate with the rich and famous? If Colombian coffee can produce fame, shouldn't one go out and buy some?

Print Media: Books, Magazines, and Posters

Book designers, of all graphic artists, often have the most difficulty making people understand what they do. In this book, for example, the designer selected the typefaces; chose the appropriate sizes of type for text, headings, captions, and so forth; and decided how much space to allow for margins and between various elements. She also devised a way to set off the artists' biographies, the "Art People," and the "Artists on Artists" stories from the text.

Cover design is another major responsibility of the graphic designer. For the cover of this book, there was first the matter of choosing one image from all the possible works of art in the world. Then the designer had to select typefaces and sizes and decide which color to set around the painting and "frame" it. An old adage says, "You can't judge a book by its cover," but to some extent you can. Readers of this book are far enough along now to have formed a good idea of what it is like. Did the book deliver what the cover suggested it would?

The design of magazine covers, while drawing on the same elements as book cover design (type, photography, illustration), differs in certain respects. For one thing, magazine covers are more influential in a reader's decision to purchase. You may be motivated to buy a particular book for any of several reasons—it's on the best-seller list, you heard about it from a friend, you are familiar with the author's work, your teacher assigned it, and so on. But buying a magazine is more often a spur-of-the-moment decision. You are dashing for the train, waiting to check out at the supermarket, faced with a boring evening when your friends are away and there's nothing on television. You scan the magazine racks looking for diversion. Chances are, you will buy the magazine whose cover attracts you.

Another difference between magazine and book cover design has to do with longevity. Books often are kept, in homes and libraries, for many years. Magazines tend to be read quickly and then thrown away. (There are exceptions: In 1982 a Connecticut couple narrowly escaped disaster when several years' worth of stored *National Geographic* issues crashed through the floor of their attic to the bedroom below, landing on the bed to which they would soon have retired.) Because of their short life span, magazines can have covers that are contemporary, following up-to-the-minute fashions and events.

When a drawn illustration is to be used for a cover, the choice of an illustrator is up to the designer of the cover or the magazine's art director— the person in charge of the visual aspects of the whole magazine. Occasionally a particular illustrator is used over and over, has a distinctive style, and therefore becomes closely associated with that magazine. There could be no better example of such a partnership than the one that existed between Norman Rockwell and *The Saturday Evening Post.*

In 1916 a very young Norman Rockwell, just twenty-two years old, presented himself at the Philadelphia offices of the *Saturday Evening Post,* a popular weekly magazine. He carried two paintings meant as potential *Post* covers and a sketch for a third. The *Post*'s art director was impressed and immediately bought the young artist's illustrations, requesting more. Rockwell's first *Post* cover appeared in May of that year, and his covers continued to appear regularly until 1963, when the artist branched out to other magazines. His last *Post* cover was a portrait of President John F. Kennedy, used as a memorial on the December 14 issue—three weeks after the president's assassination. During those forty-seven years Rockwell averaged about six covers each year—an amazing feat when one considers that each of the illustrations was a fully developed painting, often including many characters. Every Rockwell cover was greeted with delight by *Post* readers and guaranteed an increase in sales.

Rockwell's task was not an easy one; working in the magazine's format imposed many restrictions. Obviously, the image had to fit within a certain left: **329.** Norman Rockwell. *The Tom Boy*, cover for *The Saturday Evening Post*, May 23, 1953. Reprinted from *The Saturday Evening Post* © 1953 The Curtis Publishing Company.

right: **330.** Cover for *The New Yorker* magazine, June 4, 1990. Cover-drawing by Levin. © 1990 The New Yorker Magazine, Inc.

vertical framework—the shape of the magazine cover **(329)**. Space had to be left at the top for the magazine's title and the date. Sometimes "teaser" blurbs for articles were superimposed over the artwork; Rockwell once mildly complained that the blurbs always seemed to fall just over the spot where he had drawn his most interesting detail. Nevertheless, Rockwell's association with *The Saturday Evening Post* proved to be a long and happy one for all concerned. As with many enduring works of art, his illustrations offered the right style in the right medium at the right time.

Most contemporary magazines attempt, through their covers, to establish a certain "tone" or style that is to be associated in readers' minds with the magazine. Computer and electronics magazines have photographs of high-tech equipment, fashion magazines picture models wearing the latest styles, expensive cooking magazines feature elegant, beautifully composed photographs of chic food, and so forth. Some magazines shift back and forth between illustration and photography, but most stick to one or the other. A prime example of the latter preference is *The New Yorker*.

The style of *New Yorker* covers has not changed for decades. Every cover is an illustration, never a photograph. Often the subject is a timely one—as in a June (graduation month) cover showing a diploma-clutching person in cap and gown being shot out of a cannon **(330)**. Although the magazine uses many different illustrators, the style is unmistakable. Anyone familiar with that style would recognize a *New Yorker* cover, even without the title, regardless of whether it is last week's issue or a number from thirty years ago. Exactly why this is so would be difficult to analyze, because, considered individually, the products of various artists seem very different from one another. One could say there is a unifying tone of whimsicality that readers have come to identify. A *New Yorker* cover does not reflect any article inside the magazine, and there are no teaser blurbs on the cover. Readers generally do not buy an issue for any particular article or story, but simply because it is *The New Yorker*.

From the magazine cover to the poster is not a large step; in fact, some exceptional magazine covers—often *New Yorker* covers—have been trans-

Norman Rockwell

1894–1978

Norman Rockwell, chronicler of small-town America, was born in New York City and raised in a section known as the Bronx. By the age of fourteen, already determined on a career as an artist, he assumed responsibility for his own education—selecting the art schools he would attend (which eventually included the Art Students League) and finding odd jobs to support himself. One such job was as an extra, often a spear carrier, at the Metropolitan Opera, where he became rather a pet of the legendary tenor Enrico Caruso.

At eighteen Rockwell began to get his first professional commissions, most of them for illustrations in boys' magazines and children's books. Then in 1916 came the first *Saturday Evening Post* cover. After his early triumph at the *Post*, Rockwell never again lacked for assignments. His career blossomed, and he remained busy trying to keep up with the demand for his work until the onset of his last illness at the age of eighty-four.

Rockwell's great success was based on the simplest of formulas: He drew ordinary people in ordinary situations doing the sorts of things all the *Post*'s readers were accustomed to doing. He drew them with a gentle humor that poked fun at the situations while never poking fun at people. The magazine's readers could laugh at themselves, at the odd and funny plights they got themselves into, because they sensed the artist was one of *them*, subject to the same foibles as anybody else.

After leaving New York, Rockwell first lived in a suburb of the city, then for many years in Vermont. Ultimately he settled in Stockbridge, Massachusetts, the town with which he is most closely associated. His models for *Post* covers and other illustrations were the townspeople—the mayor, the barber, the village clerk, the children of the neighborhood. In the early years Rockwell painted them from life, but later he developed a system of photographing the scenes and models, then painting from the photographs. Not all Rockwell's subjects were Stockbridge villagers, however. Routinely he was called upon to paint the famous and the mighty—presidents and presidential candidates, from Eisenhower onward; heads of state; sports heroes and astronauts; and many entertainment figures, including Bob Hope, Frank Sinatra, John Wayne, even Lassie.

Rockwell married three times—the latter two marriages were apparently very happy ones—and had three sons. Apart from the sudden death of his second wife, little trouble marred a peaceful, productive life. Although the major art critics always were harsh in their assessment of Rockwell's work, he enjoyed enormous popularity with the general public. In 1969 Rockwell had his first one-artist show of paintings in New York; the local critics savaged the show, but nearly every painting sold at the preview, before the exhibit opened officially.

Actually, the problem of criticism arose only when people tried to evaluate the artist as a *painter;* few ever questioned his gifts as an illustrator. Rockwell commented once on this distinction: "Some people have been kind enough to call me a fine artist. I've always called myself an illustrator. I'm not sure what the difference is. All I know is whatever type of work I do, I try to give it my very best. Art has been my life."[1]

Norman Rockwell. *Triple Self-Portrait,*
cover for *The Saturday Evening Post,* February 13, 1960.
Reprinted from *The Saturday Evening Post*
© 1960 The Curtis Publishing Company.

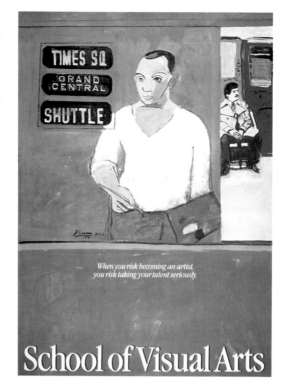

formed into posters and found their way onto home and office walls around the country. Posters are by no means new, but only since the 1960s have they been such an ever-present factor in our lives. Nowadays, it is the rare individual who has never hung up a poster from a museum exhibition, a travel poster, a poster featuring a film or music star, even an advertising poster, if it is particularly attractive. Posters are supposed to catch the eye, to create an instant impression, and perhaps to make us smile. All three qualities are present in Seymour Chwast's poster advertising *Happy Birthday, Bach* **(331)**, a book published on the three-hundredth anniversary of the composer's birth. A familiar image of Bach, known from an old painting, has been cheerfully transformed by Chwast's pen, which turns the powdered wig into a tiered birthday cake and adds a celebratory cigar. On the whole, Bach has a stuffy reputation, but not when he is interpreted by the creative poster artist.

Our next example also features a well-known image, but in this case the image is thrown into a wholly unexpected context. Although many people are familiar with Picasso's self-portrait (p. 39), few are prepared to see Picasso catching the subway at Grand Central Station in New York **(332)**. This poster's visual impact is brilliant in its simplicity, and the message it conveys is understated but clear. The School of Visual Arts teaches courses in art. Probably the bulk of its students commute by subway, and that is where the poster has been displayed. Thus, if the artist can take the subway, the subway can take you to art.

So far, our examples in this chapter have been made with conventional materials—paint, ink, pencil, pen. We turn now to the newest branch of graphic design, which depends on the medium of our age: the computer.

Graphics and the Computer

The computer has done more to influence graphic design than anything since the invention of the printing press. Each of the three tools available to the designer—type, photography, and illustration—can be manipulated in special ways when the computer's help is enlisted.

Computer-designed typography is now commonplace. Unique typefaces can be created, stored, rearranged, and redesigned with a speed and flexibility unheard of just a few years ago. The computer influences the character of mechanically produced alphabets as surely as the quill and ink influenced the design of letters centuries ago. For instance, letters designed by computer can be set against graphically exciting backgrounds (333), or even designed to move in a colorful landscape. The word "move" is significant. While most computer-designed type resembles older-style typography, the computer offers the potential of an extra dimension. If desired, computer lettering can be made to float or bounce or streak across the screen of a television set or display terminal. Quite often, computer graphics are graphics in motion.

Through computer technology images, too, can be made to streak through an apparently three-dimensional landscape. Designer/director Mario Kamberg used a glittering high-tech image, seeming to have the transparency of glass, to create a television commercial for Rockwell International (334). Unfortunately, a still image, as we must show here, cannot really convey the electric visual impact of moving graphics. They flash across our visual field like lightning—dazzling and colorful and exciting.

The computer has changed the way graphic artists in *all* media work. Even if the end result is to be a printed design—an advertisement or magazine cover, for example—some graphic designers have replaced their sketch pads with computer terminals. Designing, testing of ideas and forms and color, is done on the screen with as much flexibility as the pencil or pen could offer, but much faster. The design can then be transmitted almost instantly anywhere it needs to go—to the client, the art director, or the home office.

A major contribution of the computer to graphic design is in the field of animation—the creation of illusory movement through a series of drawn illustrations. As mentioned in Chapter 9, animation means "bringing to life." The images brought to life by computer techniques can be any of the graphic tools we have mentioned—type, photographs, illustrations. Letters can move, still photographs can move, drawn images can move, and any two or three of these can be combined so as to interact with one another.

Animated films—ambitious versions of the cartoon—have been with us for decades, but new computer technology has vastly increased their sophistication. A feature-length film called *Quest* (335), made in 1985, employed a method known as "ray tracing," which is capable of producing quite realistic effects of transparency, reflection, texture, and shadows. A scene from the film showing the Main Temple Arcade appears to have ripples and reflections in the water, shadows on the columns, and a transparent arched roof overhead. At present, ray tracing is a relatively slow technique, as computer graphics go, but by the time you read this it probably won't be any longer.

One hesitates to say too much about computer graphics, because this field is evolving so rapidly. In the short time that elapses between the writing of this book and its publication, tremendous expansion of computer graphics will undoubtedly take place. Without question we are in the middle of another revolution in graphic design.

below: **333.** Logo for ABC Television. 1987.

bottom left: **334.** Still from a commercial for Rockwell International, made on a Cray Super-Computer. Designer: Mario Kamberg.

bottom right: **335.** Main Temple Arcade, from the film *Quest: A Long Ray's Journey into Light.* A poll-computer, Chelmsford, Mass. Producer/Director: Michael Sciulli.

PART FOUR

THREE-DIMENSIONAL MEDIA

336. Alexander Liberman. *Iliad*. 1974–76.
Steel, painted orange; 36' × 54'7" × 19'7".
Storm King Art Center, Mountainville, N.Y.
(gift of the Ralph E. Ogden Foundation and by exchange).

Sculpture

The study of sculpture confronts us with the third dimension, with the concept of *depth*. This seems like an easy and obvious point, but there is more to it than you might imagine. In everyday life we are faced constantly with situations in which our brains have to make adjustments for depth. Just walking down the street requires the brain to make a thousand calculations. How far away is that building? If you misjudge the distance, you may bump into it. How high is the curb? Unless you estimate correctly, you may trip and fall. The mass media require us to make a similar set of adjustments. We see images of people on the movie screen or television set. Even though these are, in reality, flat images, we perceive the people as being full-bodied and three-dimensional. This correction for depth becomes automatic, and we don't have to think about it.

As we approach sculpture, however, we might suspend this visual over-drive and train ourselves to be more *actively* aware of depth. Heightened perception of the third dimension is crucial to our full appreciation of sculpture. Sculptures are like our selves, full-bodied and substantial. Usually they look different when viewed from different angles. The experience of looking at a flat painting on a wall is quite unlike the experience of walking up to a freestanding sculpture, circling it, observing it from various viewpoints. If a sculpture is exceptionally large, like Alexander Liberman's *Iliad* **(336)**, we need also to consider it from various *distances*, because we cannot take it in, so to speak, all in one gulp. Only when we integrate many visual perceptions do we begin to reach an understanding of the sculpture as a whole.

This chapter will explore a wide range of three-dimensional forms, from many times and places. Sculpture has one of the longest histories of any art medium, and yet it is especially vital and exciting today. A major reason for this vitality in contemporary sculpture is its use of materials and techniques that were unheard of just a century ago. We will look first at the sculptor's methods, how materials are handled, and how sculptures are designed.

Methods of Sculpture

There are four basic methods for making a sculpture: modeling, casting, carving, and assembling. Modeling and assembling are considered ***additive*** processes. The sculptor begins with a simple framework or core or nothing at all and *adds* material until the sculpture is finished. Carving is a **subtractive** process in which one starts with a mass of material larger than the planned sculpture and *subtracts*, or takes away, material until only the desired form remains. Some people consider casting to be an additive process, but in a sense this method occupies a category all its own. Casting involves a mold of some kind, into which liquid or semiliquid material is poured and allowed to harden. Often casting is used to make several identical sculptures.

Let us consider each of these methods in more detail.

MODELING

Modeling is familiar to most of us from childhood. As children we experimented with Silly Putty or clay to construct lopsided figures of people and animals. For sculpture, the most common modeling material is clay, an earth substance found in most parts of the world. Wet clay is wonderfully pliable; few can resist the temptation to squeeze and shape it. As long as clay remains wet, the sculptor can do almost anything with it—add on more and more clay to build up the form, gouge away sections, pinch it outward, scratch into it with a sharp tool, smooth it with the hands. But when a clay form has dried and been *fired*—heated to a high temperature in a kiln (Chapter 12, p. 307)—it becomes hard. Fired clay, sometimes called by the Italian name *terra cotta*, is surprisingly durable. Much of the ancient art that has survived was formed from this material.

A female figure made in Cyprus more than three thousand years ago (337) is typical of the fertility images found in most early cultures. The artist who created this little statue had learned to exploit many of the possibilities of clay. After the overall form had been shaped by the fingers, delicate lines defining the form were incised with a sharp tool. The arms and "earrings" were shaped of separate pieces of clay and then added to the main piece.

Throughout their history the Chinese have been masters of ceramic sculpture—sculpture made from clay—but not until recently has the enormous scope of their production been fully appreciated. In 1974 well diggers near the central Chinese city of Xian accidentally uncovered part of the tomb complex of the first emperor of China, Shi Huang Di. Buried since 210 B.C., guarding the tomb in military formation, were a whole army of life-size clay soldiers, horses, and attendants—at least seven thousand of them (338). The warriors' faces and bodies are modeled with amazing naturalism, and each variety of provincial headdress is rendered in specific detail. The horses stand waiting to be harnessed and ridden off into battle. More recent digs

above: 337. Female figure holding a fluttering bird (fertility image?), from Cyprus. c. 1500–1200 B.C. Terra cotta, height 8¾". The Metropolitan Museum of Art, New York (Cesnola Collection; purchased by subscription, 1874–1876).

right: 338. *Cavalryman and Saddle Horse from Earthenware Army of First Emperor of Qin.* c. 210 B.C. Terra cotta, height of man 5'10½". Cultural Relics Bureau, Beijing, and The Metropolitan Museum of Art, New York.

have unearthed a similar array of scribes, or clerks, suggesting that the entire court, represented in clay, may have gone into the emperor's tomb. We can only speculate how many sculptors labored to build this immense ceramic population, especially in view of the high quality maintained in the figures.

Clay served the Chinese tomb builders well, because of its permanence and potential for naturalism. But later artists have prized clay for other qualities. Sculptors often use clay modeling in the same way that painters traditionally have used drawing, to test ideas before committing themselves to a finished sculpture. As long as the clay is kept damp, it can be worked and reworked almost indefinitely. Even the terminology is the same; we sometimes call a clay test piece a "sketch."

Our illustration (339) shows a clay study for Eustache de St. Pierre, one of the figures in Rodin's *Burghers of Calais* (355), a life-size bronze piece. We can learn much about the sculptor's creative process by comparing the little terra cotta sketch—only about a foot tall—to the large finished work. Most obvious is the fact that the clay model is nude, while the figures in the *Burghers* are clothed. Undoubtedly Rodin wanted to explore the way this man would hold his body, to capture every line of muscle and bone, to study the movement of legs, arms, and shoulders, the curve of the back—before draping the figure in garments. In our photograph of the completed *Burghers* (355) Eustache de St. Pierre appears just to right of center, facing us. Rodin has changed the pose from that of his terra cotta study. In the modeled clay figure the arms are held out from the body, almost as though in supplication. But the bronze Eustache—more inward-looking, more self-contained—holds his arms closer to his sides. Only after many such sketches, in clay and plaster, did Rodin settle upon the final composition for his work. We are fortunate in having the clay study, not only because it helps us to understand the creative process, but also for its own sake. Despite this figure's small size, the clay modeling is wonderfully lifelike and expressive.

Rodin also made studies in plaster, and this too has traditionally been a common material for preliminary models. But in contemporary sculpture plaster has come into its own as a medium for finished work. Modern sculptors seem to like the flat, white impersonality of plaster, as well as its ready acceptance of bright color. Manuel Neri's *Red Legs* (340), modeled in plaster

left: **339.** Auguste Rodin. *Eustache de St. Pierre,* nude study for *The Burghers of Calais.* 1884–85. Terra cotta, height 12¼". Musée Rodin, Paris.

right: **340.** Manuel Neri. *Red Legs.* 1979. Plaster, dry pigment, steel armature, and Styrofoam core; 33½ × 33 × 25". Private collection, San Francisco.

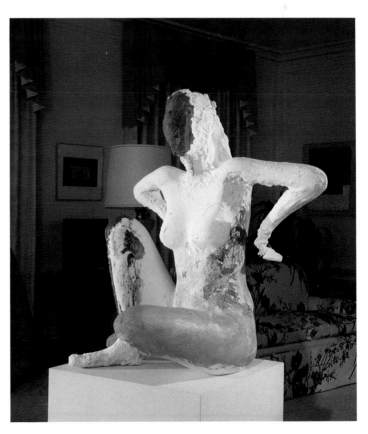

over a steel frame, or **armature,** seems almost cheerful in its vivid colors and jaunty pose. But this gaiety is in direct contradiction to the flat blue face. A face without features is depersonalized and frightening. We cannot tell where the figure is looking or what it is thinking, and it cannot speak to us. There is only that blank, staring oval of blue.

In some ways modeling is the most direct of sculpture methods. The workable material responds to every touch, light or heavy, of the sculptor's fingers, so that the maker and the made become almost one.

CASTING

In contrast to modeling, casting seems like a very *indirect* method of creating a sculpture. Sometimes the sculptor never touches the final piece at all. Metal, and specifically bronze, is the material we think of most readily in relation to casting. Bronze can be superheated until it flows, will pour freely into the tiniest crevices and forms, and then hardens to extreme durability. Even for a thin little projection, like a finger, there is no fear of it breaking off. Other materials also can be cast, including many plastics and clay.

The simplest type of casting is *solid* casting—that is, solid as opposed to hollow. You make a solid cast every time you make an ice cube. You pour liquid material (water) into a mold (the ice-cube tray), cause it to harden (by freezing), and then remove the cast (the ice cube). Novelty ice-cube trays can make cast-ice "sculptures" in the shape of hearts or flowers or any number of other shapes. Some plastics are cast by a very similar method. Liquid plastic is poured into a mold and allowed to set, after which the mold is removed.

There are three problems with solid casting. First, it uses quite a lot of material, and this can be expensive, especially with metal. Second, solid-cast objects tend to be very heavy unless they are made of lightweight plastic. Third, many materials, including metal and clay, develop cracks if cast solid. For all these reasons various methods have been developed to make *hollow* casts—that is, casts with an inner core of air.

Metal usually is cast by the **lost-wax** method, sometimes known by the French name, **cire perdue.** This is an extremely complex process. The following description and the illustrations **(341)** outline its basic principles.

1. The sculptor works either in clay or in plaster to create a full-size model of the intended sculpture **(341a)**. For the sculptor this may end the creative part; very likely specialized technicians will take over afterward to complete the casting.
2. A coating of synthetic rubber is applied to the clay or plaster model. (Earlier generations used other materials.) This rubber coating makes an outside mold of the sculpture's contours that is accurate in every detail **(341b)**. The synthetic rubber mold is removed from the outside of the model.
3. The synthetic rubber mold is now a *negative* or exterior mold of the sculpture **(341c)**. Wax is coated inside the parts of the synthetic rubber mold to a depth of about ⅛ inch. The wax layer is the exact shape and thickness that is wanted for the final metal sculpture.
4. The space inside the wax layer—what will eventually be the sculpture's hollow core—is filled with a mixture of wet plaster called **investment,** which is then allowed to dry **(341d)**. This plaster core is held in place by a series of metal pins. Then the synthetic rubber mold is removed from the outside of the wax layer. A network of wax rods is constructed all over the outside of the wax model. (Later, when the wax is melted away and the metal poured in, these rodlike channels will serve as conduits for the flow of material.)
5. The wax model, complete with rods and plaster core, is coated with another layer of investment plaster, and the assembly is placed in a kiln **(341e)**. The kiln melts away the wax—hence the term *"lost" wax*—leaving an empty space between the inner core and outer layer of plaster that is

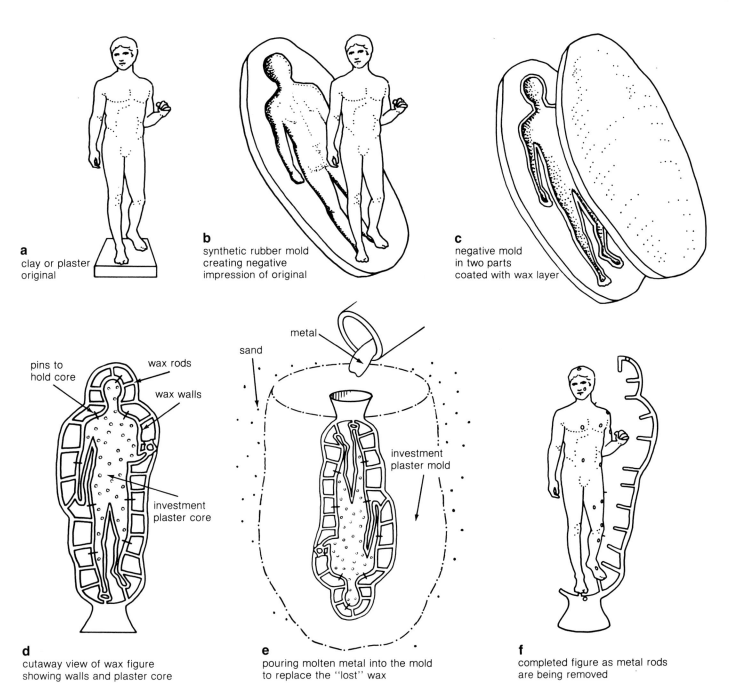

a
clay or plaster
original

b
synthetic rubber mold
creating negative
impression of original

c
negative mold
in two parts
coated with wax layer

d
pins to
hold core

wax rods

wax walls

investment
plaster core

cutaway view of wax figure
showing walls and plaster core

e
metal

sand

investment
plaster mold

pouring molten metal into the mold
to replace the "lost" wax

f
completed figure as metal rods
are being removed

341. Sketch of the major steps
in lost-wax casting.

exactly the shape and thickness of the desired sculpture. (The metal pins maintain the gap between these two sections of plaster, now that the wax is no longer there to hold them apart.) Molten metal is poured into the space that once held the wax, filling every crevice and filling all the rod-like channels. Metal, therefore, has replaced the wax, which is why casting is often known as a *replacement* method. Depending on the size of the sculpture, it may take several days for the metal to cool and set.

6. The new metal sculpture is taken from the kiln, and both inner core and outer layer of plaster are removed. Then the rods, now also metal, are cut from the sculpture (**341f**), rough spots are filed away, and the sculpture is cleaned and polished.

A common application for lost-wax casting has been the large equestrian (rider on horseback) statues we see in parks and plazas. The ancient Romans were masters of the equestrian portrait, and it remained popular for depicting military heroes well into this century. Almost no material except bronze would be strong enough, for the horse and its rider, life-size or larger, must be balanced on slender legs in an animated pose. An outstanding example is the statue of *Colleoni* (342) by the 15th-century Italian sculptor Andrea del Verrocchio. The sculptor has shaped the tense muscles and alert poses of both figures with such skill that the horse, although cast in rigid bronze, seems about to leap off its pedestal and gallop away.

Besides providing the necessary strength to make thin forms and projections, cast metal offers the sculptor two other great advantages. First, because the mold is generally reusable, one can make several identical casts of the work. Each is considered an original sculpture, just as each impression of a graphic print is considered an original work of art (Chapter 8). Second, casting makes permanent the most fleeting gesture of the sculptor's hands. The sculptor can work freely in some soft material like clay or wax, and then translate that free expression into a more durable material. Edgar Degas' *Dancer* (343) was one of about seventy wax figures, among many broken fragments, found in the artist's studio after his death. Later cast in bronze, the little *Dancer* embodies a spontaneous creative drive in the aging artist as he experimented with forms and balances. By the time he made this sculpture Degas was almost blind. The pliable wax took the imprints of his fingers as he "saw" through his hands when modeling forms. The solid bronze of the cast preserves this expression for later viewers.

Still another asset of cast bronze is its resistance to weather. If properly cleaned and cared for, a bronze sculpture installed outdoors not only will withstand the elements but will in time acquire a desirable **patina**, or surface coloring. Bronze was the preferred material of the sculptor Henry Moore (344), whose massive, organic works are displayed in outdoor spaces around the world. Moore's sculptures seem equally at home in a fountain beside a modern building or in a parkland of trees and grass.

above: 342: Andrea del Verrocchio.
Equestrian Monument of Colleoni. c. 1483–88.
Bronze, height c. 15′. Campo SS. Giovanni e Paolo, Venice.

left: 343. Edgar Degas. *Dancer: developpé en avant.*
Cast bronze, height 16″.
The Metropolitan Museum of Art, New York
(bequest of Mrs. H. O. Havemeyer, 1929).

below: 344. Henry Moore. *Reclining Figure.* 1963–65.
Bronze, length 30′.
Lincoln Center for the Performing Arts, New York.

Henry Moore

1898–1986

On the occasion of Henry Moore's eightieth birthday, art critic John Russell wrote that "it is a great thing to be before the public uninterruptedly for the best part of half a century and still stand up, erect and uncontaminated, as a completely honorable human being."[1] Few people would argue with Russell's assessment. If fate smiles on certain individuals, Moore was surely one of them, but one cannot begrudge this "completely honorable" man having enjoyed rich talents as a sculptor and draftsman, international fame, a loving family, respect from his friends, and a long, productive life.

Born in a small mining town in the north of England, Moore was the seventh child of a miner and his wife. Quite early he settled upon the career of sculptor as his goal. ("When I was 11, I was in Sunday school and I heard a story about Michelangelo. I can't remember the story, but what I retained was that Michelangelo was esteemed the greatest sculptor who ever lived. That unremarkable bit of information moved me, then and there, to decide to become a sculptor myself."[2]) After a brief stint in the army during World War I, Moore entered art school in the city of Leeds and first encountered modern art in a private collection there. Later he moved on to London's Royal College of Art.

Henry Moore was no overnight sensation; the type of sculpture he made was too new, too innovative for the public at large to accept. During the 1920s and 1930s Moore patiently laid the groundwork for what would become a world-class career. He worked steadily, exhibited often, taught first at the Royal College and later the Chelsea School of Art. In 1929 he married Irina Radetzky, a painting student, to whom he remained happily wed all his life. (Their daughter Mary was born in 1946.)

The year 1940 marked something of a turning point for Moore. England was at war, and he became an official war artist. His drawings of Londoners huddled in shelters to escape the Nazi bombing raids have become famous, both because of their unique circumstances and because the artist's sensitive rendering turned the act of hiding underground into a heroic gesture. The English people never forgot that it was Moore who showed them so poignantly in their "finest hour." After the war he was recognized as one of England's

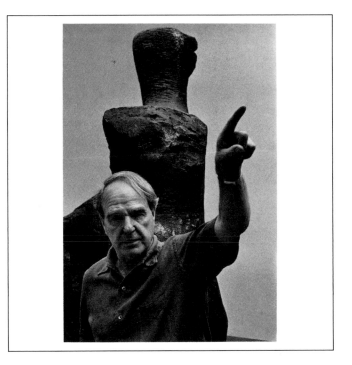

foremost artists, and his stature thereafter increased steadily.

Whether in stone or wood or metal, Moore's sculptures focused on three great themes: the family group (or mother and child), the reclining female figure, the form within a form. These sculptures are in the collections—and often adorn the outsides—of the world's great museums, as well as countless other public buildings.

Reflecting on a lifetime devoted to art, Moore retained the joy and excitement that motivated a little boy who learned about Michelangelo: "Art is not practical, and shouldn't be practical. Art is not to earn a living. It's to make the difference between us and animals, like cows. I mean a cow doesn't stop and look at a field and say, isn't it a beautiful green. Painting and sculpture . . . are there to make life more interesting, more wonderful than it would be without them."[3]

Photograph of Henry Moore, 1980.

CARVING

Carving is more aggressive than modeling, more direct than casting. In this process the sculptor begins with a block of material and cuts, chips, and gouges away until the form of the sculpture emerges. Wood and stone are the principal materials for carving, and both tend to resist the sculptor's tools. When approaching the block to be carved, the sculptor must study the grain of the material—its fibrous or crystalline structure—so as to work *with* that material. Any attempt to violate the grain could result in a failed sculpture.

Wood carving reached an especially high level of expertise in Europe during the Middle Ages and Early Renaissance. A work from 15th-century Germany shows the wood-carver's skill at its most refined. Adriaen van Wesel portrays the *Death of the Virgin* **(345)**, the death of Jesus Christ's aged mother, in an intricate oak carving just 30 inches high. Grouped around the dying Madonna are Christ's twelve Apostles, each showing by individualized facial expression, pose, and gesture his grief at parting from the beloved Mary. Although the space of the carving is shallow, only a few inches deep, the figures do not seem crowded or crammed together, so artfully has the sculptor arranged them. The grain of the oak is apparent throughout the piece, enhancing the texture created by exceptionally fine carving in the hair, faces, and drapery. Given the tendency of wood to chip and split, we marvel at this sculptor's ability to achieve sensitive detail in such a small scale.

Medieval carvers also worked extensively in stone; both the number of sculptors and their output became enormous during the great period of cathedral building in Europe from the 12th to the 15th century (p. 401). Contemporary printed sources give us some clues to the carvers' working methods and testify that at least some of them were women **(346)**—which might contradict our stereotyped idea that "heavy" work for women is a 20th-century innovation.

Stone carving presents an even greater challenge to the sculptor than does wood, because the material is scarcer, more expensive, and more resistant to the chisel. A stonecutter of present-day Italy, Pasquinio Pasquini, has spoken eloquently of the risks:

Sometimes there are surprises in the marble—there can be a defect in it. The hammer is a dangerous instrument: one wrong movement, a statue's finger breaks off, and in a moment the work of months is destroyed. If there's space

left: 345. Adriaen van Wesel. *Death of the Virgin.* 15th century. Oak, 30 × 21¼″. Rijksmuseum, Amsterdam.

right: 346. *Woman Sculptor at Work,* detail from Boccaccio's *Le livre des cleres et nobles femmes.* France, late 15th century. Manuscript illustration. Bibliothèque Nationale, Paris.

347. Gianlorenzo Bernini.
Costanza Bonarelli. c. 1635.
Marble.
Bargello, Florence.

between arm and body, that's another problem. Delicate parts won't take hammering. There are so many places where danger lurks, where we can't use power tools. Portraits are difficult; one false move banishes resemblance.[4]

Most people consider Michelangelo to have been the greatest genius of stone carving in the history of art; we will see his marble figure of *David* in Chapter 16 **(494)**. According to writings from his day, Michelangelo believed that the sculptor's task is simply to free the subject from its imprisoning block of stone. So perfectly did he visualize the figure inside a block of marble that he announced one had only to cut away those parts of the stone that *weren't* the figure. Few other sculptors would be quite so confident.

One who approached Michelangelo in skill—and took second place to no one in self-confidence—was the 17th-century Italian artist Gianlorenzo Bernini. The portrait bust of his mistress, Costanza Bonarelli **(347)**, would present sufficient answer to anyone who feels that marble cannot be warm and alive. As carved by Bernini, Costanza is not merely alive but sensual and magnetic. The slightly parted lips, the intense eyes, the disarranged bodice of the dress all suggest a woman whose emotions are barely contained within the cool white of the stone. Looking at the sculpture, we know it to be stone, but we see hair, flesh, and rumpled linen. In his writings Bernini spoke of the difficulties a sculptor faces when trying to convey personality all in one color (p. 429). In his portrait of Costanza Bonarelli he shows how he overcame those difficulties. He made Costanza live; we half expect her to breathe.

Sculptors who work in stone are harder to find today than they were in Bernini's time, but they do exist. Even artists who specialize in decidedly 20th-century materials, like steel and plastic, may go back to stone every once in a while, possibly as a way of keeping in touch with their colleagues from earlier times. No other material is so solid and yet so alive, so cold and yet so inviting to the touch, so resistant and yet so satisfying.

ASSEMBLING

Assembling is a process by which individual pieces or segments or objects are brought together to form a sculpture. Some writers make a distinction between *assembling*, in which parts of the sculpture are simply placed on or near each other, and *constructing*, in which the parts are actually joined together through welding, nailing, or a similar procedure. We have chosen to use the term *assemblage* for both types of work, because often the line separating one from the other is a fine one.

The 20th-century American sculptor David Smith came to assemblage in an unusual way. While trying to establish himself as an artist, Smith worked as a welder. Later, when he began to concentrate on sculpture, he readily adapted his welding skills to a different purpose. His mature works broke new ground in both materials and forms (**348**). Sculptures like *Becca* are of steel, which eventually became Smith's favorite material. Steel had long been used for the framework of cars, of refrigerators, of locomotives, but Smith explored its aesthetic potential. He polished the surfaces so they would shine in the sunlight when exhibited outdoors. The form of these works is also daring—slab piled upon slab, the parts joined at seemingly precarious angles. Steel, with its great strength, makes possible the dynamic balance of *Becca*, and assemblage makes possible the soaring composition.

Alice Aycock uses assemblage to create extremely complex sculptures that fulfill her own spiritual and mystical ideals. According to one art critic, her *Fantasy Sculpture I* (**349**) looks like "a kind of combination Ferris wheel and merry-go-round," but this is only the initial view. As we approach the large work, we are inevitably drawn into Aycock's world of magic, personal symbolism, and cosmic mysteries. We puzzle over the unexpected combinations of forms, the cryptic words stenciled onto the raw wood of the understructure. Unlike most sculpture of this century, Aycock's work has quite specific and very rich content. It "tells a story," and even if the story isn't fully accessible to us, we are intrigued by it.

The recent sculptures of Nancy Graves also are assembled, but by a technically more complicated process. Like many contemporary artists, Graves begins with ***found objects***—literally objects the sculptor finds here and there, in the street or the studio or the natural environment. Some of the

left: 348. David Smith. *Becca*. 1965. Stainless steel, 9′5¼″ × 10′3″ × 2′2½″. The Metropolitan Museum of Art, New York (purchase, bequest of Adelaide Milton de Groot, by exchange, 1972); on loan to Storm King Art Center, Mountainville, N.Y.

right: 349. Alice Aycock. *Fantasy Sculpture I*. 1990. Wood, steel, stone, copper, lucite, moving parts, plants; 20′6″ × 18′ × 33′. Lent by the artist for a 1990 installation at Storm King Art Center, Mountainville, N.Y.

David Smith

1906–1965

David Smith holds a special interest for students of art history because, more than most artists of past or present, he was extremely articulate about his work and wrote widely about the business of making art. The man himself was something of a paradox. Physically strong and burly, he personified what we would now call a "macho" life style, having worked as a logger, an oilman, and a welder; as a sculptor his expression depended on the physical skills of the blacksmith. But from the noisy atmosphere of the machine shop Smith produced sculptures of shimmering pure form, and this same macho hero was also a lover of classical music, a lifelong poet, a gourmet cook, and a sensitive father to two daughters.

Smith was born in Decatur, Indiana, where he remained for the first twenty years of his life. By 1926 he was in New York, studying painting at the Art Students League. He took a variety of jobs to support himself, including one that proved crucial for his later work—that of metal welder in an automobile factory. In 1927 he married the artist Dorothy Dehner; two years later the couple bought the now-famous farm in Bolton Landing overlooking Lake George, New York, where Smith worked until his death and where he displayed quantities of his large sculptures outdoors.

About 1933 Smith turned from painting and collage to sculpture. Influenced by the iron sculptures of Picasso, he focused on metal and began using his welding skills to assemble the forms. Finding a suitable place to work became a problem. As he told it: "One Sunday afternoon we were walking on a navy pier [in Brooklyn]. Down below on the ferry terminal was a long rambly junky looking shack called Terminal Iron Works. Wife said, 'David that's where you ought to be for your work.' Next morning I walked in and was met by a big Irishman named Blackburn. 'I'm an artist. I have a welding outfit. I'd like to work here.' 'Hell! yes—move in.' I learned a lot from those guys."[5]

From that point Smith worked almost exclusively in metal, soon focusing on steel. He had his first exhibition in New York in 1937, after which his reputation as a sculptor grew steadily. Whether in New York or Bolton Landing, he worked prolifically, and he also played with gusto, enjoying a wide range of friendships with many of the most successful artists of the period. After the breakup of his first marriage, Smith married Jean

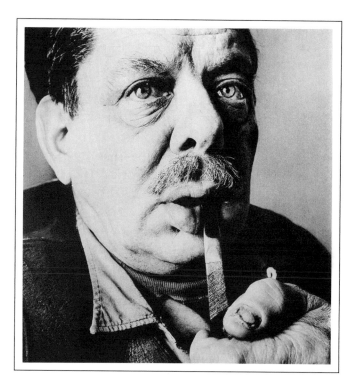

Freas in 1953, and his daughters, Rebecca and Candida, were born in the following two years. The artist's life ended prematurely when, driving near the farm, he failed to negotiate a turn in the road, crashed his truck, and was killed.

The sculpture of David Smith is represented in nearly every major collection of modern art, but the works housed indoors in museums may strike the viewer as out of place, almost uncomfortable. Smith always preferred his pieces to be displayed outdoors. He wrote: "I like outdoor sculpture and the most practical thing for outdoor sculpture is stainless steel, and I make them and I polish them in such a way that on a dull day, they take on the dull blue, or the color of the sky in the later afternoon sun, the glow, golden like the rays, the colors of nature. . . . They are colored by the sky and the surroundings, the green or blue of water. Some are down by the water and some are by the mountains. They reflect the colors. They are designed for outdoors."[6]

Photograph of David Smith by Irving Penn.

left: **350.** Nancy Graves.
*Synonymous with
Ceremony.* 1989.
Iron, stainless steel,
carbon steel, aluminum, bronze,
brass, paint, and patina;
6′9″ × 4′5″ × 2′7″.
Courtesy M. Knoedler & Co., Inc.,
New York.

right: **351.** Louise Nevelson.
Mrs. N's Palace. 1964–77.
Black-painted wood
with black mirror floor,
11′8″ × 19′11″ × 15′.
The Metropolitan Museum of Art,
New York (gift of the artist, 1985).

objects are organic (leaves, pods, and so forth), others manufactured castoffs (wheels, furniture parts, musical instruments). Once Graves has chosen the components, she has them cast in metal, assembles them into the form she wants, and finally paints them with bright-hued enamels. We see the results in a work like *Synonymous with Ceremony* (**350**), a whimsical, delicately balanced, merry construction that shows off some of its original ingredients, but joins them in wholly new ways. Graves' constructions make us want to smile, to participate in their colorful and cheerful presence.

A somewhat different use of found objects for assembling characterizes the best-known work of Louise Nevelson. Nevelson's sculptures, like *Mrs. N's Palace* (**351**), consist of odds and ends, mostly pieces of wood, that she accumulated in her studio over many years. Some of the objects are handmade, others machine products. As with Graves' components, these objects had no connection with one another until the sculptor *gave* them a connection by assembling them, setting up relationships of form that never existed before. Nevelson, however, enhanced the connection by arranging her objects into boxlike structures, then painting the whole a uniform color (often black). So assembled, the objects create a rich, intricate, serene world of their own.

Sculpture and the Third Dimension

Most of the sculptures we have looked at so far are **in the round,** or freestanding and completely finished on all sides. There is another category of sculpture, however, called **relief** sculpture, that is meant to be viewed from one side only. Relief sculptures have three-dimensional depth, but they do not occupy space as independently as sculptures in the round. Often they are used to decorate architecture or functional objects.

If you have a nickel in your pocket, take it out and look at it. On the face you'll see a profile of Thomas Jefferson and on the back an image of his home,

Louise Nevelson

1899–1988

As a sculptor and as a person, Louise Nevelson always projected the image of royalty. Many of her large works have names suggesting royal subjects—kings, queens, palaces—and the artist made it her personal trademark to dress with an exotic flamboyance suitable for an eastern princess. This preoccupation seems related to her expressed conviction that one can make one's life be anything one chooses. She said that royalty is "dressing beautifully and having comfort and great houses and great art. Who wouldn't want it? Who wants to live in a hut?"[7]

Born Louise Berliawsky in Kiev, Russia, Nevelson emigrated with her family to Rockland, Maine, in 1905. She claimed she was drawn to art as a child because the schoolhouse in Maine was always cold, and the art room was the only warm place. When she was just twenty-one she married Charles Nevelson. Decades later she would say the marriage was the only thing in her life she would have done differently, because she was not equipped for it. Nevelson's son Mike was born in 1922, but only a few years later the marriage collapsed, and the artist remained single thereafter.

Nevelson attended the Art Students League in New York for three years, then traveled to Europe, where she studied briefly with the painter Hans Hoffmann. Her first one-artist show came in 1941 at an important New York gallery. Despite favorable critical notice, many years passed before the public showed any interest in her work and it became financially sustaining. The artist felt this was because the components of her sculptures have little material value. From her earliest years in New York (where she lived until her death) she formed the habit of picking up cast-off wooden objects in the street—bits of furniture, old tools, sections of architectural elements, and the like. Her most characteristic sculptures are complex assemblages of these "found" objects in shallow, boxlike grids, many of which are wall- or room-size. The assemblages are each spray-painted a uniform color—occasionally white or gold, but most often black, which Nevelson called an "aristocratic" color.

In the late 1960s and 1970s Nevelson experimented with new materials—aluminum and steel—

and made several large outdoor sculptures that echo the feeling of her box assemblages. She also accepted an unusual commission for the complete interior design of a Christian church (Nevelson was Jewish) in New York, including architectural details, sculptural decoration, even the priest's vestments.

Louise Nevelson was always an extremely prolific worker. All through the years of struggle she continued to produce. She maintained that she had a preconceived blueprint for her life and that, by and large, she had fulfilled it. "I remember my mother telling me, 'You know, art is a very difficult life, and why do you want to choose that? You won't live as well as you could otherwise.' And I said, 'It's not how I live, it is how I finish my life.' And I did it."[8]

Photograph of Louise Nevelson.

Monticello. Both images are in **low relief,** sometimes called by the French name **bas-relief.** The subjects project very slightly from their background. Many kinds of flat surfaces serve as fields for low-relief sculpture—coins, tombstones, walls, decorative plates, book covers. The illustration here **(352)** shows the back of a throne found in the tomb of the Egyptian king, Tutankhamun (p. 376). A low relief applied to pure sheet gold depicts the young King "Tut" and his queen in graceful poses. The flowing clothes of the two monarchs are of silver, and their headdresses and jeweled collars are inset with colored glass and gemstones.

When a sculpture projects more boldly from the background, we call it **high relief** (or **haut-relief**). To fit this category, the sculptured elements should project by at least half their depth, and parts of the figures may be in the round, unattached to the background. The wood carving by Adriaen van Wesel **(345)**, with its rounded heads and torsos of the Apostles, qualifies as moderately high relief. *Mrs. N's Palace* is even higher relief; if the museum guard will let you, you can walk inside it.

Both low and high relief are evident in *The Story of Jacob and Esau* **(353)**, one panel of Lorenzo Ghiberti's famous bronze doors for the Baptistry of Florence Cathedral **(487)**. The arched openings, the figures at upper right, and some of the background figures are in low relief. But nearly all the foreground figures are in very high relief—still attached to the background, but fully round and almost freestanding. Ghiberti used these gradations in relief to create a sense of deep space, which is heightened by the receding perspective of the arches. The impression of depth is enhanced even more by the figures that overlap the frame at left and right, in such a way that they actually seem to advance into our space.

We may be tempted to think of figural relief sculpture as "primitive"— something artists of earlier centuries did before they developed the skill necessary to make fully round sculptures. This isn't true at all. The Egyptians and certainly the sculptors of the Renaissance, like Ghiberti, were quite capable of undertaking freestanding works. Moreover, in our own time sculptures still are made to decorate the walls of buildings, and a few modern artists have experimented with relief sculpture for its own sake.

Robert Longo's *Corporate Wars* **(354)**, made in 1982, is a modern version of high-relief sculpture. A huge work in cast aluminum, *Corporate Wars* depicts a hellish tangle of people in business suits—clawing, pushing, choking, and punching one another, presumably in an effort to get ahead in the corpo-

left: 352.
Tutankhamun and His Queen,
relief on the back
of the Golden Throne
found in the tomb
of King Tutankhamun.
c. 1325 B.C.
Sheet gold, silver,
colored glass, and carnelian.
Cairo Museum.

right: 353. Lorenzo Ghiberti.
The Story of Jacob and Esau,
detail from
The Gates of Paradise. c. 1435.
Gilt bronze, 31¼" square.
Baptistry, Florence.

left: **354.** Robert Longo.
Corporate Wars:
Wall of Influence. 1982.
Cast aluminum, 7 × 9 × 3'.
Collection Emily and Jerry Spiegel,
courtesy Metro Pictures, New York.

right: **355.** Auguste Rodin.
The Burghers of Calais. 1886.
Bronze, 6'10½" × 7'11" × 6'6".
Hirshhorn Museum and Sculpture
Garden, Smithsonian Insitution,
Washington, D.C.
(gift of Joseph H. Hirshhorn, 1966).

ration. Parts of the figures jut out in high relief, and some even overlap the frame of the panel. Longo's composition offers a fascinating contrast to Ghiberti's *Story of Jacob and Esau.* The Ghiberti was designed to project order and serenity. The Longo work, with its chaotically overlapping forms, erupts in violence and ugly emotions.

Although we have already looked at several examples of sculpture in the round, it will be useful here to consider one work primarily from the standpoint of its complex interaction with space. Sculpture in the round exists wholly in our world. We can walk around it and see it from every angle. This is a terrific challenge to the sculptor's compositional ability, since every viewpoint must be under control. Even when there is a definite front and back, as there usually is in figurative sculpture, all viewpoints should be interesting. And the fact that the work looks different from every angle makes the observer's experience much richer.

An excellent example of sculpture in the round is Rodin's *Burghers of Calais* (**355**), whose preliminary study we examined earlier in this chapter (**339**). Rodin made this sculpture for public display in the city of Calais, and it depicts an episode in the town's medieval history. Six men have offered to give their lives to ransom their city from the English, who hold it captive. Each of them faces certain death, but they confront their sacrifice in different ways. One is angry, one sorrowful, one merely resigned, and so on—but each is unique, facing a personal tragedy amid shared crisis. We can read the men's emotions from their various postures, facial expressions, and gestures. The six hostages march in an irregular circle, some determinedly erect, others drooping in despair. And the viewer must also walk in a circle, because there is no angle from which all faces are visible. Rodin's message is complex, so he expressed it in the complex form of sculpture in the round.

The Human Figure in Sculpture

We humans tend to be egocentric. We are interested in ourselves, in anything that touches upon our immediate concerns. Artists throughout history have expressed this egocentrism with the self-portrait. So it should come as no surprise that the human figure has always been a basic subject of sculpture.

left: 356.
Mycerinus and His Queen,
from Giza, Egypt. 2599–2571 B.C.
Slate, height 4'6½".
Museum of Fine Arts, Boston
(Harvard University–M.F.A.
Expedition).

right: 357. Praxiteles (?).
Hermes with the Infant Dionysus.
c. 330 B.C. Marble, height 7'1".
Museum, Olympia.

What could be more interesting than oneself—or a figure shaped like oneself? We respond psychologically to the sculpture of a human form much as we would to a real human being. What is that person like? Why does he or she look that way? What is that person thinking?

When children see a figure sculpture, they often arrange their bodies into the same pose as that of the sculpture. As adults we may be tempted to do the same thing, but we have learned to be more inhibited in public. We may be surprised to discover that we have the same impulse to let our bodies mimic the shape of *abstract* sculptures, but this is not really so strange. There is considerable similarity in the way naturalistic and abstract (or nonobjective) sculptures are designed. By studying the figure in sculpture, we can learn much about the way nonfigurative sculptures are designed—how the sculptor handles weights, balances, stresses, and the composition in general. Some nonobjective sculptors go back occasionally to study the human figure, in order to test their understanding of forms in space.

The sculptural treatment of figures throughout history usually has been greatly influenced by the culture in which a particular piece was made. For example, in ancient Egypt figural sculptures, especially those depicting members of the nobility, tended to be somewhat rigid and immobile. Just as the Egyptians built their pyramids for all eternity, so they meant their kings and queens to be posed in eternal serenity. In the sculpture of *Mycerinus and His Queen* **(356)** both figures stand proudly erect, facing straight ahead. Although each has the left foot planted slightly forward, there is no real suggestion of walking. The shoulders and hips are level, the arms frozen at solemn attention.

In contrast to the formal poses favored by the Egyptians, we find the **contrapposto** perfected by the Greeks in the 5th and 4th centuries B.C. Contrapposto means "counterpoise" or "counterbalance," and it is intended to be natural, curving, and relaxed, to imply motion. We have the impression the sculptor has caught the figure in the middle of a movement, and that one second earlier or later the pose would have been different. You can see this effect in *Hermes with the Infant Dionysus* **(357)**, which is probably an original by the famous Greek sculptor Praxiteles. Hermes' weight is on his right foot, so that his right hip is raised and his left leg bent and relaxed. To counterbalance this, Hermes' left shoulder is raised, and the whole figure stands in a gentle S-curve. This elegant curve was Praxiteles' trademark and has been copied ever since. We see exaggerated versions of it today in the poses of such "living statues" as fashion models and professional body builders, who use contrapposto to show off to best advantage accomplishments in fabric or muscle tissue.

Eastern art, like its Western counterpart, also presents examples of formal and informal poses. The Buddha, who exists in eternity like the monarchs of Egypt, is routinely depicted in a serene, motionless pose, his arms and legs folded, his face a study in peaceful contemplation **(358)**. But less exalted beings may be modeled in animated motion. Our illustration shows *Shukongojin* **(359)**, a guardian figure known as the "thunderbolt-bearer," who is also associated with Buddhism. This life-size figure stands in the Sangatsu-do (Third Month Hall) of the temple known as Todai-ji at Nara, in Japan. Shukongojin's role is protection. He is meant to ward off demons and evildoers, thus guarding the temple and the faith. His ferocious expression shows that early Japanese sculptors were capable of emotionalism and theatricality, while the S-curve twist to his body demonstrates mastery of the contrapposto pose.

Contemporary sculptors are less committed to specific categories of poses, yet they are no less interested in the human figure as a subject. One modern sculptor who has concentrated on the figure almost exclusively is George Segal. Segal works in plaster, and his figures are cast from living models. The "sculpting" is done by selecting, dressing, and posing his subject. After that, technology largely takes over. The artist pastes plaster-saturated cloth squares over the model to form a perfectly defined shell of the

left: 358. *Seated Buddha,* from Gandhara, India (now Pakistan). Kushan period, A.D. 2nd–3rd century. Stone, 36 × 22½″. Seattle Art Museum (Eugene Fuller Memorial Collection).

right: 359. *Shukongojin,* guardian figure. Nara period, A.D. mid-8th century. Painted clay, height 5′8½″. Sangatsu-do of Todai-ji, Nara, Japan.

body. After the plaster has hardened, the shell is removed in sections. Later, Segal reassembles the sections and uses this shell as a mold in which to make a plaster cast. Earlier works were left in the pure chalky white of the plaster, but later Segal began to paint some of his people in vivid colors, as evidenced by *Blue Girl on Park Bench* **(360)**.

Segal likes to place his figures in a setting of objects from the real world, such as the actual park bench supporting the *Blue Girl* (or the real-life bus terminal, **79)**. His expressionless people suggest isolation, boredom, and mental stagnation in a packaged society. The *Blue Girl* might be waiting for a bus, but one has the feeling that if the bus doesn't come, she will go on waiting impassively for all time. These figures are antiheroic. Just as heroic figures show us what we might aspire to be, Segal's show us what we might fear to become.

Sculpture and the Environment

The term "environmental sculpture" may cause some confusion, because it is used in at least three different ways. First, it can refer to sculptures that are large enough for viewers to enter and move about in, sculptures that create their own environments. Second, it can mean large sculptures designed for display in the outdoor environment, such as a sculpture commissioned for a city square. And third, it can be sculptures that are actually a part of the natural environment, such as the presidents' heads carved out of the natural rock of Mt. Rushmore. We will look at one or two examples of each type.

Red Grooms has made a kind of specialty of the huge-scale, zany, colorful sculptured environment depicting a place or event. His constructions—always witty and entertaining, always crammed with people, buildings, and things—resemble a cross between an amusement-park funhouse and a comic strip come to three dimensions. In 1975 Grooms lampooned New York City, with comic depictions of a subway car, the Brooklyn Bridge, and other land-

left: 360. George Segal. *Blue Girl on Park Bench.* 1980. Painted plaster and aluminum, lifesize. Collection Jeanette, Nina, and Constance Golder.

right: 361. Red Grooms. *Philadelphia Cornucopia*, detail. 1982. Mixed media. Installed at Institute of Contemporary Art, University of Pennsylvania, Philadelphia.

marks. In 1982 the city of Philadelphia requested the same madcap treatment, in honor of its three-hundredth birthday. The result was *Philadelphia Cornucopia* **(361)**, a 2,500-square-foot environment installed at the Institute of Contemporary Art. Inspired by the history, romance, and glorious tradition of the city, Red Grooms, as the saying goes, really went to town. His centerpiece is an 11-foot-tall figure of George Washington, proudly standing at the helm of a "ship of state" whose figurehead is an image of Martha Washington. Many other ghosts from Philadelphia's past rise up in colorful caricature, including Benjamin Franklin, Thomas Jefferson, Betsy Ross, and of course the artist Charles Willson Peale **(22)** in his museum.

Grooms' constructions are built of any material at hand—wire, cloth, wood, plastic, metal. And they are painted, but not with naturalistic skin tones. Grooms paints his figures the way a clown puts on makeup—the broader, the more exaggerated, the better. *Philadelphia Cornucopia* demonstrates Grooms' desire for active audience participation in large-scale works of art. Viewers are allowed to walk among the structures and interact with the outlandish creatures who dwell there. To enter this environment is to suspend judgments about reality and let the magic take over.

Also full of vivid colors, Judy Pfaff's environmental sculptures are not figurative but instead are abstract and poetic. Walking into a sculpture like *Kabuki* **(362)** is not unlike carrying around with you a vague memory of a dream whose details you can't quite recall. Everything in Pfaff's environment comes into play—the walls, ceiling, floor, and objects placed or suspended in the composition. Viewers who venture in are surrounded by a self-contained world of colors and shapes. Because the work is entirely nonrepresentational, it is even truer than usual that each viewer experiences the environment differently. Pfaff controls the visual stimuli, but she cannot control the associations we bring to her work.

362. Judy Pfaff.
Kabuki (Formula Atlantic).
1980. Mixed media.
Installation February 12
to May 3, 1981,
at the Hirshhorn Museum
and Sculpture Garden,
Washington, D.C.
Courtesy Holly Solomon Gallery,
New York.

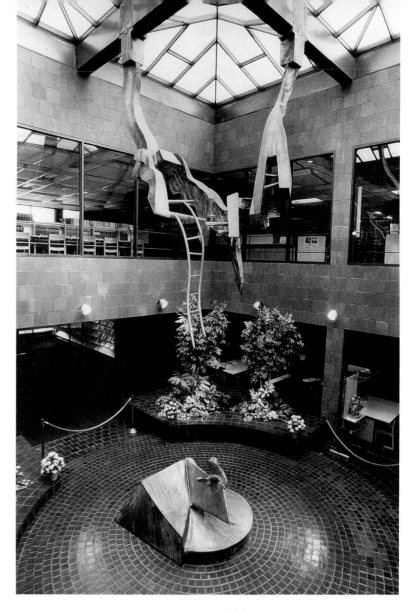

right: **363.** Richard Hunt. *Jacob's Ladder.*
1977. Bronze, overall height of space 18'.
Installed at the Carter G. Woodson
Regional Library, Chicago.

below: **364.** Robert Smithson. *Spiral Jetty.*
1970. Rock, salt crystals, earth, algae;
coil length 1500'. Great Salt Lake, Utah
(now submerged).

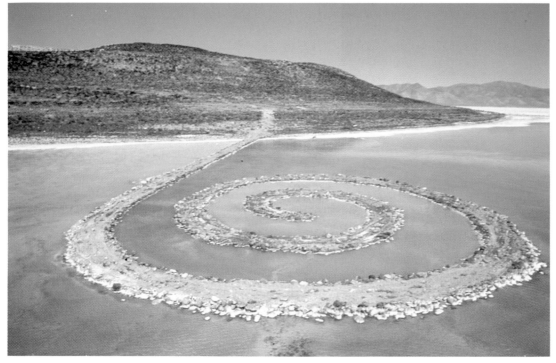

Richard Hunt's large work *Jacob's Ladder* (363) is an example of a sculpture designed both physically and iconographically to fit a particular environment. Created for the atrium of Chicago's Carter Woodson Library, the sculpture tells, in abstract terms, the story of the biblical patriarch Jacob. While traveling in the desert, Jacob fell asleep one night and dreamed of a ladder reaching from the earth to Heaven. Angels were moving up and down the ladder, and God appeared at the top, speaking to Jacob. "Jacob's ladder" thus becomes a metaphor for the gateway to Heaven.

As interpreted by Hunt, two giant bronze arms reach down from the skylight (symbolically Heaven), and one holds a curving ladder. On the floor below is a bronze structure representing an altar in the desert, with Jacob just waking from his sleep. This metaphor, however, has another layer of meaning. The Carter Woodson Library is located in a predominantly black section of Chicago, and is staffed and used mostly by blacks. Richard Hunt, who is himself black, intends his "Jacob's ladder" to represent learning, knowledge, literacy—all of which can be acquired in the library—as the gateway to the "heaven" of freedom.

Environmental sculpture on a grand scale occurs when an artist sets out to sculpt the earth itself. Robert Smithson's *Spiral Jetty* (364) is such a construction, and it has become one of the classics of modern sculpture. The *Spiral Jetty* is a 1,500-foot-long ramp of earth and rock, bulldozed into position in a secluded part of the Great Salt Lake in Utah. When the *Jetty* was constructed in 1970, the United States was actively involved in space exploration, and for the first time we could see photographs of what our planet looks like from "the outside." We became aware that Earth is always in a state of change, with forms continually building up and breaking down. Smithson's work exemplifies this process on a grand scale; although intended as a permanent structure, the *Spiral Jetty* is no longer visible, because the lake has risen to cover it. The long curl of the spiral also reminds us of old legends about the Great Salt Lake being connected by an underground canal to the Pacific Ocean. According to these legends, the flow of water back and forth created huge whirlpools in the lake, similar to the form of the spiral. Above all, the spiral is a timeless symbol. Spirals have been a recurring motif in the arts since earliest ages. Smithson took the bold step of carving a giant spiral into the very land we inhabit.

A similarly ambitious work, Christo's *Running Fence* (365), never was intended to be anything but temporary. Constructed of 18-foot-high nylon

365. Christo. *Running Fence.* 1972–76. Nylon fabric and steel poles, 18′ × 24½ miles. Installed in Sonoma and Marin Counties, California, for two weeks, fall 1976.

panels set on steel posts, the *Running Fence* meandered over the hills and fields of northern California for 24½ miles, starting at the Pacific Ocean then moving inland. It was built by Christo's team of workers, stood for two weeks, and then, as planned, was removed. All that remain are photographs, films, and preliminary drawings.

Christo's work is similar to *Conceptual Art*, which we shall explore in more detail in Chapter 17 (pp. 492–493). More important than the physical structure itself is the concept underlying it—in this case the experience of conceiving, planning, building, recording, and removing a monumental work. This artist's sculptures make a mark upon the landscape; they confront nature on a giant scale. The impulse is similar to, though grander than, that of drawing one's initials in wet concrete or painting them on a rock. And yet, after all, one cannot leave a 24½-mile fence across California. Christo deliberately chose to create a structure that had to come down, that had removal built into its concept, in order to focus attention on the process.

Motion, Light, and Time

The world we live in is preoccupied with action—change and movement and energy—so it is only natural that some of our sculpture would reflect this. **Kinetic sculpture** is a broad term generally used to describe works that incorporate motion as part of their artistic expression. The mobiles of Alexander Calder **(366)**, for instance, are light and fluid, balanced so that the slightest current of air will set them moving. In a sense they are *about* motion, which is to say their subject is constant change and a never-ending formation of new relationships in space. Implicit in these mobiles is the element of time. We said of Rodin's *Burghers* **(355)** that you have to move around the sculpture to appreciate it fully. You can also move around a Calder mobile, but *it* is moving too, so the experience of elapsed time, of changing forms and spaces, is even more complex.

Weightless as they seem to be, Calder's mobiles still have substance. If you could touch one, you would feel thin, rigid pieces of metal. Other sculptors have created works based on an element with no substance at all—light.

366. Alexander Calder. *Untitled.* 1976. Painted aluminum and tempered steel, 29'10½" × 76'. National Gallery of Art, Washington, D.C. (gift of the Collectors Committee).

367. James Turrell. *Afrum.* 1967. Xenon light. Installation 1976 at the Stedelijk Museum, Amsterdam. Collection Dr. Giuseppe Panza dì Blumo, Varese, Italy.

The light sculptures of James Turrell are designed to "make light inhabit space so it feels materially present," according to the artist. In *Afrum* (367), for instance, we see what appears to be a solid cube hovering in the air. Closer inspection, however, leads us to discover that the cube consists entirely of light. Turrell's work is based on illusion, and that illusion is very persuasive—so much so, in fact, that a 1980 exhibition of his work at the Whitney Museum of American Art resulted in two lawsuits. In both cases visitors to the exhibition leaned against what seemed to be a wall but was only a light-illusion, lost their balance, and fell to the floor.

To the person whose idea of sculpture is the stone carvings of Michelangelo and Bernini, the cast bronzes of Verrocchio or Moore, this conception of light as sculpture may be strange, even shocking. But somehow it seems appropriate that our world should produce sculptures just this transitory and just this susceptible to a modern phenomenon—the power failure.

As a matter of fact, nearly all of us have had experience making sculptures out of materials almost as insubstantial as light—snow and sand. You build a snowman or snowwoman or snowdog; the sun comes out, and it melts. You build a sand castle at the beach; the tide comes in, and it washes away. Are these really sculptures? Perhaps, by some definitions. They have form, they exist in three dimensions, they are a human creation for the purpose of aesthetic expression. The only thing unusual is that they exist for just a little while and then fade, never to be duplicated exactly.

One thing is clear: we cannot evaluate sculptures according to how long they last. Classical civilizations made sculptures to survive for all eternity, but they will not. Wood sculptures may burn, stone sculptures are eaten away by acid rain and industrial pollution. In times of war metal sculptures have sometimes been melted down to be turned into bullets. What remains, what cannot be taken away, is the sculptor's expression and the experience of the viewer—even if it lasts only for a moment.

Chapter Twelve

Crafts

The works of art considered in this chapter have certain things in common with one another, but they also share traits with other media, such as sculpture. Most of them have roots in the traditional trades of the Middle Ages—potter, glassblower, blacksmith, woodworker, weaver. It is from this background that the word "craft" derives, referring to expert work done by hand. We still describe as "well-crafted" anything finely made, including a chair, an automobile, a house, even sometimes a painting or sculpture. The specific connotation of craft, however, is an object made by hand, not by machine, and this is true of all the works shown in this chapter.

A common assumption people make about the crafts is that objects are made for some functional use, such as eating, drinking, wearing, or sitting. For this reason they have often been called the "functional arts" or the "applied arts"—that is, applied to everyday necessities. And, to be sure, many of the objects we will look at have that very reason for being. A handmade dinner plate or wine goblet is a craft object, meant to be used for eating or drinking. However, it has never been true that such pieces were supposed to be *only* utilitarian. Hand-crafted objects are made to be beautiful, to be admired for their perfection of form and materials, for the unique expression of their makers. And sometimes an object is *so* special that we are disinclined to use it for any functional purpose.

Consider, for example, our first illustration **(368)**. This "stirrup vessel," dating from about A.D. 200–500, was made by the Mochica culture of ancient Peru. The little ceramic figure was intended to hold liquids and actually has a pouring spout (the name "stirrup" comes from the arc-shaped spout), but it is so masterfully shaped that its form takes precedence over any practical use. Most people would be more likely to put it on display as an art object than to store it in a kitchen cupboard.

What, then, separates the craft object from the art object? There is no definite line. Individual observers must make up their own minds about each specific piece, whether it is "more" art or craft. Some would say that a number of the works shown in this chapter belong more properly in the previous one, as sculptures. And a few pieces in the sculpture chapter, such as the ceramic figure from China **(338)**, could be equally at home in this one. To add to the confusion, craft artists frequently move back and forth from the functional to the sculptural. It is not unusual for a potter who makes bowls, cups, vases, and similar useful objects to work also in ceramic sculpture.

What *may* help to distinguish the crafts from the other arts is their emphasis on particular materials. The traditional materials of the crafts are clay, glass, fiber, metal, and wood. Most craft artists concentrate on one material only and have learned to realize its potential for many different kinds of expression. Each of these materials has its own capabilities and limitations, and each lends itself to certain kinds of structural and decorative design. In this chapter we shall consider each of these materials in turn.

Clay

The craft of **ceramics** involves making objects from clay, a naturally occurring earth substance. When dry, clay has a powdery consistency; mixed with water it becomes **plastic**—that is, moldable and cohesive. In this form it can be modeled, pinched, rolled, or shaped between the hands. Once a clay form has been built and permitted to dry, it will hold its shape, but it is very fragile. To ensure permanence the form must be **fired** in a kiln, at temperatures ranging between about 1200 and 2700 degrees Fahrenheit, or higher. Firing changes the chemical composition of the clay so that it can never again be made plastic. A fired ceramic object, especially one fired at a high temperature, is quite durable. It can be shattered by a hard blow, but the pieces will not disintegrate. A sizable portion of the ancient art that has survived is ceramic, because—unlike wood or fiber—fired clay is highly resistant to the elements. Most large museums have very old ceramic treasures that have been patiently reassembled from the fragments discovered at archaeological sites.

Nearly every culture we know of has practiced the craft of ceramics, and civilizations in the Middle East understood the basic techniques by as early as 5000 B.C. The first ceramic ware was undoubtedly made by **pinching**—simple molding and squeezing of a lump of clay between the fingers. This method is adequate for making a small figurine or a miniature bowl, but it would be inefficient to impossible for larger items.

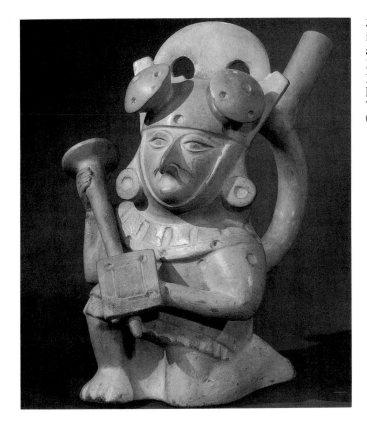

368. Stirrup vessel in the shape of a kneeling warrior with shield. Mochica culture, Peru, A.D. 200–500. Earthenware with cream slip, height 9⅛″. The Metropolitan Museum of Art, New York (gift of Nathan Cummings, 1963).

A major requirement for most ceramic objects is that they be hollow, that they have thin walls around a hollow core. There are two reasons for this. First, many ceramic wares are meant to contain things—food or liquids, for instance. Second, a solid clay piece is difficult to fire and may very well explode in the kiln. To meet this need for hollowness, ceramists over the ages have developed specialized forming techniques.

One such technique is called **slab construction.** The ceramist rolls out the clay into a sheet, very much as a baker would roll out a pie crust, and then allows the sheet to dry slightly. The sheet, or slab, can then be handled in many ways. It can be cut into pieces for assembly into a box form, curled into a cylinder, draped over a mold to make a bowl, or shaped into free-form sculptural configurations. Slab building is usually the method of choice for forming rectilinear objects.

Slab construction was used to create the little horse shown here (369). This charming figure is an example of *haniwa*—clay figures placed around Japanese burial mounds between the 3rd and the 6th centuries. *Haniwa* were made to represent many subjects—horses, warriors, birds, and elegant costumed ladies. Usually there was little attempt at naturalism; the subjects were rendered in simple, tubular forms—the word *haniwa* means "circle of clay." This figure intentionally looks more like a toy horse than a real one. The slab construction lends itself readily to the creation of these basic sculptural forms.

Coiling is another technique for making a thin, hollow form. The ceramist rolls out ropelike strands of clay, then coils them upon one another and joins them together. A vessel made from coils attached one atop the other will have a ridged surface, but the coils can be smoothed completely, to produce a uniform, flat wall. The native tribes of the southwestern United States (who never developed the potter's wheel common in most other parts of the world) made extraordinarily large, finely shaped pots by coiling. In this century their craft has been revived by a few supremely talented individuals, including the famous Pueblo potter María Martínez (370).

left: 369. *Haniwa: Horse,* from Japan. A.D. 3rd–6th century. Terra cotta, height 23½". The Cleveland Museum of Art (gift of Mrs. R. Henry Norweb).

right: 370. María Martínez. Black-on-black jar.

María Martínez

1881(?)–1980

It is a long way in miles and in time between the tiny pueblo of San Ildefonso in New Mexico and the White House in Washington, D.C. But the extraordinary ceramic artist María Martínez made that journey, and many others, in a long lifetime devoted to the craft of pottery making. María—as she signed herself and is known professionally—began her career as a folk potter and ended it as a first-ranked potter of international reputation.

A member of the Pueblo tribe, María most likely was born in 1881, but there are no records. As a child she learned to make pottery, using the coil method, by watching her aunt and other women in the community. Part of her youth was spent at St. Catherine's Indian School in Santa Fe, where she became friends with Julián Martínez. The couple married in 1904.

Although the husband worked at other jobs, the two Martínezes early formed a partnership for making pottery—she doing the building, he the decorating. Between 1907 and 1910 he was employed as a laborer on an archaeological site near the pueblo, under the direction of Dr. Edgar L. Hewett. The amazing career of María Martínez was launched in a simple way: Dr. Hewett gave her a broken piece of pottery from the site and asked her to reconstruct a whole pot in that style using the traditional blackware techniques.

About 1919 the Martínezes developed the special black-on-black pottery that was to make them and the pueblo of San Ildefonso famous. The shiny blackware—created from red clay by a process of smothering the dung-fueled bonfire used for firing—was decorated with matte-black designs. This black-on-black ware was commercially quite successful. María Martínez and her husband became wealthy by the standards of the pueblo and, as was customary, shared that wealth with the entire community.

María bore four sons who survived. Eventually they and their wives and children and grandchildren became partners in her enterprise. One shadow on her domestic life was her husband's serious alcoholism, which began early in their marriage and contributed to his death in 1943. After he was gone, María's daughter-in-law Santana took over much of the decorating of pots, later to be followed by María's son Poponi Da.

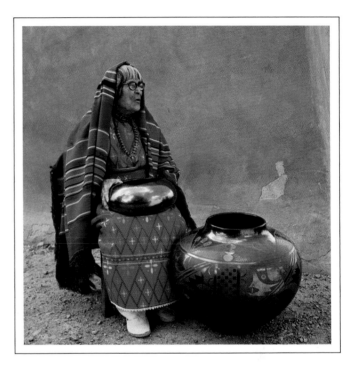

As María's fame spread, she traveled widely, giving demonstrations at many world's fairs. Among the awards she received were an honorary doctorate from the University of Colorado and the American Ceramic Society's highest honor for a lifetime of devotion to clay. Her visit to Washington during the 1930s was a highlight. President Franklin D. Roosevelt was not at home, but Mrs. Eleanor Roosevelt was, and she told María, "You are one of the important ones. We have a piece of your pottery here in the White House, and we treasure it and show it to visitors from overseas."

Undoubtedly, María's greatest achievement was in reviving and popularizing the traditions of fine pottery making among the Pueblo people. Not long before her death, according to her great-granddaughter, she said: "When I am gone, essentially other people have my pots. But to you I leave my greatest achievement, which is the ability to do it."[1]

Photograph of María Martínez.

By far the fastest method of creating a hollow, rounded form is by means of the **potter's wheel (371).** Egyptian potters were using the wheel by about 4000 B.C. Despite some modern improvements and the addition of electricity, the basic principle of wheel construction remains the same as it was in ancient times. The wheel is a flat disk mounted on a vertical shaft, which can be made to turn rapidly either by electricity or by foot power. The ceramist centers a mound of clay on the wheel and, as the wheel turns, uses the hands to shape, "open," and lift the clay form—a procedure known as **throwing.** Throwing on the wheel always produces a rounded or cylindrical form, although the thrown pieces can later be reshaped, cut apart, or otherwise altered. Two or more thrown forms can also be joined together.

The most suitable technique, therefore, is one choice the ceramist needs to make in planning a particular work; another choice is the type of clay to be used. Clays differ in their composition, and this in turn affects the character of pieces made from them. Usually a clay is categorized by its firing temperature—the optimum temperature needed to change the clay's chemical composition permanently and make it hard. **Earthenware** clays, generally red or brown, fire at the lowest temperatures. Fired earthenware objects are often called **terra cotta** ("baked earth"). They tend to be coarse and porous and will not hold liquids unless coated with a glaze (see below). **Stoneware** clays, which fire at medium temperatures, are generally brown or grayish. Much commercial dinnerware is made of stoneware, and these clays have been popular among artist-potters.

The aristocrats of clays are the pure white **porcelains,** which fire at the highest temperatures. Porcelain is the material of the finest dinnerware and in the past was used for the most elegant of commercial vases and figurines. Until recently, individual artist-potters seldom worked in porcelain because the high firing temperatures are difficult to achieve with noncommercial equipment and because porcelain clays are less plastic and thus more difficult to handle than earthenware or stoneware. In the last few years, however, additives have been developed for porcelain clays that decrease the problems, so there has been renewed interest in porcelain among craft artists. (A term often used—and misused—by commercial ceramics manufacturers is *china,* which refers to a ware not unlike porcelain but firing at a lower temperature. China clays are rarely used by the craft artist.)

While clays themselves may have interesting colors and textures, much of the potential for decoration in ceramics comes from the glaze. A **glaze** is a glasslike material usually applied to the surface of a ceramic piece and then fired on so as to fuse the glaze with the clay body. Nearly always this is a second firing, which follows the preliminary one to harden the clay. There is

left: 371. Throwing on the potter's wheel.

right: 372. *Hippopotamus,* from the tomb of Senbi at Meir, Egypt. XII Dynasty, 2000–1788 B.C. Egyptian faience, height 4⅜". The Metropolitan Museum of Art, New York (gift of Edward S. Harkness, 1917).

virtually no limit to the different effects that can be produced by combining glazes or by the various methods of applying them. While there are clear glazes, most glazes have color, and this is a major reason for their application. A secondary purpose of the glaze is to make an object watertight and nonabsorbent—especially important for cooking and eating vessels and for the more porous low-fired clays.

One of the earliest glazes, in use by 3000 B.C., is known as **Egyptian paste.** Unlike most glazes, this material is mixed into the clay rather than applied on top of it. When the piece is fired (in a single firing), a glassy coating, often turquoise in color, forms on the surface. We see this in the Metropolitan Museum's famous hippopotamus figure, affectionately known as "William" **(372).**

Conventional glazes can be applied in many ways—by pouring, dipping, or spraying, for example. When properly compounded, glazes can also be painted onto a surface with all the precision and potential for color effects available to an artist using oil paints on canvas. The best examples of this technique appear in the decorated plates from Renaissance Italy and Spain, known as *majolica* ware **(373).** Elaborate painted scenes, some of them quite naturalistic, were achieved through the use of multicolored glazes. In this type of expression the form of the ceramic piece is much less important than its decoration. The plate becomes just another surface on which to paint.

In contemporary ceramics we are more likely to find a balance of form and decoration—a blend so perfect that one could not exist without the other. This is apparent in the work of Elena Karina **(374).** Karina's forms may remind us of seashells, but if so, they are the most delicate, intricate, and complex seashells ever made. Shaped by hand from porcelain, Karina's vessels shimmer with a variable opalescent glaze that seems like a natural extension of the form.

Our next illustration, a teapot by Linda Arbuckle **(375),** brings us back to the discussion at the beginning of this chapter: Is it functional or decorative, art or craft? Ceramic teapots have been made for hundreds of years, and clay is a preferred material for teapots. This particular teapot, however, doesn't look as though it will get much day-to-day service. Arbuckle might almost be poking fun at the traditional utilitarian role of clay pots. The frivolous shape and decoration of this pot banish any ideas about clay being a heavy or ordinary material.

top left: 373.
The Calydonian Boar,
decorated plate from Urbino, Italy.
c. 1542. Majolica ware,
diameter 10¾".
Victoria & Albert Museum, London.

top right: 374. Elena Karina.
Botticelli. 1979.
Porcelain, height 13".
Collection
Mr. and Mrs. Alvin Ferst, Jr.

above: 375. Linda Arbuckle.
Onward and Upward. 1989.
Thrown terra cotta with
majolica glaze, 13 × 12 × 6".
Collection Ruth and Rick Snyderman,
Philadelphia.

Glass

If clay is one of the most versatile of the craft materials, glass is perhaps the most fascinating. Few people, when presented with a beautiful glass form, can resist holding it up to the light, watching how light changes its appearance from different angles.

While there are thousands of formulas for glass, its principal ingredient is usually silica, or sand. The addition of other materials can affect color, melting point, strength, and so on. When heated, glass becomes molten, and in that state it can be shaped by several different methods. Unlike clay, glass never changes chemically as it moves from a soft, workable state to a hard, rigid one. As glass cools it hardens, but it can then be reheated and rendered molten again for further working.

Glass as a material holds many risks, both during the creative process and afterward. The shaping of a glass object demands split-second timing—quick decisions and quick handwork—while the glass remains hot. What's more, a finished glass piece is the most fragile of all craft wares. One swift blow can shatter it irreparably. There is something almost heroic about an artist who would spend days, weeks, even months making an object that is so vulnerable.

Glassmaking is nearly as old a craft as ceramics, but it was not until the Roman era, shortly before the birth of Christ, that the first great period of glassmaking as an art began. The Roman era saw the invention of the blow-pipe—an instrument that has changed very little in two thousands years. To blow glass, the artist dips up a portion of molten glass at the end of the pipe and then blows through the pipe to produce a bubble. The bubble can be shaped or cut by various methods while it is still hot. Besides blowing, other ways of forming glass include molding, pressing, and rolling.

The Roman historian Pliny the Elder wrote of large "statues" made from glass, but almost nothing is known about them. It is assumed that they were chiseled out of solid glass blocks and then polished. Although we can only speculate about such pieces, many examples of glassware from the Roman period have survived, including what is perhaps the most famous glass object in the world—the *Portland Vase* **(376)**. The incredible virtuosity displayed in this vessel testifies to long experience in glassmaking. The vase was made in three stages. First the basic form of dark blue glass was blown, and then a layer of semi-opaque white glass was added to the outside. Next

left: 376. *Portland Vase.*
A.D. 3rd century.
Cameo-cut glass.
British Museum, London.

right: 377. Goblet, from Venice.
Early 16th century.
Cristallo with enameled
and gilt decoration, height 9¼".
The Corning Museum of Glass,
Corning, N.Y.

the vase was given over to a cameo cutter—a carver of low-relief figural designs—who patiently chipped away the white glass to create a relief design of many gradations. In some areas the dark blue shows faintly through the white to give a shaded effect. Later glass artists have tried to duplicate the remarkable cameo quality of the *Portland Vase* and have failed.

About a thousand years later, another great era of glassmaking took place in Italy. This time it centered on the city of Venice. By the year 1291 there were so many glass factories in Venice, with so many furnaces burning day and night, that the entire city seemed in danger of going up in flames. As a result, the Senate demanded that all the glass factories be removed to the island of Murano, where many remain to this day.

Venetian glassmakers excelled in decorative design and perfected many elaborate techniques. Among their specialties were enameling ("painting" with colored glass), etching with acids, gilding, trailing on thin ribbons of molten glass in preplanned designs, and combinations of these. Ornate examples of Venetian glass like this elaborately decorated goblet (**377**) were highly sought throughout Europe. Because their glasswares were such valuable trading items, Venetian glassmakers were forbidden to leave Murano, and the techniques were closely guarded secrets. Nevertheless, several of the artisans escaped, and their knowledge spread across Europe.

Contemporary glass artists, like their counterparts in ceramics, strive for a balance of form and decoration. Dale Chihuly's designs are exuberant and deliberately sculptural (**378**). Their decoration seems to evolve from the form itself, rather than being applied to an existing structure. Chihuly's blown-glass works are very thin and translucent; they have a fluid quality reminiscent of shapes in the natural world.

A special branch of glass craft, **stained glass** is a technique used for windows, lampshades, and similar structures that permit light to pass through. Stained glass is made by cutting sheets of glass in various colors into small pieces, then fitting the pieces together to form a pattern. Often the segments are joined by strips of lead, hence the term *leaded* stained glass.

Probably our most common association with stained glass is the decorated windows of churches, which often portray religious scenes. Our illustration shows a secular adaptation—Catherine Thompson's panel *The Elephant's Child* (**379**). Thompson's interest lies in narrative, or story telling, especially as it relates to fables. Here she interprets the figures of elephant, crocodile, snake, and bird from Rudyard Kipling's classic tale of how the elephant got its trunk. The artist's decorative pattern fills (sometimes overlaps) the border with luminous, jewel-like colors.

above left: 378. Dale Chihuly.
Violet and Green Persian Set.
1990. Blown glass, 18 × 32 × 32".
Courtesy the artist.

above: 379. Catherine Thompson.
The Elephant's Child. 1989.
Leaded and painted
stained-glass panel, 6'4" × 2'2".
Mountlake Terrace Public Library,
commissioned by the Mountlake
Terrace Arts Commission,
Mountlake Terrace, Wash.

Metal

From the most fragile craft material we turn to the most indestructible. Metals rust and corrode under some circumstances, but they do not shatter, chip, or rot away. Indeed, sometimes the action of the elements has a beneficial effect on metals. As was mentioned in reference to cast-bronze sculptures (p. 288), weathering may give metals a surface color, or **patina,** that is more attractive than their original appearance.

Ever since humans learned to work metals, they have made splendid art, as well as functional tools, from this versatile family of materials. Given all the sophisticated technology we have available today, we might think that metalwork would simply get better and better. Yet for sheer beauty of form and decoration, few artists have matched the skill of bronze artisans in China during the Shang and Zhou dynasties three thousand years ago.

Ornate bronze vessels were made in China as early as the 16th century B.C. The piece illustrated here **(380)** is later, dating from the Late Zhou dynasty (9th century B.C.). It is interesting to note that this work predates by hundreds of years the art of Classical Greece, which many Westerners consider to have been the beginning of all civilized art. Chapter 11 (p. 287) explained the process of lost-wax casting. The Shang and Zhou bronzes also were cast, but by a far more demanding method. Archaeologists now speculate that the Chinese metalworkers were able to build a two-piece "sandwich" mold without benefit of the wax layer to hold the two sections apart—an inexplicable and astonishing feat for that time or any other. The tiger shown here is thought to have been made as a base support for some large structure, perhaps a throne. Like most works from this period, it is covered with stylized geometric designs in relief.

One distinctive aspect of metal is that it is equally at home in the mundane and the sublime—the bridge that spans a river or the precious ring on a finger; the plow that turns up the earth or the crown on a princess' head. Whatever the application, the basic composition of the material is the same, and the methods of working it are similar.

Casting is but one of several methods for working metal. Another ancient technique is **forging**—the art of the blacksmith. Forging involves heating a chunk of metal over a fire until it is red-hot, then beating and shaping it with hammers. This is how horseshoes traditionally were made, and it is also the method of making wrought iron, as for balconies and railings.

Some metals are soft enough to be worked cold—hammered into shape without heating. This is the technique of many fine silversmiths. The artisan begins with a thin sheet of metal and, working from the back, strikes it repeatedly with small hammers, a technique known as **repoussé.** In some cases

380. *Tiger,* from China. Late Zhou period, 9th century B.C. Bronze, length 29⅝". Freer Gallery of Art, Smithsonian Institution, Washington, D.C.

the metal sheet is placed on top of a mold and hammered so as to conform to the shape of the mold. The vase illustrated (381) is a wonderful example of this technique. It was made by Tiffany and Company for the World's Columbian Exposition in 1893, and no effort was spared to make it as elaborate—and as uniquely American—as possible. Hammered into relief are flowers and plants from every region of the United States. Both the overall shape of the vase and the handles at the top were inspired by pottery forms from the ancient tribes that inhabited the Americas before the arrival of Columbus.

One of the oldest uses of metal as an expressive medium is for jewelry. This has been true since prehistoric times. Early cultures believed that wearing special stones or special metals could ward off disease and evil spirits—a practice continued today in the wearing of copper bracelets for therapeutic purposes. Apart from its supposed magical powers, metal has great symbolic value. People wear jewelry to symbolize wealth and status. They also wear jewelry to symbolize belonging—to a person (a wedding ring), to an institution (a school ring), to a group (a club or fraternity or religious ring.)

Among contemporary metal artists jewelry has been a major preoccupation—not the jewelry of the perfect one-carat diamond in a traditional setting, but far more creative forms. Any of the various metalworking techniques can be used for jewelry, and sometimes two or more are combined in the same piece. For instance, Merry Renk's necklace *Arizona Conference* (382) was created by a combination of sawing, casting, soldering, carving, and hammering. The design recalls an event in the life of the artist—a goldsmiths' conference she attended shortly before she made this piece. The flock of little silver cactus wrens is a witty reference to her fellow metalsmiths.

The use of metals for precious objects has a long history and has attracted many noted practitioners. Two names, however, stand out above the rest: Cellini and Fabergé. Benvenuto Cellini was a goldsmith and sculptor of 16th-century Italy, undoubtedly one of the greatest masters of fine gold work

left: **381.** Tiffany and Company. *Magnolia Vase*, made for World's Columbian Exposition, 1893. Silver, gold, and enamel; height 31″. The Metropolitan Museum of Art, New York (gift of Mrs. Winthrop Atwell, 1899).

right: **382.** Merry Renk. *Arizona Conference.* 1980. Necklace of silver, carved coral, sawed from sheet, cast, soldered, and hammered; 11 × 7″. Courtesy the artist.

who ever lived. His best-known piece is the *Saltcellar of Francis I* **(383)**, made for the king of France. Cellini's genius was to capture in miniature the physical perfection of figures such as Michelangelo and his colleagues would have carved on a heroic scale—and to surround them with an opulent decoration to satisfy the tastes of monarchs. Supposedly, this elegant piece was meant to dispense salt and pepper. Neptune, god of the sea, doles out the salt; the goddess Earth is custodian of the pepper. Whether the king often used Cellini's masterpiece for this purpose has not been recorded.

Peter Carl Fabergé, a Russian of French descent, established a shop in St. Petersburg (now Leningrad) in the late 19th century. About 1884 he was named official jeweler and goldsmith to the imperial family. Czar Alexander III was his first patron, followed by Czar Nicholas II. Between 1884 and 1917 Fabergé created numerous pieces in gold, enamels, and gems for his royal clients. His greatest achievement, however, was a series of objects that are unique in all the world. Only 53 are known to exist. They are the imperial Easter eggs **(384)**.

It is a Russian custom to give eggs at Easter. Czar Alexander improved upon the custom by having Fabergé construct, every year, an elaborate metal-and-jeweled egg for presentation to the empress. Each egg was as ornate and lavishly decorated as Fabergé's skilled workers could manage, and each contained a "surprise." When a tiny pearl or diamond on the outside was pressed, the egg opened to reveal a separate, gemlike little object—a portrait, a miniature basket of flowers, or, in the case of the "coronation egg" shown here, a finely detailed gold coach. Alexander's son Nicholas continued the custom, commissioning Fabergé to make Easter eggs for his empress, Alexandra, and for his mother as well. This practice was repeated yearly until the Russian Revolution of 1917 wiped out both the imperial family and Fabergé's workshop.

Wood

There are two reasons for the great popularity of wood as a craft material throughout the entire history of art. One is that it is relatively easy to work. The simplest tools will shape it, and there is no need for extreme heat, as with clay, glass, or metal. The second reason is that wood is so widely available. In most inhabited areas of the globe wood is abundant and easy to obtain.

These two qualities would make wood the ideal material were it not for certain drawbacks. Because of its organic nature, wood is not very durable. Cold and heat distort it, water rots it, and insects can eat it away. More than one collector has tried to import a gorgeous wood carving from Africa, only to find it contained an active colony of insects that left nothing but a crumbling shell. We must assume that only a tiny fraction of the wood artifacts made over the centuries have survived.

Wood carving, especially of figures, reached a high point in the United States during the 19th century. Certain types of figures flourished: cigar-store Indians and other images that adorned the fronts of shops; magnificent figureheads, usually of women with long, flowing hair, that crowned the prows of sailing ships; and ornate carrousel animals. Generations raised on look-alike merry-go-round horses can scarcely comprehend the ingenuity of carrousel figures carved a century ago. Not only horses, but lions and giraffes and elephants and camels—all were meticulously hand-carved and imaginatively painted (385). The thrill of the ride was far less important than the exotic experience of sitting atop one of these fanciful sculptures in wood.

Carving is only one of several methods for working with wood. It is a subtractive process (pieces of wood are cut away), but there are also additive processes for wood, such as nailing and gluing pieces together. One of the more interesting of these is the old technique of **inlay,** in which small pieces of wood, often with different grains and colors, are glued together to make a pattern. When this method is used to decorate a wall or the face of a piece of furniture, it is often called **marquetry.** A splendid example of this art comes from the Ducal Palace at Gubbio, in Italy (386). Small pieces of different woods have been cleverly combined to give a **trompe-l'oeil** (fool-the-eye) effect of three-dimensional space, even though the wall is absolutely flat. The open cabinet doors, the benches below them, even the shadows are all illusions! This type of visual deceit was much prized in earlier centuries, and it still astonishes us as we move closer to see that, yes, it really *is* a flat surface of wood.

For most of us, of course, wood is usually associated with furniture, which is generally constructed by a process of nailing and/or gluing. When furniture craft and fine wood carving merge, we may get a zany result like

left: 385. Carrousel figure. 19th century. Wood, length 5′2″. National Museum of American History, Smithsonian Institution, Washington, D.C. (Van Alstyne Collection of American Folk Art).

right: 386. Francesco di Giorgio of Siena. Room from the Ducal Palace, Gubbio, Italy. Late 15th century. Trompe-l'oeil inlay of walnut, oak, beech, rosewood, and fruitwoods; height of room 8′10″. The Metropolitan Museum of Art, New York (Rogers Fund, 1939).

387. Klindt Houlberg.
Phantasy Plenishing. 1980.
Wood, height 7'.
Courtesy the artist.

the bedstead illustrated here **(387)**. Klindt Houlberg's *Phantasy Plenishing* looks like a normal, well-crafted bed frame—up to about a foot from the floor. Above that the artist's imagination runs wild. One bedpost is a nude female figure, another a fantasy tree with a bird perched on top, and so on. Houlberg's work makes us realize how rich our environment could be if more everyday objects were treated with this kind of delightful expressiveness.

Fiber

The design possibilities for works of fiber are enormous. By fiber we mean a narrow strand of vegetable or animal material (cotton, linen, wool, silk) or the modern-day synthetic equivalents. Like wood, fiber is widely available and quite perishable, but the construction methods used for fiber are unique to this pliable medium.

For centuries the most common method of working with fiber has been **weaving.** Weaving involves placing two sets of parallel fibers at right angles to one another and interlacing one set through the other in an up-and-down movement, generally on a loom or frame. One set of fibers is held taut; this is called the **warp.** The other set, known as the **weft** or **woof,** is interwoven through the warp to make a fabric. Nearly all fabrics, including those used for our clothing, are made by some variation of this process.

A complex loom is a little like a computer. Much of the designing of fabric takes place when the loom is "programmed." The weaver decides in advance how the warp yarns are to be arranged on the loom and also decides on the pattern of interlacing for the weft yarns. After the planning stage, the weaving progresses more or less automatically. Amazingly intricate fabrics can be created on the loom.

Tapestry is a special type of weaving in which the weft yarns are manipulated freely to form a pattern or design on the front of the fabric. Often the weft yarns are of several colors, and the weaver can use the different colored yarn almost as flexibly as a painter uses pigment on a canvas. The weavers of ancient Peru specialized in tapestry weaves with geometric forms or stylized animal figures **(388)**. The shirt illustrated here seems even more remarkable when we consider that it was woven on the most primitive of looms.

Tapestry weaving enjoyed a "golden age" in Europe from the late 14th century through the 17th. For those who could afford it, tapestry was the art of choice. In place of the paintings we would expect to see now, the castles and great houses of Europe were hung with huge, finely woven cloth hangings, often with elaborate pictorial images designed by prominent artists. Nicolas Bataille, a master weaver of Paris, is believed responsible for the splendid *King Arthur* tapestry (389), one of nine large works depicting "heroes" venerated in the Middle Ages. With its extremely fine woven detail, the tapestry shows Arthur, the semi-legendary king who may have flourished in

above: 388. Shirt, Ica,
south coast of Peru. 13th–15th century.
Tapestry of wool and cotton, height 23½".
The Metropolitan Museum of Art, New York
(The Michael C. Rockefeller Memorial Collection,
bequest of Nelson A. Rockefeller, 1979).

left: 389. Workshop of Nicolas Bataille (?).
King Arthur with Three Cardinals,
from *The Nine Heroes.* c. 1385.
Wool tapestry, 11'6½" × 10'.
The Metropolitan Museum of Art, New York
(The Cloisters Collection, Munsey Fund, 1932,
and gift of John D. Rockefeller, Jr., 1947.

above: 390. Ruth Scheuer, designer;
Beverly Godfrey, Susan Giller, and Ruth Scheuer, weavers.
Veils. 1989. Tapestry, 5′ × 9′4″ × 5″.
© 1989 by Ruth Scheuer.

below: 391. *Norman Fleet Sailing to England,*
detail of the *Bayeux Tapestry.* c. 1073–88.
Wool embroidery on linen; height 20″, overall length 231′.
Town Hall, Bayeux, reproduced with special authorization
of the City of Bayeux.

England during the 6th century, holding court at his Round Table. So sure-handed is the composition that, seeing this work in reproduction, we can hardly recognize it as a painting made in thread.

Tapestry of this quality is a demanding art—a large work can take six months to a year to complete—so we do not see much of it anymore. However, the tradition has not completely died out. At the Center for Tapestry Arts in New York City an American weaver, Ruth Scheuer, has adapted classic French methods and standards to imagery that is very much of our own time **(390)**.

One of the most famous examples of fiber art in the Western world once hung in the Cathedral of Bayeux and now is preserved in the Town Hall of that French city. This is the *Bayeux Tapestry* **(391)**—misnamed, because it is actually a work of embroidery. (In the past, large-scale fabrics, especially those hung in buildings, often were loosely called "tapestries," regardless of the construction method.) **Embroidery** is a technique in which colored yarns are sewn to an existing woven background; frequently the sewing takes the form of decorative motifs or images, as here. The *Bayeux Tapestry* is like a long picture book—20 inches high and 231 feet long—telling the story of the conquest of England by William of Normandy in 1066. The scene illustrated, one of seventy-two separate episodes reading from left to right, shows the Norman boats setting sail to wage war on Saxon England. The fabric's pictorial design is simple and flat. The smaller boat, which is meant to be seen as farther away than the two large ones, does not contribute to any sense of spatial depth; it almost seems to be floating in the air. Despite the charming naïveté of these images, however, scholars have learned more about the events surrounding the Norman Conquest from the *Bayeux Tapestry* than they have from any of the literature of the time.

Centuries later and light-years away in expression, Lynda Benglis' *Patang* **(392)** shares one of the functions of the *Bayeux Tapestry*—to cover the bare walls of a public building. It is a work in **appliqué,** or pieces of fabric stitched onto a fabric backing, and hangs above a check-in counter at Atlanta's airport. Benglis' work makes an interesting contrast with the *Bayeux*

392. Lynda Benglis. *Patang.*
1980. Satin appliqué on canvas,
15 × 90'.
Atlanta Airport Commission,
Courtesy Paula Cooper Gallery,
New York.

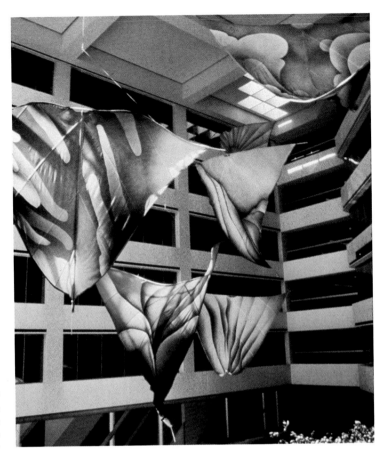

393. Ina Kozel. *Seven Sisters.* Hand-painted fabric. Installed in the Ashford-Green Building, Atlanta, 1982. Courtesy Eve Mannes Gallery, Atlanta.

Tapestry. Where the latter originally hung, high up on the walls in a dim cathedral, it is unlikely that viewers could see much of its detail, and this was apparently of little concern to its makers. *Patang,* on the other hand, was designed for maximum impact at a distance in a large, open space. Planned for this location, it presents large, bold, abstract designs in brilliant colors.

Benglis' work represents a revival of the use of fabric to decorate large expanses of wall. Fifteen years ago the architects of this building probably would have left the wall plain. Fifty years ago they might have commissioned a painter to do a mural. Today, increasingly, architects and interior designers seek the work of the fiber artist. Why is this so, why has fashion turned in this direction? We cannot say for sure, but it is certainly true that fiber brings a warmth, a softness, a flexibility to the often-forbidding steel and concrete of our world.

While fiberworks can be stretched taut or laid flat against the wall or even sculpted into three-dimensionality, we usually associate fabric with pliability. Clothing flows around our bodies as we move, sails puff out and fill with the wind, flags flutter. This association of fabric with movement is inherent in Ina Kozel's *Seven Sisters* (393). Installed in the atrium of Atlanta's Ashford-Green Building, *Seven Sisters* is an assemblage of hand-painted "kites" that swoop and pivot constantly as they are propelled by air currents. Within this six-story glass enclosure has been contained a gentle reminder of all graceful things that fly.

The illustrations in this chapter cover five different families of materials and four thousand years of human history. They are very different, yet they have certain things in common. Each of them represents a perfect use of the material from which it was made. Each has been formed with the highest possible standards of craftsmanship. Above all, each shows the striving for aesthetic satisfaction that is part of humanity.

ART PEOPLE *Aileen Osborn Webb*

The American craft movement today is remarkably healthy. Craft fairs abound in every corner of the United States throughout the summer and increasingly in other seasons as well. Major department stores sell handmade craft items in special "boutiques." Numerous craft magazines are published regularly. Organizations of craft artists are active and well-structured. This happy situation has existed for a surprisingly short time, and it exists largely through the efforts of one woman—a woman who began life as a most unlikely candidate for patron of the crafts.

Aileen Osborn was born in 1892, in the Hudson River town of Garrison, New York, to a family of great wealth and prestige. Her early years were correct for a privileged young woman of the time—private schools, a finishing school in Paris, a formal debut into society at age seventeen, marriage at twenty to an equally privileged young man, Vanderbilt Webb. For some time after the marriage, life continued as Aileen Osborn's parents, and her parents' parents, could have predicted—four children were born, lavish entertainments were planned and executed, servants were instructed, flowers were arranged. One cannot doubt that young Mrs. Webb was busy, for the management of a 102-room mansion requires energy and skill. But far more ambitious projects lay ahead for this tireless, creative woman.

It was during the 1930s, at the height of the Great Depression, that Mrs. Webb became interested in handcrafts. Cushioned herself by almost unlimited money, she nevertheless saw that many of her neighbors in the area were suffering terrible hardships. Jobs were scarce, and many families had difficulty putting food on the table. Aileen Webb reasoned that if a method could be found to popularize objects finely made by hand, this could provide employment and income for needy people. In 1932 she founded Putnam County Products, a cooperative association intended to market the wares of craftworkers. The effort was modest, but Aileen Webb had only just gotten started.

Largely through Mrs. Webb's efforts, the American Craftsmen's Council (later the American Craft Council) was founded in 1943. From this root grew many branches: the retail outlet called America House, in New York City, which sold only craft objects made by hand; the magazine *Craft Horizons* (now *American*

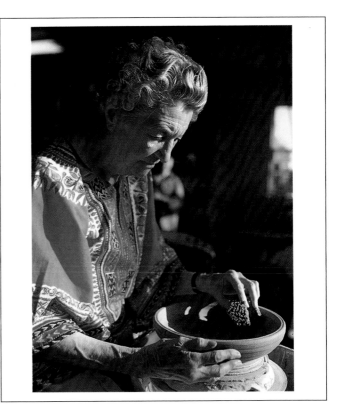

Craft), and its offspring publications; the Museum of Contemporary Crafts in New York; and eventually the World Craft Council, launched in 1964. Aileen Webb's participation in these activities was not merely that of a Lady Bountiful, writing checks; rather she was deeply involved in the day-to-day work. Until shortly before her death in 1979, at the age of 87, she appeared regularly at her American Craft Council office.

Never one to look on benignly from a distance, Aileen Webb became accomplished at enameling, woodcarving, and especially ceramics. The hands that birth and social class had designated for arranging flowers found their true expression plunged up to the elbows in potter's clay. Obviously, whatever the task to be done, Mrs. Webb plunged in up to the elbows, and every craft artist today benefits from her efforts.

Aileen Osborn Webb at her potter's wheel in Garrison, New York, 1977.

Chapter Thirteen

Architecture

Architecture satisfies a basic, universal human need for a roof over one's head. More than walls, more than a chair to sit on or a soft bed upon which to lie, a roof is the classic symbol of protection and security. We've all heard the expression "I have a roof over my head," but it would be unusual to hear someone say, "I'm all right because I have walls around me." Of course, in purely practical terms a roof does keep out the worst of the elements, snow and rain, and in warm climates a roof may be sufficient to keep people dry and comfortable. The roof seems to be symbolic of the nature of architecture.

As was discussed in Chapter 4 (p. 130), the walls and roof of a building shape space and define it. We can discuss architecture equally in terms of the spaces and volumes created within a structure and in terms of the forms that create those spaces.

More than any of the other arts, architecture demands structural stability. Every one of us daily moves in and out of buildings—schools, houses, offices, stores, churches, bus stations, banks, and movie theaters—and we take for granted, usually without thinking about it, that they will not collapse on top of us. That they do not is a tribute to their engineering; if a building is physically stable, this means it adheres faithfully to the principles of the particular *structural system* on which its architecture is based.

Structural Systems in Architecture

Any building is a defiance of gravity. Since earliest times architects have tackled the challenge of erecting a roof over empty space, setting walls upright, and having the whole stand secure. Their solutions have depended upon the materials they had available, for, as we shall see, certain materials are better suited than others to a particular structural system. There are two basic families of structural systems: the **shell** system and the **skeleton-and-skin** system.

In the shell system one building material provides both structural support and sheathing (outside covering). Buildings made of brick or stone or adobe fall into this category **(394)**. So do older (pre-19th-century) wood buildings constructed of heavy timbers, the most obvious example being the log cabin. The structural material comprises the walls and roof, marks the boundary between inside and outside, and is visible as the exterior surface. Shell construction prevailed until the 19th century, when it began to fall out of favor. Today, however, the development of strong cast materials, including many plastics, has brought renewed interest in shell structures.

The skeleton-and-skin system might be compared to the human body, which has a rigid bony skeleton to support its basic frame and a more fragile skin for sheathing. We find it in modern skyscrapers, with their steel frames (skeletons) supporting the structure and a sheathing (skin) of glass or some other light material. Also, most houses today—at least in Western cultures— are built with a skeleton of wood beams nailed together, topped with a sheathing of light wood boards, shingles, aluminum siding, or the like. Skeleton-and-skin construction is largely a product of the Industrial Revolution; not until the mid-19th century could steel for beams or metal nails be manufactured in practical quantities.

Two factors that must be considered in any structural system are *weight* and *tensile strength*. Walls must support the weight of the roof, and lower stories must support the weight of upper stories. In other words, all the weight of the building must somehow be carried safely to the ground. You can get a sense of this if you imagine your own body as a structural member. Suppose you are lying flat on your back, your body held rigid. You are going to be lifted high in the air, to become a "roof." First you are lifted by four people: One supports you under the shoulders, one under the buttocks, one holds your arms extended above your head, another holds your feet. Your weight is therefore channeled down through four vertical people to the ground, and so you can hold yourself horizontally with some ease. Next you are lifted by two people, one holding your shoulders, another your feet. A lot of your weight is concentrated in the center of your body, which is unsupported, so eventually you sag in the middle and fall to the floor. Then you are lifted by one person, who holds you at the center of your back. The weight at both ends of your body has nowhere to go, nothing to carry it to the ground, and you sag at both ends.

Tensile strength, as applied to architecture, is the ability of a material to span horizontal distances with minimum support from underneath. Returning to the analogy of the body, imagine you are not made of flesh and blood but of strong plastic or metal. Regardless of how you are held up in the air, you can stay rigid and horizontal, because you have great tensile strength.

If you keep these images in mind, you may find it easier to understand the various structural systems we shall consider below. They are introduced here in roughly the chronological order in which they were developed. As was mentioned earlier, all will be of the shell type until the 19th century.

394. Mission St. Francis of Assisi, Ranchos de Taos, New Mexico. c. 1776–80.

LOAD-BEARING CONSTRUCTION

Another term for load-bearing construction is "stacking and piling." This is the simplest method of making a building, and it is suitable for brick, stone, adobe, ice blocks, and certain modern materials. Essentially, the builder constructs the walls by piling layer upon layer, starting thick at the bottom, getting thinner as the structure rises, and usually tapering inward near the highest point. The whole may then be topped by a lightweight roof, perhaps of thatch or wood. This construction is stable, because its greatest weight is concentrated at the bottom and weight diminishes gradually as the walls grow higher.

Load-bearing structures tend to have few and small openings (if any) in the walls, because the method does not readily allow for support of material above a void, such as a window opening. This was the system used to construct the Ranchos de Taos church in New Mexico (394), a piled-up mass of adobe, or sun-dried mud. Although the Taos church is hollow, meant to contain worshippers inside, many load-bearing structures are solid all the way through, or perhaps have only small open chambers within them.

POST-AND-LINTEL

We encountered post-and-lintel construction earlier, in the discussion of Stonehenge (59). After stacking and piling, it is the most elementary structural method, based on two uprights (the posts) supporting a horizontal crosspiece (the lintel, or beam). This configuration can be continued indefinitely, so that there may be one very long horizontal supported at critical points along the way by vertical posts to carry its weight to the ground. The most common materials for post-and-lintel construction are stone and wood. Since neither has great tensile strength, these materials will yield and cave in when forced to span long distances, so the architect must provide supporting posts at close intervals.

Post-and-lintel construction has been, for at least four thousand years, a favorite method of architects for raising a roof and providing for open space underneath. Tracing its history back to the first culture we know well, we find post-and-lintel used widely by the ancient Egyptians. At Luxor on the east bank of the Nile in Egypt stand the ruins of the mighty temple of Amen-Mut-Khonsu (395), planned by the pharaoh Amenhotep III in the 14th century B.C. The heavy lintels of the colonnade are supported solidly by tall,

post-and-lintel

395. Colonnade and Court of Amenhotep III, Temple of Amen-Mut-Khonsu, Luxor, Egypt. c. 1390 B.C.

massive columns, almost too massive for the job they have to do. Perhaps the builder deliberately made the columns heavier than necessary in order to create an imposing effect.

In ancient Greece the design of post-and-lintel buildings, especially temples, became rather standardized in certain features. There were three major architectural styles, which appeared in sequence (with some overlapping), and they are known as the **Greek Orders.** The most distinctive feature of each was the design of the column (**396**). By the 7th century B.C. the **Doric** style had been introduced. A Doric column has no base, nothing separating it from the floor below; its **capital,** the topmost part between the shaft of the column and the roof or lintel, is a plain stone slab above a rounded stone. The **Ionic** style was developed in the 6th century B.C. and gradually replaced the Doric. An Ionic column has a stepped base and a carved capital in the form of two graceful spirals known as **volutes.** The **Corinthian** style, which appeared in the 4th century B.C., is yet more elaborate, having a more detailed base and a capital of delicately carved acanthus leaves.

Possibly the best-known and most impressive post-and-lintel building of all time is the Parthenon in Athens, which is in the Doric style (**397**). We have already studied the Parthenon as a religious and political structure (Chapter 3, p. 63); here we will focus on its construction. Had the Parthenon been simply an academic exercise in placing horizontal members atop vertical supports—a kind of Classical Age prefabrication—it never would have been so admired for its architectural purity. What sets it apart are the many subtle refinements in its structure.

To begin with, the Parthenon has a particularly satisfying proportion of width to length to height—many would say a "perfect" proportion. Legend claims there are no straight lines in the Parthenon, but this is probably a romantic exaggeration. Many of the lines we expect to be straight, however, are not. What the builders did was adjust the physical lines of the temple so they would appear to be straight visually. For example, tall columns that are absolutely straight may appear to bend inward at the center, so the columns on the Parthenon have been given a slight bulge, known as **entasis,** to compensate for the visual effect. Also, a long horizontal, such as the Parthenon's porch steps, may appear to sag in the middle; to correct for this optical illusion, the level has been adjusted very slightly, rising about $2\frac{1}{2}$ inches to form an arc higher at the center. A large building rising perpendicular to the ground may loom over the visitor and seem to be leaning forward; to avoid

frieze
architrave
capital

shaft

base

Doric   Ionic   Corinthian

396. Comparison of column styles in the Greek Orders.

397. Ictinus and Callicrates. Parthenon, Athens. 447–432 B.C.

this impression, the architects of the Parthenon tilted the whole facade back very slightly. Corner columns, seen against the sky, would have seemed thinner than inside columns, which have the building as a backdrop; therefore, the outside columns were made slightly heavier than all the others. These are only a few of the structural refinements that resulted in a beautiful temple.

Because the Parthenon looks so visually perfect, these optical corrections are not noticeable to the casual viewer. Precise measurements have revealed the secrets of the Parthenon's majesty. The point is, post-and-lintel construction, which at first appears to be so rudimentary, can embody the most sublime forms ever conceived by an architect's mind.

People often assume the Parthenon is a ruin simply because it is old, but this is far from true. Not only is post-and-lintel construction highly stable, but the builders who took such trouble about visual details were equally careful about structural soundness. In fact, were it not for an unfortunate incident in the 17th century, the Parthenon would stand today much as it did twenty-four hundred years ago. In 1687 the Turks, who then controlled Athens and were at war with the Venetians, used the Parthenon as an ammunition dump. The Venetians laid siege to the city, a well-placed shell ignited the ammunition, and the Parthenon blew up. No structural system yet devised can withstand the tragic consequences of conflict between nations.

The post-and-lintel system, then, offers potential for both structural soundness and grandeur. When applied to wood or stone, however, it leaves one problem unsolved, and that is the spanning of relatively large open spaces. The first attempt at solving this problem was the invention of the round arch.

ROUND ARCH AND VAULT

Although the round arch was used by the ancient peoples of Mesopotamia several centuries before the birth of Christ (450), it was most fully developed by the Romans, who perfected the form in the 2nd century B.C. To get a sense of how the arch works, we might go back to the analogy of the body. Imagine that, instead of lying flat on your back, you are bent over forward into a curve, and again you will be lifted into the air. One person will support your hands, another your feet. As long as your body follows the proper arc—that is, your two supporters stand the correct distance apart—you can maintain the pose for some time. If they stand too close together, you start to topple first one way and then the other; if they move too far apart, you have insufficient support in the middle and plunge to the floor. An arch incorporates more complex forces of **tension** (pulling apart) and **compression** (pushing together), but the general idea is the same.

round arch

barrel vault

398. Pont du Gard, Nîmes, France. A.D. early 1st century. Length 902′.

The arch has many virtues. In addition to being an attractive form, it enables the architect to open up fairly large spaces in a wall without risking the building's structural soundness. These spaces admit light, reduce the weight of the walls, and decrease the amount of material needed. As utilized by the Romans, the arch is a perfect semicircle, although it may seem elongated if it rests on columns. It is constructed from wedge-shaped pieces of stone that meet at an angle always perpendicular to the curve of the arch. Because of tensions and compressions inherent in the form, the arch is stable only when it is complete, when the topmost stone, the **keystone,** has been set in place. For this reason an arch under construction must be supported from below, usually by a wooden framework.

Among the most elegant and enduring of Roman structures based on the arch is the Pont du Gard at Nîmes, France (**398**), built in A.D. 15 when the empire was nearing its farthest expansion (see map, p. 388). At this time industry, commerce, and agriculture were at their peak. Roman engineering was applied to an ambitious system of public-works projects, not just in Italy but in the outlying areas as well. The Pont du Gard functioned as an aqueduct, a structure meant to transport water, and its lower level served as a footbridge across the river. That it stands today virtually intact after nearly two thousand years (and is crossed by cyclists on the route of the famous Tour de France bicycle race), testifies to the Romans' brilliant engineering skills. Visually, the Pont du Gard exemplifies the best qualities of arch construction. Solid and heavy, obviously durable, it is shot through with open spaces that make it seem light and its weight-bearing capabilities effortless.

When the arch is extended in depth—when it is, in reality, many arches placed flush one behind the other—the result is called a **barrel vault** or **tunnel vault.** This vault construction makes it possible to create large interior spaces. The Romans made great use of the barrel vault, but for its finest expression we look many hundreds of years later, to the cathedrals of the Middle Ages.

STRUCTURAL SYSTEMS IN ARCHITECTURE 329

399. Nave,
Cathedral of St. Sernin,
Toulouse, France.
c. 1080–1120.

round arches in the
Romanesque style

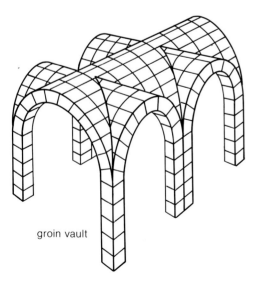

groin vault

The church of St. Sernin **(399)**, in the southern French city of Toulouse, is an example of the style prevalent throughout Western Europe from about 1050 to 1200—a style known as *Romanesque.* Romanesque builders adopted the old Roman forms of round arch and barrel vault so as to add height to their churches. Until this period most churches had beamed wooden roofs, which not only posed a threat of fire but also limited the height to which architects could aspire. With the stone barrel vault, they could achieve the soaring, majestic space we see in the *nave* (the long central area) of St. Sernin. Round arches set on half columns punctuate the ceiling, leading one's eye forward to the altar.

On the side aisles of St. Sernin (not visible in the photograph) the builders employed a series of *groin vaults.* A groin vault results when two vaults are crossed at right angles to each other, thus directing the weights and stresses down into the four corners. By dividing up a space into square segments known as *bays,* each of which contains one groin vault, the architects could cover a long span safely and economically. The arrangement of bays also creates a satisfying rhythmic pattern down the length of the structure.

POINTED ARCH AND VAULT

While the round arch and vault of the Romanesque era solved many problems and made many things possible, they nevertheless had certain drawbacks. For one thing, a round arch, to be stable, must be a semicircle; therefore, the height of the arch is limited by its width. Two other difficulties were weight and darkness. Barrel vaults are both literally and visually heavy, calling for huge masses of stone to maintain their structural stability. Also, the builders who constructed them dared not make light-admitting openings in or around them, for fear the arches and vaults would collapse, and so the interiors of Romanesque buildings tend to be dark. The *Gothic* period in Europe, which followed the Romanesque, solved these problems with the pointed arch.

400. Nave,
Chartres Cathedral, France.
c. 1194–1260.

The pointed arch, while seemingly not very different from the round one, offers many advantages. Because the sides arc up to a point, weight is channeled down to the ground at a steeper angle, and therefore the arch can be taller. The vault constructed from such an arch also can be much taller than a barrel vault. Architects of the Gothic period found they did not need heavy masses of material throughout the curve of the vault, as long as the major points of intersection were reinforced. These reinforcements, called **ribs,** are visible in the nave ceiling of Chartres Cathedral (**400**; see also **64,480**). The lighter vault also enabled builders to introduce stained-glass windows in the stone walls, and so the Gothic church is much brighter inside than its Romanesque predecessor.

Gothic builders also provided for structural reinforcement outside the churches. Given that the walls were relatively thin, and that arches tend to create a sideways or lateral thrust, there remained the danger that a large cathedral could "lean" outward and collapse. To prevent this, architects developed a system of exterior masonry columns or **piers,** joined to the body of the church by **flying buttresses,** or arched supports. In effect, the flying buttresses (visible in our exterior view of Chartres Cathedral, **480**) "hold in" the walls of the church. As the style progressed, they were increasingly carved and embellished to become decorative outside features of the buildings.

pointed arches in the
Gothic style

THE DOME

A dome is an architectural structure generally in the shape of a hemisphere, or half globe. One customary definition of the dome is an arch rotated 360 degrees on its axis, and this is really more accurate, because, for example, the dome based on a pointed arch will be pointed at the top, not perfectly hemispherical. The stresses in a dome are much like those of an arch, except that they are spread in a circle around the dome's perimeter. Unless the dome is buttressed—supported from the outside—from all sides, there is a tendency for it to "explode"—for the stones to pop outward in all directions.

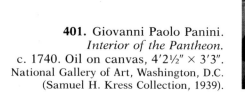

dome

401. Giovanni Paolo Panini. *Interior of the Pantheon.* c. 1740. Oil on canvas, 4'2½" × 3'3". National Gallery of Art, Washington, D.C. (Samuel H. Kress Collection, 1939).

Like so many other architectural structures, the dome was perfected under the incomparable engineering genius of the Romans, and one of the finest domed buildings ever erected dates from the early 2nd century. It is called the Pantheon **(467)**, which means a temple dedicated to "all the gods"—or, at least, all the gods who were venerated in ancient Rome. We reproduce here an 18th-century painting of the interior **(401)** because the circular building is so vast that it is impossible to find a camera angle to convey adequately its shape and scale.

As seen from the inside, the Pantheon has a perfect hemispherical dome soaring 142 feet above the floor, resting upon a cylinder almost exactly the same in diameter—140 feet. At the very top of the dome is an opening 29 feet in diameter called an **oculus,** or eye, thought to be symbolic of the "eye of Heaven." This opening provides the sole (and plentiful) illumination for the building. In its conception, then, the Pantheon is amazingly simple, equal in height and width, symmetrical in its structure, round form set upon round form. Yet because of its scale and its classic proportions, the effect is overwhelming. The fact that the Romans, in ancient times, could enclose such a huge space without interior supports today seems extraordinary.

When an architect wishes to set a round dome atop a square building, as is very often the case, the structural problems become more complex. Some transitional device is required between the circle (at the dome's base) and the square (of the building's top), preferably one that bolsters the dome. An elegant solution can be found in Hagia Sophia (the Church of the Holy Wisdom) in Istanbul (**402**; see also **473**). Hagia Sophia was built as a Christian church during the 6th century, when Istanbul, then called Constantinople, was the capital of the great Byzantine Empire (p. 493). When the Turks conquered the city in the 15th century, Hagia Sophia became an Islamic mosque, and it is now preserved as a museum. In sheer size and perfection of form it was the architectural triumph of its time and has seldom been matched since then.

The dome of Hagia Sophia rises 183 feet above the floor, with its weight carried to the ground by heavy stone piers—in this case, squared columns—at the four corners of the immense nave. Around the base of the dome is a row of closely spaced arched windows, which make the heavy dome seem to "float" upward. Each of the four sides of the building consists of a monumental round arch, and between the arches and the dome are curved triangular sections known as *pendentives.* It is the function of the pendentives to make a smooth transition between rectangle and dome.

Because domes have so much been a feature of public buildings, both religious and political, we may think of them as the capstones of "official" architecture. St. Peter's Basilica in Rome (**496**), the U.S. Capitol in Washington (**412**) and its many offshoots in the state capitals, the great cathedrals of London—all are monumental structures topped by imposing domes. One of the loveliest of all domed buildings, however, originally was constructed for a private purpose, and despite its size it has a more intimate quality. This is the famous Taj Mahal in Agra, India.

The Taj Mahal (**403**) was built in the mid-17th century by the Moslem emperor of India, Shah Jahan, as a tomb for his beloved wife, Arjummand Banu, who died at the age of thirty-nine after having borne fourteen children. Although the Taj is nearly as large as Hagia Sophia and possessed of a dome rising some 30 feet higher, it seems comparatively fragile and weightless. Nearly all its exterior lines reach upward, from the graceful pointed arches, to the pointed dome, to the four slender towers—minarets—poised at the outside corners. The Taj Mahal, constructed entirely of pure white marble, appears almost as a shimmering mirage, which has come to rest for a moment beside the peaceful reflecting pool but may float away at any time.

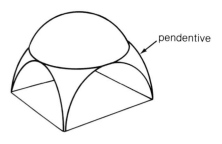

pendentive

dome with pendentives

left: 402. Interior, Hagia Sophia, Istanbul. 532–37. Height of dome 183′.

right: 403. Taj Mahal, Agra, India. 1632–53. White marble.

404. Joseph Paxton. Crystal Palace, Hyde Park, London. 1851, destroyed by fire 1936. Contemporary lithograph. New York Public Library (Astor, Lenox and Tilden Foundations).

CAST-IRON CONSTRUCTION

With the perfection of the post-and-lintel, the arch, and the dome, construction in stone and brick had gone just about as far as it could go. Not until the introduction of a new building material did the next major breakthrough in structural systems take place. Iron had been known for thousands of years and had been used for tools and objects of all kinds, but only in the 19th century did architects realize that its great strength offered promise for structural support. This principle was demonstrated brilliantly in a project that few contemporary observers took seriously.

In 1851 the city of London was planning a great exhibition, under the sponsorship of Prince Albert, husband of Queen Victoria. The challenge was to house under one roof the "Works of Industry of All Nations," and the commission for erecting a suitable structure fell to Joseph Paxton, a designer of greenhouses. Paxton raised in Hyde Park a wondrous building framed in cast iron and sheathed in glass—probably the first modern skeleton-and-skin construction ever designed **(404)**. The Crystal Palace, as Paxton's creation came to be known, covered more than 17 acres and reached a height of 108 feet. Because of an ingenious system of prefabrication, the whole was erected in just sixteen weeks.

Visitors to the exhibition considered the Crystal Palace a curiosity—a marvelous one, to be sure, but still an oddity outside the realm of architecture. They could not have foreseen that Paxton's design, solid iron framework clothed in a glass skin, would pave the way for 20th-century architecture. In fact, Paxton had taken a giant step in demonstrating that as long as a building's skeleton held firm its skin could be light and non-load-bearing. Several intermediary steps would be required before this principle could be translated into today's architecture.

Another bold experiment in iron construction came a few decades later just across the English Channel, in France, and involved a plan that many considered to be foolhardy, if not downright insane. Gustave Eiffel, a French engineer, proposed to build in the center of Paris a skeleton iron tower, nearly a thousand feet tall, to act as a centerpiece for the Paris World's Fair of 1889. Nothing of the sort had ever been suggested, much less built. In spite of loud protests, the Eiffel Tower **(405)** was constructed, at a cost of about a million dollars—an unheard-of sum for those times. It rises on four arched columns, which curve inward until they meet in a single tower thrusting up boldly above the cityscape of Paris. (The writer Guy de Maupassant claimed that he lunched in a restaurant on the tower as often as possible, because "it's the only place in Paris where I don't have to see it."[1])

The importance of this singular, remarkable structure for the future of architecture rests on the fact that it *was* a skeleton that proudly showed itself without benefit of any cosmetic embellishment. No marble, no glass, no tiles, no skin of any kind—just the clean lines drawn in an industrial-age product. Two concepts emerged from this daring construction. First, metal in and of itself can make beautiful architecture. Second, metal can provide a solid framework for a very large structure, self-sustaining and permanent. Today the Eiffel Tower is the ultimate symbol of Paris, and no tourist would pass up a visit. From folly to landmark in less than a century—such is the course of innovative architecture.

Iron for structural members was not the only breakthrough of the mid-19th century. The Industrial Revolution also introduced a construction material that was much humbler but equally significant in its implications for architecture: the nail. And for want of that simple little nail, most of the houses we live in today could not have been built.

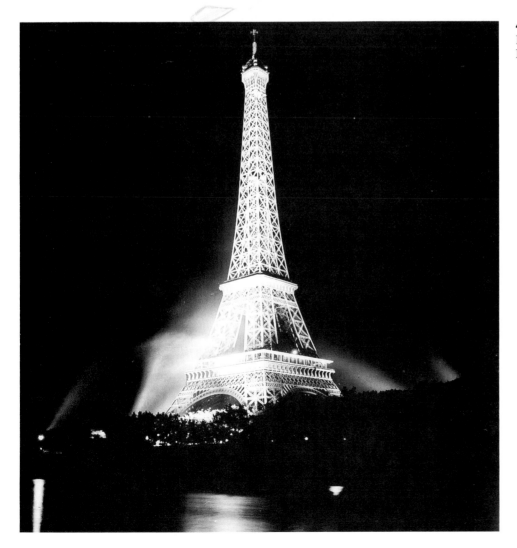

405. Alexandre Gustave Eiffel. Eiffel Tower, Paris. 1889. Iron, height 934'.

BALLOON-FRAME CONSTRUCTION

So far in this chapter the illustrations have concentrated on grand and public buildings—churches, temples, monuments. These are the glories of architecture, the buildings we admire and travel great distances to see. We should not forget, however, that the overwhelming majority of structures in the world have been houses for people to live in, or **domestic architecture.**

Until the mid-19th century houses were of shell construction. They were made of brick or stone (and, in warmer climates, of such materials as reeds and bamboo) with load-bearing construction, or else they were post-and-lintel structures in which heavy timbers were assembled by complicated notching and joinery, sometimes with wooden pegs. Nails, if any, had to be fabricated by hand and were very expensive.

About 1833, in Chicago, the technique of *balloon-frame* construction was introduced. Balloon-frame construction is a true skeleton-and-skin method. It developed from two innovations: improved methods for milling lumber and mass-produced nails. In this system, the builder first erects a framework or skeleton by nailing together sturdy but lightweight boards (the familiar 2-by-4 "stud"), then adds a roof and sheathes the walls in clapboard, shingles, stucco, or whatever the homeowner wishes. Glass for windows can be used lavishly, as long as it does not interrupt the underlying wood structure, since the sheathing plays little part in holding the building together.

When houses of this type were introduced, the term "balloon framing" was meant to be sarcastic. Skeptics thought the buildings would soon fall down, or burst just like balloons. But some of the earliest balloon-frame houses stand firm today, and this method is still the most popular for new house construction in Western countries.

The balloon frame, of course, has its limitations. Wood beams 2 by 4 inches thick cannot support a skyscraper ten or fifty stories high, and that was the very sort of building architects had begun to dream of late in the 19th century. For such soaring ambitions, a new material was needed, and it was found. The material was steel.

STEEL-FRAME CONSTRUCTION

Although multistory buildings have been with us since the Roman Empire, the development of the skyscraper, as we know it, required two late-19th-century innovations: the elevator and steel-frame construction. Steel-frame construction, like balloon framing, is a true skeleton-and-skin arrangement. Rather than piling floor upon floor, with each of the lower stories supporting those above it, the builders first erect a steel "cage" that is capable of sustaining the entire weight of the building, and then apply a skin of some other material. But if one is going to erect a building of great height, one cannot expect people to walk up ten or more flights of stairs to get to the top floors. Hence, the elevator made its appearance.

What many consider to be the first genuinely modern building was designed by Louis Sullivan and built between 1890 and 1891 in St. Louis. Known as the Wainwright Building **(406)**, it employed a steel framework sheathed in masonry. Other architects had experimented with steel support but had carefully covered their structures in heavy stone so as to reflect traditional architectural forms and make the construction seem reliably sturdy. Centuries of precedent had prepared the public to expect bigness to go hand in hand with heaviness. Sullivan broke new ground by making his sheathing light, letting the skin of his building echo, even celebrate, the steel framing underneath. Regular bays of windows on the seven office floors are separated by strong vertical lines, and the four corners of the building are emphasized by vertical piers. The Wainwright Building's message is subtle but we cannot mistake it: the nation had stopped growing outward and started growing *up*.

balloon-frame construction

steel–frame construction

Sullivan's design looks forward to the 20th century, but it nevertheless clings to certain architectural details rooted in classical history, most notably the heavy *cornice*—the projecting roof ornament—that terminates upward movement at the top of the building. In a very few decades even these backward glances into the architectural past would become rare.

Toward the middle of the 20th century skyscrapers began to take over the downtown areas of major cities, and city planners had to grapple with unprecedented problems. How high is too high? How much air space should a building consume? What provision, if any, should be made to prevent tall buildings from completely blocking out the sunlight from the streets below? In New York and certain other cities ordinances were passed that resulted in a number of look-alike and architecturally undistinguished buildings. The laws required that if a building filled the ground space of a city block right up to the sidewalk, it could rise for only a certain number of feet or stories before being "stepped back," or narrowed; then it could rise for only a specified number of additional feet before being stepped back again. The resultant structures came to known as "wedding-cake" buildings. A few architects, however, found more creative ways of meeting the air space requirement; those working in the *International* (in fact, European) style designed some of the most admired American skyscrapers, such as Lever House.

Lever House in New York **(407)**, designed by the architectural firm of Skidmore, Owings, and Merrill and built in 1952, was heralded as a breath of fresh air in the smog of look-alike structures. Its sleek understated form was widely copied but never equaled. Lever House might be compared to two shimmering glass dominoes, one resting horizontally on freestanding supports, the other balanced upright and off-center on the first. At a time when most architects of office buildings strove to fill every square inch of air space to which they were entitled—both vertically and horizontally—the elegant Lever House drew back and raised its slender rectangle aloof from its neighbors, surrounded by free space. Even its base does not rest on the ground but rides on thin supports to allow for open plazas and passageways beneath the building. Practically no other system of construction except steel frame could have made possible this graceful form.

left: **406.** Louis Sullivan. Wainwright Building, Saint Louis. 1890–91.

right: **407.** Gordon Bunshaft of Skidmore, Owings, and Merrill. Lever House, New York. 1952.

408. Verrazano-Narrows Bridge, New York. 1964. Ammann and Whitney, consulting engineers; John B. Peterkin, Aymar Embury II, and Edward D. Stone, consulting architects.

SUSPENSION

Also made feasible by steel, suspension is the structural method we associate primarily with bridges, although it has been employed for some buildings as well. The concept of suspension was developed for bridges late in the 19th century. In essence, the weight of the structure is suspended from steel cables supported on vertical pylons driven into the ground. A long bridge, such as the Verrazano-Narrows Bridge in New York **(408)**, may have only two sets of pylons planted in the riverbed, but the steel cables suspended under tension from their towers are strong enough to support a span between them more than four-fifths of a mile long. Suspension structures are among the most graceful in architecture, involving as they do long sweeping curves and the slender lines of the cables. A bridge in particular, suspended over water, may seem almost weightless when viewed from a distance, and there is a sense of flexibility—both visual and physical, because the roadbed may rise and fall several feet depending on winds and passing traffic.

TRUSS CONSTRUCTION

By contrast, the truss is one of the most rigid structural systems in architecture. It is based on the triangle, and it derives its stability from the fact that the triangle, unlike other geometric shapes, cannot be bent out of shape without changing the length of one of its legs. The truss, therefore, can be used to span horizontal distances much in the way post-and-lintel is employed, but with far less support from underneath.

Although truss construction has been known since the Middle Ages, its principles have been fully developed only in the 20th century. It is most often associated with wood, since the triangular arrangement gives that inexpensive material greater strength than it otherwise would have, but there are also trusses in iron and steel. In the Federal Correctional Institution at Bastrop, Texas **(409)**, thick wood trusses are part of a design that constitutes a startling departure from our usual image of prison architecture. The trusses support the roof and are angled so that their long sides provide a surface on which to rest solar energy collectors. Beyond this, the repeated trusses set up a rhythmic pattern that unifies the complex of the buildings.

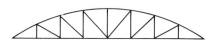

trusses

REINFORCED CONCRETE CONSTRUCTION

Concrete is an old material that was known and used by the Romans. A mixture of cement, gravel, and water, concrete can be poured, will assume the shape of any mold, and then will set to hardness. Its major problem is that it tends to be brittle and has low tensile strength. This problem is often observed in the thin concrete slabs used for sidewalks and patios, which may crack and split apart as a result of weight and weather. Late in the 19th century, however, a method was developed for reinforcing concrete forms by imbedding irons rods inside the concrete before it hardened. The iron contributes tensile strength, while the concrete provides shape and surface. In the 20th century reinforced concrete, also known as *ferroconcrete,* has been used in a wide variety of structures, often in those with free-form, organic shapes. While it may seem at first to be a skeleton-and-skin construction, ferroconcrete actually works more like a shell, because the iron rods (or sometimes a steel mesh) and concrete are bonded permanently and can form structures that are self-sustaining, even when very thin.

A special kind of ferroconcrete construction—precast reinforced sections—was used to create the soaring shell-like forms of the famous Sydney Opera House in Australia **(410).** The Opera House, which is really an all-around entertainment complex, is almost as famous for its construction difficulties as it is for its extraordinary design. So daring was its concept that the necessary technology virtually had to be invented as the project went along. Planned as a symbol of the great port city in whose harbor it stands, the Opera House gives the impression of a wonderful clipper ship at full sail. Three sets of pointed shells, oriented in different directions, turn the building into a giant sculpture in which walls and roof are one. Reinforced concrete is the sort of material that allows the builder to experiment and try new techniques, that allows the architect to dream impossible dreams.

below left: **409.** CRS Sirrine. Federal Correctional Institution, Bastrop, Tex. Completed 1979.

bottom: **410.** Joern Utzon. Sydney Opera House, Australia. 1959–72. Reinforced concrete, height of highest shell 200'.

reinforced concrete

GEODESIC DOMES

Of all the structural systems, probably the only one that can be attributed to a single individual is the geodesic dome, which was developed by the American architectural engineer R. Buckminster Fuller. Fuller's dome **(411)** is essentially a bubble, formed by a network of metal rods arranged in triangles and further organized into tetrahedrons. (A tetrahedron is a three-dimensional geometric figure having four faces.) This basic metal framework can be sheathed in any of several lightweight materials, including wood, glass, plastic, even paper.

The geodesic dome offers a combination of advantages never before available in architecture. Although very light in weight in relation to size, it is amazingly strong, because its structure rests on a mathematically sophisticated use of the triangle. It requires no interior support, and so all the space encompassed by the dome can be used with total freedom. The geodesic dome can be built in any size. In theory, at least, a structurally sound geodesic dome 2 miles across could be built, although nothing of this scope has ever been attempted. Perhaps most important for modern building techniques, Fuller's dome is based on a modular system of construction. Individual segments—modules—can be prefabricated to allow for extremely quick assembly of even a large dome. And finally, because of the flexibility in choice of sheathing materials, there are virtually endless options for climate and light control.

Fuller patented the geodesic dome in 1947, but it was not until twenty years later, when his design served as the U.S. Pavilion at the Montreal World Fair, that the public's attention was awakened to its possibilities. The dome at Expo 67, shown here, amazed the architectural world and fairgoers alike. It was 250 feet in diameter (about the size of a football field rounded off) and, being sheathed in translucent material, lighted up the sky at night like a giant spaceship set down on earth.

After Expo 67 some predicted that before long all houses and public buildings would be geodesic domes. This dream has faded considerably, but Fuller's dome has proved exceptionally well suited for government and scientific operations in arctic climates. To build a habitable structure in the freezing wastes of Antarctica, for example, one needs a lightweight material that can be shipped and assembled easily, great strength to withstand below freezing temperatures and high winds, and control of the interior environment. The geodesic dome meets all these requirements.

geodesic dome

411. R. Buckminster Fuller. U.S. Pavilion, Expo 67, Montreal. 1967. Geodesic dome, diameter 250'.

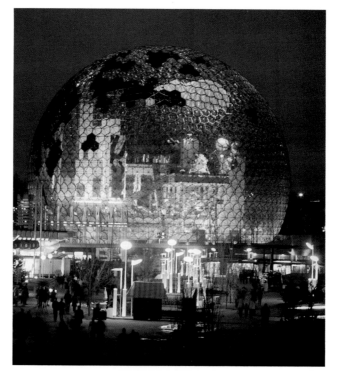

R. Buckminster Fuller

1895–1983

The term "eccentric genius" might have been coined to describe the 20th-century architect/engineer/inventor/philosopher R. Buckminster Fuller, known to his friends as "Bucky." Whether history will characterize him as more of an eccentric or more of a genius remains to be seen.

Born in a suburb of Boston, Fuller was the black sheep of a distinguished New England family. He attended Harvard University for a short time, but, as he explained afterward, "I cut classes and went out quite deliberately to get into trouble, and so naturally I got kicked out." There followed a variety of odd jobs and a stint in the Navy. After he married Anne Hewlett in 1917, Fuller went into partnership with his father-in-law, an architect, in a building-block company. The year 1922 marked a crisis in his life. The business did not prosper, and the Fullers' daughter Alexandra died on her fourth birthday. Fuller sank into a terrible depression—working all day and drinking all night. At the lowest ebb he seriously considered suicide. Then in 1927, for some reason, he reached a critical turning point. One night, he later recalled, he found himself saying, "You do not have the right to eliminate yourself. You do not belong to you. You belong to the universe." From that moment he dedicated his life to discovering "the principles operative in the universe and [turning] them over to my fellow men."

The theory Fuller eventually formulated was both simple and extraordinarily grandiose: any problem in the world can be solved by design and technology. He believed wholeheartedly that "there is absolutely nothing that cannot be done." Fuller liked to talk about our planet as "Spaceship Earth" and felt that it should be designed as efficiently as any space vehicle; one of his twenty-five books is entitled *Operating Manual for Spaceship Earth.*

The first practical application of Fuller's theories was the Dymaxion House, patented in 1927. This experimental dwelling had glass walls, rooms hung from a central mast, and such energy-efficient devices as an automatic vacuum-cleaning system. Next came the Dymaxion automobile, a three-wheeled vehicle capable of speeds up to 120 m.p.h. Neither invention achieved any popular success, but in 1947 Fuller patented the design for which he is most famous—the geo-

desic dome. Based on a system of triangles arranged into four-planed figures, or tetrahedrons, the geodesic dome could enclose a huge amount of space without interior support and allow for total climatic control. Thousands of Fuller's domes have been built around the world. One of his most ambitious projects, however—the complete enclosure of midtown Manhattan in a dome 3 miles across—was (understandably) considered impractical.

Fuller remained active until about a month before his death, at the age of eighty-seven. He traveled widely, lecturing about his theories, and particularly enjoyed speaking to college audiences, among whom he attracted rather a cult following. Education was one of his many interests, for, he said: "Every child is born a genius. It is my conviction, from having watched a great many babies grow up, that all of humanity is born a genius and then becomes degeniused very rapidly by unfavorable circumstances and by the frustration of all their extraordinary built-in capabilities."[2]

Photograph of R. Buckminster Fuller.

In this brief survey of the major structural systems we have seen that the form of architecture and its method of construction are largely determined by the materials available. Wood readily lends itself to post-and-lintel construction, balloon-frame construction, or the truss; stone works for post-and-lintel also, as well as for the arch and dome; metal allows for steel-frame construction, suspension, or reinforced concrete; and so on. But there is another factor—often a more important one—that affects the shape of architecture, and that is the purpose a building will serve. For the rest of this chapter we will look at some of the possibilities.

Purposes of Architecture

Architecture throughout the ages has been enormously diverse, but nearly every structure fits into one of just a few major categories: government buildings; other public buildings, such as libraries or museums; commercial buildings, including offices, banks, and shops; buildings for transportation—airline terminals and train stations, for example; religious buildings; and, of course, residences. In other words, nearly every structure has been designed to serve a specific purpose.

This section of the chapter will consider six types of structures—the government building, the museum, the office building, the hotel, the apartment building, and the private residence. For each category we will study three examples. These examples don't begin to cover the entire range of possibilities for any given architectural purpose. That would be impossible in a book many times this size. Rather, they have been chosen because they provide interesting comparisons with one another and because they reveal how architects have attempted to serve the purposes at hand in different times, in different places, with different personal styles.

THREE GOVERNMENT BUILDINGS

The function of government is ruling, managing, controlling, protecting the people it governs. In order to do so it must establish and maintain its legitimacy. A government that was not taken seriously by those it governs would have difficulty sustaining itself. For this reason most governments throughout history have taken pains to create outward symbols of their legitimacy, and some of the most powerful of those symbols have been in the form of official architecture. Anyone who has visited the United States Capitol building in Washington will understand this (412). Its architecture states emphatically: *Here* is something of stability and order. *Here* is a foundation on which

412. Thomas Ustick Walter. U.S. Capitol, Washington, D.C. 1865.

a nation stands. As discussed in Chapter 1, President Abraham Lincoln, during whose administration the Capitol was finished, was fully aware of the symbolic role played by government buildings.

The original Capitol building was begun in 1793, a mere four years after the new government of the United States had been established, and George Washington himself laid the cornerstone. After many embellishments, repairs (following a severe fire in the War of 1812), and additions, it assumed in 1865 the form it has now. It is easy to look back and understand why the framers of this newly independent nation would want an impressive building. Just free from Britain, just victorious in war, just come from formulating an innovative method of government—the founders celebrated their achievements in marble and stone and classical architecture. Their choice was a structure that combines the best of Greek and Roman architecture.

One of the early architects of the Capitol, Benjamin Latrobe, even designed an American "classical" column for the inside of the building (413). Based on the ancient Greeks' Corinthian style (396), the column featured corncobs and other plants native to the Americas. The Greeks had their Orders; the architects of our new nation wanted an American Order—both an architectural Order and an ordered government.

Even today, accustomed as we are to enormous sports arenas and the like, we find the Capitol awe-inspiring. To enter one climbs a steep flight of marble stairs and passes through a formal Greek-style porch, continually aware of the immense building flanking out in both directions. Above the whole is the dome, 268 feet high, circled with columns and arches, crowned by a monumental statue representing Freedom. Inside the building, under the dome, those with a taste for history may feel brushed by the ghosts of Washington, Adams, Jefferson, Madison—the nation's past standing by to oversee the nation's present. The best of government buildings, like the U.S. Capitol, represent the legitimacy and continuity of the government; at the same time they reach back to the past and forward to the future. The purpose of a government building, therefore, is not just to house the machinery of government but also to symbolize the solidity of government.

At roughly the same time that the U.S. Capitol was completed, the former mother country, across the Atlantic, also was building a structure to serve its legislative body. The Houses of Parliament in London (414), finished in 1860, aimed at quite a different architectural ideal. Washington's Capitol looked backward to Greece and Rome for legitimacy, but the Houses of Parliament sought another precedent on which to base England's national pride—the Gothic period of the Middle Ages. The Gothic style, as exemplified by Chartres Cathedral (64,400), had prevailed throughout Western Europe starting in the 13th century, but each nation, including England, claimed it as its own. For England, Gothic represented a Golden Age. In contrast to the

413. Benjamin H. Latrobe. Corncob capital, U.S. Capitol, Washington, D.C. c. 1808.

414. Charles Barry and A. W. N. Pugin. Houses of Parliament, London. 1840–60.

343

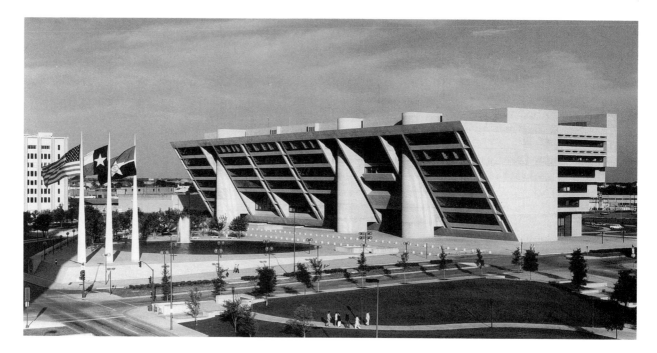

415. I. M. Pei.
City Hall, Dallas.
Completed 1977.

stately, dignified U.S. Capitol, the Houses of Parliament, with its three Gothic-Revival towers of different heights and shapes, seems to be all lightness and vertical thrust—more like a castle than a government building.

Government buildings today project many different kinds of images; they interpret in varied ways the purpose of housing the machinery of state. One of the more interesting of recent structures is the City Hall in Dallas, designed by I. M. Pei **(415)**. Its sharp diagonal overhang of glass serves a functional purpose—to keep out the relentless sun of a Texas summer. Beyond this, however, the dramatic overhang may suggest either the protective roof of government or the looming presence of Government with a capital G, depending on your point of view. Government buildings nearly always evoke powerful associations.

THREE MUSEUMS

Art museums make an interesting study in architectural design, because they are works of art meant to display other works of art. How they go about fulfilling this purpose tells us much about the nature of architecture.

One of the largest museums in the world, and probably the most famous, is the Louvre in Paris. This grand structure houses the *Mona Lisa* **(493)**, the best-known painting in the Western world, and literally millions of other priceless works of art. The Louvre, however, was not originally designed to be a public museum. Built on the site of a 13th-century castle, the Louvre was erected as a royal palace in the 16th century, and it did not assume its present role as a museum until some two hundred years later, after the French Revolution.

In company with the British Museum in London and the Metropolitan Museum of Art in New York, the Louvre exists as a kind of shrine to art—a huge, imposing, somewhat intimidating monument filled with treasures. Art lovers approach the Louvre with awe and reverence. And, until recently, many also approached it with dread, for a royal palace is not the best setting in which to view art. The classically decorated building, intended for the display of kingly power, has sapped the energy of many an art-seeking tourist. Merely finding the artworks one wanted to see required considerable stamina. The rooms are spread out, the corridors are long and were poorly marked. One could walk for (seeming) miles, only to discover one's goal was at the opposite end of the museum. Without question the Louvre needed renovation to bring it in line with contemporary museum standards, to make it "user-friendly." French President François Mitterand assigned this task to the same architect who had cast his assertive geometry on the city of Dallas: I. M. Pei.

When first unveiled, Pei's design for the Louvre **(416)** horrified traditionalists around the world. The architect proposed to set a huge glass pyramid, 71 feet tall, in the center of the Louvre's courtyard, smack among the 16th- and 17th-century wings of the museum. The clash of stark modernism against stately classicism would, it was felt, be too jarring even for the sophisticated Parisians. But when the newly designed section opened in 1989, reaction was nearly all favorable. The pyramid was a hit. Few commentators could resist making a connection with the Eiffel Tower **(405)**, finished exactly a hundred years earlier—at first considered an eyesore, later the beloved symbol of Paris.

The pyramid is only the tip of the iceberg in Pei's overall scheme. It serves as the Louvre's main entrance, opening into a vast underground hall where restaurants, shops, ticket booths, and other services are clustered. From this hall a computerized directional system points the way, efficiently and in several languages, to the desired galleries in the older building above. If, for instance, you want to find Greek antiquities or medieval sculpture or (as most tourists do) the *Mona Lisa*, you can learn the most direct route from the underground hall.

Beyond these practical improvements, Pei's design is considered a visual triumph. From inside the clear glass of the pyramid visitors can see the ornate façades of the Louvre that surround it on three sides. From outside, especially at night, the pyramid seems to float lightly in the courtyard, a glittering beacon, less an intruder than an extraterrestrial friend.

Museum architecture produces strong feelings, and our second example in this section has produced some of the very strongest feelings. In the 1950s master architect Frank Lloyd Wright set out to build a museum unlike any

416. Louvre Palace (Museum), Paris. Original buildings by Pierre Lescot, Claude Perrault, and others, c. 1541–c. 1670. Pyramid entrance and other additions by Pei Cobb Freed & Partners, completed 1989.

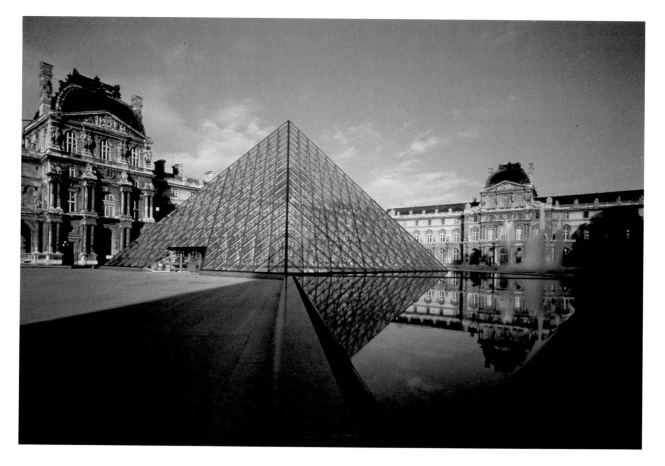

museum before, a structure that would be as much "about" art as the art inside it. His project was the Solomon R. Guggenheim Museum in New York City (417).

Wright's architecture in general is distinguished by its coherence of interior and exterior, and nowhere is this more apparent than in the Guggenheim Museum. The outside consists of a series of curves arranged into a cylinder, looking rather like a spinning top when set among the boxlike buildings around it. The cylinder shape is duplicated inside the museum (143). There is a long, curving ramp that spirals from the top of the building to the ground level, so that visitors' usual practice is to take an elevator to the top and walk down the ramp.

When the Guggenheim opened in 1959, it became the focus of much controversy. Some people said that Wright had pulled off a great joke on painters and sculptors, whom he did not much admire. It is true that Wright's building carefully *controls* the circumstances under which one may view art. The viewer cannot get very far away from any work of art because of the width of the ramp, and the ramp keeps one slightly off balance, going uphill or downhill. Also, the form of the museum itself is so intriguing that it competes with almost anything that is put inside it. Its giant "mushroom" shape seems to work best with fairly aggressive works, like Claes Oldenburg's *Knife Ship* (198) or Jenny Holtzer's neon messages (574).

In spite of these quirks, the public gradually came to accept Wright's design for what it is—a unique form, a splendid eccentricity, a museum with a dynamic tension of its own. The Guggenheim settled peaceably into the art community, and the controversy died down—for the time being. Some thirty years later it was to boil up again, this time over a plan to *change* the design.

The Guggenheim has a space problem. Although the museum owns a wonderful collection of modern art, some 80 to 90 percent of it is in storage at all times, out of reach for the people who would most like to see it. Wright's unusual design does not really allow for display of a "permanent collection," as most museums would have. Therefore, it seemed logical to build an addition and increase gallery space, but this logic faced a major obstacle. Like the Eiffel Tower and other one-of-a-kind structures, the Guggenheim has made the transition from folly to landmark. It is, in fact, an officially designated New York landmark, so any change in its basic configuration is subject to strict review. Ironically, some of the very voices that were raised against the

417. Frank Lloyd Wright. Solomon R. Guggenheim Museum, New York. 1957–59.

building to begin with now object to spoiling its "pure" design. One cannot help wondering if Wright's spirit is somewhere looking on, enjoying the joke even more.

If the Louvre looks like a royal palace and the Guggenheim looks like a spinning top, our third museum example looks like an unfinished building, or, as many have suggested, an oil refinery. Completed in 1977, the Georges Pompidou National Center for Art and Culture (418), sometimes called the "Beaubourg," shocked contemporary Parisians at least as much as the Louvre's pyramid would a generation later, and even more than the Eiffel Tower shocked their great-grandparents nearly a century before. The Eiffel Tower proudly raised its iron skeleton to the skies without benefit of any decorative skin. The Pompidou Center wears its internal organs, so to speak, on the outside of the body. Structural members, heating ducts, plumbing conduits, elevators and escalators—all the necessary items we expect to be neatly hidden away within a building's core are boldly displayed on the outside and painted in bright colors. Paris had wanted a space-age structure to house its modern art, and Paris got what it wanted—and then some.

The Pompidou Center is not just a museum of art. It is an ongoing light-and-motion show (as the elevators and escalators move visibly outside), a library, a film studio, a theater and concert hall, a mecca for all the arts. Both physically and symbolically, the Pompidou Center is meant to seem "open"— that is, open to many different types of artistic expression, open to many different people who might want to participate. Whereas the Louvre stands as a monument to reverence for art, the Pompidou Center encourages one to *live* with art.

So we have seen three museums with three different points of view. Each reflects the time and place of its building, each creates a specific ambience for viewing art. Two of them are now in transition, and—who knows?— perhaps the third will be someday. Architecture for art is never static; it is always changing.

418. Renzo Piano and Richard Rogers. Georges Pompidou National Center for Art and Culture, Paris. Completed 1977.

THREE OFFICE BUILDINGS

The architecture of commerce, like that of government, often has strong symbolic value. Its primary purpose is to house offices, but a secondary one may be to make a statement about the firm that owns the building. When a company decides to erect a new office building, its leaders give serious thought to the image that will be projected by that building and lodged in the minds of the public. Unlike the government structure, however, the office building

419. William Van Alen.
Chrysler Building, New York.
Completed 1930.

rarely seeks a model in traditional architecture, but rather attempts to convey the impression of dynamic modernism—of a company forging ahead to the future. The office building of the 20th century has therefore tended to be a creature of fashion, taking its design from the trend of the times. Three examples spanning half a century will illustrate this.

The Chrysler Building in New York, indisputably the gem of early skyscrapers, was completed in 1930 and was the first office building to rise above 1,000 feet. Its slender, elegantly pointed spire **(419)** changed the skyline of New York dramatically and still remains distinctive, in spite of later, taller buildings around it. We might list three elements that contributed to this splendid building: the great success of the automobile industry, which enabled Walter Percy Chrysler to erect a monument to his name; the relative cheapness of fine building materials and labor; and the prevalence of the style known as **Art Deco.**

Art Deco, then at the height of fashion, was marked by geometric patterns and a rich display of surface decoration. (The term "deco" came from the Exposition des Arts Décoratifs, held in Paris in 1925, where the style first appeared as a significant force.) Art Deco was definitely a product of the machine age, for its favorite materials were chrome and steel and glass and aluminum—modern materials that glitter and sparkle, preferably in elaborate combinations to dazzle the eye. Its symbolism, indeed, is razzle-dazzle, and it celebrates the speed of the automobile and the airplane, people on the move. The top of the Chrysler Building is layered in an overlapping sunburst pattern pierced with triangular windows—a streamlined, geometric sculpture cutting through the sky.

The patterned forms of Art Deco gave way in the 1940s to the pared-down, austere design aesthetic of the International Style. In a sense the roots of the International Style might be traced back to Louis Sullivan **(406)**, who insisted that "form follows function." In other words, the form of a building or any other object should be expressive of what it is supposed to do, not overlaid with arbitrary decoration. This theme was taken up by two European architects, Le Corbusier and Ludwig Mies van der Rohe, and translated into a style that dominated American architecture through the 1970s. Mies van der Rohe added another catch phrase to the history of art when he made his often-quoted statement: "Less is more." By this he meant that architects (and other designers) must strip their forms to the barest essentials, the parts necessary to the work's function, and by so doing they would achieve a more honest, satisfying design.

As mentioned earlier, the International Style was introduced to the United States by such buildings as Lever House **(407)**. Diagonally across the street from Lever House is a building many consider to be the quintessence of that style. The Seagram Building **(420)**, designed by Mies van der Rohe and Philip Johnson, is almost the direct opposite of the Chrysler Building in its design aesthetic. A stark vertical slab resting on stilts, the Seagram Building rises abruptly from the base and terminates abruptly at the top, with no attempt at accent or decoration. Its form is the extended cube, and much of its visual appeal comes from the combination of bronze-colored steel and amber glass sheathing.

For more than twenty years after the Seagram Building was completed, through the 1970s, the International Style held sway as the most luxurious and sophisticated style for skyscraper architecture. Across the United States towers of steel and glass vied with one another for height and simplicity of design. By about 1980 it became clear that some change was due, that the business firm of the 1980s and 1990s would be looking for an image quite different from "the old company that lived in a box." Architects too were ready for change, and from the evolving tastes of corporate client and architectural firm emerged a style that has been called **Postmodern.**

Postmodern architecture is practically everything the International style was not. It emphasizes curves and decorative details, not pure straight lines. It is complex rather than simple, warm rather than cool. Its structures are understood gradually, through exploration and study from many angles, in contrast to the severe box of the International Style, which could be absorbed at a glance. Sometimes the Postmodern building is even brightly colored. Several of these traits are evident in the General Foods Corporation headquarters in Rye, New York, completed in 1983 **(421)**.

One need not be a student of architecture to see the most obvious characteristics that separate the General Foods headquarters from the Chrysler and Seagram buildings. The earlier buildings are skyscrapers; General Foods hugs the ground and spreads out horizontally. Chrysler and Seagram are "city" buildings, packed in among their neighbors. General Foods is set in a suburban location and meant to be accessible to the automobile. Another clear difference is the pattern of employee traffic mandated by the architecture. We imagine employees at Chrysler and Seagram being whisked up to their offices by high-speed elevators, then whisked down again at day's end. At General Foods, employees are encouraged to walk. There are bridges and passageways and even a large glass-enclosed garden atrium in the center of the building.

In its overall style the General Foods headquarters most resembles a very grand European country house dressed in modern materials, and this is the effect the architects (and the corporate client) were after. Chief architect Kevin Roche said of the building:

> I am very interested in the idea of the corporate headquarters as a house. The house analogy really has to do with the family—the idea being that any group of people who work together become a family that can be as important to the individual as the family he or she may belong to. A working group establishes relationships similar to those of a family.[3]

This notion of office building as house, as a home away from home, has rarely been recognized in architecture, but it fits well into the patterns of modern life. Most people today do, in fact, spend the greater part of their waking lives outside the traditional home. Moreover, with the enormous increase in travel for business and pleasure, one's "home" for any given night may well be a home for hire. We therefore turn for our next group of three to an architectural category that serves the needs of travelers—the hotel.

left: 420.
Ludwig Mies van der Rohe and Philip Johnson.
Seagram Building,
New York. 1958.

right: 421. Kevin Roche John Dinkeloo and Associates. General Foods Corporation Headquarters, Rye, N.Y. 1983.

THREE HOTELS

Choosing a hotel for a brief stay is a little like choosing a costume for a masquerade party. It is temporary, it is special, it is outside everyday life. It gives one the opportunity to say, "What life do I want to live?" or "Who do I want to be?"—for a little while.

The Hotel del Coronado in San Diego is the queen of the 19th-century resort hotels. Designed by the famed architect Stanford White and completed in 1888, the "Del" wanders amiably across a pretty site overlooking the Pacific Ocean (422). In its heyday the Hotel del Coronado was a favored holiday spot for Victorian ladies and gentlemen, whose "holiday" was not the catch-as-catch-can vacation of today, but a leisurely visit of weeks or months. Daring guests could swim in the sea, but salt-water "bathing tanks" were nearby to accommodate the more timid. The very architecture of the building—rambling, unpredictable, stuck here and there with towers and porches and chimneys—speaks of a bygone time when nobody was in a hurry, when walking the grounds could be a day's activity. The del Coronado has a kind of majesty that says its visitors chose to be there and did not need to be anywhere else. Modern visitors to the "Del" may be seeking the same experience, trying to recapture a time when life was more graceful and much slower.

A few hundred miles up the California coast is the San Francisco Marriott hotel, which is a century younger and much, much faster. As a matter of fact, it is a lightning bolt in the skyline of a city that prides itself on quiet good manners and gentle Old World charm (423). Decked out in its bright blue reflective glass, the Marriott, designed by Tony Lumsden of the Los Angeles firm DMJM, prompted a *New York Times* writer to call it "a hotel only Liberace could love." The locals hold an equally colorful point of view. San Franciscans have taken to calling their new hotel "the thermometer," "the jukebox," or "the hotel designed for Cher."

To be sure, the Marriott comes as something of a shock, and it is a shock not to be missed, since the hotel is visible from nearly every part of the city. Architecture that so aggressively calls attention to itself must be reckoned with; it is bound to make a splash. Perhaps visitors who choose to stay at the hotel want the same—to make a splash, to be noticed, to stand out. Only time will show whether the passionately city-proud San Franciscans will take the Marriott to their hearts, make it their own Eiffel Tower. Meanwhile, some positive voices have been raised. One member of the city's Redevelopment Agency has said, "It's a building that's fun. We don't have many of these."[4]

422. Stanford White. Hotel del Coronado, San Diego. 1888.

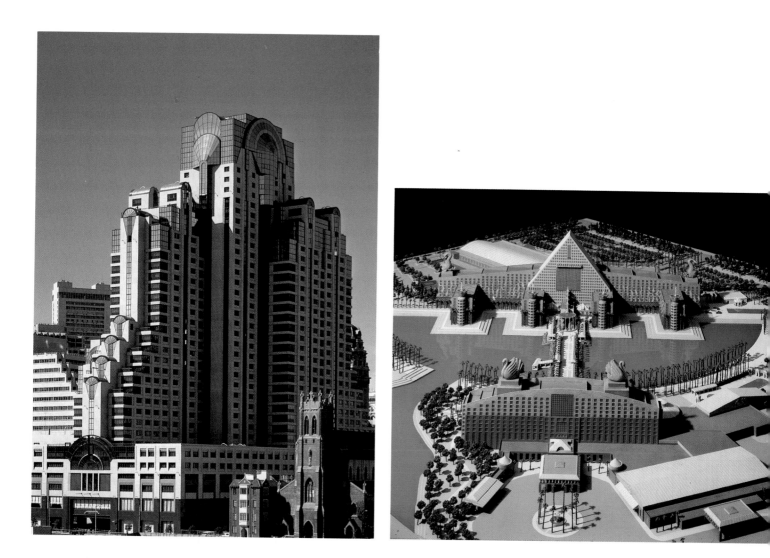

Buildings that are fun may make the people of San Francisco nervous, but they are business as usual in Orlando, Florida. And that is where the Postmodern architect Michael Graves has built not one but two new hotels—the Walt Disney World Swan Hotel and the Walt Disney World Dolphin Hotel **(424)**. At Disney World, fun is serious business. It is the whole point. A commission from Disney must be the whimsically inclined architect's dream come true, since nothing could be too far-fetched, too exaggerated, too *silly*. There are 28-ton turquoise swans standing guard. There are huge seashell fountains and giant dolphins and painted waves lapping at the hotels' windows. Inside, the potted palms are fanciful cutouts, the lights are clamped in parrots' beaks, and the sofas are more swans. Outside, of course, one is struck by the color, the nursery turquoise and pink. Color in architecture is a trademark of Postmodernism and of Graves' work, but nowhere is it more at home than here, in the fantasy world of permanent childhood. Visitors to these hotels have come to play, and if the architecture is playful at every turn, so much the better. For Disney, Graves has created "entertainment architecture," or architecture-as-theater. Nevertheless, there are classical precedents, in concept if not in kind. Referring to the 17th-century architect who also knew how to put on a good show (p. 429), Graves has said, "I wasn't thinking about Disney. I was thinking about Bernini."[5]

The delightful excesses of the Swan and Dolphin might cause an observer to say, "It's a nice place to visit, but I wouldn't want to live there." Most of us expect the places where we live, day in and out, to be more serious, more sensible and down-to-earth. As we turn to our next category of buildings, we will find that is usually true. But not always.

left: **423.** Tony Lumsden for DMJM, Los Angeles. San Francisco Marriott Hotel. Completed 1990.

right: **424.** Michael Graves. Walt Disney World Swan Hotel and Walt Disney World Dolphin Hotel, Lake Buena Vista, Fla. Completed 1990.

THREE APARTMENT BUILDINGS

Fanciful architecture was not born yesterday. A century ago the Spanish architect Antoni Gaudí was designing buildings so unusual that their like cannot be found anywhere. Gaudí's masterpiece, the Casa Milá apartment house in Barcelona (425), shows why this architect is not associated with any prevailing style, but is one of a kind. The Casa Milá seems almost to have grown on its site, carved out by wind and weather, and this was Gaudí's intention, the "natural" his obsession. The façade of cut stone swirls around windows and balconies in an irregular wavelike pattern. The chimneys on the roof—no two alike—resemble huge organic sculptures. Inside as out, there is scarcely a straight line to be found. Unlike the typical apartment building—where rooms are rectangular, boxes nesting beside, above, and under boxes—the Casa Milá has a completely unpredictable floor plan of free-form rooms clustered around interior patios. As an exercise in multiple dwelling, the Casa Milá would certainly not be for everyone, but for those with a spirit of adventure, life inside this giant cave palace could be exciting.

below: 425. Antoni Gaudí. Casa Milá, Barcelona. 1905–07.

bottom: 426. Moshe Safdie. Habitat, Montreal. 1967. Alan Douglas Carruthers/NYT Pictures.

427. Schipporeit-Heinrich, Inc.
Lake Point Tower, Chicago.
1969.

At the opposite extreme from the Casa Milá is an apartment complex that actually does consist of boxes nested together. Habitat in Montreal **(426)**, designed by Moshe Safdie, was intended as an experiment in the housing of the future, in both form and construction. Like Fuller's dome **(411)**, it was unveiled at Expo 67, the Montreal World Fair. The complex consists of 354 prefabricated concrete boxes, stacked one on top of another to form 158 apartments, each with a private entrance, windows on all sides, and a terrace—the flat roof of one dwelling providing the garden terrace for its neighbor above. In effect, every family lives in the penthouse.

When it first opened, Habitat was considered exciting as a concept but rather sterile as a living environment. It is, after all, so *boxy*. But Habitat has aged well in the quarter-century since, as residents have impressed their human stamp on technology. Some families have added sun porches, some skylights, one a fireplace with a chimney; everywhere there are trees, plants, and flowers. All these touches have turned the apartment house of the future into a sought-after home for the present.

Our final example in this section is exactly contemporary with Habitat but miles away in design sensibility. If Habitat is a box, then Lake Point Tower in Chicago **(427)** is a bottle, perhaps a bottle with a screw cap on top. A sentinel on the shores of Lake Michigan, Lake Point Tower stacks its residents efficiently in seventy stories of curving glass, affording spectacular views of the lake and the city. This apartment building functions as a kind of vertical suburb, with restaurants, stores, an indoor park, even a "country" club. Like the office skyscrapers considered earlier, Lake Point Tower is a creature of the elevator and of crowded downtown spaces. Its sleek and glittering design makes a virtue of high-density housing for the urban environment.

Apartment houses have been with us at least since the time of the ancient Romans, and as space on our planet gets tighter and tighter, they will no doubt proliferate. For the time being, however, most people's dream remains the one-family house, and so we turn to this type of structure for our last group of three.

THREE HOUSES

Ever since humans came down from the trees or out of their caves, most of the architecture built has been in the form of houses. Needless to say, dwellings from different times and places have displayed enormous variety. Each of the three houses considered here reflects a special point of view about what it means to dwell within a building, what kind of roof one should have over one's head.

Master architects usually make their reputations on the "big" commissions—the office buildings, museums, airport terminals, hotels—and only incidentally design private houses. But for the man whom many consider to have been America's greatest architect, the reverse is true. Although he did design important public buildings, Frank Lloyd Wright will always be remembered as the master builder of houses.

Wright's theory of domestic architecture was characterized by two related principles: first, a house should blend with its environment; second, the interior and exterior of a house should be visually and physically integrated. The Kaufmann House in Bear Run, Pennsylvania, usually known as "Fallingwater," is considered to be Wright's masterpiece (**428**). Sited beside a waterfall, it was designed to take best advantage of the surrounding landscape. Much of the house is built of stone, quarried from the immediate area, so that it seems to grow up from the site, rather than being set down upon it. One departure from this use of natural materials comes in the three terraces of reinforced concrete, two of them **cantilevered** over the waterfall. A cantilever is a horizontal form supported at only one end, jutting out into space at the other. Reinforced concrete, with its high tensile strength, makes such a construction possible, and Wright was among the first to exploit the cantilever for domestic architecture. Although not strictly "natural," the concrete cantilevers emphasize the waterfall and make it seem a natural extension of the house. Wright's architecture, then, blends with the natural surroundings and at the same time makes use of them.

428. Frank Lloyd Wright. "Fallingwater" (Kaufmann House), Bear Run, Pa. 1936–37.

Frank Lloyd Wright

1867–1959

Many critics consider Frank Lloyd Wright to have been the greatest American architect of his time; certainly few would dispute the claim that he was the greatest designer of residential architecture. To see a Wright-designed building from the first decade of this century is to be shocked by how remarkably modern it seems.

Wright had very little formal education. He attended high school in Madison, Wisconsin, but apparently did not graduate. Later, he completed the equivalent of about one year's course work in civil engineering at the University of Wisconsin, while holding down a job as a draftsman. In 1887 he moved to Chicago and eventually found work in the architectural firm headed by Louis Sullivan, the great designer of early office buildings. Before long Wright had assumed responsibility for fulfilling most of the residential commissions that came into the company, and in 1893 he opened a firm of his own.

During the next two decades Wright refined the principles of the "Prairie houses" that are his trademark. Most are in the Midwest, and they echo that flat expanse of the Great Plains—predominantly horizontal, stretching out over considerable ground area but usually in one story. All expressed Wright's special interest in textures and materials; he liked whenever possible to build with materials native to the immediate surroundings, so that the houses blend with their environments. Interiors were designed on an open plan, with rooms flowing into one another (an unusual practice for the time), and the inside and outside of the house were also well integrated. These ingredients added up to what Wright always referred to as "organic" architecture.

For most of his long life Wright's personal situation was far from tranquil. His parents seem to have had a bitterly unhappy marriage, and they divorced in 1885, when Wright was seventeen—an extraordinary event for that era. Wright himself had a troubled marital history. His first marriage ended when he eloped to Europe with Mamah Brothwick, the wife of a former client, leaving his own wife and six children behind. Five years later, back in Wisconsin, Brothwick was brutally murdered by a deranged servant while Wright was out of the house. This tragedy sent the architect off on a period of wandering through faraway parts of the

world. A final marriage in the late 1920s lasted out his lifetime and appears to have given him his first real happiness.

Although he is best known for his domestic architecture, Wright also designed many large-scale commercial and public buildings, including the Solomon R. Guggenheim Museum in New York. His innovative design for the Imperial Hotel in Tokyo, planned to be stable in an area plagued by earthquakes, proved successful when the hotel survived without damage a devastating quake just a year after it was completed.

Wright was the author of several books on his theories of architecture, and always he focused on the organic nature of his work and on his own individuality. "Beautiful buildings are more than scientific. They are true organisms, spiritually conceived, works of art, using the best technology by inspiration rather than the idiosyncrasies of mere taste or any averaging by the committee mind."[6]

Photograph of Frank Lloyd Wright.

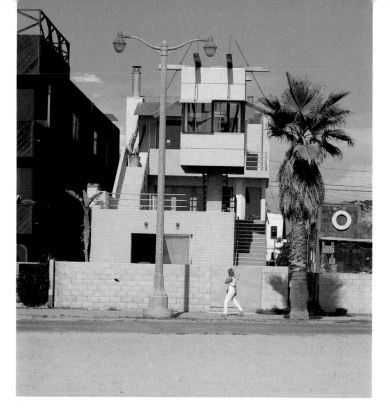

429. Frank O. Gehry
& Associates.
Norton House,
Venice, Calif. 1985.

Our second example would seem, at first glance, not to blend with any-thing whatsoever, but a longer view would show that the Norton house, de-signed by Frank Gehry **(429)** does blend—sort of—with its eclectic neighbors overlooking the beach in Venice, California. Venice is a community of mil-lionaires and beachcombers, where typical vehicles are the Mercedes-Benz and the skateboard. Gehry's design seems to have borrowed a little from each extreme, but it is nonetheless a presence unto itself. This architect likes to take risks and he likes the concept of the "little jewel," the small one-family house. He happily indulges in Postmodern design, and the Norton house dis-plays a coat of many colors—blue and green and yellow tiles on the front, red and orange on the street side. Its most distinctive feature is the tiny sus-pended study, joined to the main house by a ladder staircase, patterned after a lifeguard station from the beach and offering superb views of the ocean. Gehry's architecture takes some getting used to; it is so fresh and innovative, but at the same time so very human. It is hard to imagine that anyone living in such a house could ever be bored.

There are houses . . . and there are houses. Wright's "Fallingwater" is a house, and so are log cabins and cottages. And so is Casa Grande **(430)**, the centerpiece of William Randolph Hearst's fabulous California estate known as San Simeon. In 1919 the newspaper magnate, who owned an immense ranch on a site overlooking the Pacific Ocean, had become tired of "camping out," as he put it. He therefore hired the San Francisco architect Julia Mor-gan to "build something a little more comfortable." Morgan, who had been the first woman ever to earn an architectural degree from the prestigious Ecole des Beaux-Arts in Paris, was known for her tenacity, her determination to see a project through to its completion. She would need every bit of that tenacity, for Hearst's project consumed the next eighteen years of her life.

Morgan's supervision of the design was comprehensive. She had first to build wharves at oceanfront to accommodate ships bringing the building materials, as well as roads to transport materials to the site. Next she de-signed, and supervised the building of, three immense Mediterranean-style guest houses. Eventually she would add hothouses for plants; kennels; two huge swimming pools (one outdoor, one in); a newspaper office and tele-phone switchboard; a mile-long pergola (a vine-covered archway) so that visitors could ride their horses even in bad weather without getting wet; and an elephant house and bear and lion pits for Hearst's private zoo.

But Casa Grande, the main residence, was Morgan's triumph—and Hearst's as well, for he took an avid interest in the construction. Casa Grande—the translation "big house" is something of an understatement—was intended to have the look and impact of a cathedral. It has more than a hundred rooms, the more public rooms designed on an enormous scale, and is fronted by two 137-foot-high towers copied from the Cathedral of Ronda in Spain. One observer described its architecture as "Bastard-Spanish-Moorish-Romanesque-Gothic-Renaissance-Bull Market-Damn the Expense" style.[7] By all reports, however, Hearst loved it, and so do the tourists who now flock to see its splendors.

When filmmaker Orson Welles made his thinly disguised biographical movie about Hearst, *Citizen Kane* (307), he called the estate "Xanadu," a reference to the domain of the legendary Chinese emperor Kublai Khan. Hearst himself really was a kind of emperor—an emperor of newspapers. The "something a little more comfortable" that Julia Morgan made may seem to us a palace, but for Hearst it was home.

Architecture touches us more directly than any of the other arts. As we move through our everyday lives, we are influenced continually by the structures we enter, leave, or pass by. A huge, forbidding structure makes us feel uncomfortable; a warm and welcoming one makes us feel secure. Moreover, when we seek to learn about other cultures—far away or long ago—it is often their architecture that we study most closely. The people who built the Parthenon, the Taj Mahal, the Eiffel Tower—yes, even the Casa Grande at San Simeon—were telling us much about their way of life and the values they considered to be important. A society's choice of materials, structural systems, and styles of architecture makes a fundamental statement. Architecture tells us who we are. It shows us the face we want to present to the world.

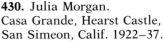

430. Julia Morgan.
Casa Grande, Hearst Castle,
San Simeon, Calif. 1922–37.

Chapter Fourteen

Environmental Design

When Buckminster Fuller proposed to build a 3-mile-wide geodesic dome over the whole midtown area of Manhattan Island, he probably knew that his idea would never be put into practice. Fuller was a visionary, and visionary plans usually falter before the realities of everyday life. In the abstract, however, the dome concept had its attractions. Think of it: The business district of New York City no longer would be plagued by the stifling heat of August or the cold and slush of January. Snow removal—a huge expense in the city's budget—would become a thing of the past. Individual buildings would not need to be heated or cooled; the entire atmosphere under the dome would be climatically ideal year-round. Air pollution, too, would become obsolete. No more would prevailing winds carry the smoke from factories to the west of the city into its heart, and whatever exhaust fumes were produced inside the dome could be vacuumed away efficiently. Hence, there would no doubt be a decrease in respiratory ailments, along with a reduction in medical costs and therefore in medical insurance premiums. Flying insects, such as flies and mosquitoes, could be all but eliminated, as could New York's perennial pigeon problem. There would be no more gloomy Mondays. Workers returning from their weekends would be greeted by a light (artificially lighted, if necessary), cheerful environment. Perhaps depressions would lift, psychological problems diminish, crime rates plummet. . . . One could go on listing the possibilities.

In proposing to "dome" Manhattan, Fuller was responding to an impulse that has tempted many artists—the urge to design an entire environment, to improve the quality of life by total design. *Environmental design* can be defined as large-scale planning to improve the aesthetic quality of the surroundings in which we live and make them more habitable. This type of design may involve architects, urban planners, landscape designers, and even psychologists and sociologists. While modern technology has greatly expanded the potential scope of the environmental designer, the concept of environmental design has actually been with us for thousands of years.

Environmental Design in History

The planned environment may seem as new as today, but we have only to look back to the ancient city of Babylon to realize how long humans have sought to order their space. Babylon was a city of Mesopotamia (the ruins are in modern Iraq, near Baghdad), and it was built over a period of many years—from the 18th to the 6th century B.C. Its history includes several famous rulers, from Hammurabi (who wrote an exemplary legal code) to Nebuchadnezzar (under whose reign was built the Ishtar Gate, **450**).

According to the old writings, Babylon was constructed as a square, bisected by the Euphrates River **(431)**. Its perimeter was about 60 miles. Double walls with fortified gates surrounded the city, and outside the walls was a large water-filled moat. The Greek historian Herodotus wrote that Babylon "surpasses in splendor any city of the known world." It had broad, even streets, crossing each other at right angles, and a covered bridge spanned the river. In one sector of the city were the legendary Hanging Gardens of Babylon, one of the Seven Wonders of the Ancient World; in another was the tower that probably inspired the biblical story about the Tower of Babel. All told, the planners of Babylon seem to have thought of everything important that touched upon their way of life: the security of the city, convenience of movement, and a pleasant visual aspect.

Like the Babylonians the ancient Greeks and Romans—master designers—favored the **grid** system for city planning. Streets crossed at right angles, with broader avenues allocated for the passage of many chariots. The Romans also pioneered in a surprisingly modern approach to high-density living in downtown areas—apartment houses of four and five stories. But after the Roman Empire and through the Middle Ages, environmental design

431. Plan of Babylon, as rebuilt by Nebuchadnezzar. c. 604–561 B.C.

as such was apparently not considered a priority. Cities grew up as they would, following the contours of the landscape and of well-traveled paths, with major access routes leading to the churches and markets. Not until the Renaissance did total design again excite the interest of artists.

Several artists of the Renaissance, including Michelangelo and Leonardo da Vinci, turned their attention to the concept of "ideal" cities and large urban spaces. One Renaissance architect, Antonio Filarete of Florence, actually planned such a city in detail, naming it Sforzinda after his patron, the duke Francesco Sforza. Sforzinda was to have broad, straight streets, large public spaces, and housing and work areas for every level of society. Filarete's plan was never realized, but during the 15th and 16th centuries a number of European cities, most notably Rome, were substantially rebuilt in an effort to eliminate the crowded, dirty, and disorganized conditions that had developed during the Middle Ages.

In the 17th century the quest for large, well-planned urban spaces gathered momentum. One such example, designed by the Italian architect and sculptor Gianlorenzo Bernini, was the plaza in front of St. Peter's Basilica at the Vatican in Rome. St. Peter's—the heart of the Roman Catholic Church—had been under construction since 1450, on the site once occupied by a 4th-century church. This site is the presumed burial place of the Apostle Peter, the first pope. In the mid-16th century Michelangelo designed the dome and the main section of the church containing the altar **(496)**. The remainder of the basilica and the façade were completed in the first quarter of the 17th century by the architect Carlo Maderno. There remained the problem of creating a suitable plaza in front of the church, and this problem was addressed immediately after the election of Pope Alexander VII in 1655. As the story goes, before the sun set on the first day of his papacy, Alexander sent for Bernini.

Bernini's challenge was to design an enclosed area capable of holding the enormous crowds that converge on St. Peter's to receive the pope's blessing on ceremonial occasions, particularly on Easter Sunday. His solution was a structure consisting mainly of a double set of roofed colonnades (rows of columns) creating a wedge-shaped space in front of the church and then bulging into an enormous oval that encompasses the plaza **(432)**. Thus enclosed, the space can hold as many as two million people. The colonnades are symbolic of the "arms of the church" reaching out to embrace the faithful. Atop them are scores of monumental marble statues of the saints carved by Bernini's assistants following his designs.

Besides providing a suitable and awe-inspiring setting for the pope's appearances, Bernini had another architectural goal in mind. He felt that

432. Gianlorenzo Bernini. Plaza and colonnades, St. Peter's Basilica, Vatican, Rome. 1656–63.

433. The Mall, Washington, D.C., viewed from the steps of the Lincoln Memorial, with the reflecting pool, the Washington Monument, and the Capitol dome in the distance.

Maderno's façade was too wide and too low, that its proportions were incorrect. Since he could not adjust the proportions physically, he did so visually. The colonnades, like pincers, visually "squeeze" the façade to make it seem taller and narrower. In all, Bernini's design was a brilliant conclusion to what had been a somewhat disjointed architectural scheme, for it pulled together into one cohesive unit all the diverse elements in the papal enclave. It is an environmental solution to an architectural problem.

Beginning in the late 18th century and continuing through the 19th, two extremely ambitious city-planning projects were carried out. Both involved great capital cities, and both took place in the aftermath of political revolution. Moreover, both were based on a combination of the grid plan, with streets at right angles to one another, and the **radial** plan, in which streets radiate outward on the diagonal from central points like the spokes in a wheel. The two cities in question were Washington, D.C., and Paris.

The construction of Washington was an adventure, and one at first plagued by tremendous difficulties. In its conception it reflected the ideals of the newly independent United States. Just as the founders of the young country set out to construct a totally new model of government, so too they set out to build, from the ground up, a grand and glorious capital city on an unoccupied spot—a spot, in fact, consisting principally of swampland. George Washington chose the site, and his selection had more to do with political considerations than with physical ones. The area of the city was then roughly equidistant from the northernmost and the southernmost states. In terms of climate, however, the first president's choice was not a happy one; a swamp is a swamp. Letters written by the early government leaders are filled with complaints about the city's oppressive heat in summer, the mosquitoes, the generally unhealthful atmosphere. Not until the advent of modern air conditioning did Washington become a truly comfortable place to be.

To design the city, the president called in Pierre Charles L'Enfant, a young French engineer who had volunteered his services in the American Revolution. L'Enfant's plan is surprisingly ambitious and innovative, considering that he worked in a time when most cities had rather narrow and often winding streets. At the very center of the original city limits stands the Capitol building **(412)**. From the Capitol, running along a north-northwest axis, is the main thoroughfare, Pennsylvania Avenue, which is 160 feet wide and leads directly to the White House. The Capitol also serves as the eastern anchor of the Mall **(98,433)**, a parklike section lined with museums and

434. Place de l'Etoile, Paris, as it appeared about 1870. Engraving.

government buildings. The Mall has three main focal points, arranged in an east-west row: the Capitol at the east, the Washington Monument in the center, and the Lincoln Memorial at the west, on the banks of the Potomac River. (Not all of these buildings existed in L'Enfant's plan. Lincoln had not yet been born when the plans were drawn up.) The president and the Congress can look at each other from their windows, and now the Congress can look down The Mall for inspiration from Washington and Lincoln.

L'Enfant's design provided for several elements deemed desirable for an important capital city—broad, ceremonial avenues, imposing vistas, open public areas, major buildings as focal points. All these are possible when one is building from "scratch" and has a master plan. It is far more difficult to impose such an order on an existing city, one that has grown up haphazardly over the centuries. To a large extent, however, the city of Paris did this.

The transformation of Paris from a medieval town to a city of many monuments, stately public buildings, and majestic avenues took place over several centuries. Nearly always the construction was undertaken to satisfy grandiose, ego-enhancing ambitions of a monarch. The last Bourbon kings of France, in the 17th and 18th centuries, made a number of major contributions in and around Paris, including Louis XIV's conception for the gigantic Versailles Palace and gardens (**511,512**). During the French Revolution, beginning in 1789, the mood ran more to tearing down than to building up. The main square of Paris, the Place de la Concorde, became the headquarters of the guillotine, the device invented as a "humane" method of severing heads. In the Place during the Revolution more than 2,500 people were executed, among them the king and queen.

A mere fifteen years after the Revolution began, Napoleon came to power in France, styled himself emperor, and set out to create a regime equal in glory to the empire of ancient Rome. To this end he ordered built numerous monuments, streets, plazas, gardens, and bridges. His projects included first one and then a second huge triumphal arch, modeled on Roman designs. The Arc de Triomphe at the Place de l'Etoile is the grander of the two (**434**), placed in the center of a circle that interrupts Paris' main avenue, the Champs-Elysées. Later, during the third quarter of the 19th century and under the rule of Napoleon III, the first emperor's nephew, more grand-scale city planning was undertaken. Large sections of the city were flattened to allow for the construction of diagonal avenues radiating outward from important monuments. At the Place de l'Etoile, as shown in the illustration, *six* major thoroughfares intersect to create a focal point for the arch—and a traffic problem of staggering proportions.

Both Washington and Paris demonstrate that when it comes to environmental design the grand and the efficient do not always coexist. Washington, too, has traffic problems. To anyone not intimately familiar with the city, the business of getting around by car can be formidable. Generously proportioned boulevards tend to stop abruptly—at one of those majestic focal points!—and though they pick up on the other side of the monument, one often has no clear idea how to *get* to the other side. Neither city, in fact, was conceived with the automobile in mind.

The automobile is but one of many developments that have changed the character of environmental design. Others include the challenge of cities housing millions of people, the blight of urban slums, air pollution, the concentration of office buildings, mass transportation and communication, limited natural resources, and the desire for open space on a crowded planet. Environmental designers of the 20th century have far more complex problems to solve than their predecessors ever dreamed of.

Environmental Design for the Modern World

To compare the environmental designs of our own age with those of previous ones, we might look at a 20th-century architect's scheme for the same city in which Louis XIV and Napoleon erected their tributes to kingly power. The architect who in 1925 planned a drastic renovation of Paris was Charles Edouard Jeanneret, known as Le Corbusier, designer of Notre-Dame-du-Haut at Ronchamps (161,162).

Le Corbusier, in his way, could be just as grandiose as a king or an emperor. What he proposed for Paris involved no less than leveling a large area in the center of the city—600 acres—and starting all over again. His design for a new Paris (435) would have concentrated the central Parisian population into sixteen tall, glass-sheathed skyscrapers with open spaces around them. The old public spaces would be abolished; for example, Le Corbusier wrote that his dream was "to see the Place de la Concorde empty once more, silent and lonely." In this vision of the ideal city, the automobile would rule. Motorized traffic would be given a priority, and pedestrian traffic would cease to exist.

Not being a king, Le Corbusier had neither the power nor the funds to put his idea into practice, and subsequent generations have expressed gratitude that this is so. The trouble with Le Corbusier's plan—and Fuller's dome plan for Manhattan—is that it ignores how people *do* live and *want* to live,

435. Le Corbusier.
Drawing of the "Voisin"
[neighbor] Plan for Paris. 1925.
Fondation Le Corbusier, Paris.

436. Thomas Jefferson. University of Virginia, Charlottesville. 1817–26.

and reflects instead one artist's idea of how people *should* live. And people, by and large, resist doing what they "should" do. A population such as that of Paris, accustomed to small, individual houses and used to living an energetic life in the streets and squares, would take up arms before being stacked into vertical towers of glass. The more far-sighted contemporary environmental designers strive to understand the fabric of people's lives and make their plans an enhancement, not a restructuring of modern civilization.

Today's environmental design is as varied as the populations it attempts to serve. At its best, it asks many questions before attempting to provide answers. Where is this environment—city, suburbs, or country? What are its geographical location and climate? Who lives in the environment—children, teenagers, young adults, middle-aged adults, elderly people, or a mixed group? How do they move about—on foot, on bicycle, by car, or by mass transit? What do they do in the environment—eat, sleep, work, study, play, or some combination of these? What is the image to be projected by this environment? How do the people who plan it, and those who will use it, feel about themselves, and what do they want to show to the world?

To see how designers have grappled with these questions, we will look at a few environmental designs in three important categories, the first of which should be familiar to readers of this book.

DESIGN FOR LEARNING: THREE COLLEGE CAMPUSES

Thomas Jefferson referred to the college campus as an "academical village." This term is apt, because a campus typically possesses most of the characteristics we would find in a traditional village. It is self-contained. It provides nearly all the essentials for daily life—sleeping and eating facilities, work spaces, health care, provision for goods and services, places for social gathering. Its inhabitants interact closely with one another and have common interests and goals.

The stereotypical view of a college campus evokes the "halls of ivy"— that is, imposing, monumental buildings, perhaps in the Gothic style, possibly with ivy growing thickly up the walls. As a matter of fact, some campuses do look like this, at least in their older sections. But campus design is just as diversified as any other; the personality of each college is unique.

There could hardly be a more challenging or interesting task for the environmental designer than planning a college campus. After all, it is much like designing a city from the ground up, and few people in history have had the opportunity to do that. The campus will, presumably, endure for many hundreds of years. It will serve as a working environment and home away from home for a constantly changing population of students and professors. It must be comfortable and efficient, but above all it must express the special personality of the college. It must say through its design: This is who we are. Let us see how three designers tackled this challenge.

Jefferson was not trained as an architect, much less as an environmental designer—if such a term could have existed in the early 19th century. In his day, however, the educated person was expected to be informed on many subjects. Honored now as drafter of the Declaration of Independence and third president of the United States, Jefferson drew more satisfaction from being a cultivated student of the arts and sciences. His great pride was the college he established and whose architecture and overall layout he designed—the University of Virginia (436).

Jefferson's plan for the University of Virginia combined the qualities we admire in the man himself: idealism and practicality. Idealism was embodied in the veneration of knowledge; practicality in the belief that one's surroundings when pursuing knowledge should be comfortable and conducive to study. The university is organized around a rectangle, with a large, grassy lawn at its center. Its focus is the Rotunda, the library, which is modeled after the Pantheon in Rome (401,467), for Jefferson's ideals were rooted in the traditions of ancient Greece and Rome. Strung out along the two sides of the lawn are ten "pavilions," each meant to house the professor of one branch of learning and his college of students. This situation was intended to provide natural and spirited communication between teacher and pupils. (In Jefferson's time education was based on the tutorial system. Each subject had one distinguished professor, around whom students grouped.)

The pavilions are not identical, but each is based on a specific classical prototype, some in the Doric style, some the Ionic (396). Joined to one another by roofed colonnades, the pavilions are planned for an elegant balance between ready access and studious seclusion. Behind the pavilions are formal gardens, then another range of buildings on each side, including "hotels" meant as dining rooms. Overall, Jefferson's design expresses magnificently his concept of "who we are." The "we" in this case—the students and faculty of the University of Virginia—are rational, orderly, dedicated to learning, and enlightened heirs to the great legacy of Greece and Rome.

Just over half a century later, and a continent apart from Virginia, another great university, a very different one, was established and designed. Its patron was Leland Stanford, once governor of California, who endowed the university in memory of his dead son. (We met Governor Stanford earlier in this book, in connection with a bet on his racehorse that inspired Eadweard Muybridge's serial photographs, p. 254.)

In contrast to the University of Virginia, Stanford University is not classical in its design aesthetic. Rather, it draws its inspiration from the Romanesque monastery cloister, but even more specifically from California history. During the 18th and early 19th centuries Spanish Franciscan priests had established a series of mission churches up and down the coast of California. It is this "mission-style" architecture, with its low buildings and red-tiled roofs, that Stanford University emulates (437). Seen from a distance, the

437. Charles A. Coolidge. Stanford University, Palo Alto, Calif. Begun 1886.

438. Skidmore, Owings & Merrill. United States Air Force Academy, Colorado Springs, Colo. 1956–63.

university looks rather like a Mediterranean village, growing naturally from the landscape. Its basic motif is not the square post-and-lintel of Jefferson's design, but the graceful arch. For Stanford University, "who we are" is identified with the West, with California, with the legacy of Spanish colonists.

Yet another half century or so brings us to our third campus design—in this instance a design rooted in time and technology rather than place. The U.S. Air Force was organized as an independent branch of the military in 1947, and in 1954 it established its own service academy **(438)**. Rejecting the architectural examples of its kin—the army academy at West Point (Gothic) and the naval academy at Annapolis (Classical)—the U.S. Air Force Academy sought an environment that would speak to the present and the future. The architectural firm of Skidmore, Owings & Merrill designed for the Colorado Springs site a campus that is consciously modern, sleek as an airplane, boasting of speed, progress, and technological power. For the students and faculty of the Air Force Academy, obviously, "who we are" is a people meant to fly, to be the wave of the future.

Design of the "academical village" is not static. Over the years needs change, student populations grow, buildings must be added. Even Jefferson foresaw this, leaving the grassy central rectangle at the University of Virginia open on one end for possible future expansion. Nevertheless, design of the campus does afford the rare opportunity for total, harmonious environmental planning. Quite different are the challenges for a designer working within an existing city.

DESIGN FOR THE CITY

As often as not, the urban environmental designer is brought in to "fix" something that is already there but has gone wrong. Few American cities were actually planned (Washington being a major exception). Mostly, the cities just grew, with individual districts taking shape as the need presented itself. Trouble arose when that need no longer applied.

A problem often addressed by urban planners is the rejuvenation of decaying sections of the city, especially waterfront areas. So many of the old cities in the United States were founded initially as major ports, but with the decline of the shipping trade the waterfront sections fell into disrepair. Designers have confronted this question. What do you do with a seaport that is no longer a seaport? In New York and Baltimore, in Boston and San Francisco, the answer has been to turn a waterfront area into a community center.

Boston's harbor renewal is a good example **(439)**. Decrepit buildings in a once-seedy part of town have been renovated to house restaurants, shops, and artists' studios. Charming pedestrian walkways make the area a pleasant place by day or night. A neighborhood that good Bostonians once skirted and tourists avoided has become a focus of the city's social life.

Port cities are not the only ones with decaying older sections. Many cities in the interior of the country have seen their downtown areas become shabby and deserted as a result of a post-World War II trend—the flight from the cities to the suburbs. The burgeoning of huge shopping malls in the suburbs has caused many downtown stores to close for lack of customers. Then, as stores and restaurants have moved out of the inner city, downtown areas have become unpleasant places to be, especially at night, and so increasing numbers of residents have also fled to the suburbs. Many large cities have found that a formerly bustling district in the heart of town has become desolate, run-down, and dangerous.

Dayton, Ohio, is one of a number of cities that has taken active steps to remedy this problem. In downtown Dayton stand many fine old buildings, constructed between 1902 and 1904, that once housed such facilities as a farmer's market and government offices. These buildings now form the center of Arcade Square (440). This project, undertaken in the late 1970s, involved a partnership between the City of Dayton and a private corporation

above: 439.
Boston waterfront district, Quincy Market.

left: 440.
Lorenz & Williams, Inc.
Rotunda, Arcade Square,
Dayton, Ohio. 1902–04
(rebuilt late 1970s).

367

backed by individual and business funds. The result is an exciting mix of the old and the new. While the basic architectural character of the buildings has been retained, the interiors have been substantially remodeled to allow for retail stores, restaurants, and apartments. So far, the outcome has been promising, largely because of the civic leaders' quest for excellence. As *Progressive Architecture* commented, "Not every city, of course, has officials with the sensitivity and/or the wisdom to hire talented design people and listen to them. It is much to the credit of both this city and this developer that, for the most part, they listened."[1]

Renewal is one solution to keeping the city alive and thriving, but innovative new construction is another. In New York the Citicorp atrium **(441)** represents a particularly creative use of urban space, for it gives city workers a planned and streamlined version of exactly the sort of space they are used to occupying. The Citicorp tower is an office building in midtown Manhattan. On its ground and below-ground levels is a three-tiered area that merges with the outdoors and that includes many restaurants, shops, bookstalls, sitting areas, "green spots" of plantings, and walkways. Here New Yorkers can stroll through to take a shortcut, meet their friends, get a meal or a snack, browse in the shops, or simply "hang out." The realities of city life—the way people do live, not how someone believes they should live—are given a splendid setting.

Then what of the realities of suburban life? The most stunning reality is the very phenomenon the planners in Dayton, Ohio, were trying to counteract. As an exercise in environmental design, in total planning, in response to ultramodern life styles, one could hardly top the suburban mall.

DESIGN FOR THE SUBURBS: THE MALL

"I shop; therefore I am." This witty paraphrase of René Descartes' famous philosophical statement ("I think, therefore I am") sums up the essence of the mall. Once upon a time people shopped only when they needed something. Now people visit the mall as an integral part of life, as entertainment. The mall has become the equivalent of the village green, a gathering place as comprehensive as the old medieval cathedral. Even if you don't need anything, even if you aren't going to shop today—come to the mall.

Chapter 3 of this book, in its discussion of Chartres Cathedral (p. 65), pointed out the vital role played by the cathedral in people's daily lives.

441. Hugh Stubbins and Associates, and Emery Ross and Sons. Atrium, Citicorp Building, New York. Completed 1977.

442. West Edmonton Mall, Alberta, showing the lagoon with submarines.

Today, that role has largely been assumed by the mall. Nearly all the social activities one could want are satisfied within the enclosed environment of the mall—sports and entertainment, music and dramatic performances, socializing with friends, having a meal or a snack, and of course buying, or simply admiring, an endless array of consumer goods. The people of medieval Europe walked, so their obvious gathering place was the cathedral in the center of town. The people of suburban North America drive cars; their obvious gathering place is the mall.

One of the world's largest malls is located in West Edmonton, Alberta, in Canada **(442)**. Its dimensions stagger the imagination. Housed under one roof is a complex the size of 108 football fields, including 11 department stores and more than 800 shops. If you are hungry, you can choose from among some 110 restaurants. For entertainment you might visit the zoo, the ice-skating rink, the huge "waterpark" with its elaborate swimming pool, or the canal with its submarines. No matter what the weather outside—and Edmonton has a brutal winter climate—you can pursue whatever activities you fancy under the roof. One can't help but think Buckminster Fuller would have loved it. The mall is, after all, one version of life inside the dome.

If we try to envision the environmental design of the future, we will be in precisely the position of Pierre L'Enfant, who laid out the city of Washington without knowing about the automobile. We don't know what lies ahead. We don't know what factors will influence human life fifty or a hundred years hence. Yes, certain things probably can be taken for granted. Population will increase, and there will be a greater need for housing. Industrial pollution must be eliminated or counteracted. But how will the dominance of the computer affect life and the environment? How will space travel influence future generations? Must we plan now for the colonization of the moon and of distant planets? Should the L'Enfant of our day set out to plan a capital city in the "swampland" of our galaxy? Environmental design is among the most dynamic and most perplexing of all the arts, because the environment keeps changing before our very eyes.

PART FIVE

ARTS IN TIME

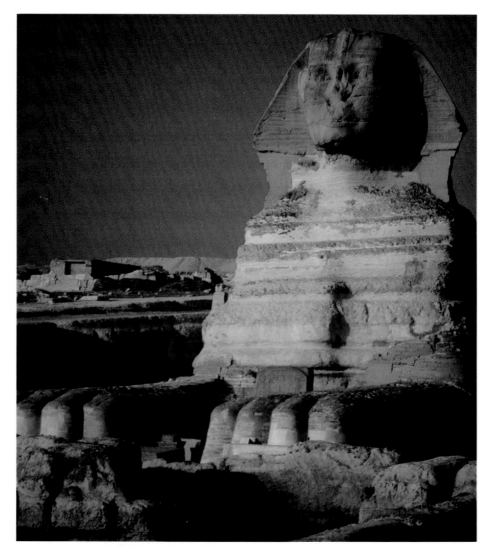

443. *The Great Sphinx.*
c. 2530 B.C. Stone, height 65'.
Giza, Egypt.

Chapter Fifteen

The Ancient World to the Middle Ages

A major factor in the understanding and appreciation of art is knowledge of its time frame—when a work of art was made and under what circumstances, how cultural factors of the time may have influenced the artists. For this reason the final part of this book has been devoted to a brief chronological survey, tracing the major movements in Western art from earliest times to the present. The three chapters here should help to place works of art discussed throughout the text in their historical context. Chronologies in the chapters list significant dates and show parallels for artworks and events around the world. As we study the arts in time, however, it should be remembered that the works illustrated could also be considered primarily for their themes, their design components, and their media.

Some of the earliest surviving works of art have already been presented in this book—the cave paintings of southern Europe **(3)** and the figurines made by very early peoples **(58)**. For the most part these are isolated examples, deriving from cultures that were essentially nomadic, oriented toward hunting to meet their needs for food. Not until we come to two cultures, both in the Middle East, do we find a coherent, reasonably intact artistic production about which we know a great deal. These are the ancient cultures of Egypt and Mesopotamia—the ancestors of Western art and civilization.

The Egyptians and Mesopotamians built their societies around mighty rivers, which enabled them to develop agriculture and therefore establish permanent settlements. This permanence, in turn, led to the development of architecture, the standardization of religions and rituals, and the creation of a social climate in which art could flourish. Our brief survey of Western art history, therefore, begins in the regions of these mighty rivers—the Nile in Egypt, the Tigris and Euphrates in Mesopotamia.

Egypt

The principal message of Egyptian art is continuity—a seamless span of time reaching back infinitely into history and forward into the future. The Sphinx **(443)**, the symbol of this most important characteristic of Egyptian art, is the essence of stability, order, and endurance. Built about 2530 B.C. and towering to a height of 65 feet, it faces into the rising sun, seeming to cast its immobile

CHRONOLOGY

STYLE/PERIOD	POLITICAL/SOCIAL EVENTS AND PERSONALITIES	MONUMENTS/MAJOR ARTISTS

30,000–3,000 B.C.

STYLE/PERIOD	POLITICAL/SOCIAL EVENTS AND PERSONALITIES	MONUMENTS/MAJOR ARTISTS
Old Stone Age, 30,000–10,000 New Stone Age, 10,000–4,000		*Venus of Willendorf*, 30,000–10,000 **(58)** cave paintings, France and Spain, 15,000–10,000 **(3)**

3,000–800 B.C.

STYLE/PERIOD	POLITICAL/SOCIAL EVENTS AND PERSONALITIES	MONUMENTS/MAJOR ARTISTS
Cycladic culture, Aegean, c. 3000–1100 Sumerian culture, Mesopotamia, c. 2800–c. 1720 Old Kingdom, Egypt, 2686–2181 Middle Kingdom, Egypt, 2133–1991 Minoan culture, Crete, c. 2000–1100 Assyrian Empire, Mesopotamia, c. 1760–612 New Kingdom, Egypt, 1567–1085 Mycenaean culture, Greece, c. 1600–1100	Hammurabi, king of Babylonia, c. 1750–1708 Amenhotep IV, pharaoh of Egypt, *c. 1353–c. 1336 Tutankhamun, pharaoh of Egypt, *c. 1334–c. 1325 Fall of Troy (Trojan Horse), c. 1184	Square Temple, Tell Asmar, Iraq, c. 2900–2600 **(448)** *Great Sphinx*, Egypt, c. 2530 **(443)** Great Pyramids, Egypt, c. 2500 **(67)** Stonehenge, England, c. 2000–1500 **(59)** Temple of Amen-Mut-Khonsu, Egypt, c. 1390 **(395)**

800 B.C.–A.D. 1

STYLE/PERIOD	POLITICAL/SOCIAL EVENTS AND PERSONALITIES	MONUMENTS/MAJOR ARTISTS
Zhou Dynasty, China, 1045–256 Geometric period, Greece, c. 800–c. 650 Etruscan style, Italy, 6th cent. Archaic period, Greece, c. 650–c. 500 Classical period, Greece, c. 500–c. 400 Hellenistic period, Greece, c. 400–c. 150	Sargon II, king of Assyria, c. 722–705 Nebuchadnezzar II, king of Babylon, 605–562 Rome founded, c. 753 Buddha, c. 563–483 Confucius, c. 551–479 Pericles, ruler of Athens, c. 449–429 Augustus, emperor of Rome, 27 B.C.–A.D. 14	Palace of Sargon II, Iraq, c. 721–705 **(449)** Ishtar Gate, Babylon, c. 575 **(450)** Parthenon, Athens, 447–432 **(62,397,456,583)** Great Stupa, India, 3rd cent. B.C.–A.D. 1st cent. **(63)** Great Wall of China begun, c. 228 **(68)** Pont du Gard, France, 1st cent. **(398)** *Laocoön Group*, late 2nd cent. **(461,580)** *Augustus of Prima Porta*, c. 20 **(69)** Phidias (d. 432) Praxiteles (c. 390–c. 330)

A.D. 1–800

STYLE/PERIOD	POLITICAL/SOCIAL EVENTS AND PERSONALITIES	MONUMENTS/MAJOR ARTISTS
Roman Empire, 31 B.C.–c. 500 Maya culture, Mexico & Central America, c. 300–1500 Gupta Period, India, 320–647 Byzantine Empire (Europe-Asia), c. 400–1453 Tang Dynasty, China, 618–907 Islamic Empire, c. 622–900 Nara Period, Japan, 645–794	Jesus Christ (c. 4 B.C.–c. A.D. 29) Pompeii destroyed, 79 Constantine, emperor of Rome, 306–337 Nomadic migrations, Europe, 4th–5th cent. Justinian, emperor of Byzantium, 527–565 Mohammed (c. 570–632)	Colosseum, Rome, 72–80 **(466)** Pantheon, Rome, 118–125 **(401,467)** San Vitale, Ravenna, 527–547 **(471)** Hagia Sophia, Istanbul, 532–537 **(402,473)** Sutton Hoo Ship Burial, 625–633 **(474)** *Book of Kells*, mid-8th cent. **(476)**

A.D. 800–1400

STYLE/PERIOD	POLITICAL/SOCIAL EVENTS AND PERSONALITIES	MONUMENTS/MAJOR ARTISTS
Romanesque period, Europe, c. 1050–c. 1200 Gothic period, Europe, c. 1200–c. 1500 Song Dynasty, China, 960–1279 Inca Empire, Peru, c. 1100–1532 Kamakura Period, Japan, 1185–1333	Charlemagne, Holy Roman Emperor, 800–814 Crusades, Europe, 1096–1270 Magna Carta, England, 1215 Marco Polo journeys to China, 1271–1295 Black Death in Europe, 1348–1357	Li Cheng (d. 967) *Bayeux Tapestry*, c. 1073–1088 **(391)** St. Sernin, Toulouse, France, c. 1080 **(479)** Chartres Cathedral, France, c. 1194–1260 **(64,400,480)** Duccio (active 1278–1318) Giotto (c. 1267–1337)

*Egyptian dates vary according to which of several systems has been used to translate them into our calendar. Therefore, other sources may show different dates.

444. *Palette of King Narmer,*
from Hierakonpolis. c. 3100 B.C.
Slate, height 25″.
Egyptian Museum, Cairo.

gaze down the centuries for all eternity. The Sphinx has the body of a reclining lion and the head of a man, thought to be the pharaoh Chefren, whose
pyramid tomb is nearby **(67)**. Egyptian kings ruled absolutely and enjoyed a
semidivine status, taking their authority from the sun-god, Ra, from whom
they were assumed to be descended. Power and continuity both are embodied in this splendid monument.

An even earlier relic from Egyptian culture, the so-called *Palette of King
Narmer* **(444)**, illustrates many characteristics of Egyptian art. The Greek
philosopher Plato wrote that Egyptian art did not change for ten thousand
years; while this may be something of an exaggeration, there were many
features that remained stable over long periods of time. The palette (so
named because it is thought to have been a slab for mixing cosmetics) com-
memorates a victory by the forces of Upper Egypt, led by Narmer, over those
of Lower Egypt, resulting in a unified kingdom. Narmer is the largest figure
and is positioned near the center of the palette to indicate his high status. He
holds a fallen enemy by the hair and is about to deliver the death blow. In the
lowest sector of the tablet are two more defeated enemies. At upper right is a
falcon representing Horus, the god of Upper Egypt. In its organization of
images the palette is strikingly logical and balanced. The central section has
Narmer's figure just to left of the middle, with his upraised arm and the form
of a servant filling the space, while the falcon and the victim complete the
right-hand side of the composition.

Narmer's pose is typical of Egyptian art and of art styles in other ancient cultures. When depicting an important personage, the Egyptian artist
strove to show each part of the body to best advantage, so it could be "read"
clearly by the viewer. Thus, Narmer's lower body is seen in profile, his torso
full front, his head in profile, but his eye front again. This same pose recurs
throughout most two-dimensional art in Egypt. It is believed that the priests,
who had much control over the art, established this figure style and decreed
that it be maintained for the sake of continuity. Obviously, it is not a posture
that suggests much motion, apart from a stylized gesture like that of
Narmer's upraised arm. But action was not important to Egyptian art, no

more in the smaller objects than in official sculptures **(356)** or large monuments. Order and stability were its primary characteristics, as they were the goals of Egyptian society.

Egyptian painting reveals the same clear visual design and illustrative skill as the works in stone. A wall painting from Thebes **(445)**, depicting a hunting scene, poses the main figure very much like the figure of Narmer, although the two works are separated in time by some 1,650 years. Again the hunter's body is stylized: his head, eyes, torso, and legs are each shown from the most advantageous viewpoint. In keeping with the Egyptians' love of exact detail, this painter draws the birds and other creatures with almost biological precision. If we recognize the species, we can identify them. Even the fish are rendered meticulously; we don't see them as we would through a blur of water, but rather as we *know* the fish to look.

We know other things as well. We know that the hunter, probably a nobleman, is the most important figure in the composition, because he is the biggest. (This is called **hierarchical scale.**) Apart from clues provided by clothing, we know that he is a man and the figure at right is a woman. By convention, regardless of race or complexion, the Egyptians painted men darker (reddish) and women lighter (yellowish).

Above all, this work is beautifully composed. The artist has balanced the dominant figure of the hunter against a richness of sea, plant, and animal life. No area is left "empty." Our eyes find some subject of interest in every

The Ancient Near East

part of the painting, yet it doesn't seem crammed or busy or chaotic. In this
instance the Egyptians' art shows both unity and a plentiful variety.

One brief period in the history of Egyptian culture stands apart from
the rest and therefore has fascinated scholars and art lovers alike. This was
the reign of the pharaoh Amenhotep IV, who came to power about 1353 B.C.
For a civilization that prized continuity above all else, Amenhotep was a
genuine revolutionary. He changed his name (to Akhenaten), moved his capital, attempted to establish monotheism (belief in one god) among a people
who had traditionally worshiped many gods, and fostered a new, more relaxed style in art.

Nowhere is this more apparent than in the famous portrait bust of his
queen, Nefertiti **(446)**. While enchanted by Nefertiti's beauty, the modern
viewer is perhaps even more taken by how contemporary she seems, how she
appears to bridge the gap of more than three thousand years to our own
world. Despite her regal headdress and elongated neck, Nefertiti might be a
model in this month's fashion magazine. When the opportunity presented
itself, the Egyptian sculptor was capable of great humanity and warmth, of
letting a subject's real characteristics transcend convention.

We are fortunate that so much art from ancient Egypt has been preserved. That it has been is partly owing to Egypt's hot, dry climate, partly
because the Egyptians buried the finest of their art with their dead. Custom
decreed that an important personage, especially a king, must be fitted out
lavishly for the afterlife, with furnishings, jewelry, and artifacts of all kinds,

447. Burial mask of the pharaoh Tutankhamun. c. 1325 B.C. Gold, inlaid with blue glass and semiprecious stones; height 21¼". Cairo Museum.

made from the richest materials available. These objects were supposed to remain entombed with the dead pharaohs for all eternity. From earliest times, however, grave robbers have coveted that buried treasure—and not for its artistic merits. Most of the royal tombs uncovered in the Valley of the Kings, across the Nile from Luxor, were found nearly empty, stripped of their wealth. Only in this century, in 1922, did the full splendor of Egyptian art reveal itself to modern eyes. For in that year archaeologists located the one tomb that had remained sealed, virtually intact—the tomb of the boy-king Tutankhamun **(576)**.

King "Tut," as the 1922 newspapers quickly dubbed him, was married as a young child to a daughter of Akhenaten and Nefertiti, and he succeeded Akhenaten to the throne. Crowned in about 1334 B.C. at the age of nine, he died just nine years later. Modern scholars knew of his existence and sought his tomb, wondering whether it, too, had been pillaged by grave robbers. One man in particular, an Englishman named Howard Carter, had spent ten years searching and was running out of time. His sponsor, the Earl of Carnarvon, intended to withdraw financial support. Three weeks before the deadline, Carter's workers found the entrance to the tomb. With Lord Carnarvon behind him, Carter made a hole in the door and stuck in a lighted candle. Unable to stand the suspense, Carnarvon cried out, "Can you see anything?" "Yes," replied Carter, "wonderful things!"

Yes, the diggers had found wonderful things—things that had remained untouched even by light for more than three thousand years. Although a very young king, Tutankhamun had been sent into the hereafter in extraordinary style. His tomb was a veritable warehouse of priceless objects, made with superb craftsmanship, created from alabaster, precious stones, and above all gold—gold in unimaginable quantities. We saw the back of the pharaoh's throne, with its relief sculpture in gold, in Chapter 11 **(352)**. Tutankhamun's body, mummified to preserve it from decay, was encased in three coffins, nested one inside the other, the innermost being of solid gold. But perhaps most splendid of all the artworks is Tutankhamun's burial mask, which rested atop the mummy's head and shoulders **(447)**. Also of solid gold, ornamented with blue glass and semiprecious gems, the mask is thought to be a faithful depiction of Tutankhamun (insofar as the mummy remains agree), if somewhat idealized. The sculptor's hand was sure in molding the soft gold into a vibrant likeness.

In a sense, Carter and his party were grave robbers themselves. They did not sell the gold or melt it down, but they did remove it. The objects from Tutankhamun's tomb are in the Cairo Museum and they have toured the world. We can see them, we can marvel at their beauty, and we rejoice in this. But that is not what their makers intended.

Mesopotamia

At the same time that ancient Egypt was flourishing, another great civilization had established itself to the east, in Mesopotamia, roughly in the area of modern-day Syria and Iraq. The two cultures had contact with one another but maintained their separate identities, and their styles in art were quite different. Mesopotamia occupied a large, flat area made fertile by its two rivers, the Tigris and the Euphrates. Many archaeologists and historians believe that the biblical Garden of Eden was located here, at a point near where the rivers join before flowing into the Persian Gulf.

Unlike Egypt, which was protected on two sides by the sea and elsewhere by the desert, Mesopotamia had few natural defenses against invasion. Successive waves of people conquered the region—the most important being the Sumerians, the Assyrians, and the Babylonians. Judging by the surviving art, each culture centered around the temple as a place of worship and a focus of daily life.

The unique character of **Sumerian** art is exemplified by a group of marble statues from the Abu Temple at Tell Asmar, approximately contemporary with the Sphinx **(448)**. The tallest figure is Abu, the god of vegetation, and just to the right is a mother goddess, while the rest of the statues represent priests and worshipers. No real attempt has been made to carve these figures naturalistically; the bodies are extremely stylized and some of the figures seem rather like decorated cylinders. Each has the hands clasped in the ritual Sumerian gesture of worship. The male figures show the heavily textured

448. Group of votive statuettes, from the Square Temple of the god Abu, Tell Asmar, Iraq. c. 2900–2600 B.C. Marble, height of tallest figure 30″. Iraq Museum, Baghdad, and Oriental Institute, University of Chicago.

left: 449. Outer Portal of the Citadel, Palace of Sargon II, Dur Sharrukin, Iraq. c. 721–705 B.C.

right: 450. Ishtar Gate (restored), from Babylon. c. 575 B.C. Enameled sun-dried brick, height 48'9". Near Eastern Museum, State Museums, Berlin.

beards characteristic of this art, and the lips are curved upward as though to smile—a convention that means the persons depicted are alive, not dead, though not necessarily happy. The most extraordinary and riveting feature of each statue is the eyes, which are enormous, especially in the two gods. Outlined in black and inset with colored stones and shells, the eyes apparently served as the medium of communication between the worshipers and their gods. They give to these sculptures an exotic appearance very different from that of most Western art from ancient times.

Mesopotamia's history over the centuries was a turbulent one marked by almost continual warfare and conquest. A major goal of architecture, therefore, was the erection of mighty citadels to ensure the safety of temples and palaces. Such a citadel was that of the **Assyrian** ruler Sargon II, built at Dur Sharrukin in the 8th century B.C. One of its gates **(449)** shows the monumental stone slabs that protected the entrance, which have been carved into guardian demons meant to impress—and possibly to intimidate—any visitor to the citadel.

The **Babylonians,** who followed the Assyrians, surely must be ranked among the great architects of the ancient world **(431)**, although far less of their production remains than does that of Greece and Rome. We get some idea of their skill from the Ishtar Gate (reconstructed in a German museum), which was built in the 6th century B.C. under the great king Nebuchadnezzar II **(450)**. Made of thousands of glazed mud bricks, the gate has two massive towers flanking a central arch—the latter proving that, although the Romans developed the arch extensively, the Babylonians had discovered its uses earlier. On ceremonial occasions Nebuchadnezzar would sit under the arch in majesty to receive his subjects. The walls of the gate are decorated with processions of glazed ceramic animals, probably meant as spirit-guardians.

Both Mesopotamia and Egypt had access to the Mediterranean Sea, the "highway" of the ancient world. If we were to sail northwest from Egypt, or west-northwest from Mesopotamia, we would reach the Aegean Sea, an arm of the Mediterranean separating Greece from what is now Turkey. Around the Aegean we find a third focus of early artistic production.

The Aegean

The artistic cultures of the Aegean parallel in time those of Egypt and Mesopotamia, for the earliest begins about 3000 B.C., when Old Kingdom Egypt
and the Sumerian civilization were becoming established. There were three
major Aegean cultures: the *Cycladic*, centered on a group of small islands in
the Aegean; the *Minoan*, based on the island of Crete at the southern end of
the Aegean; and the *Mycenaean*, on the mainland of Greece.

Cycladic art is a puzzle, because we know almost nothing about the
people who made it. Nearly all consists of nude female figures like the one we
saw in Chapter 2 **(42a)**—simplified, abstract, composed of geometric lines
and shapes and projections. The figures vary in size from the roughly 2-foot
height of our example to approximately life-size, but they are much alike in
style. Presumably they were meant as fertility images, although they are a far
cry from the fleshier "Venuses" found earlier in the north **(58)**. To modern
eyes the Cycladic figurines seem astonishingly sophisticated in their ability
to reduce anatomical forms to the essence of shape.

The **Minoan** culture on Crete can be traced to about 2000 B.C. and centers around the great city of Knossos. We take the name from a legendary
king called Minos, who supposedly ruled at Knossos and whose queen gave
birth to the dreaded creature, half-human, half-bull, known as the Minotaur.
The Minoans, being island dwellers, were a seafaring people, and much of
their art depicts sea creatures—fishes and dolphins and octopuses. Usually
the art is cheerful, lighthearted, and colorful. It is believed the Minoans worshiped a female deity, and this may be the identity of the *Snake Goddess*
(451), one of two similar figures discovered at the Palace of Knossos. With her
bared breasts, tiny waist, and elaborate skirt, this figure resembles then-
fashionable ladies of the court, yet she holds a wriggling snake in each hand.
Some writers have suggested she is a priestess associated with a snake-
handling cult, or perhaps a queen. In any event, the little terra-cotta statuette
is unlike female depictions we would find in any other ancient culture.

Mycenaean culture, so called because it formed around the city of Mycenae, flourished on the south coast of the Greek mainland from about 1600 to
1100 B.C. Like the Minoans, the Mycenaeans built palaces and temples, but
they are also noted for their elaborate burial customs and tombs—a taste
apparently acquired from the Egyptians, with whom they had contact. It
seems probable that Egypt was also the source of the Mycenaeans' great
supplies of gold, for they alone among the Aegean cultures were master goldsmiths. Burial places in and around Mycenae have yielded large quantities of
exquisite gold objects, such as the *rhyton*, or drinking cup, in the shape of a
lion's head **(452)**. The craftsmanship of this vessel is wonderful, contrasting
smooth planar sections on the sides of the face with the more detailed snout
and mane. The Mycenaeans also used gold for death masks, jewelry, and
weapons.

Mycenaean civilization was the last of those we identify as *pre-Hellenic*,
or "pre-Greek." Of course, the Aegean peoples lived in or near Greece, but
when we speak of "ancient Greece" we do not mean them. We mean a culture
that took root on the Greek mainland starting about 1100 B.C., spread
through much of the eastern Mediterranean world, survived for only a few
hundred years, and created art that remains a standard against which all
other art is measured.

above: 451. *Snake Goddess*,
Minoan, from Crete. c. 1600 B.C.
Terra cotta, height 17½".
Heraklion Museum, Crete.

below: 452. Rhyton in the shape
of a lion's head, from Mycenae.
c. 1550 B.C. Gold, height 8".
National Museum, Athens.

Greece

No doubt a major reason we so admire the ancient Greeks is that they seem
to have excelled at everything. Their political ideals serve as a model for
contemporary democracy. Their poetry and drama and philosophy survive

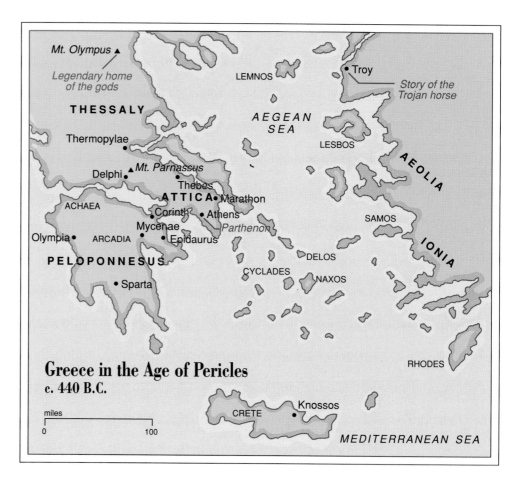

Greece in the Age of Pericles
c. 440 B.C.

miles
0   100

as living classics, familiar to every serious scholar. Their architecture and sculpture have influenced most later periods in the history of Western art and continue to do so.

It is assumed the Greeks' genius shone equally in painting, but we know very little about this because most painted works have been lost. We would know even less were it not for the large number of painted clay vases that were produced from about the 8th century B.C.. In Chapter 11 we noted that terra cotta (baked clay) is an extremely durable material; it can shatter but will not disintegrate, and so the pieces can be reassembled. For this reason a large quantity of Greek art has survived to our day.

Few cultures can match the Greeks in the elaborate painting of vases, which represent a major part of their artistic output. These terra cotta vessels served as grave monuments, storage urns for wine or oil, drinking cups, and so forth. An early example is the so-called *Dipylon Vase* (453), named for the cemetery in Athens where it was found. Made in the 8th century B.C., the *Dipylon Vase* offers a superb example of the **geometric style** of vase painting, the first clearly defined style we know the Greeks to have followed. The reason for this term is obvious. Much of the vase's decoration consists of geometric lines and patterns, including the "meander" pattern that runs around the top just under the rim. Images of people are little more than stick figures, yet they are integrated wonderfully in the overall geometric design.

The *Dipylon Vase* provides an interesting commentary on the burial customs of the Greeks, especially as contrasted with the Egyptians. The pharaoh Tutankhamun's tomb (576) was elaborately fitted out for a busy and prestigious afterlife, since that is what the Egyptians expected. The Greeks, on the other hand, were not so optimistic. To them, life beyond the grave was a gray and shadowy place, of little interest. A funerary urn like the *Dipylon Vase* was placed above the burial spot to receive liquid offerings and was intended to show the respect of the deceased's relatives and friends. A funeral procession is painted on the vase. But there is no provision for enjoyment of the next world, only a recognition of the one left behind.

Through later centuries Greek vase painting prospered and developed. Our next illustration (454) shows a *kylix* (a drinking cup) representing *Eos and Memnon*. The painting is done in the **red-figure style,** which developed late in the 6th century B.C. A background of black was created from glaze, leaving the figures in the natural red color of the clay. Sometimes details were added with white highlights. Given what sounds like a difficult technique, the painting is remarkably fine. Eos, the goddess of dawn, holds the body of her dead son, Memnon, who has been killed by the hero Achilles. There is a suggestion of depth in the overlapping of Memnon's body in front of Eos, as well as in the crossed legs; the dangling arms of the body visually balance Eos' outspread wings. The finely drawn textures of gown, hair, and wings reveal the great skill of the vase painter's brush. As a mark of the esteem in which vase painters were held, and the pride they took in their work, this kylix is signed by the painter, Douris.

Douris worked at the beginning of an era known to us as the **Classical period,** the 5th and 4th centuries B.C. At that time Greece consisted of several independent city-states, often at war among themselves or with their neighbors. Chief among the city-states—from an artistic and cultural point of view, if not always a military one—was Athens.

Like many Greek cities, Athens had been built around a high hill, or **acropolis.** Ancient temples on the Acropolis had crumbled or been destroyed in the wars. About 449 B.C. Athens' great general Pericles came to power as head of state and set about rebuilding. He soon embarked on a massive construction program, meant not only to restore the past glory of Athens but to raise it to a previously undreamed-of splendor.

Pericles' friend, the sculptor Phidias, was given the job of overseeing all architectural and sculptural projects on the Acropolis. The work would continue for several decades, but it took an amazingly short time given the ambitious nature of the scheme. By the end of the century the Acropolis probably

left: **453.** *Dipylon Vase.*
8th century B.C.
Terra cotta, height 40½".
The Metropolitan Museum of Art,
New York (Rogers Fund, 1914).

right: **454.** Douris.
Eos and Memnon,
interior of an Attic red-figure
kylix. c. 490–480 B.C.
Terra cotta, diameter 10½".
Louvre, Paris.

ART PEOPLE *Pericles*

His enemies called him "onionhead." Contemporary writers tell us that Pericles had an unusually high, sloping brow reaching up to a domed crown of the head, and that he is always portrayed wearing a helmet to cover this supposed deformity. For modern students, however, the term "onionhead" may take on another meaning. We peel away layer after layer, yet we never fully understand this complex man who is so admired 2,400 years after his death.

Pericles was born about 495 B.C., son of the Athenian general Xanthippus. Being of a noble family, he received a thorough education, first from Damon, the master of music—"music" in those times understood to include reading, writing, mathematics, singing, and poetry. Later he studied with the master philosopher Anaxagoras. Under these teachers Pericles developed habits of independent thought, enormous self-discipline, and (even his rivals admitted) unblemished integrity. After an early military career, he became active in the democratic government of Athens. About 449 B.C. Pericles was elected head of state, a post he held until his death.

An arranged marriage to a cousin produced two sons but little domestic happiness. All sources agree that the companion of Pericles' heart was the beautiful and brilliant Aspasia, a *hetaera,* or upper-class courtesan, with whom he lived openly for many years. Aspasia was possessed of wit and charm that drew to her side (and therefore to Pericles' side) the great artists and thinkers of the day, even Socrates himself. She seems also to have been a clever political advisor.

According to the ancient biographer Plutarch, Pericles excelled not only as a general and statesman but also as an orator, whose "tongue was armed with thunder and lightning." But for our purposes in this book another trait stands out: Pericles had both the means and the vision to become an incomparable patron of the arts.

Soon after taking power in Athens, Pericles assigned his friend, the sculptor Phidias, the task of rebuilding the temples on the Acropolis—but rebuilding them on a far more elaborate scale. Under Pericles' sponsorship, Plutarch remarks, "many edifices, each of which would seem to have required the labor of several successive ages, were finished during the administration of one prosperous man."[1] The jewel of these was, of course, the Parthenon (**456**), built with hand labor and embellished with many sculptures in just fifteen years.

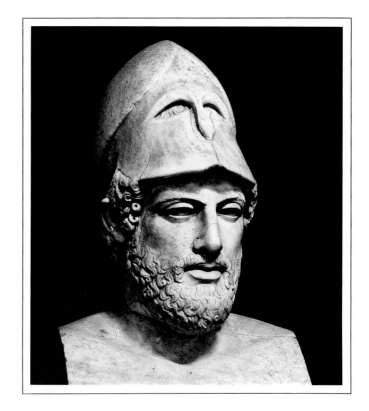

Pericles took a lively interest in the other arts as well. The theater, offering both dramas and comedies, prospered in that time, and Pericles saw to it that all citizens received free tickets. He built a music hall, the Odeum, and personally judged the musical contests held each year. This exhilarating climate for the arts continued until a plague swept Athens in 430 B.C. Although Pericles recovered from the disease, he was weakened and died the next year.

We who so highly value the Parthenon, even in its ruined state, cannot imagine it not existing, yet Pericles' building program was not universally popular. Critics charged he had emptied the treasury to serve his own ambitions. But Pericles' ambitions were not for himself. They were for Athens, for her glory in those times and her glory down through the ages. He spoke of it this way: "What I would prefer is that you should fix your eyes every day on the greatness of Athens as she really is, and should fall in love with her."[2]

Pericles. Roman copy after a Greek original of c. 429 B.C., probably by Kresilas. Marble. Vatican Museums, Rome.

looked much like the reconstruction shown here (455). The large columned building at lower right in the photo is the Propylaea, the ceremonial gateway to the Acropolis through which processions winding up the hill would pass. At left in the photo, the building with columned porches is the Erechtheum, placed on the spot where Erechtheus, the legendary founder of the city, supposedly had lived.

But the crowning glory of the Acropolis was and is the Parthenon (456). In previous chapters we have considered the Parthenon as a monument to religious devotion (62) and as an example of post-and-lintel architecture (pp. 326–328). Here let us examine it as the pinnacle of Greek art in what we have come to think of as its Golden Age.

Dedicated to the goddess Athena *parthenos,* or Athena the warrior maiden, the Parthenon is a Doric-style temple (p. 327) with columns all around the exterior and an inner row of columns on each of the short walls. The roof originally rose to a peak, leaving a triangular area or **pediment** (visible in the reconstruction) at each end. The pediments were decorated with sculptures, as was the **frieze,** the narrow band running all around the building just under the roof. In the manner of Greek temples, the Parthenon was painted in vivid colors, principally red and blue (583). Architects Ictinus and Callicrates, working under direction from Phidias, completed the structure in just fifteen years.

The inner chamber of the Parthenon, called the **cella,** once housed a monumental statue of the goddess, made by Phidias himself of gold and ivory

below: 455. Model reconstruction of the Acropolis, Athens, viewed from the northwest. Royal Ontario Museum, Toronto.

bottom: 456. Ictinus and Callicrates. Parthenon, Athens. 447–432 B.C.

and standing 30 feet tall atop its pedestal. Contemporary sources tell us Phidias was an artist of unsurpassed genius, but we must take their word for it, since neither the Athena statue nor any of his original sculptures are known to survive (although copies exist). Many other sculptures from the Parthenon have been preserved, however, and these were probably made by Phidias' students, under his supervision.

One existing sculpture group, now in the British Museum (p. 501), depicts *Three Goddesses* **(457)**. In Pericles' time this group stood near the far right side of the pediment; if you imagine the figures with their heads intact, you can seen how they fit into the angle of the triangle. Carved from marble and now headless, these goddesses still seem to breathe and be capable of movement, so convincing is their roundness. The draperies flow and ripple naturally over the bodies, apparently responding to living flesh underneath.

The Parthenon sculptures represent a high point in the long period of Greek experimentation with carving in marble. We can trace this evolution from the 6th to the 2nd century by comparing three treatments of a favorite Greek sculpture type—the nude male figure. While many marble statues were of females, the most typical Greek figure is male, a nude superbly proportioned to indicate an ideal of physical perfection.

The Greeks' approach to sculpture was a radical departure from artistic precedents in other parts of the Mediterranean world. Egyptian sculptures more often were attached to a background; Greek figures generally are free-standing, in the round. Egyptian figures usually were clothed; the Greeks introduced total nudity in the male figure and in later centuries moved toward increasing nudity in female statues **(26)**. Most of the Egyptian sculptures we know are of pharaohs, their queens, their children, and other members of the court. The Greeks seem to have been far more interested in physical beauty than in high status. To be sure, some of their finest sculptures represent gods, but they are gods in human form—magnificent human form. And many are depictions of anonymous young men, to whom scholars have given the name **kouros,** meaning "youth" or "boy."

The reasons for this new approach to sculpture are clear from Greek philosophy and literature. Whereas the Egyptians emphasized continuity of the state, the Greeks sought perfection of the state *through* perfection of the individual. The ideal human body symbolized an ideal divine soul, dedicated to the highest principles. If perfection could be chiseled into marble, then perhaps the sought-after perfection in human affairs could be attained.

Three figures, made over a period of about 150 years, will show the enormous progress of Greek sculptors in striving toward an ideal of naturalism and physical perfection. The first is a *kouros* that dates from the early **Archaic** period, around 600 B.C. **(458)**. This work is a fairly crude attempt at freeing the nude body from its original block of stone. We can almost envision the cube of marble the sculptor began with from the square appearance of the form. Although more than 6 feet tall, the figure seems puny and underdeveloped, its torso too small and slender, its shoulders too narrow. The hair is a stylized braid, the eyes blank and staring, the feet featureless slabs with rigid cylinders for toes. Nevertheless, this sculptor has made great strides toward a natural approach, especially when we compare the *kouros* to earlier Egyptian figural statues **(356)**. The musculature of arms and legs has been studied carefully, the legs separated from one another, the arms separated from the body.

Another *kouros,* carved some seventy-five years later but still in the Archaic period **(459)**, shows considerable progress toward naturalism. This body is far better proportioned, the hips and torso broader, the arms and legs well-developed. We can easily believe a human body might be shaped like this, which is hard to imagine of the earlier *kouros.* In spite of these advances, however, the sculpture retains a blocklike quality, is still imprisoned in the cube of stone. The left foot is set slightly forward to suggest motion, but we do not really believe in that motion because the hips and shoulders are level and the arms held rigidly at the sides. If you try to assume this pose, you will find it almost impossible, for when you take a step forward with one foot, the opposing hip and shoulder go up, and your arms move in counterbalance. There is no indication of this in the statue. On the *kouros'* face is an expression that has been dubbed the "archaic smile"—a rather forced grimace apparently meant to convey animation. (Compare the "smiles" on the Sumerian figures **[448]**, which indicate the people are alive, not dead.)

Now let us compare the *Spear Bearer* by the great sculptor Polyclitus **(460)**, carved yet another seventy-five years or so later, in the **Classical** period of the 5th century B.C. (Like so many Greek statues, the original bronze of the *Spear Bearer* has been lost and is known to us only through later, and probably inferior, Roman copies in marble.) Here we find the *contrapposto* of a figure in motion (p. 298). With the weight on the right foot, the left knee is bent, the left hip and shoulder rise, the arms reach outward from the body, and the whole form stands in a relaxed S-curve suggestive of movement. The musculature of a well-developed body has been carefully observed and recorded. Gone is the archaic smile, to be replaced by a natural, pensive ex-

left: 458. *Kouros.* c. 600 B.C. Marble, height 6′1½″. The Metropolitan Museum of Art, New York (Fletcher Fund, 1932).

center: 459. *Kroisos (Kouros from Anavysos).* c. 525 B.C. Marble, height 6′4″. National Museum, Athens.

right: 460. *Doryphorus (Spear Bearer).* Roman copy after a Greek original of c. 450–440 B.C. by Polyclitus. Marble, height 6′6″. National Museum, Naples.

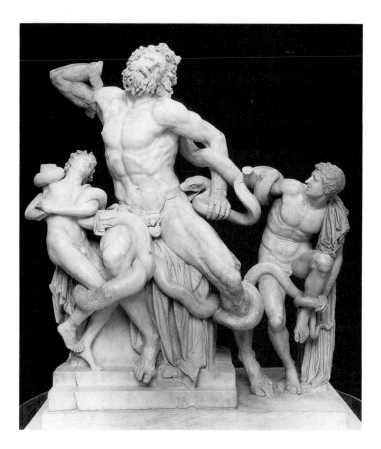

461. Agesander, Athenodorus, and Polydorus of Rhodes. *Laocoön Group.* Late 2nd century B.C. Marble, height 8′. Vatican Museums, Rome.

pression. We must consider this sculpture in terms of what the Greeks had set out to do. They intended to show a perfectly formed body, at the peak of its youthful strength, rendered in as lifelike a manner as possible. At this they succeeded admirably.

The last phase of Greek art, occurring roughly in the 3rd and 2nd centuries B.C., is known as *Hellenistic*—a term that refers to the spread of Greek culture eastward to Mesopotamia and Egypt. Hellenistic sculpture tends to be more dramatic and emotional than that of the Classical 5th century; it has more of a tendency to push out into space and is more dynamic. One of the best-known examples of this style is the *Laocoön Group* **(461)**, dated to the late 2nd century B.C. (see also the Epilogue, **580**).

Laocoön was a priest of the sun-god, Apollo, and his story involves one of the most famous events in Greek mythology. In the last year of the war between the Greeks and the Trojans, the Greeks devised a fabulous ruse to overrun the city of Troy. They built a giant wooden horse, concealed inside it a large number of Greek soldiers, and wheeled it up to the gates of Troy, claiming it was an offering for the goddess Athena. While the people of Troy were trying to decide whether to admit the horse, their priest, Laocoön, suspected a trick and urged the Trojans to keep the gates locked. (Here is the source of the well-known warning about "Greeks bearing gifts.") This angered the sea-god, Poseidon, who held bitter feelings toward Troy, and he sent two dreadful serpents to strangle Laocoön and his sons. The sculpture depicts the priest and his children in their death throes, entwined by the deadly snakes.

Compared to statues from the Classical period, such as the *Spear Bearer*, the *Laocoön Group* seems almost theatrical. Its subject matter, filled with drama and tension, would have been unthinkable three centuries earlier. The Classical sculptor wanted to convey an outward serenity, and thus showed the hero in perfection but not in action, outside of time, not throwing the spear but merely holding it. Hellenistic sculptors were far more interested than their predecessors in how their subjects reacted to events. Laocoön's reaction is a violent, anguished one, and the outlines of the sculpture reflect this. The three figures writhe in agony, thrusting their bodies outward in different directions, pushing into space. Unlike the dignified reserve of earlier figures, this sculpture projects a complicated and intense movement.

According to legend, the Trojans disregarded Laocoön's warning and brought the wooden horse into their city. That night the Greek soldiers slipped out of the horse, pillaged Troy, and destroyed it. Only a few of the Trojans escaped, including Aeneas, who sailed away and, after many adventures, landed at the mouth of the Tiber River and founded the city of Rome. Whether or not one chooses to believe the old myths, it is nevertheless true that the history of art and civilization now shifts westward, to the great empire that conquered Greece and virtually all of the Mediterranean world.

Rome

To understand the art of Rome we need to backtrack slightly to a people who inhabited the Italian peninsula from about the 7th century B.C. or earlier— the Etruscans. When the Roman Empire was established and its art began to flower, it drew on not only the traditions of the conquered Greeks but also styles of art nurtured on home soil.

If we learned much about the Egyptian and Greek cultures from their burial customs, we can learn even more about the Etruscans on that subject. At the risk of being too casual, we might say that the Etruscans loved a good funeral. Apparently, they had a rather cheerful idea of death and the afterlife, markedly in contrast to the Greeks. In Chapter 3 we saw an Etruscan sarcophagus, or burial coffin (96), on which sculptured images of a dead couple recline gracefully, enjoying a pleasant life beyond the grave. Wall paintings from Etruscan tombs testify to that same optimistic point of view.

At Tarquinia, on the west coast of Italy above Rome, are many tombs containing a wealth of frescoed murals. Our example, from the Tomb of the Leopards (462), shows a merry scene, part of the funeral banquet. The young man at left holds a cup, while the other two play, respectively, a double pipe (the Etruscans' favorite instrument) and a lyre. When compared to the figure-painting style of the Greeks during this period, as in Douris' vase painting (454), the Etruscan work seems stylized and relatively crude. Yet how lively the figures are, how colorful and animated. We sense their dancing movements from the swirl of the draperies, the vigor of the poses. There is warmth and humanity in these painted people, and even humor—a quality we seldom find in the art of the Greeks.

462. *Cup Bearer and Musicians,* from the Tomb of the Leopards, Etruscan Necropolis, Tarquinia. c. 480–470 B.C. Fresco, height 3′6″.

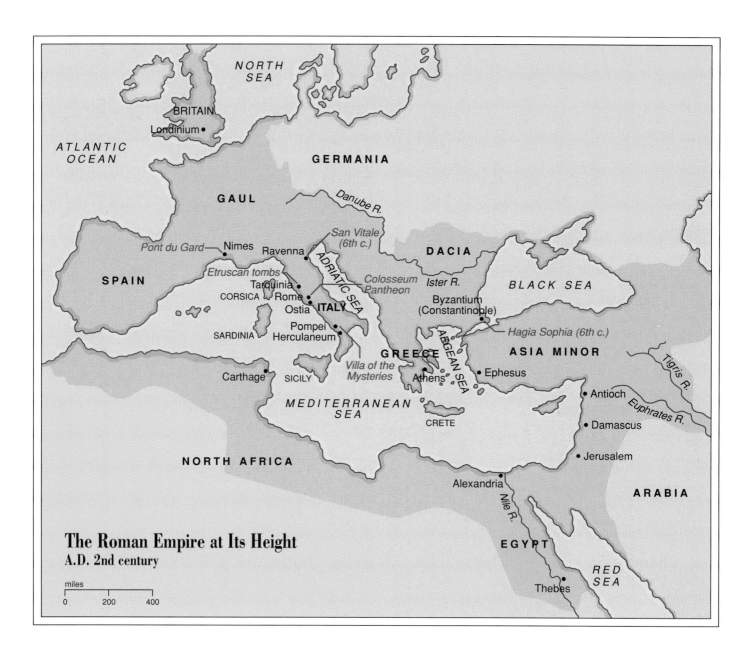

The Roman Empire at Its Height
A.D. 2nd century

miles
0   200   400

The Etruscans flourished in Italy for at least two hundred years. By the early 5th century B.C., however, they came under increasing pressure of domination by the Romans, and eventually they were absorbed into the Roman Empire, as were the Greeks.

There can be no doubt that the Romans greatly admired the work of their conquered subjects. They made numerous copies of Greek sculptures (including our example of the *Spear Bearer*), and imitated the Greek style for much of their "official" sculpture, such as emperor figures. The *Augustus of Prima Porta* (69), for instance, surely derives from Greek precedents. But it may have been Etruscan art, with its very evident warmth and humanity, that inspired a special category of sculpture in which the Romans came to excel—the portrait bust of an ordinary citizen.

One such example (463) is a portrait of a Roman husband and wife who are fully realized as individuals. Obviously, we cannot know what these people actually looked like, but it is safe to assume the sculptor made a good likeness, with a minimum of idealizing. The husband is old, the creases in his face well defined, his expression patient; we might read from his image a long experience in the trials of the world and gentle resignation to those trials. His wife seems stronger, less marked by pain, and her supportive clasp of the husband's hand is touching. Scholars have read into this pose the highly esteemed Roman virtues of *fides* (faith or fidelity) and *concordia* (harmony). Whereas the Greek sculptures and many of the Roman ones seem to exist in a world apart, these portrait busts are wonderfully accessible. They allow us to identify with people who have been dead for two thousand years.

Like other ancient cultures, the Romans often applied sculpture to architecture, in the form of carved figures in relief. However, our next example, the Column of Trajan **(464)**, is unique. Trajan came to power as emperor of Rome in A.D. 98. His role was not only political but also military—expanding the empire's territories and protecting it from outside invaders. Early in his reign Trajan went to war against the Dacians, a people of central Europe who had made periodic raids against the empire. His victory was celebrated by the erection of a triumphal column in the city of Rome.

Trajan's column stands 115 feet tall including its base, and in Roman times it was capped by a monumental statue of the emperor. An overall photograph does not do it justice. We show a closeup of the bottom section to focus on details, because the main feature of Trajan's column is a spiral sculptured band in low relief, running around and around the column, telling the story of Trajan's Dacian campaign. The relief band is about 50 inches high. If we could unwrap it from the column and stretch it out, it would be 656 feet long—about the length of two football fields.

The sculptured band takes the form of **continuous narrative,** beginning at the bottom with Trajan setting out for war, ending at the top with his conquest of the Dacians. In between are some 150 episodes, each self-contained yet flowing smoothly into the next. Needless to say, Trajan is the hero of the story, appearing prominently in most of the scenes, but he has a large supporting cast of characters. In all, more than 2,500 human figures are

left: 463. *Double Portrait of Gratidia M. L. Chrite and M. Gratidius Libanus.* Last quarter of 1st century B.C. White marble with traces of color, height 23¾". Vatican Museums, Rome.

below: 464. Column of Trajan, Rome, detail of lowest section. A.D. 106–113. Marble; height of frieze band 4'2", height of column 97', on 18' base.

carved into the relief, to say nothing of horses, chariots, boats, and all the paraphernalia of war. For a parallel to this achievement we must look nearly a thousand years later, to the *Bayeaux Tapestry* (**391**), in which many episodes of a historical event are stitched into cloth, not carved into marble.

The anonymous sculptor (or sculptors) who made the Trajan Column's relief had superior gifts at both storytelling and composition. Figures and architectural details are arranged to keep the narrative flowing, to provide basic information about what is going on in each scene. Although the relief is fairly shallow (compare **353**), we get a real sense of spatial depth, even when many figures are clustered together. Perhaps most striking is the fineness of the carving, which gives convincing realism to draped clothing and armor, faces and hair and musculature, bricks and waves in the water. Moreover, the precise carving is carried through to the very top of the column. This last fact raises an intriguing question: *Why?* Why should the sculptor lavish so much attention on a work that no one could see? Above the third or fourth turn of the spiral, the Trajan carvings become a blur to anyone standing on the ground. Today we have high-powered glasses and even cranes that could ride us up beside the column. The ancient Romans did not. How strange it seems that we, nearly two thousand years later, have a much better view of this work than the sculptor's own contemporaries.

The Romans were equally masterful at painting, but were it not for a tragedy that occurred in A.D. 79, we would know little more about Roman painting than we do about the Greek. In that year Mt. Vesuvius, an active volcano, erupted and buried the town of Pompeii, about a hundred miles south of Rome, along with the neighboring town of Herculaneum. The resulting lava and ashes spread a blanket over the region, and this blanket acted as a kind of time capsule. Pompeii lay undisturbed, immune to further ravages of nature, for more than sixteen centuries. Then in 1748 excavations were undertaken, and their findings were made public by the famous German archaeologist Joachim Winckelmann. Within the precincts of Pompeii the diggers found marvelous frescoes that were exceptionally well preserved. Pompeii was not an important city, so we cannot assume that the most talented artists of the period worked there. In fact, there is some evidence to suggest that the fresco painters were not Roman at all, but immigrant Greeks. Nevertheless, these wall paintings do give some indication of the styles of art practiced within the empire at the time.

One fresco, from a house known as the Villa of the Mysteries (**465**), shows a scene believed to represent secret cult rituals associated with the

465. Wall painting, from the Villa of the Mysteries, Pompeii. c. 50 B.C. Fresco.

wine-god Dionysus. The figures stand as though on a ledge, in shallow but convincing space, interacting only slightly with one another. Although the artist has segmented the mural into panels separated by black bands, the figures overlap these panels so freely that there is no strong sense of individual episodes or compartments. Rather, the artist has established two rhythms—one of the figures and another of the dividing bands—both contributing to a strong design unity.

For all their production in sculpture and painting, the Romans are best known for their architecture and engineering. We saw one of their engineering masterpieces, the Pont du Gard (398), in Chapter 13. But the most familiar monument—indeed, for many travelers the very symbol of Rome—is the Roman Colosseum (466).

The Colosseum was planned under the Emperor Vespasian and dedicated in A.D. 80 as an amphitheater for gladiatorial games and public entertainments. A large oval covering 6 acres, the Colosseum could accommodate some fifty thousand spectators—about the same number as most major-league baseball stadiums today. Few of the games played inside, however, were as tame as baseball. Gladiators vied with one another and with wild animals in extraordinarily bloody and gruesome contests, made possible because an extensive system of sewers under the Colosseum could drain away the gore. On special occasions the whole structure could be filled with water for quite realistic naval battles.

While the Colosseum served as headquarters for some rather bloodthirsty activity, its architectural achievement represented the highest ideals of the Romans. Even in its ruined state this structure displays the genius of the Romans as builders. The Colosseum rises on three tiers of arches, each of the levels distinguished from the next by a different style of column between the arches—Doric on the lowest level, Ionic on the second, and Corinthian on the third (396). Around the base are eighty arched openings for entry and exit; it is said that the entire building could be emptied in a matter of minutes. Above all, the structure is logical and coherent. Roman architects tell us in visual detail exactly how the building is organized—which parts are separate from other parts, where to enter, where to go, and so on. The exterior view gives us a clear sense of the inside, the walkways, the scheme as a whole. Today the Colosseum seems romantic; tourists dream of exploring it by moonlight. In its prime, it must have been the crown of the empire.

466. Colosseum, Rome.
A.D. 72–80.
Concrete; height 160′,
diameters 620′ and 513′.

Second only to the Colosseum for architectural grandeur in Rome is the Pantheon **(467)**, the temple to "all the gods." The Pantheon was built in the reign of Trajan's successor, the emperor Hadrian, who had an avid interest in architecture and apparently took a hand in the design. In form the building is simple though massive: a cylinder, topped by a hemispherical dome, fronted by a columned rectangular porch **(468)**. From the outside it may seem clumsy, almost like an immense oil-storage drum with a classic temple porch stuck incongruously on one end. What we see today, however, is not quite what the architects intended. In Roman times the surrounding streets were much lower; a flight of steps leading to the porch was exposed, and this probably contributed to the design harmony. Still, we might suspect that the Pantheon's architects deliberately kept the exterior plain so as not to spoil the "surprise." For the truly spectacular effect of the building comes from walking inside, from suddenly being within the huge space the walls enclose.

The interior of the Pantheon, as we saw from Panini's painting in Chapter 13 **(401)**, is impressive even by today's standards—142 feet high and 140 feet across. Around the base are seven niches that originally held statues (visible in the painting, but now gone) of the "sky" gods: the Sun, the Moon, Mercury, Venus, Mars, Jupiter, and Saturn. Above this level the dome stretches up in a perfect half sphere, carved out with recessed squares called **coffers,** which lighten the dome both visually and structurally. As noted in Chapter 13, the only opening is a 29-foot-wide **oculus,** or eye, at the very top of the dome. Visitors familiar with today's giant indoor spaces, such as the sports stadiums, should bear in mind that the Romans did not have space-age materials. The Pantheon is built of simple concrete. And we can marvel at the engineering genius needed to enclose a space of this size in concrete—and keep it enclosed for nearly two thousand years.

The Pantheon has been in use continually to the present day. Early in the 7th century it became a Christian church, which it remains. This fact points up the first of two changes that will lead our brief chronological survey of art into new areas. One is the increasing importance of the Christian faith; the other, the shift in power within the Roman Empire from the city of Rome to the East.

right: 467. The Pantheon, Rome. A.D. 118–125.

below: 468. Section drawing of the Pantheon.

section of the Pantheon

The Early Christians and Byzantium

469. *Gravestone of Severa,
with Adoration of the Magi,*
from the Catacomb of Priscilla,
Rome. A.D. c. 330.
Marble, height 12⁹⁄₁₆″.
Vatican Museums, Rome.

According to tradition, Jesus, known as the Christ or "anointed one," was born in the year we call A.D. 1. In time his followers would become so influential in world affairs that our common calendar refers to dates as being "B.C." (before Christ) or "A.D." (*anno Domini,* the year of our Lord). As a matter of fact, the 6th-century calendar makers who devised this plan were wrong in their calculations. Jesus probably was born between four and six years earlier than they had supposed—but we still use the calendar.

The faith Jesus preached spread throughout the Mediterranean world—that is to say, through the Roman Empire—at a surprisingly rapid rate. By about the year 111 the Emperor Trajan felt it necessary to issue an order to his provincial governors allowing them to punish citizens who openly practiced Christianity. The new religion presented a threat to the empire for several reasons, including the fact that it challenged the concept of emperor worship built into the older Roman faith. For more than three hundred years Christians were actively persecuted under the banners of Rome. As a result, they took their religion underground—quite literally. In complex networks of dugout tunnels called **catacombs** the early Christians retreated from danger, buried their dead, and sometimes assembled for worship. Their art was for the most part simple, capable of being hidden away. The gravestone of a Christian named Severa **(469)**, found in a catacomb, shows a portrait of the deceased at left, the three Wise Men bringing gifts to the child Jesus at right, and the inscription *in deo vivas* ("live in God").

The lot of the Christians changed abruptly in the early 4th century when the Emperor Constantine came to power. Far more than his predecessors, Constantine was sympathetic to the Christian religion, and he was baptized in that faith just before he died. Two actions by Constantine would have profound effect on the art and culture of the time. In 313 the emperor issued an edict of tolerance for all religions. The Christians could come out from their underground hiding places and begin to build real churches. Then in 330 Constantine abandoned Rome and moved his capital eastward. He named his new capital city after himself—Constantinople—but the ancient world knew it as Byzantium.

Byzantine art differs from its Greek and Roman precursors in two distinct ways. First, it is an art based on Christianity. No longer was art diffused into the portrayal of many gods and ideals. One god, one faith, one tradition—these became the standards of Byzantine art. Second, Byzantine art has an Eastern flavor in both style and materials. The Byzantine style is essentially flat, with an emphasis on elaborate decoration rather than naturalistic depiction. And, whereas the Greek or Roman artist might prefer to work in paint or marble, the Byzantine artist concentrated on the art of **mosaic**—small stones or pieces of tile or glass arranged in a pattern.

470. *Empress Theodora and Retinue.* c. 547. Mosaic. San Vitale, Ravenna.

We see an excellent example of this mosaic art in the portrait panel of *Empress Theodora* **(470)**, wife of the 6th-century emperor Justinian. The *Theodora* mosaic is especially splendid in its rich, vibrant colors and sumptuous decorative details. Many scholars feel the panel was intended to reinforce the royal status of—perhaps even give religious status to—the queen, who was of low birth and had been an actress before her marriage. Thus, Theodora is garbed in purple, the color of royalty, and there is a lavish use of gold throughout the picture. The "halo" effect around the queen's head has suggested to some writers that she was supposed to be identified with the Virgin Mary, mother of Jesus.

The design character of Byzantine art is well illustrated by this mosaic. Theodora is meant to be in procession, with her retinue trailing behind her, but we get little sense of this movement. Also, while the artist has used some overlapping, especially in the attendants at right, all the figures appear to be in the same plane, and that plane is identical with the ornately decorated background. But neither motion nor a sense of rounded figures in depth was important to the Byzantine artist and the intended audience. Far more compelling was the impression of quiet dignity, the appearance of an empress in majesty accepting the homage of her subjects, and these qualities are conveyed splendidly. The effect seems even more remarkable when we remember this image was put together from tiny pieces, like a giant picture puzzle.

Theodora's mosaic is housed in a building that represents one of the high points of Byzantine architecture—the church of San Vitale **(471)**, built in the early 6th century. At this point Eastern styles in art and architecture had spread westward; San Vitale is in the Italian city of Ravenna. Its ground plan **(472)** reveals its somewhat unusual spatial organization—unusual, that is, for a church in Western Europe. Most Early Christian churches were simple rectangles; later, churches in the West adopted the cross plan, consisting of a long main section intersected by a shorter section at right angles to the first. In either of these plans one enters through a door at one end, and straight ahead at the other end is the altar. The axis, or main line of sight, is from door to altar, horizontally through the church. San Vitale, with its Eastern character, is not like that. It is a central-plan church, built in the form of an octagon, and so the focus of attention is in the center of the building, immediately under the dome. The major axis, therefore, is vertical, from floor to dome (or earth to Heaven), with the altar off to one side. The central plan remained a feature of Eastern churches long after the cross plan had become firmly established in the West.

San Vitale is fairly small, a perfect little jewel of a church. At least five of its size could be contained within another Byzantine church built just at the same time—the magnificent Hagia Sophia in Constantinople (473). We saw the interior of Hagia Sophia in Chapter 13 (402). Our view of the outside gives a better sense of the building's massive scale and helps to show why it is considered the masterpiece of Byzantine architecture. The mighty dome, floating 183 feet above floor level, dominates the landscape, testifying as much to the glory of the empire as to the faith celebrated within. In time that faith would change. The pointed towers at the four corners, called **minarets,** are not original but were added in the 15th century when Hagia Sophia became an Islamic mosque.

above left: 471.
Exterior of apse, San Vitale, Ravenna. c. 527–47.

above: 472.
Plan of San Vitale, Ravenna.

left: 473. Hagia Sophia, Istanbul. 532–37.
Height of dome 183'.

Byzantine art would continue to flourish in Eastern Europe for another thousand years. Meanwhile, however, great changes were underway in the western portion of the continent. By the time San Vitale and Hagia Sophia were built, the old Roman Empire had effectively ceased to exist. New groups of people were settling and establishing their own cultures throughout Western Europe. Inevitably, they brought with them their own styles of art. It is to these people that we now turn our attention.

The Middle Ages in Europe

The authors of history books give us labels, convenient terms for naming things. Some time ago historians agreed that the "old" world ended just about when Hagia Sofia was built, in the mid-6th century. They also agreed that the "new" world began some eight hundred years later with the Renaissance. Nowadays such tidy cubbyholes seem naive, but labels can be hard to shake off. Although we may no longer refer to these periods as old and new, we still call the intervening time "middle."

The same historians who coined the undistinguished term "Middle Ages" gave a bad reputation to the first few centuries, dubbing them "Dark Ages." If taken literally, this name would imply that a great cloud descended over Europe, causing a gloom and stillness in art as well as life. Now we know that the cloud was imposed by our own ignorance, that the period in question seemed "dark" only because our vision was limited, our knowledge scant. Both art and life went on with a great deal of vigor, but their traces were hard to find. Little by little the cloud has lifted. As we learn more about the "Dark Ages," they do not seem very dark at all.

THE "DARK" AGES

The kingdoms of the early Middle Ages in Europe were inhabited by descendants of migratory tribes that had traveled southward and westward on the continent during the 4th and 5th centuries. Ethnically Germanic, these peoples emerged, for the most part, from the north-central part of Europe, or what today we would call northern Germany and Scandinavia (map p. 397). The Romans referred to them as "barbarians"—and with some justification, for, being nomadic, they had a considerably lower level of culture than did the settled citizens of the empire. Moreover, it was continual invasion by the

474. Purse cover, from the Sutton Hoo Ship Burial. 625–33. Gold with garnets and enamels, length 7½". The British Museum, London (reproduced by courtesy of the Trustees).

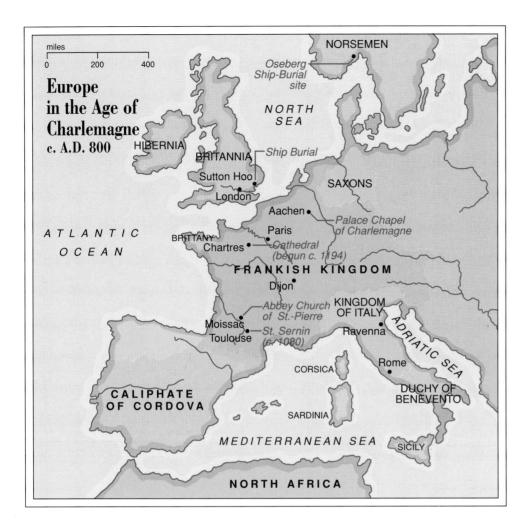

Europe
in the Age of
Charlemagne
c. A.D. 800

"barbarians" that brought about the empire's ultimate collapse, near the end of the 5th century.

By the year 600 the migrations were essentially over, and kingdoms roughly approximating the nations of modern Europe had been established. For purposes of this discussion, we will focus initially on the peoples who settled in three areas—the Angles and Saxons in Britain, the Norsemen in Scandinavia, and the Franks in Gaul (modern France).

On the island of Britain north of London (then Londinium) was Sutton Hoo, where the grave of an unknown 7th-century East Anglian king has been found. Objects discovered at the burial site include a superb gold and enamel purse cover **(474)**, with delicately made designs. The motifs are typical of the *animal style* prevalent in art of northwestern Europe at that time—a legacy, very likely, from the migratory herdsmen who were these people's ancestors. The term "animal style" came to refer not only to the actual depiction of animals but also to the intricate tracery of lines and bands that often accompanies the animal images. We see this tracery clearly in the upper left and right medallions of the Sutton Hoo purse cover.

Animal-style art also flourished in Scandinavia. A particularly rich trove of carved-wood objects was found at Oseberg in southern Norway, in a buried Viking ship dating from the early 9th century. The Oseberg ship, itself made of wood and decorated with a wonderfully carved prow, is believed to have been a luxury vessel intended for cruising the coastline and rivers. Among its contents was a splendid animal head **(475)** that adorned the top of a post—the sort of post probably carried in religious processions. The animal style is evident in the ribbonlike tracery of the creature's head and neck—astonishingly skillful for carving in wood.

475. *Animal Head,*
from Oseberg Burial Ship.
c. 825. Wood,
overall height c. 18″.
University Museum of
National Antiquities, Oslo.

476. *Portrait of Christ* page, from the *Book of Kells.* c. 800. Illumination, color on vellum; 13 × 9⅝". The Board of Trinity College, Dublin.

Animal style also appears in paintings of this time. Such painting as we know from the early Middle Ages is mostly in the form of manuscripts, and mostly done in the service of the Christian Church. Christianity centers on the Bible, a collection of sacred writings put down over many centuries and collected into one book (the word "bible" comes from the Greek and Latin words for "book"), probably in the 8th century. For the teaching and practice of faith, it was essential to possess a Bible, and in this era, long before the invention of the printing press, manuscripts had to be copied laboriously by hand. Most of the work was done by monks, who toiled in special writing centers known as *scriptoria.* Gradually, the practice evolved of decorating, or *illuminating,* the prose manuscripts with drawings, paintings, and elaborate capital letters.

Among the most famous of the early illuminated manuscripts is the *Book of Kells*, probably made in the mid-8th century in Scotland or Ireland. The *Portrait of Christ* page **(476)** shows the lengths to which these miniaturists would go in richness of color and ornamental design. (The page is only 13 inches high, requiring exceptional attention to fine detail.) Christ's figure is obviously central to this image, yet the animal-style decoration all but takes over the composition. The head is flanked by richly drawn peacocks, and elaborate interlacings of lines and bands fill the decorative borders, even appearing in Christ's hair. Few periods in the history of art have indulged in such lavish ornamentation.

Across the English Channel in France a different style of art was taking root, a style called *Carolingian*, after the emperor Charlemagne. Charlemagne, or Charles the Great, was a powerful Frankish king whose military conquests eventually gave him control over most of Western Europe. On Christmas Day of the year 800 the Pope crowned Charlemagne Holy Roman Emperor—making him the first of many rulers to bear that title. The title is significant because it united two major forces. Charlemagne was *Roman* in that he thought of himself as inheriting the legacy of the old Roman Empire. He was called *holy* for being a Christian king, the dominant Christian king.

Carolingian art derives more from Roman traditions than from the styles of the northern peoples. To see the contrast of Carolingian painting with animal-style examples, we need only look at another manuscript illumination, this one made in the early 9th century. The *St. Matthew* page from *The Gospel Book of Archbishop Ebbo* **(477)** depicts that saint hard at work transcribing what would become the first book of the Bible's New Testament. Everything about Matthew suggests a frenzy of creative inspiration, from the agitated drapery of his clothing to the intense concentration on his face. Even his feet and toes seem tensed by the effort of his project. Although this portrait of the Gospel writer may seem stylized and even exaggerated to our eyes, it is remarkably naturalistic when compared with the Christ page from the *Book of Kells*. There is some attempt to place Matthew in a natural setting and an absence of the intricate decoration that marks animal-style art.

Charlemagne seems to have been very much aware of past glories in the old Roman Empire, and he wished to imitate or surpass them in his own reign, his own empire. Following the example of many Roman emperors before him, he took an active interest in artistic and cultural matters. At his capital, Aachen, Charlemagne ordered built a splendid Palace Chapel to be his personal place of worship **(478)**. The architecture of the chapel gives several clues to his ambitions. Its basic design is modeled after San Vitale in Ravenna **(471)**, which Charlemagne apparently had seen and admired. Very likely he wished to copy the perfection of that octagonal church, to match the architectural ideals of Byzantium. At the same time, however, the details of the Palace Chapel are much heavier, more solid, more *Roman*, especially the robust Roman arches. Charlemagne—the Frankish king from the north—intended to be a Roman emperor, even to the design of his holy place.

left: 477.
St. Matthew the Evangelist,
from *The Gospel Book of Archbishop Ebbo.*
Before 823.
Illumination, $10\frac{1}{4} \times 7\frac{7}{8}''$.
Bibliothèque de la Ville, Epernay.

right: 478. Palace Chapel of Charlemagne, Aachen. 792–805.

Some writers consider Charlemagne's coronation day to be the end of the "Dark Ages." The emperor was crowned not by his own people but rather by the Pope, the leader of the Christian religion, and he was crowned *Holy* Roman Emperor. For the first time a political ruler had the sanction of the Church of Rome, and this opened a new chapter in European history.

The Christian faith was not the only one practiced in Europe. Older religions retained their adherents in the north, Jews were settled throughout Europe, and the Islamic Empire took control of Spain in the early 8th century. But Christianity was dominant, and the next several centuries would bring its greatest period of strength—and its greatest period of building.

AN ERA OF FAITH: THE HIGH MIDDLE AGES

The Middle Ages was a time of intense religious preoccupation in Europe. It was during this era that most of the great cathedrals were built. Also, a major portion of the art that has come down to us is associated with monasteries, churches, and cathedrals.

Historians generally divide the art and architecture of the high Middle Ages into two periods: the **Romanesque,** from about 1050 to 1200, based on southern styles from the old Roman Empire; and the **Gothic,** from about 1200 into the 15th century, which has more of a northern flavor. (The term "Gothic" derives from the Goths, who were among the many nomadic tribes sweeping through Europe during the 4th and 5th centuries. It was applied to this style by later critics in the Renaissance, who considered the art and architecture of their immediate predecessors to be vulgar and "barbarian.")

Although there was no sharp dividing line between the Romanesque and the Gothic, we can find many differences in their characteristic styles. These differences should be evident as we compare examples from each, first in architecture, then in sculpture.

In Chapter 13 we studied the interiors of two grand French cathedrals—St. Sernin in Toulouse and Chartres **(399,400)**. Now let us consider the outsides of these two structures, in views focused toward the *apse*—the main altar area—of each.

479. St. Sernin, Toulouse, France, view toward the apse. c. 1080.

480. Chartres Cathedral, France, view toward the apse. c. 1194–1260.

The Cathedral of St. Sernin is a splendid example of the Romanesque style **(479)**. Although the interior of the nave **(399)** soars upward to a breathtaking height, from the outside the church seems to hug the ground—solid, durable, *Roman*. The plan is absolutely symmetrical, with a single tower rising from the center. (The tower is of a later date and has some Gothic influence.) Arches around the windows are classic round Roman arches, and they are arranged in a regular, logical progression, with columns in between (compare the Colosseum, **466**). Also, we see a minimum of decorative detail on the façade; all the statuary is inside the building. This cathedral was meant to turn inward, to gather worshipers inside its core and shelter them there. St. Sernin gives us an impression of stability, of a church firmly rooted and dependable, representing a faith meant to endure forever.

Chartres Cathedral **(480)**, some 300 miles to the north and begun a century or so later, is very different in its lofty Gothic design. As St. Sernin hugs the earth, Chartres reaches upward to the heavens. As St. Sernin appears solid and durable, Chartres was intended to seem weightless. From the outside, Chartres looks to be all points and spires and intricate decorative detail. The exterior of the cathedral is embellished with more than two thousand carved figures **(482)**—not visible in this overall photograph—which serve as a transition between the town and the church, a welcoming committee, so to speak, for the faithful as they enter.

Chartres has two tall spires, notable for their very different designs and the consequent lack of symmetry. Its arches are not the round ones of a Romanesque building, but rather the pointed arches developed in the Gothic period **(400)**. Another innovation of Gothic architecture was the flying buttress (p. 331), an exterior support meant to control the outward thrust of thin masonry walls built very high. The flying buttresses around the apse of Chartres are plainly visible in the photograph **(480)**. All in all, the Gothic cathedral, as interpreted at Chartres, reveals an architecture of soaring ambitions, celebrating a faith that simultaneously reaches outward to the townspeople and up to the skies.

The sculpture of the high Middle Ages offers similarly interesting comparisons between the Romanesque and Gothic styles. As suggested earlier, most of it focused on religious themes and was made to embellish church buildings. The sculptors who created these carvings were itinerant stonecutters, who traveled about Europe from job to job, working on whichever church was currently in progress. Judging by the sheer number of sculptures, there must have been virtual armies of skilled carvers.

left: 481.
Tomb of Abbot Durandus,
column relief
at St.-Pierre de Moissac,
France. c. 1100.

right: 482.
Melchisedek, Abraham,
and Moses,
column sculptures
from North Porch
of Chartres Cathedral.
13th century.

At Moissac, in southwestern France, is the abbey church dedicated to St. Peter, or in French St.-Pierre, built from the late 11th century onward. The memorial portrait of its abbot, *Durandus* (481), is carved as a column relief and is in the Romanesque style. Durandus' figure stands contained within the round Roman arch, his shoulders and vestments echoing the arch. His pose is fully frontal, almost perfectly symmetrical. The low-relief carving and delicate lines were influenced by manuscript illumination styles (compare 476), with their flattened, decorative imagery. Romanesque sculptors were more interested in relating the carving to the architecture than in creating rounded, naturalistic forms.

Barely a hundred years later the stonecarvers of the Gothic period had "opened up" their figures, to give them more volume and greater independence from the architectural supports. The illustration shows a group of column sculptures from the north porch of Chartres Cathedral, representing the Old Testament prophets Melchisedek, Abraham, and Moses (482). Each of the figures is attached to a column, but they are not imprisoned by the columnar structure. They are convincingly rounded bodies, individuals with their own personalities, looking out, perhaps, to greet the visitors who will pass through the cathedral's doors.

The medieval carver's task was not only artistic but also instructional. For a largely illiterate populace, the sculptors had to interpret the Bible stories clearly, to make the figures recognizable. For example, in this grouping from Chartres, the figure of Abraham is identified by his son Isaac held before him. The most familiar story about Abraham tells of God testing the prophet by asking that he sacrifice the child (see also 486). Similar clues are provided for the other figures. Beyond the teaching function, however, these personalizing touches may cause us to relate to the sculptures more actively. They seem less like architectural enrichment, more like people.

Our comparison of Romanesque and Gothic sculptures shows the trend toward naturalism, toward greater volume and roundness. Sculptures were beginning to come down off the wall and inhabit their own space. Much the same tendency is evident in painting of the period, as the decorative flatness of manuscript styles gave way to a search for pictorial depth. This trend would accelerate in the 14th century, for we are approaching the era when naturalism in art would be more important than ever before or since.

TOWARD THE RENAISSANCE

Claus Sluter, a Dutch sculptor who worked in France in the late 14th century, brought his figures even farther off the wall than had the artisans of Chartres. Sluter's most ambitious project was the so-called *Moses Well* (483), a six-sided stone pedestal featuring life-size portraits of six Old Testament prophets, carved in very high relief. The view illustrated here shows Moses on the right, Isaiah on the left. Perhaps the word "portraits" seems unusual, since no one really knows what the patriarchs looked like. But Sluter has taken pains to depict them as individual personalities, vibrant and animated, so that we feel he has captured the character of each. The prophets do not stand rigidly, bonded to their background, but instead reach out to interact with one another and with the viewer.

The prophets at Chartres (482), while fully rounded, have a columnar aspect. Their bodies are compressed—shoulders rigid, arms close to the torso, legs straight—and their garments fall in orderly pleats. If one could take them down from the columns, they would still look rather like columns themselves. But Sluter's figures have a presence of their own, independent of any backing. Their heads lean forward, shoulders twist, arms are bent at the elbow—in short, we sense that they *could* walk down off the wall.

Beside the Chartres sculptures, Sluter's figures are monumental, seeming especially massive because they are encased in a heavy swirl of drapery. This last point is the key to why the *Moses Well* appears in this chapter rather than the next one. Sluter's work serves as a bridge between the art of the Middle Ages and the art of the Renaissance. In true Renaissance style the sculptor has carved lifelike, mobile figures; yet so profuse is the mountain of drapery that we have limited sense of the body underneath. It remained for the next generation to strip away the garments and study the human form.

483. Claus Sluter.
Moses Well. 1395–1406.
Stone, height of figures c. 6'.
Chartreuse de Champmol, Dijon.

Our two final artists in this chapter could easily be placed in the one that follows, as masters of the Renaissance. Like Claus Sluter, both were transitional artists, both were influential in making the shift from art styles of the Middle Ages to the quite different styles of the Renaissance. We place them here mainly because their major sources of inspiration were the vestiges of Byzantine art to the east and the medieval Gothic tradition to the north. Succeeding generations of artists would look to Greece and Rome.

Duccio was an artist of Siena, in Italy. His masterpiece was the *Maestà Altar*, a multisection panel meant to be displayed on the altar of a church, of which we illustrate the part showing *Christ Entering Jerusalem* (484). What is most interesting about this painting is Duccio's attempt to create believable space in a large outdoor scene—a concern that would absorb painters of the next century. Christ's entry into the city, celebrated now on Palm Sunday, was thought of as a triumphal procession, and Duccio has labored to convey the sense of movement and parade. A strong diagonal thrust beginning at the left with Christ and his disciples cuts across the picture to the middle right, then shifts abruptly to carry our attention to the upper left corner of the painting—a church tower that is Christ's presumed goal. The architecture plays an important role in defining space and directing movement. This was Duccio's novel, almost unprecedented, contribution to the art of the period, the use of architecture to enclose and demarcate space rather than to act as a simple backdrop.

Duccio's contemporary, a Florentine artist named Giotto, made an even more remarkable break with art traditions of the Middle Ages. Most of Giotto's best work was in fresco (Chapter 7), and the most notable examples are in a small church in Padua, called the Arena Chapel. *The Lamentation* (485),

484. Duccio.
Christ Entering Jerusalem,
detail of *Maestà Altar.*
1308–11. Panel, 40 × 21".
Cathedral Museum, Siena.

a work depicting Mary, St. John, and others mourning the dead Christ, illustrates Giotto's highly original use of space in painting. The scene has been composed as though it were on a stage and we the viewers are an audience participating in the drama. In other words, space going back from the picture plane seems to be continuous with space in front of the picture plane, the space in which we stand. Accustomed as we are now to this "window" effect in painting, it is difficult to imagine how revolutionary it was to medieval eyes, used to predominantly flat, decorative space in painting **(476,477)**. Moreover, Giotto seems to have developed this concept of space largely on his own, with little artistic precedent. The figures in *The Lamentation* are round and full-bodied, clustered low in the composition to enhance the effect of an event taking place just out of our reach.

Giotto's grouping of the figures is unusual and daring, with Christ's body half-hidden by a figure with its back turned. This arrangement seems casual and almost random, until we notice the slope of the hill directing attention to Christ's and the Virgin's heads, which are the focal point. Yet another innovation—perhaps Giotto's most important one—was his interest in depicting the psychological and emotional reactions of his subjects. The characters in *The Lamentation* interact in a natural, human way that gives this and the artist's other religious scenes a special warmth.

Neither Duccio nor Giotto had an especially long career. Each did his most significant work in the first decade of the 14th century. Yet in that short time the course of Western art history changed dramatically. Both artists had sought a new direction for painting—a more naturalistic, more human, more engaging representation of the physical world—and both had taken giant steps in that direction. Their experiments paved the way for a flowering of all the arts that would come in the next century and that its practitioners would name a "rebirth"—the Renaissance.

485. Giotto. *The Lamentation.* 1305–06. Fresco, 7'7" × 7'9". Arena Chapel, Padua.

Renaissance to Revolution

This chapter encompasses about four hundred years in the history of Western art—from the beginning of the 15th century to near the end of the 18th. The title "Renaissance to Revolution" is appropriate, because the period begins with the emergence of the Renaissance in Italy and concludes with three revolutions—the French, the American, and the Industrial—all of which occurred at roughly the same time. One could argue, however, that the title "Revolution to Revolution" would have done just as well, for in a real sense the Renaissance was a revolution in the world of art. Nearly everything about art changed, and changed quickly—the types of art being made, the way works of art looked, the materials used, the role of the artist, the identities and influence of patrons, and the artistic precedents that served as inspiration.

Before discussing the components of this "revolution" that was the Renaissance, we might address the question of why it occurred, especially why it occurred at the time and place it did. Italy in the 15th century offered a perfect combination of circumstances. For one thing, the conditions for artistic patronage were unusually favorable. Italy had developed powerful city-states engaged in extensive trade and banking. The members of the merchant class, at the head of this commerce, had a great deal of money to spend, were well educated, and were highly motivated for reasons of prestige and temperament to invest in art. Also, the Christian church was centered in Italy, and it provided another important source of patronage.

Besides the abundance of customers for art, there was ready inspiration for art. During this period a growing interest in the past led to the excavation of Classical Greek and Roman ruins, which revealed architecture and sculpture that had not been seen for centuries. Many of the leading artists of the Renaissance studied these works and took them as models.

Finally, we might be tempted to say that the Renaissance began in Italy in the 15th century because Michelangelo, Leonardo, Raphael, and others were there. But perhaps another age with the same social and historical advantages would have spawned artists of equal genius. We cannot know for sure, but the problem is intriguing. Let us now sum up the changes that took place in art; we will refer to them again as they are illustrated in specific examples. Some have already been mentioned in previous chapters.

The types of art made during the Renaissance included all those that had been popular during the Middle Ages—sculpture, architecture, tapestry, and so forth—but there was a much greater emphasis on painting. Throughout the medieval period, painting had taken rather a back seat to the other arts. Although miniatures and frescoes continued to be made, artists of the Middle Ages showed little interest in the "easel painting," the precious object to be hung on the wall for its own sake. But in the Renaissance painting came to life, with an energy perhaps never before seen. The Renaissance has been called "the age of painting"; this may be an overstatement in view of the splendid sculpture and architecture it produced, but the phrase is certainly true when we compare the Renaissance to the several centuries preceding it.

For the first time since the Classical periods of Greece and Rome the quest for "realism"—the faithful representation of the natural world— dominated art. Painters and sculptors dissected corpses to better understand the mysteries of human anatomy. Elaborate studies of perspective were undertaken (p. 133) to create the illusion of accurate three-dimensional space. It was during the Renaissance that the notion of art as mirror of the physical world became set, a notion that persists in some people's minds even today.

Since painting was newly popular, artists took great interest in its physical properties, and the materials of that medium changed radically. Oil paint, which was introduced in northern Europe (perhaps by Jan van Eyck, **236**), soon eclipsed the more cumbersome tempera (Chapter 7, p. 198). New techniques of fresco painting were perfected. On the whole, there was a great deal of experimentation with materials, some of it rewarding, some of it disastrous. Leonardo da Vinci, whose curiosity about the world seems to have been boundless, was most prone to try new techniques, and some of his best-known works have deteriorated badly **(152,581)**. Nevertheless, the experimentation led to some extraordinary developments.

The changing role of the artist is a fascinating aspect of the Renaissance. Up until that time the vast majority of Western artists had been anonymous. In isolated cases we may have a name; we know, for example, that

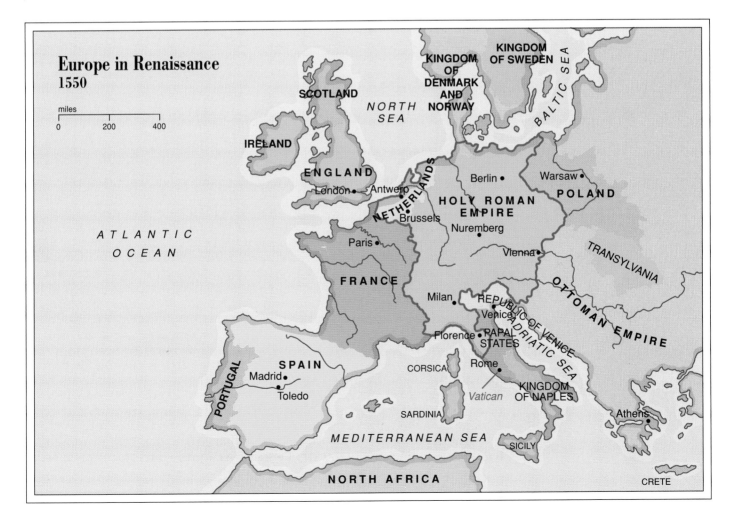

CHRONOLOGY

Style/Period	Political/Social Events and Personalities	Monuments/Major Artists
1 4 0 0 – 1 6 0 0		
Aztec Empire, Mexico, c. 1350–1521 Ming Dynasty, China, 1368–1644 Muromachi Period, Japan, 1392–1573 Renaissance, Italy, c. 1400–c. 1600 Renaissance, Northern Europe, c. 1500–c. 1600 Benin "classical" period, Africa, 1550–1680	Joan of Arc burned at the stake, 1431 Printing press invented, c. 1450 Lorenzo de' Medici, ruler of Florence, 1469–1492 Christopher Columbus landed in the Americas, 1492 Henry VIII, king of England, 1509–1547 Martin Luther, beginning of Protestant Reformation in Europe, 1517 William Shakespeare, 1564–1616	St. Peter's, Vatican, Rome, c. 1450–1663 **(432,496)** Sistine Chapel frescoes, Rome, 1508–1512 **(495)** Jan van Eyck (1370?–1440?) Donatello (1386–1466) Masaccio (1401–1428) Sandro Botticelli (1444?–1510) Hieronymus Bosch (c. 1450–1516) Leonardo da Vinci (1452–1519) Albrecht Dürer (1471–1528) Michelangelo (1475–1564) Raphael (1483–1520) Titian (c. 1490–1576) El Greco (1541?–1614)
1 6 0 0 – 1 7 0 0		
Baroque Period, Europe Colonial Period, North America Edo Period, Japan, 1615–1868 Qing Dynasty, China, 1644–1912	Catholic Counter Reformation in Europe *Mayflower* landed on coast of North America, 1620 Louis XIV, king of France, 1643–1715	Taj Mahal, India, 1632–1653 **(403)** Cornaro Chapel, Rome, 1645–1652 **(505,506)** Versailles Palace, France, 1661–1688 **(511,512)** Peter Paul Rubens (1577–1640) Gianlorenzo Bernini (1598–1680) Diego Velázquez (1599–1660) Rembrandt (1606–1669) Jan Vermeer (1632–1675)
1 7 0 0 – 1 8 0 0		
Rococo Style, Europe Colonial Period, North America Edo Period, Japan, 1615–1868 Qing Dynasty, China, 1644–1912	Louis XV, king of France, 1715–1774 Louis XVI, king of France, 1774–1792 American Declaration of Independence, 1776 American Revolution, 1775–1783 French Revolution, begun 1789	Antoine Watteau (1684–1721) Jean Baptiste Siméon Chardin (1699–1779) François Boucher (1703–1770) Jean Honoré Fragonard (1732–1806) Francisco de Goya (1746–1828) Jacques Louis David (1748–1825) Elisabeth Vigée-Lebrun (1755–1842)

Praxiteles was a great genius of Greek sculpture, and we know what his work looked like **(357)**. Beyond that, we have little information about the man himself. Even this much is an advantage over our knowledge of most artists in the 13th and 14th centuries. The medieval artist, in general, was considered a skilled craftsman, little more. A talented wood- or stone-carver might be given the same respect that today is accorded to a first-rate carpenter—valuable, indispensable when needed, forgotten when the job is finished. Of course, there were exceptions, and a few names have come down to us, but not many. It is for this reason that none of the artists' biographies in this book predate the 15th century.

Starting with the great masters of the Renaissance we suddenly have rather complete portraits of the artists—who they were, how they lived and worked, what they thought about art and life in general. For the first time artists were considered a breed apart, comprising a class of their own that transcended the social class determined by birth—not nobility, not bourgeoisie, not clergy, but a separate and elite category of people respected not because of who they were, but because of what they could *do*. They lived in the courts of the nobles and popes, they moved freely in good society, their company was sought after, their services in demand. That role has remained essentially unchanged into the 20th century.

As mentioned earlier, the character of art patronage reflected the changing times. Before the Renaissance only two groups of people could afford to be art patrons—the nobility and the clergy. Both continued to be active sponsors of art, but they were joined in the 15th century by a new merchant class, very rich, socially ambitious, fully able to support extravagant spending on art. These were the forerunners of today's corporate patrons of the arts. The climate could not have been more fertile for a flowering of art: the best artists were available, and virtually unlimited funds existed to support them.

One more element is needed to complete our picture of the Renaissance artist—the changing sources of inspiration. The Renaissance individual was very much aware of being part of a Golden Age, an age of reason and enlightenment and achievement. Only twice, to anyone's knowledge, had such a situation existed before. Renaissance artists cast their eyes backward to those they considered their natural teachers—the great masters of Greece and Rome. To their everlasting credit these later artists were not satisfied merely to imitate, but forged a new style of art that at least equaled the standards of the Classical world. With this preamble, then, let us look at the artists of the Renaissance.

The Renaissance in Italy

In 1401 the city of Florence announced an artistic competition, the winner of which would be awarded the commission for making sculptured bronze doors to decorate the Baptistry of the Cathedral. At least six artists were invited to submit trial pieces. The subject was to be the sacrifice of Isaac, from the biblical story in which God tested the faith of Abraham by requiring him to slay his son, Isaac. (At the last moment the Lord, convinced of Abraham's obedience, spared the boy.) Among those submitting designs to the competition was a twenty-three-year-old goldsmith, Lorenzo Ghiberti. Ghiberti's trial panel **(486)** shows a strong sense of composition; its action is

486. Lorenzo Ghiberti. *Sacrifice of Isaac.* 1401. Gilt bronze, 21 × 17½". National Museum, Florence.

compact, with a subtle curving rhythm from lower right to upper left, and the figures of Abraham and Isaac at middle right are emphasized to create a focal point. Isaac's nude body reveals Ghiberti's admiration for ancient statues and is a true Renaissance figure. Ghiberti won the prize and spent much of the next two decades working on the doors.

Shortly after the doors were installed, Ghiberti was asked to make another set, this time for the east side of the Baptistry, and this time without any need to prove himself in competition. The east doors were more than twenty-five years in the making, and finally were installed in 1452. So marvelous were their design and craftsmanship that Michelangelo termed them the "Gates of Paradise," and so they have been called ever since (487).

Between the time of the first competition and the completion of the "Gates of Paradise"—half a century—Ghiberti's style had matured considerably. We saw one panel of the later doors in Chapter 11 (353). The artist had made extensive studies of perspective, allowing him to create the illusion of spatial depth on the shallow bronze doors. And he is in full control of three-dimensional volumes; some of the figures on the east doors are virtually in the round. The composition is simplified, less cluttered, easier to understand. In the span of time from the trial panel to the "Gates of Paradise," Ghiberti made the transition from the first gropings of the Renaissance to a more assured style that foreshadowed the sculptures of Michelangelo's generation.

While Ghiberti was working on the first set of bronze doors for the Baptistry, he was assisted by, among others, the young sculptor Donatello. Donatello was born in Florence about 1386 and was apprenticed to Ghiberti by the age of seventeen. During his long career he worked in many different styles and in all the sculptural media then available—wood, stone, and metal. An early work, the statue of *St. Mark* in Florence (488), depends on Donatello's familiarity with two sources of inspiration—ancient Greek and Roman sculptures and the Scriptures. The figure is as naturalistic as any of

left: 487. Lorenzo Ghiberti. "Gates of Paradise," east doors of the Baptistry, Florence. 1425–52. Gilt bronze, height 18'6".

right: 488. Donatello. *St. Mark.* 1411–13. Marble, height 7'9". Or San Michele, Florence.

489. Masaccio.
The Tribute Money. c. 1427.
Fresco, 8'2¾" × 19'8¼".
Brancacci Chapel, Sta. Maria
del Carmine, Florence.

the Greek statues, yet there is a stamp of individual personality in both face and body that may have come from Donatello's reading of Mark's Gospel.

St. Mark shows many of the characteristics that came to typify Donatello's work and helps to explain why some writers consider Donatello to be the founder of modern sculpture. This statue is enclosed within a niche but is by no means dependent on the architectural framework for support. For the first time in centuries we see a sculpture that is totally self-sustaining—fully rounded and capable of standing on its own. Moreover, Donatello's figure is remarkably lifelike. St. Mark seems caught in the act of movement, and his body underneath the garments seems real, substantial, made of flesh and bone. If you compare this statue to the figures on Sluter's *Moses Well* (**483**), carved a mere decade earlier, you will appreciate Donatello's originality. Sluter's prophets are wrapped in massive drapery that has a life of its own, independent of the body. But St. Mark's clothing responds to the form underneath. Where the left knee bends outward, the robe falls back; where the right arm is pressed to the body, the sleeve wrinkles. We know that if St. Mark moved, the garments would move with him.

At the same time that Donatello was exploring the potential for naturalism and animation in sculpture, the first painters of the Renaissance were grappling with the problems of conveying these qualities on a flat surface. Among the first of those who could indisputably be called a Renaissance artist was the young genius known as Masaccio, whose name has been variously translated as "wicked Tom" and "slovenly Tom." Masaccio lived for only twenty-seven years, and there are just four works that can be attributed to him definitely. Nevertheless, his contribution to the development of Early Renaissance art was immense.

Masaccio's best-known painting is *The Tribute Money* (**489**), a fresco in the Brancacci Chapel in Florence. The story related in this fresco is taken from the Gospel of St. Matthew and concerns an event in the life of Christ. Christ's disciples, especially Peter, had questioned whether it was proper to pay taxes to the Roman government, considering that Christ was the Messiah and above such authority. But Christ pointed out the difference between earthly and spiritual obligations and counseled that the taxes be paid, saying "Render therefore unto Caesar the things which are Caesar's; and unto God the things that are God's" (Matthew 22:21). He urged Peter to go and catch a fish, which would have a coin in its mouth, and to pay the tax collector.

To portray this fairly complicated story Masaccio has employed a device known as *continuous narrative.* Three different parts in the sequence of events are shown in the same painting. In the center, Christ is conferring with his disciples and instructing Peter to pay the tax. At left, Peter goes fishing and finds the coin; at right, he turns the coin over to the Roman tax

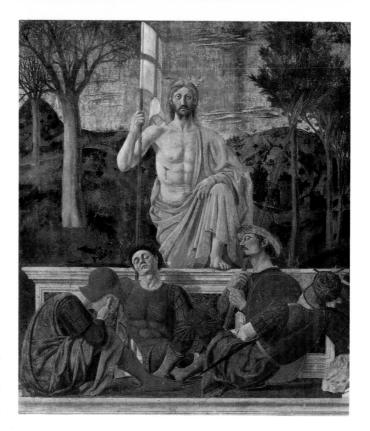

490. Piero della Francesca. *The Resurrection.* c. 1460. Fresco, 9'6" × 8'4". Gallery, Palazzo del Commune, Borgo San Sepolcro, Italy.

collector. Such a running narrative might have seemed awkward were it not for Masaccio's compositional powers. The most important scene is the conference among Christ and his twelve Apostles, just off center in the composition. Here the figures are drawn together in dramatic tension by their grouping and their gestures. The fishing segment is least important to Masaccio; he thrusts it far to the left in his composition. For the paying of the tribute money, the climax of the event, Masaccio has separated the two key figures—Peter and the tax collector—by an architectural background.

All of Masaccio's figures are well constructed, standing in relaxed *contrapposto* poses (p. 298). This effect is especially apparent in the legs of the tax collector in his two appearances. Like Donatello's *St. Mark,* the figures have real, living bodies under their garments, bodies that seem to have the muscle and bone to move. A comparison of this work with Duccio's *Christ Entering Jerusalem* **(484),** painted just a little over a century earlier, will show that great strides had been made in using linear perspective to depict architecture in three-dimensional space. Also, Masaccio's shading and treatment of drapery give convincing roundness to the bodies. The figures have a dignity and gravity that mark them as true products of the Renaissance.

Masaccio's art had a profound influence on another Florentine painter, who came into prominence about a generation later—Piero della Francesca. In Piero's fresco *The Resurrection* **(490)** we can see the artist's debt to Masaccio in the sure handling of linear perspective and the wonderful roundness of the bodies. Piero, however, was a skilled mathematician, and that is one of the things that sets his composition apart from the work of the earlier master. This picture is constructed as a triangle, with Christ's head at the apex. The triangle moves down to the two lower corners of the painting and cuts across the bottom, pulling the figures of Christ and the sleeping soldiers into one coherent group. There is a pronounced vertical axis from Christ's face straight down to the bottom of the painting. In spite of this structure, the picture does not seem rigid. The poses of the soldiers, as they lie sprawled in sleep, are by no means stiff. Also, Piero has introduced elements of asymmetrical balance to offset the predominantly symmetrical balance of the triangle. Christ's upraised arm with the banner juts out to one side of the central axis while his bent left knee pushes out to the other side. At their best, Renaissance painters imposed an order, often a geometrical order, on their compositions, but they did not let that order overwhelm their art.

Yet another Florentine painter, a quarter-century younger than Piero, was Sandro Botticelli. Botticelli was rather more sophisticated and worldly than most of his artist-contemporaries. While he painted many religious subjects, his earlier works took their subjects from Greek and Roman culture and the Classical myths. Also, he had a special fascination with detail and with the depiction of women as graceful, exquisite beings, so weightless they often seem about to float out of the paintings. Early in his career Botticelli had the great fortune to enjoy the patronage of the Medici, the ruling merchant family of Florence. At the beginning of this text, in Chapter 1, we pointed out that Botticelli's *Primavera* (13) was painted for a villa belonging to the Medici. Apparently, two large works were commissioned from Botticelli for that same villa, and the other was *The Birth of Venus* (491).

Venus was the Roman goddess of love and beauty. According to legend, she was born from the sea, and so Botticelli depicts her floating upward on a shell. Two Zephyrs, or wind gods, blow her gently toward the shore, where a figure representing spring waits ready to clothe Venus in a flowing garment. The portrayal of Venus, a pagan goddess, gave Botticelli a justification for doing what no artist, insofar as we know, had done since classical times—creating a large-scale female nude. Venus' pose is modeled after a Roman sculpture of the goddess, which Botticelli had studied in the Medici collection, but her lightness, her fragile quality, her delicate beauty and billowing hair—these are Botticelli's own.

As we can see in *The Birth of Venus*, Botticelli has mastered the technique of painting round, full-fleshed bodies. However, he is not nearly as interested as later artists would be in depicting deep, three-dimensional space. The space in *The Birth of Venus* is actually quite shallow, with the sea and horizon and trees serving as a backdrop, almost a stage set, and the figures are all set in the same plane. These characteristics mark Botticelli as an artist of the Early Renaissance. Painters of the next generation would strive to set their figures naturally in a deeper landscape.

We come now to a period known as the **High Renaissance**—a brief but glorious time in the history of art. In barely twenty-five years, from shortly

491. Sandro Botticelli.
The Birth of Venus. c. 1480.
Tempera on canvas, 6'7" × 9'2".
Uffizi, Florence.

before 1500 to about 1525, some of the most celebrated works of Western art were produced. Many artists participated in this brilliant creative endeavor, but the giants among them were unquestionably Leonardo da Vinci and Michelangelo.

The term "Renaissance man" is applied to someone who is very well informed about, or very good at doing, many different, often quite unrelated, things. It originated in the fact that several of the leading figures of the Renaissance were artistic jacks-of-all-trades. Michelangelo was painter, sculptor, poet, architect—incomparably gifted at all. Leonardo was painter, inventor, sculptor, architect, engineer, scientist, musician, and all-around intellectual. In our age of specialization these accomplishments seem staggering, but during the heady years of the Renaissance nothing was impossible.

Leonardo is the artist who most thoroughly embodies the term "Renaissance man"; many people consider him to have been the greatest genius who ever lived. Leonardo was possessed of a brilliant and inquiring mind that accepted no limits. Throughout his long life he remained absorbed by the problem of how things work, and how they might work. A typical example of his investigations is the well-known *Study of Human Proportions* (492), in which the artist sought to establish ideal proportions for the human body by relating it to the square and the circle. Above and below the figure is Leonardo's eccentric mirror writing, which he used in his notes and journals.

Leonardo's interest in mathematics is also evident from his careful rendering of perspective. In Chapter 4 we examined his masterpiece, *The Last Supper* (152), which uses one-point linear perspective to organize the many figures in the composition and set them into deep space. Yet another interest, experimental painting techniques, served the artist less well in *The Last Supper*. As we shall see in the Epilogue, the fresco has suffered severe deterioration and is undergoing a major restoration effort (581).

492. Leonardo da Vinci.
*Study of Human Proportions
According to Vitruvius.*
c. 1485–90.
Pen and ink, $13\frac{1}{2} \times 9\frac{3}{4}''$.
Academy, Venice.

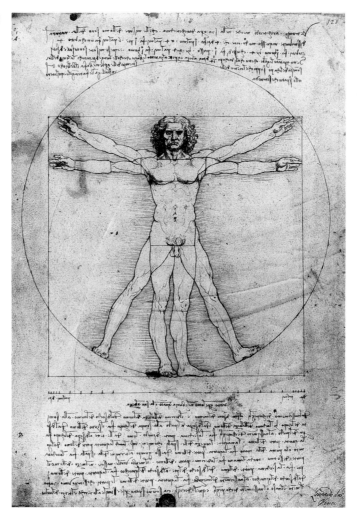

Leonardo da Vinci

1452–1519

No clues are offered by the scant knowledge about Leonardo's origins to explain what spawned perhaps the most complex imagination of all time. Leonardo was the illegitimate son of a peasant woman known only as Caterina and a fairly well-to-do notary, Piero da Vinci. He was raised in his father's house at Vinci and, when he was about fifteen, apprenticed to the Florentine artist Andrea del Verrocchio, in whose workshop he remained for about ten years.

In 1482 Leonardo left Florence for Milan, where he became official artist to Lodovico Sforza, duke of that city. There the artist undertook many projects, foremost among them his famous painting of the *Last Supper,* for which he used an experimental mural technique that caused the painting to deteriorate badly soon after its completion (Epilogue, **581**). Leonardo remained with Sforza until the latter's fall from power in 1499, after which he returned to Florence.

Sketches and written records indicate that Leonardo worked as a sculptor, but no examples remain. Only about a dozen paintings can be definitely attributed to him, and several of these are unfinished. There are, however, hundreds of drawings, and the thousands of pages from his detailed notebook testify to the man's extraordinary genius. If Leonardo completed relatively few artistic works, this can only be ascribed to the enormous breadth of his interests, which caused him repeatedly to turn from one subject to another. He was a skilled architect and engineer, engrossed in the problems of city planning, sanitary disposal, military engineering, and even the design of weapons. He made sketches for a crude submarine, a helicopter, and an airplane—with characteristic thoroughness also designing a parachute in case the airplane should fail. He made innovative studies in astronomy, anatomy, botany, geology, optics, and above all mathematics. His contemporaries reported his great talent as a musician—he played and improvised on the lute—as well as his love of inventive practical jokes.

In 1507 Leonardo was appointed court painter to the King of France, Louis XII, who happened to be in Milan at the time. Nine years later the aging artist was named court painter to Louis's successor, Francis I. Francis seems to have revered him for his towering reputation as an artist and his crisp intellect, but to have

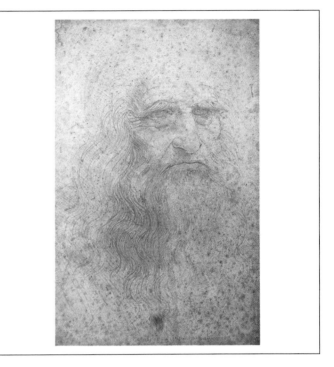

expected little artistic production from the old man. The king provided comfortable lodgings in the city of Amboise, where Leonardo died.

Solitary all his life, Leonardo did not marry, and he formed very few close attachments. His obsession seems to have been with getting it all down, recording the fertile outpourings of his brain and hand. In his *Treatise on Painting,* assembled from his notebook pages and published after his death, he advised painters to follow his method: "You should often amuse yourself when you take a walk for recreation, in watching and taking note of the attitudes and actions of men as they talk and dispute, or laugh or come to blows with one another . . . noting these down with rapid strokes, in a little pocket-book which you ought always to carry with you . . . for there is such an infinite number of forms and actions of things that the memory is incapable of preserving them."[1]

Leonardo da Vinci. *Self-Portrait.* c. 1512. Chalk on paper, 13 × 8¼". Biblioteca Reale, Turin.

493. Leonardo da Vinci. *Mona Lisa.* c. 1503–05. Oil on panel, 30¼ × 21″. Louvre, Paris.

Despite his vast accomplishments, Leonardo often had difficulty completing specific projects. Many of his most ambitious works were left unfinished, including his best-known painting, the *Mona Lisa* (**493**). The *Mona Lisa* has been the object of special fascination ever since it was painted. Songs, poems, and treatises have been written about the sitter's smile, and her image often turns up in remarkably unexpected contexts (p. 275, **544**). Just what is so magical about this painting is hard to define. Certainly the "mysterious" smile on the woman's face contributes to the *Mona Lisa*'s special aura, but it alone is not sufficient to explain the painting's fascination. For this work Leonardo was in masterful control of a newly developed technique known as *sfumato* (deriving from the Italian for "smoke"), which involves painting in thin glazes to achieve a hazy, cloudy atmosphere and a sense of three-dimensional form. Behind the model is a fantasy landscape, vague and undefined, another element of the painting's mystery. Some of the intrigue of the *Mona Lisa* must lie in its contradictions. It presents to us a Florentine matron, not at first glance beautiful, posed almost rigidly in the exact center of the painting, showing little of her emotions. Yet further acquaintance with the subject reveals beauty so unique as to ignore conventional ideas of beauty, a pose that is not rigid but serene, and a personality which, though elusive, draws us to her.

During the years when Leonardo was painting the *Mona Lisa*, Michelangelo, a quarter-century younger, also was in Florence, at work on one of the projects for which he is best known. That two such extraordinary figures could live and work in close proximity, surrounded by numerous others of scarcely lower stature, demonstrates how remarkable a time the High Renaissance was.

By the age of twenty-five Michelangelo had established his reputation as a sculptor. A year later he received the commission for, and began work on, a colossal image of the biblical hero David (494), the young Hebrew shepherd who killed the giant Goliath with a single stone from his slingshot. The *David* statue reveals Michelangelo's debt to Classical sculptures; we might compare it to the Roman copy of the Greek *Spear Bearer* (460). *David* is not, however, a simple restatement of Greek art. The Greeks knew how bodies looked on the outside. Michelangelo knew how they looked on the inside, how they worked, because he had studied human anatomy and had dissected corpses. He translated this knowledge into a figure that seems made of muscle and flesh and bone, though all in marble.

There are other characteristics that make *David* a Renaissance sculpture, not a copy of a Greek one. For one thing, it has a tension and energy that is missing from Greek art. Some writers have suggested that the statue is a self-portrait—not so much that it duplicates Michelangelo's features, but that it expresses the creative tension of its maker. The hands especially are taut and strong, held at the ready for action. Another Renaissance quality is the expression on David's face. Classical Greek statues generally bore an expression of beatific calm, showing the subject to be above earthly concerns. But David is young and vibrant—and angry, angry at the forces of evil represented by the giant Goliath. Michelangelo equated perfect beauty with perfect truth and honor; he seems to have found these qualities in the story of David and to have embodied them in his statue of the young conqueror.

Four years after the completion of *David*, Michelangelo was in Rome, working on sculptures for the tomb of Pope Julius II (to be completed in the Pope's lifetime). Julius interrupted this project and persuaded, some would say coerced, his young artist to undertake another commission, the fresco

494. Michelangelo. *David.* 1501–04. Marble, height 18′. Academy, Florence.

Michelangelo

1475–1564

He is beyond legend. His name means "archangel Michael," and to his contemporaries and those who came after, his stature is scarcely less than that of a heavenly being. He began serious work as an artist at the age of thirteen and did not stop until death claimed him seventy-six years later. His equal may never be seen again, for only a particular time and place could have bred the genius of Michelangelo.

Michelangelo Buonarroti was born in the Tuscan town of Caprese. According to his devoted biographer and friend, Giorgio Vasari, the young Michelangelo often was scolded and beaten by his father for spending too much time drawing. Eventually, however, seeing his son's talent, the father relented and apprenticed him to the painter Domenico Ghirlandaio. At the age of fourteen Michelangelo was welcomed into the household of the wealthy banker Lorenzo de' Medici, who operated a private sculpture academy for promising young students. There he remained until Lorenzo's death, after which Michelangelo, just seventeen years old, struck out permanently on his own.

He traveled to Venice and Bologna, then finally to Rome, where he attracted the first of what would become a long list of patrons among the clergy. A *Pietà* (Virgin mourning the dead Christ) made in 1500 and now in the Vatican established his reputation as a sculptor. From that time until his death he never lacked for highly placed patrons. He served—and survived—six popes, and in between accepted commissions from two emperors, a king, and numerous members of the nobility. All his life he struggled to keep a balance between the work he wanted to do and the work demanded of him by his benefactors. His relationships with these powerful figures were marked continually by squabbles about his payment, insults given and forgiven, flight from the scene of a particular commission followed by penitent return to continue with the work.

Michelangelo served these masters, at various times, as painter and architect, but he always considered himself above all to be a sculptor. Much of his time was spent supervising the quarrying of superior stones for sculptural projects. His greatest genius lay in depictions of the human figure, whether in marble or in paint. Vasari writes that "this extraordinary man chose

always to refuse to paint anything save the human body in its most beautifully proportioned and perfect forms." To this end he made extensive anatomical studies and dissected corpses to better understand the inner workings of the body.

Michelangelo never married, though he formed a number of passionate attachments during his life. These inspired the artist, always a sensitive and gifted poet, to write numerous sonnets. One of his most poignant verses, however, was not addressed to a loved one but to his friend Vasari, a few years before his death:

> The course of my long life has reached at last
>> In fragile bark o'er a tempestuous sea,
>> The common harbor, where must rendered be
>> Account of all the actions of the past. . . .
> Painting and sculpture satisfy no more
>> The soul now turning to the Love Divine,
>> That oped, to embrace us, on the cross its arms.[2]

Anonymous artist. *Portrait of Michelangelo.* 16th century. Staatliche Museen Preussischer Kulturbesitz, Berlin.

decoration of the ceiling in the Sistine Chapel at the Vatican **(495)**. So great was the power of the Papacy and of patronage in those times that even an artist of Michelangelo's stature could be readily controlled, and Michelangelo writhed under this system.

Chapter 7 explained some of the difficulties of the fresco technique. Paint must be applied to the fresh plaster just when it has the proper degree of dampness; only a small area can be covered at a time; and the painting must be done directly, with no allowance for correction of mistakes. Add to these problems the fact that Michelangelo had to cover an area 44 by 128 feet (700 square yards), working on a scaffolding 68 feet above the floor, lying

495. Michelangelo.
Ceiling, Sistine Chapel.
1508–12. Fresco, 44 × 128'.
Vatican, Rome.

above: The entire ceiling
before cleaning and restoration.

left: A partial view
of the ceiling after cleaning
completed 1990.
© Nippon Television Network
Corporation, Tokyo, 1990.

419

always on his back in a cramped position with paint and plaster dripping into his face, and you can appreciate how arduous was his task.

Even more overwhelming than the physical difficulties was the challenge of making a coherent composition in such a huge area. Because the artist was Michelangelo, the composition is not merely coherent but is one of the great masterpieces of all time. Michelangelo organized the ceiling into a painted architectural framework of squares, rectangles, and triangles. These segments depict Old Testament stories of the creation of the world, the creation of Adam (34) and of Eve, the Fall of Man, and other biblical events. The figures have the same anatomical fullness and muscular energy as Michelangelo's sculptures. A thorough restoration completed in 1990 has cast new light on the artist's use of colors.

Just as Pope Julius II had urged Michelangelo to work as a painter, one of Julius' successors, Pope Paul III, encouraged the sculptor to work as an architect. In 1546 Paul named Michelangelo the official architect of the new St. Peter's—the basilica (or ceremonial cathedral) that is the "headquarters" of the Roman church (496). By the time he began work on this project he was

left: 496. Michelangelo.
St. Peter's, apse and dome. 1546–64.
Vatican, Rome.

below: 497. Andrea Palladio.
Villa Rotonda, Vicenza. Begun 1550.

498. Giorgione. *The Tempest.* c. 1505. Oil on canvas, $32\frac{1}{4} \times 28\frac{3}{4}''$. Academy, Venice.

an old man, well into his seventies and physically tired, but his creative vigor was undiminished. Michelangelo designed a majestic cross-shaped structure that now comprises the *apse* of St. Peter's (the section containing the altar) and topped it with a towering dome, which he did not live to see completed. (The building was substantially enlarged over the next hundred years; Bernini's colonnade, which we saw in Chapter 14 **[432]**, was added in the 17th century.) Even at his advanced age Michelangelo did not relax his lifelong perfectionism. He studied the engineering problems of the huge building, and he mastered them. Today Michelangelo's dome stands as the world symbol for the Roman Catholic Church.

Although Michelangelo could be pressed into service as an architect, other 16th-century artists specialized in this field. Foremost among them was Andrea Palladio, architect of the Villa Rotonda **(497)**, near Vicenza—the architect's birthplace. The Villa Rotonda, strange as it may seem to modern tastes, was planned as a country house for its owners. Like most of his contemporaries, Palladio looked to ancient Greece and Rome for inspiration, and he apparently believed that the Roman nobility lived in houses of this sort. The villa is absolutely symmetrical all around. Its basic structure is a square, with identical Greek-style porches on each of the four sides, not unlike the entrances to Greek temples **(456)**. At the very center is a round salon (the word "rotonda" refers to a round room) reaching up through the building and capped with a low dome. Palladio's architecture epitomizes the "classic" style that would send out echoes for centuries to come. Across the United States, even in small towns, you can see banks and government buildings that resemble the Villa Rotonda.

Besides Leonardo and Michelangelo, three other painters, each just a few years younger than Michelangelo, made far-reaching contributions to the art of the High Italian Renaissance. They are Giorgione, Raphael, and Titian.

The iconography of Giorgione's painting *The Tempest* **(498)** is unknown. Even the artist's contemporaries seem not to have known what story he was depicting or to have been able to identify the nude woman nursing a child at right and the soldier (or shepherd) at left. Most likely Giorgione was making reference to some event in Greek or Latin poetry, or perhaps he was trying to evoke a classical mood. But regardless of the meaning of its subject, *The*

Tempest makes an important contribution to Renaissance art in the way it is composed. Artists of earlier generations, even up to Botticelli (491), would compose a scene by concentrating on the figures and painting the landscape as a kind of backdrop. Giorgione, however, has started by constructing a landscape and then placing his figures in it naturally. This approach paved the way for the great landscape paintings of the centuries to follow. In *The Tempest*, as the title implies, the subject is really the approaching storm, which closes in dramatically over the city while the two foreground figures are still bathed in sunlight. Giorgione's principal interest seems to have been the contrast of bucolic foreground against the city rendered in careful perspective, with the two drawn together by the violent effects of nature. The storm and the lush vegetation create a world in which nature dominates, not people, and the painting evokes a powerful, compelling mood of apprehension and anticipation.

Raphael also was capable of placing figures in a believable setting, as we saw in his brilliant fresco *The School of Athens* (233). But for the painting illustrated here, *Pope Leo X with Two Cardinals* (499), the artist has deemphasized the architectural setting and moved in close to create a true and perceptive portrait. As Julius II had been Michelangelo's great patron, Leo X was Raphael's. Leo was the son of Lorenzo de' Medici (Chapter 1, pp. 14–15), and the cardinals on either side of him are his nephews. Raphael has not flattered the pope. The pontiff we see is seriously overweight and has a puffy face and rather coarse features. Despite its unflinching realism, the portrait conveys Leo's majesty and power, emanating not just from the office but from the man.

Even before Raphael painted the portrait of Leo X, the artist Titian, Raphael's contemporary, had declined to become the pope's official artist. Possibly Titian hoped that a career of greater scope awaited him. If so he was not disappointed, for Titian eventually achieved an international reputation,

499. Raphael.
Pope Leo X with Two Cardinals.
c. 1518. Oil on wood, 5'5⅝" × 3'8⅞".
Uffizi, Florence.

500. Titian. *Portrait of a Man.*
Mid-16th century.
Oil on canvas, 32 × 26".
The National Gallery, London
(reproduced by courtesy
of the Trustees).

numbering among his many royal patrons King Philip II of Spain, King Francis I of France, and the Holy Roman Emperor Charles V.

In the service of his noble clients Titian painted many grand and heroic pictures, but his influence on later artists derives largely from the more intimate portraits, such as the *Portrait of a Man* shown here **(500)**. The artist had at his command a wide repertoire of poses—copied by artists even today—that flattered his sitters and bestowed on them a self-assured dignity. Among Renaissance artists, Titian is thought of as the greatest colorist. The lush blue sleeve in this portrait, for instance, is iridescent with tonal shadings and highlights. The sleeve is treated with such importance, it seems almost to form a pedestal for the sitter's head.

By the time of Titian and his contemporaries, the style that can be identified as Renaissance had begun to spread outward from the Italian peninsula. When Renaissance ideals penetrated the North—Germany, Switzerland, northern France, and the Netherlands—they changed the look of art and swept away the last vestiges of the Middle Ages.

The Renaissance in the North

The first half of the 16th century was a time of tremendous spiritual, intellectual, and artistic upheaval in northern Europe. The Protestant Reformation was in full swing, bringing with it the establishment of new Christian denominations—Anglican, Lutheran, and Calvinist—which would split away large numbers of people from the Church of Rome. Literary and philosophical explorations emphasized the Greek and Roman classics, and gave rise to the movement known as *humanism*. And Renaissance styles in art, which had appeared in Italy a century earlier, now sprang up in the North. All this activity can be traced in part to the new ease of communication. The printing press, developed in the mid-15th century, made possible a dramatic increase in the spread of books and artistic images. Travel throughout Europe became far more common, not just for trade, but for pleasure and study. Many Northern artists made pilgrimages to Rome and Florence to examine the work of their Italian contemporaries.

501. Hans Holbein the Younger. *Henry VIII*. 1540. Panel, 32½ × 29″. National Gallery, Rome.

We have already seen several works by two of the greatest Northern masters, Jan van Eyck **(94,236)** and Albrecht Dürer **(55,182,253)**. Here we turn to Hans Holbein the Younger, a German artist who was among the first of the true cosmopolitans—well educated, well traveled, at home in many cities. Holbein was born in Augsburg, in southern Germany, but lived for many years in Switzerland. After traveling extensively in France, Italy, and the Netherlands, he eventually settled in London, where he became court painter to King Henry VIII. It is largely through Holbein that we have a visual record of that most intriguing of monarchs **(501)**. The painting shows two characteristics of the style that made Holbein one of the greatest portraitists ever. On the one hand, every aspect of the subject's appearance is rendered in careful detail, from the hairs in his beard to the textures of skin, clothing, and fur. On the other, the artist has penetrated surface appearance to give us an imposing character study. He has posed the monarch full front, so that he dominates and fills the picture space, the very image of arrogant kingship at the height of its powers. Henry confronts and overwhelms the viewer—much as he must have confronted the papacy, his own ministers in England, and, for that matter, all six of his wives.

Pieter Bruegel the Elder, an artist who worked in Antwerp and Brussels, also was well educated and well traveled, but his work took an opposite path from that of Holbein. Whereas Holbein concentrated on extravagant portraits of the nobility, Bruegel is best known for his animated genre scenes of the peasantry at work and play. *Peasant Wedding* **(502)** depicts the celebration, held in a barn, after the nuptials of a young couple. Just to right of center a hanging cloth, on which is suspended something like a crown, isolates the bride, who sits looking rather pleased with herself—presumably because she has made a good match. There is disagreement about which figure is the groom; some art historians identify him as the man in dark clothing leaning backward just at the center of the composition.

Bruegel employed an interesting compositional device for this painting. The table, slanting diagonally from lower right to upper left, pulls together a large number of people in conviviality but without confusion. His special genius, however, lies in painting these people as *types*—as "cheerful peasants"—yet also as individuals. If you examine each character, you begin to speculate about emotions, thoughts, reactions. The bagpiper at center left: Surely he wishes he could stop playing and eat some of the delicious food going by. The pair at far right: Are they discussing the details of the marriage contract and assessing the match? The couple immediately to the bride's left, variously identified as her parents or the groom's: They don't look especially happy. In fact, they look downright grim. Have they made a poor bargain, or are they pessimistic about the outcome of this marriage? All in all, *Peasant Wedding* is a marvelous study in personality and in visual organization.

Once the Northern Renaissance caught up with its Italian predecessor, the North never again lagged behind. Starting with the 17th century, although there continued to be regional styles, art developments throughout western Europe moved forward at the same pace.

17th-Century Europe: Post-Renaissance and Baroque Styles

The Protestant Reformation in northern Europe was extremely successful and drew large numbers of people away from the Roman Catholic Church. Deeply wounded, the Church of Rome regrouped itself and struck back. The Catholic Counter-Reformation, begun in the second half of the 16th century and continuing into the 17th, aimed at preserving what strength the Church still had in the southern countries, and perhaps recovering some lost ground in the North. Spain and Italy were the two major centers of the Counter-Reformation, and some artists were deeply involved in its activities.

502. Pieter Bruegel the Elder. *Peasant Wedding.* c. 1565. Oil on panel, 3'8⅞" × 5'4'. Kunsthistorisches Museum, Vienna.

Our first two artists in particular are associated with the Counter-Reformation and can serve as a transition from the 16th century to the 17th. They are difficult to categorize, because their styles, while very different from those of the High Renaissance, do not fit either with the Baroque style we shall consider presently. Some writers label their work **Mannerist**—a term that implies a dramatic use of space and light and a tendency toward elongated figures.

The first of the two artists was the Italian master Tintoretto, born in Venice. His *Last Supper* (**503**) makes an interesting comparison with Bruegel's *Peasant Wedding*. Like Bruegel, Tintoretto has organized a large group of people by means of a table set in a sharply diagonal composition. The mood of the two paintings, however, could hardly be more different. Bruegel's atmosphere is one of light-hearted—perhaps slightly vulgar—celebration. But Tintoretto's picture portrays a religious subject, and he has given it a dramatic and mystical treatment.

The scene of the *Last Supper* takes place a few days before Christ's death and depicts the moment when Christ breaks bread and gives it to his disciples to eat—the basis for the sacrament of Holy Communion. Christ's head is brilliantly lighted, and clouds of angels waft toward him, making it clear that a supernatural event is taking place in this ordinary setting. The serving attendants, who are tied to earthly concerns, go about their business, oblivious to the spiritual drama, but Christ's disciples are very much caught up in the great mystery. Small halos of light form around all their heads to indicate their holiness—except for Judas, who will soon betray Christ, and who sits alone on the opposite side of the table.

The artist most closely associated with the Catholic Counter-Reformation was Domenikos Theotokopoulos, known as El Greco. Born on the Greek island of Crete (hence, "the Greek"), El Greco traveled as a young man to Venice and Rome, where he studied the works of Michelangelo and Titian. Eventually he moved on to Spain, settling permanently in Toledo, an intensely Catholic center of the Counter-Reformation. One of his most important commissions, executed for a chapel in that city, was *The Burial of Count Orgaz* (**504**). The count in question, an extremely pious man, had actually died and been buried some 250 years earlier, but El Greco depicts the burial as though it were taking place at the time of the painting. The nobility and clergy of Toledo, many of them El Greco's patrons, are portrayed as graveside mourners. So holy was Count Orgaz, that St. Stephen and St. Augustine have

503. Tintoretto.
The Last Supper. 1592–94.
Oil on canvas, 12′ × 18′8″.
San Giorgio Maggiore, Venice.

504. El Greco.
The Burial of Count Orgaz.
1586. Oil on canvas,
16′ × 11′10″.
Santo Tomé, Toledo, Spain.

miraculously appeared to lower the body into its tomb. At the center of the composition, above the mourners' heads, an angel holds a wispy white form, meant to represent the count's soul, conveying it to Heaven.

Catholic Spain turned its eyes upward, to the heavens rather than the earth, and forward, to eternal life rather than the earthly one. *The Burial of Count Orgaz* illustrates this tendency perfectly, with a sharply divided composition. The living are grouped in a static row, earthbound, the line of their heads forming a barrier between earth and sky, life and the hereafter. Above them, the heavens open into a turbulent vision of Paradise. The figures of Christ and the Virgin, saints and angels, are dramatically elongated and flamelike. Below all is stillness and sorrow; above, movement and ecstasy.

Tintoretto's and El Greco's works have some elements in common, especially in their emphasis on the spiritual, but we cannot link them with each other or with the products of other artists as constituting a particular style, as we could with the Renaissance. The last half of the 16th century and beginning of the 17th was a period of much experimentation in art, but no single coherent trend. Not until about the second decade of the 17th century can we again see a definite style and give it a label. That label is *Baroque.*

Baroque art differs from that of the Renaissance in several important respects. Whereas Renaissance art stressed the calm of reason and enlightenment, Baroque art is full of emotion, energy, and movement. Colors are more vivid in Baroque art than in Renaissance, with greater contrast between colors and between light and dark. In architecture and sculpture, where the Renaissance sought a classic simplicity, the Baroque favored ornamentation, as rich and complex as possible. Baroque art has been called dynamic, sometimes even theatrical. This theatricality is clearly evident in the work of the Baroque's leading interpreter, the artist Gianlorenzo Bernini.

Bernini would have been a fascinating character in any age, but if ever an artist and a style were perfectly suited for one another, this was true of Bernini and the Baroque. With a taste for drama and overstatement, a flair for the grand gesture, Bernini found great success in an era that appreciated such expression (432). Bernini's background was in the theater, in stage and scene design; he was also an unsurpassed sculptor and architect. All these talents were brought to bear in his masterpiece, the Cornaro Chapel in the church of Santa Maria della Vittoria in Rome (505). The chapel itself, shown here in an 18th-century painting, is a brilliantly integrated scheme of architecture, painting, sculpture, and lighting. On the ceiling is painted a vision of heaven, with angels and billowing clouds. At either side of the chapel sit sculptured figures of the Cornaro family, donors of the chapel, in animated conversation, watching the drama before them as though from opera boxes. The whole arrangement is lighted dramatically by sunlight streaming through a concealed yellow-glass window.

The centerpiece of the chapel is Bernini's sculptured group known as *St. Teresa in Ecstasy* (506). Teresa was a Spanish mystic, founder of a strict order of nuns, and an important figure in the Counter-Reformation. She claimed to be subject for many years to religious trances, in which she saw visions of Heaven and Hell and was visited by angels. It is in the throes of such a vision that Bernini has portrayed her. Teresa wrote:

left: 505. Anonymous artist. *Cornaro Chapel, Santa Maria della Vittoria, Rome.* 18th century. Oil on canvas. Staatliches Museum, Schwerin, Germany.

right: 506. Gianlorenzo Bernini. *St. Teresa in Ecstasy.* 1645–52. Marble and gilt bronze, life-size. Cornaro Chapel, Sta. Maria della Vittoria, Rome.

Gianlorenzo Bernini

1598–1680

Gianlorenzo Bernini falls into a category we find fascinating in all the arts—the youthful prodigy. Born in Naples, he trained with his father, Pietro, a talented sculptor, and by the age of seventeen he had received a commission from the Pope. Too late in history to be a man of the Renaissance, Bernini was nonetheless a Renaissance man—sculptor, painter, architect, stage designer, playwright, composer of music, and, by all accounts a great wit. He lived into his eighties and displayed throughout his life enough energy and enthusiasm and inventiveness for a dozen ordinary people.

Nearly all of Bernini's life was spent in Rome, and he outdid even his great predecessor Michelangelo in papal patronage, serving seven popes over a period of half a century. Master always of the grand design, he executed many huge projects, including the Cornaro Chapel group with *St. Teresa in Ecstasy* and the piazza and colonnade of the Vatican. Several outdoor fountains in Rome—elaborate figural sculptures—are also of his design. This last is typical of Bernini, for, grand showman that he was, he loved to incorporate such effects as light, smoke, or in this case water in his creations. Often he was called upon to plan important public events, such as state funerals or celebrations in honor of the saints.

As a sculptor, Bernini excelled at the portrait bust—the head and shoulders likeness in marble of an individual. One of the loveliest of these depicts Costanza Bonarelli (347), the wife of Bernini's assistant who was also Bernini's mistress. Sometime in the mid-1630s the current pope, Urban VIII, urged the artist to terminate this relationship and take a wife. So in 1639 Bernini, then forty-one years old, married a young woman half his age, Caterina Tezio. The story is told that Bernini felt compelled to give away the portrait bust of Costanza Bonarelli, which until then he had kept in his home. The artist's wife eventually bore him eleven children, nine of whom survived to maturity.

Bernini's fame as an architect and sculptor spread throughout Europe. In 1665 Louis XIV, king of France, summoned the artist to Paris to work on a new design for the Louvre palace. The trip was not a success. Bernini's plan for the Louvre was rejected, and

the artist alienated his hosts by expressing his preference for Italian art and contempt for French art. He returned to Rome, where he remained until his death.

One major work did result from Bernini's sojourn in Paris—a splendid portrait bust of Louis carved after Bernini had made numerous sketches of the king going about his daily activities. It was in Paris, too, that the artist reportedly explained the problems of portrait sculpture: "If a man whitened his hair, beard, eyebrows and—were it possible—his eyeballs and lips, and presented himself in this state to those very persons that see him every day, he would hardly be recognized by them. . . . Hence you can understand how difficult it is to make a portrait, which is all of one color, resemble the sitter."[3]

Gianlorenzo Bernini. *Self-Portrait.* c. 1625. Oil on canvas. Galleria Borghese, Rome.

Beside me, on the left hand, appeared an angel in bodily form, such as I am not in the habit of seeing except very rarely. . . . He was not tall but short, and very beautiful; and his face was so aflame that he appeared to be one of the highest rank of angels, who seem to be all on fire. . . . In his hands I saw a great golden spear, and at the iron tip there appeared to be a point of fire. This he plunged into my heart several times so that it penetrated to my entrails. When he pulled it out, I felt that he took them with it, and left me utterly consumed by the great love of God. The pain was so severe that it made me utter several moans. The sweetness caused by this intense pain is so extreme that one cannot possibly wish it to cease. . . . This is not a physical, but a spiritual pain, though the body has some share in it—even a considerable share.

Bernini shows the saint in a swoon, ready for another thrust of the angel's spear. She falls backward, yet is lifted up on a cloud, the extreme turbulence of her garments revealing her emotional frenzy. We can almost hear the moans Teresa spoke of in describing her passionate experience. The angel, wielding his spear, has an expression on his face of tenderness and love; in other contexts he might be mistaken for a Cupid. A work like *St. Teresa in Ecstasy* could never have emerged from the Renaissance. Artists of the Renaissance looked backward to the cool, restrained style of Greece in the Classical period. But the Baroque artist was far more interested in the later Hellenistic period of Greek art, typified by the *Laocoön Group* **(461)**. Both in composition and in the intensity of emotion portrayed, there is a kinship between the *Laocoön* and *St. Teresa* sculptures.

The Baroque fondness for dramatic composition and lighting revealed in the Cornaro Chapel also is apparent in works by two of Bernini's contemporaries—Artemisia Gentileschi and Caravaggio. In Gentileschi's *Judith and Maidservant with the Head of Holofernes* **(507)**, pose, gesture, and light are used much as they would be in the theater. The artist took her subject from the biblical story of Judith. According to the Scripture, Judith, a pious and beautiful Israelite widow, volunteered to rescue her people from the invading

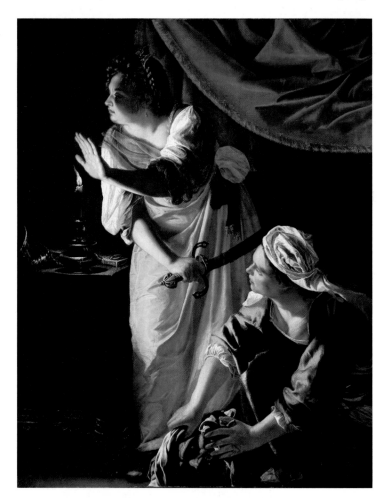

507. Artemisia Gentileschi. *Judith and Maidservant with the Head of Holofernes.* c. 1625. Oil on canvas, $6'\frac{1}{2}'' \times 4'7\frac{3}{4}''$. The Detroit Institute of Arts (gift of Mr. Leslie H. Green).

508. Caravaggio. *The Deposition.*
1604. Oil on canvas,
9′9⅛″ × 6′7¾″.
Pinacoteca, Vatican, Rome.

armies of the Assyrian general Holofernes. Judith charmed the general, accepted his invitation to a banquet, waited until he drank himself into a stupor, then calmly beheaded him, wrapped up his head in a sack, and escaped.

Other of Gentileschi's paintings show the decapitation in progress. Here she focuses on the moments after the gory deed is done. She poses Judith tensely, caught in the wavering light from a single candle, one hand still clutching the bloody sword, the other poised in a gesture of silence. These Baroque devices heighten the sense of danger, the urgency of deeds committed in the dark of night.

Caravaggio, too, focuses on a suspended moment after violent death. His magnificent *Deposition* (**508**) shows the crucified Christ being removed from the Cross and prepared for burial. The body is lowered by two of Christ's followers—his disciple St. John and the Jewish ruler Nicodemus, to whom Christ had counseled that a man must be "born again" to enter Heaven. The group also includes the three Marys—Christ's mother, the Virgin Mary, at left; Mary Magdalene, center; and Mary Cleophas, at right—who look on in despair. Caravaggio's structure is a strong (though complex and twisting) diagonal leading from the upraised hand at top right down through the cluster of figures to Christ's face. The light source seems to be coming from somewhere outside the top left edge of the picture. Light falls on the participants in different ways, but always enhances the sense of drama. Mary Magdalene's face, for example, is almost totally in shadow, but a bright light illuminates her shoulder to create a contrast with the bowed head. Light also catches the pathetic outstretched hand of the Virgin. Christ's body is the only figure lit in its entirety; the others stand in partial darkness.

When one sees this painting, the most immediate impact comes from the stark dead-white of Christ's form, in contrast to the vivid garments and flesh tones of the others. The viewer's experience of this poignant scene is intensified by the fact that we observe it from "a worm's-eye view," from a position below that of the participants in the drama, who stand on a stagelike slab. Certain elements of the composition almost seem to project forward out of the painting—the corner of the slab, Christ's feet, Nicodemus' elbow. Because the deposition group breaks out of the picture plane, we are drawn into the scene, we become a part of it.

We might compare Caravaggio's *Deposition* to a work painted just a few years later, *The Raising of the Cross* (509) by the Flemish artist Peter Paul Rubens. Although he spent most of his life in Antwerp (in modern Belgium), Rubens had traveled to Italy and studied the works of Italian masters, including Caravaggio. There are similarities between these two paintings—in the sharply diagonal composition and dramatic lighting—but we also find several differences in the two master's styles. Caravaggio's figures seem almost frozen in a moment of anguish, but Rubens' painting teems with movement and energy, each of the participants balanced precariously and straining at his task. While the Caravaggio group projects from the picture plane, its action is contained on four sides within the frame of the canvas. Rubens' figures, in contrast, burst outside the picture in several directions, suggesting that the action continues beyond the painting. In addition, Rubens, like other Northern artists, is far more interested than Caravaggio in textural details—precise rendering of foliage, hair, the curly dog, and so on. Rubens' lifelike treatment of musculature in the bodies recalls Michelangelo's paintings on the Sistine Chapel ceiling (34,495), but the writhing S-curve of Christ's body is typically Baroque.

509. Peter Paul Rubens. *The Raising of the Cross.* 1609–10. Oil on panel, 15'2" × 11'2". Antwerp Cathedral.

In all the history of art, one of the most civilized figures was the Flemish painter Peter Paul Rubens. Rubens was born in the German town of Siegen, but he returned with his mother at the age of ten to her native Antwerp (then in the Spanish-controlled Netherlands, now a city of Belgium) after the death of his father. There he was placed as a page in a wealthy home—a post that seems to have taught him the tact and courtly manners that would serve him well in the years to come. Coupled with these was an innate intelligence and pleasant disposition, all of which contributed to an enormously productive, rewarding life.

Rubens began his art studies in Antwerp. At the age of twenty-two, however, he set out for Italy, where he was to remain for eight years. During this time he traveled widely through all the major cities, studied the works of the great Italian masters, and was employed as court painter by the Duke of Mantua.

When the final illness of Rubens' mother called him home in 1608, the artist fully expected to return to Italy. But several inducements persuaded him to remain in Antwerp, which became his base for the rest of his life. For one thing, he was immediately successful as an artist and found many lucrative commissions. For another, the political and intellectual climate satisfied him. Perhaps most important, Rubens met, fell in love with, and married a young woman of Antwerp, Isabella Brant. This union lasted for seventeen years, produced three children, and was an extremely happy one. Rubens painted their wedding portrait, a detail of which is shown here.

In an atmosphere of domestic fulfillment, Rubens settled down to work. He became court painter to the Archduke Albert and his wife (also named Isabella), who were at the time rulers of the Netherlands. Over many years he also served them as political emissary and diplomat to foreign courts, often being entrusted with the most secret of negotiations. Artistic commissions poured in from all parts of Europe. Rubens was able to fulfill them mainly because he had a well-organized studio and many assistants. For certain large works, Rubens would make preliminary drawings, assistants would execute routine parts of the canvas, and then the master would make corrections and provide finishing touches.

Rubens' personal life took a stunning blow in 1626, when his wife died suddenly. Four years later, however, the artist remarried. His second wife was Hélène Fourment, and at the time of their marriage she was sixteen, Rubens fifty-three. This marriage, too, seems to have been a most successful one and produced five children. It was cut short by the artist's death, at sixty-three, from heart failure caused by gout.

The workshop approach perfected by Rubens occasionally got him into trouble. In 1621 he was forced to write this letter to a dissatisfied client: "I am quite willing that the picture painted for My Lord Ambassador Carleton be returned to me and that I should paint another . . . making rebate as is reasonable for the amount already paid, and the new picture to be entirely by my own hand without admixture of the work of anyone else, which on the word of a gentleman I will carry out."[4]

Peter Paul Rubens. *The Honeysuckle Bower* (*Self-Portrait with Wife*), detail. c. 1609. Oil on canvas, 5'10½" × 4'5½". Bayerische Staatsgemäldesammlungen, Munich.

510. Nicolas Poussin.
The Rape of the Sabine Women.
c. 1636–37.
Oil on canvas, 5'1" × 6'10½".
The Metropolitan Museum of Art,
New York
(Harris Brisbane Dick Fund, 1946).

Baroque painting in mid-17th century France seems relatively subdued in contrast to the work of Southern artists of this period and even to that of Rubens. This was due to the French interest in Classical Greek and Roman art, particularly evident in the paintings of Nicolas Poussin. Poussin, born a Frenchman, spent much of his career in Rome, but he struck a different path from that of the Italian artists. His *Rape of the Sabine Women* **(510)** depicts a famous episode in Roman myth. Romulus, the legendary founder and first king of Rome, was concerned that the men of his city had no wives and so could not establish families. To remedy this problem, he announced a festival and invited the people from the neighboring town of Sabina to attend. Poussin shows us the climax of this event. Romulus, standing at upper left on the steps of the temple, gives a signal—opening his cloak—and each of the Roman men seizes a Sabine woman to carry off, killing the Sabine men.

Despite the violent and dramatic nature of the occasion, Poussin's treatment seems curiously restrained and reflects his admiration for Classical art. Poussin based his background on what he believed to be authentic Roman architecture, and he modeled his figures after ancient Greek and Roman sculptures. The two women at left, with their arms upraised, strike us more as carefully posed statues than as terrified maidens about to be carted away into wedlock by rather brutish strangers. There is little sense of continuous action. We almost have the impression that these are actors, arranged into a living tableau with appropriate facial expressions, who will momentarily break the pose and go about their business. Poussin's art is above all rational and intellectual. He wants us to understand the dramatic import of the scene from his careful composition and ordering of the figures, not from any overt display of passion. The "classicizing" tendencies of Poussin had much influence on French artists for the next century.

To grasp fully the flavor of the Baroque in France, we should look once again at a king who for all time exemplifies the term "absolute monarch"— Louis XIV. In Chapter 3 we discussed how his portrait by Rigaud **(70)** both captured and enhanced the ideal of regal power. But in Louis's reign official portraiture was, so to speak, just the tip of the iceberg. Every aspect of the king's life and environment was calculated to present the image of divine rule. Louis's statement *"L'Etat c'est moi"* ("I am the state") was not just an expression of ego. It was the truth.

Louis ascended the throne of France in 1643, at the age of four. He assumed total control of the government in 1661 and reigned, in all, for seventy-two years. During that time he made France the artistic and literary center of Europe, as well as a political force to be reckoned with. Showing the unerring instincts of a master actor, he created an aura around his own person that bolstered the impression of divinity. Each day, for example, two ceremonies took place. In the morning half the court would file into Louis's chambers, in full pageantry, to participate in the king's *lever*—the king's "getting up." At night the same cast of characters arrived to play ritual roles in the king's *coucher*—his "going to bed."

A life in which the simple act of climbing in and out of bed required elaborate ceremony must surely also need an appropriate setting, and Louis did not neglect this matter. He summoned Bernini from Rome to Paris to work on completion of the Louvre palace (although the final design of the building was the work of others). But Louis's real love was the Palace of Versailles, in a suburb of the capital, which he substantially rebuilt and to which he moved his court in 1682. It was from this remarkable structure that the power of kingship flowed forth.

In all, Versailles occupies an area of about 200 acres, including the extensive formal gardens (511). The complex embraces several grand chateaux, used at various times by one or the other of Louis's mistresses and their children, who were accorded quasi-royal status. There were also the Orangerie, a massive and elegant building in which the king kept his orange trees, and the king's stables—capable, it is said, of accommodating some twelve thousand horses. A system of reservoirs, constructed at huge expense, provided water for innumerable fountains and a mile-long "Grand Canal." Louis's plans greatly expanded the Menagerie, or zoo, which provided rooms for dining overlooking the animals' cages.

The palace itself, redesigned and enlarged during Louis's reign, is an immense structure, more than a quarter of a mile wide. Of the countless rooms inside, the most famous is the Hall of Mirrors (512), 240 feet long and

below: 511. Pierre Patel. Bird's-eye view of the château and park of Versailles, 1668, viewed from the East.
Musée du Château, Versailles.

right: 512. Jules Hardouin-Mansart and Charles Lebrun. Hall of Mirrors, Versailles Palace. Begun 1676. Length 240', height 43'.

lined with large reflective glasses. In Louis's time the Hall of Mirrors was used for the most elaborate state occasions, and even in our own century it has served as backdrop for momentous events. The treaty ending World War I was signed in the Hall of Mirrors.

At the beginning of this discussion we said the Baroque style was characterized by ornamentation, dynamism, theatricality, and overstatement. What could better exemplify this style than the reign of Louis XIV and the Palace of Versailles?

The French court clearly was a model of pomp and pageantry, and the Spanish court to the south was eager to emulate that model. King Philip IV of Spain reigned for a shorter time than his French counterpart and could not begin to match Louis in either power or ability. Philip had one asset, however, that Louis never quite managed to acquire—a court painter of the first rank. That painter was one of the geniuses of Spanish art—Diego Velázquez.

In his capacity as court painter Velázquez created his masterpiece, *Las Meninas (The Maids of Honor)* **(513)**. At left we see the artist, working on a very large canvas, but we can only guess at the subject he is painting. Perhaps it is the young princess, the *infanta*, who stands regally at center surrounded by her attendants (*"las meninas"*), one of whom is a dwarf. Or perhaps Velázquez is actually painting the king and queen, whom we see reflected in a mirror on the far wall. Their participation is clear, but where are they standing? Possibly they are outside the picture, standing next to us, the observers. This ambiguity is part of the picture's fascination, as is the dual nature of the scene. Although it shows a formal occasion, the painting of

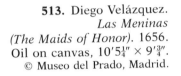

513. Diego Velázquez. *Las Meninas (The Maids of Honor).* 1656. Oil on canvas, 10′5¼″ × 9′¾″. © Museo del Prado, Madrid.

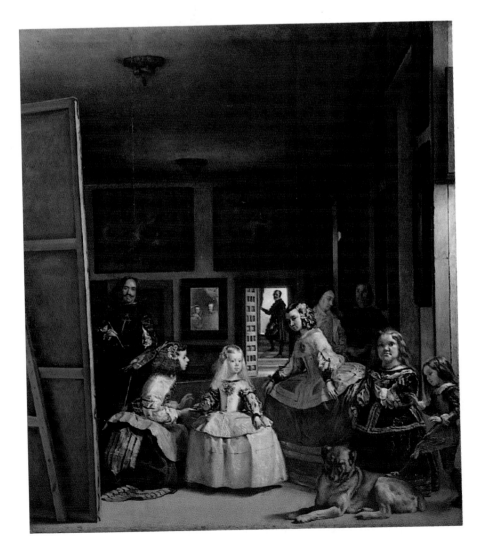

ARTISTS ON ARTISTS *Picasso on Velázquez*

Almost exactly three hundred years after Velázquez painted *Las Meninas*, another Spaniard undertook the same subject. Here are all the familiar elements of Velázquez' masterpiece: the easel at left with a large work in progress, the little *infanta*, the maids in waiting, the dog, the dwarf, the mysterious figure at the open door in the background. It is unmistakably *Las Meninas*—and unmistakably Picasso.

One cannot resist the temptation of thinking Picasso had a wickedly good time with this painting, sparring against his great compatriot. His free play with Velázquez' forms is endlessly inventive. The figure of the artist, not conspicuous in the original, now looms large and has taken on a jaunty, convivial air. The dog becomes a pale dachshund, the maid behind the *infanta* a cartoon horse, the two figures at right playing-card images. With his impish sense of fun—and, no doubt, a vigorous competitive spirit—Picasso has sought out minor details in the Velázquez (such as the ceiling fixtures) and sifted them through his own style to pull our eyes into every part of this busy composition. Picasso is paying witty tribute to his great predecessor, while at the same time making sure—as always—that we know who holds the brush now.

Pablo Picasso. *Las Meninas (after Velázquez).*
1957. Oil on canvas, 6'4⅜" × 8'6⅜".
Museo Picasso, Barcelona.

an official portrait, Velázquez has given the scene a warm, "everyday" quality, almost like that of a genre painting. Some experts believe Velázquez is painting the king and queen, and the little *infanta* has just wandered in.

Like Caravaggio, Velázquez uses light to create drama and emphasis, but light also serves here to organize and unify a complex space. The major light source comes from outside the top right corner of the painting, falling most brilliantly on the *infanta*, leaving the others in various degrees of shadow. Another light source illuminates the mysterious figure in the open doorway at back. Velázquez may have put him there to direct attention to the reflected images of the king and queen. Light also strikes the artist's face and the mirror reflection. What could have been a very disorderly scene has been pulled together by the device of spotlighting, much as a designer of stage lighting would control what the audience sees. The theatricality of the Baroque is more subtle in Velázquez than in Bernini, but it is no less skillful.

To end this discussion of 17th-century art, we move north, to the Netherlands. The Dutch Baroque, sometimes called the "bourgeois Baroque," is quite different from Baroque movements in France, Spain, and Italy. In the North, Protestantism was the dominant religion, and the outward symbols of faith—imagery, ornate churches, and clerical pageantry—were far less important. Dutch society, and particularly the wealthy merchant class, centered not on the church but instead on the home and family, the land and the community. We see this focus in the work of two great Dutch artists with very different styles—Rembrandt and Jacob van Ruisdael.

In this book, we have already considered several works by Rembrandt (**218,240,263**, p. 205). He was master of so many media that we return to him again and again in discussions of art. For most people, though, Rembrandt's special appeal lies in his portraits, and especially his self-portraits. He did more of these than practically any other artist. Through them we trace not only his maturation as a painter but his path through life as a human being—from rather humble beginnings to a period of great prosperity and happiness to the disappointments of his later life (p. 205).

The portrait shown here **(514)** represents a high point in the artist's life and is among the most charming of his self-explorations. Rembrandt portrays himself and his wife, Saskia van Uijlenburgh, as an elegant and worldly young Amsterdam couple. Both are dressed in fine clothing, with Rembrandt in the guise of a cavalier; his pose and the elaborate treatment of the sleeve may have been influenced by Titian **(500)**. The two are surrounded by splendid material possessions, and the artist lifts his wine glass high as though to say, "This is the good life!" And so it was for an artist of Rembrandt's incomparable talents.

The 17th century was the great age of landscape painting in the Netherlands. Of course, Rembrandt drew and painted many landscapes **(218)**, but his style in this area as in every other was a personal one. More typical of the Dutch landscape painting was the work of Jacob van Ruisdael. Van Ruisdael's *Extensive Landscape with a View of the Town of Ootmarsum* **(515)** shows not only the famed flatness of the Dutch landscape, but also the artist's reaction to that flatness as an expression of the immense, limitless grandeur of nature. The artist makes a contrast between the land—where human order has been established in the form of buildings and cultivation—and the sky, with its billowing clouds, yielding to the wind, which mere people can never tame. The horizon line is set quite low, and, significantly, only the church steeple rises up in silhouette against the sky, perhaps symbolizing that humankind's one connection with the majesty of nature is through the church.

Despite this emphasis on the church building, Van Ruisdael's art is essentially secular, as is that of Velázquez and Rembrandt. Although religious subjects continued to appear in art—and do so even now—never again would religious art dominate as it did in the Renaissance and Italian Baroque periods. No doubt this is largely because of the change in sponsorship; popes and cardinals became less important as patrons, while kings, wealthy merchants, and the bourgeoisie became more so. We can follow this increasing secularization of art as we move out of the 17th century into the 18th.

The 18th Century

The first half to three-quarters of the 18th century is often thought of as the age of **Rococo**—a development and extension of the Baroque style. The term "rococo" was a play on the word "baroque," but it also refers to the French words for "rocks" and "shells," forms that appeared as decorative motifs in architecture, furniture, and occasionally in painting. Like the Baroque, Rococo is an extravagant, ornate style, but there are several points of contrast. Baroque, especially in the South, was an art of cathedrals and palaces; Rococo is more intimate, suitable for the aristocratic home and the drawing room (although there are a number of very grand Rococo buildings). Baroque colors are intense; Rococo leans more toward the gentle pastels. Baroque is large in scale, massive, dramatic; Rococo has a smaller scale and a light-

left: **514.** Rembrandt.
Self-Portrait with Saskia. c. 1634.
Oil on canvas, 5'3½" × 4'3½".
Gemäldegalerie Alte Meister
Staatliche Kunstsammlungen, Dresden.

below: **515.** Jacob van Ruisdael.
*Extensive Landscape with a View
of the Town of Ootmarsum.* 1660s.
Oil on canvas, 23¼ × 28⅞".
Bayerische Staatsgemäldesammlungen, Munich.

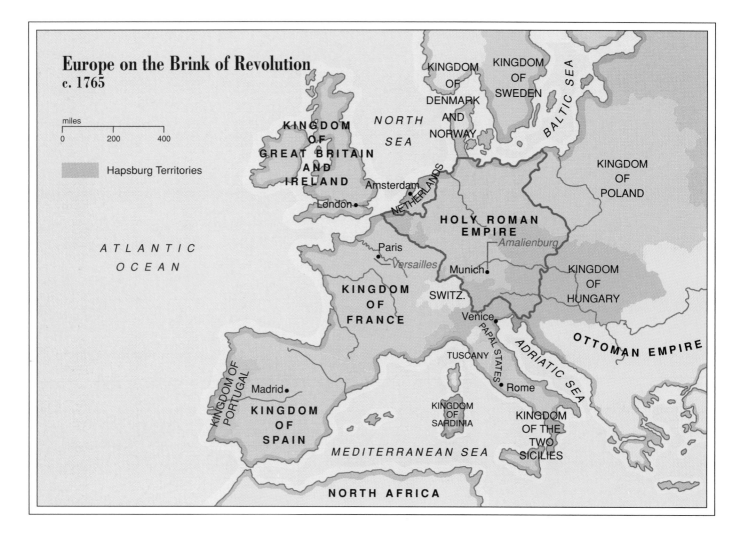

Europe on the Brink of Revolution
c. 1765

hearted, playful quality. And, as suggested earlier, the Baroque—at least in its origins—was a religious art; Rococo is far more secular and, in its extreme forms, charmingly romantic.

The Rococo style of architecture originated in France but was soon exported. We find some of the most developed examples in Germany, especially in Bavaria. The Mirror Room of the Amalienburg, a little house in Nymphenburg Park near Munich (516), should demonstrate amply why the word "rococo" has come to mean "elaborate and profuse." Designed by a Frenchman, François Cuvillies the Elder, the Mirror Room is a perfect riot of sinuous, twisting, almost visibly *growing* decorative forms. The line between walls and ceiling has been obscured deliberately to create the illusion of "sky" above the room. Large arched mirrors multiply the effect of playful design everywhere the eye might focus. Rococo was above all a sophisticated style, and the Amalienburg shows us the height of that sophistication.

Sophistication was paramount in painting as well. The art of Antoine Watteau is typical of the carefree, aristocratic impulse of the Rococo. In *Gersaint's Signboard* (517) Watteau gives us a picture of fashionable French society out for a day of shopping—shopping for pictures to decorate the opulent home. All is elegance, verging on the pretentious—the men in their powdered wigs, the women in their silks, everyone maintaining a pose of bored nonchalance. At right the gallery owner, Gersaint, displays a painting to prospective customers, while the adjacent group seems more taken with a smaller work of art. At left, paintings are being crated, presumably for shipment to purchasers. Watteau celebrates in painting a class of people whose most serious concern was maintaining a chic life style.

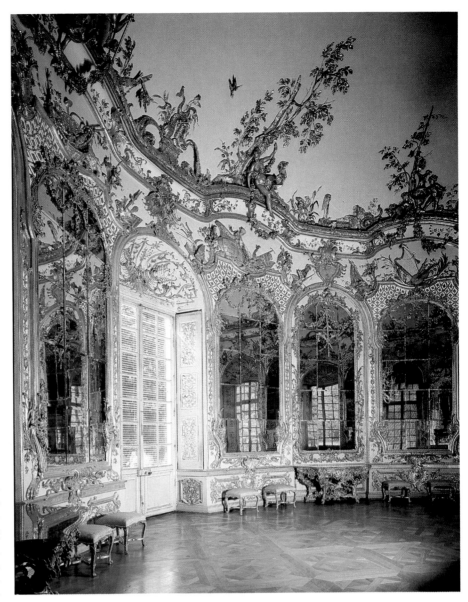

right: **516.**
François Cuvillies the Elder.
Mirror Room, Amalienburg.
1734–39. Nymphenburg Park, Munich.

below: **517.** Antoine Watteau.
Gersaint's Signboard. 1720–21.
Oil on canvas, 5'3⅞" × 10'1".
Staatliche Museen, Berlin.

Somewhat outside this predominant trend toward aristocratic art was another French artist, younger by about fifteen years than Watteau, the painter Jean Baptiste Siméon Chardin. Chardin specialized in the still life **(171)** and the middle-class genre scene. His works have a quiet, meditative appeal and show ordinary people in ordinary activities. Pictures of children at play, as in *The House of Cards* **(518)**, were a favorite theme. Here the boy, dressed in the very proper middle-class attire of the day, is caught up in the concentration of building his card house. There is a tension between his still pose and the precarious balance of the cards. Like the card house, Chardin's picture is perfectly but precariously balanced. The boy leans into his project, and Chardin's masterfully calculated light strikes three areas—the face, the upright cards, and the half-open drawer—to create a tight triangle of interest **(519)**. The fact that this triangle is balanced on one of its points adds subtly to the tension of the moment.

Two painters in particular, also French, have become almost synonymous with the Rococo. To admirers their art is sumptuous and delightful; to detractors it is frivolous and decadent. The first is Jean-Honoré Fragonard, whose work we saw in Chapter 4 **(138)**. The other is François Boucher. In Boucher's paintings all the people are pretty. The women are frequently nude and, if so, are very pink and voluptuous. (Fragonard's women are more often clothed but equally pink.) If the women are dressed, they are stunningly dressed. Everybody is in love.

Boucher's art suited perfectly the ideals of the French court presided over by Louis XV, great-grandson of the builder of Versailles. Form without substance, beauty without character, extravagance with little regard for paying the bills—such was the reign of Louis XV, and so it was chronicled by Boucher. In 1759 Boucher painted the *Marquise de Pompadour* (**520**), Louis's mistress and influential advisor. How beautiful she looks, how romantic—posed languidly in her lace-frilled dress, resting lightly against a classical statue. Boucher flattered her physically (she was a good deal fatter and less gifted with regular features), and he failed to record the steely political brain that lurked behind the soft face. During the reign of Louis XV, the government of France was on the brink of collapse. The king himself is reputed to have said, *"Après moi, le déluge"* ("After me, the flood"). But for a little while—with Louis XV on the throne, the Marquise de Pompadour at his side, and Boucher at his easel—appearances were kept up.

The lower classes did not participate in this world. They could not afford to wear lace-frilled dresses and had no time to be charmingly in love. Many, in fact, were on the brink of starvation. Louis—if he really said it—was right. The flood was coming. France would endure only one more self-indulgent Louis before taking up arms.

Louis XVI, grandson of his predecessor, came to power in 1774. His queen, Marie Antoinette, probably never did say "The people have no bread? Let them eat cake!" However, history has marked her forever with the callous attitude implied by this remark. In a portrait done by Elisabeth Vigée-Lebrun, her favorite painter, the queen certainly does not look preoccupied

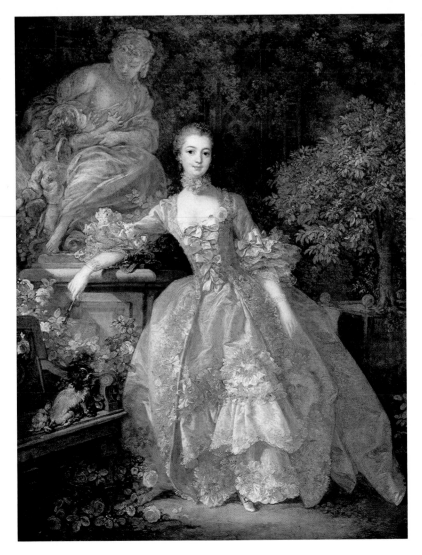

520. François Boucher.
Marquise de Pompadour. 1759.
Oil on canvas, $35\frac{7}{8} \times 27\frac{1}{4}''$.
The Wallace Collection, London.

with the suffering of her oppressed subjects **(521)**. Gowned sumptuously in red satin, she poses in a setting so regal as to seem almost defiant. Marie Antoinette might be saying, "Everything is all right, the monarchy is intact, nothing to worry about." Her surroundings are indeed regal—a grand salon in the Palace of Versailles, with the Hall of Mirrors visible at left. And the queen sits among her children, the supposed future of the nation, arranged in sentimental attitudes. Her son, the *dauphin* (or crown prince) points to the empty cradle of Marie's youngest child, who has just died.

Vigée-Lebrun always flattered her sitters, and never more so than in this portrait. Such extravagant flattery, however, did not enhance the queen's popularity in a nation on the brink of financial disaster. Vigée-Lebrun herself tells us that when the large canvas was carried into the palace, she heard angry voices crying "Voilà la déficite" ("There is the deficit").

Although Vigée-Lebrun later made several copies of her own portraits of the queen, she never again painted Marie Antoinette from life. Within two years revolution had swept the country, ultimately destroying the monarchy and the aristocracy. The artist fled and took refuge outside France. The queen died by the guillotine.

521. Elisabeth Vigée-Lebrun. *Marie Antoinette and Her Children.* 1787. Oil on canvas, 8′8″ × 6′10″. Palace of Versailles, France.

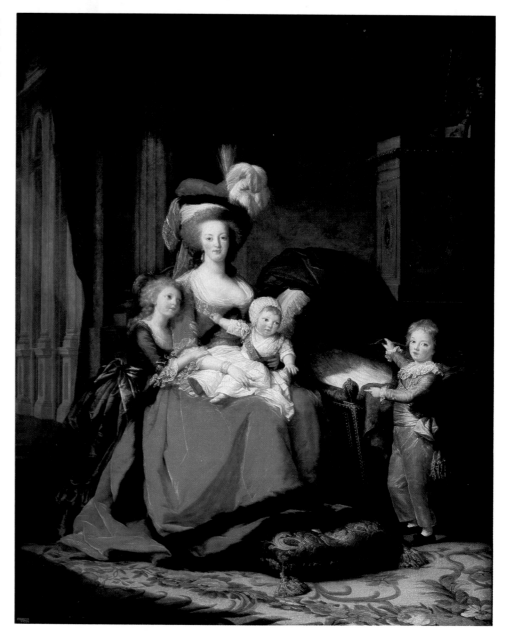

Elisabeth Vigée-Lebrun

1755–1842

From her self-portrait she gazes directly at us, her viewers—calm, self-possessed, sure of her talent, sure of her place in the world. Her brush is poised over the canvas; we have momentarily interrupted her work on a portrait of her great patron, the Queen of France. She will not be interrupted for long. Throughout her remarkable life, Elisabeth Vigée-Lebrun knew where she was going and remained steadfast on that path.

Born in Paris, the daughter of a portrait painter, Elisabeth Vigée was convent-educated and encouraged from an early age to draw and paint. At eleven she began serious art studies. After her father's untimely death, Elisabeth resolved to work as a painter, and by age fifteen she was her family's chief financial support. Patrons flocked to her studio, eager to have their portraits done by the young artist, and her fees multiplied.

One dark spot was her mother's remarriage, to a man who seems mainly to have coveted his step-daughter's income. Because of this unpleasant circumstance, Elisabeth made the one real mistake of her life. Although she "felt no manner of inclination for matrimony," she succumbed to her mother's urgings and accepted the proposal of Jean Baptiste Pierre Lebrun, hoping "to escape from the torture of living with my stepfather." Alas for the twenty-year-old artist, she had merely "exchanged present troubles for others." Lebrun was "quite an agreeable person," but, his wife soon discovered, "his furious passion for gambling was at the bottom of the ruin of his fortune and my own." The happiest result of the union was the birth of Vigée-Lebrun's only child, her daughter Julie.

Neither marriage nor motherhood interfered with the artist's burgeoning career and social life. By all evidence she was lovely, witty, charming, and perfectly at home in any company. Quite independent of her husband, she entertained a growing circle of aristocratic friends, many of whom commissioned portraits. In 1779 a summons came from the Palace of Versailles. Marie Antoinette sought her services, and Vigée-Lebrun made the first of some twenty portraits of the queen. The two women became friends—a splendid advantage for the artist initially, but a dangerous liability as resentment of the monarchy grew. When revolution came in 1789, Vigée-Lebrun fled the country, taking Julie with her. Lebrun was left behind forever.

Then commenced Vigée-Lebrun's twelve years of "exile" from France. And what an exile it was! She

traveled first to Rome and Vienna, then to St. Petersburg and Moscow, spending six years altogether in czarist Russia. Wherever she went she was treated like visiting royalty, entertained lavishly, invited to join the local painters' Academy. Wherever she went she was overwhelmed with portrait commissions. Kings and queens, princesses, counts, duchesses—she painted them all, in between the elaborate dinners and balls to which they invited her. In her memoirs she tells us she missed painting Catherine the Great because the empress died just before the first scheduled sitting.

In 1801, the furies of the revolution having abated, Vigée-Lebrun returned to Paris. She had not, however, quite satisfied her urge to travel. Only after a three-year stay in London and two visits to Switzerland did she finally settle down to write her memoirs and paint the survivors of the French nobility. She died in her eighty-seventh year, having painted more than 660 portraits. Her memoirs conclude with these words: "I hope to end peacefully a wandering and even a laborious but honest life."[5] And she did.

Elisabeth Vigée-Lebrun. *Self-Portrait at the Easel.* c. 1789. Oil on canvas. Uffizi, Florence.

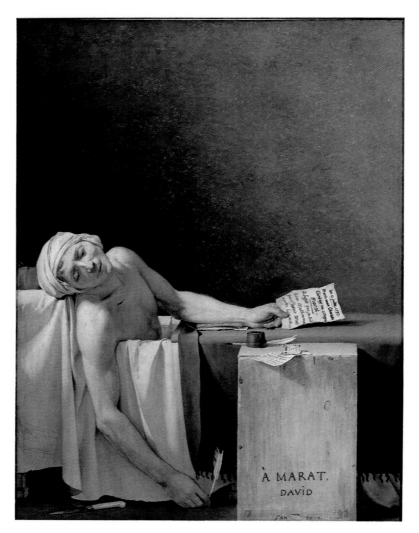

522. Jacques Louis David. *The Death of Marat.* 1793. Oil on canvas, 5'5" × 4'2½". Musées Royaux des Beaux-Arts de Belgique, Brussels.

Revolution

Repeatedly in this book we have pointed out that art responds to the culture from which it emerges. To get a sense of how dramatic was the revolution that shook France in 1789 (and its implications for much of Western civilization), we might compare Vigée-Lebrun's painting with a work done in France six years later, when the revolution had reached its height.

Jacques Louis David began his artistic career under the patronage of Louis XVI, but as the revolutionary impulse spread he switched allegiances, eventually becoming an important propagandist for the anti-aristocracy forces. What many consider to be David's finest picture was made to support the leaders and goals of the revolution. Its subject is Jean-Paul Marat, a major figure in the Reign of Terror, who was responsible for the death by guillotine of hundreds of people. Because of a painful skin ailment Marat spent his days in the bathtub, which was fitted out with a writing desk so he could work, and there he received callers. A woman named Charlotte Corday, incensed by Marat's excesses with the guillotine, gained entry to his apartments and stabbed him to death. As a memorial to his friend, David painted *The Death of Marat* **(522)**.

In lesser hands Marat's demise could have been laughable—a naked man murdered in his tub by a furious woman caller. But David has invested the scene with all the pathos and dignity of Christ being lowered into his tomb. (Compare Caravaggio's *Deposition,* **508.**) Marat is shown, in effect, as a kind of secular Christ martyred for the revolution. All the forms are concentrated in the lower half of the composition, and light bathes the fallen leader in an unearthly glow, both of these devices contributing to the sense of tragedy. It is probably safe to conclude that David's purpose in this work was to transform a man whom many considered Satan himself into a sainted hero.

The French Revolution was built on goals like those David attributed to Marat—liberty, equality, fraternity, and participation by all levels of society in the government and economy of France. In practice, however, the noble ideals of the revolution soon disintegrated into wholesale slaughter of aristocrats (including the royal family) and, in time, of anyone who disagreed with those momentarily in power. Art such as David's projected the *image* the leaders of the revolution wished to have of themselves, just as Vigée-Lebrun's art had projected the image desired by the French monarchs.

Two other revolutions occurred at more or less the same time as that in France. The first was the American Revolution, preceding the French by thirteen years, in which a small group of colonies in an untamed land broke free of England to create what is now the United States. The other was the Industrial Revolution—not a political uprising but an economic and social upheaval. The Industrial Revolution began slowly in the last half of the 18th century and, many would argue, is still going on.

It is difficult to overestimate the impact—social, economic, and ultimately political—of the change from labor done by hand to labor done by machine. Within the space of a few decades the machine drastically altered a way of life that had prevailed for millennia. People who had formerly worked in their homes or on farms suddenly were herded together in factories, creating a new social class—the industrial worker. Fortunes were made virtually overnight by members of another new class—the manufacturers. Naturally, all this upheaval was reflected in art. At the beginning of the 19th century, then, Western civilization faced a totally new world.

ART PEOPLE *Vincenzo Perugia*

At 7:20 on the morning of August 21, 1911, three members of the maintenance staff at the Louvre paused briefly in front of the *Mona Lisa*. The chief of maintenance remarked to his workers, "This is the most valuable picture in the world." Just over an hour later the three men again passed through the Salon Carré, where Leonardo's masterpiece hung, and saw that the painting was no longer in its place. The maintenance chief joked that museum officials had removed the picture for fear he and his crew would steal it. That joke soon proved to be an uncomfortably hollow one. *Mona Lisa* was gone.

Thus begins the story of the most famous art theft in history, of the most famous painting in the world, and of the man who would inevitably become the most famous art thief of all time: Vincenzo Perugia.

French newspapers announced the catastrophe under the banner headline "Unimaginable!" All during the weeks that followed, rumors abounded. A man carrying a blanket-covered parcel had been seen jumping onto the train for Bordeaux. A mysterious draped package had been spotted on a ship to New York, a ship to South America, a ship to Italy. The painting had been scarred with acid, had been dumped in the sea. All clues, however far-fetched, were followed up, but no trace of *Mona Lisa* could be found.

More than two years would pass before the thief surfaced. Then, in November of 1913, an art dealer in Italy received a letter from a man who signed himself "Leonard." Would the dealer like to have the *Mona Lisa?* Would he. Of course it was a joke. But was it? The dealer arranged to meet "Leonard" in a hotel room in Florence. "Leonard" produced a wooden box filled with junk. The junk was removed, a false bottom came out of the box, and there, wrapped in red silk and perfectly preserved, was the smiling face of *Mona Lisa*. The dealer swallowed his shock and phoned for the police.

"Leonard" was actually an Italian named Vincenzo Perugia—a house painter who had once done some contract work in the Louvre. As he told the story of the theft, it was amazingly simple. On the morning in question Perugia, dressed in a workman's smock, walked into the museum, nodded to several of the other workers, and chose a moment when no one else was in the Salon Carré to unhook the painting from the wall. Then he slipped into a stairwell, removed the picture from its frame, stuck it under his smock, and walked

out. Stories that Perugia had accomplices have never been proved.

What were the thief's motives? And why, after pulling off what can only be described as the heist of the century, did he so naively offer the painting to the Italian dealer? Perugia claimed he was motivated by patriotism. *Mona Lisa* was an Italian painting by an Italian artist. Believing (mistakenly) that it had been stolen by Napoleon to hang in France, he wanted to restore it to its rightful home. At the same time, however, he expected to be "rewarded" by the Italian government for his heroic act and thought $100,000 would be a good amount. No one shared this point of view.

Perugia was tried, convicted, and sentenced to a year in prison. After his release he served in the army, married, settled in Paris, and operated a paint store. Soon Perugia, who had so briefly captured the world's headlines, settled back into the obscurity from which he had emerged.

And *Mona Lisa?* After a triumphal tour of several Italian museums, she was returned to France. She hangs—at least as of this writing—safely in the Louvre. Romantics say her smile is even more enigmatic than before.

"Mug shot" of Vincenzo Perugia (with the name misspelled) after his arrest in 1913.

Chapter Seventeen

The Modern World

A chapter covering art of the 19th and 20th centuries presents certain difficulties, not the least of which is its title. Many writers designate the art of this period as "modern," a term that means "characteristic of the present or of the recent past," and so we have chosen to call it. However, this poses a problem: When did "modern" start? There are those who would say that truly modern art did not exist until the Impressionists in the 1870s, or until the period just before World War I, or even until the late 1940s. Moreover, we must remember that people in other periods of history undoubtedly thought of their own art as "modern," and perhaps even called it that. Very likely the period we call "modern" will be given an entirely different name by future generations.

Whatever we call it, we cannot ignore the fact that the art produced during the 19th and 20th centuries offers a variety of expression unprecedented in the history of art. If you flip through the chapter quickly, you will see an amazing range of styles—works so diverse they seem to have little in common with one another. Our discussion begins with a portrait of a woman, to our eyes not markedly different from paintings of the previous four hundred years. It ends with a work *by* a woman in which there is no tangible substance at all, nothing to hang on the wall or place on a pedestal. No wonder many people find "modern" art bewildering.

Despite the dizzying variety and complexity of modern styles, we have one great advantage in approaching the art of this period. We live now. About three-quarters of the art we shall consider in this chapter was made during the lifetimes of people still alive today. While we can have only limited success in getting "inside" the minds of Michelangelo or Rembrandt—or those of the audiences for whom they worked—we inhabit the same world as contemporary artists and, as a result, often share their sensibility. It is not inconceivable that you could meet and talk with several of the artists whose work is illustrated here, could question them about their inspirations, their goals, their reasons for working the way they do. Throughout this text it has been stressed that art is a product of the culture that produces it. In this chapter, then, and especially in the latter part of the chapter, we come to *our* art, the art of our own culture. We see works made by artists who have walked the same streets we have, watched the same television programs, felt the same tides of history washing over us. If we take the trouble to look and study, we may find that this is the art with which we feel the closest connection.

CHRONOLOGY

Style/Period	Political/Social Events and Personalities	Major Artists

1800–1850

Neoclassicism, France, early 19th century	Napoleon I, emperor of France, 1804–1814	Jacques Louis David (1748–1825)
Romanticism, France, early 19th century	War of 1812, United States, 1812–1814	Katsushika Hokusai (1760–1849)
Realism, France, mid-19th century	invention of photography by Daguerre, 1837	Jean Auguste Dominique Ingres (1780–1862)
Federal style and Greek Revival, United States		Théodore Géricault (1791–1824)
Edo Period, Japan, 1615–1868		Ando Hiroshige (1797–1858)
Qing Dynasty, China, 1644–1912		Eugène Delacroix (1798–1863)
		Honoré Daumier (1808–1879)

1850–1900

Impressionism, France, c. 1875–1900	Victoria, queen of England, 1837–1901	Edouard Manet (1832–1883)
Post-Impressionism, France, c. 1880–1900	Admiral Perry visited Japan, 1853	James Abbot McNeill Whistler (1834–1903)
	First public showing of motion pictures, 1895	Edgar Degas (1834–1917)
		Paul Cézanne (1839–1906)
		Auguste Rodin (1840–1917)
		Claude Monet (1840–1926)
		Berthe Morisot (1841–1895)
		Pierre-Auguste Renoir (1841–1919)
		Thomas Eakins (1844–1916)
		Paul Gauguin (1848–1903)
		Vincent van Gogh (1853–1890)
		Georges Seurat (1859–1891)
		Henri de Toulouse-Lautrec (1864–1901)

1900–1945

Expressionism, Europe, c. 1900–1920	Wright Brothers' first flight, 1903	Edvard Munch (1863–1944)
Fauvism, France, begun 1905	Armory Show, New York, 1913	Alfred Stieglitz (1864–1946)
Cubism, France, c. 1907–1914	World War I, 1914–1918	Wassily Kandinsky (1866–1944)
Dada, Europe, c. 1916–1922	Russian Revolution, 1917	Käthe Kollwitz (1867–1945)
Surrealism, Europe, begun 1924	Bauhaus, Germany, 1919–1933	Frank Lloyd Wright (1867–1959)
	Tutankhamun's tomb found, 1922	Henri Matisse (1869–1954)
	Great Depression, 1929–1941	Piet Mondrian (1872–1944)
	Spanish Civil War, 1936–1939	Paul Klee (1879–1940)
	Television broadcast from New York World's Fair, 1939	Pablo Picasso (1881–1973)
	World War II, 1939–1945	Edward Hopper (1882–1967)
		Georgia O'Keeffe (1887–1986)
		Marcel Duchamp (1887–1968)
		Norman Rockwell (1894–1978)
		Alexander Calder (1898–1976)
		Henry Moore (1898–1986)
		Alice Neel (1900–1984)

1945–present

Abstract Expressionism, c. 1945–1960	atomic bombs dropped on Japan, 1945	Pablo Picasso (1881–1973)
Op Art, 1960s	Korean War, 1950–1953	R. Buckminster Fuller (1895–1983)
Pop Art, 1960s	Vietnam War, c. 1961–1973	Henry Moore (1898–1986)
Minimal Art, 1960s	first walk on moon, 1969	Louise Nevelson (1899–1988)
New Realism, 1970s–1990s		David Smith (1906–1965)
Neo-Expressionism, 1980s–1990s		Lee Krasner (1908–1984)
Conceptual Art, 1970s–1990s		Jackson Pollock (1912–1956)
Computer Art, 1980s–1990s		Robert Rauschenberg (b. 1925)
Performance Art, 1970s–1990s		Andy Warhol (1930–1987)
		Frank Stella (b. 1936)
		David Hockney (b. 1937)

To get to the art of the present we begin at the turn of the 19th century, when the seeds of most modern art movements were sown. The center of Western art was France, and so it remained (with a few digressions) until the onset of World War I.

France, Early 19th Century: Neoclassicism, Romanticism, Realism

As we have seen in earlier chapters, most periods in the history of art had one dominant style—the High Renaissance style or the Baroque style, for instance—that major artists of the time followed. But French art of the early 19th century is not like that. It is customarily divided into three broad categories: classic, romantic, and realist. The fact that artists of the first rank were working in each of these styles gives a hint of the great diversity that was soon to come.

Representing the classic style—or, as it is usually called, **Neoclassical** ("new classical")—was the work of Jean Auguste Dominique Ingres; we saw one of his drawings in Chapter 6 **(211)**. Ingres was a pupil of Jacques Louis David **(522)**, and he inherited his master's admiration of ancient Greek and Roman art, as well as David's preference for sharp outline, reserved emotions, and studied (often geometric) composition—all characteristics of the Neoclassical style. We see these qualities in *La Grande Odalisque* **(523)**. "Odalisque" is a French word derived from the Turkish, meaning a concubine in a harem. (Matisse would later use the same term to describe his model in the painting on this book's cover.) It is typical of Ingres that, in portraying the nude figure, he placed it in an exotic situation. The nude was acceptable to contemporary standards of morality only when separated from everyday life. This nude, while unquestionably sensual, seems also rather distant and aloof. In Classical Greek art **(460)** and in much art of the High Renaissance **(493)** a cool detachment was deemed ideal. The Neoclassical style followed this trend. Ingres has outlined this figure very clearly, isolating it from its background, and the composition is perfectly balanced—the drape at right offsetting the raised torso on the left. Although a classicist, Ingres was capable of

523.
Jean Auguste Dominique Ingres.
La Grande Odalisque.
1814. Oil on canvas,
2'11¼" × 5'3¾".
Louvre, Paris.

524. Eugène Delacroix. *Liberty Leading the People, 1830.* 1830. Oil on canvas, 8′6″ × 10′10″. Louvre, Paris.

certain romantic touches. Here the figure of the odalisque has been considerably adjusted in its proportions. The long curving spine gives the figure an unearthly elegance, and the graceful arm that connects the two halves of the composition surely outreaches that of any human female.

Ingres's lifelong rival was Eugène Delacroix, champion of the **Romantic** movement. We can get as clear a picture of the differences between the two men by comparing their drawings **(211,118)** as we can in a comparison of the paintings shown here. The Romantic ideal stressed drama, turbulent emotions, and complex composition, all of which are evident in Delacroix's masterpiece, *Liberty Leading the People* **(524)**. In 1830 France was rocked by a brief uprising of the people, an aftershock of the French Revolution forty years earlier. Although not personally involved, Delacroix chose to depict an imaginary moment in this uprising as a statement of sympathy with the democratic ideals of the Revolution. Prominent in the composition is the figure of a woman, symbolizing Liberty and France—powerful, striding across the barricades, holding aloft the tricolor flag of France. Participants in the uprising stream behind her, following her lead—the artist does not tell us where, but presumably to the abstract goal of Freedom.

If we compare this passionate scene to the polished perfection of Ingres, the differences are obvious. Ingres's figure is motionless, languid; Delacroix's composition seethes with energy and violence. Ingres's *Odalisque* is beautifully contained within the frame of the picture, whereas Delacroix's figures marching toward us in a diagonal movement seem about to burst out of the composition, giving the impression of one frame in a continuous drama.

Ingres's outlines are clear and refined; Delacroix's free brush strokes give us a sense of blurred motion, of flickering light and confusion. Yet, in spite of its dynamism, Delacroix's composition is every bit as carefully composed as that of Ingres. The composition is stable, based on a triangle, with the apex in the hand and flag of Liberty, and the two sides moving down through the upraised rifle at left, the boy's arm and pistol at right. In their concern for the structure of painting Ingres and Delacroix were not as far apart as they appeared, but—because of the bitterness of their rivalry—neither would have admitted it.

The **Realist** movement in French art came somewhat later than Neoclassicism and Romanticism and was, in effect, a reaction against both. Realist artists sought to depict the everyday and the ordinary, rather than the heroic or the exotic. Their concerns were very much rooted in the present. One of the leaders of the Realist movement was Gustave Courbet, who in 1855 exhibited a huge painting, *The Artist's Studio* **(525)**, subtitled *A Real Allegory Summing Up Seven Years of My Life as an Artist.* To this day, more than a century later, art historians debate the meanings of the "allegory," or symbolic story.

At the center of the canvas sits Courbet himself, at work on a landscape painting. Although a great many people crowd into the studio, the artist seems aloof from them, as though his aesthetic concerns are all-consuming. A little boy (usually identified as Innocence) gawks up at the work in progress. Behind the artist stands a nude model, whom some consider to be his Muse, or inspiration, others the personification of Truth (that is, the "naked truth"). All the figures to the left of the composition are common people; they are "types," not individuals, derived from Courbet's origins in a rural village. At right are the artist's "intellectual" friends, many of them identifiable figures—his patrons, other artists, writers, and so on. Perhaps Courbet is saying the artist represents a special elite, fed by his origins and by his comrades, but apart from them, alone with Innocence and Truth. We know from Courbet's work as a whole that here the artist was trying to make a particular point—that everyday activities, such as an artist working at his easel or peasants toiling in the fields, were fit subject matter for grand-scale art. In an age when only paintings of religious or historical or mythological scenes were considered "great art," this was a revolutionary idea.

525. Gustave Courbet.
The Artist's Studio:
A Real Allegory Summing Up
Seven Years of My Life
as an Artist. 1855.
Oil on canvas,
11'9¾" × 19'6⅝".
Musée d'Orsay, Paris.

Each of the three paintings we have considered so far in this chapter has included a nude or seminude woman. Why are the women unclothed? Their nudity has a specific, accepted purpose—the exotic (Ingres's odalisque is a harem woman); the heroic (Delacroix's Liberty is bare-breasted as a mythical Amazon); the allegorical (Courbet's model may be the nude figure of Truth). These conventions satisfied contemporary tastes. But eight years after Courbet exhibited *The Artist's Studio,* a painting was placed on display in Paris that portrayed female nudity without any apparent justification at all. It caused a terrific scandal—the first of many artistic scandals that would shock the art world in the decades to come. The artist responsible for setting off this earthquake was a mild, conventional, well-to-do gentleman: Edouard Manet.

France, Late 19th Century: Manet

In 19th-century France the mark of an artist's success was acceptance at the annual "Salon," a state-sponsored exhibition of paintings. Artists submitted their work for consideration by an official jury, whose members varied from year to year but tended to be conservative, if not downright stodgy. Art critic John Russell has described an ideal Salon painting of the period as containing the following ingredients:

> . . . a knight in armor, a group of cardinals, some tropical vegetation, some counterfeit stained glass, a medieval feast with every dish and goblet shown in meticulous detail, a distant view of Constantinople through a window in the background, and in the foreground, three or four naked women, dancing.[1]

Russell wrote this description with tongue in cheek, but there can be no doubt the Salon pictures followed a predictable formula.

In 1863 the Salon jury rejected four thousand of the submitted paintings, which caused such an uproar among the spurned artists and their supporters that a second official exhibition was mounted—the "Salon des Refusés" (showing of those who had been refused). Among the artists who were refused were Whistler and Cézanne. Among the works in the "refused" show—

526. Edouard Manet. *Le Déjeuner sur l'herbe.* 1863. Oil on canvas, 7′ × 8′10″. Musée d'Orsay, Paris.

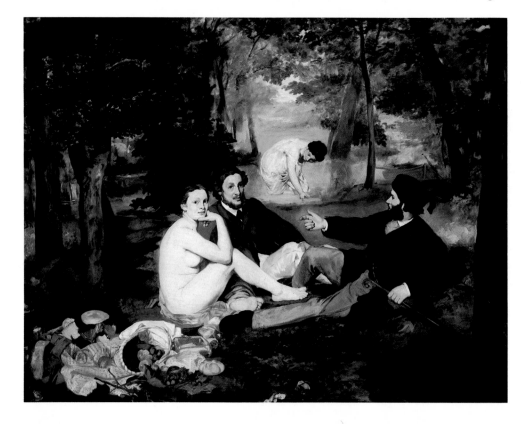

and soon the most notorious among them—was Edouard Manet's painting *Le Déjeuner sur l'herbe* (526).

Luncheon on the Grass, as it is usually translated, shows a kind of outdoor picnic. Two men, dressed in the fashions of the day, relax and chat in a woodland setting. Their companion is a woman who has, for no apparent reason, taken off all her clothes. In the background another woman, wearing only a filmy garment, bathes in a pool. With this one painting Manet had broken several "rules" held dear by French artists and art lovers alike, and it would be difficult to decide which transgression shocked the public most.

The nude woman is not a goddess, not a harem slave, not an allegorical figure. Then why is she naked, and why sitting nonchalantly with two men who are clothed? Why does she gaze out at the viewer so calmly and matter-of-factly? Nudity in some classical guise was quite acceptable to Manet's audience, but nudity for its own sake was not. With the wisdom of hindsight we can now understand that Manet regarded the nude figure as a study in painted form, an exercise to display his newfound insights into light and shape. His contemporaries had no such understanding. To make matters worse, Manet had "borrowed" certain compositional elements from well-known masterpieces of the past—not an unusual practice among artists but considered presumptuous in the hands of such a "bad" painter as Manet.

Bad, indeed, his technical skills must have seemed to the Salon jurors, for Manet was breaking new ground in the way he interpreted forms on canvas. The artist simplified round, three-dimensional shapes into a series of flat planes. He took a fresh look at the way light strikes a subject, concentrating on brilliant highlights and deep shadow, all but eliminating the middle transitional tones. The image seems to have been caught in an instantaneous flash of brilliant light.

Today's viewer sees *Le Déjeuner sur l'herbe* as one of the first steps toward concerns that would dominate 20th-century art, especially in the use of light and shadow and in the de-emphasis of absolute naturalism. Manet's contemporaries, on the whole, thought him just a clumsy painter. Poor Manet was subjected to a storm of outrage and scorn from critics and the art-viewing public alike. We find it ironic, therefore, that little over a hundred years later, when a major Manet exhibition was organized in Paris and then moved to the United States, *Le Déjeuner sur l'herbe* was not included in the traveling show. The painting is considered priceless—and far too precious to leave France.

Impressionism and Post-Impressionism

During the years following Manet's sensation in the Salon des Refusés, young French artists increasingly sought alternatives to the Salon. One group in particular looked to Manet as their philosophical leader, although he never consented to exhibit with them. The group was formed in 1874 and staged private showings each year until 1886. Because of the diversity of their techniques, the artists had difficulty finding a name for their association. Then a critic, after seeing a painting by Claude Monet (a member of the group) entitled *Impression: Sunrise,* scornfully dubbed the artists "impressionists." Rather than taking offense, the group happily adopted the name; their work was known thereafter as **Impressionism.**

The Impressionists attempted to paint what the eye actually sees, rather than what the brain interprets from visual cues. For example, if you look at a house in the distance and you know intellectually that the house is painted a uniform color of yellow, you might "see" all one shade of yellow, because your brain tells you that is correct. In purely visual terms, however, your eyes register many variations of yellow, depending on how light strikes the house and the shadows it creates. This is what the Impressionists were

Edouard Manet

1832–1883

Edouard Manet was a gentleman. That old-fashioned word aptly describes one of the most civilized, elegant figures in the history of art. Unfortunately for Manet, through most of his career he was also a gentleman scorned. Few artists have had to endure as much public derision and abuse as Manet did, and few have been as poorly equipped to tolerate abuse as he. To the end of his life he sought popular success for his art, but always it eluded him.

Manet was born in Paris of well-to-do parents. At first he contemplated a naval career, but after two unsuccessful attempts to gain admittance to the naval academy, he turned to painting. He studied at the Ecole des Beaux-Arts and also in the studio of the painter Thomas Couture, but the major influences on his work were Dutch and Spanish art, particularly the paintings of the great Spanish artist Diego Velázquez. In 1859, when he was just twenty-seven, Manet submitted work to the Salon, the annual government-sponsored art exhibition. This submission was rejected, but two years later Manet placed two paintings in the Salon, one of them a portrait of his parents. Then in 1863 came the great scandal of *Le Déjeuner sur l'herbe*, which was rejected by the Salon, hung in the Salon des Refusés, called "immodest" by the French emperor, and heaped with abuse by critics and the public alike. Nevertheless, Manet continued to send paintings to the Salon each year, considering it the only true "field of battle" for an artist.

Surprisingly little is known about Manet's private life. He married Suzanne Leenhoff, who had been his piano teacher, in 1863. Though he earned little money from his art, his private means were sufficient to enable him to live comfortably. From time to time he traveled in Europe, but he always returned quickly to Paris, his spiritual as well as actual home. Manet was the quintessential Parisian. The well-dressed, well-mannered, well-spoken artist played an important role in intellectual society of the time. His closest friends were the writer-journalist Emile Zola and the poet Charles Baudelaire. Although he never exhibited with the Impressionist painters—most of whom were younger than he—Manet was considered by the Impressionists to be their natural leader.

Sometime in the early 1880s Manet was struck by a serious illness, the exact nature of which is unknown.

This illness resulted in the amputation of a gangrenous leg, and ultimately in his death at the age of fifty-one. As has happened with so many artists, recognition came to Manet just a bit too late. Seven years after his death, his painting *Olympia* was accepted by the Louvre.

Manet never got over his surprise at the public's contempt for his art, nor his bitterness about the rejection. In 1878 he wrote to Edgar Degas: "If there were no rewards, I wouldn't invent them: but they exist. And one should have everything that singles one out . . . when possible. It is another weapon. In this beastly life of ours, which is wholly struggle, one is never too well armed. I haven't been decorated? But it is not my fault, and I assure you that I shall be if I can and that I shall do everything necessary to that end."[2]

Henri Fantin-Latour. *Edouard Manet.*
1867. Oil on canvas, 46 × 35½".
Art Institute of Chicago (Stickney Fund).

above: 527.
Pierre-Auguste Renoir.
Piazza San Marco. 1881.
Oil on linen, 25⅝ × 32″.
Minneapolis Institute of Arts
(John R. van Derlip Fund).

left: 528. Detail of Renoir's
Piazza San Marco, 527.

after—the true visual impression, not the version that is filtered through the knowing brain.

If you look closely at a small section of an Impressionist painting, you will see many individual brush strokes of varying colors, placed side by side with no blending—a jumble of color daubs. But when you move farther away, your eyes "mix" the colors to produce a recognizable subject with shimmering effects of light. Pierre-Auguste Renoir's painting of the *Piazza San Marco* illustrates this effect (527,528). As rendered in the Impressionist style, St. Mark's is not the massive Byzantine cathedral we may know it to be, but a light-as-air palace wavering in the heat of a Venice summer.

Claude Monet, who gave Impressionism its name, is perhaps the artist who best typifies that style. (Despite the similarity of the names, Manet and Monet were not related.) Monet preferred to work outdoors, in daylight, and labored diligently to record on canvas the exact "impression" created by light striking a surface. Best known of Monet's paintings—and those showing the most developed Impressionist style—were the canvases of the water gar-

above: **529.** Claude Monet.
Pool of Waterlilies. 1900.
Oil on canvas, 35⅜ × 39¾".
The Art Institute of Chicago
(Mr. and Mrs. Lewis Larned Coburn
Memorial Collection).

left: **530.** Berthe Morisot.
La Lecture. 1888.
Oil on canvas, 29¼ × 36½".
Museum of Fine Arts, St. Petersburg, Fla.

den he built outside his home, the famous "water lilies" series **(529)**. Although we can identify trees, reeds, a bridge, the floating lily pads, our overall impression is of shimmering light and color, the sparkling effect produced by sunlight reflecting off the water. Monet's technique of combining many small, vivid brush strokes of pure color gives a dazzling brilliance.

Another artist associated with the Impressionist group, and one firmly dedicated to its goals, was Berthe Morisot. Morisot had an early success in the Salon and exhibited in this "establishment" forum several years running, but after she took up with the Impressionists she refused ever again to submit work to the Salon. Like Monet's, Morisot's paintings are suffused with light; they sparkle with the immediacy of the quick glimpse. Morisot, however, was not so committed as Monet to painting outdoors. Often she posed her figures in a charming room or on a balcony, as in *La Lecture* **(530)**. Her brushwork is somewhat freer than Monet's, and is sometimes described as "nervous," with its long flamelike flicks of color. But according to Edgar Degas, an artist whose praise was highly valued by his colleagues and followers, Morisot's airy style "conceals the purest draftsmanship."

Degas was well equipped to comment on Morisot's draftsmanship, being the finest, most sure-handed draftsman of the Impressionist group. Considering his great interest in line, some critics question whether he can be called an Impressionist at all. Yet Degas's concerns were similar to those of Renoir and Monet and Morisot—to record the fleeting moment, to capture on canvas an instantaneous perception of the eye. As we have noted in other chapters, Degas was absorbed by the unusual angle of sight, the "peephole" view of a scene, and his composition was strongly influenced by the complex spatial relationships in Japanese prints **(146)**. *The Tub* **(531)**, a work of the mid-1880s, shows the artist in masterful control of these effects. We see a nude at her bath, viewed from above. We glimpse her as though we are quickly looking in a window while passing by. She is crouched rather awkwardly, scrubbing her shoulder, her body almost filling the left side of the canvas. On the right is a table or shelf that increases the picture's spatial ambiguity. We assume that it is above the figure, but the space is so compressed that the left and right sections might be in the same plane. These spatial relations appear to be haphazard, but actually they reflect a meticulously planned composition. To appreciate the originality of Degas's conception, we might speculate how Ingres or Delacroix might have posed a nude bathing, barely half a century earlier.

531. Edgar Degas. *The Tub.* 1886. Pastel, $23\frac{1}{2} \times 32\frac{1}{8}''$. Musée d'Orsay, Paris.

The Impressionists profoundly influenced the major artists who followed them, especially in the lightness and brightness of colors. However, the work of the members of this next generation is so diverse in so many respects that no one stylistic label seems to fit all of them, and they generally are known as the **Post-Impressionists.** They include Vincent van Gogh, Paul Cézanne, Paul Gauguin, and Georges Seurat **(137,215)**.

We have already seen several works by Van Gogh in this book **(2,20,21, 45,219)**. His style is characterized by intense, high-key colors; loose brushwork, often with a heavy impasto; a swirling, agitated composition; and a subject matter emphasizing those things closest to him—the landscapes he inhabited, buildings in which he dwelled, his friends, himself. Among his best-known paintings is *The Artist's Room at Arles* **(532)**, a study of his own bedroom in the little yellow house **(2)**. Van Gogh identified so closely with the bedroom that it is virtually a self-portrait. The narrow room, empty except for the bed, two straight chairs, a small table, and, significantly, several paintings on the wall, speaks eloquently of a lonely artist dedicated to his work. The composition is an unusual one. Nearly half the canvas is devoted to bare floor and the blank footboard of the bed. All the main items of interest—Van Gogh's toilet articles on the table, his clothes on a peg, his looking glass, the pillows on his bed, and above all his paintings—are clustered (we might even say crammed) into the top half of the composition. The artist might be showing us that he lived in a tiny, compressed world—the world of his mind, his body, and his extraordinary art.

Paul Cézanne took a different approach in building on the work of the Impressionists. His search was for a solidity and a geometric order in the visual world, and he explored this problem in landscapes **(83)**, in figural compositions **(104)**, in still lifes, even in portraits (p. 85). A solitary and uncommunicative figure nearly all his life, Cézanne had enormous influence on artists of succeeding generations.

Paul Gauguin worked in the Impressionist style early in his career, but he soon became dissatisfied. Like Van Gogh and Cézanne, he felt the need for more substance, more solidity of form than could be found in optical percep-

532. Vincent van Gogh.
The Artist's Room at Arles.
1888–89. Oil on canvas, 29 × 36".
The Art Institute of Chicago
(Helen Birch Bartlett
Memorial Collection).

ARTISTS ON ARTISTS *Fitch on Van Gogh*

Here is Van Gogh's bedroom —an image familiar to anyone who knows the artist's work. There is the bed on the right, with its prominent footboard. There are his paintings on the walls, the clothes on pegs, the looking glass, the window, the two chairs, the sharply up-tilted floor. But, wait. What is wrong with this picture? Someone has added two enormous boots to the left half of the canvas. And someone has put the figure of Van Gogh into his own bed. This is not Van Gogh's painting of the bedroom at Arles, but a painting by the contemporary American artist Rik Fitch, done almost exactly a hundred years later.

In December of 1988 Rik Fitch began what he calls a "search for Van Gogh." Fitch's aim was "to play with the artist's style, his myth, and also to reach into the unknown being of the artist." The search would be a long and deep one, involving more than a year of intense work and scores of canvases.

None of Fitch's paintings are exact copies of any particular Van Gogh work. To be sure, the style and subject matter are unmistakably Van Gogh, but Fitch often combines imagery from two or more Van Gogh canvases, then adds inventions and interpretations of his own. The resulting expression is altogether new. Where did the boots come from? They are adapted from a still life Van Gogh painted a year or two before

he made the bedroom scene. Some critics think the boots are a kind of self-portrait, as the bedroom is as well. They are symbols of his life and personality. By joining the two, Fitch intensifies the projection of Van Gogh's "self." And to make the self-portrait theme even more compelling, Fitch puts Van Gogh in his bed. The viewer wonders: Is Vincent dead or just sleeping? Fitch will only reply, "Oh, yes, that is the question."

Rik Fitch. *It Feels So Good To Take Them Off.* 1989.
Oil on canvas, 24 × 32". Courtesy the artist.

tions of light. Beyond this, Gauguin was interested in expressing a spiritual meaning in his art. All these he sought on the sun-drenched islands of the South Pacific. Gauguin's paintings made in Tahiti have brilliant high-keyed colors, thus revealing his debt to the Impressionists. But to this color effect he has added his own innovations: flattened forms and broad color areas, a strong outline, a taste for the exotic, an aura of mystery, and an interest in the primitive.

Paul Gauguin

1848–1903

When Gauguin set sail from France in 1891, headed for the remote island of Tahiti in the South Pacific, he wrote a new chapter in the legend of the romantic, bohemian artist. To this day the legend persists. Many people want an artist to be—and Gauguin himself perhaps wanted to be—a dramatic, tormented soul who turns away from the comforts of modern civilization, who is not subject to society's conventions, who thrives in an exotic climate.

Paul Gauguin's origins gave but little hint of what was to come. Born in Paris, he spent part of his childhood in Peru, then returned with his family to France. After a stint in the merchant marine, he settled down and established himself as a stockbroker in Paris. When his career prospered, he married a young Danish woman, Mette Gad, who eventually bore him five children. Sometime in this period he took up painting as a hobby.

Over the years this hobby gradually came to be an obsession. In 1883, when he was thirty-five, Gauguin suddenly announced to his wife that he intended to quit his job and become a full-time painter. His attempts to support himself in this profession were not rewarding; eventually, Gauguin's wife rejoined her family in Denmark, taking the children, and the couple never lived together again. In 1886 Gauguin made the first of three visits to Brittany, the westernmost province of France. By this time he had already begun to establish his style of painting in broad shapes and flat color areas. A year later the artist journeyed to the island of Martinique, in the Caribbean, where the lush tropical colors heightened his palette even further. Late in 1888 Gauguin paid a brief—and disastrously unpleasant—visit to Van Gogh in the south of France. Finally, disillusioned with Western society and its values, Gauguin departed for Tahiti.

In Tahiti, Gauguin "went native." He lived in a grass hut and took as his *vahine*, or woman, a thirteen-year-old Tahitian girl, who gave birth to his son. At first all seemed idyllic, but even in the tropics one could not live for free, and Gauguin's finances were tight. He returned to Paris in 1893, hoping to sell his paintings, but the trip was not a success. Two years later Gauguin again set sail for Tahiti—never to return home.

During the second Tahitian period, Gauguin's fortunes went from bad to ghastly. He was wracked by a severe case of syphilis, suffered from a broken ankle that would not heal, and was desperately poor. At lowest ebb he attempted suicide, but the arsenic he swallowed was vomited up, causing him great agony. In 1901 he made his final voyage, to the Marquesas Islands, where—after a series of strokes—he died, penniless and completely alone. Three years after his death a memorial exhibition of Gauguin's work was organized in Paris. The show was a triumph. Gauguin was recognized as one of the great artists of his time.

Through all his ordeals, Gauguin seems to have considered the sacrifice worth it—necessary to achieve the vision he sought in art. As he wrote to his wife, "I am a great artist. . . . I am a great artist and know it. It is because of what I am that I have endured so many sufferings so as to pursue my vocation, otherwise I would consider myself a rogue."[3]

Paul Gauguin. *Les Miserables (Self-Portrait.)*
1888. Oil on canvas, 28 × 35".
Rijksmuseum Vincent van Gogh, Amsterdam.

Nafea Faaipoipo (When Are You To Be Married?) **(533)** was painted soon after the beginning of Gauguin's first long stay in Tahiti, and it shows all these characteristics. The figures of the two young women are so flat that we feel we almost could cut around them like paper dolls and pull them out of the painting. Strong outlines define them; this is especially apparent in the skirt and face of the woman at left. The landscape is rendered in broad, flat color areas receding backward: green grass of the foreground, a large yellow middle ground, deep blue shadow under the trees, purple mountain in the background. We know that the women of Tahiti, especially the young girls, were usually slender and lithe. Gauguin has given them a heavy, monumental solidity in keeping with his interest in broad form, and perhaps also because it fulfilled his fantasies about what a "noble savage" ought to look like. Mystery and magic are conveyed by the stylized gesture of the woman at right and the secretive expressions of both women. Perhaps the magic was more in Gauguin's mind than in the subjects he painted. Nevertheless, in the South Pacific he found the ideal environment to foster his unique artistic vision.

When Gauguin moved to this remote island thousands of miles from France, he still kept in touch with his colleagues and dealers in Paris—an indication that we are approaching 20th-century standards of travel and

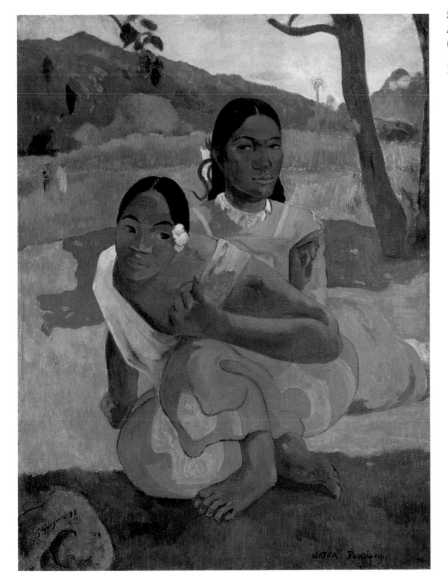

533. Paul Gauguin.
Nafea Faaipoipo
(When Are You To Be Married?).
1892. Oil on canvas, 41¼ × 30½".
Rudolf Staechelin Foundation, Basel.

communication. Of course, artists always have traveled. Even the ancient Greek sculptors occasionally set out on the "wine-dark sea" celebrated by the poet Homer. But at the turn of the 20th century, travel across the great oceans had become so convenient and commonplace as to be taken for granted. This ease of movement gave rise to a new phenomenon—transatlantic cultivation of the arts. American artists and writers flocked to London and Paris to learn from the masters there. European artists and writers flocked to the United States, where they found an eager market among certain discerning collectors. Two worlds were rapidly becoming one.

Bridging the Atlantic: Late 19th Century

Since the early days of the Colonies, American artists had journeyed to Europe, the better to learn their craft. Toward the end of the 19th century, however, the pace of this traveling accelerated. Some artists based in the United States, including Winslow Homer (258) and Thomas Eakins (113, 125, 126), made brief visits to Europe and then returned home. Others, born in the United States and considered to be American artists, actually spent much of their working lives in Europe. This latter group includes Mary Cassatt (217, 266), Maurice Prendergast (241), James Abbott McNeill Whistler, and John Singer Sargent.

Whistler was born in Massachusetts but eventually settled in London. His most famous painting (534) has been done a great injustice—and become a cliché—through generations of use on Mother's Day cards, advertisements, and comic posters, thus earning the unfortunate title *Whistler's Mother*. But the artist himself wondered aloud why anyone should care about the identity of the model; his own title, *Arrangement in Gray and Black, No. 1*, speaks far more to Whistler's intent. This image, which has entered the public consciousness as an expression of a son's devotion to his aged mother, actually was meant, and succeeds, as a subtle study of formal composition, light, and color. Whistler's harmony of values—principally soft black and grays—gives the painting a warm, mellow quality. But even more striking is the composition's exquisite visual balance—the elderly woman arranged in profile at right, balanced against the drape at left, the perfect placement of the picture on the wall a bit off center, even the second picture barely visible at upper right. If any of these elements were changed or removed, Whistler's elegant composition would fall apart. (Indeed, the drape at left is often cropped out in commercial reproductions; you can see how awkward the picture becomes if you cover this portion with your hand.) *Arrangement in Gray and Black* demonstrates a new interest among artists in using the visual elements for their own sake, not just to serve the needs of a particular subject matter.

Although John Singer Sargent was an American citizen, he actually spent very little time in the United States. Born in Italy to American parents, Sargent established his primary studio in London, with only occasional trips to New York and Boston. He made his reputation early as a portrait painter, and throughout his career he remained wildly in demand by the rich and fashionable on both sides of the Atlantic. The best of Sargent's portraits succeed because they create an aura of elegance and aristocratic glamour. A typical example is the notorious *Madame X* (535), painted in 1884. This portrait of Mme Gautreau, an American society woman, caused a scandal when it was exhibited in Paris, in equal parts because of the subject's low-cut dress—quite daring for a "nice" woman of the time—and her haughty expression. A century later, however, we see both of these factors as contributing to the effectiveness of the picture. Mme Gautreau's pose, the essence of grace, is enhanced by the elegant full profile of her head. The abundance of creamy white skin contrasts dramatically with the velvety tones of her dress. Shocking as the portrait might have been, we can well imagine that wealthy women of the period would pay handsomely to be made to look like this.

If Paris was startled by *Madame X*, worse upsets were soon to come. Change was everywhere, signaled by the Impressionists and the Post-Impressionists. How far and how fast art was moving will be obvious when we look at the next "portrait" illustrated here, a work painted just twenty-one years after *Madame X*.

France, Early 20th Century: Fauvism, Cubism, and Other Movements

A public that could be shocked by *Madame X*—to our eyes a lovely but rather conventional painting—was hardly prepared for the explosion that shook the art world soon afterward. In 1903 the Salon d'Automne (autumn salon) was organized in Paris as an alternative to the establishment Salon. Two years later the Salon d'Automne exhibited the work of a new group of artists whose style caused a critic to label them *fauves*—"wild beasts"—and the label stuck. Among the artists who evoked this angry response was an unlikely candidate for wildness—Henri Matisse.

left: 534.
James Abbott McNeill Whistler. *Arrangement in Gray and Black, No. 1 (The Artist's Mother).* 1871. Oil on canvas, 4'9" × 5'4½". Musée d'Orsay, Paris.

right: 535. John Singer Sargent. *Madame X (Mme Pierre Gautreau).* 1884. Oil on canvas, 6'10¼" × 3'11¼". The Metropolitan Museum of Art, New York (Arthur Hoppock Hearn Fund, 1916).

536. Henri Matisse.
The Green Stripe (Mme Matisse).
1905. Oil on canvas, 16 × 12¾″.
Royal Art Museum, Copenhagen.

The Matisse painting illustrated here **(536)** is technically a portrait of the artist's wife, but it is usually known by a more descriptive title, *The Green Stripe*. Mme Matisse is portrayed recognizably, though the contours of her face are flattened and her features abstracted. Most remarkably, the artist, building on precedents Gauguin had explored a generation earlier **(533)**, has painted this image in purely arbitrary colors, that is, colors unrelated to the natural appearance of his wife. While the left side of the face is rendered in close-to-normal flesh tones, the right side is a harsh greenish-yellow, and the hair is purplish-blue. The background is divided into sections of green, red-orange, and rose-violet; these sections do not define a setting, but are simply color patches. Most startling of all, Matisse has drawn a vivid green stripe down the middle of the subject's face, from her hair to her neckline. Three-quarters of a century later, we are accustomed to the use of color for its own sake and can scarcely comprehend how outrageous this painting must have seemed to Matisse's audience. Its clear message is that color need not be subordinated to nature. With *The Green Stripe* color became a tool, one of many tools in the artist's kit, to be used as the artist sees fit.

The Fauve movement did not last very long, a mere three years or so. Matisse went on to explore other aspects of painting, as did his fellow exhibitors at the 1905 Salon d'Automne. Yet the Fauve experiment was crucial for the development of modern art, in that it broke once and for all a longstanding taboo about the boundaries and conventions of art. Never again would artists feel they must confine themselves to replicating the "real" colors of the natural world, although they might do so if they wished. The artistic bag, so to speak, was open.

No sooner had the color rule been broken than artists began to break more daringly than ever before with conventions of shape and space. At the forefront of this experimentation was an artist, just a dozen years younger than Matisse, who broke nearly every rule art had long followed and who emerged as one of the greatest masters of all time: Pablo Picasso. Many consider a painting done relatively early in the artist's career to be pivotal in the development of 20th-century art. That painting is called *Les Demoiselles d'Avignon* **(537)**.

Les Demoiselles d'Avignon was not Picasso's title but was given to the painting years later by a friend of his. It translates literally as "the young women of Avignon" and refers to the prostitutes of Avignon Street, a notorious district of Barcelona. In early sketches for the painting Picasso included a sailor entering at left to purchase the prostitutes' services, but in the finished canvas the sailor has been omitted. Picasso had become so involved with the formal components of his painting—the relations of form and space—that he all but forgot its original content.

If these are prostitutes, then how extraordinary they are! They are far from enticing. Picasso has chopped them up into planes—flat, angular segments that still hint at three-dimensionality but have no conventional modeling. Almost as an affront to traditional pictures of curvaceous nude bathers, the artist has defined his nudes in sharp geometric shapes. Figure and ground lose their importance as separate entities; the "background"—that is, whatever is not the five figures—is treated in much the same way as the women's bodies. As a result, the entire picture appears flattened; we have no sense of looking "through" the painting into a world beyond, as with Delacroix **(524)** or even Manet **(526)**.

To many people who see *Les Demoiselles* for the first time, the faces cause discomfort. The three at left seem like reasonable enough, if abstract, depictions of faces, except for the fact that the figure at far left, whose face is in profile, has an eye staring straight ahead, much as in an Egyptian painting. But the two faces at right are clearly masks—images borrowed from "primitive" art—and they create a disturbing effect when set atop the nude bodies of European females.

537. Pablo Picasso.
Les Demoiselles d'Avignon. 1907.
Oil on canvas, 8' × 7'8".
Collection, The Museum
of Modern Art, New York
(acquired through
the Lillie P. Bliss Bequest).

In *Les Demoiselles* Picasso was experimenting with several ideas that he would explore in his art for years to come. First, there was the inclusion of nontraditional elements. Picasso had recently seen sculptures from ancient Iberia (Spain before the Roman Empire), as well as art from Africa. In breaking with Western art conventions that reached back to ancient Greece and Rome, Picasso looked for inspiration from other, equally ancient, traditions. Second, there is the merging of figure and ground, reflecting the assumption that all portions of the work participate in its expression. And third, there is fragmenting of the figures and other elements into flat planes, especially evident in the breasts of the figure at upper right and the mask just below. This last factor proved especially significant for an artistic journey on which Picasso was soon to embark—the movement known as **Cubism.**

Picasso's partner in this venture was the artist Georges Braque. Braque met Picasso in 1907 and saw *Les Demoiselles* in Picasso's studio. By all reports, Braque was at first dismayed and puzzled by the painting, but later he came to understand Picasso's goals. Both artists had been strongly influenced by the late works of Paul Cézanne **(83)** and by Cézanne's idea that natural forms could be reduced to geometric solids—the cone, the sphere, and the cylinder. Picasso and Braque also were interested in the inherent geometry of forms, but they took as their starting point an angular, rather than a curved, solid—the cube.

In 1909 Braque and Picasso began working closely together, and they continued to do so for several years. By 1910 their experiments were so closely intertwined that the two artists' styles became virtually one, and it is sometimes difficult to tell their work apart (Chapter 2, p. 53; **52,53**). Cubism is an art of facets, like the facets in a diamond. As is evident in Braque's painting of 1911, *The Portuguese* **(538)**, forms are flattened into planes, broken apart, and reassembled to make a striking visual (but abstract) reality. We see the same form from several angles simultaneously; top, bottom, side, and frontal views may be combined into one image. Figure and ground are treated in the same way and have equal weight in the composition, blending

left: **538.** Georges Braque. *The Portuguese.* 1911. Oil on canvas, $45\frac{7}{8} \times 32\frac{1}{8}''$. Kunstmuseum, Basel.

right: **539.** Erich Heckel. *Woman (Portrait of the Artist's Wife).* 1920. Oil on canvas, $31\frac{1}{2} \times 27\frac{1}{2}''$. © The Detroit Institute of Arts (City of Detroit Purchase).

together into a coherent whole. As Cubism developed, both Braque and Picasso began introducing bits of the "real world" into their canvases—stenciled letters and numbers (as here) or even pasted-on newspaper and fabrics. The psychological tension produced in the viewer by merging "real" with "not-real" (the illusory world of paint on canvas) would have important implications for the artists of the Dada movement (p. 473) and for many artists of the later 20th century.

Cubism was a final, dramatic declaration of independence from Renaissance ideals of natural representation and linear perspective (p. 133). Braque's painting is clearly *not* an attempt to show us exactly what his model looked like. Instead, it is a study of forms for their aesthetic possibilities, a statement that a work of art has its own reality and need not be a mirror of the natural world. Neither Braque nor Picasso completely abandoned naturalism. Some of Picasso's works after Cubism (36) are as faithful representations of the natural world as anyone could ask for. However, with Cubism the principle was firmly established that a painting is *paint on canvas*—an arrangement of shapes and colors and lines chosen to suit the artist's expressive purpose, whatever that might be.

Early 20th Century: Expressionism

If Picasso and Braque in this period were experimenting with a purely visual reality, some of their contemporaries were more interested in exploring a psychological one. During the first two decades of this century a movement developed in Germany that came to be known as *Expressionism*. Centered around a group of artists based in Dresden who called themselves **Die Brücke** ("the bridge"), Expressionism had many roots. It was strongly influenced by Van Gogh and Gauguin, took its intense color effects from Fauvism, and admired the stark, emotional works of the Norwegian artist Edvard Munch (269). At the time when Expressionism flourished, Sigmund Freud was active in Vienna, publishing his new theories about the role of the unconscious, the meaning of dreams, and the practice of psychoanalysis. The Expressionists were entirely in sympathy with Freud's goal of probing the unconscious and hoped to take the process one step further—to translate their inner explorations into a meaningful art.

Erich Heckel, a leader of *Die Brücke*, gives us an image of loneliness and sorrow in the painting he called, simply, *Woman* (539). The model for this work was the artist's wife, Siddi, but this is by no means a portrait. Instead, the woman is meant to represent the suffering that Heckel considered to be universal, the ultimate sadness he saw in the human condition. She poses against a turbulent background—wildly colored flowers and a figure of a nude male bather, which Heckel had painted on his studio walls—but the woman does not see her surroundings. She shrinks into herself, and her heavy-lidded eyes look inward. The clasp of her hands is touching, for it shows her helplessness and vulnerability. If we compare this painting to Munch's *Sin* (269) of some thirty years earlier, the differences are striking. Munch's woman is beautiful and ripely sexual; her eyes gaze inward but also out, toward some dreadful vision. Heckel's woman is gaunt, almost starved into the angular lines often used by the Expressionists to show anguish. And she is alone, she stands for Everywoman and Everyman—alone. Whereas Munch's torment seems personal and individual, the Expressionists were pessimistic about life itself.

The painting styles of the Expressionist artists are often dissimilar, but their thread of connection is the desire or need to probe their deepest emotions and to express those emotions in their work. Other artists generally associated with the Expressionist movement include Käthe Kollwitz (46,222, p. 189), Paula Modersohn-Becker (93), Gustav Klimt (142), Oskar Kokoschka (237), and Emil Nolde (256).

Synthesis and Awakening: The Armory Show

European art, by the second decade of the 20th century, had run through a series of "isms"—Impressionism, Post-Impressionism, Fauvism, Cubism, Expressionism. The artists connected with these styles certainly were aware of each other's work and were influenced by one another. But each group tended to exhibit with other members of that group—Impressionists with Impressionists, Cubists with Cubists, and so on. Never had the various movements been brought together in one place to make the statement that *here* is modern art—or, rather, here are the many directions of modern art. Moreover, this extraordinary activity in European art had gone mostly unnoticed in the United States. Some few American artists and collectors had followed the new styles, but the public at large was unaware of them. All this changed abruptly in 1913. In that year a show of European and American art was organized by a group of progressive American artists. The show opened at the 69th Regiment Armory in New York, and, although there have been many art exhibitions in many armories, this one is still known as the Armory Show.

European art of the previous four decades was well represented, and the show caused an immediate sensation. So abusive was the press in its criticism that the general public became intrigued and flocked to the Armory to laugh at the art (and its makers). The critics singled out one work in particular for their greatest scorn, and that work soon became the star attraction. It is a Cubist-derived painting by Marcel Duchamp known as *Nude Descending a Staircase* (**540**).

As in a more "orthodox" Cubist painting, Duchamp has taken an image, here the nude figure, and flattened it into planes, which are then reshuffled

540. Marcel Duchamp. *Nude Descending a Staircase No. 2.* 1912. Oil on canvas, 4′10″ × 2′11″. Philadelphia Museum of Art (Louise and Walter Arensberg Collection).

and rearranged. However, he has also repeated the image many times over, creating a sharp, choppy rhythm that makes the figure appear to descend the staircase. When we first look at *Nude Descending a Staircase,* we may be tempted to echo the comment of a viewer at the Armory Show, who called the painting "an explosion in a shingle factory." But on closer inspection the forms begin to emerge, although they are abstracted: the rounded shape moving diagonally across the center of the canvas is a hip, the lower section of the painting a series of repeated legs. Duchamp had adopted the rather static forms of Cubism and set them in motion.

Another artist represented in the Armory Show was the Romanian-born sculptor Constantin Brancusi. Brancusi worked briefly in the studio of the great French sculptor Auguste Rodin **(339,355)** but soon departed with the now-famous statement, "No other trees can grow in the shadow of an oak tree." By 1910 Brancusi's work had become very abstract, as evidenced by *The Kiss* **(541)**—one of a long series of sculptures on this theme. *The Kiss* represents two of Brancusi's main preoccupations—fidelity to materials and a search for the essence of form. Here Brancusi's material is stone, and he has carved it in such a way that we are very much aware of its nature as stone, not as an attempt to mimic flesh. So highly simplified is the shape that the kiss itself, the union of two souls and bodies, becomes more important than the individuals who take part in it. Even sex differences between the two are barely suggested (the woman, at right, by longer flowing hair and a rounded breast). Brancusi said: "Simplicity is not an end in art, but one arrives at simplicity in spite of oneself, in approaching the real sense of things."

We can see how far Brancusi has moved from the style of his teacher—how nearly he had arrived at simplicity—by comparing a work of Rodin's, also called *The Kiss,* carved just about a decade earlier **(542)**. Rodin's version of the same subject is far more naturalistic, the figures modeled to a smooth perfection and grace. The embrace of the lovers is both romantic and erotic—qualities missing from Brancusi's interpretation.

left: 541. Constantin Brancusi.
The Kiss. 1910.
Stone, height 19¾".
Musée National d'Art Moderne, Paris.

right: 542. Auguste Rodin.
The Kiss. 1886–98.
Marble, height 5'11¼".
Musée Rodin, Paris.

543. Wassily Kandinsky.
Picture with an Archer.
1909. Oil on canvas, 5'9" × 4'9".
The Museum of Modern Art, New York
(fractional gift of Mrs. Bertram Smith
to The Museum of Modern Art, New York).

The Armory Show introduced not only French artists to the United States, but Russian as well, most notably Wassily Kandinsky, whose early gouache painting we saw in Chapter 7 **(245)**. Born in Moscow, Kandinsky spent long periods of time in both Paris and Munich. He was influenced by the Post-Impressionists and the Fauves, but by about 1905 he had begun to move toward a much greater abstraction than that attempted by either group. *Picture with an Archer* **(543)**, painted in 1909, is roughly contemporary with both Matisse's *Green Stripe* and Picasso's *Les Demoiselles d'Avignon*, yet it is remarkably different in approach. Neither Picasso nor Matisse ever completely abandoned figural references in their work, but Kandinsky strove increasingly to eliminate representation. His canvases explode with color and energy derived from his own emotional experience—an expression of "inner necessity"—and he considered subject matter "detrimental" to this expression. For this artist, "The harmony of color and form must be based solely upon the principle of proper contact with the human soul."

While the Armory Show attracted much negative criticism, it was a commercial success; about 350 works were sold. Moreover, the show firmly established the position of modern art and introduced its principles to the United States. As we have seen, Marcel Duchamp was the most controversial figure in the show, exhibiting a work influenced by Cubism. Within a very short time, however, Duchamp had shifted his interest to quite a different mode of expression. He became a leader in the first of two movements that, in their own ways, were fully as revolutionary as Cubism.

Europe During and After World War I: Dada and Surrealism

During World War I in Europe there arose an art movement known as *Dada*, which came into being as a reaction against the unprecedented carnage of world war. The artists associated with Dada felt that any civilization that could tolerate such brutality must be swept away, and all of its institutions, including traditional art, along with it. Dada, therefore, was anti-everything, even anti-meaning (the name "dada" is said to have been chosen at random from a French dictionary). Representative of Dada's art is Duchamp's work known as *L.H.O.O.Q.* **(544)**. Duchamp selected the one painting that for the Western world symbolizes art with a capital *A* and gleefully drew a moustache and goatee on a reproduction of *Mona Lisa*. As if that irreverence were not enough, he penciled in the letters at the bottom, which, when pronounced the French way, make a vulgar pun suggestive of nymphomania. *L.H.O.O.Q.* is thus a kind of artistic blasphemy—poking fun at one of the most cherished institutions of art.

Duchamp's friend, the French-Cuban artist Francis Picabia, followed a similar artistic path. He, too, began his career with Cubist-inspired paintings, and he, too, became caught up in the Dada movement. Picabia exhibited several works at the Armory Show, and he journeyed to New York for the exhibition. In the United States Picabia found himself both impressed and amused by Americans' obsession with the machine. The result was a series of works featuring machine symbolism, including *Machine Tournez Vite* **(545)**. In true Dada fashion, *Machine Tournez Vite* ridicules a basic human activity—sexual union—by equating it with the meshing of machine gears "turning quickly." A legend at the bottom of the picture identifies the smaller wheel at lower left as "woman," the larger wheel as "man." The Dada world considered nothing sacred; everything was a potential subject for ironic humor.

Surrealism, as we have seen (p. 91), is an art based on the unconscious, often taking its subject matter and its imagery from dreams and fantasies.

left: **544.** Marcel Duchamp. *L.H.O.O.Q.* 1919. Rectified ready-made, pencil on reproduction of Leonardo's *Mona Lisa;* 7¾ × 4⅞". Private collection.

right: **545.** Francis Picabia. *Machine Tournez Vite.* c. 1916–17. Gouache, 19¼ × 12⅝". Private collection.

Conceived as a reaction to the more "intellectual" art movements, such as Cubism, Surrealism—according to its manifesto published in 1924—aimed at "pure psychic automation by which one intends to express verbally, in writing, or by other method, the real functioning of the mind." Artists who worked in the Surrealist mode are generally separated into two categories—those whose imagery is predominantly figural, including Salvador Dali **(89)** and René Magritte **(193)**; and those following a more abstract style, such as Joan Miró.

Possibly the most famous of all Surrealist works is Dali's *Persistence of Memory* **(546)**, a small painting that many people call simply "the melted watches." Dali's art, especially here, offers a fascinating paradox: His rendering of forms is precise and meticulous—we might say *super*realistic—yet the forms could not possibly be real. *Persistence of Memory* shows a bleak, arid, decayed landscape populated by an odd, fetal-type creature (some think representative of the artist) and several limp watches—time not only stopped but melting away. Perhaps in this work Dali's fantasy, his dream, is to triumph once and for all over time. Earlier in this book we have seen images connected with "time running out"—in the egg timer and clock of Audrey Flack's *Marilyn* **(57)** and the bedside clock of a dying Edvard Munch (p. 229). Dali's melted watches cannot move, so the artist may hope to capture time and gain artistic immortality.

Joan Miró's *Carnival of Harlequin* **(547)**, representing the abstract phase of Surrealism, shows us not the oddly distorted landscape of a Dali work but rather a completely invented landscape—and one teeming with life. Miró's fantasy world is aswarm with odd little creatures—animals and fish and insects and perhaps a snake or two—as well as nameless abstract forms that participate in the artist's madcap party. Much of Miró's imagery suggests a cheerful sexuality, as though the whole space of the universe were occupied with lighthearted erotic play and reproduction. In contrast to the utter stillness of Dali's *Persistence of Memory*, Miró's *Carnival* is all movement. There are even a few musical notes at the top to accompany the dance. As interpreted by Miró, Surrealism's dreams are lively ones.

While both Dada and Surrealism, as movements, were relatively short-lived, they had great influence on artistic developments in the second half of this century. Meanwhile, another aesthetic—one equally dedicated to altering the course of modern art—had taken root in Germany. It centered on what is perhaps the most famous of all art schools: The Bauhaus.

546. Salvador Dali.
The Persistence of Memory. 1931.
Oil on canvas, 9½ × 13".
Collection,
The Museum of Modern Art,
New York (given anonymously).

Between the World Wars: 1918–1938

The **Bauhaus** was founded as a school of design in 1919 in Weimar, Germany. It moved to Dessau in 1925 and then briefly to Berlin, before being closed by the Nazis in 1933. Throughout its short existence, a mere fourteen years, it had an enormous impact on all the art and design of its time, and the influence of the Bauhaus continues to be felt in many fields. Actually, the Bauhaus was less important as a school than as an *idea*. Although its faculty included some of the most noteworthy names in 20th-century art and architecture, it produced few students of particular talent. But many of the principles that guided its curriculum are alive and well today.

Architect Walter Gropius founded the Bauhaus, and he was also the prime theorist in the development of the school's philosophy. Briefly, the Bauhaus hoped to erase the lines separating painters, sculptors, architects, craftsmen, and industrial designers. All artists and designers, whatever their form of expression, were considered essentially craftsmen, committed to using materials and forms in the most straightforward manner, without artificially applied decoration. The word "Bauhaus" translates roughly as "building house," and its leaders sought to "build" a new guiding principle of design compatible with 20th-century technology. In its later years the school focused more and more on architecture and industrial design, with a view toward reconciling aesthetic design to the capabilities of machine production. Structures, rooms, furniture, and everyday household objects were stripped of superficial embellishment, pared down to the lines necessary for functional use.

Despite this emphasis on industrial design, the painting faculty retained a strong voice. Wassily Kandinsky taught at the Bauhaus for eleven years, and he is only one of several noted artists whose names are associated with the school. Another was Josef Albers, who later emigrated to the United States. Albers' most representative work was done in the 1950s and 1960s, so he will be considered later in this chapter **(554)**.

Also on the painting faculty was the Swiss artist Paul Klee. Klee's work is among the most difficult to categorize in the history of art. Most art historians consider him among the great painters of the century, yet he fits no niche or "ism"; there is really no one like Klee. A common first reaction to a

547. Joan Miró.
Carnival of Harlequin. 1924–25.
Oil on canvas, $26 \times 36\frac{3}{8}''$.
Albright-Knox Art Gallery,
Buffalo, N.Y.
(Room of Contemporary
Art Fund, 1976).

548. Paul Klee.
*Dance You Monster
to My Soft Song!* 1922.
Watercolor and oil transfer
drawing on plaster-grounded
gauche mounted on gouache-
painted paper,
gauze support; 13¾ × 11½".
Solomon R. Guggenheim Museum,
New York.

Klee painting is, "That looks like a child's drawing!" And, indeed, the artist took much of his inspiration from the art of children, but behind the childlike imagery is a technique and sensibility of great sophistication. The apparent playfulness masks a deeply complex, subtle imagination. *Dance You Monster to My Soft Song!* **(548)**, a mixed-media watercolor, was done two years after Klee joined the Bauhaus staff. Here the delicate line drawing is masterfully controlled to express the idea of a quite friendly monster dancing away to the tune played by a little girl at a transparent piano. Klee's genius lies in combining inventive imagery with a sure command of line, color, and design.

Except for Dada and Surrealism, few major art movements emerged during the period between the world wars, although individual artists pursued their own styles. Piet Mondrian was at work in Holland **(119,203)**, Henry Moore in England **(344)**, and Marc Chagall in France **(90)**. In the United States Edward Hopper painted his lonely, penetrating visions of the American scene **(201)**, while the Mexican muralists were creating grand-scale images of the social scene both above and below the border **(234)**. Of course, Picasso and Matisse continued to develop their art throughout the period.

Following World War I Europe remained in a state of social and economic turmoil, joined by the United States in 1929, when the entire Western world plunged into the Great Depression. World War II, beginning in 1939 in Europe, 1941 for the United States, brought organized activity in Western art almost to a standstill. Certainly art was made during the war years, but attention was focused on the conflict, and many of the artists were on the battlefield. When the Western nations emerged from war in 1945, it was discovered that the art capital of the Western world had moved—from Paris to New York.

Art Since 1945

NEW YORK: 1945–1960

In the aftermath of World War II most of Western Europe was completely devastated. The United States, while exhausted, was not. No bombs had fallen or battles been fought in New York, as they had in London and Paris and Amsterdam and most of the cities in Germany. When the time came to resume the normal activities of life, New York became the center of a vibrant art revival. Many of the most progressive European artists had immigrated to the United States, and they served as teachers and inspiration for a new generation of artists—most of them American—who gravitated to New York. In fact, painters associated with the first major postwar art movement are referred to as the **New York School.**

Not a school in the sense of an institution or of instruction, the New York School was a convenient label under which to lump together a group of painters also known as the **Abstract Expressionists.** Primary among them were Jackson Pollock and Willem de Kooning; the group also included Franz Kline and Lee Krasner. Abstract Expressionism had many sources—Surrealism, Cubism, the early works of Kandinsky **(543)**, and in some cases even Eastern art. The artists involved had less in common than seems apparent at first. One unifying thread is that their paintings, on the whole, are very large in scale, tending to overwhelm the viewer in their dynamic—even violent—presence. Most of the works are entirely nonrepresentational, but de Kooning for one retained figural elements in many of his paintings and thus fits better the technical definition of "abstract." Abstract Expressionism was characterized by bold, passionate painting—sometimes achieved with sweeping brush strokes, at other times produced by hurling paint on the canvas, as Pollock did. The sheer power and energy of this technique caused it to be known as **action painting.**

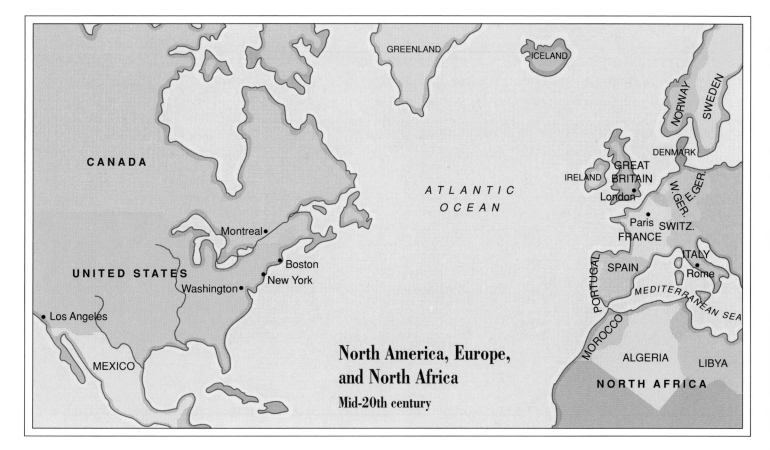

North America, Europe, and North Africa
Mid-20th century

The quintessential Abstract Expressionist was Jackson Pollock, who had perfected his technique of "drip painting" by the late 1940s (pp. 48–49, and **47**). *Blue Poles* **(549)** shows Pollock's typically dense interweaving of lines and colors, here punctuated by the almost vertical "poles," which are themselves criss-crossed with intricate patterns of dripped and spattered paint. Even in reproduction this canvas vibrates with energy, so that one can imagine the impact of the 7-by-16-foot painting on a viewer standing before it.

Lee Krasner, who was married to Pollock, came to Abstract Expressionism at about the same time as her husband. Krasner's work, as exemplified by *The Bull* **(550)**, has bolder areas of color and is often characterized by bulbous shapes that seem to burst out at the viewer. There is a fierce quality

above: 549. Jackson Pollock. *Blue Poles.* 1952. Oil, enamel, and aluminum paint, glass on canvas; 6'11½" × 16'½". Australian National Gallery, Canberra (purchased 1973).

right: 550. Lee Krasner. *The Bull.* 1958. Oil on cotton duck, 6'5" × 5'10⅛". Courtesy Robert Miller Gallery, New York.

Lee Krasner

1908–1984

In October of 1983 the first major retrospective exhibition of paintings by Lee Krasner opened at the Museum of Fine Arts in Houston. Later, the same show toured the United States. Krasner did not live to see it arrive in New York—once the hub of the Abstract Expressionist movement—because she died just eight months after the Houston opening. Amazingly, this remarkable woman, whom critics now consider to be "an artist of the first rank," expressed little bitterness about the fact that she worked so long under the shadow of Abstract Expressionism's "golden boy"—Jackson Pollock.

Krasner, born Lenore, was the sixth child of Russian immigrant parents who had settled in Brooklyn. By the age of thirteen she had decided to become an artist. She enrolled first at Cooper Union, later at the Art Students League in New York. She also studied for several years with the painter Hans Hofmann, from whom she learned the principles of Cubism, and under whose tutelage she took her first steps toward Abstract Expressionism. Like many other young artists of the Depression period, Krasner supported herself by working for the government-sponsored Federal Art Project. Her first exhibition—part of a group show—came in 1937, in New York.

In 1942 Krasner, having heard about the work of Jackson Pollock, went to his studio one day and introduced herself. Soon the couple were living together, and in 1945 they married. This union proved to be a successful working partnership. Wherever they lived, in New York or at their house on Long Island, Krasner and Pollock maintained joint studios. While their painting styles usually remained separate, the two seemed to sustain and encourage each other's work.

Unfortunately for Krasner, the climate of the times was not receptive to a woman who painted in such an assertive style as Abstract Expressionism. Of the New York School of artists she later said, "There were very few painters in that so-called circle who acknowledged I painted at all." Krasner was relegated to the status of "Pollock's wife." Not long afterward, in 1956, she became "Pollock's widow," when her husband was killed in a car crash.

Gradually, after Pollock's death, the critics began to take a fresh look at the work of Lee Krasner, to evaluate it for its own sake. Through it all she continued

to paint and to exhibit. And she remained true to the principles of Abstract Expressionism. Other fashions came and went, but this artist continually sought the development of her personal style. By the late 1970s "Pollock's widow" was again Lee Krasner.

Krasner's ideas about painting were her own, not an echo of Pollock's. "Painting, for me, when it really 'happens' is as miraculous as any natural phenomenon—as, say, a lettuce leaf. . . . One could go on forever as to whether the paint should be thick or thin, whether to paint the woman or the square, hard-edge or soft, but after a while such questions become a bore. . . . The painting I have in mind . . . transcends technique, transcends subject and moves into the realm of the inevitable—then you have the lettuce leaf."[4]

Lee Krasner. *Self-Portrait.*
c. 1930. Oil on linen, 30⅜ × 25⅛".
Courtesy Robert Miller Gallery, New York.

above: **551.** Willem de Kooning.
Composition. 1955.
Oil, enamel, and charcoal on canvas;
6'7⅛" × 5'9⅛".
Solomon R. Guggenheim Museum,
New York.

left: **552.** Franz Kline. *Chief.* 1950.
Oil on canvas, 4'10⅜" × 6'1½".
Collection, The Museum of Modern Art,
New York (gift of
Mr. and Mrs. David M. Solinger).

in Krasner's work, deriving from the strong colors and tensely drawn—not spattered—lines. In *The Bull* the rhythms are mostly circular, except for the totem-like image at right.

As mentioned earlier, Willem de Kooning often used figural images in his paintings, especially in his famous "Woman" series **(48)**. However, he, too, could work in an entirely nonrepresentational mode, as evidenced by *Composition* **(551)**. A saturated blood-red dominates this canvas, seeming to spill out from between the jagged lines and patches of other colors, taking on the intensity of a scream. Abstract Expressionism as interpreted by de Kooning is emotion exploding before your eyes.

Krasner, de Kooning, and Pollock usually worked in color, but other Abstract Expressionists—notably Franz Kline—are more closely identified with the bold use of black. Kline's painting *Chief* (**552**), named after a locomotive that passed through the Pennsylvania town where the artist was born, resembles an actual locomotive only in its raw, almost menacing power. Above all, Kline's art is based on the gesture—the tense sweep of a broad brush held at arm's length, the dramatic contrast of black against white in large scale.

Another form of abstraction that came into prominence in the postwar period is known as **Color Field** painting. As the name implies, imagery is reduced to a large "field" or area of color, in some cases one pure color filling the entire canvas. In contrast to the dynamic emotionalism of Abstract Expressionism, Color Field paintings have a meditative tranquillity that draws the viewer in and invites contemplation. The work of Mark Rothko in the late forties through the sixties (**553**) usually features one or more soft-edged color rectangles floating in the larger color rectangle of the canvas. The inner rectangle has sides parallel to the canvas edges, and its boundaries are blurred and gently blended, causing the inner sections to float. Very large scale is also characteristic of Rothko's work, so the viewer is enveloped in an atmosphere of sensuous color.

553. Mark Rothko.
Orange and Yellow. 1956.
Oil on canvas, 7'7" × 5'11".
Albright-Knox Art Gallery,
Buffalo, N.Y. (gift of Seymour
H. Knox, 1956).

Superficially the work of Josef Albers (554) seems much like that of Rothko, especially when reproduced in a book. In fact, the two artists' paintings have very little in common. Rothko's canvases are huge, Albers' rather small. Rothko's edges are soft and blurred, Albers' precise. Most important, Rothko's expression is emotional, Albers' more intellectual. In the 1950s Albers began a long series of paintings—finally there were hundreds—all entitled *Homage to the Square*. All are "nests" of three or four squares centered in the canvas. What varies is the color, and this was Albers' chief preoccupation. Albers hoped to show the dynamic interaction of colors—how they work together when placed side by side, how some colors advance while others recede, how colors intensify or deintensify each other (pp. 117–127). By restricting himself to the square, he avoided distractions of form, so that the viewer can concentrate on the pure, saturated color. Because it is a series, *Homage to the Square* makes the point that there is no one "best" way a painting can be done, but many different possibilities.

By the time Rothko and Albers painted the works shown here, in the mid-1950s, abstractionism had held sway for more than fifteen years, and the art world was ready for a change of pace. The return of representational art was signaled by two artists who appeared on the scene about 1955—Robert Rauschenberg (74) and Jasper Johns.

Jasper Johns chose as his subjects some of the most familiar images one could imagine—the American flag, a map of the United States, numbers, letters of the alphabet. All are rendered accurately, in true proportions, but in a freely brushed, painterly style. His *Target with Four Faces* (555) may remind us of a shooting gallery in an amusement park. The inclusion of actual three-dimensional heads with the painting owes a debt to Dada, which often pushed into the third dimension, and to the earlier collage work of Picasso and Braque. Here the target is drawn precisely, the four identical faces seem waiting for bullets to hit them, yet there is no sense of menace in this work. By painting the target so matter-of-factly, Johns has taken away the menace. The target and faces are no longer objects to be shot at, but images to be studied for their own visual interest. This artist seeks the familiar, strips it of its familiar associations, and shows it to us as art. With his targets and other known images, Johns anticipated what would become one of the most important art styles of the 1960s—Pop Art.

left: **554.** Josef Albers. *Homage to the Square: Ascending.* 1953. Oil on composition board, 43½″ square. Whitney Museum of American Art, New York (purchase).

right: **555.** Jasper Johns. *Target with Four Faces.* 1955. Assemblage: encaustic and collage on canvas with objects, 26″ square, surmounted by four tinted plaster faces in wood box with hinged front; overall dimensions with box open 33⅝ × 26 × 3″. Collection, The Museum of Modern Art, New York (gift of Mr. and Mrs. Robert C. Scull).

ART STYLES OF THE SIXTIES

Pop Art was both startling and controversial. As Dada had done nearly half a century earlier, it broke the rules about what constituted fitting material for serious art. Pop drew its subject matter from the most mundane objects of mass-produced culture—billboards, commercial packages, and the like. Andy Warhol's *200 Campbell Soup Cans* **(174)** was but one example of this trend. Roy Lichtenstein, whose still life we saw earlier **(109)**, often based his imagery on the comic book. Many of Lichtenstein's paintings **(556)** are huge, meticulously rendered frames adapted from comic strips, accurate down to the dialogue in "balloons" and the dot pattern of cheap newspaper reproduction. The artist did not hesitate to introduce a touch of irony by poking fun at himself and the art world in proclaiming this work a "masterpiece." Pop Art attempted to show that a detached look at the overfamiliar objects of daily life could give them new meaning as visual emblems.

Coexisting with Pop was the movement known as ***Op Art,*** or art based on optical principles. Op Art deals in complex color interactions, to the point where colors and lines actually seem to vibrate before the eyes. We have already seen this effect in the work of Bridget Riley **(164)**, who was also part of the Op movement. In Richard Anuszkiewicz' painting *Splendor of Red* **(557)** red and blue lines radiate outward from a central diamond shape of intense red. As a viewer looks at the painting, the lines begin to pulsate, and a halo forms around the red diamond. The Op artists were exploring visual phenomena in a wholly new way, generating a clash between what the eye records and the brain perceives. Some critics dismissed the paintings as "just designs," but in fact Op works suggest a new approach to painting—as a challenging optical experience.

A third movement of the sixties was ***Minimal Art,*** which reduced the art elements to a "minimum"—simple (often geometric) shapes and sometimes color. Minimal Art can be seen as a kind of celebration of the artist's basic materials. A painting is paint on canvas, a sculpture is metal or stone or wood or similar material. By stripping art down to these substances, the Minimal artist attempted to reaffirm the worth of art for its own sake, not as a reflection of anything else. In sculpture, an excellent example of the Mini-

left: **556.** Roy Lichtenstein. *Masterpiece.* 1962. Oil on canvas, 4'6" square. Private collection, New York.

right: **557.** Richard Anuszkiewicz. *Splendor of Red.* 1965. Liquitex on canvas, 6' square. Yale University Art Gallery, New Haven, Conn. (gift of Seymour H. Knox).

mal is Tony Smith's *Die* **(558)**, a 6-foot cube of plain black steel that Smith ordered by telephone from the foundry. *Die* cannot be said to have much emotional content. It has no color, no variations of texture, no movement, no rhythm, no focal point. What is does have is *scale*, and that scale gives it a presence, a monumentality. *Die* conveys the idea that form can exist for its own sake in art.

In painting, the Minimal style is often referred to as "hard-edge." Lines are drawn as though with a ruler, colors are pure and unshaded, shapes are precise. Frank Stella's *Sinjerli Variation IV* **(559)** illustrates these characteristics. Its shapes are as regular as those drawn with a compass and a protractor, its rhythms simple and repetitive. Geometric shape in one way or another has been a part of painting for centuries. For example, Raphael based many of his compositions on the triangle **(111)**, and Hopper structured a picture around a series of rectangles **(202)**. The Minimalists stripped away such figural references and concentrated on geometry alone.

The decade of the sixties was a time of testing, a time of breaking rules, in many spheres—political, social, economic, artistic. Then emerged the sexual revolution, the struggle for racial equality, the peace movement, the feminist movement, the space age, and the computer era. In art a similar kind of testing took place. Merely the fact that there coexisted three art movements—radically different in philosophy and visual effect—demonstrates the vitality of art and the quest for new frontiers. During the following decades, then, artists as well as those in other fields had to confront a basic question: If all the rules have been broken, where does one go next?

CURRENT TRENDS

A good way to introduce the art of the present time is to consider another work by Frank Stella, this one made thirteen years after *Sinjerli Variation IV*. Stella's *Pergusa* **(560)** still shows the artist's preoccupation with interwoven, curvilinear forms, yet he has transformed hard-edged geometry into a more painterly and complicated tracery that is wonderful in its variety. Creative artists, in general, build on what they have done before. Stella has taken his Minimal expressions of the sixties and developed them into a joyous visual

below: 558. Tony Smith. *Die.* 1962. Steel, 6' cube. Private collection, New York.

right: 559. Frank Stella. *Sinjerli Variation IV.* 1968. Fluorescent acrylic on canvas, diameter 10'. Collection Mr. and Mrs. Burton Tremaine.

exuberance for the eighties. *Sinjerli*'s movement is slow and measured; our eyes move rhythmically around and through its precise curves. But *Pergusa* is alive with movement, a roller-coaster ride of shapes. There is another big difference between the two works. *Sinjerli* of the sixties is two dimensional—as flat as a bull's-eye. *Pergusa* of the eighties has moved out into the third dimension. It has elements of relief attached to the background surface and projecting to almost 2 feet.

Like many works of contemporary art, *Pergusa* is difficult to categorize. It looks like a painting when reproduced in this book, and sections of it are painted, but it has more depth than many sculptures. Strictly speaking, it is neither a painting nor a sculpture, but a little of both. Stella's prints (273) show a similar versatility in the combination of several techniques. As we move into the nineties, we see an increasing trend toward a "no-holds-barred" approach to material and method. For the contemporary artist any medium, any process, is fair game if it results in the desired expression.

The variety of options extends also to the styles in which contemporary artists work. Earlier periods in the history of art often pitted fashion against anti-fashion. As recently as the 1950s, when Abstract Expressionism held sway, few important museums or galleries would mount shows by contemporary artists working in a naturalistic style, because such work was considered old-fashioned, even trivial. Now the situation has changed dramatically. A tour of the major galleries in New York or San Francisco or Chicago will reveal an astonishing range of styles—all fashionable, all taken seriously by critics and the art-viewing public. The art of the eighties and nineties can be said to offer something for nearly everyone. Abstraction, realism, large, small, painting, sculpture, mixed media, art object, no art object—each has its adherents. Beyond this, the individual art viewer can enjoy a variety of styles, just as one might enjoy having Mexican food one night, Italian food the next night, and so on. The artistic "menu" is a varied and exciting one. In the next few pages, then, we will look at some of the styles of today.

560. Frank Stella.
Pergusa. 1981.
Mixed media on etched magnesium panel,
6'1" × 7'8" × 2'.
Collection Graham Gund,
Cambridge, Mass., courtesy
M. Knoedler & Co., New York.

Jasper Johns is another artist who, like Stella, has developed his style into a new expression. In 1987 he exhibited four large paintings in a series called *The Seasons*, of which we illustrate *Winter* (**561**). Johns is still dealing in what we might call the "givens"—the images and ideas that are so ingrained in our consciousness and our everyday life that we take them for granted. Earlier his "givens" were targets and flags and numbers; now he touches upon the most fundamental rhythms of life itself, as felt through the changing seasons of the year. Depiction of the seasons has many precedents in the history of art; we saw an early example in the Limbourgs' *Très Riches Heures* (**76**). *The Seasons* series is considered to be autobiographical, but, since Johns is a private and introspective person, his allusions to himself are often puzzling. Crowded into the right side of *Winter* is a shadowy figure, surely symbolic of the artist, which may remind you of Edvard Munch's claustrophobic self-portrait (p. 229). The snowman at left is an emblem of winter, and the cut-off circular form at bottom left may serve as an echo of Johns' earlier paintings, such as *Target*. We sense the artist taking stock, sifting through his artistic attic, reworking the imagery that has developed in his art and life for thirty years.

Abstraction is still an important current in present-day art, and among the most innovative of its practitioners is Elizabeth Murray. *Painter's Progress* (**562**) is typical of Murray's exuberant shaped canvases, rather like a brilliantly colored Cubist painting in which the facets have been cut apart and allowed to slip and slide and collide with one another. Here the basic form is a painter's palette, shattered and then reassembled. As in a Cubist work, we can find references to the human figure, but Murray's forms are not only more joyous but more outward-turning, seeming to ricochet off each other like a vivid musical animation.

Existing side by side with abstract art is what many would consider its antithesis—art that attempts to duplicate faithfully forms in the natural world. The **New Realism,** as it is sometimes called, almost certainly derives

left: 561. Jasper Johns. *Winter,* from *The Seasons.* 1987. Oil on canvas, 6'3" × 4'2". Courtesy Leo Castelli Gallery, New York.

right: 562. Elizabeth Murray. *Painter's Progress.* 1981. Oil on canvas, in 19 parts; 9'8" × 7'9". Collection, The Museum of Modern Art, New York (acquired through the Bernhill Fund and gift of Agnes Gund).

563. Philip Pearlstein.
Model Seated on a Rocking Rattan Lounge. 1984.
Oil on canvas, 6 × 5'.
Courtesy Hirschl & Adler Modern,
New York.

some of its inspiration from the Pop Art of the 1960s, but it is more likely to focus on the human figure, and it lacks the association with commercial, mass-produced culture that was so important to Pop. Audrey Flack **(57)** is one of the best-known New Realist painters. Some of the artists, including Flack, work from photographs, projecting a photographic image onto a canvas and then painting with an airbrush over the image. The paintings that result have such photographic accuracy that the term ***Photorealism*** was coined.

Another prominent artist of the New Realist style is Philip Pearlstein, who paints the nude figure in a *super*realistic way that might more accurately be described as "naked" **(563)**. Pearlstein's nudes, both male and female, are captured with meticulous, almost brutal accuracy, with all their bulges, wrinkles, warts, hairs, and general imperfections. The "peephole" point of view, in which we see the models at odd angles and oddly cut off by the edges of the canvas, is reminiscent of works by Degas **(531)**. In recent years Pearlstein has taken to painting his nudes against elaborate backgrounds, such as intricate, colorful Oriental rugs. The interplay of visual textures becomes extremely important, and one cannot help but wonder at the artist's amazingly naturalistic rendering. Pearlstein's figures are not lovely in the sense that fashion models are lovely, but his pictures fascinate in their stark, uncompromising look at the real.

Relatively few artists aim for such an extreme of realism, but many work in a basically representational style. Of these, one of the most difficult to pin down is Jennifer Bartlett. To get a meaningful sense of her range, the viewer should see a wide selection of her works, and here we can show only one. Bartlett's sources are eclectic—everything from Impressionism to the various styles of the 1960s—and her subjects are equally wide-ranging. She has worked in practically every known medium: oil, pastel, charcoal, fresco,

564. Jennifer Bartlett. *Old House Lane #9.* 1986. Pastel on paper, 2'6" × 11'. Courtesy Paula Cooper Gallery, New York.

ceramic, enamel, steel plates, wood, and so on. *Old House Lane #9* **(564)**, painted in 1986, is a pastel, and like others of Bartlett's recent paintings it has a large horizontal format. Critics often use the word "mysterious" to describe Bartlett's work, and we may apply this adjective to *Old House Lane #9*. A white picket fence, sun-splashed and viewed from different angles, is its subject. Ordinarily, "white picket fence" comes right behind "Mom" and "apple pie" as a symbol of domestic tranquillity, but this fence is painted so aggressively that it stands as a barrier. The house barely seen in each section is on the other side of the fence, but we cannot tell if we are inside the fence looking out, or outside looking in.

Earlier in this book we encountered the work of Sandro Chia **(140)**, who is often referred to as one of the "new" Expressionists, or **Neo-Expressionists.** This movement was spearheaded by a group of European artists, principally Germans and Italians, who were young children during and after World War II. Their art reflects the consciousness of nations that fought the great war, lost, and began to pick up the pieces afterward.

Neo-Expressionist art is basically representational and often contains figures, but its intensity of form and energy makes it quite different from the New Realist paintings just discussed. Neo-Expressionist works are full of passion and symbolism, occasionally even story line. Sometimes there is a jarring, unsettling note, as in the paintings of Georg Baselitz **(565)**, which may look as though they have been hung upside down.

Best known of the German Neo-Expressionists is Anselm Kiefer, whose enormous paintings often include direct references to the horrors of Nazi power under Adolf Hitler and the atrocities of World War II. *Interior* **(566)**, for example, was copied from a photograph of Hitler's Chancellery (or office of state), a building designed by the ambitious Nazi architect Albert Speer. In

565. Georg Baselitz. *Nachtessen in Dresden.* 1983. Oil on canvas, 9'2" × 14'9". Collection Doris and Charles Saatchi, London, courtesy Xavier Fourcade, Inc., New York.

Kiefer's work the Chancellery, rendered in dramatic perspective, is abandoned and decaying. A fire burns in the center of the room; perhaps it will destroy the building and the regime it represents. Most critics have read Kiefer's work as a kind of exorcism—an attempt to drive out the evil spirits of Germany's past. And, to be sure, the artist's vast theatrical spaces, almost like stage sets, are empty. The actors are gone.

By the mid-1980s several American (New York–based) artists had become associated with the Neo-Expressionist movement. Whether they would label themselves as Neo-Expressionist remains unclear, but without doubt their work is strong, often disturbing, and expressive. Foremost among the group are Julian Schnabel, David Salle, and Eric Fischl.

Schnabel frequently paints on unconventional surfaces with unconventional materials; we saw his drawing/painting on velvet in Chapter 6 **(230)**. For an exhibition in 1986, Schnabel took painted muslin stage backdrops he had obtained from the Japanese Kabuki theater, stretched them like ordinary plain canvas, and added his own painted touches to produce works like *Rebirth I (The Last View of Camilliano Cien Fuegos)* **(567)**. In *Rebirth I* the blossoming trees are from the theater backdrop, turned upside down; Schnabel has painted in the eyes and the horizontal lines. The intense eyes seem to be peering straight at us over a peaceful landscape. In current art we will find two important trends, both manifest in this work of Schnabel's: **reference** to already existing art, and **transformation** of already existing art to make a fresh statement.

right: 566. Anselm Kiefer. *Interior.* 1981. Oil, paper, and straw on canvas; 9'5¼" × 10'2½". Collection Stedelijk Museum, Amsterdam.

below: 567. Julian Schnabel. *Rebirth I: (The Last View of Camilliano Cien Fuegos).* 1986. Oil and tempera on muslin, 12'4" × 11'2". Courtesy Pace Gallery, New York.

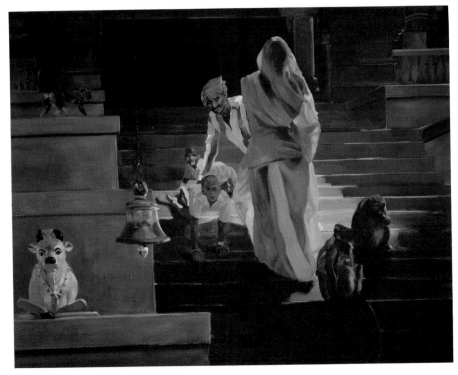

above: 568. David Salle.
Tennyson. 1983.
Oil and acrylic on canvas
with wood, 6'6" × 9'8".
Courtesy Mary Boone Gallery, New York.

left: 569. Eric Fischl.
On the Stairs of the Temple. 1989.
Oil on linen, 9'7" × 11'8".
National Gallery of Art,
Washington, D.C.,
courtesy Mary Boone Gallery, New York.

Besides "references," two other words you are likely to hear in connection with contemporary art are *quotation* and *appropriation*—that is, quoting from or appropriating images from other types of art or media. Nowhere is this tendency more marked than in the work of David Salle **(568)**. Salle's sources are diverse: traditional master artworks, Pop Art, television, magazine layout and graphic design, Dada, photography. Often his images are traced, rather than freely drawn or painted. He may stencil letters onto a painting, as here, or he may borrow a fragment from another painting or a photograph for inclusion in his own visual expressions. Not even Salle's dealers profess to understand what his art is all about. Perhaps Salle is closer to Dada than to any other form of art, for in Dada the imposition of the word "Tennyson" over the traced figure of a nude would not *have* any meaning. It would simply be presented as an image to look at.

Recent works by Eric Fischl show an appropriation not of subject matter or form, but rather of style. In a series of paintings resulting from a trip to

India, Fischl evokes the heroic, allegorical style of such 19th-century French artists as Delacroix and Courbet **(524,525)**, even to the majestic composition and dramatic lighting. *On the Stairs of the Temple* **(569)** shows a veiled woman descending the stairs, a turbaned man, two apparently crippled boys, a pair of monkeys, a hanging bell, a small white cow figure. In a 19th-century painting all these images would *mean* something, there would be a story or moral or allegory. In Fischl's work they probably do *not* mean anything. The allegory is presented for its own visual sake, with no hidden significance. The heroic style in itself is reason enough for art.

Neo-Expressionist art has no monopoly on references and quotations. Pat Steir, an American artist not associated with the group, has carried the idea of artistic quotation to marvelous heights in a complex work known as *The Brueghel Series* **(570)**. Steir, who lives part of the year in Holland, conceived the project after viewing a still-life painting of flowers by Jan Brueghel the Elder in a Dutch museum. Having bought a poster of the Brueghel painting, she then cut the poster into small pieces and used each piece as the basis for a separate painting. When hung together in a prearranged pattern, the sixty-four panels—completed over a period of two years—echo the form of the original flower painting. Each panel, however, is executed in a different style, which explains the work's subtitle, *A Vanitas of Style*. In effect, *The Brueghel Series* is a painting about painting, about all the rich variety of styles that have been practiced by artists for the last several

570. Pat Steir.
The Brueghel Series
(A Vanitas of Style).
1982–84. Oil on canvas;
64 panels, each $28\frac{1}{2} \times 22\frac{1}{2}''$.
Courtesy the artist
and Michael Klein, Inc., New York.

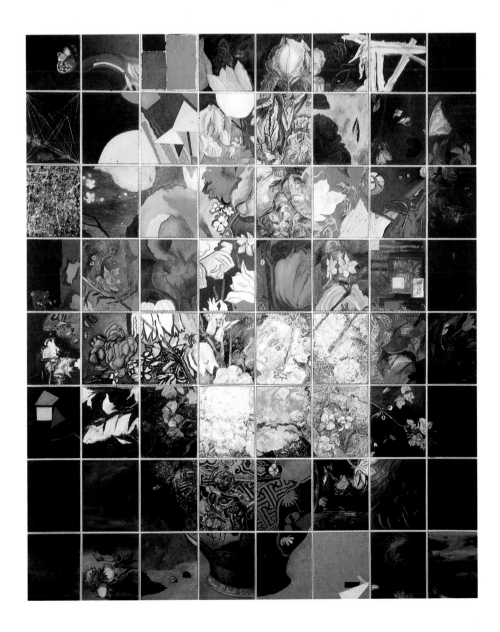

centuries, ranging from Rembrandt to Steir herself. A small book reproduction of this work—which in life is nearly 20 feet tall—makes it difficult to identify the individual styles, but we might recognize the style of Jackson Pollock (far left, third from top); of Franz Kline (top row, second from right); and of Piet Mondrian (top row, third from left). Other artists represented include Botticelli, Picasso, Watteau, Matisse, O'Keeffe, Degas, and Gauguin. Taken as a piece, *The Brueghel Series* is a wonderful summation of the best in Western art history. Each panel is unique, yet the styles have been blended into a coherent whole.

It could be said that *The Brueghel Series* was motivated by the underlying *concept* the artist developed while studying the Brueghel flower painting and cutting apart the poster—the concept that many different artistic styles could be quoted and merged into one complex image. Steir's work, however, has physical substance. True **Conceptual Art** has no permanent physical presence, because it is based primarily or solely on an idea. A good example of this type of expression can be found in the work of Sol LeWitt.

We show no illustration of LeWitt's conceptual work *Ten Thousand Lines About 10 Inches (25 cm) Long, Covering a Wall Evenly.* There is nothing to show, no permanent image. The work exists only as an idea, and it is the idea that can be transferred to a gallery or sold to a collector. Suppose a collector decides to "buy" *Ten Thousand Lines* (at a price that may range upward of thirty thousand dollars). What the collector gets is a certificate entitling him or her to have a draftsman—not LeWitt, not necessarily a trained artist—come into the collector's home and draw ten thousand lines on a blank wall, using a ruler and a pencil. If the collector subsequently "sells" the work, the wall must be painted over and the certificate transferred to the new owner. Or, suppose a museum owns the work. It can display the work whenever it wishes to, then simply have the wall painted over to make room for a new exhibit. There is no storage problem. Needless to say, each time the work is redrawn on a wall, it looks different, and that is perfectly compatible with the tenets of conceptual art. The appearance doesn't matter; only the idea matters.

Another artist who has sometimes been associated with Conceptual Art—although he himself disclaims the connection—is Christo. Christo's works *do* have physical substance. What sets them apart from more conventional artworks is that they retain their physical substance for only a short time. In 1969 Christo's workers wrapped and tied a section of the Australian coastline with a million square feet of polypropylene fabric—and then took it down. In 1972 workers strung a huge orange curtain between two mountains in Colorado—and then took it down. In 1976 hundreds of workers installed an 18-foot-high white nylon fence across 24½ miles of the California countryside—and then took it down **(365)**. In 1985 a team of three hundred workers transformed the historic Pont Neuf across the Seine in Paris into a giant surprise package by wrapping the bridge in 440,000 square feet of polyamide fabric. And then, inevitably, they took it all down, leaving the bridge as before. All of Christo's works are conceived as *projects,* and the existence of a tangible object is only part of each project. One of the artist's most ambitious projects was the *Surrounded Islands.*

The highlight of the *Surrounded Islands* project **(571)** came in 1983, when eleven small islands in Biscayne Bay, next to Miami, Florida, were "skirted" in pink polypropylene cloth—6.4 million square feet of it. For a few days a string of rather untidy, trash-strewn islands were transformed into bright pink flowers shimmering on the blue water. Then Christo's workers removed the pink fabric, leaving the islands in their previously unsurrounded state. Why would the artist do this? Why would anyone want to create a large, important work that is doomed to be dismantled?

For Christo, the project is what matters, and the actual time when the installation remains in place—a few days or weeks—is only part of that project. It begins with the first glimmer of an idea about the project and extends indefinitely into the future. After the idea, there is a thinking through of the project. Next come the drawings to test possibilities for what the project's installation will look like **(572)**. Then bureaucracy gets involved. For the *Surrounded Islands* it became necessary to deal with the Army Corps of Engineers, the City of Miami, and platoons of local residents, just in order to get the necessary permits to install the work. In the end Christo engaged two lawyers, a marine biologist, a marine engineer, several other engineers, two ornithologists (biologists specializing in the study of birds), and an expert in marine mammals. Again, Christo considers this part of the operation intrinsic to the overall project.

At first the local people were hostile to Christo's project. Soon, however, nearby residents became intrigued with the idea. Not least of the factors responsible for the change of heart was the influx of many, many tourist dollars as the project progressed. By the day of the installation, the *Miami Herald* was cheering, "Go for it, Christo!" As the project took shape, was realized, and was disassembled, practically no one was disappointed.

Yet another part of the project—and one that no doubt prompted the support of local residents—is the fact that Christo's works often leave the natural landscape in better condition than it was in before. Christo's people clean up after themselves. More than 4 tons of trash was carted away in preparation for the *Surrounded Islands,* and the materials of the project were removed without a trace. There were even some surprising results that Christo himself could not have predicted. The manatee, a local mammal that is a species of sea-cow, increased its mating behavior. (Could anyone have anticipated a bumper crop of baby manatees?) Local birds seemed happier; the pink plastic kept people and boats away. Tides were unaffected, because the gossamer fabric allowed the water to ripple underneath.

left: **571.** Christo.
Surrounded Islands. 1980–83.
Biscayne Bay,
Greater Miami, Florida.
Copyright © 1980–83
Christo/C.V.J. Corporation.

right: **572.** Christo.
Surrounded Islands,
Project for Biscayne Bay,
Greater Miami, Florida. 1983.
Drawing in two parts: pencil,
charcoal, pastel, crayon,
enamel paint, fabric sample,
and aerial photograph;
1'3" × 5'5" and 3'6" × 5'5".
Copyright © 1982
Christo/C.V.J. Corporation.

Christo

b. 1935

Who *is* that wrapped man?

The photographer poses a figure outdoors in New York City, all trussed up like a mummy. Is this human package the artist who once wrapped a wall in Rome, a girl in London, a walkway in Kansas City, a tree in Holland, a monument in Milan, a floor in Chicago? The artist who once wrapped a whole section of the Australian coast (cliffs and all) in plastic sheeting? The artist who wrapped a historic bridge in Paris with 10 acres of silky Champagne-colored fabric? The artist who plans to wrap the Whitney Museum in New York and a government building in Berlin (but hasn't yet)? Has the wrapper been wrapped? If so, then this is the artist who calls himself, simply, Christo.

Despite the very public nature of his work, the man himself is something of a mystery. Christo Javecheff was born in 1935 in Bulgaria, a country of eastern Europe. He studied at the Fine Arts Academy in Sofia, his nation's capital, then traveled by way of Prague and Vienna to Paris, crossing the border from the then-communist bloc into the West by a method he calls "a long story." It was in Paris, in 1958, that Christo began wrapping things, at first on a modest scale. As he tells it, he began with small objects, the objects he found in his studio, such as chairs and tables and bottles. In Paris, too, Christo met Jeanne-Claude de Guillebon, who became his wife and later his business manager and partner. Their son Cyril was born in 1960.

The first of the large-scale wrapped projects was made in Cologne, Germany, in 1961, when Christo allowed his own art exhibition to spill outside a gallery beside the Rhine harbor onto the docks. A stack of oil barrels and other harbor paraphernalia, plus rolls and rolls of industrial paper piled on the dock, soon became the *Dockside Packages*. Other ambitious wrappings followed. In 1964 Christo moved his base to New York City, but his projects keep him traveling constantly, often to far points of the globe.

For Christo, projects may have a beginning, but they don't really have an end. Even though the physical structure—the wrapping or other construction—is invariably taken away after a few days or weeks, the project remains active. Projects whose physical form has been realized, including the *Running Fence* **(365)** and the *Surrounded Islands* **(571)**, live in the sketches

and films and photographs and recounting of their history.

Christo's most recent project was *The Umbrellas*, which called for planting 1,340 blue umbrellas at a site in Japan and 1,760 yellow umbrellas in California. Installed in November 1991, *The Umbrellas* took an unpredictable and tragic turn when one of the 485-pound yellow ones came loose in a freak accident and killed a passerby. The shocked artist had the entire installation dismantled immediately.

Some observers have criticized the artist for the transitory nature of his works. But Christo has a ready reply: "I am an artist, and I have to have courage. . . . Do you know that I don't have any artworks that exist? They all go away when they're finished. Only the sketches are left, giving my works an almost legendary character. I think it takes much greater courage to create things to be gone than to create things that will remain."[5]

Annie Leibovitz. *Christo, New York City*. 1981. Photograph.

Finally it was all over but the telling and the showing—and that, too, is part of the project. Christo lectures widely on college campuses and in other forums. Pictures and films of his projects are widely available. And the concept remains—a mental perception of what art can be. As one critic wrote, "Where other artists put nature in a frame, Christo goes boldly to the landscape itself, bringing to it elegant artistic effects that recall our attention to the splendors of natural environment (or what's left of it) in the same romantic spirit as the painters of the 19th-century West." In a sense, Christo's installations *remind* us to look at the landscape we so often take for granted.

Another important result of Christo's projects is that they get so many people involved—from the volunteers who help construct them to the bureaucrats who must approve them to the onlookers and those who hear about the projects afterward. A huge project like the *Surrounded Islands* cannot help but attract attention, both on the spot and through the media. Thus it reaches more people than could ever see a single painting hanging in a museum. If art is about communication, then clearly Christo has found an effective way to communicate, through art, with an enormous audience.

To conclude our discussion of contemporary art, we look at three artists who help to illustrate the range of today's work. One does painting, the second does words, and the third does anything she pleases.

The English artist Howard Hodgkin carries on the tradition of luxuriantly painted everyday life left off by Matisse **(cover)**. Like Matisse, Hodgkin focuses on his own world of people and places, and like Matisse he has been drawn by the exotic richness of North Africa. *In Tangier* **(573)** creates an immediate and engulfing sense of the tropics, with its lush central palm tree and hot colors. We feel rather than see the landscape of Tangier, that most romantic of Moroccan cities. Hodgkin himself has said, "I am a representational painter, but not a painter of appearances. I paint representational pictures of emotional situations."[6] Few artists today dare to be so *painterly*, to take so much pleasure in pure color and form. Some art critics (and many artists) have been saying for decades that painting is dead, that it is an outdated concept. Hodgkin's critical and popular success shows this is not true.

One artist who *has* forsaken painting is the American Jenny Holzer. Holzer, who was chosen to represent the United States at the 1990 Venice Biennale, the prestigious international art show held every two years, practices the art of words. Specifically, she deals in slogans—short, pithy state-

573. Howard Hodgkin.
In Tangier. 1987–90.
Oil on wood, 5′4½″ × 5′10½″.
Courtesy M. Knoedler & Company,
New York.

ments like: "Lack of charisma can be fatal," and "Money creates taste," and "A name means a lot by itself," and "You are trapped on the earth so you will explode." Quite a lot of people think Holzer's slogans are trite and childish, and grumble that they might have come out of a fortune cookie, but this criticism doesn't bother Holzer in the least. She has said, "I want to make art that's understandable, has some relevance and importance to almost everyone. . . . I like fooling with different presentations and modes. I like to make it turn purple and go upside down."[7]

Holzer's art is unabashedly popular. Set into gaudy electronic letters that flash or travel in a running band, her slogans might seem most at home in New York's Times Square or on the strip in Las Vegas—and in fact they *have* appeared in both places. But one of Holzer's best-known sites was the Guggenheim Museum in New York, where her installation took over the museum for two months in 1989–90 **(574)**.

As noted in other chapters, the Guggenheim **(143,417)** may not be the most hospitable setting for every type of art, but Holzer's moving red, yellow, and green slogans fit in as though the museum had been designed for that purpose. (One critic remarked that the museum "never looked better"—all the while allowing that the architect, Frank Lloyd Wright [p. 355] might be spinning in his grave.) This art, obviously derived from television and advertising and computers, speaks directly to our time.

Finally, as mentioned at the beginning of this chapter, we come to an artist whose work has no physical substance at all. During the 1970s the phenomenon known as **performance art** emerged. Performance art undoubtedly took its inspiration from the "Happenings" of the 1950s and 1960s, one of which is described on page 77. **Happenings** are difficult to define; they are visual events in which some activity occurs, often with several people participating, often with audience involvement. They may include music, dance, mime, art, reading, or none of these. Imprecise as it may sound, Happenings are things that happen.

574. Jenny Holzer. *Selections from Truisms, Inflammatory Essays, The Living Series, The Survival Series, Under a Rock, Laments, and new writing.* Installation, December 12, 1989–February 11, 1990. Extended helical tricolor L.E.D. electronic display signboard, 11″ × 162′ × 4″. Solomon R. Guggenheim Museum, New York (partial gift of the artist, 1989).

575. Laurie Anderson
in performance, *Empty Places.*
1989.

Performance artist Laurie Anderson developed this idea considerably through the 1980s. In *Empty Places*, a performance work first presented in 1989, the artist herself is at the center of the action **(575)**. She tells stories and she sings, sometimes in her own clear soprano voice, sometimes through an electronic device that alters the sound. She plays a keyboard and a violin (Anderson is a classically trained violinist). Meanwhile, on a series of screens—two of them 20 feet tall—are projected still and moving images that change at a dizzying pace. The slides and films, most of which were shot by Anderson, may be keyed to the stories and the music (or they may not). In broadest terms, the theme of *Empty Places* is the American scene, but it is a scene filtered through the artist's own experience. And the title? Anderson says, "An empty place is a place for potential."

Perhaps it is slightly incorrect to say Anderson's art has no physical presence, although it is certainly true that you could not buy it or hang it on the wall. In performance art the art is the artist. What a far cry this is from the art of the Middle Ages, when artists were often anonymous. Their art endures, but the artist's names have been forgotten. In contrast, performance art places the artist at the very center. If you take away the artist, there is no more art. Performance art is the triumph of the artist.

So that is the scope of modern art—from Ingres to Anderson in less than two hundred years. It should be clear now that the question we addressed in Chapter 2 of this book—what is art?—has no convenient answer. It would be almost impossible to construct a meaningful definition of art that would encompass all the works discussed in this chapter. Beyond this, we could be almost certain that a definition formulated now would prove inadequate five or ten years hence. It may seem to us that performance artists like Laurie Anderson have broken all the rules, lowered all the barriers to expression in art. But we must remember that the public so outraged by Manet's *Le Déjeuner sur l'herbe* and Matisse's *Green Stripe* also thought that *those* artists had broken all the rules. The trouble is, no one ever knows what rules are left.

Artists always seem to be one step ahead of everybody else. If we choose to follow them in their explorations—if we choose to live with art—we may sometimes find the experience unsettling, but we will not find it dull. Living with art is an ongoing adventure.

ART PEOPLE   *Dorothy and Herbert Vogel*

Art collectors are rich. Art collectors are glamorous. Art collectors are members of the upper classes or the nobility, or else they are important business leaders. Everybody knows these facts, but apparently nobody bothered to inform Dorothy and Herbert Vogel of New York City. The Vogels—she a retired librarian, he a retired postal worker—are not rich, and their life style is modest. They are the sort of people one can't help but call "ordinary." One fact about the Vogels is undeniably *extra*ordinary: They have been collecting art on an ambitious scale for more than twenty-five years.

Everybody in the fashionable art world of New York, it seems, knows the unfashionable Herbert and Dorothy. The Vogels attend as many openings as possible, they regularly visit several artists' studios, they study the art seriously—and they buy. Their small Manhattan apartment eventually became crammed to ceilings with some seventeen hundred original works of art, emphasizing the Minimal, Conceptual, and Postmodern artists. This collection was acquired almost entirely on Herbert's salary from the post office. Dorothy's income pays the couple's living expenses.

The odds against two such . . . well, *ordinary* . . . people becoming important art collectors seem formidable. Herbert, the son of a tailor, grew up in New York and started work for the post office after high school and the army. Dorothy, born in Elmira, New York, earned a master's degree in library science and took a librarian's job in Brooklyn. The couple met at a singles' party, dated for a year, then married in 1962. Their plunge into the art world was led by Herbert, who had taken some art courses at New York University, had made friends with young artists, and aspired to be an artist himself. Soon Herbert got Dorothy involved, and the two decided collecting would be more to their taste.

The Vogels began slowly. Rushing from their respective jobs in the evening, they would rendezvous in a subway station, then go off to a gallery to study the art and consider possible purchases. At first, dealers and gallery habitués wondered, "Who on earth *are* those people?" The Vogels do not look like one's usual image of collectors. Soon, however, their clever and persistent buying attracted attention; soon their appearance in a gallery created a stir. As their collection grew, so did their reputation. Artists accept them as friends because their love of the work is so sincere.

No doubt an important factor in the Vogels' success has been their single-mindedness. Dorothy and Herbert have no children, though they have turtles and fish in quantity and—as of this writing—eight cats (Picasso, Renoir, Manet . . .). Nearly all their time is devoted to the collection. They are shrewd buyers, stretching their limited budget to the utmost. Often they buy the work of a particular artist before that artist "hits" and becomes too expensive.

The value of the Vogels' collection was demonstrated in 1992, when the National Gallery of Art in Washington announced that it would acquire the collection as a part-purchase, part-donation. Once the artworks were moved out for inventory, Dorothy and Herbert sensibly arranged to have their apartment painted—for the first time in decades—and *un*sensibly went right on buying art.

Most people pretty much live out the lives they were born to, but Herbert and Dorothy Vogel obviously are made of stronger stuff. The postal worker and the librarian—together they invented a special life for themselves, a life with art. Seeing them, talking with them—one cannot doubt they are enjoying every moment of it.

Photograph of Dorothy and Herbert Vogel, with Tiffany.

Keeping the Art We Live with: Conservation and Restoration

Torrential rains had fallen on Italy for many days. The earth was wet; rivers were swollen. Just before dawn on the morning of November 4, 1966, the Arno River overflowed its banks, engulfing the countryside. Citizens of Florence awakened to find their city under water—in several places under 14 feet of water and mud. Also under water were thousands of works of art, a large portion of them priceless and irreplaceable masterpieces from the Renaissance. Overnight, Florence, the great repository of Italian art, had become the watery graveyard of Italian art.

The great flood of 1966 woke up not only the Florentines, who survived by clinging to the rooftops and upper stories of their houses, but also awakened art lovers around the world to a fact that no one likes to dwell on: Art is destructible. Disasters, both natural and unnatural, can take away forever the splendid works of art we consider essential to our cultural heritage. How would our culture be impaired without a *Mona Lisa*? a *Starry Night*? a *David*? Would some necessary piece of our civilization be lost? We already know what it means to live with a badly damaged Parthenon **(456)**, because that destruction happened so long ago, three hundred years ago, and we are used to it. The trouble is, most of us tend to be complacent, to assume that works of art will always stay the same as they are now, during our lifetimes. No doubt the citizens of Florence and those who admire the art housed in Florence thought the same thing, but they were wrong. Keeping the art we live with—keeping it in the highest possible state of preservation—requires vigilance and care, and sometimes it requires repair work. That is the subject of this essay.

Artworks at Risk: The Dangers

To begin our discussion, we might pose the question: What *are* the sorts of phenomena that threaten our works of art? The list is a long one:

Item: The tomb of King Tutankhamun in Egypt, sealed and intact for more than 32 centuries, has begun to show serious deterioration since it was opened in 1922 **(576)**. Although its precious contents **(352,447)** have been removed to museums, the wall paintings obviously must stay where they are. Increased humidity from the breathing of some 2,500 visitors a day has caused a growth in bacteria, which are eating away the paint.

576. Wall paintings in the tomb of King Tutankhamun, Egypt, showing bacterial damage suffered since 1922.

Item: In 1987 a man who claimed to be disgusted with the "political, social, and economic conditions in Britain" entered London's National Gallery and fired a shotgun blast into a large and priceless drawing by Leonardo da Vinci.

Item: The 1989 earthquake in San Francisco damaged or destroyed about ten million dollars worth of artworks, including a rare statue of the Hindu god Nagaraja, dating from the 2nd century.

Item: Security at the Taj Mahal in India **(403)** now includes barbed wire, extra guards, and a ban on cameras. The Taj is menaced by the triple threat of air pollution, terrorist bombings (a camera might conceal an explosive device), and vandals who consider it a romantic gesture to scratch their initials deep into the marble walls.

Item: Anonymous "collectors" routinely plunder works of art that are left unguarded. In 1989 one such art lover sawed off the head from a statue of the war god Mars on the Triumphal Arch of Septimius Severus in Rome. No doubt the head will turn up someday at auction, or find its way into private ownership.

Item: The *David* sculpture of Michelangelo **(494)**, which is marble, needed only a cleaning after the flood in Florence, but an important work by Donatello, a wood sculpture of *Mary Magdalene*, was badly damaged.

Item: In 1975 a Dutch mental patient carried a knife into the Rijksmuseum in Amsterdam and managed to gouge twelve deep slashes into Rembrandt's painting *The Night Watch* before a guard was able to pull him off **(577)**. Fifteen years later another Dutch citizen, said to be "confused," sprayed the painting with chemicals from a hand pump.

Item: The popular uprising that brought an end to communism in Romania in 1989 also brought tragedy to that nation's art collection. During the last days of the totalitarian regime, the National Museum became a battleground. Fire and bullet holes took a heavy toll on the artworks.

Item: Many of the sculptures on the Acropolis in Athens have been removed to museums and replaced with cheap copies, because that city's devastating air pollution was eating the originals to dust.

To sum up, then, the disasters that can befall art divide into two categories: those caused by nature—floods, earthquakes, tornadoes; and those caused by people—wars, pollution, terrorism, vandalism, even simple overexposure. In our time, sad to say, human damage has unquestionably taken the lead.

The struggle to protect artworks from damage must rely on two approaches: *conservation*, which means preserving works of art in their present state and preventing any damage or any further damage; and *restoration*, which means employing modern techniques to correct existing damage and put artworks back in their original condition. Both of these activities sound idealistic and sensible, but in practice they frequently open a Pandora's box of troubles. Nearly every decision about conservation or restoration is controversial, and nearly every decision makes *somebody* angry. As often as not, there are at least two sides to every art-preservation issue.

Conservation

Possibly the most famous—or notorious—incident involving art conservation occurred early in the 19th century. At that time Greece, and all the surviving art treasures of ancient Greece, were under the control of the Turks. The British ambassador to the Sultan of Turkey was a man named Thomas Bruce, the seventh Earl of Elgin. With the Sultan's permission, Lord Elgin arranged for the removal of numerous sculptures from the buildings on the Acropolis, including the Parthenon, and had them shipped back to England at his own expense. Although he claimed his motives were pure, that he intended to protect the precious legacy of Greek art, many felt that Lord Elgin's goal was the aggrandizement of Great Britain and (not incidentally) of Lord Elgin. The sculptures ended up in the British Museum, where they remain today and are known as the "Elgin marbles." Even at the time Lord Elgin's act caused a good deal of scandal, and it is still a source of international friction. The Greeks want their sculptures back. The British refuse to give them up. Who is right? A good lawyer could argue either side. On the one hand, the sculptures are undeniably Greek. They were carved *in* Athens *for* Athens, and Lord Elgin's action in cutting them off the architecture could be

577. Rembrandt.
Sortie of Captain Banning Cocq's Company of the Civic Guard (The Night Watch), detail; photographed the day after it was slashed on September 14, 1975. Rijksmuseum, Amsterdam.

viewed as vandalism and theft. On the other hand, the sculptures have remained safe in London for nearly two hundred years and are in a high state of preservation **(578)**. Anyone who wishes can go to the British Museum and look at them. By contrast, the sculptures Lord Elgin left behind on the Acropolis have deteriorated badly from exposure to the elements.

Fortunately, most issues of conservation are not as dramatic as the controversy over the Elgin marbles, but the problem of keeping artworks intact, especially architecture and outdoor sculptures, becomes increasingly acute as our industrial society progresses. The enemies of outdoor art are almost invisible but nonetheless treacherous: acid rain, automobile emissions, pollutants from factory smokestacks. Our illustration **(579)** shows two photographs of the same sculpture, taken about sixty years apart, in 1908 and 1969. In the later photo, the sculpture is almost unrecognizable. Chemists have coined the term "stone leprosy" to describe such effects of air pollution, which is no less damaging to buildings than to sculpture. There is no easy answer to this problem. Either we must accept the gradual decay of everything we keep outdoors, or we must accept the urgent need to curtail pollutants in the air.

Artworks housed in museums and other "safe" locations can be considered reasonably immune to destruction. Most large museums have elaborate systems of temperature, humidity, and light control, as well as tight security. Still, accidents can happen, and there remains the backlog of artworks that have been permitted to deteriorate over the centuries. That is where the restorers come in.

Restoration

Restoration is even more controversial than conservation, and its major area of contention usually revolves around the question: How much? Or, more broadly, how much restoration work should be done, and what kind, and who decides? In a crisis like the slashing of Rembrandt's *Night Watch*, few arguments will arise. Museum curators knew what *The Night Watch* looked like moments before the knife attacked the canvas, and restorers had only to put it back the way it was before. Of course, the word "only" is relative and should not degrade the work of enormously skilled restorers, who took the deeply scarred and torn painting and returned it to a state where inspection from even a few inches away does not reveal the slash marks **(240)**. The chemical stains from the 1990 incident were even easier to repair.

above: 578. Caryatid from the Erechtheum, Athens, part of the "Elgin marbles." The British Museum, London.

right: 579. Photographs of sandstone sculpture, Herten Castle, Westphalia, Germany, taken in 1908 and 1969.

580. Agesander, Athenodorus, and Polydorus of Rhodes.
Laocoön Group,
with early restorations
(now removed).
Late 2nd century B.C.
Vatican Museums, Rome.

Arguments are more likely to rage when nobody knows exactly what a particular work of art looked like in its original state. The *Laocoön* statue from 2nd-century B.C. Greece is often given as the extreme example of restoration gone wild, and also of the tendency for restorations to mirror the prevailing fashions of a given period. When the statue was found in Italy in 1506, it was already damaged; the right arms of all three figures in the group were missing. Since then, no fewer than six restorers have, so to speak, taken a crack at repairing the sculpture, with mixed results. The first major restoration was done in 1532–33, at which time the figures were provided with outstretched arms much like those in our illustration (580; compare 461). Art historians generally agree that restorers of the Renaissance thought of themselves as "remodelers," rather than mere repair technicians, so they considered it entirely correct to do over a statue to their own satisfaction. From that point the story becomes complicated.

New plaster arms were made in the 17th century, but they were superseded by marble arms attached in the 18th century. During the 19th century earlier versions of the two sons' arms were replaced, as was a terra cotta version of the 16th-century arm made for Laocoön. To satisfy the prudish sensibilities of the 19th century, "fig leaves" were added to cover the men's nakedness. Finally, in 1954 a thorough study of the statue was undertaken, and all the restorations were removed in 1960. As of that date—that is, as of the mid-20th century—classical experts feel the *Laocoön* is as close as possible to the sculptors' original intent. Naturally, the 21st century may have different ideas.

Unwise restorations have been the plague of many a great work of art, and there can be no better example than Leonardo da Vinci's famous depiction of *The Last Supper* (152). Painted to decorate the wall of a monastery in Milan, *The Last Supper*, which shows Christ and the twelve Apostles, has become for Christians around the world as much a religious image as a masterpiece of art. Countless reproductions of the painting have appeared on

Bibles, Mass cards, pamphlets, and prints to hang on the wall. These reproductions probably bear little resemblance to Leonardo's original image. And no wonder, considering the painting's checkered history.

Leonardo worked on *The Last Supper* during the years 1495–97. Always a great one for experiment and innovation, he eschewed the established fresco technique (Chapter 7) in favor of a medium he devised for this project—the details of which will probably never be known. For once, Leonardo's genius let him down. What may have been his greatest work soon became a ruin. Within ten years the painting was said to be flaking badly; within about fifty years the biographer Giorgio Vasari wrote that "Nothing is visible but a dazzling mass of blots." The first major restoration was undertaken in 1726, and five others followed. Each of these restorers did more harm than good. One used a harsh solvent that dissolved Leonardo's colors. Another applied a strong glue that attracted dirt. Yet another restorer managed to give one of the Apostles six fingers on one hand.

To make matters worse, the physical environment of *The Last Supper* could scarcely be more precarious. Sharp variations in heat and humidity all but force the paint off the wall, bringing deep cracks in a surface that is really too thin to support a painting. Sometime in the 18th century well-meaning friars in the monastery installed a curtain across the mural—which had the effect of trapping moisture on the wall and scraping off yet more paint each time the curtain was drawn back. French soldiers of Napoleon occupied the monastery in 1796, and they took turns throwing rocks at the mural and climbing ladders to scratch out the Apostles' eyes. A bomb fell on the monastery during World War II, missing the wall by a yard. It's a miracle that anything is left at all, and little is left.

Finally, nearly five hundred years after Leonardo put down his brushes, sensible measures were taken to save the mural. A Milanese restorer, Dr. Pinan Brambilla Barcilon, began a major restoration in 1977 (581). Dr. Brambilla had three major assets that earlier restorers lacked: modern technology in the form of microscopes, chemicals, and measuring devices; generous financial support (from the Olivetti Corporation); and a sincere respect for Leonardo's creation. Through sensitive probing she was able to determine what was Leonardo's work and what was somebody else's—and remove the latter. In areas where nothing is left of Leonardo's paint, she did not attempt

581. Leonardo da Vinci. *The Last Supper,* photographed during restoration, 1990; see also **152.** Refectory Santa Maria delle Grazie, Milan.

to reconstruct the imagery. Dr. Brambilla simply painted in a neutral color. The restored mural surely will not look much like popular reproductions, but it is *all* Leonardo.

Curiously in view of the *Last Supper*'s status as a treasured artwork, Dr. Brambilla's restoration has not attracted much criticism, negative or otherwise. This is not true of another major enterprise, underway about the same time and completed in 1990. It should be safe to say that no restoration project in history has generated as much controversy as the cleaning of Michelangelo's ceiling frescoes in the Sistine Chapel of the Vatican (34,495).

If art were a religion, one of its major deities might well be the Sistine Chapel frescoes of Michelangelo. One cannot overestimate the importance—the reverence—accorded this one stunning work of art. It is as though the hand of an angel laid down the paint, and lowly mortals dare not ever touch what Michelangelo made. Unlike Leonardo, Michelangelo used a tried-and-true fresco technique for the Sistine paintings. They were and are excellently preserved. The only problem was, they had become very dirty. A simple cleaning seemed in order, but nothing can be simple when an artwork of this magnitude is involved.

Art historians around the world took to their battle stations. Their cries were many and varied, but the conflict boiled down to this: How much is too much? How much cleaning would strip away the dirt and yet leave every particle of paint that was placed by Michelangelo's brush? Did the restorers go far enough? Did they go too far? Certainly the changes after cleaning are dramatic (495,582). Some critics say the cleaning has restored clarity and vibrancy to the frescoes. Others say the restorers scrubbed away not only the dirt but also the subtle shading and modeling, the essence of Michelangelo's genius, leaving a flat, lifeless, postcard-type image. During the long period of restoration, opinion gradually shifted toward the positive. Perhaps observers needed time to adjust to a Michelangelo they had never seen before—the painter of vivid and clear colors. But no matter how many art historians vote yea, and how many nay, the basic question cannot be answered: Does this restoration produce what the artist wanted, or does it produce what contemporary tastes want to see? We will never know.

How much restoration is too much? For an interesting exploration of this question, we might once again consider the Parthenon (62,456). This ancient Greek temple is currently undergoing major restoration, but in this instance the restorers intend merely to hold the line, to keep the Parthenon

582. Michelangelo. Detail of ceiling frescoes, Sistine Chapel, before and after 1980s restoration. Vatican, Rome.

583. Artist's rendering of a corner of the Parthenon, Athens, as it may have looked in the 5th century B.C.

the way it is, to prevent further damage. No responsible person has ever proposed restoring the Parthenon to its original state. Not only would major architectural work be needed, but the Parthenon would have to be painted in the vivid hues we assume it displayed originally **(583)**. Few of us nowadays are prepared to confront a bright red and blue Parthenon. That would be too much! Better to save what we have, to save what we are used to.

The idea of saving brings us back to the disaster in Florence. On the morning after the flood, art students in the city formed a human chain to pull the precious works of art out of the water and move them to higher ground. Within twenty-four hours restorers and conservators from around the world had begun arriving, eager to begin the work of saving what could be saved. In the United States art lovers formed the Committee to Rescue Italian Art (CRIA), which raised huge donations to fund the restoration.

Much was saved. To be sure, many works of art, especially the most vulnerable books and manuscripts, were lost forever to the flood, but far more were rescued. The work of restoration goes on and will continue until every piece that suffered damage has been returned to the best possible state of preservation. Florence was under water, but Florence did not drown.

Perhaps most important, the great flood of 1966 taught lessons that will not be forgotten. New methods were developed to protect artworks from natural disasters. New restoration techniques were invented on the spot to meet the urgent need, and those techniques will guide restorers of the future. They will help us to keep the art we live with—to keep it safe for the generations to come.

Pronunciation Guide

This guide is meant to provide the reader with an acceptable pronunciation for names and other words that may be unfamiliar to native speakers of English. It is not perfect. It ignores the nasal sounds of the French *en, in, ain*, as well as the guttural German consonants, giving instead the nearest English equivalents. These sounds are difficult to render phonetically and difficult to pronounce for those who have not studied the languages. However, no reader should be embarrassed by using the pronunciations here.

In many cases there are two or more pronunciations for a particular artist's name, both or all of which are in common use and considered "correct." The pronunciations in this guide are those most often heard among English-speaking North Americans, and a few alternates have been provided. Some instructors may prefer variant pronunciations of certain artists' names; these may be equally correct but inadvertently omitted from the list.

The phonetic system employed for this guide is meant to be as simple as possible. Its conventions include:

an—plan, tan
ay—play, day, stay
ah—spa, hurrah
eh—pet, get
er—her, fur
oh—toe, show, go
ohn—phone, moan
uh—bus, fuss

Akhenaten   ah-keh-NAH-ten
Anuszkiewitz, Richard   ah-NUHS-keh-vitz
Aphrodite   aph-roh-DYE-tee
auteur   oh-TER
Baldovinetti, Alesso   ah-LESS-oh bal-doh-veen-ETT-ee
Balla, Giacomo   JAH-koh-moh BAH-lah
bas-relief   BAH ree-leef
Bernini, Gianlorenzo   jahn-loh-REN-zoh bayr-NEE-nee
Bosch, Hieronymus   heer-AHN-ih-mus bosh
Botticelli, Sandro   SAN-droh boht-ee-CHEL-ee
Boucher, François   frahn-SWAH boo-SHAY
Brancusi, Constantin   KAHN-stan-teen BRAHN-koosh
  (more often in the U.S.: brahn-KOO-see)
Braque, Georges   zhorzh brahk
Bruegel, Pieter   PEE-tur BROO-g'l (often: BROY-g'l)
camera obscura   KAM-er-uh ob-SKOOR-uh
Caravaggio   kah-rah-VAH-jyoh
Cellini, Benvenuto   ben-ven-OO-toh chel-EE-nee
Cézanne, Paul   say-ZAN
Chardin, Jean Baptiste Siméon   zhahn ba-TEEST
  see-may-OHN shar-DAN
Chartres   SHAR-tr'
Chia, Sandro   SAN-droh KEE-ah
chiaroscuro   kee-ah-roh-SKOOR-oh
Cimabue   chee-mah-BOO-ay
cire perdue   seer payr-DOO
contrapposto   kohn-trah-POH-stoh
Corbusier, Le   luh kohr-boo-ZYAY
Courbet, Gustave   goos-TAHV koor-BAY
Daguerre, Louis Jacques Mandé   loo-ee ZHAHK
  man-DAY dah-GAYR

Dali, Salvador   sal-vah-DOHR DAH-lee, or dah-LEE
Daumier, Honoré   ohn-ohr-AY dohm-YAY
David, Jacques Louis   zhahk loo-EE dah-VEED
Degas, Edgar   ed-GAHR deh-GAH
de Kooning, Willem   VILL-um duh KOON-ing
Delacroix, Eugène   uh-ZHAYN duh-lah-KRWAH
Derain, André   ahn-DRAY deh-RAN
Donatello   dohn-ah-TELL-oh
Dubuffet, Jean   zhahn dyu-boo-FAY
Duccio   DOO-chyoh
Duchamp, Marcel   mahr-SELL doo-SHAHN
Dufy, Raoul   rah-OOL dyu-FEE
Dürer, Albrecht   AHL-brekht DOOR-er
Eakins, Thomas   AY-kins
Fabergé, Peter Carl   fab-er-ZHAY
Fauve   fohv
Fragonard, Jean-Honoré   zhahn ohn-ohr-AY
  frag-oh-NAHR
Gaudí, Antoni   ahn-TOH-nee gow-DEE
Gauguin, Paul   goh-GAN
Gentileschi, Artemisia   ahr-tuh-MEE-zhyuh
  jen-till-ESS-kee
Géricault, Théodore   tay-oh-DORE zheh-ree-COH
Ghiberti, Lorenzo   loh-REN-zoh ghee-BAYR-tee
Giacometti, Alberto   ahl-BAYR-toh jah-coh-MET-ee
Giorgione   johr-JYOHN-ay
Giotto   JYOH-toh
gouache   gwahsh
Goya, Francisco de   frahn-SISS-coh day GOY-ah
  (in Spain: frahn-THEES-coh)
haut-relief   OH ree-leef

507

Hiroshige, Ando ANH-doh heer-oh-SHEE-gay
Hokusai, Katsushika kat-s'-SHEE-kah HOH-k'-sahy
Holbein, Hans hahns HOHL-byne
Houdon, Jean Antoine zhahn ahn-TWAHN oo-DOHN
Ingres, Jean Auguste Dominique zhahn oh-GOOST dohm-een-EEK AN-gr'
intaglio in-TAHL-yoh (sometimes anglicized to in-TAG-lee-oh)
Kandinsky, Wassily vah-SEE-lee kan-DIN-skee
Klee, Paul klay
Klimt, Gustav goos-TAHV kleemt
Knossos KNAH-sohs
Kokoschka, Oskar koh-KOHSH-kah
Kollwitz, Käthe KAY-tuh KOHL-vitz
Laocoön lay-AH-coh-un
Lascaux las-COH
Laurencin, Marie lohr-ahn-SAN
Lautrec, Henri de Toulouse- ahn-REE deh too-LOOS loh-TREK
L'Enfant, Pierre Charles pyayr shahrl' lahn-FAHN
Leonardo da Vinci lay-oh-NAR-doh dah VEEN-chee (often in U.S.: lee-oh-NAR-doh)
Limbourg lam-BOOR
Magritte, René reh-NAY ma-GREET
Manet, Edouard ayd-WAHR ma-NAY
Mantegna, Andrea ahn-DRAY-ah mahn-TAYN-yah
Mapplethorpe, Robert MAY-p'l-thorp
Marisol mah-ree-SOHL
Masaccio mah-ZAH-chyoh
Matisse, Henri ahn-REE ma-TEES
Medici, Lorenzo de' loh-REN-zoh deh MED-ee-chee
mezzotint MET-zoh-tint
Michelangelo my-kel-AN-jel-oh, or mee-kel-AN-jel-oh
Mies van der Rohe, Ludwig LOOT-fik mees van der ROH-eh
Miró, Joan hwahn meer-OH
Modersohn-Becker, Paula MOH-der-zun BEK-er
Mondrian, Piet peet MOHN-dree-ahn
Monet, Claude moh-NAY
Morisot, Berthe bayr-t' mohr-ee-ZOH
Munch, Edvard ED-vahrd moonk
Muybridge, Eadweard ED-werd MY-bridj
Mycenae my-SEEN-ay, or my-SEEN-ee
Nebuchadnezzar neb-uk-ad-NEZ-zer

Piero della Francesca PYAYR-oh DEL-lah fran-CHESS-kuh
pointillism PWAN-teel-ism (sometimes anglicized to POYN-till-ism)
Pollock, Jackson PAHL-uck
Polyclitus pahl-ee-KLY-tus
Pompeii pahm-PAY, or pohm-PAY
Pont du Gard pohn dyu GAHR
Poussin, Nicolas nee-coh-LAH poo-SAN
Praxiteles prak-SIT-uh-leez
Raphael RAFF-yell, or RAF-fy-ell, or raf-fy-YELL
Renoir, Pierre-Auguste pyayr oh-GOOST reh-NWAHR
repoussé reh-poo-SAY
Rigaud, Hyacinthe ee-ah-SANT ree-GOH
Rococo roh-coh-COH
Rodin, Auguste oh-GOOST roh-DAN
Rousseau, Henri (le Douanier) ahn-REE roo-SOH (luh dwan-YAY)
St. Sernin san sayr-NAN
Salle, David SAL-lee
San Vitale san vee-TAHL-ay
Seurat, Georges zhorzh syu-RAH
Siqueiros, David Alfaro see-KAYR-ohs
Sotatsu, Nonomura noh-noh-MOOR-ah SOH-taht-s'
Stieglitz, Alfred STEEG-litz
Titian TISH-an, or TEE-shan
trompe-l'oeil trump-LOY
Tutankhamun toot-an-KAH-mun
Van Eyck, Jan yahn van IKE
Van Gogh, Vincent van GOH (in the U.S.; the Dutch pronunciation is nearly impossible to render phonetically for English speakers)
Van Ruisdael, Jacob YAH-cub van ROYS-dahl
Vasari, Giorgio JORE-jyoh va-SAHR-ee
Velázquez, Diego DYAY-goh vay-LASS-kess (usually, in the U.S.; in Spain, vay-LATH-keth)
Vermeer, Jan yahn vayr-MEER, or vayr-MAYR
Verrocchio, Andrea del ahn-DRAY-uh del vayr-OHK-yoh
Versailles vayr-SYE
Vigée-Lebrun, Elisabeth vee-ZHAY leh-BRUN
Vuillard, Edouard ayd-WAHR vwee-AHR
Watteau, Antoine ahn-TWAHN wah-TOH, or vah-TOH
Willendorf VILL-en-dohrf

Bibliography
and Suggested Readings

General References

Baker, Joan Stanley. *Japanese Art.* London: Thames and Hudson, 1984.

Beardsley, John, and Jane Livingston. *Hispanic Art in the United States.* New York: Abbeville Press, 1987.

Bechett, Wendy. *Contemporary Women Artists.* New York: Universe, 1988.

Canaday, John. *What Is Art? An Introduction to Painting, Sculpture & Architecture.* New York: Knopf, 1980.

Cummings, Paul. *Artists in Their Own Words.* New York: St. Martin's, 1982.

De la Croix, Horst, and Richard G. Tansey. *Gardner's Art Through the Ages,* 8th ed., 2 vols. New York: Harcourt Brace Jovanovich, 1986.

Dwyer, Jane Powell, and Edward B. Dwyer. *The Traditional Art of Africa, Oceania, and the Americas.* San Francisco: Fine Arts Museum of San Francisco, 1973.

Fine, Elsa H. *Women and Art: A History of Women Painters and Sculptors from the Renaissance to the Twentieth Century.* Montclair, N.J.: Allanheld & Schram, 1978.

Fleming, William. *Arts and Ideas,* 7th ed. New York: Holt, Rinehart and Winston, 1986.

Furst, Peter T., and Jill L. Furst. *North American Indian Art.* New York: Rizzoli, 1982.

Goldwater, Robert, and Marco Treves, eds. *Artists on Art: From the Fourteenth to the Twentieth Century.* New York: Pantheon, 1974.

Gombrich, E. H. *The Story of Art,* 15th ed. Englewood Cliffs, N.J.: Prentice-Hall, 1989.

Harris, Ann Sutherland, and Linda Nochlin. *Women Artists: 1550–1950.* New York: Knopf, 1977.

Hartt, Frederick. *Art: A History of Painting, Sculpture, Architecture,* 3rd ed., 2 vols. Englewood Cliffs, N.J.: Prentice-Hall, 1989.

Honour, Hugh, and John Fleming. *The Visual Arts: A History,* 2nd ed. Englewood Cliffs, N.J.: Prentice-Hall, 1986.

Janson, H. W. *History of Art,* 4th ed. rev. by Anthony Janson. Englewood Cliffs, N.J.: Prentice-Hall, 1991.

Johnson, Ellen H., ed. *American Artists on Art: From 1940 to 1980.* New York: Harper & Row, 1982.

Jones, Lois Swan. *Research Methods and Resources: A Guide to Finding Art Information.* Dubuque, Iowa: Kendall/Hunt, 1985.

Lee, Sherman. *A History of Far Eastern Art,* 4th ed. Englewood Cliffs, N.J.: Prentice-Hall, 1982. New York: Abrams, 1982.

Mendelowitz, Daniel M. *A History of American Art.* New York: Holt, Rinehart and Winston, 1970.

Piper, David, ed. *Random House Library of Painting and Sculpture,* 4 vols. New York: Random House, 1981.

Rawson, Jessica. *Ancient China: Art and Archaeology.* New York: Harper & Row, 1980.

Chapter One
Living with Art

Arnheim, Rudolf. *Visual Thinking.* Berkeley: University of California Press, 1980.

Bishop, Robert. *American Folk Sculpture.* New York: Dutton, 1983.

Edwards, Betty. *Drawing on the Right Side of the Brain.* Los Angeles: Tarcher, 1979.

Four Americans in Paris: The Collections of Gertrude Stein and Her Family. New York: Museum of Modern Art, 1970.

Hemphill, Herbert W., and Julia Weissman. *Twentieth Century American Folk Art and Artists.* New York: Dutton, 1974.

Lipman, Jean, and Tom Armstrong, eds. *American Folk Painters of Three Centuries.* New York: Hudson Hills and Whitney Museum of American Art, 1980.

Livingston, Jane, and John Beardsley. *Black Folk Art in America, 1930–1980.* Washington, D.C.: Corcoran Gallery of Art, 1982.

Stein, Gertrude. *The Autobiography of Alice B. Toklas.* New York: Random House, 1955.

Chapter Two
What Is Art?

Blocker, H. Gene. *Philosophy of Art.* New York: Scribner's, 1979.

Hammacher, A. M., and Renilde Hammacher. *Van Gogh: A Documentary Biography.* New York: Macmillan, 1982.

Nelson, George. *How to See: A Guide to Reaching Our Manmade Environments.* Boston: Little, Brown, 1979.

Chapter Three
Themes and Purposes of Art

Bradley, William. *Art: Magic, Impulse, and Control: A Guide to Viewing.* Englewood Cliffs, N.J.: Prentice-Hall, 1973.

Clark, Kenneth M. *Civilization: A Personal View.* New York: Harper & Row, 1970.

Elsen, Albert E. *Purposes of Art,* 4th ed. New York: Holt, Rinehart and Winston, 1981.

Hawkins, Gerald S. *Stonehenge Decoded.* New York: Delta, 1965.

Kris, Ernst, and Otto Kurz. *Legend, Myth, and Magic in the Image of the Artist.* New Haven, Conn.: Yale University Press, 1979.

Lisle, Laurie. *Portrait of an Artist: Georgia O'Keeffe.* New York: Seaview Books, 1980.

Pfeiffer, John E. *The Creative Explosion: An Inquiry into the Origins of Art and Religion.* Ithaca, N.Y.: Cornell University Press, 1985.

Rauschenberg, Robert. *An Interview with Robert Rauschenberg by Barbara Rose.* New York: Elizabeth Avadon Editions, 1987.

Wheat, Ellen Harkins. *Jacob Lawrence: American Painter.* Seattle: Seattle Art Museum, 1986.

Chapter Four

The Visual Elements

Chapter Five

Principles of Design in Art

Albers, Josef. *Interaction of Color*, rev. ed. New Haven, Conn.: Yale University Press, 1975.

Birren, Faber. *Color and Human Response*. New York: Van Nostrand Reinhold, 1978.

Boase, T. S. R. *Giorgio Vasari: The Man and the Book*. Princeton, N.J.: Princeton University Press, 1979.

Ellinger, Richard. *Color, Structure and Design*. New York: Van Nostrand Reinhold, 1980.

Ernst, Bruno. *The Magic Mirror of M.C. Escher*. New York: Ballantine, 1977.

Gill, Robert W. *Basic Perspective*. London: Thames and Hudson, 1980.

Itten, Johannes. *The Art of Color*. New York: Van Nostrand Reinhold, 1973.

———. *Design and Form: The Basic Course at the Bauhaus and Later*. New York: Van Nostrand Reinhold, 1975.

Pile, John F. *Design: Purpose, Form and Meaning*. New York: Norton, 1982.

Richardson, John Adkins, Floyd W. Coleman, and Michael J. Smith. *Basic Design: Systems, Elements, Applications*. Englewood Cliffs, N.J.: Prentice-Hall, 1984.

Chapter Six

Drawing

Betti, Claudia, and Teel Sale. *Drawing: A Contemporary Approach*, 2nd ed. New York: Holt, Rinehart and Winston, 1986.

Chaet, Bernard. *The Art of Drawing*, 2nd ed. New York: Holt, Rinehart and Winston, 1983.

David Hockney: A Retrospective. Los Angeles: Los Angeles County Museum of Art, 1988.

Edwards, Betty. *Drawing on the Artist Within*. New York: Simon & Schuster, 1986.

Goldstein, Nathan. *The Art of Responsive Drawing*, 3rd ed. Englewood Cliffs, N.J.: Prentice-Hall, 1984.

Mendelowitz, Daniel M. *A Guide to Drawing*, 3rd ed. New York: Holt, Rinehart and Winston, 1982.

Nicolaides, Kimon. *The Natural Way to Draw: A Working Plan for Art Study*. Boston: Houghton Mifflin, 1975.

Chapter Seven

Painting

Blunden, Maria, and Godfrey Blunden. *Impressionists and Impressionism*. New York: Rizzoli, 1980.

Chaet, Bernard. *An Artist's Notebook: Techniques and Materials*. New York: Holt, Rinehart and Winston, 1979.

Cockcroft, Eva, John Weber, and James Cockcroft. *Toward a People's Art: A Contemporary Mural Movement*. New York: Irvington, 1987.

Godley, John. *The Master Forger: The Story of Han van Meegeren*. New York: Wilfred Funk, 1950.

Goldman, Shifra M. *Contemporary Mexican Painting in a Time of Change*. Austin: University of Texas Press, 1981.

Goldstein, Nathan. *Painting: Visual and Technical Fundamentals*. Englewood Cliffs, N.J.: Prentice-Hall, 1979.

Mayer, Ralph. *The Artist's Handbook of Materials and Techniques*. New York: Viking, 1981.

Chapter Eight

Prints

Gelman, Barbara, ed. *The Wood Engravings of Winslow Homer*. New York: Bounty Books, 1969.

Hoffman, Detlef. *The Playing Card: An Illustrated History*. Greenwich, Conn.: New York Graphic, 1973.

Mayor, A. Hyatt. *Prints and People*. Princeton, N.J.: Princeton University Press, 1980.

McShine, Kynaston, ed. *Andy Warhol: A Retrospective*. New York: Museum of Modern Art, 1989.

Peterdi, Gabor. *Printmaking*. New York: Macmillan, 1980.

Pratt, John Lowell, ed. *Currier and Ives: Chronicles of America*. Maplewood, N.J.: Hammond, 1968.

Saff, Donald, and Deli Sacilotto. *Printmaking: History and Process*. New York: Holt, Rinehart and Winston, 1978.

Salamon, Ferdinando. *The History of Prints and Printmaking from Dürer to Picasso*. New York: American Heritage, 1972.

Chapter Nine

The Camera Arts

Bernard, Bruce. *Photodiscovery: Masterworks of Photography 1840–1940*. New York: Abrams, 1980.

Four Screenplays of Ingmar Bergman, trans. Lars Malmstrom and David Kushner. New York: Simon & Schuster, 1960.

Gutman, Judith Mara. *Through Indian Eyes*. New York: Oxford University Press, 1982.

Horan, James D. *Mathew Brady: Historian with a Camera*. New York, Bonanza, 1955.

Lax, Eric. *Woody Allen: A Biography*. New York: Knopf, 1991.

Livingston, Jane. *Lee Miller: Photographer*. New York: The California/International Arts Foundation, 1989.

Mast, Gerald. *A Short History of the Movies*. New York: Macmillan, 1986.

Newhall, Beaumont. *The History of Photography*. New York: Museum of Modern Art, 1982.

Newhall, Beaumont, and Nancy Newhall, eds. *Masters of Photography*. New York: A & W, 1983.

The New York Times Film Reviews, 1913–1970, 1-Vol. Selection. New York: Arno Press, 1971.

Shipman, David. *The Story of Cinema*. New York: St. Martin's, 1986.

Spoto, Donald. *The Dark Side of Genius: The Life of Alfred Hitchcock*. Boston: Little, Brown, 1983.

Szarkowski, John. *Looking at Photographs: One Hundred Pictures from the Collection of the Museum of Modern Art*. New York: Museum of Modern Art, 1973.

Truffaut, François. *Hitchcock*, rev. ed. New York: Simon & Schuster, 1983.

Tucker, Anne, ed. *The Woman's Eye*. New York: Knopf, 1973.

Upton, Barbara, and John Upton. *Photography*. Glenview, Ill.: Scott Foresman, 1989.

Chapter Ten

Graphic Design

Buechner, Thomas S. *Norman Rockwell: A Sixty Year Retrospective*. New York: Abrams, 1972.

Deken, Joseph. *Computer Images: State of the Art*. New York: Stewart, Tabori and Chang, 1983.

Glaser, Milton. *Graphic Design*. Woodstock, N.Y.: Overlook, 1983.

Hall, Jim. *Mighty Minutes: An Illustrated History of Television's Best Commercials*. New York: Harmony, 1984.

Heller, Steven, ed. *Innovators of American Illustration*. New York: Van Nostrand Reinhold, 1986.

Johnson, Steward J. *The Modern American Poster*. New York: Museum of Modern Art, 1983.

Chapter Eleven
Sculpture

Beardsley, John. *A Landscape for Modern Sculpture: Storm King Art Center*. New York: Abbeville Press, 1985.

————. *Earthworks and Beyond*. New York: Abbeville Press, 1989.

Gray, Cleve, ed. *David Smith by David Smith*. New York: Holt, Rinehart and Winston, 1968.

Kaprow, Allan. *Assemblage, Environments and Happenings*. New York: Abrams, 1966.

Lipman, Jean. *Calder's Universe*. Philadelphia: Running Press, 1989.

Wilkin, Karen. *Smith*. New York: Abbeville Press, 1984.

Chapter Twelve
Crafts

Charleston, Robert J., ed. *World Ceramics*. New York: McGraw-Hill, 1968.

Held, Shirley. *Weaving: A Handbook of the Fiber Arts*, 2nd ed. New York: Holt, Rinehart and Winston, 1978.

Nelson, Glenn C. *Ceramics: A Potter's Handbook*, 5th ed. New York: Holt, Rinehart and Winston, 1984.

Nordness, Lee. *Object U.S.A.* New York: Viking, 1970.

Waller, Irene. *Textile Sculptures*. London: Studio Vista, 1977.

Westbrook, Adele, and Ann Yarowski, eds. *Design in America: The Cranbook Vision, 1925–1950*. New York: Abrams, 1983.

Chapter Thirteen
Architecture

Boutelle, Sara. *Julia Morgan, Architect*. New York: Abbeville Press, 1988.

Fuller, R. Buckminster, and Robert W. Marks. *The Dymaxion World of R. Buckminster Fuller*. New York: Reinhold, 1960.

Hitchcock, Henry Russell. *In the Nature of Materials: The Buildings of Frank Lloyd Wright, 1887–1941*. New York: Da Capo, 1975.

Le Corbusier. *Towards a New Architecture*. New York: Praeger, 1959.

Risebero, Bill. *Modern Architecture and Design: An Alternative History*. Cambridge, Mass.: MIT Press, 1983.

Safdie, Moshe. *Form and Purpose: Is the Emperor Naked?* Boston: Houghton Mifflin, 1982.

Scully, Vincent J. *Modern Architecture: Innovation and Tradition*. New York: Rizzoli, 1985.

————. *Pride of Place: Building the American Dream*. Boston: Houghton Mifflin, 1986.

Torre, Susana. *Women in American Architecture*. New York: Whitney Library of Design, 1977.

Chapter Fourteen
Environmental Design

Bacon, Edmund N. *Design of Cities*. New York: Penguin, 1976.

Bennett, Corwin. *Spaces for People: Human Factors in Design*. Englewood Cliffs, N.J.: Prentice-Hall, 1977.

Mehrabian, Albert. *Public Places and Private Spaces: The Psychology of Work, Play and Living Environments*. New York: Basic Books, 1980.

Rudofsky, Bernard. *Streets for People: A Primer for Americans*. New York: Doubleday, 1969.

Chapter Fifteen
The Ancient World to the Middle Ages

Cowen, Painton. *Rose Windows*. San Francisco: Chronicle, 1979.

Edwards, I. E. S. *Tutankhamun: His Tomb and Its Treasures*. New York: Metropolitan Museum of Art, 1977.

Mendelssohn, Kurt. *The Riddle of the Pyramids*. New York: Praeger, 1974.

Stokstad, Marilyn. *Medieval Art*. New York: Harper & Row, 1986.

Swann, Wim. *The Gothic Cathedral*. Garden City, N.Y.: Doubleday, 1969.

Chapter Sixteen
Renaissance to Revolution

Chambers, D. S. *Patrons and Artists in the Italian Renaissance*. Columbia: University of South Carolina Press, 1971.

Cuttler, Charles D. *Northern Painting: From Pucelle to Bruegel*. New York: Holt, Rinehart and Winston, 1968.

Hartt, Frederick. *History of Italian Renaissance Art*, 3rd ed. Englewood Cliffs, N.J.: Prentice-Hall, 1987.

Held, Julius S., and Donald Posner. *17th and 18th Century Art*. New York: Abrams, 1979.

Leonardo da Vinci. *Notebooks*, ed. E. MacCurdy. New York: Braziller, 1955.

Levey, Michael. *Rococo to Revolution*. New York: Praeger, 1966.

Panofsky, Erwin. *The Life and Art of Albrecht Dürer*. Princeton, N.J.: Princeton University Press, 1955.

Vasari, Giorgio. *Lives of the Artists*, trans. George Bull. New York: Penguin, 1966.

Walton, Guy. *Louis XIV's Versailles*. Chicago: University of Chicago Press, 1986.

Chapter Seventeen
The Modern World

Anderson, Laurie. *United States*. New York: Harper & Row, 1984.

Arnason, H. H. *History of Modern Art: Painting, Sculpture, Architecture, Photography*. New York: Abrams, 1986.

Ashton, Dore. *The New York School: A Cultural Reckoning*. New York: Penguin, 1980.

Battcock, Gregory. *Super Realism: A Critical Anthology*. New York: Dutton, 1975.

————. *Minimal Art: A Critical Anthology*. New York: Dutton, 1968.

Brettell, Richard, et al. *The Art of Paul Gauguin*. Washington, D.C.: National Gallery of Art, 1988.

Chicago, Judy. *The Dinner Party: A Symbol of Our Heritage*. Garden City, N.Y.: Doubleday, 1979.

Dachy, Marc. *The Dada Movement*. New York: Rizzoli, 1990.

Diamonstein, Barbaralee. *Inside New York's Art World*. New York: Rizzoli, 1980.

Hughes, Robert. *The Shock of the New*. New York: Knopf, 1981.

Kaprow, Allan. *Assemblage, Environments and Happenings*. New York: Abrams, 1966.

Rosenblum, Robert. *Cubism and Twentieth-Century Art*. Englewood Cliffs, N.J.: Prentice-Hall, 1976.

Roskill, Mark, ed. *The Letters of Vincent Van Gogh*. New York: Atheneum, 1977.

Rubin, William, ed. *Pablo Picasso: A Retrospective*. New York: Museum of Modern Art, 1980.

Rubin, William S. *Dada and Surrealist Art*. New York: Abrams, 1969.

Seitz, William C. *Abstract Expressionist Painting in America*. Cambridge, Mass.: Harvard University Press, 1983. Washington, D.C.: National Gallery of Art, 1983.

Notes to the Text

Chapter One

1. Adapted from Sidney J. Parnes and Harold F. Harding, eds. *A Source Book for Creative Thinking* (New York: Scribner's, 1962); and Daniel M. Mendelowitz, *Children Are Artists*, 2d ed. (Stanford, Calif.: Stanford University Press, 1963).
2. Quoted in Dora Jane Hamblin, "A Bright and Happy Four-Hundredth-Birthday Year for the Remarkable Uffizi," *Smithsonian* (November 1982), p. 71.
3. Arthur Schlesinger, Jr., "The Arts' Key Role in Our Society," *The New York Times* (September 20, 1985), p. A31.
4. "More Corporations Becoming Working Museums," *The New York Times* (September 15, 1985), p. 60.
5. Mark Roskill, ed., *The Letters of Vincent van Gogh* (New York: Atheneum, 1977), p. 188.
6. P. Huisman and M. G. Dortu, *Lautrec by Leutrec* (New York: Viking, 1964), p. 164.

Chapter Two

1. Douglas C. McGill, "Artists and Officials Argue over Removing Sculpture," *The New York Times* (March 7, 1985), p. B1.
2. Ibid.
3. "Intrusive Arc," *The New York Times* (May 31, 1985), p. A26.
4. Isabel Wilkerson, "Obscenity Jurors Were Pulled 2 Ways," *The New York Times* (October 10, 1990), p. A12.
5. For more detail about *The Polish Rider* and the Rembrandt Research Project, see Anthony Bailey, "A Young Man on Horseback," *The New Yorker* (March 5, 1990), pp. 45–77.
6. "A Picture over the Sofa," *The New York Times* (December 1, 1981), p. B2.
7. Michael Brenson, "Art People," *The New York Times* (November 12, 1982).
8. Catherine Barnett, "Mischief with Mummies," *Art & Antiques* (September 1988), p. 71.
9. Robert Goldwater and Marco Treves, eds., *Artists on Art: From the Fourteenth to the Twentieth Century* (New York: Pantheon, 1972), p. 421.
10. Ibid., p. 417.
11. Quoted in Irving Sandler, *The Triumph of American Painting: A History of Abstract Expressionism* (New York: Harper & Row, 1976).
12. Goldwater and Treves, p. 82.
13. Vincent van Gogh, *The Complete Letters*; quoted in Ronald Pickvance, *Van Gogh in Saint-Rémy and Auvers* (New York: The Metropolitan Museum of Art and Harry N. Abrams, Inc., 1986), p. 219.

Chapter Three

1. Paul Zanker and John Pollini, quoted in "Scholar-Detectives Learn How Augustus Idealized His Image," *The New York Times* (January 10, 1984), p. C3.
2. Charles Blitzer and the Editors of Time-Life Books, eds., "Age of Kings," *Great Ages of Man: History of World's Culture* (New York: Time-Life, 1967), p. 62.
3. Black Mountain College Records, 1946; quoted in Ellen Harkins Wheat, *Jacob Lawrence: American Painter* (Seattle: Seattle Art Museum, 1986), p. 73.
4. Henry Kamm, "Rauschenberg Show Heralds Union of the Arts in Berlin," *The New York Times* (March 10, 1990), p. 11.
5. Robert Rauschenberg, *An Interview with Robert Rauschenberg by Barbara Rose* (New York: Elizabeth Avadon Editions, 1987), p. 59. Information in this biography is adapted from *Robert Rauschenberg* (Washington, D.C.: National Collection of Fine Arts, 1976).
6. Gerstle Mack, *Paul Cézanne* (New York: Knopf, 1936), p. 199.
7. Exhibition catalogue statement, Anderson Galleries, January 29, 1923; quoted in Laurie Lisle, *Portrait of an Artist: Georgia O'Keeffe* (New York: Seaview Books, 1980), p. 66.
8. Kathleen Jessie Paine, *William Blake* (New York: Praeger, 1970), p. 148.

Chapter Four

1. Goldwater and Treves, op. cit., p. 74.
2. Benoit B. Mandelbrot, "Fractals and an Art for the Sake of Science," in *LEONARDO, Computer Art in Context, Supplemental Issue* (1989), pp. 21–22.
3. Peter de Polnay, *Enfant Terrible: The Life and Work of Maurice Utrillo* (New York: Morrow, 1969), p. 190.

Chapter Five

1. John Russell and the Editors of Time-Life Books, eds., *The World of Matisse* (New York: Time-Life, 1969), p. 9.
2. Goldwater and Treves, op. cit., p. 413.
3. Ibid., pp. 203–204.

Chapter Six

1. Martha Kearns, *Käthe Kollwitz: Woman and Artist* (Old Westbury, N.Y.: Feminist Press, 1976), p. 48.
2. Ibid., p. 164.
3. B. J. Roche, "The Soul of a New Machine: David Hockney and His Art for the Faxes," *The Washington Post* (September 3, 1989), p. G5.
4. Grace Glueck, "Leo Castelli Takes Stock of 30 Years Selling Art," *The New York Times* (February 5, 1987), p. C19.

Chapter Seven

1. Barbaralee Diamonstein, *Inside New York's Art World* (New York: Rizzoli, 1979), pp. 261–262.
2. Joan Kinnear, *The Artist by Himself* (New York: St. Martin's, 1980), p. 101.
3. John Godley, *The Master Forger: The Story of Han van Meegeren* (New York: Wilfred Funk, 1950), p. 191.

Chapter Eight

1. Elizabeth Ripley, *Hokusai: A Biography* (Philadelphia: Lippincott, 1968), p. 24.
2. Ibid., pp. 62, 68.
3. Kinneir, op. cit., p. 107.
4. Piri Halasz, "An Artist's World of Passion, Pain and Weird Beauty," *Smithsonian* (December 1978), p. 94.
5. Gretchen Berg, "Andy: My True Story," *Los Angeles Free Press* (March 17, 1967), p. 3; quoted in *Andy Warhol: A Retrospective*, Kynaston McShine, ed. (New York: Museum of Modern Art, 1989), p. 460.
6. Ibid.

Chapter Nine

1. *David Hockney: A Retrospective* (Los Angeles: Los Angeles County Museum of Art, 1988), p. 58.
2. Sue Davidson Lowe, *Stieglitz: A Memorial Biography* (New York: Farrar Straus Giroux, 1983), pp. xxiii, 441.
3. Glenn Collins, "A Portraitist's Romp Through Art History," *The New York Times* (February 1, 1990), p. C17.
4. Jane Livingston, *Lee Miller: Photographer* (New York: The California/International Arts Foundation, 1989), p. 35.
5. *The New York Times Film Reviews, 1913–1970* (New York: Arno Press, 1971), p. 6.
6. François Truffaut, *Hitchcock*, rev. ed. (New York: Simon and Schuster, 1983), p. 256.
7. Donald Spoto, *The Dark Side of Genius: The Life of Alfred Hitchcock* (Boston: Little, Brown, 1983), p. 73.
8. Vincent Canby, "Film: Woody Allen's Fond Remembrances of 'Radio Days,'" *The New York Times* (January 30, 1987), p. C10.
9. Kerry Green, "Nam June Paik," *Video Systems* (July 1982), p. 53.

Chapter Ten

1. Donald Walton, *A Rockwell Portrait* (Kansas City: Sheed Andrews & McMeel, 1978), p. 7.

Chapter Eleven

1. John Russell, "Henry Moore at Eighty—Many Happy Returns," *Smithsonian* (August 1978), p. 75.
2. Carll Tucker, "Henry Moore," *Saturday Review* (March 1981), p. 44.
3. Ibid., p. 46.
4. Israel Shenker, "A Sculptor's Heaven on Earth Is Italy's City of Holy Stone," *Smithsonian* (February 1989), p. 108.
5. Cleve Gray, ed., *David Smith by David Smith* (New York: Holt, Rinehart and Winston, 1972), p. 25.
6. Ibid., p. 123.
7. Vicki Goldberg, "Louise Nevelson," *Saturday Review* (August 1980), p. 36.
8. Diamonstein, op. cit., p. 271.

Chapter Twelve

1. Susan Peterson, *The Living Tradition of María Martínez* (New York: Kodansha International, 1977), p. 191.

Chapter Thirteen

1. Quoted in Stanley Meisler, "Long Live Paris, with Her Pleasures and Complexities," *Smithsonian* (August 1991), p. 44.
2. *The New York Times* (July 3, 1983), p. 17.
3. "Symbol and Workplace: An Interview with Kevin Roche," *Architectural Record* (September 1984), p. 106.
4. Katherine Bishop, "Grimaces Over a Dab of Glitz in Skyline," *The New York Times* (December 8, 1989), p. A20.
5. Patricia Leigh Brown, "Disney Deco," *The New York Times Magazine* (April 8, 1990), p. 21.
6. Frank Lloyd Wright, *A Testament* (New York: Horizon Press, 1957), p. 64.
7. Quoted in Patricia Failing, "She Was America's Most Successful Woman Architect," *ARTnews* (January 1981), p. 70.

Chapter Fourteen

1. "Under Glass," *Progressive Architecture* (November 1980), p. 106.

Chapter Fifteen

1. *Life Stories of Men Who Shaped History, from Plutarch's Lives*, Eduard C. Lindeman, ed. (New York: The New American Library, 1950), p. 73.
2. Thucydides, *The Peloponnesian War*, trans. Rex Warner (Baltimore: Penguin, 1954), pp. 118, 121.

Chapter Sixteen

1. Quoted in Robert Wallace and the Editors of Time-Life Books, eds., *The World of Leonardo* (New York: Time Incorporated, 1966), p. 17.
2. Goldwater, op. cit., pp. 60–61.
3. Ibid., p. 134.
4. Ibid., pp. 145–146.
5. *Memoirs of Madame Vigée Lebrun*, trans. Lionel Strachey (New York: Braziller, 1989), pp. 20, 21, 214.

Chapter Seventeen

1. John Russell and the Editors of Time-Life Books, eds., *The World of Matisse* (New York: Time-Life, 1969), p. 17.
2. Nicholas Wadley, *Manet* (London: Paul Hamlyn, 1967), pp. 25–26.
3. Daniel Guérin, ed., *The Writings of a Savage: Paul Gauguin* (New York: Viking, 1974), p. 54.
4. Barbara Rose, *Lee Krasner: A Retrospective* (Houston: Museum of Fine Arts; New York: Museum of Modern Art, 1984), p. 134.
5. Steven R. Weisman, "Christo's Intercontinental Umbrella Project," *The New York Times* (November 13, 1990), p. C13.
6. John Russell, "A Hodgkin Original," *The New York Times Magazine* (November 11, 1990), p. 57.
7. Grace Glueck, "And Now, a Few Words From Jenny Holzer," *The New York Times Magazine* (December 3, 1989), p. 110.

Glossary

Words in *italics* are also defined in the glossary.
Numbers in **boldface** following the definitions
refer to the numbers of figures in the text
that best illustrate the definitions.

abstract Characteristic of art in which natural *forms* are not rendered in a *naturalistic* or *representational* way, but instead, are simplified or distorted to some extent, often in an attempt to convey the essence of form. Compare *nonobjective*. **(42)**

Abstract Expressionism Painting style of the late 1940s and 1950s in which *abstract* or *nonobjective forms* were used to convey emotional *content*. Abstract Expressionism emphasized spontaneity and often employed bold colors and/or strong *value* contrasts; the paintings were usually quite large in *scale*. Because this art often involved energetic physical movement by the artist, it is also referred to as *action painting*. **(47)**

acrylic A plastic substance commonly used as a *binder* for paints and as a *casting* material for sculpture.

action painting Any painting style calling for vigorous physical activity; specifically, *Abstract Expressionism*.

aesthetic Pertaining to the beautiful, as opposed to the useful, scientific, or emotional. An aesthetic response is an appreciation of such beauty.

afterimage An image that persists after the visual stimulus for that image has been removed. In colors, the tendency of the eyes to see a *hue* after having looked for a time at the *complementary* hue. **(136)**

aquatint An *intaglio printmaking* method in which areas of tone are created by dusting resin particles on a plate and then allowing acid to bite around the particles. Also, a *print* made by this method. **(259)**

arch A curving architectural *form* usually made of bricks or other masonry, often in the shape of a semicircle but sometimes rising to a point at the top. **(398)**

Archaic style In Greek art, the style prevalent from the 8th to the 6th century B.C. **(458)**

armature A rigid framework, often of wood or steel, used to support a sculpture or other large work while it is being made.

Armory Show An art exhibition held in 1913 at the 69th Regiment Armory in New York, at which avant-garde European art was introduced to the United States.

Art Deco An art style of the 1920s and 1930s based on modern materials (steel, chrome, glass) and repetitive geometric patterns. **(419)**

Art Nouveau An art style of the 1890s featuring curvilinear shapes based on plant forms.

assemblage The technique of creating a sculpture by joining together individual pieces or segments, sometimes "found" objects that originally served another purpose. Also, a sculpture made by this method. **(351)**

asymmetrical Not *symmetrical*. **(178)**

atmospheric perspective A device for suggesting three-dimensional depth on a two-dimensional surface. Forms meant to be perceived as distant from the viewer are blurred, indistinct, and misty.

auteur A filmmaker who exercises maximum control over a film's production and imparts an individual style to a film, often drawing upon personal imagery, dreams, obsessions, fears, memories, or loves as subject matter.

axis A straight line, often an imaginary vertical line.

Baroque A style dominant in European art during the 17th century, characterized by strong colors and *value* contrasts, bold *scale*, dramatic use of light, elaborate ornamentation, great emotionalism, even theatricality. **(505)**

barrel vault A *vault*, or masonry roof, based on an extension of the round *arch*; in effect, many round arches placed one behind the other. **(399)**

bas relief Also known as low relief, sculpture in which figures project only slightly from a background, as on a coin. **(352)**

Bauhaus A school of design in Germany from 1919 to 1933, best known for its attempts to adapt design principles to machine technology.

binder A substance in paints that causes particles of *pigment* to adhere to one another and to a *support*.

calligraphy The art of "beautiful writing." Specifically, a style of decorative penmanship highly developed in Asia, featuring a flowing, controlled line, often with gradations from thick to thin. **(210)**

cantilever A horizontal architectural *form* projecting beyond its supports. **(428)**

cartoon 1. A simple drawing with humorous or satirical *content*. 2. A preparatory drawing for a *mural*, *tapestry*, or other large work.

casting The process of making a sculpture or other object by pouring liquid material—clay, metal, plastic—into a mold and allowing it to harden.

ceramic Made from fired ("baked") clay.

chiaroscuro Literally, "light-dark." In two-dimensional art, the use of different *values* to create *modeling* and to simulate the effects of light and shadow in nature. **(128)**

chroma See *intensity*.

cire-perdue See *lost wax*.

Classical style In Greek art, the style of the 5th century B.C. Loosely, the term "classical" is often applied to all the art of ancient Greece and Rome, as well as to any art based on logical, rational principles and deliberate *composition*. **(460)**

collage A work of art made by pasting bits of paper, cloth, or other material onto a flat surface. **(172)**

Color Field painting A style of painting prominent from the 1950s through the 1970s, featuring large "fields" or areas of color, meant to evoke an *aesthetic* or emotional response through the color alone. **(553)**

color wheel A circular arrangement of *hues* based on some particular color theory. Often, an arrangement of the hues in a rainbow, plus intermediary colors. **(130)**

514

complementary colors *Hues* directly opposite one another on the *color wheel* and therefore assumed to be as different from one another as possible. When placed side by side, complementary colors are intensified; when mixed together, they produce a *neutral*. **(130)**

composition The organization of lines, shapes, colors, and other art elements in a work of art. More often applied to two-dimensional art; the broader term is *design*.

computer art Art generated electronically, within the computer. **(223)**

conceptual art An art form in which the underlying idea or concept and the process by which it is achieved are more important than any tangible product.

content The message conveyed by a work of art—its subject matter and whatever the artist hopes to convey by that subject matter.

continuous narrative A device by which two or more episodes in an event are portrayed in the same work of art. **(489)**

contrapposto Literally, "counterpoise." A method of portraying the human figure, especially in sculpture, so that it is apparently relaxed and mobile. The result is often a graceful S-curve. **(357)**

cross-cutting In filmmaking, a technique of alternating two or more scenes or *shots* to advance the action.

cross-hatching An area of closely spaced lines intersecting one another, used to create a sense of three-dimensionality on a flat surface, especially in drawing and *printmaking*. See also *hatching, stippling*. **(106)**

Cubism A style of art pioneered in the early 20th century by Pablo Picasso and Georges Braque. In the most developed type of Cubism, *forms* are fragmented into *planes* or geometric facets, like the facets in a diamond; these planes are rearranged to foster a pictorial, but not *naturalistic*, reality; forms may be viewed simultaneously from several vantage points; figure and background have equal importance; and colors are deliberately restricted to a range of *neutrals*. **(52,53)**

Dada A movement that emerged during World War I in Europe that purported to be anti-everything, even anti-art. Data poked fun at all the established traditions and tastes in art with works that were deliberately shocking, vulgar, and nonsensical. **(544)**

daguerreotype The earliest form of photograph, invented by Louis Jacques Mandé Daguerre, in which the photographic image is made permanent on a copper plate.

design The planned organization of lines, shapes and masses, colors, textures, and space in a work of art. In two-dimensional art, often called *composition*.

distemper A painting *medium* in which the *binder* is water-soluble glue; also known as poster paint.

dome An architectural structure generally in the shape of a hemisphere or half globe; theoretically, an arch rotated 360 degrees on its vertical *axis*. **(402)**

drypoint An *intaglio printmaking* technique, similar to *engraving*, in which a sharp needle is used to draw on a metal plate, raising a thin ridge of metal that creates a soft line when the plate is printed. Also, the resultant *print*. **(259)**

earthenware *Ceramic* ware, usually coarse and reddish in color, fired in the lowest temperature ranges.

edition In *printmaking*, the number of images made from a single plate and authorized by the artist.

encaustic A painting *medium* in which the *binder* is hot beeswax. **(232)**

engraving An *intaglio printmaking* method in which a sharp tool called a burin is used to scratch lines into a metal plate. Also, the resultant *print*. **(259)**

entasis In *Classical* architecture, the slight swelling or bulge built into the center of a column to make the column seem straight visually.

environmental art 1. Art that is large enough for viewers to enter and move about in. 2. Art designed for display in the outdoor environment. 3. Art that actually transforms the natural landscape. **(364)**

etching An *intaglio printmaking* method in which lines and image areas are created by first coating a plate with an acid-resistant substance, then scratching through the substance with a sharp needle, and finally immersing the plate in acid, which "bites" depressions into the exposed sections. Also, the resultant *print*. **(259)**

Expressionism Any art that stresses the artist's emotional and psychological expression, often with bold colors and distortions of form. Specifically, an art style of the early 20th century followed principally by certain German artists. See also *Abstract Expressionism*. **(256)**

Fauvism A short-lived painting style in early-20th-century France, which featured bold, clashing, arbitrary colors—colors unrelated to the appearance of *forms* in the natural world. Henri Matisse was its best-known practitioner. The word *fauve* is usually translated as "wild beast." **(536)**

ferroconcrete Reinforced concrete; a building material that has metal rods or steel mesh embedded in concrete to provide strength. **(410)**

figure-ground relationship In two-dimensional art, the relationship between the principal *forms* and the background. Figure-ground ambiguity suggests equal importance for the two. **(121)**

flashback In filmmaking, a cut to a scene or episode that is supposed to have taken place before the main action of the film.

foreshortening A method of portraying *forms* on a two-dimensional surface so that they appear to project or recede from the *picture plane*. **(158)**

forging Shaping metal with hammers while it is hot; the method for making wrought iron.

form 1. The physical appearance of a work of art—its materials, style, and *composition*. 2. Any identifiable shape or mass, as a "geometric form."

fresco A painting *medium* in which colors are applied to wet plaster, thus bonding the image with the painting surface; most often used for *murals*. **(233)**

Futurism Art movement founded in Italy in 1909 and lasting only a few years. Futurism concentrated on the dynamic quality of modern technological life, emphasizing speed and movement. **(165)**

genre Art that depicts the casual moments of everyday life and its surroundings. **(76)**

geodesic dome An architectural structure invented by R. Buckminster Fuller, based on triangles arranged into tetrahedrons (or four-faceted solids). **(411)**

glaze 1. A coating of glassy, often colored material bonded by heat onto a *ceramic* object. 2. Paint applied in a very thin layer.

golden section Also called the "golden mean," a system of proportions developed by the ancient Greeks in which sections of a line or shape were related to one another according to an "ideal" expressed algebraically as $a:b = b:(a + b)$. **(196)**

Gothic A style of architecture and art dominant in Europe from the 12th to the 15th century. Gothic architecture features pointed *arches*, ribbed *vaults*, and often large areas of stained glass. **(400)**

gouache A painting *medium* similar to *watercolor* but with the addition of an opaque white. **(245)**

groin vault A *vault*, or masonry ceiling, resulting when two *barrel vaults* intersect. Often used in medieval architecture to roof a square area.

ground 1. A substance applied to a painting or drawing *support* in preparation for the *pigmented* material. 2. The preparatory substance used as a coating for a *printmaking* plate. 3. The background in a work of two-dimensional art. See also *primer, figure-ground relationship*.

happening An event performed by artists, usually spontaneous and unrehearsed, that may include music, dance, mime, art, reading, or any combination of these.

hard-edge A style of art, principally painting, of the mid-20th century in which *forms* are depicted with precise, geometric lines and edges. **(559)**

hatching An area of closely spaced parallel lines used to create a sense of three-dimensionality on a flat surface, especially in drawing and *printmaking*. See also *crosshatching, stippling*. **(106)**

haut-relief Also known as high relief, sculpture in which figures are attached to a background but project substantially from that background, usually by at least half their normal depth. **(354)**

Hellenistic style In Greek art, the style of the 3rd and 2nd centuries B.C., characterized by drama and emotionalism and, in sculpture, a tendency for *forms* to push out boldly into space. **(461)**

hue The property of a color that distinguishes it from others in the *color wheel;* the name of a color. **(130)**

iconography Loosely, the "story" depicted in a work of art; people, places, events, and other images in a work, as well as the symbolism and conventions attached to those images by a particular religion or culture.

illumination Hand-drawn decoration or illustration in a manuscript, especially prevalent in medieval art. **(476)**

impasto A thick application of paint to canvas or other *support*. **(237)**

Impressionism An art style of the late 19th century, principally in France, in which artists tried to capture in paint the fleeting effects—or impressions—of light, shade, and color on natural *forms*. **(528)**

inlay In woodworking, a technique in which small pieces of wood, often with varying grains and colors, are glued together to make a pattern. **(386)**

intaglio Any *printmaking* technique in which the lines or image areas to be printed are recessed below the surface of the printing plate. The intaglio techniques are *aquatint, drypoint, etching, engraving,* and *mezzotint*. **(250)**

intensity The degree of purity or brilliance of a color. Also known as *chroma* or *saturation*. **(131)**

isometric perspective A system for depicting three-dimensional depth on a two-dimensional surface, especially common in Eastern art. Isometric perspective resembles *linear perspective* in some ways, except that parallel lines do not converge. Instead, they are parallel to one another, but at an angle to the *picture plane*. **(156)**

kinetic Of or relating to movement. Kinetic art is art that incorporates movement as part of its expression. **(163)**

kore Greek for "maiden"; an ancient Greek sculpture of a young woman, usually clothed.

kouros Greek for "youth" or "boy"; an ancient Greek sculpture of a nude young man. **(459)**

linear perspective System for depicting three-dimensional depth on a two-dimensional surface. Linear perspective has two main precepts: 1) *forms* that are meant to be perceived as far away from the viewer are made smaller than those meant to be seen as close; 2) parallel lines receding into the distance converge at a point on the horizon line known as the *vanishing point*. **(149)**

linocut Also known as linoleum cut, a *relief printmaking* technique in which a block of linoleum is carved so as to leave image areas raised above the surface of the block; in function, similar to a common rubber stamp. Also, the resultant *print*. **(257)**

lintel A beam; a horizontal architectural member usually supported by vertical posts. See also *post-and-lintel*. **(395)**

lithography A *planographic* (or flat-surface) *printmaking* technique, based on the premise that oil and water do not mix. Image areas are drawn in greasy crayon on a stone or plate, and the greasy ink used in this method adheres to those areas. **(250)**

lost-wax casting Also known by the French term *cire-perdue*, a method for *casting* metal sculptures and other objects. Positive and negative *molds* are built around a layer of wax that exactly duplicates the shape and size of the desired sculpture. When this arrangement is heated, the wax melts out (is "lost") and then molten metal is poured into the mold to replace it. **(341)**

Mannerism A term sometimes applied to art of late 16th and early 17th-century Europe, characterized by a dramatic use of space and light and a tendency toward elongated figures. **(504)**

mass Three-dimensional *form*, often implying bulk, density, and weight.

medium 1. The material used to create a work of art. 2. The *binder* for a paint, such as oil. 3. An expressive art form, such as painting, drawing, or sculpture.

metalpoint A drawing technique, especially popular in the *Renaissance*, in which the drawing material is a thin wire of metal. See also *silverpoint*. **(213)**

mezzotint An *intaglio printmaking* method in which the printing plate is first roughened all over with a sharp tool called a rocker to create a pattern of burrs. *Values* from light to medium dark are created by smoothing away the burrs in relative degree. Also, the resultant *print*. **(259)**

Minimal Art A style of painting and sculpture in the mid-20th century in which the art elements are restricted to an extreme "minimum"—lines, simple (often geometric) shapes, and sometimes color. **(558)**

mixed media Descriptive of any work of art employing more than one *medium*—for example, a work that combines painting, *collage*, and *screenprinting*.

mobile A sculpture that incorporates movement, usually effected by air currents. **(366)**

modeling 1. In sculpture, shaping a *form* in some *plastic* material, such as clay, wax, or plaster. 2. In drawing, painting, or *printmaking*, the illusion of three-dimensionality on a flat surface created by simulating effects of light and shadow. **(128)**

mold A hollow or negative *shape* used for *casting* liquid clay, metal, or *plastic*.

monochromatic Having only one color. Descriptive of work in which one *hue*—perhaps with variations of *value* and *intensity*—predominates.

monotype A *printmaking* method in which only one impression results. **(272)**

mosaic An art form in which small pieces of tile, glass, or stone are fitted together and embedded into a background to make a pattern or image. Often used for floor and wall decoration. **(470)**

mural Any large-*scale* wall decoration in painting, *fresco, mosaic,* or other *medium*. **(234)**

naturalistic Descriptive of a work of art that closely resembles *forms* in the natural world. Synonymous with *representational*.

nave The long central section of a church or cathedral where the congregation stands or sits. **(400)**

Neoclassicism "New" classicism—a style in 19th-century Western art that referred back to the *Classical* styles of Greece and Rome. Neoclassical painting is marked by sharp outline, reserved emotions, deliberate (often geometric) *composition*, and cool colors. **(523)**

Neo-Expressionism "New" Expressionism—a term originally applied to works by some European artists, primarily German and Italian, who came to maturity in the post-World War II era; expanded in the 1980s to include certain American artists. Neo-Expressionist works have much emotion and symbolism, sometimes unconventional *media*, and often intense colors and turbulent composition. **(566)**

neutral Having no *hue*—black, white, or gray; sometimes a tannish color achieved by mixing two *complementary* colors.

New York School See *Abstract Expressionism*.

nonobjective Descriptive of works of art that have no reference to the natural world of images. Composed of lines, shapes, and sometimes colors, chosen and arranged for their own expressive potential. Synonymous with *nonrepresentational*. Compare *abstract, stylized*.

nonrepresentational See *nonobjective*.

Op Art Short for optical art, a style popular in the 1960s and based on optical principles. Op Art deals in complex color interactions, to the point where colors and lines seem to vibrate before the eyes. **(164)**

optical color mixture The tendency of the eyes to blend patches of individual colors placed near one another so as to perceive a different, combined color. Also, any art style that exploits this tendency, especially the *pointillism* of Georges Seurat. **(137)**

painterly Descriptive of paintings in which *forms* are defined principally by color areas, not by lines or edges.

palette 1. A surface used for mixing paints. 2. The range of colors typically used by an artist or group of artists.

pastel 1. A soft, chalky crayon used for drawing; also, the resultant drawing. 2. A light-*value* color.

patina A surface coating that develops on metals, particularly copper and bronze, through exposure to weather and oxides, or by the deliberate application of chemicals.

pediment The triangular area above the porch on a Greek temple, often decorated with sculptures. **(455)**

pendentive In architecture, a curving, triangular section that serves as a transition between a *dome* and the four walls of a rectangular building. **(402)**

performance art Similar to a *happening*, art in which there is no concrete object, but rather, a series of events performed by the artist in front of an audience, possibly including music, sight gags, recitation, audio-visual presentations, or other elements.

perspective Any system for depicting the illusion of three-dimensional space on a two-dimensional surface. See *atmospheric perspective, isometric perspective, linear perspective*. **(149)**

Photorealism A painting style of the mid-20th century in which people, objects, and scenes are depicted with such naturalism that the paintings resemble photographs. **(563)**

pictorial space The illusory space in a painting or other work of two-dimensional art that seems to recede backward into depth from the *picture plane*; the "window" effect in a painting.

picture plane An imaginary flat surface that is assumed to be identical to the surface of a painting. *Forms* in a painting meant to be perceived in deep three-dimensional space are said to be "behind" the picture plane. The picture plane is commonly associated with the foreground of a painting.

pigment A coloring material made from various organic or chemical substances. When mixed with a *binder*, it creates a drawing or painting *medium*.

plane A flat surface. See *picture plane*.

planography A *printmaking* technique in which the image areas are level with the surface of the printing plate; *lithography*. **(250)**

plastic 1. Capable of being molded or shaped, as clay. 2. Any synthetic polymer substance, such as *acrylic*.

pointillism An art style of the late 19th century, particularly associated with Georges Seurat, in which small patches or "points" of color are placed close together to build *form*. See also *optical color mixture*. **(137)**

Pop Art An art style of the 1960s, deriving its imagery from the popular, mass-produced culture. Deliberately mundane, Pop Art focused on the overfamiliar objects of daily life to give them new meanings as visual emblems. **(174)**

porcelain A *ceramic* ware, usually white, firing in the highest temperature ranges and often used for fine dinnerware, vases, and sculpture.

post-and-lintel In architecture, a structural system based on two or more uprights (posts) supporting a horizontal crosspiece (lintel or beam). **(395)**

Post-Impressionism A term applied to the work of several artists—French or living in France—from about 1885 to 1900. Although all painted in highly personal styles, the Post-Impressionists were united in rejecting the relative absence of *form* characteristic of *Impressionism*. The group included Vincent van Gogh, Paul Cézanne, Paul Gauguin, and Georges Seurat.

primary color A *hue* that, in theory, cannot be created by a mixture of other hues. Varying combinations of the primary hues can be used to create all the other hues of the spectrum. In pigment the primaries are red, yellow, and blue. **(130)**

primer A preliminary coating applied to a painting *support* to improve adhesion of paints or to create special effects. A traditional primer is gesso, consisting of a chalky substance mixed with glue and water. Also called a *ground*.

print An image created from a master wood block, stone, plate, or screen, usually on paper. Prints are referred to as multiples, because as a rule many identical or similar impressions are made from the same printing surface, the number of impressions being called an *edition*. A print is considered an original work of art and, today, is customarily signed and numbered by the artist. See *relief, intaglio, lithography, screenprinting*. **(250)**

printmaking The art of making *prints*.

proportion Size relationships between parts of a whole, or between two or more items perceived as a unit; also, the size relationship between an object and its surroundings. Compare *scale*. **(193)**

radial Projecting outward from a central core like the spokes in a wheel. **(186)**

Realism Broadly, any art in which the goal is to portray forms in the natural world in a highly *representational* manner. Specifically, an art style of the mid-19th century, identified especially with Gustave Courbet, which fostered the idea that everyday people and events are fit subjects for important art. **(525)**

refraction The bending of a ray of light, for example, when it passes through a prism. **(129)**

registration In *printmaking*, the precise alignment of impressions made by two or more printing blocks or plates on the same sheet of paper, as when printing an image in several colors.

relief Anything that projects from a background. 1. Sculpture in which figures or other images are attached to a background but project from it to some degree. See *bas-relief, haut-relief*. 2. A *printmaking* technique in which portions of a block meant to print are raised above the surface. See *woodcut, linocut, wood engraving*. **(250)**

Renaissance The period in Europe from the 14th to the 16th century, characterized by a renewed interest in *Classical* art, architecture, literature, and philosophy. The Renaissance began in Italy and gradually spread to the rest of Europe. In art, it is most closely associated with Leonardo da Vinci, Michelangelo, and Raphael.

representational Descriptive of a work of art that closely resembles *forms* in the natural world. Synonymous with *naturalistic*.

Rococo A style of art popular in Europe in the first three-quarters of the 18th century. Rococo architecture and furnishings emphasized ornate but small-*scale* decoration, curvilinear *forms*, and *pastel* colors. Rococo painting, also tending toward the use of pastels, has a playful, light-hearted, romantic quality and often pictures the aristocracy at leisure. **(516)**

Romanesque A style of architecture and art dominant in Europe from the 9th to the 12th century. Romanesque architecture, based on ancient Roman precedents, emphasizes the round *arch* and *barrel vault*. **(399)**

Romanticism A movement in Western art of the 19th century, generally assumed to be in opposition to *Neoclassicism*. Romantic works are marked by intense colors, turbulent emotions, complex *composition*, soft outlines, and sometimes heroic subject matter. **(524)**

salon 1. A fashionable gathering of artists, writers, and intellectuals held in a private home. 2. In France, a state-sponsored exhibition of art, held in Paris, controlled by the Academy of Fine Arts. Starting in 1863, opposition to the restrictive, overly conservative jurying of the Salon resulted in alternative exhibitions.

sarcophagus A stone or *ceramic* coffin, sometimes decorated with sculpture. **(96)**

saturation See *intensity*.

scale Size in relation to some "normal" or constant size. Compare *proportion*.

screenprinting A *printmaking* method in which the image is transferred to paper by forcing ink through a fine mesh in which the areas not meant to print have been blocked; a stencil technique. **(250)**

secondary color A *hue* created by combining two *primary colors*, as yellow and blue mixed together yield green. In pigment the secondary colors are orange, green, and violet. **(130)**

serigraphy See *screenprinting*.

sfumato From the Italian word for "smoke," a technique of painting in thin *glazes* to achieve a hazy, cloudy atmosphere, often to represent objects or landscape meant to be perceived as distant from the *picture plane*. **(493)**

shape A two-dimensional area having identifiable boundaries, created by lines, color or *value* changes, or some combination of these. Broadly, *form*.

shot In filmmaking, any continuous sequence of movie frames, with the camera rolling.

silkscreen See *screenprinting*.

silverpoint A variation of *metalpoint* in which the drawing material is a thin silver wire.

simultaneous contrast The tendency of *complementary colors* to seem brighter and more intense when placed side by side.

slab construction In *ceramics*, a construction method in which objects are formed from sheets of clay rolled out as with a rolling pin.

solvent Also known as a *vehicle*, the liquid used to thin paints and to clean brushes after painting; for example, water or turpentine.

still life A painting or other two-dimensional work in which the subject matter is an arrangement of objects—fruit, flowers, tableware, pottery, and so forth—brought together for their pleasing contrasts of shape, color, and texture. Also, the arrangement of objects itself. **(171)**

stippling A pattern of closely spaced dots or small marks used to create a sense of three-dimensionality on a flat surface, especially in drawing and *printmaking*. See also *cross-hatching, hatching*. **(106)**

stoneware *Ceramic* ware, usually gray or tan in color, fired in the medium temperature ranges.

style A characteristic, or a number of characteristics, that we can identify as constant, recurring, or coherent. In art, the sum of such characteristics associated with a particular artist, group, or culture, or with an artist's work at a specific time.

stylized Descriptive of works based on *forms* in the natural world, but simplified or distorted for *design* purposes. See also *abstract*.

support The surface on which a work of two-dimensional art is made; for example, canvas, paper, or wood.

Surrealism A painting style of the early 20th century that emphasized imagery from dreams and fantasies, as well as an intuitive, spontaneous method of recording such imagery. **(546)**

suspension A structural system in architecture, most common in bridges, in which the weight of a horizontal member is suspended from steel cables supported by uprights called pylons. **(408)**

symbol An image or sign that represents something else, because of convention, association, or resemblance.

symmetrical Descriptive of a design in which the two halves of a composition on either side of an imaginary central vertical *axis* correspond to one another in size, shape, and placement. **(176)**

tapestry A type of weaving in which the crosswise yarns are manipulated freely to create patterned or pictorial effects.

tempera A painting *medium* in which the *binder* is egg yolk. **(235)**

tensile strength In architecture, the ability of a material to span horizontal distances with minimum support from underneath.

terra cotta Italian for "baked earth." A *ceramic* ware, usually reddish, fired in the low temperature ranges and somewhat porous and fragile; *earthenware*. **(369)**

throwing Forming rounded *ceramic* objects on the potter's wheel. **(371)**

triptych A three-part work of art; especially a painting, meant for placement on an altar, with three panels that fold together.

trompe-l'oeil French for "fool-the-eye." A painting or other work of two-dimensional art rendered in such an extremely *naturalistic* manner that the viewer is "tricked" into thinking it is three-dimensional. **(41)**

truss In architecture, a structural system, used principally with wood and metal, based on the triangle. **(409)**

value The relative lightness or darkness of a *hue*, or of a *neutral* varying from white to black. **(127)**

vanishing point In *linear perspective,* the point on the horizon line where parallel lines appear to converge. **(149)**

vault A masonry (brick or concrete) roof or ceiling, especially in medieval architecture. See also *groin vault, barrel vault.* **(399)**

vehicle See *solvent.*

video art Any art form based on television. **(318)**

volume Similar to *mass,* a three-dimensional *form* implying bulk, density, and weight; but also a void or empty, enclosed space.

wash Ink or *watercolor* paint thinned so as to flow freely onto a *support.*

watercolor A painting *medium* in which the *binder* is gum arabic.

woodcut A *relief printmaking* method in which a block of wood is carved so as to leave the image areas raised from the background. Also, the resultant *print.* **(250)**

wood engraving Similar to *woodcut,* a *relief printmaking* process in which the image is cut on the end grain of a wood plank, resulting in a "white-line" impression.

Index

All references are to page numbers.
Numbers in **boldface** indicate an illustration on that page.

Photographic Credits

All references are to figure numbers. The following abbreviations have been used throughout:

AR: Art Resource, New York
ARS: Artists Rights Society, New York
PR: Photo Researchers, New York
RMN: Service de Documentation Photographique de la Réunion des Musées Nationaux, Paris

Chapter 1: 3, Jean Vertut, Issey-les-Moulineaux, France; **7,** © Craig Aurness/West Light, Los Angeles; **10,** Chevojon Frères/ARS; **11,** © 1991 M.C. Escher, Cordon Art-Baarn-Holland; **13,** Scala/AR; **14,** Steve Kagan/NYT Pictures; **19,** from *Perception* by Irwin Rock © 1984 Scientific American Books, Inc.; **p. 20,** Service Photographique; **p. 25,** © 1988 Juliet Man Ray.

Chapter 2: 26, Alinari/AR; **29,** Copyright 1991 Richard Serra/ARS, N.Y., and Jack Manning/NYT Pictures; **32,** Tony Jerome/NYT Pictures; **34,** Alinari/AR; **36, 39,** RMN; **41,** Courtesy Brooke Alexander, New York; **52,** David Heald, © 1990 Solomon R. Guggenheim Foundation.

Chapter 3: 59, Fritz Henle/PR; **60,** A. Singer, courtesy Department of Library Service, American Museum of Natural History; **62,** George Holton/PR; **63,** Archeological Survey of India, Janpath, New Delhi; **64,** French Government Tourist Office, New York; **66,** AR; **67,** Hirmer Fotoarchiv, Munich; **68,** Uniphoto Inc.; **70,** © RMN; **76,** Giraudon/AR; **79,** © George Segal/VAGA New York 1990; **95,** Giraudon/AR; **96,** Soprintendenza Archeologica per l'Etruria Meridionale; **98,** Richard Strauss.

Chapter 4: 99, Norrine Betjemann, courtesy Janet Fleischer Gallery; **102,** © the Estate of Tseng Kwong Chi, 1991; **107, 115, 118,** Giraudon/AR; **121,** © M.C. Escher Heirs, Cordon Art BV, Baarn, The Netherlands; **122,** © George W. Gardner, Hillsdale, N.Y.; **124,** Christopher Springman/TIME Magazine; **128,** Giraudon/AR; **132,** from the jacket of *The Fractal Geometry of Nature,* by Benoit B. Mandelbrot, published by W. H. Freeman and Company, New York; **133,** John Betancout, courtesy Galeria Botello, Hato Rey, Puerto Rico; **134,** Copyright 1991 ARS/ADAGP; **141,** courtesy Maxwell Davidson Gallery, New York; **142,** reproduced with permission of Galerie Welz, Salzburg; **143,** Robert E. Mates; **144,** John Webb FRPS, Cheam, Surrey, England; **148,** from Dorothy Dunn, *American Indian Painting of the Southwest and Plains Areas,* University of New Mexico Press, 1968; **150, 152, 158,** Alinari/AR; **161,** Doisneau/PR; **162,** French Government Tourist Office, New York; **163,** Rob Cornfelder, George Rickey Workshop, East Chatham, N.Y.; **p. 106,** Alinari/AR; **p. 135,** Sidney Janis Gallery, N.Y.; **p. 142,** Le Fevre Gallery, London; **p. 146,** Alinari/AR.

Chapter 5: 167, courtesy the artist; **168,** © 1990 The Art Institute of Chicago, All Rights Reserved; **170,** George Holton/PR; **172,** George Holzer; **173,** courtesy Elizabeth Benton; **176,** reproduction authorized by the Instituto Nacional de Bellas Artes y Litteratura; **177,** © 1990 The Art Institute of Chicago, All Rights Reserved; **179,** Robert E. Mates; **180,** from *Prairie Fires and Paper Moons* by Hal Morgan and Andreas Brown, pub. David Grodine, Boston; **185,** Otto E. Nelson, New York; **186,** Alinari/AR; **188,** Philadelphia Museum of Art; **189,** © Museo del Prado, All Rights Reserved; **191,** Jim Strong; **192,** VAGA; **195,** Hirmer Fotoarchiv, Munich; **197,** © 1989 Annie Leibovitz/

Contact Press Images; **198,** David Heald; **201,** Geoffrey Clements, New York; **205,** The Nelson-Atkins Museum of Art, Kansas City, Mo.; **206,** courtesy Robert Miller Gallery, New York; **p. 155,** Magnum Photos, New York.

Chapter 6: 225, copyright 1991 ARS N.Y./SPADEM.

Chapter 7: 233, Scala/AR; **238,** AR; **239,** courtesy Robert Miller Gallery, New York; **246,** courtesy Acquavella Galleries, Inc., New York; **249,** courtesy Bernice Steinbaum Gallery, New York; **p. 203,** courtesy Robert Miller Gallery, New York; **p. 212,** Yale Joel, Life Magazine, © Time, Inc.

Chapter 8: 260, The Bettmann Archive; **262,** courtesy Kennedy Galleries, Inc., New York; **263,** Giraudon/AR; **265,** courtesy Getler/Pall Gallery, New York.

Chapter 9: 284, courtesy Pace/MacGill Gallery, New York; **288,** for the estate of Diane Arbus, Ellis J. Freedman; **290,** PR; **292,** courtesy Pace/MacGill Gallery, New York; **295,** UPI/Bettmann Newsphotos; **297,** NYT Pictures; **304, 305,** Museum of Modern Art Film Stills Archive; **306,** courtesy Turner Entertainment Company; **307,** Museum of Modern Art Film Stills Archive; **308,** Janus Films; **309,** Museum of Modern Art Film Stills Archive; **310,** courtesy Turner Entertainment Company; **311,** Brian Hamill, from Jack Rollins and Charles H. Jaffe Productions; **312,** Museum of Modern Art Film Stills Archive; **314,** © Touchstone Pictures/Amblin Entertainment, Foto Fantasies; **315,** CBS Entertainment, a Division of CBS, Inc.; **317,** David Plastik/Retna, Ltd.; **318,** David Allison; **p. 263,** The Bettmann Archive.

Chapter 10: 323, 331, courtesy the Pushpin Group, New York; **333,** © 1987 Capital Cities/ABC Inc.; **p. 275 right,** Nencioli/LIRE.

Chapter 11: 338, Seth Joel; **340,** Anne Kohs and Associates, Inc., San Francisco; **342,** Alinari/AR; **344,** Jacqui Wong, New York; **347,** Alinari/AR; **348,** David Finn; **349,** Jerry L. Thompson; **352,** Lee Boltin Picture Library; **353,** Alinari/AR; **354,** courtesy Metro Pictures, photo D. James Dee; **357,** Hirmer Fotoarchiv, Munich; **359,** courtesy Sakamoto Photo Research Laboratory; **363,** © Michael Melford 1989; **364,** Gian Franco Gorgoni © 1984 Contact Press; **365,** Jeanne-Claude Christo; **p. 289,** Sanford H. Roth, Rapho/PR; **p. 293,** courtesy Condé Nast Publications; **p. 295,** Lynn Gilbert, courtesy Pace Gallery, New York.

Chapter 12: 370, Jerry Jacka, Phoenix; **371,** Ellen Grossman; **374,** Bill Scott; **375,** Linda Arbuckle with technical assistance of Robert Lyon; **379,** Michael Seidl; **382,** Robert Boni; **384,** Larry Stein; **390,** Elijah Cobb; **p. 309,** Jerry Jacka, Phoenix; **p. 323,** Jerry Cook.

Chapter 13: 394, Marc Treib, Berkeley, Calif.; **395,** Hirmer Fotoarchiv, Munich; **397,** William Katz/PR; **398,** French Government Tourist Office, New York; **399,** Jean Roubier; **400,** Rapho/PR; **402,** Hirmer Fotoarchiv, Munich; **403,** Comstock; **405,** French Government Tourist Office, New York; **406,** Hedrich-Blessing, Chicago; **407,** Ezra Stoller, ESTO; **408,** Chris Minerva/FPG International; **409,** Joe Aker; **410,** Dennis Halinan/FPG

International; **411,** David Maclean/Shostal Associates, New York; **412, 413,** Library of Congress, Washington, D.C.; **414,** Brown Brothers; **416,** Koji Horiuchi/Pei Cobb Freed & Partners; **417,** Robert E. Mates; **418,** French Government Tourist Office, photo François Darras; **419,** Brown Brothers; **420,** © 1958 Ezra Stoller, ESTO; **421,** Robert Livieri; **422,** Culver Pictures; **423,** Russell Abraham Photographers, San Francisco; **424,** William Taylor; **425,** © MAS, Barcelona; **427,** courtesy Lake Point Tower Marketing; **428,** Bill Hedrich, Hedrich-Blessing, Chicago; **429,** Timothy Hursley; **430,** Special Collections, California Polytechnic State University; **p. 341,** Theo Westenberger/Liaison, New York; **p. 355,** UPI/Bettmann Newsphotos.

Chapter 14: 433, Ewing Galloway; **434,** The Bettmann Archive; **436,** Jack Mellott; **437,** Edward W. Souza, courtesy Stanford University, News and Publications Service; **438,** U.S. Air Force; **439,** Richard Wood/The Picture Cube; **440,** Gregory Glass; **441,** courtesy Citicorp; **442,** Enrico Ferorelli/DOT.

Chapter 15: 443, Comstock; **447,** Lee Boltin Picture Library; **449,** Oriental Institute, University of Chicago; **451, 452,** Hirmer Fotoarchiv, Munich; **454,** © RMN, Mr. Chuzeville; **456,** William Katz/PR; **459,** Hirmer Fotoarchiv, Munich; **460,** Alinari/AR; **462,** Hirmer Fotoarchiv, Munich; **464,** Alinari/AR; **465,** Scala/AR; **466, 467,** Alinari/AR; **470,** Scala/AR; **471,** Alinari/AR; **473,** Ara Güler, Istanbul; **478,** Foto Marburg/AR; **479,** © ND-Viollet; **480,** © Collection Viollet; **481, 482,** Foto Marburg/AR; **483,** RMN; **484, 485,** Scala/AR; **p. 382,** Alinari/AR.

Chapter 16: 486, Anderson/AR; **487, 488,** Scala/AR; **489,** Antonio Quattrone, Florence, courtesy Olivetti; **490,** Alinari/AR; **491, 492,** Anderson/AR; **493,** Scala/AR; **494,** Alinari/AR; **495 above,** Scala/AR; **496,** Francesco Ricceri, Fabbrica di San Pietro; **497, 498,** Alinari/AR; **499,** Scala/AR; **501,** Giraudon/AR; **503,** Scala/AR; **504,** Lauros-Giraudon/AR; **505, 506,** Alinari/AR; **508,** Scala/AR; **509,** © Frans Claes, Antwerp, courtesy Belgian National Tourist Office, New York; **511,** RMN; **512,** Lauros-Giraudon/AR; **516,** BSV/L. Weiss, 1984; Bayerischen Verwaltung der Staatlichen Schlosser, Garten und Seen Museumsabteilung; **521,** RMN; **pp. 415, 429, 445,** Scala/AR; **p. 448,** The Bettmann Archive.

Chapter 17: 523–526, RMN; **530,** Hirschl and Adler Galleries, Inc., New York; **531,** RMN; **533,** Hans Hinz, Allschwil; **534,** RMN; **536,** Hans Petersen, Copenhagen; **548, 551,** Robert E. Mates, New York; **556,** courtesy Leo Castelli Gallery, New York; **558,** courtesy Xavier Fourcade, Inc., New York; **559,** courtesy Leo Castelli Gallery, New York; **564,** Geoffrey Clements; **565,** Bruce C. Jones, New York; **571, 572,** Wolfgang Volz/photo Eeva-Inkerti, © Christo; **574,** © 1990 The Guggenheim Foundation, photo David Heald; **575,** Martha Swope Associates/William Gibson; **p. 461,** Hubicki, Ripton, Vt.; **p. 494,** © 1981 Annie Leibovitz/Contact Press Images; **p. 498,** Duane Michaels.

Epiloque: 576, Egyptian Tourist Authority; **577,** UPI/Bettmann Newsphotos; **579,** Schmidt-Thomsen, Landschafts-Verband Westfalen-Lippe, Munich; **580,** Anderson/AR; **581,** Ing. C. Olivetti & C., S.p.A.; **582,** courtesy NTV-Tokyo; **583,** Ecole nationale supérieure des Beaux-Arts, Paris.